T4-AJR-274

HILDEGARD OF BINGEN
AND HER GOSPEL HOMILIES

Previously published volumes in this series are listed at the back of this book.

VOLUME 12

HILDEGARD OF BINGEN AND HER GOSPEL HOMILIES

Speaking New Mysteries

by

Beverly Mayne Kienzle

BREPOLS

British Library Cataloguing in Publication Data

Kienzle, Beverly Mayne.
    Hildegard of Bingen and her gospel homilies : speaking new mysteries. – (Medieval
women : texts and contexts ; 12) 1. Hildegard, Saint, 1098–1179. Expositiones
evangeliorum. 2. Bible – Criticism, interpretation, etc. – Early works to 1800.
3. Mysticism – History – Middle Ages, 600–1500 – Sources.
I. Title II. Series
220.6-dc22

ISBN-13: 9782503517773

D/2009/0095/62
ISBN: 978-2-503-51777-3

Printed in the E.U. on acid-free paper

In memory of my dearest Auntie
Ann Cary Cleveland

For my beloved Edward and Kathleen
In gratitude for their love and support

And for my dear feline companions,
Walter, Basile, Athena, Tecla, Cecilia, and Stella

CONTENTS

Abbreviations

CCCM   Corpus Christianorum, Continuatio Mediaeualis (Turnhout: Brepols, 1966–)

CCSL   Corpus Christianorum, Series Latina (Turnhout: Brepols, 1954–)

CSEL   Corpus scriptorum ecclesiasticorum Latinorum (Vienna, 1866–)

MGH   Monumenta Germaniae Historica (Hannover, 1826–)
SS   Scriptores

PL   *Patrologiae cursus completus, series latina*, ed. by J.-P. Migne, 221 vols (Paris: Garnier, 1844–64)

SBOp   Bernard of Clairvaux, *Sancti Bernardi Opera*, ed. by J. Leclercq, H. Rochais, and C. H. Talbot, 8 vols (Rome: Editiones cistercienses, 1957–77)

SC   Sources chrétiennes

Hildegard of Bingen's Works

Cause   *Cause et cure*, ed. by Laurence Moulinier and Rainer Berndt, Rarissima mediaevalia Opera latina, 1 (Berlin: Akademie Verlag, 2003)

De reg. Bened.   *De regula Sancti Benedicti*, ed. by Hugh Feiss, in *Opera minora*, pp. 67–97

Epistolarium, I	*Hildegardis Bingensis Epistolarium, Pars prima*, I–XC, ed. by L. Van Acker, CCCM, 91 (Turnhout: Brepols, 1991)
Epistolarium, II	*Hildegardis Bingensis Epistolarium, Pars secunda*, XCI–CCLR, ed. by L. Van Acker, CCCM, 91A (Turnhout: Brepols, 1993)
Epistolarium, III	*Hildegardis Bingensis Epistolarium, Pars tertia*, CCLI–CCXC, ed. by Monika Klaes, CCCM, 91B (Turnhout: Brepols, 2001)
Expl. Atha.	*An Explanation of the Athanasian Creed*, trans. by Thomas M. Izbicki, Peregrina Translations Series (Toronto: Peregrina, 2001)
Expl. Rule	*Explanation of the Rule of Benedict by Hildegard of Bingen*, trans. by Hugh Feiss, Peregrina Translations Series, 15 (Toronto: Peregrina, 1990)
Expl. Symb.	*Explanatio Symboli Sancti Athanasii*, ed. by Christopher P. Evans, in *Opera minora*, pp. 109–33
Expo. Euang.	*Expositiones euangeliorum*, ed. by Beverly M. Kienzle and Carolyn A. Muessig, in *Opera minora*, pp. 185–333
LDO	*Hildegardis Bingensis Liber diuinorum operum*, ed. by Albert Derolez and Peter Dronke, CCCM, 92 (Turnhout: Brepols, 1996)
Letters	Hildegard of Bingen, *Letters*, trans. by J. L. Baird and R. K. Ehrman, 3 vols (Oxford: Oxford University Press, 1994–2004)
Life of Hildegard	*The Life of the Saintly Hildegard by Gottfried of Disibodenberg and Theodoric of Echternach*, trans. by Hugh Feiss (Toronto: Peregrina, 1996)
Opera minora	*Hildegardis Bingensis Opera minora*, ed. by Peter Dronke, Christopher P. Evans, Hugh Feiss, Beverly Mayne Kienzle, Carolyn A. Muessig, and Barbara Newman, CCCM, 226 (Turnhout: Brepols, 2007)

Ordo	*Ordo virtutum*, ed. by Peter Dronke, in *Opera minora*, pp. 503–21
Sciuias	*Hildegardis Bingensis Sciuias*, ed. by Adelgundis Führkötter and Angela Carlevaris, CCCM, 43, 43A (Turnhout: Brepols, 1978)
Scivias (Eng.)	*Scivias*, trans. by C. Hart and J. Bishop (New York: Paulist Press, 1990)
Solut.	*Solutiones quaestionum XXXVIII, PL* 197 (1855): 1037–54
Symph.	*Symphonia armonie celestium reuelationum*, ed. by Barbara Newman, in *Opera minora*, pp. 371–477
V. Disib.	*Vita sancti Disibodi episcopi, PL* 197 (1855): 1093–1116
V. Hild.	*Vita sanctae Hildegardis*, ed. by M. Klaes, CCCM, 126 (Turnhout: Brepols, 1993)
V. Rup.	*Vita sancti Ruperti ducis, confessoris Bingensis, PL* 197 (1855): 1083–92
Vite mer.	*Hildegardis Bingensis Liber vite meritorum*, ed. by Angela Carlevaris, CCCM, 90 (Turnhout: Brepols, 1995)

Secondary Works

Angesicht	'*Im Angesicht Gottes suche der Mensch sich selbst': Hildegard von Bingen (1098–1179)*, ed. by Reiner Berndt (Berlin: Akademie Verlag, 2001)
Context	*Hildegard of Bingen: The Context of her Thought and Art*, ed. by Charles Burnett and Peter Dronke (London: Warburg Institute, 1998)
Umfeld	*Hildegard von Bingen in ihrem historischen Umfeld*, ed. by Alfred Haverkamp (Mainz: von Zabern, 2000)
Voice	*Voice of the Living Light: Hildegard of Bingen and her World*, ed. by Barbara Newman (Berkeley: University of California Press, 1998)

PREFACE

This volume represents the second part of a three-stage undertaking: the critical edition of Hildegard of Bingen's *Expositiones euangeliorum*, edited with Carolyn A. Muessig and George Ferzoco, was published in 2007, and an English translation will be published by Cistercian Publications. The Latin texts cited in the present volume are translated to facilitate reading for an English-speaking audience. The translations are mine, unless indicated otherwise.

Many are interested in the history of women's ministry and eager to know about the preaching and exegesis of an extraordinary twelfth-century woman, especially when restrictions on women's voices still operate in the twenty-first century. An article in *The New York Times* on 26 August 2006 reported on the 'stained-glass ceiling', the 'long-standing limits, preferences and prejudices' that meet contemporary women seeking positions of leadership in large congregations in the United States. Even in denominations that have ordained female ministers for decades, women find resistance to their authority, particularly when they take on the task of biblical interpretation in preaching. The article reports that clergy state: 'People in the pews often do not accept women in the pulpit.' One pastor tells that, 'Names and nomenclatures in the black church are so important: as a woman you teach but don't preach. Yet the teaching sounds just like preaching.' A Methodist pastor told the reporter that, 'a man in the congregation covered his eyes whenever she preached'. Moreover, parishioners have asked her, 'Timothy says women can't preach, so how can you?' The latter statement refers to I Timothy 2. 12, which reads: 'I permit no woman to teach or have authority over men.' The worlds and personal situations of Hildegard of Bingen and contemporary women ministers in the United States differ vastly, yet the struggle to overcome Pauline injunctions and the misogyny that accompanies their interpretation establishes a bond between twenty-first-century women pastors and the twelfth-century seer and exegete. Moreover, the controversy over nomenclatures that the woman pastor references in *The New York Times* played a role in Hildegard's day and before her.

The idea for this book arose out of my search for evidence of women preaching in the Middle Ages. The long process of writing has often brought to mind Hildegard's autobiographical reflections on the labour of composition. I attest to 'sweating out' the book over a period of about ten years, as Hildegard said about *Sciuias*, and to times when I have found myself 'a shadow of health and strength', as well as 'frequently worn down by tribulations', as she remarked when writing the *Liber uitae meritorum*.

I owe much gratitude to the people and institutions who have supported me. A Fellowhip from the National Endowment for the Humanities[*] and the generosity of William A. Graham, Dean of Harvard Divinity School, allowed me to take a full year of leave in 2006–07 and complete the manuscript. A research leave in spring 2002 from Harvard Divinity School provided the time to ground the meticulous research of tracing Hildegard's sources. Funding from the Harvard University Provost's Fund for Interfaculty Collaboration for an interdepartmental grant, 'Art, Theology, Mysticism and Female Monasticism in the Rhineland during the later Middle Ages', 2004–06, directed by Jeffrey Hamburger, made possible collaborative research, reciprocal teaching, and a 2005 excursion to Germany with students for the magnificent exhibition, *Krone und Schleier* — an experience that broadened my perspective on Hildegard's cultural world. The Provost's Fund for Interfaculty Collaboration, the Houghton Library, and the Harvard Divinity School brought together scholars of liturgical manuscripts and sequences for a conference at Houghton Library, organized by Jeffrey Hamburger: 'Leaves from Paradise: The Cult of John the Evangelist at the Dominican Nunnery of Paradies bei Soest', Harvard University, 23 October 2006. Discussions there with various participants, especially Susan Boynton and Erika Kihlman, provided the key to my understanding of Hildegard's method of glossing.

Invited lectures gave me opportunities to discuss my work and shape my ideas. Reiner Berndt invited me to the 1998 conference in Mainz, '"Im Angesicht Gottes suche der Mensch sich selbst": Hildegard von Bingen (1098–79)', where I had the opportunity to meet and discuss the beginnings of my work with a number of Hildegard specialists. Invitations to 'Medieval Monastic Preaching' (1997) and 'Medieval Monastic Education and Formation' (1999), organized by Carolyn A. Muessig at Downside Abbey, Stratton on the Fosse, sponsored by the Newman

---

[*] Any views, findings, conclusions, or recommendations expressed in this book do not necessarily reflect those of the National Endowment for the Humanities.

Fellowships Trust, Downside Abbey, the British Academy, and the Department of Theology and Religious Studies, University of Bristol, facilitated fruitful discussion with attendees on the monastic context of the *Expositiones euangeliorum*. A lecture at Princeton in December 2003, invited by E. Ann Matter on behalf of the Delaware Valley Medieval Association, made possible a productive exchange of ideas with the participants. The University of Bristol invited me as Benjamin Meaker Professor in July 2004 to spend time in residence and teach a master class on 'Text and Image in Hildegard of Bingen's *Sciuias, Expositiones euangeliorum et altera opera*', which provided further occasion for exchange with Carolyn Muessig and her students. During the same period, I participated in the conference, 'Envisaging Heaven in the Middle Ages', organized by Ad Putter and Carolyn Muessig at the Centre for Medieval Studies, University of Bristol. The number of participants involved in Hildegardian studies, including Bernard McGinn, Barbara Newman, Stephen D'Evelyn, Carolyn Muessig, and George Ferzoco, assured a fruitful discussion of my work. Another July 2004 conference furthered my thinking on Hildegard's sense of authority: 'Charisma and Religious Authority: Jewish, Christian, and Muslim Preaching, 1200–1600', organized by Miri Rubin and Katherine Jansen at Queen Mary College, London. A conference in Mazamet (Tarn – France) in May 2007, 'Écrire l'histoire d'une hérésie', provided another occasion for discussing Hildegard's writings against heresy.

I have benefited enormously from the suggestions and comments of colleagues and reviewers. My expression of gratitude to them follows a largely chronological course. Barbara Newman first alerted me to the need for work on the *Expositiones* and generously offered advice over the duration of the project. François Bovon guided my early work on the history of exegesis and provided pre-print sections of his commentary on the Gospel of Luke, remarkable for his extensive treatment of the reception of the gospel texts in patristic and some medieval commentators. He and Kevin Madigan have invited me to discuss the *Expositiones* in their classes on the reception of the Gospel of Luke. Annewies van den Hoek guided me in my explorations of Origen's works. Constant Mews, whom I met in Mainz in 1998, has shared his expansive knowledge of German monastic culture, sent pre-print versions of several articles, and generously provided feedback on the book. Bernard McGinn graciously exchanged ideas and sent copies of articles on spiritual exegesis and Hildegard's visionary exegesis. Carolyn A. Muessig, my co-editor of the *Expositiones*, read an early version of the manuscript and signalled several directions for development. She and George Ferzoco provided important insights on the Riesenkodex that bear on the analysis of the *Expositiones*. Jeffrey Hamburger has shared his abundant knowledge of medieval German culture and kindly read portions of the book manuscript. I have benefited greatly from the collaborative research projects he has organized. Richard Emmerson lectured on *Sciuias* in my classes at Harvard Divinity School and Harvard Extension, which provided the occasion for fruitful discussion on the interpretation of that work's layered texts and the implications for the *Expositiones*. Stephen D'Evelyn, while a Visiting Scholar in Harvard's Classics Department, worked as a research assistant for me and as a teaching assistant in my 2005 course on 'Hildegard and the Gospels'. A valuable conversation partner, Stephen also researched parallels between the *Expositiones* and the *Symphonia* and the *Cause et cure*, as well as manuscript catalogues from libraries with which Hildegard could have had some contact. Anne Brenon, Peter Biller, Ylva Hagman, and Daniela Müller discussed with me the chapter on heresy. Fiona Griffiths read the entire manuscript in an early and lengthier form and offered valuable comments from the perspective of her work on Herrad of Hohenbourg. She offered me a pre-print version of her book on Herrad. Karin Grundler-Whitacre advised me on some difficult passages in German scholarship. Cynthia Bland-Biggar and Norman Sheidlower also read the lengthy version of the manuscript, and Cynthia offered suggestions on parallels with Julian of Norwich. Julie Hotchin sent a pre-print version of her article on the monastery at Lippoldsberg, and Alison Beach kept me apprised of recent work on Admont. Discussions with Susan Boynton, Erika Kihlman, and other participants at 'Leaves from Paradise' helped to shape my views on Hildegard's technique of glossing. Both provided me copies of their own works and read my chapters on monastic education. Nicholas Watson gave me the intellectual boost and advice needed to complete the last phases of the manuscript. Reviewers and editors for Brepols provided careful scrutiny that is much appreciated.

My students have been eager participants in the ongoing intellectual exchange about the *Expositiones*. Some did transcription exercises; others have read parts of early versions of the book and have written papers or done conference presentations on selected homilies. I mention specific contributions in footnotes to the volume, and I broadly acknowledge several who took special interest in some phase of the project, with apologies to anyone I may not have mentioned: Rita Bodlak, Robert Canavello, Sarah Castricum, Nicholas Cohen, Matthew Cressler, Robert Davis, Jennifer De LaGuardia, Annalese Duprey-Henry, Leonardo Espinosa, Kyle Highful, Danielle Joyner, Jaehyun Kim, Christine Libby, Juan Miguel Marin, Fay Martineau, Zachary Matus, Jess Michalik, Amy Nelson, Carlos Parra, Audrey Pitts, John F. Rhilinger, Katherine Shaner, Henry Shapiro, Norman Sheidlower, William E. Smith, III, Tiffany Sprecher, Charles Stang, Travis Stevens, Audrey Walton, Annelies Wouters, Wendy Wyche.

The staff at Harvard Divinity School has supported my work in many ways. My faculty assistants, Katherine Lou and Michael Zaisser, have helped with editing and organizing various phases of the project. I am also grateful to the staff in the Information Technology Department for finding a computer monitor that allows me to see two pages side-by-side, the Andover-Harvard Library for much research assistance, and the Operations Department, which secured for me the perfect orthopedic chair for long hours of work.

I express thanks to friends who have followed the progress of the book over the years; several of them are recognized among my colleagues. Christopher Jarvinen has supported my research generously. Anita Dana visited my classes to discuss her wonderful visionary paintings and offered the permission to use the illustration on the cover. Arnold Reif and I have shared frustrations and found laughter together as we discussed the unfolding of long projects in progress over the same decade. Hellen Dayton painted me a beautiful icon for the healing of hands in pain. Jan and Eugene Ward have discussed the book's progress during my visits at their home in Louisville. Friends at St Stephen's Church, Cohasset, Massachusetts, who listened and participated keenly to a presentation I made there, followed the book's progress with great care and attention during the year my husband was their interim priest. Six cats — Walter, Basile, Athena, Tecla, Cecilia, and Stella — have sat by the computer and on the many papers and books that belong to the project, challenging me to take a few minutes off, weigh my thoughts, receive their warm affection, and think better for it.

Finally, I am grateful to my closest family members who supported the course of the project for so many years: my auntie, Ann Cary Cleveland; my daughter, Kathleen Cary Kienzle, who took on various tasks from photocopying the enormous pages of the *Glossa ordinaria* to typing excerpts from the *Cause et cure*; and most of all, my dear husband, Edward, who has listened, commented, researched, read, proofread, and provided unfailing encouragement and joy. He has cheerfully carried my books, with all the strong love and support that that symbolizes, since we met in 1963: through high-school corridors, across university campuses, in and out of the places we have lived during almost forty years of marriage.

VISIONARY AUTHORITY, EXEGESIS, AND PREACHING

The catholic faith now totters among the people and the Gospel limps in their midst; the most steadfast volumes that the most learned doctors expounded with utmost diligence are melting away out of shameful disgust; and the life-giving food of divine Scripture has grown tepid. Therefore, I speak through a person not versed in the Scriptures and not instructed by an earthly teacher; but I who am speak new secrets through this person and many deep meanings that up to this point have lain hidden in volumes.[1]

The voice of God charged Hildegard of Bingen (1098–1179) with restoring the faltering faith of her era through the revelation of hidden mysteries in the Scriptures. Although untaught by earthly masters, she was to continue the exegetical tradition of the most learned teachers. Hildegard composed a vast corpus of diverse works, all deeply rooted in Scripture and in monastic thought and life; in addition, she founded monasteries at Rupertsberg (*c.* 1150) and Eibingen (1165). Hildegard was above all a learned Benedictine who lived and performed exegesis in the observance of the *Rule*, internalized what she heard and read, and enriched the readings and teachings of the liturgy with other sources and her creative imagination to produce a magnificent, organically coherent, vision of the world in her written works, illustrations, and liturgical songs.

Yet what lay between this divine commission to scriptural interpretation and its implementation? How did a medieval woman access the 'steadfast volumes' of

---

[1] *Sciuias*, III.11, p. 586, lines 379–91: 'Sed nunc catholica fides in populis uacillat et euangelium in eisdem hominibus claudicat, fortissima etiam uolumina quae probatissimi doctores multo studio enucleauerant in turpi taedio diffluunt et cibus uitae diuinarum Scripturarum iam tepefactus est: — unde nunc loquor per non loquentem hominem de Scripturis, nec edoctum de terreno magistro, sed ego qui sum dico per eum noua secreta et multa mystica quae hactenus in uoluminibus latuerunt, uelut homo facit qui limum sibi primum componit et deinde ex eo quasque formas secundum uoluntatem suam discernit.'

the doctors and come to interpret the Scriptures in writing and preaching? The present volume explores those questions as it focuses on Hildegard of Bingen as exegete and preacher. Surprisingly little attention has been paid to the central role of exegesis in the seer's works. Her visionary treatises — *Sciuias, Liber uitae meritorum*, and *Liber diuinorum operum* — dazzle with remarkable visions, while they also contain substantial passages of exegesis. In addition, Hildegard's other works expound biblical passages: the *Ordo uirtutum*, the first extant morality play; the lives of saints Disibod and Rupert; the *Cause et cure* (*Causes and Cures*), a medical work on the humours; the liturgical songs of the *Symphonia*; commentaries on the *Rule of Benedict* and the Athanasian Creed; the *Solutiones quaestionum XXXVIII* (*Solutions for Thirty-Eight Questions*); and over three hundred letters, including several that preserve sermons she delivered.[2]

With the image of reflection from the 'Living Light', Hildegard of Bingen explained to the learned monk Guibert of Gembloux around 1175 how she came to comprehend the Scriptures: 'Just as the sun and moon and stars are reflected in water, so too the Scriptures, sermons, virtues, and certain human deeds are resplendent in that light.'[3] Such exegetical understanding permeates all her works, most notably the *Expositiones euangeliorum*, homilies on the Gospels that establish Hildegard as the only known systematic female exegete of the Middle Ages. The *Expositiones*, which Johannes Trithemius (1462–1516) described as 'quite obscure' and 'intelligible only to the learned and devout',[4] represent for the most part Hildegard's preaching, teaching, and exegesis to her nuns at Rupertsberg whom she served as *magistra*: teacher and superior. They offer an extraordinary testimony to a medieval woman instructing her community on the Scriptures for the liturgical year.

Hildegard's exposition of 'new secrets' was not confined to the written word, nor did it remain within the confines of her monasteries. The *Expositiones* and the commentaries on other texts undoubtedly took root in Hildegard's practice of teaching and preaching as the spiritual head of her religious community. Her secretary Volmar

---

[2] Hildegard's works will be cited in accordance with the list of abbreviations.

[3] *Epistolarium*, II, 103R, p. 261, lines 78–83: 'Lumen igitur quod uideo, locale non est, sed nube que solem portat multo lucidius, nec altitudinem nec longitudinem nec latitudinem in eo considerare ualeo, illudque umbra uiuentis luminis mihi nominatur, atque ut sol, luna et stelle in aqua apparent, ita scripture, sermones, uirtutes et quedam opera hominum formata in illo mihi resplendent.'

[4] Johannes Trithemius, *Catalogus illustrium uirorum, Johannes Trithemii Opera historica*, vol. I, ed. by Marquand Freher (Frankfurt, 1601; repr. Frankfurt/Main: Minerva, 1966), p. 138: 'Liber super Euangelios Dominicalibus homelias LVIII composuit ualde obscuras et nisi deuotis eruditis intelligibles.'

praised her 'new interpretation' and her 'unheard-of sermons on the feast days of saints'.[5] She expressed her concern to construct fortifications, a 'moat and wall', with the words of the Scriptures to defend her sisters against the aerial spirits.[6] Furthermore, as God's voice called her to revive the faith by continuing the exegesis begun by the Church Fathers, the seer undertook journeys to preach and give spiritual advice in Rhineland monasteries and cathedrals, presumably in their chapter houses. By the 1160s and 1170s, Hildegard expanded her exegetical and preaching mission and allied with Ekbert and Elisabeth of Schönau in writing against the Cathars in the Rhineland. Hildegard's public mission remains unrivalled, as far as we know, among women of the High Middle Ages and invites comparison with the apostolate of Catherine of Siena (1347–80) in the fourteenth century. The tensions surrounding women's preaching and interpretation of the Word over the centuries make Hildegard's preserved sermons and her preaching journeys to religious communities all the more remarkable. Furthermore, although medieval women gained acceptance as preachers in a few cases, no other woman to our knowledge composed a work of systematic exegesis like the *Expositiones euangeliorum*.

The Expositiones euangeliorum

The *Expositiones euangeliorum*, the fifty-eight homilies Hildegard of Bingen composed for her sisters at Rupertsberg, expound twenty-seven gospel pericopes — selections used for the liturgy on Sundays and feast days.[7] How and when would Hildegard have interpreted these texts? She probably spoke to her sisters in the chapter house, in accordance with Benedictine liturgical practice, with the scriptural text either before her or recited from memory, section by section.[8] Some of

---

[5] *Epistolarium*, II, 195, p. 443, lines 19–21.

[6] *V. Hild.*, II.12, pp. 37, 29–32; *Life of Hildegard*, p. 60.

[7] *Expo. Euang.*, pp. 185–333, edition based on Wiesbaden, Hessisches Landesbibliothek, Handschrift 2 (Riesenkodex, *R*), fols 434ʳ–461ᵛ, and London, British Library, MS Additional 15102 (*L*), fols 146–91ʳ (a 1487 copy). The *Expositiones quorumdam evangeliorum quas divina inspirante gratia Hildegardi exposuit*, in *Analecta Sanctae Hildegardis opera Spicilegio Solesmensi parata*, ed. by Jean-Baptiste Pitra, Analecta Sacra, 8 (Paris, 1882) pp. 245–327, presents the *Expositiones* as fifty-nine homilies, counting one more *expositio* than the number found in manuscripts *R* and *L* by dividing *Expositio* 2 into two texts (pp. 320–22). Citations of biblical verses throughout this volume are from *Biblia Sacra iuxta Vulgatam versionem*, 3rd edn (Stuttgart: Deutsche Bibelgesellschaft, 1983).

[8] On sermons and chapter talks in Benedictine houses, see Jean Leclercq, 'Recherches sur d'anciens sermons monastiques', *Revue Mabillon*, 36 (1946), 11–14; and *The Love of Learning and*

the *Expositiones* had been written at least in part by the time Hildegard wrote the prologue to the *Liber uitae meritorum*, which was completed around 1163, for there she refers to 'certain expositions'.[9] Two of the *Expositiones* may be dated approximately by intratextual references: one alludes to heretics and another to schism, which may place them respectively to 1163, when heretics suspected of Catharism were burned in Cologne, and somewhere between 1159 and 1177, a period of schism.[10] Four *Expositiones* (1–4) may have been delivered to the religious at Disibodenberg around 1170.[11]

If the chronology set by the *Vita Hildegardis* obtains for the *Expositiones*, then Hildegard wrote the collection of *Expositiones* after the *Symphonia* and extended her oeuvre of liturgically linked compositions with gospel commentaries and explanations of other texts: the *Rule of Benedict* and the Athanasian Creed. Furthermore, if Hildegard gave the *Expositiones* their final form after she composed the *Symphonia*, it is plausible to assume that the content of the *Expositiones* took shape as Hildegard composed her other works. The evidence for the working habits of medieval preachers indicates a pattern of drafts, compositions, and revisions, which allows for assuming that the writing of the *Expositiones* would have accompanied, followed, or perhaps even preceded the treatment of certain themes or pericopes in Hildegard's other works.[12] The *magistra* would have added to them and filled out her coverage of the liturgical year.

What gospel texts did Hildegard select and why? The *Expositiones euangeliorum* expound six pericopes from the Gospel of Matthew, with one being a parable and the others narratives from Jesus's life. Three texts come from Mark and relate to

the Desire for God, trans. by C. Misrahi, 3rd edn (New York: Fordham University Press, 1982), pp. 168–69.

[9] *Vite mer.*, I, p. 8, lines 6–13: 'postquam eadem uisio subtilitates diuersarum naturarum creaturarum, ac responsa et admonitiones tam minorum quam maiorum plurimarum personarum, et symphoniam harmonie celestium reuelationum, ignotamque linguam et litteras cum quibusdam aliis expositionibus, in quibus post predictas uisiones multa infirmitate multoque labore corporis grauata per octo anos duraueram, mihi ad explanandum ostenderat'.

[10] See *Expo. Euang.*, 54 and 55, pp. 323–27. In *Expositio* 54 Hildegard attacks the Cathars' docetic tendencies; see pp. 323–24, lines 1–12 and 21–29. In *Expositio* 55 for references to schism, see p. 326, lines 28–29.

[11] *Epistolarium*, I, 77, 77R, pp. 174, lines 225–27: 'hec uerba in magnis egritudinibus uidi et audiui, ut ea in loco uestro uiua uoce proferrem iussa sum'; *V. Disib.*, *PL* 197: 1093–1116.

[12] *The Sermon*, dir. by Beverly M. Kienzle, Typologie des Sources du Moyen Âge Occidental, 81–83 (Turnhout: Brepols, 2000), pp. 172–73, 974–78. See Barbara Newman, 'Introduction', *Symph.*, p. 350, on the composition of the *Symphonia*.

Jesus's ministry, Resurrection, and Ascension. Thirteen are devoted to Lukan passages; roughly half are parables and the others correspond to episodes in the life of Christ. Five *Expositiones* are based on Johannine pericopes, comprising the Gospel's beginning, two miracle stories, the Nicodemus episode, and the Good Shepherd passage. The chart below identifies each passage in the four Gospels, with the parables listed in the right-hand column. The choice of texts reflects the lectionary selections, but the proportion of Lukan pericopes and particularly parables may reflect Hildegard's attention to gospel passages that lend themselves especially well to her narrative exegesis.

Matthew 1. 18–21 (*Expo. Euang.* 5, 6) The annunciation and the birth of Jesus	Matthew 20. 1–16 (*Expo. Euang.* 22, 23) The labourers in the vineyard
Matthew 2. 1–12 (*Expo. Euang.* 12, 13) The wise men	
Matthew 2. 13–18 (*Expo. Euang.* 10, 11) The flight into Egypt and the massacre of the innocents	
Matthew 4. 1–11 (*Expo. Euang.* 24, 25) The temptation in the wilderness	
Matthew 8. 1–13 (*Expo. Euang.* 18, 19) Healing the leper and the centurion's servant	
Mark 7. 31–37 (*Expo. Euang.* 49, 50) Healing the deaf mute	
Mark 16. 1–7 (*Expo. Euang.* 28, 29) The Resurrection	
Mark 16. 14–20 (*Expo. Euang.* 32, 33) The Ascension	
Luke 1. 57–68 (*Expo. Euang.* 41, 42) The nativity of John the Baptist	Luke 14. 16–24 (*Expo. Euang.* 39, 40) The great supper
Luke 2. 1–14 (*Expo. Euang.* 7, 8) Christmas	Luke 15. 11–32 (*Expo. Euang.* 26, 27) The prodigal son
Luke 2. 22–32 (*Expo. Euang.* 20, 21) The purification	Luke 16. 1–9 (*Expo. Euang.* 1, 2) The dishonest steward
Luke 2. 42–52 (*Expo. Euang.* 14, 15) Jesus in the temple	Luke 16. 19–31 (*Expo. Euang.* 37, 38) Lazarus and the rich man
Luke 5. 1–11 (*Expo. Euang.* 43, 44, 45) The miraculous catch	Luke 18. 10–14 (*Expo. Euang.* 51, 52) The Pharisee and the publican
Luke 19. 1–10 (*Expo. Euang.* 57, 58) Zacchaeus	Luke 21. 29–31 (included in 21. 25–33) The fig tree (*Expo. Euang.* 53, 54, 55, 56)
Luke 19. 41–47 (*Expo. Euang.* 46, 47, 48) Jesus expels the money changers	
John 1. 1–14 (*Expo. Euang.* 9) The prologue	
John 2. 1–11 (*Expo. Euang.* 16, 17) The wedding at Cana	

John 3. 1–15 (*Expo. Euang.* 34, 35, 36) Nicodemus	
John 6. 1–14 (*Expo. Euang.* 3, 4) Feeding the five thousand	
John 10. 11–16 (*Expo. Euang.* 30, 31) The good shepherd	

Are there any similar homilies outside this collection of fifty-eight? Two additional Hildegardian writings bear the title *expositio*. Both expound Matthean passages: the first a simple catechetical explanation of the Lord's Prayer (Mt 6. 9–13); the second a teaching on the institution of the Eucharist (Mt 26. 26–29) with the incarnation and passion.[13] These two *expositiones* employ the sort of progressive exegesis that Hildegard develops in the *Expositiones euangeliorum*. However, each of these two homilies constitutes a single reading of the pericope, whereas in the *Expositiones euangeliorum* all but one pericope receive multiple interpretations that the *magistra* set forth in two to four texts. We are left to wonder if the collection was still in progress near the time of Hildegard's death and what sort of reading Hildegard might have offered had she completed parallel commentaries for the two Matthean texts.

Do the *Expositiones euangeliorum*, like Hildegard's treatises, open with a visionary preface that introduces God's voice speaking to the seer? Neither the *Expositiones euangeliorum* nor the two other homilies on Matthean texts open with a prefatory vision. What would explain the striking absence of such a visionary foreword? It may relate to the genre of the texts as running commentaries. It may also reflect their composition as a series of single expositions rather than one sequential work. Finally, the lack of a visionary mandate before the texts probably indicates that Hildegard felt no need to justify her authority for the scriptural commentary that she delivered regularly within a monastic community.

The Exegetical Visions: 1141, 1163, 1167

Although the *Expositiones euangeliorum* lack a visionary preface, God's voice in visions commanded Hildegard to undertake exegesis. The gift of the Holy Spirit, visionary and prophetic, grounded her exegetical authority. Scholars have examined

---

[13] *Epistolarium*, III, 383, 386, pp. 144–45, 149–51. On twelfth-century commentaries, see Nikolaus M. Häring, 'Commentary and Hermeneutics', in *Renaissance and Renewal in the Twelfth Century*, ed. by Robert L. Benson and Giles Constable with Carol D. Lanham, Medieval Academy Reprints for Teaching (Toronto: University of Toronto Press, 1991), pp. 173–200 (p. 189).

the accounts of her visions to determine what sort of experience she had.[14] Rarely does anyone underscore the exegetical mandate the seer received in the three decisive visions of 1141, 1163, and 1167. In 1141 Hildegard experienced a crucial turning point when a powerful vision instructed her to make known the revelations of divine light that she began receiving as a child.[15] The spirit filled her with light and heat, as if the sun shone its rays upon her. A voice from heaven stated the order to 'speak and write' three times. The self-portrait accompanying the Prologue to *Sciuias* depicts the *magistra*, clearly awake and lucid enough to write, as she receives the Spirit's inspiration, depicted by tongues of fire.[16] Hildegard refused the divine command for some time and was struck by severe illness. Counselled by Volmar and by one of her sisters, Richardis, Hildegard received permission from Abbot Kuno (1136–55) to accept the divine order.[17] As Barbara Newman states, 'What had begun as a child's idiosyncrasy, now became a prophetic mission.'[18]

From this divine calefaction, the *magistra* attained the sudden understanding of the spiritual sense of the Scriptures: 'And suddenly I knew the meaning of the exposition (*intellectum expositionis*) of the Psalter, the Gospels, and other catholic books from the volumes of the Old as well as the New Testaments.'[19] Hildegard

---

[14] See Madeline Caviness, 'Hildegard as Designer of the Illustrations to her Works', in *Context*, pp. 29–62 (p. 33), on views that Hildegard experienced migraine headaches that influenced the visual form of the visions.

[15] In the autobiographical account Hildegard composed, she states that she received a vision of light at age three. *V. Hild.*, II.2, pp. 22–23, lines 45–47: 'ac tercio etatis mee anno tantum lumen uidi, quod anima mea contremuit, sed pre infantia de his nichil proferre potui'; *Life of Hildegard*, p. 44. To Guibert of Gembloux, she specifies no age but *infantia* for receiving visions: *Epistolarium*, II, 103R, p. 261, lines 62–65: 'Ab infantia autem mea, ossibus et neruis et uenis meis nondum confortatis, uisionis huius munere in anima mea usque ad presens tempus semper fruor, cum iam plus quam septuaginta annorum sim.'

[16] *Sciuias*, p. 4, lines 43–47: 'Visiones uero quas uidi, non eas in somnis, nec dormiens, nec in phrenesi, nec corporeis oculis aut auribus exterioris hominis, nec in abditis locis percepi, sed eas uigilans et circumspecta in pura mente, oculis et auribus interioris hominis, in apertis locis, secundum uoluntatem Dei accepi.' See the discussion of mystical experience and the self-portrait in Richard Emmerson, 'The Representation of Antichrist in Hildegard of Bingen's *Scivias*', *Gesta*, 41 (2002), 95–110 (pp. 105–06).

[17] *Sciuias*, p. 5, lines 84–85: 'testimonio cuiusdam nobilis et bonorum morum puellae et hominis illius, quem [. . .] quaesieram et inueneram'.

[18] Barbara J. Newman, 'Hildegard of Bingen: Visions and Validation', *Church History*, 54 (1985), 163–75 (p. 166).

[19] *Sciuias*, pp. 3–4, lines 24–33: 'Factum est in millesimo centesimo quadragesimo primo Filii Dei Iesu Christi incarnationis anno, cum quadraginta duorum annorum septemque mensium

specifies that she did not possess a command of 'the interpretation of the words in the text, the division of syllables, the cases and tenses'.[20] This statement arguably refers not simply to schooling in grammar, as many have observed, but also to exegetical training or education in interpreting the sacred page (*interpretationem uerborum textus eorum*). Hildegard probably distinguished between exegetical training including syntactical analysis, which was acquired in the schools (*interpretationem uerborum textus*), and the spiritual understanding of Scripture (*interior intelligentia*) that came from her instant enkindling.[21]

Hildegard made clear in her letter to Guibert of Gembloux that she wrote precisely what she saw and heard in her visions: 'And the things that I write, I see and hear through visions, and I write no words other than those that I hear.'[22] Moreover, Hildegard emphasized her extraordinary memory; although untaught about the substance of her visions, she retained their every detail:

> Whatever I have seen or learned from this vision I hold in my memory for a long time, so that I remember that I saw and heard it at some time. I see and hear and know simultaneously, and I learn as if in an instant what I know. But what I do not see, I do not know, because I am untaught.[23]

essem, maximae coruscationis igneum lumen aperto caelo ueniens totum cerebrum meum transfudit et totum cor totumque pectus meum uelut flamma non tamen ardens sed calens ita inflammauit, ut sol rem aliquam calefacit super quam radios suos ponit. Et repente intellectum expositionis librorum, uidelicet psalterii, euangelii et aliorum catholicorum tam ueteris quam noui Testamenti uoluminum sapiebam.'

[20] *Sciuias*, p. 4, lines 33–35: 'non autem interpretationem uerborum textus eorum nec diuisionem syllabarum nec cognitionem casuum aut temporum habebam'.

[21] See also *Epistolarium*, I, 1, p. 4, lines 17–19: 'Scio enim in textu interiorem intelligentiam expositionis librorum, uidelicet psalterii, euangelii et aliorum uoluminum, que monstrantur mihi de hac uisione.'

[22] *Epistolarium*, II, 103R, p. 262, lines 88–90: 'Et ea que scribo, illa in uisione uideo et audio, nec alia uerba pono quam illa que audio.' Barbara Newman analyzes this description in terms of Augustine's writing on visions in *De Genesi ad litteram*. See Newman, 'Hildegard of Bingen: Visions and Validation', pp. 168, 170; Kent Kraft, 'The Eye Sees More than the Heart Knows: The Visionary Cosmology of Hildegard of Bingen' (unpublished doctoral dissertation, University of Wisconsin, 1977).

[23] *Epistolarium*, II, 103R, pp. 261–62, lines 84–88: 'Quicquid autem in hac uisione uidero seu didicero, huius memoriam per longum tempus habeo, ita quod, quoniam illud aliquando uiderim et audierim, recordor. Et simul uideo et audio ac scio, et quasi in momento hoc quod scio disco. Quod autem non uideo, illud nescio, quia indocta sum.'

The seer's assertion, 'indocta sum', affirms to Guibert, who was educated in Paris, that her knowledge came from her visions and not from school texts. Later the seer expanded the range of enlightenment brought in the 1141 vision, when she added the writings of prophets, saints, and philosophers to the list of texts she understood: 'By that vision I understood the writings of the prophets, the Gospels, and of other saints and certain philosophers, without any human teaching, and I expounded on certain of those.'[24] Which saints and philosophers Hildegard comprehended remains a matter for conjecture. A letter expounding the book of Ezekiel testifies to her comprehension of that prophet's book, and her biographer Theodoric compares her to Daniel when she wondrously interprets letters found on an altar cloth.[25]

---

[24] *V. Hild.*, II.2, p. 24, lines 88–90: 'In eadem uisione scripta prophetarum, euangeliorum, et aliorum sanctorum, et quorundam philosophorum, sine ulla humana doctrina intellexi, ac quedam ex illis exposui.' On philological evidence for Hildegard's knowledge of certain philosophical texts, see Peter Dronke, 'Introduction', *LDO*, pp. xiii–xxxv; and the earlier 'Problemata Hildegardiana', *Mittellateinisches Jahrbuch*, 16 (1981), 97–131 (pp. 107–14), where Dronke suggests that Hildegard's cosmology may have been influenced by a knowledge of various texts: Lucan, namely the notion of 'cosmic sympathy'; Seneca's *Quaestiones naturales*, II.6; Cicero's *De natura deorum*; or Origen's *De principiis*. Dronke also points out (ibid., p. 107) that Hildegard's claim to understanding texts without formal training recalls similar words from Augustine (*Confessiones*, IV.16) on his intuitive comprehension of Aristotle's categories. On Hildegard's representation of the figure of Philosophy, see Barbara J. Newman, *Sister of Wisdom: St. Hildegard of Bingen's Theology of the Feminine* (Berkeley: University of California Press, 1997), pp. 83–87. Constant J. Mews, 'Hildegard and the Schools', in *Context*, pp. 89–110 (pp. 99–100), points out that in writing to Bernard, who was pursuing Abelard, Hildegard was careful not to describe herself as learned.

[25] On Ezekiel, see *Epistolarium*, I, 84R, p. 190, lines 7–11. *V. Hild.*, I.9, p. 16, lines 3–5; *Life of Hildegard*, p. 79. On the rich depiction of Ezekiel in Hildegard's culture, see Anne Derbes, 'The Frescoes of Schwarzrheindorf, Arnold of Wied, and the Second Crusade', in *The Second Crusade and the Cistercians*, ed. by Michael Gervers (New York: St Martin's Press, 1992), pp. 141–54; and Wilhelm Neuss, *Das Buch Ezechiel in Theologie und Kunst bis zum Ende des XII. Jahrhunderts, mit besonderer Berücksichtigung der Gemälde in der Kirche zu Schwarzrheindorf; ein Beitrag zur Entwicklungsgeschichte der Typologie der christlichen Kunst, vornehmlich in den Benediktinerklöstern, von dr. theol. Wilhelm Neuss [. . .] Mit 86 abbildungen, gedruckt mit Unterstützung der Provinzialverwaltung der Rheinprovinz.*(Münster in Westf.: Aschendorff, 1912), pp. 114–31, 265–97. I am grateful to Jeffrey Hamburger for introducing me to Neuss's work. The Daniel motif also appears in the work of Hildegard's near contemporary, the learned Rupert of Deutz. In the prologue to *De uictoria Dei*, Rupert recounts that he explained the vision of Daniel to his abbot, who was so pleased with the interpretation that he requested Rupert to compose a work on the victory of the word of God. *De uictoria Dei*, ed. by R. Haacke, MGH, Quellen zur Geistesgeschichte des Mittelalters, 5 (Weimar: Herman Böhlaus Nachfolger, 1970), Prologus, pp. 1–3. Theodoric probably reveals a debt to Rupert of Deutz and perhaps the intent to place Hildegard squarely in Rupert's visionary footsteps.

St Augustine asserts that Daniel saw images in the spirit and understood them intellectually, as when he received a revelation about the content and the meaning of the dream of King Nebuchadnezzar.[26] Similarly, Hildegard provides a visual copy and a verbal description of the image; then, through the Voice from heaven, she comments upon it, much as if the Voice were exegeting a text, or even preaching a sermon on the vision. The exegesis of the vision prompts Richard Emmerson to argue that the visions as we have them in *Sciuias* reflect the product of 'retrospective interpretation', which took shape over a long period of time, as Hildegard discussed and received assistance with the description of her vision.[27] The same argument can be made for her other works that result from visionary enlightenment.

Hildegard recounted two additional visions that furthered her understanding of Scripture: a powerful 1163 vision, described in the prologue to the *Liber diuinorum operum*, opened her first understanding of Genesis 1 and John 1 even while it shook her profoundly and made her ill; and a gentler 1167 vision, portrayed in the *Vita Hildegardis*, heightened her comprehension of those texts to such a degree that she could no longer refrain from writing the *Liber diuinorum operum*.[28] The

---

[26] Daniel 2–4. Augustine of Hippo, *De Genesi ad litteram libri duodecim*, 12. 9, ed. by J. Zycha, CSEL, 28.1 (Vienna, 1894). See Claire L. Sahlin, *Birgitta of Sweden and the Voice of Prophecy* (Woodbridge: Boydell and Brewer, 2001), pp. 69–70.

[27] See Emmerson's application of Peter Moore's analysis in 'The Representation of Antichrist', pp. 105–06. Peter Moore, 'Mystical Experience, Mystical Doctrine, Mystical Technique', in *Mysticism and Philosophical Analysis*, ed. by S. Katz (New York: Sheldon, 1978), pp. 101–31 (pp. 108–09), distinguishes the four elements of 'raw experience', 'incorporated interpretation', 'reflexive interpretation' (including elements 'spontaneously formulated either during the experience itself or immediately afterwards'), and 'retrospective interpretation'. On the primacy of the visions, see also Caviness, 'Hildegard as Designer', pp. 29–41; Madeline Caviness, 'Artist: "To See, Hear, and Know All at Once"', in *Voice*, pp. 110–24 (p. 112).

[28] Hildegard states in the Prologue that she was sixty-five years old (hence 1163) when she felt compelled to write down these visions, the first of which occurred in 1163, when she had just completed the *Vite mer*. See *LDO*, p. 45, lines 5–14: 'qui primus annus exordium presentium uisionum fuit, cum sexaginta quinque annorum essem, tanti misterii et fortitudinis uisionem uidi, ut tota contremiscerem et pre fragilitate corporis mei inde egrotare inciperem. Quam uisionem tandem per septem annos scribendo uix consummaui. Itaque in millesimo centesimo sexagesimo tercio Dominice incarnationis anno [. . .] uox de celo facta est ad me, dicens.' *V. Hild.*, II.16, p. 43, lines 1–10: 'Subsequenti demum tempore mysticum et mirificam uisionem uidi, ita quod omnia uiscera mea concussa sunt et sensualitas corporis mei extincta est, quoniam scientia mea in alium modum conuersa est, quasi me nescirem. Et de Dei inspiratione in scientiam anime mee quasi gutte suauis pluuie spargebantur, quia et Spiritus Sanctus Iohannem euangelistam imbuit, cum de pectore Iesu profundissimam reuelationem suxit, ubi sensus ipsius sancta diuinitate ita tactus est, quod absconsa mysteria et opera aperuit, "In principio erat uerbum", et cetera'; *Life of Hildegard*, pp. 66–67.

seer consistently avoided claiming her own learning as the source for her understanding of Scripture. She protested repeatedly that she was unlearned (*indocta*),
and she and Theodoric place her in the line of Daniel, Ezekiel, and John the Evangelist as an interpreter of divinely revealed images.

Hildegard's description of her 1141 vision places it into the Augustinian category of *uisio intellectualis*, with no connection to the senses or to images that the
spirit perceives.[29] Clearly her visions are not corporeal, that is Hildegard does not
associate them or their origin with any physical object. In this she differs from her
Benedictine predecessor, Rupert of Deutz (1070–1129/30). While a series of
visions stimulated Rupert's lifelong devotion to exegesis, as they did for Hildegard,
in his case the cross arguably served as a catalyst to conversion and ordination. After kissing a wooden cross adorned with an image of Christ, Rupert saw the Saviour
with inner eyes. A subsequent mystical experience filled him with something like
liquid gold and set him on the path of writing without ceasing. Moreover, unlike
Hildegard, Rupert states that his vision came to him in a dream.[30]

For later visionaries such as Gertrude the Great and Julian of Norwich, the link
between the physical and mystical held tightly. Hildegard's contemporary Elisabeth
of Schönau meditated on the passion of Christ and received visions in response to
liturgical singing. Gertrude the Great (1256–1301/02), author of the *Legatus diuinae
pietatis* (*Herald of Divine Love*), meditated on an image of the crucifix in her prayerbook, which led to the vision of an arrow coming forth and piercing her heart.[31]
Julian of Norwich (*c*. 1342–*c*. 1416), during a serious illness, gazed upon a crucifix
held up by her parish priest and received a series of visions from God, which she
called showings.[32] Both Gertrude and Julian exemplify the tendency for women and
men to meditate on the passion. The focus on the human suffering of Jesus took hold

---

[29] See Bernard McGinn, 'Hildegard of Bingen as Visionary and Exegete', in *Umfeld*, pp.
321–50 (pp. 329–31). See also Bernard McGinn, *The Presence of God: A History of Western
Christian Mysticism*, 4 vols (New York: Crossroad, 1996), II: *The Growth of Mysticism*, 333–36.

[30] Rupert of Deutz, *De gloria et honore Filii hominis super Mattheum*, ed. by R. Haacke,
CCCM, 29 (Turnhout: Brepols, 1979), p. 378, lines 603–09; p. 379, line 630; p. 382, lines
742–46; pp. 651–53 (dream). Gregory the Great, *Dialogues*, Book 4, cap. 48, *PL* 77: 409–12, states
that it is difficult to discern whether dreams are God-sent visions or demon-inspired illusions. See
Sahlin, *Birgitta of Sweden*, p. 64.

[31] Gertrude of Helfta, *The Herald of Divine Love*, trans. by Margaret Winkworth (New York:
Paulist Press, 1993), Book 2.5, pp. 101–02.

[32] Julian of Norwich, *A Book of Showings to the Anchoress Julian of Norwich*, ed. by Edmund
Colledge and James Walsh, 2 vols (Toronto: Pontifical Institute of Mediaeval Studies, 1978), I,
128, 180.

in the twelfth century and became increasingly realistic and dramatic in the late Middle Ages.[33] In contrast, relatively little of this contemplation on the passion appears in Hildegard's works.[34] That the seer attributes her exegetical authority to intellectual and not corporeal visions such as those of her male predecessor Rupert of Deutz makes her claim and practice of exegetical knowledge all the more remarkable.

Women, the Spirit, and the Terminology for Preaching

Why did Hildegard's descriptions of her visionary knowledge avoid any claim that her own learning was the source for her comprehension of Scripture? Such a claim reflects the contemporary monastic tension with the schools; in addition, it undoubtedly shielded her from suspicions of transgressing gender bounds on religious discourse. Guibert of Gembloux replied to Hildegard's description of her Spirit-given exegetical understanding with the assertion, through the voice of a 'certain monk', that the gift of the Spirit freed Hildegard from the scripturally based restrictions on women's speech:

> The apostle does not allow a woman to teach in the Church; but this woman, through receiving the Spirit, has been freed from that condition and instructed by the Spirit's teaching. In her heart through her own wisdom she has learned by experience what is written: 'Blessed is the person whom you have instructed, Lord, and you have taught him from your law' (Ps 93. 12).[35]

---

[33] See Giles Constable, 'The Ideal of the Imitation of Christ', in *Three Studies in Medieval Religious and Social Thought* (Cambridge: Cambridge University Press, 1995), pp. 143–248 (pp. 158, 162–64, 181, 209–10). Rachel Fulton, *From Judgment to Passion: Devotion to Christ and the Virgin Mary 800–1200* (New York: Columbia University Press, 2002), esp. pp. 142–92. Hildegard's contemporary, Aelred of Rievaulx compares the Cistercian Order to the cross: 'Iam ipsa crux Christi sit quasi speculum Christiani [. . .]. Ordo noster crux Christi est.' *Sermones I–XLVI: Collectio Claraeuallensis prima et secunda*, ed. by G. Raciti, CCCM, 2A (Turnhout: Brepols, 1989), pp. 87–88. On female visionaries' responses to Christ's face, notably Gertrude of Helfta, Mechthild of Hackeborn, and Julian of Norwich, see Jeffrey Hamburger, 'Vision and the Veronica', in *The Visual and the Visionary: Art and Female Spirituality in Late Medieval Germany* (New York: Zone, 1998), pp. 350–70.

[34] I am grateful to Felix Heinzer for highlighting this contrast between Hildegard and Elisabeth in his lecture, 'Unequal Twins: Hildegard of Bingen and Elisabeth of Schonau — Visionary Attitude and Monastic Culture in Twelfth-Century Germany', 23 October 2006, Humanities Center Seminar on Medieval Studies, Harvard University.

[35] Guibert of Gembloux, *Epistolae quae in codice B. R. Brux. 5527–5534 inueniuntur*, ed. by A. Derolez, E. Dekkers, and R. Demeulenaere, CCCM, 66, 66A (Turnhout: Brepols, 1988–89), I, 18, p. 232, lines 240–44: 'Mulierem in ecclesia docere non permittit apostolus; sed hec, per

Guibert refers to the injunction against women teaching in the public venue of the Church; a summary of I Corinthians 14. 33b–35.[36] He probably expressed his own view under the cloak of anonymity. The freedom Hildegard enjoyed from the 'condition' imposed by Pauline injunctions proves quite unusual by medieval norms. The utterance of a religious discourse by a woman to an audience has provoked controversy for centuries.[37] Guibert's remark about Hildegard probably indicates that someone objected to her teaching and preaching.[38] Moreover, her biographer Theodoric declares not that she preached but that she 'announced the things which God wanted' and 'proclaimed' things which pertained to the good of souls.[39]

Are these cautious semantics particular to Hildegard's biography? In fact, other biographies of medieval women saints demonstrate a similar strategy to skirt the terminology of preaching.[40] The biographer of Leoba (d. 779) recorded that she 'spoke' 'wise counsels', gave 'spiritual instruction' to her nuns, 'discussed spiritual matters' with princes and prelates, and sometimes 'held a conversation' with the

---

assumptionem spiritus ab hac conditione soluta et per eius magisterium erudita, corde in sapientia propria didicit experientia quod scriptum est: "Beatus homo quem tu erudieris, Domine, et de lege tua docueris eum".' This statement has erroneously been attributed to Robert of Val-Roi, whose words are reported on pp. 229–30 in the same letter. On p. 230, line 158, Guibert introduces the thoughts of a certain other person, 'alius quidam'.

[36] Current biblical scholars identify the passage as an interpolation by a later author or scribe. See Karen King, 'Afterword; Voices of the Spirit: Exercising Power, Embracing Responsibility', in *Women Preachers and Prophets Through Two Millennia of Christianity*, ed. by B. Kienzle and P. J. Walker (Berkeley: University of California Press, 1998), pp. 335–43 (p. 336).

[37] For a fuller treatment of this topic, see Beverly M. Kienzle, 'Sermons and Preaching', in *Women and Gender in Medieval Europe: An Encyclopedia* (New York: Routledge, 2006), pp. 736–40; the articles in *Women Preachers and Prophets*, ed. by Kienzle and Walker; Alcuin Blamires, 'Women and Preaching in Medieval Orthodoxy, Heresy, and Saints' Lives', *Viator*, 26 (1995), 135–52; Alistair Minnis, 'De impedimento sexus: Women's Bodies and Medieval Impediments to Female Ordination', in *Medieval Theology and the Natural Body*, ed. by P. Biller and A. J. Minnis, York Studies in Medieval Theology, 1 (Woodbridge: York Medieval Press, 1997), pp. 109–39; Claire Waters, *Angels and Earthly Creatures: Preaching, Performance and Gender in the Later Middle Ages* (Philadelphia: University of Pennsylvania Press, 2004).

[38] See Newman, 'Hildegard of Bingen: Visions and Validation', p. 171, on Hildegard's detractors.

[39] *V. Hild.*, III.17, pp. 54–55; *Life of Hildegard*, p. 79.

[40] In medieval discussions, that discourse itself was variously termed teaching or preaching, yet the two are separated only with difficulty. See Beverly Mayne Kienzle, 'Preaching as Touchstone of Orthodoxy and Dissidence in the Middle Ages', *Medieval Sermon Studies*, 43 (1999), 18–53 (pp. 33–40); Kienzle, 'Preface: Authority and Definition', in *Women Preachers and Prophets*, ed. by Kienzle and Walker, pp. xiii–xiv.

brothers at Fulda.[41] The *Vita* of Liutberga (d. 870) recounts briefly that she gave any spare time she had to instructing the women who came to her cell.[42] Such semantic strategies reflect centuries of tension over women's leadership in the Church and the development in the Middle Ages of legislated prohibitions against women's speech, repeating Pauline injunctions.[43]

Do we know anything about other nuns preaching in Hildegard's day? Nuns at the Benedictine double monastery of Admont in Austria preached in their chapter meeting on feast days when the abbot or his deputy was unable to be present. Two manuscripts of feast-day sermons from Admont feature portraits of nuns, one holding a book and the other preaching. Abbot Irimbert (1172–76) praised the nuns' skill in exegesis and probably benefited from their input in composing his scriptural commentaries.[44] At other monasteries in Germany and Austria, women taught and learned from *magistrae* and collaborated with men on the production of manuscripts if not sermons.[45] In contrast, Hildegard's contemporary Sigewize tried to emulate the *magistra*'s preaching and was judged to be possessed.[46]

---

[41] Rudolf of Fulda, *The Life of Saint Leoba*, in *The Anglo-Saxon Missionaries in Germany*, trans. and ed. by C. H. Talbot (New York: Sheed and Ward, 1954), pp. 212, 218, 223.

[42] *Vita S. Liutberga*, in *Annales, chronica et historiae aevi Carolinii et Saxonici*, ed. by Georg H. Pertz, MGH SS, 4 (Hannover, 1902), pp. 158–64.

[43] See Ann Graham Brock, *Mary Magdalene, The First Apostle: The Struggle for Authority*, Harvard Theological Studies, 51 (Cambridge, MA: Harvard University Press, 2003); Karen King, 'The Gospel of Mary Magdalene', in *Searching the Scriptures: A Feminist Commentary*, ed. by Elisabeth Schüssler Fiorenza, vol. II (New York: Crossroad, 1994), pp. 601–34; King, 'Prophetic Power and Women's Authority: The Case of the *Gospel of Mary* (Magdalene)', in *Women Preachers and Prophets*, ed. by Kienzle and Walker, pp. 21–41; and King, 'Afterword: Voices of the Spirit', pp. 335–43. See Elisabeth Schüssler Fiorenza, *In Memory of Her: A Feminist Theological Reconstruction of Christian Origins* (New York: Crossroads, 1983), p. 51.

[44] See Alison I. Beach, *Women as Scribes: Book Production and Monastic Reform in Twelfth-Century Bavaria* (Cambridge: Cambridge University Press, 2004); Stephan Borgehammar, 'Who Wrote the Admont Sermon Corpus — Gottfried the Abbot, his Brother Irimbert, or the Nuns?', in *De l'homélie au sermon: Histoire de la prédication médiévale*, ed. by Jacqueline Hamesse and Xavier Herman, Textes, Études, Congres, 14 (Louvain-la-Neuve: F.I.D.E.M., 1993), pp. 47–52; and F. P. Knapp, *Admonter Predigten und Bibelkommentare, Die Literatur des früh- und Hochmittelaters in den Bistümern Passau, Salzburg, Brixen und Trient von den Anfängen bis zum Jahre 1273* (Graz: Akademischer Druck, 1994), pp. 74–78.

[45] *Manuscripts and Monastic Culture: Reform and Renewal in Twelfth-Century Germany*, ed. by Alison I. Beach, Medieval Church Studies, 13 (Turnhout: Brepols, 2007).

[46] Barbara J. Newman, 'Three-Part Invention: The *Vita S. Hildegardis* and Mystical Hagiography', in *Context*, pp. 189–210; Barbara J. Newman, 'Possessed by the Spirit: Devout Women,

Did the cloister then provide women greater freedom for intellectual activity? Within communities of religious women, teaching and learning apparently took place in greater freedom than outside convent walls. Herrad of Hohenbourg (d. after 1196), an Augustinian canoness, compiled a manual for the education of religious women that consists of carefully arranged and edited excerpts for texts read in the schools. While the learned canoness made no teaching or preaching journeys outside the monastery, as far as we know, she drew heavily on the works of preachers and cast her work to some degree in the genre of a sermon.[47] Caroline Bynum, writing about thirteenth-century nuns at Helfta, suggests that women who 'grew up in monasteries were less likely to be influenced by the contemporary stereotype of woman as morally and intellectually inferior'.[48] Gertrude of Helfta provided spiritual advice to visitors, even in oral discourses which may be considered a form of preaching.[49] Her writing and the community's production of texts also constitute an interesting parallel to Hildegard, her texts and images. Expanding research on religious women, notably in German-speaking lands, no longer makes it valid to see Hildegard as completely unique or a phenomenon without context.[50]

Visionaries from the Rhineland and other parts of Europe followed Hildegard's precedent, at the same time that women outside religious orders came under increasing suspicion.[51] Visionaries claimed their revelations as direct authorization to make themselves heard through written or spoken sermons. Italian saints such as Rose of Viterbo, Umiltà of Faenza, and Angela of Foligno illustrate a variety of ways in which women were called by the Spirit to express their voices.[52] Catherine

Demoniacs, and the Apostolic Life in the Thirteenth Century', *Speculum*, 73 (1998), 733–70 (pp. 753–55).

[47] Fiona Griffiths, *The Garden of Delights: Reform and Renaissance for Women in the Twelfth Century* (Philadelphia: University of Pennsylvania Press, 2006).

[48] Caroline Walker Bynum, *Jesus as Mother: Studies in the Spirituality of the High Middle Ages* (Berkeley: University of California Press, 1982), p. 185, suggests that women who grew up in the cloister were more confident than those who grew up in the misogynist world.

[49] See Gertrude of Helfta, *Herald of Divine Love*, Book 1, pp. 53–54.

[50] Griffiths, *Garden of Delights*, pp. 12–15, on women in the Empire.

[51] Walter Simons, *Cities of Ladies: Beguine Communities in the Medieval Low Countries, 1200–1565* (Philadelphia: University of Pennsylvania Press, 2001).

[52] On female Franciscan preaching, see Bert Roest, 'Female Preaching in the Late Medieval Franciscan Tradition', *Franciscan Studies*, 62 (2004), 119–54; Roberto Rusconi, 'Women's Sermons at the End of the Middle Ages: Texts from the Blessed and Images of the Saints', in *Women Preachers and Prophets*, ed. by Kienzle and Walker, pp. 173–95, plates 9.12 and 9.13; *Medieval*

of Siena, who joined a lay order in her native city, developed a community-based apostolate that became more and more public. She achieved a level of recognition that provides an interesting comparison to Hildegard, as she advocated a new crusade while trying to gain peace between Pope Gregory XI and the city of Florence. She finally persuaded the Pope to leave Avignon for Rome, and after his death and the beginning of the Great Schism (1378), she served as adviser to his successor in Rome, Urban VI.[53]

The tensions surrounding women's religious speech over the centuries, be it preaching, prophecy, or teaching, make Hildegard's preserved sermons and her travels to preach to other communities all the more remarkable. Even within supportive religious environments, no other women and indeed few men achieved the level of Hildegard's literary and artistic production. In the twelfth-century Rhineland, where visions and erudition were not out of the ordinary, Hildegard was exceptional in regard to her extensive *opera* and her preaching in cathedrals and other religious houses. The visionary understanding of Scripture inspired and underlay all her writings, but most notably the *Expositiones euangeliorum*.

Review of Scholarship

The present volume is the first comprehensive study of the *Expositiones euangeliorum*. The lack of scholarly attention to the *Expositiones* may indicate that readers have shared the sentiments of the scholarly abbot Johannes Trithemius, who found the *Expositiones* 'very obscure and intelligible only to the devout and learned'

Women's Visionary Literature, ed. by Elizabeth Alvilda Petroff (New York: Oxford University Press, 1986), p. 236; Catherine Mooney, 'The Authorial Role of Brother A. in the Composition of Angela of Foligno's Revelations', in *Creative Women in Medieval and Early Modern Italy: A Religious and Artistic Renaissance*, ed. by E. Ann Matter and John Coakley (Philadelphia: University of Pennsylvania Press, 1990), pp. 34–63.

[53] See F. Thomas Luongo, *The Saintly Politics of Catherine of Siena* (Ithaca: Cornell University Press, 2006); Renate Blumenfeld-Kosinski, *Poets, Saints, and Visionaries of the Great Schism, 1378–1417* (University Park: Pennsylvania State University Press, 2007), pp. 46–54; John Coakley, *Women, Men, and Spiritual Power: Female Saints and their Collaborators* (New York: Columbia University Press, 2006), pp. 170–92; Karen Scott, 'Urban Spaces, Women's Networks, and the Lay Apostolate in the Siena of Catherine Benincasa', in *Creative Women in Medieval and Early Modern Italy*, ed. by Matter and Coakley, pp. 105–19; Scott, 'Mystical Death, Bodily Death: Catherine of Siena and Raymond of Capua on the Mystic's Encounter with God', in *Gendered Voices: Medieval Saints and their Interpreters*, ed. by Catherine M. Mooney (Philadelphia: University of Pennsylvania Press, 1999), pp. 136–67.

('ualde obscuras et nisi deuotis et eruditis intelligibiles'). Nonetheless, Trithemius also found the texts 'very subtle, difficult and profound' ('multum subtiles, difficiles et profundas'). Hildegard, in his view, could not have possibly written herself the homilies, letters, and saints lives. He concluded that her secretary must have either had them written, or written them himself.[54]

A handful of scholars include the *Expositiones* in broader studies and fewer have attempted to penetrate their 'very obscure' commentary.[55] A more extensive review of related scholarship precedes the Select Bibliography for this volume. Here I shall discuss only the work most relevant to the *Expositiones*.

Peter Dronke analyzes three *expositiones*, focusing on allegories that he considers '"Platonic" in more than one sense', those where Hildegard constructs 'fables' of microcosm and macrocosm.[56] He identifies some possible sources,[57] and he

---

[54] Johannes Trithemius, *Opera historica*, ed. by Freher: *Catalogus illustrium virorum*, I, 138; *Chronica insignis monasterii Hirsaugiensis*, II, 134: 'In octo et quinquaginta Euangelia dominicalia per circulum anni homilias, totidem multum subtiles, difficiles et profundas'; *Chronicon monasterii Sponheimense*, ad annum 1179, II, 257: 'Inter caetera uero eius uolumina, magnum in eodem loco uolumen, et epistolas eius ad diuersos, Homilias, uitas sanctoruum et alia quae diuinitus edocta edidit, continet; quod moniales istius loci manu eam propria manu scripsisse falso confirmant, cum et latini sermonis fuerit ignara, et ad scribendum propter crebras infirmitates et humidum caput penitus indisposita. Nihil enim eorum, quae ibi ostenduntur hodie, propria manu scripsisse credendum est; quippe cum nesciret scribere; sed praefatus monachus omnia uel scripsit uel scribi procurauit.'

[55] Newman, *Sister of Wisdom*, pp. 94–95, on John 2. 4; pp. 171–72 on John 1. 14; p. 184 on Matthew 1. 18–21. Fabio Chávez-Alvarez, *'Die brennende Vernunft': Studien zur Semantik der 'rationalitas' bei Hildegard von Bingen* (Stuttgart-Bad Cannstatt: Friederich Frommann, Günther Holzboog, 1991). Reviewed by John van Engen, *Speculum*, 69 (1994), 757–58. Hildegard Gosebrink, *Maria in der Theologie Hildegards von Bingen* (Würzburg: Echter, 2004). Michael Embach, *Die Schriften Hildegards von Bingen: Studien zu ihrer Überlieferung und Rezeption im Mittelalter und in der Frühen Neuzeit* (Berlin: Akademie, 2003). Uwe Brunn, *Des contestataires aux 'cathares': Discours de réforme et propagande antihérétique dans les pays du Rhin et de la Meuse avant l'Inquisition*, Collection des Études Augustiniennes: Moyen Âge et Temps Modernes, 41 (Paris: Institut d'Études Augustiniennes, 2006).

[56] Peter Dronke, 'Platonic-Christian Allegories in the Homilies of Hildegard of Bingen', in *From Athens to Chartres: Neoplatonism and Medieval Thought: Studies in Honour of Edouard Jeauneau*, ed. by Haijo Jan Westra (Leiden: Brill, 1992), pp. 381–96 (p. 383). Ernest Benz, *Die Vision: Erfahrungsformen und Bilderwelt* (Stuttgart: Klett, 1969) also discusses Hildegard's *Lehrvisionen* and compares them to those of St John in the Book of Revelation, Hermas, Julian of Norwich, and Swedenborg. See Newman, 'Hildegard of Bingen: Visions and Validation', p. 169.

[57] Dronke studies the *expositiones* on Luke 2. 1–14; John 1. 1–14; Matthew 20. 1–16; and Luke 15. 11–32, in 'Platonic-Christian Allegories', pp. 385–96.

observes 'the technique of systematic allegorising' in the homilies, for which he proposes the distinctions of microcosmic or psychological interpretations, and macrocosmic or cosmological.[58] He remarks that Hildegard turns the parable of the householder (Mt 20. 1–16) 'into a new kind of *figura*': the opening of the Old Testament is what she sees fulfilled in the New Testament narrative; she 'achieves a *tour de force* of recounting two disparate narratives simultaneously'.[59] Elsewhere Dronke points to Hildegard's mention of Origen in one of the *Expositiones* and suggests that 'hints' of her interpretations can be found in earlier works.[60] Dronke allows for Hildegard's reliance on 'traditional allegorical meanings',[61] but he does not explore the influence of liturgical reading and Hildegard's aural reception of the texts, whereas Sr Angela Carlevaris, in 'Ildegarda e la patristica' (1998), asserts that Hildegard gained access to her sources primarily through the liturgy.[62]

The 1998 anniversary of Hildegard's birth generated much research, including two further articles relevant to the *Expositiones*.[63] Bernard McGinn asserts that what makes Hildegard genuinely unique is not her visionary experience but her exegesis. Based on a survey of exegetical material in the visionary works, he argues that a new shape of commentary in the *Liber diuinorum operum* reveals a Hildegard emboldened after the 1167 vision she recounted in the *Vita*.[64] McGinn also considers

---

[58] Dronke looks briefly at the *Expositiones* in 'The Allegorical World Picture of Hildegard of Bingen: Revaluations and New Problems', in *Context*, pp. 1–16 (pp. 3–6), where he proposes five techniques of Hildegard's allegory: (1) establishment of allegorical correspondence; (2–4) self-revelation: gradual, direct, and allegory within allegory; and (5) allegoresis — allegorical reading of the sacred text.

[59] Dronke, 'Platonic-Christian Allegories', p. 391.

[60] Dronke, 'Problemata Hildegardiana', p. 114.

[61] Dronke, 'Platonic-Christian Allegories', p. 384.

[62] Angela Carlevaris, 'Ildegarda e la patristica', in *Angesicht*, pp. 65–80.

[63] On the anniversary volumes, see Franz J. Felten, 'Hildegard von Bingen, 1098–1998 — oder Was bringen Jubiläen für die Wissenschaft?', *Deutsches Archiv für Erforschung des Mittelalters*, 59 (2003), 165–94.

[64] McGinn, 'Hildegard of Bingen as Visionary and Exegete', p. 343. Sixteen per cent of passages in *Sciuias* and 8 per cent in the *Vite mer.* contain exegetical material appearing as 'piecemeal' commentary, that is generally serving as proof texts. That percentage increases to 25 in the *LDO*, John 1. 1–14, Revelation 6. 2–8, Revelation 12. 13–16, Genesis 1. 1–2/3, and II Thessalonians 2. 2–7. Moreover, numerous letters of Hildegard's tackle exegetical questions, and in many Hildegard evokes her visionary authority. On the exegetical material in the visionary works, see McGinn, 'Hildegard of Bingen as Visionary and Exegete', p. 343, and on the letters of the first two volumes of the *Epistolarium*, see ibid., pp. 336, 344, n. 71.

Hildegard in the context of Origen's reception and signals a few references that point to Hildegard's probable familiarity with Origen.[65] Joop van Banning establishes a classification for the level of scriptural interpretation that predominates in each of the *Expositiones*. He considers Hildegard's exegesis in the light of patristic biblical interpretation and the concerns of modern interpreters of Scripture, and he proposes three *expositiones* that argue for expanding the understanding of Hildegard's allegory beyond the Platonic categories suggested by Dronke.[66]

Chapter Outline

Clearly the obscurities of the *Expositiones euangeliorum* need clarification, for these texts constitute the centrepiece of the *magistra*'s exegesis and preaching. The present volume focuses on the *Expositiones* and situates the interpretation of Scripture at the core of Hildegard's thought and writings. The visions that led to the writing of *Sciuias* and the *Liber diuinorum operum* produced exegetical understanding that extended into the *Expositiones euangeliorum* and other works.

Chapter 1 surveys the political and cultural history of Hildegard's era to elucidate how her cultural milieu prepared and received her vocation as exegete and preacher. Struggles over reform and the Investiture Controversy occurred while monasteries and learning flourished in German-speaking lands. Visionary authority established precedent, and monastic communities, including houses of Benedictine and Augustinian women, devoted themselves to learning. Hildegard's early life and the assessment of her education must be understood in the light of the method and content of monastic learning. The chapter follows the course of Hildegard's works with an emphasis on the visionary understanding that drove her exegesis and preaching.

Chapter 2 considers Hildegard's access to patristic sources through the 'ear of the heart', the Divine Office, and the 'eye of the mind', written sources available to her through the monastic network of intellectual exchange. Her praise for patristic exegetes weighs against her criticism of contemporary teachers for their

---

[65] Bernard McGinn, 'The Spiritual Heritage of Origen in the West', in *Origene maestro di vita spirituale: Milano, 13–15 settembre 1999*, ed. by Luigi F. Pizzolato and Marco Rizzi (Milan: Vita e Pensiero, 2001), pp. 263–89 (pp. 279–82).

[66] Joop van Banning, 'Hildegard von Bingen als Theologin', in *Angesicht*, pp. 243–68, which will be discussed and compared to my interpretations in later chapters. Readers should note that van Banning's chart, p. 260, uses the numbering of the Pitra edition.

ignorance of the true inner knowledge of Scripture. The *magistra*'s articulation of the spiritual interpretation of Scripture, inherited from Origen, balances the procedure of explication according to the four senses of Scripture: literal-historical, allegorical, tropological, and anagogical. Echoes of Origenist language and themes sound in the *Expositiones*, and several homilies illustrate the impact of Gregory the Great on Hildegard's exegesis. In only a handful of *Expositiones* does the seer stress the literal sense of the pericope.

Chapter 3 centres on Hildegard's method of exegesis and education. A brief explanation of the *magistra*'s technique of commentary and the genre of the homily precedes the discussion of medieval monastic liturgy and education. Hildegard employs several specific types of glossing and incorporates them into a continuous narrative. The nearly contemporary homilies from Admont bear comparison to Hildegard's *Expositiones*. Even though both collections accent the tropological meaning of the Gospels, Hildegard's approach differs markedly from that of the Admont homilist(s). Moreover, the *magistra* develops and extends the voice of biblical characters. In Hildegard's dramatic narrative exegesis, the story unfolds like the acts of a drama voiced and performed by Hildegard herself as *magistra*, narrator, and interpreter.

Chapter 4 deals with Hildegard's remarkable historical vision: in many of the *expositiones*, she creates a three-act drama of salvation history. Hildegard's theology and representation of salvation history builds on Augustine's theology of history and bears comparison to several of her near contemporaries. Several *expositiones* reveal a Trinitarian framework; others span the course of history in one text; still more treat the three acts of salvation history separately. Several *expositiones* either evoke the end times or the vision of the heavenly Jerusalem.

Chapter 5 introduces the *Ordo uirtutum* and the literary and visual representations of the theme of virtue and vice. Comparisons between the *Expositiones* and the *Ordo* follow: semantic parallels reflect the notion of the virtues' battle against vices; and selected homilies indicate correspondences in theme and structure. Several specific virtues such as Fides, Humilitas, and Caritas reveal similar or complementary presentations in the two works. Hildegard uses the virtues as attributes, discusses them as abstractions, and in some cases, assigns them speaking roles in the *Expositiones*. Finally, certain *expositiones* centre on vices, whose personifications do not play a role in the *Ordo uirtutum*.

Chapter 6 explores Hildegard's anti-Cathar writings and the role that opposition to the Cathar heresy played in her theology of creation and Christology. Hildegard's anti-heretical and notably anti-Cathar writing is much more significant than previously recognized. The *magistra*'s exegesis undergirds the theology of creation and Christology which she opposes to Cathar beliefs; it also grounds the objections she makes to Cathar practices. She speaks through the image of the *uir preliator* (Is 42. 13), who defends the goodness of creation and the life-giving power of the Spirit.

In conclusion, writings from the 1170s, the last decade of Hildegard's life, demonstrate the intellectual confidence of age that she describes with the metaphor of marrow. The distinctive features of her exegesis stand out from the tradition of commentary by her predecessors and compare fruitfully with the preaching of her contemporary, Bernard of Clairvaux. Finally, the *Expositiones*, as a twelfth-century text written for a female audience, merits comparison with the earlier *Speculum uirginum* and the later *Hortus deliciarum* of Herrad of Hohenbourg, while it stands apart as an exegetical work composed by a woman.

Chapter 1

HILDEGARD'S MISSION, ITS BACKGROUND, AND ITS IMPLEMENTATION

For by the one thousand and one hundredth year after the incarnation of Christ, the teaching of the apostles and the burning righteousness which he had established in Christians and in the spiritual began to slacken and turn to wavering. It was in those times I was born.[1]

To understand why Hildegard described the time of her birth as a period when righteousness began to slacken and waver requires some examination of the power struggles between the Church and the Empire during the many decades of the Investiture Controversy. Those struggles were tightly intertwined with the history of Disibodenberg, the monastery where Hildegard was immured, and the family of Jutta of Sponheim, Hildegard's *magistra* there. The dynamics of political struggle as well as ecclesiastical reform and growth lie behind the urgency of Hildegard's prophetic claim to speak of 'new mysteries' in the Scriptures while the faith 'tottered' and the Gospel 'limped'.[2] This chapter looks briefly at the Investiture Controversy before tracing the progress of monastic reform and education — the religious culture that contributed to Hildegard's call to exegesis and preaching and to the implementation of her exegetical and homiletic mission. From *Sciuias* to the *Liber diuinorum operum*, to the *Expositiones* and the preaching journeys outside Rupertsberg, Hildegard expanded her writings and her audience.

---

[1] *V. Hild.*, II.2, p. 22, lines 41–44: 'Nam post incarnationem Christi anno millesimo centesimo doctrina apostolorum et ardens iusticia, quam in christianis et spiritualibus constituerat, tardare cepit et in hesitacionem uertebatur. Illis temporibus nata sum.' My translation. Compare *Life of Hildegard*, pp. 43–44; *Jutta and Hildegard: The Biographical Sources*, trans. by Anna Silvas (University Park: Pennsylvania State University Press, 1999), p. 158.

[2] *Sciuias*, III.11, p. 586, lines 379–91.

The Investiture Controversy, Jutta, and Hildegard

Distinctions between ecclesiastical and secular authority had been complicated since the Carolingian era, when bishops were accorded temporal rights. Kings sided with one episcopal faction or another during the eleventh century and came into conflict with the papacy. Pope Gregory VII (1073–85) delimited a structure for Christian society with all lay persons placed below the ecclesiastical hierarchy.[3] He and his advisors attempted to rein in the nobility and to assert the primacy of the Church in choosing and investing bishops, including the Bishop of Rome. The long and widespread conflict brought violent consequences in Hildegard's Germany, which was divided among five powerful duchies: Franconia, Swabia, Saxony, Bavaria, and Lotharingia.[4] Quarrels between Gregory VII and Emperor Henry IV (1056–1106) had a direct impact on Ruthard, the Archbishop of Mainz (1089–1109);[5] he was exiled in the very year of Hildegard's birth. Ruthard's exile must have represented acutely for the seer the downturn she decried.[6] Not until

---

[3] Giles Constable, *The Reformation of the Twelfth Century* (Cambridge: Cambridge University Press, 1996); Jeffrey B. Russell, *Dissent and Order in the Middle Ages: The Search for Legitimate Authority* (New York: Maxwell Macmillan, 1992).

[4] On the Investiture Controversy in Germany, see Alfred Haverkamp, *Medieval Germany 1056–1273*, trans. by Helga Braun and Richard Mortimer, 2nd edn (Oxford: Oxford University Press, 1992).

[5] Haverkamp, *Medieval Germany*, pp. 104–05, 112–16. Henry IV was excommunicated by Gregory VII in 1076. Papal supporters elected an anti-king in 1077, and civil war resulted. Henry IV took Rome in 1084, forcing the Pope into exile in Salerno. Pope Urban II, elected in 1088, re-entered Rome in 1093 and renewed Gregory VII's reform measures, including the ban on lay investiture.

[6] The *Chronicles of Disibodenberg* record Ruthard's exile and the refounding of the Church and describe the Emperor as a perverse man whom the Church disciplined with right cause. *Chronicles of Disibodenberg*, in *Jutta and Hildegard*, trans. by Silvas, p. 14. In addition, Ruthard split with Henry IV over protection of the Jews in Mainz who were persecuted in the pogroms of 1096. Henry IV allowed those forcibly baptized to return to Judaism. Relatives of the Archbishop and even Ruthard himself were reported to have profited from the wealth of Jews who were murdered. See Haverkamp, *Medieval Germany*, pp. 125, 215–19, on Jewish communities along the Rhine in the late eleventh and twelfth centuries. See also *Jutta and Hildegard*, trans. by Silvas, pp. 14–15, n. 26. In 1096, Ruthard himself granted brief refuge at Rudesheim to the Jewish *parnas* of Mainz, Kalonymous ben Meshullam, but he reversed his decision and the rabbi and others perished. See Robert Chazan, *In the Year 1096 [. . .] The First Crusade and the Jews* (Philadelphia: Jewish Publication Society, 1996), pp. 38–41. There are conflicting accounts on the cause of R. Kalonymous's death. See also Angela Carlevaris, 'Sie kamen zu ihr, um sie zu befragen: Hildegard und die Juden',

1105 did the Archbishop, whom Hildegard characterized as 'pious, humble, and contrite of heart', return and resume the project of refounding Disibodenberg as a Benedictine monastery.[7] The new church was dedicated in 1108, around the time that Hildegard's parents were making the decision about their precocious child.[8]

Mechthild and Hildebert, who ranked in the lower free nobility, reportedly recognized the predictive ability of their five-year-old daughter when she foretold accurately that the offspring of a pregnant cow would be white and covered with spots of a different colour.[9] They devoted their young daughter, born in 1098 at Bermersheim (near Mainz), to a religious life and placed her in the care of the holy woman Jutta. Paternal ties between Hildegard's father and Jutta's father, the Count of Sponheim, probably facilitated an arrangement for the young girl to reside at Sponheim, or in special quarters with her own family. Jutta and Hildegard were immured at the Benedictine monastery of Disibodenberg on All Saints' Day, 1 November 1112, when Hildegard was fourteen or fifteen.[10] Jutta's renown influenced other noble parents to vow their daughters to her, her enclosure expanded to become a *schola*, and a small women's Benedictine community developed in dependence on the Abbot of Disibodenberg with Jutta as superior.[11] Hildegard remained under Jutta's tutelage for around thirty years, until her teacher's death

in *Umfeld*, pp. 117–28 (p. 119), who notes the events at Rudesheim not far from Eibingen, where Hildegard was to found her second monastery in 1165.

[7] *Chronicles of Disibodenberg*, in *Jutta and Hildegard*, trans. by Silvas, pp. 17–19. V. Disib., PL 197: 1114: 'quidam Moguntiae sedis archiepiscopus, pius, humilis, contritusque corde'.

[8] Sabina Flanagan, *Hildegard of Bingen, 1098–1179: A Visionary Life*, 2nd edn (London: Routledge, 1998), pp. 31, 44. Flanagan distinguishes between oblates and children who were entrusted to a monastery by vow of their parents. Mews, 'Hildegard and the Schools', p. 92, n. 20, suggests that noble children could be brought up in the monastery but later make the choice whether to remain or not.

[9] Bruno, priest of St Peter in Strasbourg, *Acta inquisitionis de virtutibus et miraculis S. Hildegardis*, ed. by Petrus Bruder, *Analecta Bollandiana*, 2 (1883), 116–29 (pp. 124–25); *Jutta and Hildegard*, trans. by Silvas, p. 267. On the canonization proceedings, see Barbara J. Newman, 'Hildegard and her Hagiographers: The Remaking of Female Sainthood', in *Gendered Voices*, ed. by Mooney, pp. 16–34.

[10] *Jutta and Hildegard*, trans. by Silvas, p. 54, scrutinizes the evidence of these suppositions. See also John Van Engen, 'Abbess: "Mother and Teacher"', in *Voice*, pp. 30–51 (p. 32), who signals the six years between Hildegard's oblation and her immurement at Disibodenberg and asserts that Hildegard 'remained connected to her familial household in some way'.

[11] See Guibert of Gembloux, 'Letter to Bovo', in *Jutta and Hildegard*, Silvas, pp. 99–117 (pp. 109–11). Guibert of Gembloux, *Epistolae*, II, 38, pp. 367–79.

in 1136, whereupon Hildegard became the *magistra*, shining above the others in 'merit and holiness'.[12]

Through her family's ties to the Count of Sponheim, Hildegard's interests were allied with forces that supported the reform impetus and the Pope in opposition to the Salian dynasty (the four kings who reigned from 1024 to 1125: Conrad II, Henry III, Henry IV, Henry V). Lothar III (crowned as Emperor Lothar III in Rome in 1133) was related to Sophia, the mother of Jutta, Hildegard's *magistra*. Jutta's father opposed the Salian dynasty and her brother Meinhard participated in the 1125 election of Lothar.[13] Moreover, Jutta's father and brother supported the Hirsau monastic reforms. Meinhard founded a monastery at Sponheim in 1124 and endowed Disibodenberg with property in honour of his sister's vow. According to Johannes Trithemius, Meinhard's daughter Hiltrude became a sister at Rupertsberg who was highly praised by her *magistra* Hildegard.[14]

Monastic Reform and Learning

The reform measures initiated by Gregory VII emphasized the moral responsibility of the clergy, a concern that profoundly influenced Hildegard's own calling to advocate reform. At the same time, the reform impetus fostered a monastic culture

---

[12] Guibert of Gembloux, 'Letter to Bovo', in *Jutta and Hildegard*, trans. by Silvas, p. 111. Guibert of Gembloux, *Epistolae*, II, 38, p. 375, lines 297–99.

[13] Henry V had revolted against his father and led an army into Rome to subdue the forces of Urban II; he died without a son in 1125. The German princes claimed their right to elect the king and in the same year chose Lothar von Supplinburg, Duke of Saxony. Lothar III expectedly met opposition from the Salian dynasty but continued to uphold papal interests, placing himself on the side of Bernard of Clairvaux and Norbert of Xanten in support of Innocent II's claim to the papacy against Anacletus II in the early 1130s. Haverkamp, *Medieval Germany*, pp. 125–28, 133–37.

[14] The endowment to Disibodenberg appears in an 1128 charter of Adalbert, Archbishop of Mainz. Trithemius mentions Hiltrude in the *Chronica insignis monasterii Hirsaugiensis*, in *Johannes Trithemii Opera historica*, II, 156: '1177: Anno Conradi abbatis primo, qui fuit dominicae natiuitatis 1177. apud Bingos, in monasterio sancti Ruperti, 15. calendas Decembris obiit sancta Hiltrudis uirgo monialis nostri ordinis, filia Meginhardi comitis de Spanheim et soror domini Crastonis secundi abbatis monasterii mei Spanheimensis; cui B. Hildegardis magistra eius, testimonium sanctitatis et in uita et post obitum perhibuisse dicitur'. See *Jutta and Hildegard*, tran. by Silvas, p. xx, on the material in Trithemius and the entry in *Chronica insignis monasterii Hirsaugiensis* cited above. A shorter entry appears in the *Chronicon monasterii Sponheimensis*, in *Johannes Trithemii Opera historica*, II, 256.

which promoted learning and respected the authority of visionary experience.[15] The best-known proponent of monastic reform, William, Abbot of Hirsau (1069–91), promoted a renewal of monastic life in Germany that spurred the foundation of forty houses between 1080 and 1120.[16] Hirsau-influenced monasticism extended into present day Austria, Thuringia, and northward to the Weser valley. William of Hirsau's biographer, Haimo, acclaimed the reformer for the revitalization of monasticism in the Teutonic regions.[17] The chronicler Bernold of Constance (d. 1100) wrote from St Blasien in Swabia that in the year of William of Hirsau's death (1091), a community life that modelled itself on the apostles flourished among clerics, monks, and lay people. William and other reformers, including Ulrich of Zell (d. 1073), Siegfried of Schaffhaussen (d. c. 1098), and Altmann of Passau (d. 1091), supported women's religious communities, whether through the foundation of dependent daughter houses or of double monasteries (women living in proximity to men and under the same authority).[18]

Numerous examples from German monasteries demonstrate the value of learning and visionary gifts;[19] saints' lives and other texts transmit models for education and reform. Otloh of St Emmeram (c. 1010–c. 1070), mentor and friend of William of Hirsau and a scribe himself, authored the *Liber uisionum* (*Book of Visions*) and the *Liber de admonitione clericorum et laicorum* (*Admonition to Clergy and Laity*).[20]

---

[15] On Benedictine monasticism and the perception of a crisis, see John Van Engen, 'The "Crisis of Cenobitism" Reconsidered: Benedictine Monasticism in the Years 1050–1150', *Speculum*, 61 (1986), 269–304. Van Engen asserts that the false perception of decline was based on too literal a reading of the Benedictine's critics without sufficient consideration of the context. The black monks suffered no decline in numbers during the first half of the twelfth century and only later lost their central position in the Church.

[16] Constable, *Reformation of the Twelfth Century*, p. 44. See also Haverkamp, *Medieval Germany*, p. 190; *Hirsau, St. Peter und Paul, 1091–1991: Geschichte, Lebens- und Verfassungsformen eines Reformklosters*, ed. by Klaus Schreiner, vol. II, Forschungen und Berichte der Archäologie des Mittelalters in Baden-Württemberg, 10 (Stuttgart: Theiss, 1991).

[17] Constable, *Reformation of the Twelfth Century*, p. 44. See also Haverkamp, *Medieval Germany*, p. 190.

[18] Julie Hotchin, 'Female Religious Life and the *cura monialium* in Hirsau Monasticism, 1080 to 1150', in *Listen Daughter: The 'Speculum virginum' and the Formation of Religious Women in the Middle Ages*, ed. by Constant J. Mews (New York: Palgrave, 2001), pp. 61–78.

[19] On the visionaries, see Constant J. Mews, 'Hildegard, Visions and Religious Reform', in *Angesicht*, pp. 325–42; and Mews, 'Hildegard and the Schools', p. 109, n. 96.

[20] Otloh composed the *Vita* of St Wolfgang (Bishop of Regensburg, 972–74), a reformer whose dreams ordered him to urge houses of canonesses living under the Augustinian rule to adopt

The *Liber uisionum* comprises a series of visions, including four revelations that Otloh himself experienced.[21] Otloh structures his book by recounting a vision, then asserting the value of recording it for purposes of edification, *ad edificationem fidelium*. The narrative structure that Otloh employs — vision followed by commentary — bears comparison to Hildegard's organization of her visionary works.[22] However, Otloh generally limits his moral commentary to brief remarks such as 'Those who want to heed the few things I have said earlier will grasp from them not a small matter for edification.'[23] Otloh's *Liber de admonitione clericorum et laicorum* advocates teaching in the method of Christ, using gospel parables to illustrate how to combat vices or practise virtues. Otloh discusses several parables briefly with their moral lessons, including four that Hildegard explains in the *Expositiones*: Lazarus and the rich man (Lk 16. 19–31), the unjust steward (Lk 16. 1–9), the Pharisee and the publican (Lk 18. 10–14), and the great banquet (Lk 14. 16–24).[24] Hildegard makes similar observations on the moral and didactic impact of parables.[25] Moreover, Otloh, like Hildegard, assigns virtues to several Old Testament figures in accordance with established motifs, such as patience for Job.[26]

the more stringent Benedictine observance. Adam S. Cohen, *The Uta Codex: Art, Philosophy, and Reform in Eleventh-Century Germany* (University Park: Pennsylvania State University Press, 2000), p. 17. On Otloh as scribe, see Beach, *Women as Scribes*, p. 22 and sources cited in n. 85.

[21] Otloh of St Emmeram, *Liber visionum*, ed. by Paul Gerhardt Schmidt, MGH, Quellen zur Geistesgeschichte des Mittelalters, 13 (Weimar: Nachfolger, 1989), pp. 31–115 (pp. 33–34). Otloh hails a precedent in Book Four of Gregory the Great's *Dialogues*. On the *Liber visionum* in the context of monastic reform, see Ellen Joyce, 'Speaking of Spiritual Matters: Visions and the Rhetoric of Reform in the *Liber visionum* of Otloh of St Emmeram', in *Manuscripts and Monastic Culture*, ed. by Beach, pp. 69–98; C. Stephen Jaeger, *The Envy of Angels: Cathedral Schools and Social Ideals in Medieval Europe, 950–1200* (Philadelphia: University of Pennsylvania Press, 1994), pp. 213–14.

[22] Constant Mews makes this suggestion in 'Hildegard, Visions and Religious Reform'.

[23] Otloh, *Liber visionum*, ed. by Schmidt, p. 79: 'qui predictis cupiunt intendere paucis, non paruam possunt exinde capescere causam edificationis'; p. 90: 'Hec igitur ego ita euenisse audiens literis tradere curaui, sperans exinde aliquem posse edificari.'

[24] Otloh of St Emmeram, *Liber de admonitione clericorum et laicorum*, PL 146: 244–62 (cols 252–54).

[25] *Solut.*, XXXV, PL 197: 1037–54 (col. 1052); Hildegard tells a parable (*parabolam*) herself in Letter 80R, *Epistolarium*, I, pp. 181–82.

[26] Otloh, *Liber de admonitione clericorum et laicorum*, PL 146: 251–55. Such moral interpretations of biblical personages derive from patristic sources such as Jerome's *Liber interpretationis hebraicorum nominum* or Isidore of Seville's *De uita et obitu patruum*. Isidore, PL 83: 129–56, develops longer moralizations than the simple associative lists in Jerome, *Liber interpretationis*

Otloh of St Emmeram's works do not stand alone in signalling the esteem accorded to education and visionary gifts for men and women in German monasteries. The biographer of Theoger of St Georgen (d. 1119) praises Theoger for his instruction of boys and girls (*pueros et puellas*) and affirms that both women and men were 'taught by divine revelation'. The chronicler of Petershausen, a community of men and women reformed by Hirsau, recounts numerous visions. He reports that the nun Regilinda experienced a vision of a heavenly garden and the procession of saints. Another vision narrated in the chronicle occurred in a dream to the monk Bernard and appears in the manuscript with an illustration, a significant example of a visionary text and image in the same manuscript that pre-dates Hildegard's works.[27] Herluca of Epfach (d. 1127), a disciple of William of Hirsau, became a recluse and experienced visions with clear lessons for clerical reform. Her biographer, Paul of Bernried, reports that she envisioned the chastisement of corrupt clergy. The coupling of vision and reform message provides an antecedent for Hildegard's visionary wrath against immoral clergy.[28]

The best known of Hildegard's German predecessors, the learned Rupert of Deutz, authored influential biblical commentaries. Rupert asserted that a vision constituted the source for his understanding of Scripture, an important precedent for Hildegard's claim of divine inspiration for her exegetical understanding. Rupert speaks explicitly of his conversion, when he comprehended the inner meaning of the Son of God on the cross and subsequently received a series of visions. He was

---

nominum hebraicorum, ed. by P. de Lagarde, CCSL, 72 (Turnhout: Brepols, 1959), pp. 59–161. Gregory the Great's *Moralia in Iob* disseminated widely the patristic association of Job with patience: Gregory the Great, *Moralia in Iob Libri I–IX*, ed. by Marcus Adriaen, CCSL, 143 (Turnhout: Brepols, 1979), 2, 18, p. 80, lines 34–39; 28, 4, pp. 1403–04, lines 7–12.

[27] *Vita Theogeri*, ed. by Philipp Jaffé, in *Annales et chronica aevi Salici, Vitae aevi Carolini et Saxonici*, ed. by Georg Pertz, MGH SS, 12 (Stuttgart, 1856), pp. 449–79, at 1, 20, p. 458. *Casus Monasterii Petrishusensis*, ed. by Otto Abel and Ludwig Weiland, MGH SS, 20 (Hannover, 1868), pp. 621–83, at Pref. 9, p. 625; V, 20, p. 673; III, 18, pp. 651–53 (dream). Mews, 'Hildegard, Visions and Religious Reform', p. 335, points out that this invites comparison with Hildegard's use of text and image.

[28] Paul de Bernried, *Vita B. Herlucae*, in *Acta SS*, April II (Brussels, 1865), pp. 552–55. On Herluca and her contact with the Archbishop of Ravenna (1118–44), see Beach, *Women as Scribes*, p. 37. Haverkamp, *Medieval Germany*, p. 194. Mews, 'Hildegard, Visions and Religious Reform', p. 341, notes that by the mid-twelfth century, Hirsau was experiencing internal quarrels and Cistercian abbots were ordered not to accept monks from Hirsau. Hildegard corresponded with the monks of Hirsau in 1153–54 and thereafter with Abbot Manegold, elected in 1156. See *Epistolarium*, II, 119–36, pp. 292–309; *Letters*, II, pp. 64–77.

filled with waves (*inundationes*) of the Spirit, the living matter and true life (*res uiua et uera uita*), which he describes as a substance, heavier than gold and sweeter than honey (*auro grauius, melle dulcius*), and again, as beautiful like liquid gold (*aurum liquidum*).[29] Rupert arguably gained authority from his vision for greater creativity in his exegesis. Still Rupert's vision and the other visionary texts described above demonstrate that when Hildegard began relaying the content of her visions, the religious culture around her was already marked by a high level of monastic literacy and, furthermore, accustomed to assertions of visionary authority to convey reform messages and exegetical understanding.

Education in Monasteries for Women

To what extent did this monastic literacy extend to women's communities? Indeed, the central role of education in Hirsau foundations followed a long tradition of learning in female monasteries that branched out from Merovingian Gaul and Anglo-Saxon double monasteries to missionary nuns on the German frontier. The number of religious communities for women in German lands, notably houses of canonesses, grew significantly from the late ninth to the eleventh centuries, before the upsurge of the twelfth-century 'renaissance'. Houses for noble women at Essen, Herford, Gandersheim, and Quedlinberg provided training in reading, writing, and scriptural study. The material evidence for the learning and influence of noble women in German religious houses speaks unambiguously. The 2005 exhibition *Krone und Schleier* brilliantly displayed manuscripts from the imperial houses of Essen, Gandersheim, and Quedlinberg, as well as other *Stift* churches: liturgical books, scriptural commentaries, Latin grammar texts, and the *Homerus latinus* —

---

[29] Rupert of Deutz, *De gloria et honore Filii hominis super Mattheum*, p. 378, lines 603–09; p. 379, Pref. 9; p. 625, V, 20; p. 673, III, 18; pp. 651–53 (dream). On Rupert's visions, see Fulton, *From Judgment to Passion*, pp. 300, 309–15, and p. 95, n. 214; McGinn, *Presence of God*, II, 328–33; John Van Engen, *Rupert of Deutz* (Los Angeles: University of California Press, 1983), pp. 51–54; Newman, 'Visions and Validation', pp. 172–73; Robert Lerner, 'Ecstatic Dissent', *Speculum*, 67, (1992), 33–57. In demonstrating the power of the Holy Spirit through history, Rupert also tells of the young Waldrada, who received the visit of the Holy Spirit while awake and renounced a marriage agreement to become a recluse. Rupert of Deutz, *De glorificatione Trinitatis et processione Spiritus Sancti*, 2. 18, *PL* 169: 13–202 (cols 48–49); Mews, 'Hildegard, Visions and Religious Reform'.

the Latin prose paraphrase of the *Iliad*.[30] This visual evidence supports the observation that Alison Beach makes about women scribes in German monasteries: 'Education was a hallmark of noble piety.'[31] While Hildegard valued the simplicity of Benedictine life, she clearly inherited this dual esteem for learning and nobility.

The life and activity of learned monasteries, notably in southern Germany, had suffered from the destruction wrought by recurring Magyar invasions, which were halted by Otto I in 955. Rebuilding proceeded through sharing of resources among monastic libraries and intense scribal activity.[32] The restoration provided momentum for wider adoption of the Benedictine *Rule*, a movement that had germinated earlier in influential monasteries such as Gorze.[33] Benedictine reformers strove not only to restore intellectual life but also to impose the Benedictine *Rule* on canonesses, whose way of life had allowed wealth, power, and the freedom to leave the monastery.[34] The magnificent Uta Codex, produced at Regensburg in the early eleventh century for Abbess Uta of Niedermünster, illustrates the ideals of Benedictine spirituality; to ensure the implementation of those ideals in daily life, Uta commissioned a *Rule of Benedict* with feminine grammatical forms.[35] Women played a role as producers and consumers of books during the rebuilding as in earlier eras.[36] While the Benedictine culture of the Hirsau network stands within this broad

---

[30] *Krone und Schleier: Kunst aus Mittelalterlichen Frauenklöstern*, Kunst- und Ausstellungshalle der Bundesrepublik Deutschland, Bonn und dem Ruhrlandmuseum Essen (Munich: Hirmer; Bonn and Essen: Kunst- und Ausstellungshalle der Bundesrepublik Deutschland, Bonn und dem Ruhrlandmuseum Essen, 2005), pp. 230–46.

[31] Beach, *Women as Scribes*, p. 19, and pp. 8–31 on background.

[32] Beach, *Women as Scribes*, pp. 21–22, 32 on Wessobrun, p. 104 on Schäftlarn.

[33] Beach, *Women as Scribes*, p. 24, n. 100, p. 33, n. 5.

[34] See Beach, *Women as Scribes*, p. 133; Griffiths, *Garden of Delights*; Carolyn A. Muessig, 'Learning and Mentoring in the Twelfth Century: Hildegard of Bingen and Herrad of Hohenburg', in *Medieval Monastic Education*, ed. by G. P. Ferzoco and C. A. Muessig (London: Leicester University Press/Continuum, 2000), pp. 87–104 (p. 94); and for a broad discussion, Jo Ann McNamara, *Sisters in Arms: Catholic Nuns through Two Millennia* (Cambridge, MA: Harvard University Press, 2000), p. 179.

[35] Uta also commissioned a Rule of Caesarius (of Arles), written for his sister Caesaria and her nuns. On the Uta Codex, its dating, and the efforts to reform the canonesses and advocate Benedictine ideals, see Cohen, *The Uta Codex*, pp. 10–18, 22–23, 196, and passim; Beach, *Women as Scribes*, pp. 24–25.

[36] Beach, *Women as Scribes*, pp. 32–64 on Diemut of Wessobrun, pp. 65–103 on the nuns of Admont, pp. 104–27 on Schäftlarn, where the nuns copied books for the monks' use.

tradition of women's learning, it also holds some degree of prominence in light of the intellectual engagement allowed to women religious in other circumstances.[37]

The widely diffused *Speculum uirginum*, probably authored by a twelfth-century monk of Hirsau, constitutes a guide for religious women in the form of dialogue and illustration.[38] The double monastery of Admont in modern-day Austria educated male and female students in separate *scholae*; they exchanged books from their respective libraries and collaborated in the transcription, production, and composition of sermons and biblical commentaries.[39] Lippoldsberg, a northern German Benedictine monastery influenced by Hirsau customs, possessed an extensive library including patristic and contemporary writings on theology and biblical commentary as well as classics in the liberal arts. Gunther, the spiritual director at Lippoldsberg, commissioned an illuminated gospel book for the monastery around 1160. Its dedicatory leaf speaks to the collaboration between men and women religious; it depicts a male cleric extending his right hand toward a nun while he gives a blessing with his left hand. The scene takes place before an image of the monastery's patron, St George; looking on are a cleric and female Benedictines in prayer.[40]

Gunther, an Augustinian canon from Hamersleben, transformed Lippoldsberg and its library after his appointment in 1138 — a significant example of how the Benedictine and Augustinian networks of houses overlapped. This frequent overlapping in affiliation and service of spiritual direction stands in contrast to the tension over the interpretation of poverty in Benedictine and Augustinian houses.[41]

---

[37] Beach, *Women as Scribes*, p. 133, contrasts Hirsau monasteries with the restricted role given women at Schäftlarn and Premonstratensian houses, perhaps because of the emphasis there on apostolic preaching.

[38] See the fine essays in *Listen Daughter*, ed. by Mews, and Figs 2 and 3 in the same volume.

[39] Alison I. Beach, 'Listening for the Voices of Admont's Twelfth-Century Nuns', in *Voices in Dialogue: Reading Women in the Middle Ages*, ed. by Linda Olson and Kathryn Kerby-Fulton (Notre Dame: University of Notre Dame Press, 2005), pp. 187–98. See also Christina Lutter, *Geschlect und Wissen, Norm und Praxis, Lesen und Schreiben: Monastische Reformgemeinschaften im 12. Jahrhundert* (Vienna: Oldenbourg, 2005).

[40] I am grateful to Julie Hotchin for a pre-print copy of her article 'Women's Reading and Monastic Reform in Twelfth-Century Germany: The Library of the Nuns of Lippoldsberg', in *Manuscripts and Monastic Culture*, ed. by Beach, pp. 139–90.

[41] Haverkamp, *Medieval Germany*, p. 193, asserts that Tenxwind and Hildegard held different views of God, the *pauper Christus* serving as model for Tenxwind and the *rex potentissimus* for Hildegard. See Haverkamp, *Medieval Germany*, pp. 201, 334 on Tenxwind, pp. 191–93 on the canons, and Haverkamp, 'Tenxwind von Andernach und Hildegard von Bingen', in *Institutionen, Kultur und Gesellschaft im Mittelalter, Festschrift für Josef Fleckenstein* (Sigmaringen: Thorbecke,

Tenxwind (d. *c.* 1152), learned *magistra* of the Augustinian house at Andernach, clashed with Hildegard over issues of social class and the attire of the nuns at Rupertsberg. She criticized Hildegard's restriction of Rupertsberg to noble nuns, as well as the sisters' display of extravagant hair, silk veils, and gold filigree crowns on feast days as they 'stood in the church'. Hildegard defended her nuns' attire and noble origin, asserting that all persons are loved by God but are not equal in rank. 'Who would gather all his livestock indiscriminately into one barn?', she asked. People of diverse status, if herded together, would 'slaughter one another out of hatred'.[42] Hildegard saw the social order as part of God's design.[43] Doubtless she also wanted to promote an audience of literate women who could both understand her and assist with the production of her writings.

Hildegard and Tenxwind, despite their profound differences in social outlook, shared a tradition of learning and a pattern of life, as did their respective orders: first as recluses living within a male community and then as superiors of their respective monasteries at Rupertsberg and Andernach.[44] Tenxwind's mother, Benigna, had

---

1984), pp. 515–48 (pp. 543–45), where he argues that Tenxwind's letter was toned down for the *Epistolarium*. See also Franz J. Felten, 'Zum Problem der sozialen Zusammensetzung von alten Benediktinerklöstern und konventen der neuen religiösen Bewegung', in *Umfeld*, pp. 189–235; Giles Constable, 'Hildegard's Explanation of the Rule of St. Benedict', in *Umfeld*, pp. 163–87 (pp. 169–72); Constant J. Mews, 'Hildegard, the *Speculum virginum* and Religious Reform', in *Umfeld*, pp. 236–67 (pp. 236–41).

[42] *Epistolarium*, I, 52–52R, pp. 125–30; *Letters*, I, 127–30. I am grateful to Felix Heinzer for signaling the phrase in Tenxwind's letter, 'in ecclesia stare', which may suggest that the nuns were so attired in a procession in the church but not in the choir.

[43] Felten, 'Zum Problem der sozialen Zusammensetzung von alten Benediktinerklöstern und Konventen der neuen religiösen Bewegung', argues that female convents promoted a self-definition rooted in nobility in order to distinguish themselves not simply from Augustinians but from other new and suspect forms of community life and to exclude the daughters of the ministerial class from membership. Maria Arduini, in her discussion of the theme of poverty and power in Rupert of Deutz, finds Hildegard's views on social class shocking. Arduini cites a passage that appears in Ep. 47, *PL* 198: 233D–234A, but not in the corresponding *Epistolarium*, I, 23, pp. 61–66, where the text of the famous letter to the prelates of Mainz ends with *deuicta cadat* at a point that corresponds to *PL* 198: 221D. In the extended *PL* text, the *magistra* remarks: 'Quoniam qui divitem et pauperem in una sede sedere faceret, dives hoc facere dedignaretur et pauper inde terreretur.' (A CETEDOC search shows no such passage in the *Epistolarium* or other works.) Maria Ludovica Arduini, *Rupert von Deutz (1076–1129) und der 'status Christianitas' seiner Zeit: Symbolisch-prophetische Deutung der Geschichte* (Cologne: Böhlau, 1987), p. 322.

[44] The establishment of female monasteries correlated in some measure to the attitudes that surfaced at the Second Lateran Council (1139) in its condemnation of canonesses for lack of

founded Springiersbach (for men and women) in the diocese of Trier around 1100; her son Richard served as provost and sent women from Springiersbach to found Andernach, establishing his sister as *magistra* in 1128.[45] Erkenbert, a Benedictine from Worms, founded the important Augustinian community of St Mary Magdalen at Frankenthal. He became its second provost in 1135 and appointed his (former) wife Richlind as *magistra* of a women's community there.[46] Manegold (d. *c.* 1103) left his marriage and in 1094 became a canon at Lautenbach, an Augustinian house. His wife and daughters, renowned for their knowledge of Scripture, attracted their own disciples.[47] Manegold eventually served as provost at Marbach, the male community that maintained a spiritual and intellectual relationship with the canonesses of Schwartzenthann in Alsace. The Guta-Sintram codex (1154) stands as verbal and visual testimony to their collaboration. One illustration depicts the Virgin Mary, flanked by the canoness Guta and the canon Sintram, while another portrays St Augustine, sitting between canons and canonesses, under a banner reading: 'Let poverty be sweet, the mind chaste, and the will one.'[48]

In the last quarter of the twelfth century, the Augustinian canoness Herrad of Hohenbourg compiled the *Hortus deliciarum*, or *Garden of Delights*, to provide a manual for religious women. The *Hortus* is a compilation of excerpts from authors read in the curriculum at cathedral schools, including the works of Herrad's contemporaries, notably the *Historia scholastica* of Peter Comestor, which she uses extensively, and the *Sententiae* of Peter Lombard.[49] The *Hortus* differs markedly in content and outlook from Hildegard's decidedly monastic scepticism towards the schools. Nonetheless, the works of the two authors merit comparison: the *Hortus* bears witness to the continuance of the Augustinian interest in women's education just as Hildegard's works demonstrate the vitality of the Benedictine tradition.[50]

---

discipline and its ruling (Canon 27) against men and women singing together in the same choir. Griffiths, *Garden of Delights*, pp. 49, 59, n. 71.

[45] Mews, 'Hildegard, Visions and Religious Reform', p. 340; Hotchin, 'Female Religious Life and the *cura monialium*', p. 65.

[46] Mews, 'Hildegard, Visions and Religious Reform', p. 340.

[47] Mews, 'Hildegard, Visions and Religious Reform', p. 340, n. 10; Griffiths, *Garden of Delights*, pp. 33–34, 145–46.

[48] Fiona Griffiths, 'Brides and *dominae*: Abelard's *Cura monialium* at the Augustinian Monastery of Marbach', *Viator*, 34 (2003), 57–88.

[49] Griffiths, *Garden of Delights*, pp. 72–75, 111, 116, 119.

[50] For a recent look at the extensive bibliography on canonesses, consult Griffiths, *Garden of Delights*, pp. 29–48.

How the seer's development of her exegetical method reflects her education within a women's community will be explored in greater depth in Chapter 3.

'Speak and Write': From Vision to Exegesis and Preaching

In 1141, approximately five years after Jutta's death, Hildegard experienced the forceful vision that instructed her to 'speak and write' what she heard and saw.[51] How Hildegard moved from that moment into international prominence remains somewhat imprecise. The *magistra* provides her own account of her prophetic call and its exegetical and homiletic consequences in the *Vita Hildegardis*, the product of Hildegard and three others: Gottfried of Disibodenberg (d. 1176), Guibert of Gembloux (1124/5–1213), and Theodoric of Echternach (d. post 1192). Hildegard herself began organizing the writing of her *Vita*, which Barbara Newman terms 'autohagiography', the product of Hildegard's direct collaboration with her hagiographers. Theodoric included the texts of her visions and incorporated especially in Book Two an autobiographical narrative, which is divided into segments.[52]

The seer compares herself to Moses, Joshua, Jeremiah, Susannah, St John the Evangelist, and, for her physical suffering, St Lawrence. Hildegard attests that like St John, she received knowledge from the Spirit of God in the form of 'soft raindrops'. With that knowledge she built a 'moat and wall' with the Scriptures to protect her sisters against the spirits of the air.[53] In her autobiography, Hildegard describes a revelation that involves preaching or teaching: Noble nuns in the room of a tower listen 'to the words of God' from her mouth. In another tower are common folk, who 'loved the words of God' that she spoke 'from true vision'.[54] These visions clearly stake out authority for interpreting the Scriptures and preaching that interpretation.[55] Furthermore, in *Sciuias* Hildegard in God's voice had

[51] *Sciuias*, pp. 3–4, lines 24–33.

[52] Gottfried served as provost of Rupertsberg after Volmar's death in 1173; Guibert was secretary to Hildegard; Theodoric compiled the *Vita* from various sources. Newman, 'Three-Part Invention' and 'Hildegard and her Hagiographers'. See also *Jutta and Hildegard*, trans. by Silvas, pp. 122–25, on the biographers.

[53] *V. Hild.*, II.16, pp. 66–67. For Hildegard's self-comparisons, see *V. Hild.*, II.5, 7, 9, 12, pp. 28–29, 32, 34, 38; *Life of Hildegard*, pp. 50, 54, 56, 60.

[54] *V. Hild.*, II.15, p. 42, lines 11–14, 17–22; *Life of Hildegard*, pp. 65–66.

[55] In my view, both Gottfried and Theodoric are intent on staking out Hildegard's prophetic and visionary authority. Newman in contrast emphasizes the elements of bridal mysticism in Theodoric's work: 'Hildegard and her Hagiographers', pp. 25–27.

criticized contemporary exegetes for their neglect of patristic commentary and identified herself as the one to revive and continue the teaching of the doctors.[56]

In the face of Hildegard's bold claims, Gottfried of Disibodenberg takes care to document how the seer's prophetic voice passed through layers of ecclesiastical authority.[57] He recounts that Pope Eugene III sent a delegation to Disibodenberg to inquire into Hildegard's writing. Gottfried further relates that the Pope then requested a copy of the seer's work and read from it publicly, whereupon Bernard of Clairvaux and others urged him to confirm the 'great grace' manifested in Hildegard. According to Gottfried's account, Eugene sent letters to Hildegard, granted her 'permission (*licentia*) to make known whatever she had learned through the Holy Spirit and encouraged or urged (*animauit*) her to write'.[58] Hildegard repeats and strengthens this story in the *Vita*, where she states that Pope Eugene sent her letters and 'instructed' (*precepit*) her to write what she saw and heard in her visions.[59] What Gottfried expresses as permission and encouragement from Eugene III, Hildegard presents as a papal mandate. Hildegard and her biographer look back around twenty-five years at the events of 1146/47 and report Pope Eugene's acts and attitudes as authorization, whether permission or mandate, for the seer to proceed with her writing.

Scholars question the veracity of Gottfried's and Hildegard's accounts; John Van Engen calls their story the 'myth of authorization'. Van Engen points to two series of events: first, Hildegard's letter to Bernard of Clairvaux in early 1147 and his reply, briefer than the version edited around 1170 for the definitive letter collection; and second, Hildegard's sending of a letter with part of the *Sciuias* to Eugene III, who spent the winter of 1147–48 (30 November–13 February) in Trier. From the letter and the autobiographical narrative, one may conclude that Eugene III sent a delegation to Disibodenberg to investigate Hildegard's writings and bring her work back to him in Trier. Eugene issued a charter of protection for Disibodenberg with no reference to Hildegard or the women's community. Hildegard in turn wrote Eugene again to seek his approval and protection, but he sent no written reply. Instead, Volmar drafted a letter in the Pope's name around 1170, when he also revised the letter from Bernard of Clairvaux. Van Engen argues that

---

[56] *Sciuias*, III.11, p. 586, lines 379–91.

[57] Newman, 'Hildegard and her Hagiographers', p. 22, notes Gottfried's insistence on the 'ecclesiastical chain of command'.

[58] My translation. See *V. Hild.*, I.4, pp. 9–10; *Life of Hildegard*, pp. 29–30.

[59] *V. Hild.*, II.2, p. 24, lines 95–102; *Life of Hildegard*, p. 46.

these later letters reflect Hildegard's 'self-understanding', which 'claimed or imagined' approval from Bernard and Eugene.[60]

Van Engen clearly presents the case against any formal authorization for Hildegard to write. However, it is worth noting that neither Bernard nor Eugene forbade her literary activity. Ecclesiastical intervention against unauthorized and thereby suspicious preaching or teaching was escalating.[61] Already in the 1140s, Everwin of Steinfeld had written to Bernard about the heretics in the Rhineland and Bernard had travelled to Occitania in 1145 in dogged pursuit of heresy. Inappropriate activities of women dissidents figured on the list of censurable behaviour. Moreover, in 1147 Bernard also targeted the unauthorized preaching of the renegade Cistercian Ralph, who was stirring up anti-Jewish hatred in the Rhineland.[62] In such a climate, I would argue that the absence of critique from Bernard implied at least his tacit approval.[63]

Does Bernard's letter to Hildegard in its unrevised form reveal anything further about his opinion of Hildegard? The abbot wrote: 'Ceterum, ubi interior eruditio est et unctio docens de omnibus, quidnos aut docere aut monere?' ('Besides, when there is inner enlightenment and anointing that teaches about all things, what is there for us to teach or advise?').[64] The phrase *unctio docens de omnibus* alludes to I John 2. 27:

> et vos unctionem quam accepistis ab eo manet in vobis et non necesse habetis ut aliquis doceat vos sed sicut unctio eius docet vos de omnibus verum est non est mendacium et sicut docuit vos manete in eo.

[60] John Van Engen, 'Letters and the Public Persona of Hildegard', in *Umfeld*, pp. 375–418 (pp. 379–89).

[61] Debates over monks' preaching and Benedictine defense of its appropriateness did not extend to women. On these debates in Germany, see Brunn, *Des contestataires aux 'cathares'*, pp. 94–97; Van Engen, *Rupert of Deutz*, pp. 271–74; Griffiths, *Garden of Delights*, p. 124.

[62] Beverly Mayne Kienzle, *Cistercians, Heresy and Crusade (1145–1229): Preaching in the Lord's Vineyard* (Woodbridge: Boydell and Brewer, 2001), p. 45.

[63] McGinn, 'Hildegard of Bingen as Visionary and Exegete', p. 335, is of the opinion that 'there is no reason to think that he did not really approve'. McGinn cites Jean Leclercq's opinion in *Women and St. Bernard* (Kalamazoo: Cistercian Publications, 1989), pp. 62–67, where Leclercq calls Bernard and Hildegard's correspondence a 'joust of humility'. For another opinion, that Bernard cautions Hildegard, see Guy Lobrichon, 'Les Joyaux de la charité: Bernard, Hildegarde, et les amitiés spirituelles du XII⁰ siècle', in *Spiritualität im Europa des Mittelalters: L'Europe spirituelle au Moyen Âge: 900 Jahre Hildegard von Bingen, 900 ans l'abbaye de Cîteaux*, ed. by Stephan Grätzel, Philosophie im Kontext, Interdisziplinäre Studien, 4 (St Augustin: Gardez, 1998), pp. 17–26.

[64] *Epistolarium*, I, 1R, p. 6, lines 12–13. The apparatus biblicus for the letter does not identify the Johannine echoes. The text of the longer, later letter is noted in the apparatus criticus.

[and the anointing which you received from him abides in you and you have no need that anyone should teach you; but just as his anointing teaches you about all things and is true and is not a lie, and just as it has taught you, abide in him.]

It also echoes I John 2. 20: 'sed vos unctionem habetis a Sancto et nostis omnia' ('but you have anointing from the Spirit and you know all things').[65] Bernard employs the notion of *unctio* as teacher of all ten times in his various works, citing I John 2, and he evokes *unctio* even more often in the general sense of teaching or anointing from the Spirit. Bernard at times employs *eruditio* alone to contrast spiritual with 'book' learning, and furthermore, he speaks of *spiritualis eruditio*, the equivalent of *interior eruditio*, or the enlightenment of the inner person.[66] The notions of *interior eruditio* and *unctio* represent spiritual enlightenment in the context of his writings.[67] Therefore, when the abbot employed this scriptural allusion, he acknowledged Hildegard's gift from the Spirit with respect and not with the ambiguity or condescension that Van Engen sees.[68] With no objection from Eugene III and the recognition that Bernard of Clairvaux gave to the power of the Spirit within her, Hildegard felt empowered to express her voice publicly in writing.

From Vision to Writing: Sciuias, Liber uitae meritorum, Liber diuinorum operum

The *magistra* had begun to produce her first work, *Sciuias*, after the divine command in 1141. Hildegard discloses in the *Liber uitae meritorum* that she 'sweated over' the 'true visions' of her first book for ten years. As she sweated, her contemporaries awaited the final product. Archbishop Arnold of Cologne wrote the seer around 1150 and expressed his impatience at waiting for the book she wrote 'under

---

[65] Leclercq, *Women and St. Bernard*, pp. 65–66, notes that this text was 'dear to Bernard'.

[66] A CETEDOC search produced seventy-seven hits for *unctio** in Bernard's works. Two of numerous examples for *eruditio* follow. Ep. 108.2, *SBOp*, VII, 278: 'Nec enim hanc lectio docet, sed unctio; non littera, sed spiritus; non eruditio, sed exercitatio in mandatis Domini.' *In Ascensione Domini*, 6. 6, *SBOp*, V, 163, lines 13–15: 'Nam de ignorantia, fratres, quaenam excusatio nobis, quibus numquam doctrina caelestis, numquam divina lectio, numquam spiritualis eruditio deest?'

[67] The term *interior eruditio* echoes Hildegard's words in her letter to Bernard. *Epistolarium*, I, 1, p. 4, line 17: *interiorem intelligentiam*. Leclercq, *Women and St. Bernard*, pp. 65–66, states that Bernard 'respected the working of grace within' Hildegard, and that, in writing to Hildegard, Bernard was pointing out 'the contrast between the power of the Spirit and his own inability'.

[68] Van Engen, 'Letters and the Public Persona of Hildegard', p. 382, describes the letter as 'certainly ambiguous, probably condescending, and ironic'.

the inspiration of the Holy Spirit'.[69] However, conflicts and sorrow interrupted the last few years of writing *Sciuias*. The Abbot of Disibodenberg resisted Hildegard's plan to move to Rupertsberg and relented only after her illness and inability to write proved the rightness of her case.[70] Once at Rupertsberg, Hildegard faced another major crisis when Hartwig, Bishop of Bremen, ordered Hildegard to release his sister Richardis as well as her niece Adelheid. Both Richardis and Adelheid had been elected to prestigious posts in Saxony: Richardis as Abbess of Bassum and Adelheid as Abbess of Gandersheim.[71] Hildegard's insinuations of material gain and even simony in the elections probably refer to family ties and the donations that would come to Hartwig and his diocese from the elections if his sister and her niece held posts as abbess.[72] Hildegard's protests to Hartwig fell on deaf ears, and her grief at losing a beloved friend was compounded when Richardis died in 1152.[73] The *Vita Hildegardis* states that Richardis sought the 'honour of this world' (*honorem seculi huius*) on account of the 'elegance of her family' (*propter elegantiam generis sui*), a phrase that may in part disculpate Richardis, who submitted to family pressure.[74]

Does *Sciuias* show evidence of Hildegard's homiletic disposition? In fact, the seer instructs all orders of society on a wide variety of topics and admonishes them

---

[69] *Epistolarium*, I, 14, pp. 31–32; *Letters*, I, 14, p. 52: 'ipsa diuino Spiritu inspirata'.

[70] *V. Hild.*, II.5, pp. 27–28, lines 14–38; *Life of Hildegard*, p. 49. The marchioness of Stade, mother of Richardis, purchased a tract of land for her in 1147.

[71] Adelheid was then in her grandmother's care after her mother's (Liutgard of Stade) divorce and remarriage to King Eric of Denmark. The family connections of the two high-placed women, particularly in the case of the child Adelheid, argue for the motivation, or at least influence, of Hartwig, an opponent of the powerful Henry the Lion, to secure the position of abbess for family members who would hold allegiance to him. Gandersheim had been the object of an early eleventh-century jurisdictional dispute between Hildesheim and Mainz. See Henry Mayr-Harting, *Ottonian Book Illumination* (London: Harvey Miller, 1999), I, 103.

[72] Scholars hold varying views on Hartwig and Richardis's motives, and Hildegard's views of both. Flanagan, *Hildegard of Bingen*, pp. 172–76, discusses the events and texts and concludes that the allegations of simony pertain to an election made against God's will and do not indicate that the election was won with bought votes (pp. 173–74). Various letters pertain to this episode in Hildegard's life. See Joan Ferrante's account of them in 'Correspondent: "Blessed Is the Speech of Your Mouth"', in *Voice*, pp. 91–109 (pp. 103–04).

[73] Hartwig admitted his error and revealed that Richardis was intending to return to Rupertsberg. *Epistolarium*, I, 13, p. 29; *Letters*, I, 49–50.

[74] *V. Hild.*, II.5, p. 29, lines 82–90; *Life of Hildegard*, p. 51. Writing to Hartwig soon after Richardis's death, Hildegard praises her friend. *Epistolarium*, I, 13R, pp. 30–31; *Letters*, I, 51.

on appropriate conduct in view of the approaching end times. Much of the material resembles the contemporary sermon in content as in form; the text constitutes a lengthy exhortation that incorporates various sub-genres and addresses lay people and ecclesiastics.[75] The final evocations of the end times, akin to the eschatological warnings of sermons, include a horrific vision of Antichrist taking birth from *Ecclesia* herself.[76] The decade-long composition of *Sciuias*, the interruptions and the process of 'sweating out' the meaning of the visions, perhaps accounts for the various genres. The images and the commentary, which often differs from the illuminations, constitute a sort of primary text upon which ensue further explanations in a different mode. The whole creates a vast didactic edifice.[77] One wonders if the second type of commentary was added to complete the vision with relevant exegetical material or moral exhortation, the sort of reflection on Scripture that Hildegard makes in the *Expositiones*.[78] The example of Julian of Norwich two centuries later provides an interesting parallel. Julian wrote a short version of her *Showings* and then expanded on her visions over a period of around twenty years, probing their

[75] See Kienzle, 'The Twelfth-Century Monastic Sermon', in *The Sermon*, dir. by Kienzle, pp. 271–72, 281–85.

[76] See Emmerson, 'Representation of Antichrist'.

[77] The original manuscript of *Sciuias*, produced by the nuns at Rupertsberg during Hildegard's lifetime, contained thirty-five images. Those were most likely prepared under Hildegard's supervision. The manuscript, formerly Wiesbaden, Hessisches Landesbibliothek, Handschrift 1, has been lost since the end of World War II, when it disappeared from storage in Dresden. Fortunately, a photographic copy was made in 1927. Those original photographs are reproduced in Maura Böckeler, *Wisse die Wege. Scivias: Nach dem Originaltext des illuminierten Rupertsberger Kodex* (Salzburg: Müller, 1928). The nuns at Eibingen also prepared a colour facsimile by hand (1927–33). On the illustrations of Hildegard's works, consult Caviness, 'Hildegard as Designer'; Caviness, 'Artist'; Madeline Caviness, 'Hildegard of Bingen: Some Recent Books', *Speculum*, 77 (2002), 113–20, a review of recent work that pertains to the *Sciuias* illuminations, including Lieselotte E. Saurma-Jeltsch, *Die Miniaturen im Liber 'Scivias' des Hildegard von Bingen: Die Wucht der Vision und die Ordnung der Bilder* (Wiesbaden: Reichert, 1998), who argues (pp. 6–11) that the manuscript postdates Hildegard's death; and Keiko Suzuki, *Bildewordene Visionen oder Visionserzählungen: Vergleichende Studie über die Visionsdarstellungen in der Rupertsberger 'Scivias' — Handschrift und im Luccheser 'Liber diuinorum operum' — Codex der Hildegard von Bingen*, Neue Berner Schriften zur Kunst, 5 (Bern: Lang, 1998). See also Klaus Niehr, Review of Saurma-Jeltsch and Suzuki, *Zeitschrift für deutsches Altertum*, 129 (2000), 215–22; and Emmerson, 'Representation of Antichrist'. I am grateful to Jeffrey Hamburger for references to Saurma-Jeltsch, Suzuki, and Niehr.

[78] On the inseparability of text and image in *Sciuias* and the possible primacy of the images, see Caviness, 'Hildegard as Designer', pp. 30–32; and Emmerson, 'Representation of Antichrist'.

theological meaning to produce the 'long text'.[79] Hildegard probably recorded her visions, visual and verbal, and then laboured at understanding them.

The second work in her trilogy, *Liber uitae meritorum*, begun in 1158, reveals a sermon-like tone and content which invite comparison with preaching. Inspired by a vision she received at age sixty, the *magistra* began to write it down at sixty-one. She toiled over it for five years, approximately 1158–63. Volmar witnessed and assisted with the work, as did 'a certain girl' (*testimonio cuiusdam puelle mihi assistentis*), probably another nun who served as amanuensis after Richardis left.[80] An autobiographical segment of the *Vita* describes how she completed the *Liber uitae meritorum* under duress: 'Although I was frequently worn down by tribulations [. . .], I brought to a conclusion the *Book of Life's Merits* which had been divinely revealed to me by God.'[81] Hildegard retains in the *Liber uitae meritorum* the somewhat homiletic structure of vision followed by lengthy commentary that is evident in *Sciuias*. Through the work's six visions, the figure of a man, superimposed on the universe, looks in four directions and describes what he sees. The *magistra* explains that the man, the *uir preliator* in Isaiah 42. 13, represents God and Christ.[82] Following a description of the visions, Hildegard highlights vices, specifying the remedial virtues along with the corresponding punishment and penance. The emphasis here lies on the negative features of salvation history, and the virtues play a smaller role than in *Sciuias*. Thirty-five vices appear with their corresponding punishment and penance. The result is a 'drama of human life' in

---

[79] Nicholas Watson, 'The Composition of Julian of Norwich's Revelation of Love', *Speculum*, 68 (1993), 637–83, argues that Julian wrote the 'short text' several years after her visions and not shortly thereafter. Scholars concur that Julian wrote the more reflective and theological long text at least twenty years after the visions. I am grateful to Cynthia Bland-Biggar for her suggestions on Julian. The most recent critical edition of the short and long texts is by Nicholas Watson and Jacqueline Jenkins, *The Writings of Julian of Norwich: A Vision Showed to a Devout Woman and a Revelation of Love* (University Park: Pennsylvania State University Press, 2006). Barbara Newman reflects on the creative process in Julian and Hildegard in *God and the Goddesses: Vision, Poetry, and Belief in the Middle Ages* (Philadelphia: University of Pennsylvania Press, 2003), pp. 302–03.

[80] *Vite mer.*, p. 9, lines 26–29. She acknowledges the same nun in the preface of the *LDO*, p. 46, lines 29–30: 'testificante etiam eadem puella cuius in superioribus uisionibus mentionem feci'.

[81] *V. Hild.*, II. 12, lines 38-40: 'Quamuis autem huiusmodi tribulationis frequenter fatigarer, tamen librum Vite meritorum diuinitus michi per gratiam Dei ad finem perduxi.'

[82] See Annelies Meis, '*Symphonia Spiritus Sancti*: Acercamiento al dilema de la razón humana en LVM de Hildegard von Bingen (1098–1179)', *Teología y Vida*, 46 (2005), 389–426 (pp. 391, 424). *Vite mer.*, I, XX–XXI, p. 21, lines 373–79; XXII, p. 22, lines 405–07. The explanation extends through the remainder of the first book.

which 'human reason struggles between vice and virtue'.[83] Less studied by modern scholars than *Sciuias*, the *Liber uitae meritorum* found a contemporary audience among the monks at Villers and Gembloux, where it served for refectory reading, an indication that it reflects features of oral discourse.[84]

Hildegard dates to 1163 her second major exegetical vision, one that stirred her thoughts about her next work, the *Liber diuinorum operum* or *De operatione Dei*, the most exegetical of the three major treatises. She states that she had barely (*uix*) completed the work after seven years.[85] In the *Vita Hildegardis*, the *magistra* recounts how the third exegetical vision (1167), that of John the Evangelist, compelled her to 'explore every statement and word of this Gospel regarding the beginning of the work of God'.[86] 'Soft raindrops' extinguished her corporal sensuality (*sensualitas corporis mei*) and turned her knowledge to another mode (*in alium modum*), unknown to her.[87] Hildegard also perceived a connection between John 1 and Genesis 1: 'I saw that the same explanation must apply to the beginning of the other Scripture which was not yet revealed.'[88] The *Liber diuinorum operum* follows the quasi-homiletic style of vision followed by commentary as it explains the spiritual significance of creation: the interrelationship of the human microcosm,

---

[83] Meis, '*Symphonia Spiritus Sancti*', pp. 391, 424.

[84] Guibert of Gembloux, *Epistolae*, I, 23, p. 253, lines 56–61; Hildegard, *Letters*, II, 108a, p. 46. See the discussion in Embach, *Die Schriften Hildegards von Bingen*, pp. 120–24.

[85] See *LDO*, p. 45, lines 5–14, and p. 10, note 28, above.

[86] The beloved disciple's memory enjoyed great favour in German religious communities, and later women visionaries claimed the authority of his inspiration. See Jeffrey F. Hamburger, *St John the Divine: The Deified Evangelist in Medieval Art and Theology* (Berkeley: University of California Press, 2002), who focuses on the period after Hildegard. See also *Leaves from Paradise: The Cult of John the Evangelist at the Dominican Convent of Paradies bei Soest*, ed. by Jeffrey Hamburger (Cambridge, MA: Houghton Library, 2008), on the sequence 'Verbum Dei Deo natum' and its cultural context.

[87] *V. Hild.*, II.16, p. 43, lines 1–10: 'Subsequenti demum tempore mysticum et mirificam uisionem uidi, ita quod omnia uiscera mea concussa sunt et sensualitas corporis mei extincta est, quoniam scientia mea in alium modum conuersa est, quasi me nescirem. Et de Dei inspiratione in scientiam anime mee quasi gutte suauis pluuie spargebantur, quia et Spiritus Sanctus Iohannem euangelistam imbuit, cum de pectore Iesu profundissimam reuelationem suxit, ubi sensus ipsius sancta diuinitate ita tactus est, quod absconsa mysteria et opera aperuit, "In principio erat uerbum", et cetera'; *Life of Hildegard*, pp. 66–67.

[88] *V. Hild.*, II.16, p. 44, lines 23–26: 'Vidique, quod eadem explanatio initium alterius scripture que necdum manifestata erat esse deberet'; *Life of Hildegard*, pp. 61, 67. On John 1, see *LDO*, I.4.105, pp. 248–64; on Genesis 1, II.1.17–49, pp. 285–344.

body and soul, with the macrocosm of the universe.[89] Ten visions, comprised in three books, advance from the creation through the history of salvation. The percentage of the text devoted to exegesis increases significantly as compared to *Sciuias*.[90] Hildegard had nearly but not completely finished the book in 1170. Final changes to the work were probably finished in 1174 and incorporated into its earliest manuscript.[91]

Rupertsberg and the Expositiones euangeliorum

While writing the visionary works and expanding her practice of written biblical commentary, Hildegard also established new houses for her nuns and a venue for practising oral exegesis. After disputes with Disibodenberg, she obtained permission to found Rupertsberg, where she and her nuns settled around 1150; then in 1165 Eibingen was founded across the Rhine from Bingen. How the *Expositiones* relate to Hildegard's other writings during this period may be indicated in the prologue to the *Liber uitae meritorum*, where the *magistra* lists various works written after the *Liber uitae meritorum*: 'after that vision, the subtleties of the various creatures of nature, and responses and admonitions for many lesser and greater persons, and the symphony of the harmony of celestial revelations, and an unknown language and writings, with certain other expositions'.[92] The 'certain other expositions' undoubtedly include the *Expositiones euangeliorum*. The *Vita Hildegardis* more or less echoes the list: the *Vita* recounts that after composing the *Symphonia* and the *lingua ignota*, Hildegard expounded some gospel passages (*euangelia quedam exposuit*) and wrote other allegorical or typological explanations (*typicas*

---

[89] The Lucca manuscript (Biblioteca Governatina, MS 1942), which probably was made as part of an effort to canonize Hildegard in the 1220s, contains remarkable illustrations. Caviness, 'Artist', p. 112, argues that the illuminations were based on designs that Hildegard devised. See also Caviness, 'Hildegard as Designer', pp. 34–42. On the canonization effort, see Flanagan, *Hildegard of Bingen*, pp. 11–12.

[90] From 16 per cent of passages in *Sciuias* and 8 per cent in the *Vite mer.* to 26 per cent in the *LDO*: McGinn, 'Hildegard of Bingen as Visionary and Exegete', p. 343.

[91] Peter Dronke, *LDO*, p. xii, has identified Letter 217 as a cover letter for the codex. Dronke and Derolez believe that the manuscript in question is the uncorrected version of the oldest manuscript of the *LDO* (Gent, University Library, MS 241). It represents a direct copy from Hildegard's wax tablets and shows the modifications suggested by her collaborators and correctors.

[92] *Vite mer.*, I, p. 8, lines 6–13; see p. 4, note 9, above.

expositiones).[93] Numerous textual parallels between the *Expositiones* and the *magistra*'s other compositions, notably *Sciuias*, the *Symphonia*, and the *Liber diuinorum operum*, reinforce the argument that the seer was working on the *Expositiones* in near proximity to other works.[94]

What further does the manuscript tradition of the *Expositiones* reveal about the texts? The division of the *Expositiones* in their most important manuscript, Wiesbaden, Hessisches Landesbibliothek, Handschrift 2 (Riesenkodex), poses interesting questions as to why the homilies fall into two distinct groupings in the Riesenkodex with two different manuscript headings.[95] *Expositiones* 5–58 are headed *Incipiunt expositiones euangeliorum quas diuina inspirante gracia Hildegardis exposuit*, proclaiming that they were composed with divine inspiration. *Expositiones* 1–4 constitute a separate group following the rubric *Expositio euangeliorum per Hildegardem exposita*, and they appear to have been added at a later date. In the Riesenkodex, the four homilies follow directly Hildegard's *Vita* of Disibod, which is preceded by eight letters between Hildegard and Abbot Kuno, and Hildegard and Abbot Helenger of Disibodenberg.[96] The four *expositiones* may then represent the substance of the *magistra*'s preaching at Disibodenberg around 1170. Abbot Helenger wrote to Hildegard (Letter 77), requesting that she send whatever she knew about the life of Disibod; he further entreated the seer to bestow her wisdom upon her former monastery as a symbol of reconciliation.[97] When the *magistra*

---

[93] *V. Hild.*, II.1, p. 20, lines 16–17. *Life of Hildegard*, p. 41 translates this as 'authoritative explanations'.

[94] Consult the apparatus criticus of the *Expositiones*.

[95] I am indebted to George Ferzoco and Carolyn Muessig for this important insight on the manuscript. The following argument is based on Ferzoco's contribution to the Introduction to *Expo. Euang.*, pp. 144–50. On the Riesenkodex, see also Albert Derolez, *LDO*, pp. xcvii–ci, and L. Van Acker, *Epistolarium*, I, pp. xxvii–xxix.

[96] *Epistolarium*, I, 74, 74R, 75, 75R, 76, 75R, 77, 77R, pp. 160–75. The first set of homilies appears on fols 434ra–436va under a title written in the original hand on fol. 434ra: *Expositio euangeliorum per Hildegardem exposita*. The homilies in the second series, found on fols 436vb–461vb, are given under the rubric *Incipiunt expositiones euangeliorum quas diuina inspirante gracia Hildegardis exposuit*. A scribal addition, probably made in the eighteenth century, placed the title, *Liber expositionis quorundam Euangeliorum*, at the top of folio 434ra and created the perception that the two sets of homilies constituted one work. Ferzoco notes further that on fol. 436va, fifth line from bottom, an ornate final 'm' supports the consideration that this is considered the end of a work. On fol. 437ra, the initial letter of *Expositiones* is perhaps the most ornate letter of the entire codex and is also the second largest letter of the codex (with the largest being the first letter of *Sciuias*).

[97] *Epistolarium*, I, 77, p. 167, lines 21–26: 'quoniam ex debito debetis, quia cum sororibus uestris a nobis quamuis corpore sed non spiritu, ut ueraciter speramus et scimus, egressa estis — si

replied to Helenger, she stated that she 'was ordered to deliver' her words aloud in Disibodenberg.[98] Certainly the four *expositiones*, Letter 77R, and the *Vita Disibodi* evidence thematic connections related to monastic life and practice. *Expositio* 3 on John 6. 1–14 points several times to an audience of monks and nuns (*monachi et uirgines*), the only such references in the *Expositiones*. *Expositio* 3 echoes the *Rule* and evokes a vision of unity in the Church. *Expositio* 4 interprets the same pericope tropologically with a focus on the monastic virtues of humility, discretion, and temperance, and it incorporates language reminiscent of the *Rule*.[99] If these *expositiones* indeed were delivered at Disibodenberg in 1170, a sister or Volmar himself could have taken them down to preserve them.

Do Hildegard's secretaries and biographers give testimony to the *magistra's* strength as exegete and preacher? Volmar praised the seer's exegesis for the community at Rupertsberg — her 'new interpretation' and her 'new and unheard-of sermons on the feast days of saints'.[100] Theodoric compared her to Moses, St John the Evangelist, and Deborah.[101] The biographer avoids the verb *praedicare* (to preach) and uses synonyms such as *exhortari* (to exhort). He notes that the mellifluous *magistra* 'explained certain Gospels and composed other authoritative explanations',[102] an indication that groups the *Expositiones euangeliorum* with other commentaries — surely those on the Athanasian Creed and the *Rule of Benedict*. With language from the Song of Songs, Theodoric describes Hildegard opening to the Holy Spirit's gift; the image in Song 5. 4–6, the bride trembling at the touch of the beloved's hand and opening the locked door, describes the receiving of visionary understanding and the explanation of thorny problems in Scripture. As Theodoric writes, she 'opened the lock', 'at one time orally and at another

---

ueraciter in uera caritate, que est initium omnium bonorum, conuenerimus, uel si qua radix alicuius dissensionis inter nos adhoc lateat manifestetis'.

[98] *Epistolarium*, I, 77R, p. 174, lines 226–27: 'ut ea (=uerba) in loco uestro uiua uoce proferrem iussa sum'; *V. Hild.*, II.10, p. 34, lines 1–8: 'Cumque in his doloribus adhuc laborarem, in uera uisione admonita sum ut ad locum in quo oblata Deo eram irem et uerba que Deus michi ostenderet proferrem; quod feci ac in eodem dolore ad filias meas redii. Ad alia quoque loca congregationum iter arripui ac uerba que Deus iussit ibi explanaui. In his omnibus uas corporis mei quasi in clybano coctum est, sicut et Deus multos probauit, quos uerba sua proferre iussit, unde laus sibi sit.' *V. Disib.*, PL 197: 1093–1116.

[99] See the apparatus fontium for *Expos.* 3 and 4, *Expo. Euang.*, pp. 195–98, 199–202, and the Introduction, p. 164.

[100] *Epistolarium*, II, 195, p. 443, lines 19–21.

[101] *V. Hild.*, II, Prologus, p. 17, II.6, p. 30; *Life of Hildegard*, pp. 37–38, 52.

[102] *V. Hild.*, II.1, p. 20, lines 16–17; *Life of Hildegard*, p. 41.

in writing'.[103] Theodoric lauds Hildegard as a preacher and exegete who removed vanities from the hearts of her nuns 'with the exhortations of the Sacred Scriptures'.[104] Moreover, he indicates that Hildegard preached to audiences beyond her sisters when she 'delivered exhortations' to crowds of both sexes, 'suitably adjusted to the life of both'. Her focus remained exegetical as she 'proposed and resolved [...] questions regarding the Holy Scriptures'.[105] These statements cast Hildegard as an exegete and a capable preacher who knew how to reach her audience.

Did Hildegard's exegesis reach an audience beyond her own community? The seer's reputation for exegetical insight is evidenced by her *Solutiones quaestionum XXXVIII*, a treatise she sent to Guibert of Gembloux for the monks at Villers. Guibert invokes the power of the Holy Spirit's breezes to catch the sails of Hildegard's boat and guide her through the sea of problems to be resolved in Scripture.[106] Guibert of Gembloux describes the activities of the *magistra* and her nuns at Rupertsberg, where he served as Hildegard's secretary and stayed from June 1177 until after her death in 1179. He testifies to the intellectual and spiritual work of the community and his relationship to Hildegard, reading and discussing her works.[107] Moreover, the seer sent other letters to churchmen grappling with exegetical questions.[108]

---

[103] *V. Hild.*, II.3, p. 25, lines 4–23, at lines 20–21: 'nunc uoce, nunc litteris'; *Life of Hildegard*, pp. 46–47. The same passage from the Song is used by the monks of Sylvanès in a letter to Bishop Gaucelin of Lodeve around 1165, praising his ability to open up the mysteries of thorny problems in Scripture. See Beverly Mayne Kienzle and Susan Shroff, 'Cistercians and Heresy: Doctrinal Consultation in Some Twelfth-Century Correspondence from Southern France', *Cîteaux: commentarii cistercienses*, 41 (1990), 159–66.

[104] *V. Hild.*, II.12, p. 37, lines 6–8: 'et cum uanitates, que per deceptionem Sathane oriebantur in cordibus puellarum suarum, remouit exhortacionibus sanctarum scripturarum'; *Life of Hildegard*, pp. 47, 59, 60.

[105] *V. Hild.*, II.4, p. 25, lines 4–6: 'confluebant ad eam undique utriusque sexus populorum examina, quibus per gratiam Dei utriusque uite affatim accomoda impendebat exhortamina'; p. 26, lines 7–8: 'Ad salutem enim animarum suarum proponebat eis et soluebat questiones sanctarum scripturarum'; *Life of Hildegard*, p. 47.

[106] *Solut.*, PL 197: 1037–54. See Ann Clark Bartlett, 'Commentary, Polemic, and Prophecy in Hildegard of Bingen's "Solutiones triginta octo quaestionum"', *Viator*, 23 (1992), 153–65.

[107] Guibert of Gembloux, 'Letter to Bovo', in *Jutta and Hildegard*, trans. by Silvas, pp. 100–02, par. II, III; Guibert of Gembloux, *Epistolae*, II, 38, pp. 367–69, lines 30–87.

[108] On Ezekiel 1, see *Epistolarium*, I, 84R, pp. 190–94. On Song 4. 6, see *Epistolarium*, III, 380, pp. 138–39. On Psalm 103. 8, see *Epistolarium*, III, 380, pp. 133–34. On the Trinity, see the correspondence on the Trinity with Odo of Soissons and with Eberhard of Bamberg: *Epistolarium*,

Hildegard's Travel and Preaching outside Rupertsberg

Hildegard's written admonitions extended to audiences outside her community, but what of her preaching? She directed not only her written words but her live speech beyond the confines of her own monastery and neighbouring Disiboden-berg. Was she unique in this teaching and preaching outside her own communi-ties? The *Vita* of an anonymous *magistra* from Admont shows that the emulation accorded to Hildegard as a woman of great scriptural learning, even if without equal, was not without parallel. The *Vita* praises the unnamed *magistra*'s eloquence and erudite teaching in her home monastery. Moreover, as the *magistra* was second to none in learning, she was sent to other places to provide an example for edifica-tion (*aliquotiens ad alia loca edificationis exemplo transmittebatur*).[109] Her travel may be construed as a scriptural teaching tour that bears comparison to Hilde-gard's preaching journeys. The Admont *magistra*'s peregrinations signal the impor-tance of biblical learning for women in that region and to some degree constitute a parallel to Hildegard: a *magistra* gained renown from home and then undertook a tour to other monasteries for teaching, spiritual advising, or preaching.

From the Rupertsberg, Hildegard journeyed to other audiences, primarily monastic communities whom she admonished about monastic and clerical reform. These travels have been described as preaching 'tours' and generally have been dated as follows: the first between 1158 and 1161 when she had reached the age of sixty; the second intervening in 1160 when she preached in the cathedral at Trier; the third between 1161 and 1163; and the fourth in 1167–70, when she was around seventy and had just suffered a serious illness.[110]

I, 40, 40R, pp. 102–05; 30, 30R, pp. 83–88. McGinn discusses these in 'Hildegard of Bingen as Visionary and Exegete', pp. 333–34. Bartlett highlights the tension between cloister and schools in 'Commentary, Polemic and Prophecy', passim.

[109] Lutter, *Geschlect und Wissen*, pp. 226–29 (p. 227): 'In silentio persistebat reverenter usque ad tempus loquendi, quod praenominatur regulariter; quanta gravitate, quanta affabilitate loquens omnes nos admonuit; et totus sermo illius inter nos de praeteritis, de futuris, de fidelium gloria, de eternitate sanctorum fuit. Et quia in divinis cultibus, studiis quoque liberalibus nulli secunda habe-batur, aliquotiens ad alia loca edificationis exemplo transmittebatur [...]. Sermo autem illius iuxta praeceptum apostoli erat "in gratia sale conditus"; id est graciosus, acceptus, ordinatus, temperatus, praestans audientibus edificationem, non immemor originis, nam ex illustrissimis Salzpurgensis ecclesie ministri oriunda exstitit, ibique in superiori castro eius urbis educata aliquos annos iuventutis sue exegit.'

[110] See Eduard Grönau, *Hildegard von Bingen 1098–1179, Prophetische Lehrerin der Kirche an der Schwelle und am Ende der Neuzeit* (Stein am Rhein: Christiana, 1985), pp. 250–84; Newman,

What do medieval sources reveal about these journeys? In the *Vita*, Hildegard states that she was admonished by a vision to go to Disibodenberg ('the place where I was offered to God'). Furthermore, she records that she returned home and then, 'also journeyed to the locations of other congregations and there explained the words which God has ordered'.[111] The letters corroborate a visit to Disibodenberg in 1170. Elsewhere in the *Vita*, she speaks more boldly about a journey: 'In the midst of all this, it was shown me in true vision that I would go to see certain communities of spiritual men and women and openly declare to them what God had shown me.' Suffering from pain and 'for fear of the people', Hildegard hesitated, although she was commanded by God to settle quarrels. Finally, she obeyed and her pain was relieved. The next autobiographical passage recounts the soothing of her soul by a vision, after which she composed the *Life of St Disibod*.[112] These passages in the *Vita* follow the exorcism of the demon possessing Sigewize and its utterance of heretical ideas; the timing may indicate that the preaching to 'certain communities' involved, at least in part, the intent to combat Catharism. In any case, both the first and second remarks in the *Vita* are linked to the composition of the *Life of St Disibod*, which was requested by the Abbot of Disbodenberg when she went to that abbey in 1170. They may refer to one and the same journey, which she undertook after visiting Disibodenberg.

Theodoric, the third of the *magistra's* biographers, cites twenty-one places where Hildegard preached: the five cathedral cities of Cologne, Trier, Metz,

---

Sister of Wisdom, pp. 11–12; Flanagan, *Hildegard of Bingen*, pp. 172–73; Régine Pernoud, 'Die predigten Hildegards von Bingen', in *Tiefe des Gotteswissens — Schönheit der Sprachgestalt bei Hildegard von Bingen. Internationales Symposium in der Katholischen Akademie Rabanus Maurus, Wiesbaden-Naurod vom 9. bis 12. September 1994*, ed. by Margot Schmidt (Stuttgart, 1995), pp. 181–92; Pernoud, 'The Preaching Peregrinations of a Twelfth-Century Nun', in *Wisdom which Encircles Circles*, ed. by A. E. Davidson (Kalamazoo: Medieval Institute Publications, 1996), pp. 15–26.

[111] *V. Hild.*, II.10, p. 34, lines 1–5: 'Cumque in his doloribus adhuc laborarem, in uera uisione admonita sum, ut ad locum in quo oblata Deo eram irem et uerba que Deus michi ostenderet proferrem; quod et feci ac in eodem dolore ad filias meas redii. Ad alia quoque loca congregationum iter arripui ac uerba que Deus iussit ibi explanaui'; *Life of Hildegard*, p. 57.

[112] *V. Hild.*, III.23, p. 66, lines 20–28: 'Inter hec in uera uisione michi ostensum fuit, quod quasdam congregationes spiritualium hominum, uirorum ac mulierum, inuiserem eiusque uerba que Deus michi ostenderet aperte manifestarem [. . .] has uias, quas Deus michi precepit, cum negligerem propter populi timorem, dolores michi corporis sunt augmentati nec cessabant, quousque obediui [. . .]. Post hec ab abbate meo et fratribus humillima instantia et deuotione coacta sum, ut uitam sancti Disibodi [. . .] ut Deus uellet scriberem'; *Life of Hildegard*, p. 92. *V. Hild.*, III.25, p. 67, lines 1–3. See *Epistolarium*, I, 77R, pp. 168–74.

Würzburg, and Bamberg, where she 'announced' to the clergy and people 'the things which God wanted'; and sixteen monasteries, where she 'proclaimed' 'things which pertained to the good of souls as God had revealed to her'. The list is presumed not to be complete, because it omits Kirchheim at the least.[113]

No evidence remains for the Bamberg and Würzburg preaching, although Hildegard corresponded with Eberhard of Bamberg on the interpretation of the Trinity.[114] Extant letters indicate that local clergy requested the texts for the Trier, Cologne, and Kirchheim sermons. The provost of St Peter's in Trier petitioned Hildegard on behalf of the entire city's clergy for a sermon delivered there at Pentecost in 1160.[115] That sermon calls upon Church leaders to reform, but does not allude to heresy.[116] Philip, dean of the cathedral at Cologne and later the archbishop, wrote to ask for a sermon Hildegard delivered there in 1163. He alludes twice to the oral discourse the seer pronounced in his city: Hildegard 'revealed the words of life' (*uerba uitae [. . .] nobis aperuistis*) and 'spoke aloud' (*uiua uoce [. . .] dixistis*).[117] Moreover, Philip identifies the Holy Spirit as the source for Hildegard's authority.

> Because we esteem your maternal piety, we want to inform you that after your recent visit to us at God's command when, through divine inspiration, you revealed the words of life to us, we were greatly astonished that God works through such a fragile vessel, such a fragile sex, to display the great marvels of his secrets. 'But the Spirit breathes where it will' (Jn 3. 8).

---

[113] *V. Hild.*, III.17, pp. 54–55; *Life of Hildegard*, p. 79.

[114] *Epistolarium*, I, 31–31R, pp. 82–88; *Letters*, I, pp. 94–99.

[115] *Epistolarium*, II, 223R, pp. 490–96; *Letters*, III, pp. 18–23. See Flanagan, *Hildegard of Bingen*, p. 167, for a brief mention.

[116] *Epistolarium*, II, 223R, pp. 490–96; *Letters*, III, pp. 18–23. See Flanagan, *Hildegard of Bingen*, p. 167, for a brief mention.

[117] *Epistolarium*, I, 15R, pp. 34–47. Philip of Heinsberg, later the Archbishop of Cologne, was a friend of Hildegard's who intervened in the dispute over the man buried at Rupertsberg, and according to Guibert of Gembloux, visited Hildegard rather frequently (*sepius*). See Guibert of Gembloux, *Epistolae*, II, 26, p. 280, lines 376–78; Silvas in *Jutta and Hildegard*, p. 91, translates *sepius* as 'constantly'. Philip's family founded the Premonstratensian house at Heinsberg in *c.* 1150. See Shelley Amiste Holbrink, 'Women in the Premonstratensian Order of Northwestern Germany 1120–1250', *Catholic Historical Review*, 89 (2003), 387–408 (pp. 388, 395, 397, 400). From Holbrink's analysis it is clear that close ties existed between Heinsberg and Steinfeld, where Everwin, author of the famous letter to Bernard of Clairvaux, served as prior. The link between those two houses and Philip's patronage of Heinsberg could have made Everwin's letter accessible to Philip, who could have at the least discussed it with Hildegard when the crisis over Cathars in Cologne arose during the 1160s. See Brunn, *Des contestataires aux 'cathares'*, pp. 131–60, on Everwin's letter.

For since it is abundantly clear that the Spirit has chosen a dwelling that pleases it in your heart, understandably we come to you in admiration as if to the living temple of God to offer up prayers, and we seek responses of truth from your heart, as from the very oracle of God.[118]

The Cologne sermon was delivered sometime in 1163. A 1220 reference from Gebeno, prior of Everbach, attests to the sermon's influence. He wrote to Hildegard's daughters about the Cathars at their request; in developing his own arguments, he cites Hildegard's letter to Cologne.

Werner of Kirchheim addressed a letter to Hildegard in 1170, similar to Phillip's, requesting a copy of the words she interpreted for 'us and many more' in that city (*nobis et aliis quam plurimis in Kirchheim presentibus [...] aperuistis*).[119] This probably refers to a sermon delivered at Kirchheim that denounces clerical corruption.[120] Hildegard's defense of orthodoxy and her calls for clerical reform doubtless contributed to her voice being heard among ecclesiastical audiences.

The various terms that these churchmen and Theodoric employ for Hildegard's discourse reflect the broad range of words that designate the act of preaching, particularly when the speech act does not come from the mouth of an authorized cleric. When a medieval author describes the religious discourse of a woman to an

---

[118] *Epistolarium*, I, 15, p. 33, lines 5–24: 'Quia maternam pietatem uestram diligimus, uobis notum facimus quia, postquam nuper a nobis recessistis, cum per diuinam iussionem ad nos uenistis, ubi uerba uite, prout Deus uobis inspirauit, nobis aperuistis, in maximam admirationem, ducti sumus pro eo quod Deus in tam fragili uase, in tam fragili sexu hominis tanta mira secretorum suorum operatur. Sed "Spiritus ubi uult spirat". Nam, ex multis rerum indiciis manifestum sit, quod in precordiis uestris placitam sibi sedem elegerit, merito et nos in admirationibus nostris ad uos quasi ad uiuum Dei templum preces oblaturi accedimus, et de corde uestro, sicuti reuera de Dei oraculo, ueritatis responsa flagitamus. Beatitudinem enim uestram quam intime exoramus, ut desideria nostra, quoniam ad curam animarum respiciunt, intentius Deo commendetis, et si quid adherens Deo animus uester, ut assolet, in uera uisione de nobis peruiderit, litteris nobis intimare curetis. Rogamus etiam, ut ea que uiua uoce nobis prius dixistis, litteris quoque commendetis et nobis transmittatis, quia, dum carnalibus concupiscentiis dediti sumus, spiritalia, que nec frequenter uidemus nec audimus, facile per negligentiam obliuioni tradimus.'

[119] *Epistolarium*, II, 149, pp. 332–33, lines 18–23: 'Adhuc uos unam petitionem petere praesumimus, scilicet ut que uos, Spiritu sancto docente, nobis et aliis quam plurimis in Kirchheim presentibus, de negligentia sacerdotum quam in diuino sacrificio habent aperuistis, materna pietate nobis scribere et transmittere non negligatis, ne a memoria nostra labantur, sed ut ea attentius pre oculis semper habeamus.'

[120] Flanagan, *Hildegard of Bingen*, p. 172, points out that Werner's letter gives the evidence for Hildegard's presence at Kirchheim. Newman, *Sister of Wisdom*, pp. 241–42, discusses the letter to Werner of Kirchheim.

audience, which in other circumstances and from a male voice would be termed a sermon or a homily, he often has recourse to the verbs 'announce' (*annuncio*), 'proclaim' (*proclamo*), 'exhort' (*exhortor*), and the like instead of 'preach' (*praedicare*). The same semantic shifting occurs in descriptions of the speech of lay persons and heretics. Terminology by itself does not declassify Hildegard's utterances from being considered sermons or instances of preaching.[121]

Likewise, the epistolary form of the discourses from Trier, Kirchheim, and Cologne does not imply that they were never sermons. The transmittal of sermons in the form of letters was not an uncommon occurrence in twelfth-century monastic circles.[122] Sermons, letters, and exegetical discourses showed common characteristics. Certain features in the opening and closing of letters, in conformity with the *ars dictaminis*, marked the epistolary genre. Letters and sermons both employed direct address, while sermons revealed other signs of orality such as exhortation.[123]

In addition to the cathedral cities, Theodoric lists sixteen places where Hildegard addressed monastic congregations: Disibodenberg, Siegburg, Eberbach, Hirsau, Zwiefalten, Maulbronn, Rothenkirchen, Kitzingen, Krauftal, Hördt, Höningen, Werden, Andernach, Marienberg, Klause, and Winkel. An examination of the *Hildegardis Epistolarium* shows letters between Hildegard and correspondents at most of the monasteries listed. Letter 77R corroborates the visit to Disibodenberg, as does the *Vita Hildegardis*.[124] In certain additional cases, the letters indicate clearly that Hildegard was physically present at a given monastery. Abbess Hazzecha of Krauftal (Ep. 159, *c.* 1160–61) recalls Hildegard's 'friendly visit' and inspired words but does not describe the circumstances of her utterances, that is whether they were private or communal. The provost of Hördt thanks the

---

[121] Kienzle, 'Conclusion', in *The Sermon*, dir. by Kienzle, p. 970.

[122] Kienzle, 'Twelfth-Century Monastic Sermon', pp. 275, 280.

[123] On monastic letters, see Giles Constable, *Letters and Letter Collections*, Typologie des Sources du Moyen Âge Occidental, 17 (Turnhout: Brepols, 1976); Beverly Mayne Kienzle, 'New Introduction' for re-edition of *The Letters of St. Bernard of Clairvaux*, trans. by Bruno Scott James (Stroud: Sutton, 1998), pp. vii–xvii.

[124] *Epistolarium*, I, 77, 77R, p. 174, lines 226–27: 'ut ea (=uerba) in loco uestro uiua uoce proferrem iussa sum'; *V. Hild.*, II.10, p. 34, lines 1–8: 'Cumque in his doloribus adhuc laborarem, in uera uisione admonita sum ut ad locum in quo oblata Deo eram irem et uerba que Deus michi ostenderet proferrem; quod feci ac in eodem dolore ad filias meas redii. Ad alia quoque loca congregationum iter arripui ac uerba que Deus iussit ibi explanaui. In his omnibus uas corporis mei quasi in clybano coctum est, sicut et Deus multos probauit, quos uerba sua proferre iussit, unde laus sibi sit.' *V. Disib.*, *PL* 197: 1093–1116.

magistra for visiting two times and writes to her (Ep. 138, *c.* 1160) that he and his brothers were 'consoled through the organ of your voice and made worthy to hear the voice of Lord Christ, who dwells in you'.[125]

Is there other evidence of Hildegard's contact with the places Theodoric lists? The letters confirm the communication between Hildegard and most of the other monasteries that Theodoric names, including Siegburg, Eberbach, Hirsau, Zwiefalten, Maulbronn, Rothenkirchen, Kitzingen, Andernach, Zwiefalten, and Hirsau. In most instances, the writers simply ask for advice in general or plead for written counsel, but some point to closer contact. Sophia, Abbess of Kitzingen, refers to her visit to Hildegard. The Abbot of Rothenkirchen indicates he has witnessed Hildegard's prophetic gift and asks for written consolation.[126] He does not specify the circumstances of his witness to the seer's prophecy. Zwiefalten, a Hirsau monastery with an impressive library, and both a women's and a men's community, owned a manuscript containing some of Hildegard's letters and recorded the death of a female scribe from its community.[127]

At the minimum, an oral tradition about the *magistra*'s preaching at Hirsau and Zwiefalten must have existed, for Johannes Trithemius includes those visits in his *Chronica insignis monasterii Hirsaugiensis*. Trithemius, as Anna Silvas notes, consulted documents now unavailable and was familiar with oral tradition from Hildegard's milieu. Some of his information proves erroneous, but as Silvas puts it, he 'is invaluable in giving us the whole texture and colour' of regional tradition.[128] Trithemius alone provides an account of Hildegard's visit to Hirsau. He reports her preaching journey in the year 1160 when Manegold was Abbot of Hirsau.

---

[125] For Krauftal, see *Epistolarium*, II, 159–62, pp. 355–65, at Ep. 159, p. 355; *Letters*, II, 107–13, at p. 107. For Hördt, see *Epistolarium*, II, 137–38, pp. 310–12, at Ep. 138, pp. 311–12; *Letters*, II, 77–78, at p. 78.

[126] For Kitzingen, see *Epistolarium*, II, 150–52, pp. 337–40; *Letters*, II, pp. 94–96. For Rothenkirchen, see *Epistolarium*, II, 191–91R, pp. 431–33; *Letters*, II, pp. 157–58. For Siegburg, see *Epistolarium*, II, 205–06R, pp. 459–63; *Letters*, II, pp. 186–88. For Eberbach, see *Epistolarium*, I, 81–84R, pp. 183–201; *Letters*, I, pp. 178–91. For Maulbronn, see *Epistolarium*, II, 171–73R, pp. 389–95; *Letters*, II, pp. 130–33. For Andernach, see *Epistolarium*, I, 52–52R, pp. 125–130; *Letters*, I, pp. 127–30. I have not identified letters for Höningen, Werden, Marienberg, Klause, or Winkel. For Wechterswinkel, see *Epistolarium*, II, 231–35, pp. 506–11; *Letters*, III, pp. 31–35.

[127] Letters to the monks and nuns of Zwiefalten include *Epistolarium*, II, 241–50R, pp. 519–32; *Letters*, III, pp. 40–48. On the monastery and its library, see Constant J. Mews, 'Monastic Educational Culture Revisited: The Witness of Zwiefalten and the Hirsau Reform', in *Medieval Monastic Education*, ed. by Ferzoco and Muessig, pp. 182–97.

[128] *Jutta and Hildegard*, trans. by Silvas, p. xx.

Several letters attest to a close relationship between Hildegard and Manegold, but none of those mentions a visit. Two of the letters are addressed to the entire congregation, but they are dated prior to Manegold's abbacy. Several of the sixteen letters to Abbot Manegold concern his difficulties with the monks and establish that Hildegard's was closely involved in advising him.[129] The episode in Trithemius deserves citing in its entirety; although not a contemporary account, it furnishes the only description of Hildegard speaking at another monastery.[130]

> The seer, compelled by the Holy Spirit, announced the Word of God in person at many places. She came to Hirsau, and Manegold and the congregation of monks received her joyously, as if she were an angel from heaven. After the customary prayer, seated in the middle of the brothers, she opened her mouth in the name of Christ. She conveyed so fervently, soberly, and prudently to the listeners the Word that the Holy Spirit entrusted to her that all turned around in great surprise. A miracle happened: while she was speaking the Word outwardly, in effect the Holy Spirit was working inwardly in the hearts of those listening. The Spirit so filled all with the grace of compunction that they were compelled to shed tears out of deepest feeling before the gentleness of her thought. Among the other things said in her most gentle speech, she foretold to the brothers that unless they guarded carefully against the plots of the ancient enemy, they would undergo some tribulation in a short space of time. That very thing happened the same year in the pernicious discord that sprung up at the devil's instigation between Manegold and the congregation. Instructed by the Holy Spirit, she reproached all at the same time about those things that concerned the community, concerning both hidden and obvious failings, and with most prudent reasoning she displayed those things that were displeasing to divine majesty either in their conversion or their way of life. From there she journeyed and was present at the monastery of our order in Zweifalten and announced equally to the nuns and the monks in that place the things that the Holy Spirit commanded to her. In many monasteries and places in Swabia also, she turned many from wickedness by her admonitions and revealed the word of the Lord by the witness of miracles.[131]

---

[129] *Epistolarium*, II, 119–36, pp. 292–309; *Letters*, II, pp. 64–77. The letters are dated from the 1150s to 1165, coinciding with Manegold's abbacy.

[130] I analyse this episode from the perspective of performance theory in 'Performing the Gospel Stories: Hildegard of Bingen's Dramatic Exegesis in the *Expositiones euangeliorum*', in *Visualizing Medieval Performance: Perspectives, Histories, Contexts*, ed. by Elina Gertsman (Aldershot: Ashgate, 2008), pp. 121–40.

[131] Johannes Trithemius, *Chronica insignis monasterii Hirsaugiensis*, p. 145: 'Anno Manegoldi abbatis 3, qui fuit dominicae natiuitatis (sicut diximus) 1160, S. Hildegardis uirgo Christi, monasterii diui confessoris Ruperti, iuxta Bingios abbatissa, per spiritum sanctum coacta multis in locis uerbum Dei hominibus personaliter annunciauit. Inter caetera uero loca quae sua praesentia sanctificauit, etiam ad Hirsaugiam uenit, quam abbas Manegoldus et conuentus fratrum cum inaestimabili gaudio, tanquam angelum Domini de coelo uenientem susceperunt. At illa post

This slice of hagiography recalls in its generic features the accounts of preaching journeys by male saints such as Bernard of Clairvaux, who converted many through preaching and miracles as he travelled.[132] Trithemius, however, describes Hildegard's preaching in monasteries and not cities and towns, although he alludes to 'other places'. Note the varying terminology he employs for Hildegard's speech acts: she 'announced the Word of God', 'opened her mouth in the name of Christ', 'conveyed the word', 'spoke the word', 'foretold', and 'uttered talks (*colloquia*) of her sweetest speech'. Nowhere does Trithemius use the verb *praedicare* (to preach); however, the word *colloquia* is probably synonymous with *collationes*, the informal talks, not in a Eucharistic context, that were delivered in monastic chapter houses.[133] When Trithemius describes Hildegard sitting in the midst of the brothers, he and I picture her sitting in the chapter house, with the monks on three sides of the room nearly encircling her. The fact that he does not use the verb *praedicare* does not indicate that the same speech act, if uttered by a male, would not be described with the verb *praedicare*.[134]

Trithemius's account suggests that Hildegard engaged in continuing travel with visits to Hirsau, Zwiefalten, and other places around 1160. The chronology that Trithemius uses for Hildegard's preaching corresponds to the dating of the epistolary attestations from Krauftal and Hördt. The whole of those visits would

orationem consuetam in medio fratrum sedens, os suum in Christi nomine aperuit, et uerbum quod Spiritus Sanctus illi commiserat, tan feruenter, sobrie, ac prudenter audientibus intimauit, ut omnes in stuporem uerterentur. Mira res accidit. Dum illa foris loqueretur uerbum, Spiritus Sanctus in cordibus audientium intus operabatur effectum; tantaque omnes gratia compunctionis perfudit, ut lachrymas fundere ex intimo affectu prae dulcedine mentis cogerentur. Inter caetera dulcissimi sermonis sui colloquia, fratribus praedixit, quoniam nisi caute insidias hostis antiqui praecauerent, in breui temporis spacio tribulationem aliquam experirentur. Quod eodem anno accidit in dissensione illa perniciosa quae inter abbatem Manegoldum et conuentum, diabolo procurante, fuit exorta, de qua suo loco dicemus. Omnes simul in his quae communitatem concernebant, de occultis et manifestis defectibus per spiritum sanctum edocta redarguit, et que in eorum conuersione seu conuersatione diuinae maiestati displicerent, prudentissima ratione ostendit. Inde progressa monasterium Zuuifaltense nostri ordinis adiit, et tam monialibus quam monachis ibidem similiter quae Spiritus sanctus ei mandauerat, annunciauit. In multis quoque Sueuiae monasteriis et locis, uerbum Domini attestatione miraculorum populis aperuit, et suis admonitionibus plures ab iniquitate auertit.'

[132] Kienzle, *Cistercians, Heresy and Crusade*, pp. 97–103, on Bernard of Clairvaux's preaching tours in Occitania.

[133] Kienzle, 'Conclusion', in *The Sermon*, p. 970.

[134] Kienzle, 'Preaching as Touchstone', pp. 33–40; Kienzle, 'Preface: Authority and Definition', pp. xiii–xiv.

plausibly constitute a preaching 'tour', as would the travels Hildegard made around 1170 after her visit to Disibodenberg. It is not clear whether her descriptions in the *Vita* pertain to one and the same journey occurring after the trip to Disibodenberg, or to two different journeys, although scholars have generally taken them as testimony to two 'tours'.

Taking into account the aforementioned travels and the requests from clergymen in Trier (1160), Cologne (1163), and Kirchheim (1170), we find evidence for Hildegard's preaching travels around 1160 and around 1170, and for a trip to Cologne in 1163. The view that the *magistra* made four preaching tours seems to be based on a conjectured itinerary including the places that Theodoric names for her visits and the letters she exchanged with the monasteries that her hagiographer names. However plausible the reconstructed itineraries may be, they are not found in medieval sources. There is no convincing reason to doubt Theodoric's list of monasteries that Hildegard visited; however, there are not corroborating texts for all the sites, nor is there evidence for weaving all the visits together into four tours.[135]

The range of Hildegard's travels remains impressive. Scholars draw on the list of places she visited not only for evidence of her preaching, but also for indications of libraries she could have visited, such as St Maximin in Trier, or works that she might have known and consulted.[136] The scriptorium at St Maximin produced masterpieces of Ottonian book illumination, such as the *Codex Egberti*, a pericopes book, and two tenth-century pandects containing the *Moralia in Iob* of Gregory the Great.[137] However, Hildegard's access to the sources at Trier could derive from her frequent exchange with the clergy there and does not depend solely on her physical presence in that city.[138]

Theodoric extends Hildegard's preaching to another audience when he extols her as a preacher to Jews who sought her out with questions: 'she exhorted them

---

[135] Franz Felten is critical of scholars who repeat the notion of the four tours with no examination of evidence. He considers the tours to be a product of late nineteenth- or early twentieth-century writers, but I have not yet located where the idea begins or found the sort of analysis of the relevant texts that I do above. Felten, 'Hildegard von Bingen, 1098–1998', pp. 169, 184–86, criticizes Newman's conclusions on Hildegard's preaching in 'Three-Part Invention', esp. pp. 204–05.

[136] See Dronke, *LDO*, pp. xiii–xxxv; and Dronke, 'Platonic-Christian Allegories', p. 384, n. 11, pp. 391–93.

[137] Mayr-Harting, *Ottonian Book Illumination*, II, 209.

[138] On Hildegard's contact with the clergy in those cities, see Rudolf Holbach, 'Hildegard von Bingen und die kirchlichen Metropolen Mainz, Köln und Trier', in *Umfeld*, pp. 71–115.

to the faith of Christ with words of loving admonition'.[139] Is this plausible? First, does evidence point to Hildegard's interaction with people from outside the monastery? Several letters do attest to people visiting Hildegard at Rupertsberg to seek her advice.[140] Spiritual advice, when delivered orally in a quasi-public setting, served as a sort of preaching and was qualified as such in some cases.[141] Similarly, the content of exegetical consultations or discussions was sometimes recorded, whereupon the written form was referred to as a sermon; such examples are found in the works of Bernard of Clairvaux.[142] To my knowledge, no texts of that sort are identified for Hildegard, but they may exist among the letters. Furthermore, the community around Rupertsberg took part in some of the monastery's activities, as when Hildegard describes the participation of all the residents of Bingen in the funeral of the man she agreed to have buried at Rupertsberg.[143]

Given that Hildegard did have some interaction with visitors and townspeople, could they have included Jews? Angela Carlevaris evaluates Theodoric's statement and cites Hildegard's profound interest in exegesis of the Old Testament, examples of twelfth-century Christian scholars consulting rabbis, and the tradition of Jewish erudition in Mainz. She concludes that 'it seems not impossible' that Jewish scholars who lived not far from Rupertsberg could have come to see Hildegard.[144]

The presence of a Jewish community in Bingen and in nearby cities gives Theodoric's assertion plausibility beyond hagiographic convention. Jews lived in Bingen at least as early as the mid-twelfth century, when Benjamin of Tudela made

---

[139] *V. Hild.*, II.4, p. 26, lines 15–17: 'Sed et Iudeos, dum ad se uenirent causa interrogationis, conuictos de lege sua ad Christi fidem exhortabatur uerbis pie admonitionis'; *Life of Hildegard*, p. 47.

[140] Van Engen points this out in 'Letters and the Public Persona of Hildegard', pp. 41–42, and posits that Hildegard's description in the *Vita Disibodi* of the saint's reception of visitors corresponds to her own practice.

[141] Among numerous parallels are the words of advice given to others by Gertrude of Helfta, where her utterances are not called sermons, even when heard outside the walls; or the *uitae* of Italian male hermit saints, whose cave-based exhortations were called unhesitatingly preaching or sermons. See Gertrude of Helfta, *Herald of Divine Love*, I, 53–54; George Ferzoco, 'Preaching by Thirteenth-Century Italian Hermits', in *Medieval Monastic Education*, ed. by Ferzoco and Muessig, pp. 148–58.

[142] See Jean Leclercq, 'Études sur S. Bernard et le texte de ses écrits', *Analecta Cisterciensia*, 9 (1953), 45–83 (pp. 55–62); and Kienzle, 'The Monastic Sermon', p. 291.

[143] *Epistolarium*, I, 23, p. 62, lines 52–53: 'cum tota Pinguiensi processione sine contradictione cuiusdam apud nos sepultus esset'. *Letters*, I, 77.

[144] See Carlevaris, 'Sie kamen zu ihr, um sie zu befragen'.

note of their presence in the diary of his travels from Zaragossa (1160–73).[145] From at least the eleventh century onward, Jewish communities maintained a strong presence in and around the cities of Speyer, Worms, and Mainz — the archepiscopal see for Hildegard's monastery. Many noted scholars and rabbis taught at Mainz, among them martyrs of the First Crusade.[146] Mid-twelfth-century scholars at Mainz included Elieser ben Nathan, Kalonymos ben Jehuda, and Eljakim ben Josef. A monk of St Eucharius and St Matthias in Trier notes his collaboration with a Jew on the life of St Matthias he composed.[147] It is possible that Hildegard participated in dialogue with Jews to some degree.

However, no other source alludes to Hildegard addressing Jews or receiving visits from them. Theodoric's claim, particularly the assertion of Hildegard's preaching to Jews, may reflect hagiographic exaggerations. Hildegard's emulated predecessor, Rupert of Deutz, debated in Münster with a Jew named Herman in 1128. Herman eventually converted, then became prior of the Premonstratensian house of Scheda. A treatise on his conversion, *Opusculum de conversione sua*, is attributed to him.[148] Rupert's precedent for debate with Herman may have influenced Hildegard's biographer.

---

[145] *The World of Benjamin of Tudela: A Medieval Mediterranean Travelogue*, ed. by Sandra Benjamin (Madison: Fairleigh Dickinson University Press; London: Associated University Presses, 1995). Richard Gottheil and Wilhelm Bacher, 'Benjamin of Tudela', in *The Jewish Encyclopedia*, 12 vols (New York: Funk and Wagnalls, 1925), III, 34–35.

[146] Jewish presence in Cologne may pre-date settlement in Mainz. Matthias Schmandt, 'Cologne, Jewish Centre on the Lower Rhine', in *The Jews of Europe in the Middle Ages (Tenth to Fifteenth Centuries): Proceedings of the International Symposium held at Speyer, 20–25 October 2002*, ed. by Christoph Cluse, Cultural Encounters in Late Antiquity and the Middle Ages, 4 (Turnhout: Brepols, 2004), pp. 367–77 (pp. 367–69); Werner Transier, 'The ShUM Communities: Cradle and Center of Jewry along the Rhine in the Middle Ages', in *The Jews of Europe in the Middle Ages*, ed. by Historisches Museum der Pfalz, Speyer (Speyer: Hatje Cantz, 2005), pp. 59–67; Chazan, *In the Year 1096*, passim; Gotthard Deutsch and Siegmund Salfeld, 'Mayence', in *Jewish Encyclopedia*, VIII, 386–91 (pp. 386–90).

[147] See Carlevaris, 'Sie kamen zu ihr, um sie zu befragen', pp. 126–27.

[148] Herman Judaeus, *Opusculum de conversione sua*, ed. by Gerlinde Niemeyer, MGH, Quellen zur Geistesgeschichte des Mittelalters, 4 (Weimar: Herman Böhlaus Nachfolger, 1963), pp. 69–128. See Van Engen, *Rupert of Deutz*, p. 243; Haverkamp, *Medieval Germany*, p. 219; Karl F. Morrison, *Conversion and Text: The Cases of Augustine of Hippo, Herman-Judah, and Constantine Tsatsos* (Charlottesville: University Press of Virginia, 1992); Jean-Claude Schmitt, *La Conversion d'Hermann le Juif: Autobiographie, histoire et fiction* (Paris: Seuil, 2003).

Spirit, Song, and Sermons: 'Prosimetric' Preaching

Hildegard's liturgical songs offer many textual parallels with the *Expositiones* that point to their composition during the years Hildegard spent at Rupertsberg. Hildegard considered her musical ability as a divine gift just as she attributed her understanding of the Scriptures to the Spirit's enlightenment.[149] Moreover, she compared singing to teaching, when she described teachers as those who 'sing righteousness into the hearts of human beings'.[150] Even though Hildegard did not study music formally, she received extensive training to sing the Psalter. She and Jutta could hear the monks at Disibodenberg singing the Divine Office day and night. Hildegard composed for the Office,[151] and Margot Fassler asserts that Hildegard, as religious superior of her community, would have intoned her own elaborate responsories and thus asserted her leadership in liturgy as another dimension of her theological teaching.[152]

Unlike Augustine, Hildegard was not bothered by the pleasures of music. He had spoken of the melody of the Psalms as being seductive while the words were wholesome.[153] For Hildegard, music belonged to the realm of the spirit. Musical harmony represented celestial harmony, and liturgical singing brought together

---

[149] *V. Hild.*, II.2, p. 24, lines 92–94; *Life of Hildegard*, pp. 44–45. Guibert of Gembloux describes Hildegard's composition of music in *Epistolae*, I, 18, p. 231, lines 207–14. I am grateful to Felix Heinzer for pointing out the issues in interpreting this passage, notably lines 212–14: 'prosis ad laudem Dei et sanctorum honorem compositis, in ecclesia publice decantari facit'. Barbara Newman cites it as proof that Hildgard intended her music to be sung for the Mass and Divine Office at Rupertsberg. Hildegard of Bingen, *Symphonia: A Critical Edition of the 'Symphonia armonie celestium revelationum'* [*Symphony of the Harmony of Celestial Revelations*], ed. and trans. by Barbara Newman, 2nd edn (Ithaca: Cornell University Press, 1998), p. 12.

[150] *LDO*, III.2.10, pp. 367–68, lines 43–45: 'Qui autem per doctrinam omnipotentis Dei officium suum exercent alios docendo, fistulis sanctitatis resonant, cum per uocem racionalitatis iusticiam in mentes hominum canunt.' I am grateful to Jess Michalik for finding this passage.

[151] Barbara Newman, *Symphonia*, pp. 12–17, observes that the number of compositions in her work reflects the frequency of usage in the Office: of the seventy-seven compositions, forty-three are antiphons and eighteen are responsories.

[152] See Margot Fassler, 'Composer and Dramatist: "Melodious Singing and the Freshness of Remorse"', in *Voice*, pp. 149–75 (pp. 153–56); and *Symphonia*, ed. and trans. by Newman, pp. 12–32, on the monastic and theological context of Hildegard's lyrics.

[153] Augustine of Hippo, *Confessionum Libri XIII*, ed. by Luc Verheijen, CCSL, 27 (Turnhout: Brepols, 1981), 10.33, pp. 181–82; *Symphonia*, ed. and trans. by Newman, p. 27.

body and soul and mirrored the dual nature of Christ.[154] She extends the allegory of music and the Spirit further to assert that music springs from the Church through the Holy Spirit, just as Jesus was born from Mary through the Spirit.[155]

The lives of regional saints — Matthias, Boniface, Eucharius, Maximin, and Ursula and her companions — are commemorated in the lyrics of the *Symphonia*.[156] Moreover, Hildegard composed lyrics and *Vitae* for Disibod and Rupert, both of which must have been read aloud, at least at Rupertsberg. The lyrics may have been received by hearers much as sermons on the saints were. One may also imagine that the lyrics belonged to a broader textual context that was not completed or preserved. Boundaries between and among medieval genres are fluid. Peter Dronke argues from manuscript evidence that Hildegard intended for the *lectio* of her *Vita Ruperti* to be followed by the performance of three lyrics, in what Dronke calls prosimetric hagiography.[157] The *Vitae* could have been read, or preached in part, or may even reflect a discourse previously preached.[158] One could arguably consider the whole as prosimetric preaching.

Hildegard affirms in the *Symphonia* that the Spirit, in alliance with Wisdom, instructs the learned: 'Tu etiam semper educis doctos per inspirationem Sapientie letificatos' ('You direct the learned, made glad through the inspiration of

---

[154] *Sciuias*, III.13.12, p. 631; *Scivias* (Eng.), p. 533. *Symphonia*, ed. and trans. by Newman, p. 27.

[155] *Epistolarium*, I, 23, pp. 64–65, lines 126–31; *Letters*, I, 76–80. See *Symphonia*, ed. and trans. by Newman, p. 27.

[156] The saints figure respectively in *Symph.* 44–54, pp. 430–49; 60–64, pp. 458–66.

[157] Peter Dronke states on the *Vita Ruperti*: 'It would seem that Hildegard intended her prose *vita* of her convent's patron saint (PL 197: 1083–92) to have as its climax three lyrical compositions in Rupert's honour: the sequence "O Ierusalem, aurea civitas", and the antiphons "O felix apparicio" and "O beatissime Ruperte". In the Wiesbaden "Riesenkodex" (Hess. Landesbibl. 2), fol. 404[rb], the transition is seamless. The last words of the prose *Vita* (cf. PL 197: 1092A), which here read *per nos precio nostro comparavimus*, are followed without a break by: "Et quia beatus Robertus (sic) uere beatus et uere sanctus est, hec in celesti armonia / audiui et didici: O Ierusalem, aurea ciuias [. . .]". If, as appears most probable, Hildegard here conceived the *lectio* of a prose Life culminating in the performance of three lyrics, then — even if this sequence is repetitionless and the antiphons are not "measured" — her contribution to prosimetric hagiography is as individual as those she made to all her other fields of endeavour', p. 159 in Review of Bernhard Pabst, *Prosimetrum: Tradition und Wandel einer Literaturform zwischen Spätantike und Spätmittelalter* (Cologne: Böhlau, 1994), *Mittellateinische Jahrbuch*, 31 (1996), 155–59. I am grateful to Stephen D'Evelyn for his insights on prosimetry and this reference.

[158] Kienzle, 'Twelfth-Century Monastic Sermon', pp. 291–95; Kienzle, 'Conclusion', in *The Sermon*, pp. 965–67.

Wisdom'). In the same sequence, 'O ignis Spiritus Paracliti' (*Symphonia*, 28), Hildegard praises the Holy Spirit for the power to give life (*uiuificando formas*), to heal (*ungendo [. . .] fractos, tergendo [. . .] uulnera*), to infuse virtues (*infusio cordium in bono odore uirtutum*), to guide the lost (*perditos requirit*) and free the captive (*solue legatos*), to unite in harmony (*omnes componis et colligis*), and to impart greenness, the life-giving force of the Spirit (*De te [. . .] terra uiriditatem sudat*). Thus the Spirit taught Hildegard to comprehend the Scriptures, to translate her visions into exegesis and preaching, and to compose music. For all these gifts and the others she enumerates, the Spirit merits great praises, the sort that Hildegard composed for her sisters to sing: 'Vnde laus tibi sit'.[159]

Conclusion

Hildegard claimed divine authority to 'speak and write' what she 'heard and saw'. She bolsters the divine command she received in 1141 with further accounts of visionary understanding of Scripture and descriptions of a world that needed her voice. She was born into a world where righteousness was slackening and wavering, such that the archbishop of her diocese was exiled and the founding of Disiboden-berg, where she was immured in 1112, was delayed by several years. At the time she received her divine call, God's voice informed her that the insights of the greatest doctors of the Church were shamefully neglected, and God ordered her to revive and reveal the secrets and mysteries that were lying hidden in books. God's command in *Sciuias* to recover the patristic commentaries on Scripture served as the impetus for her continuing education in biblical interpretation. The fact that Hildegard did not receive her learning in a school allowed her to assert that she was *indocta*; the attitude that the monks demonstrated toward the schools allowed them to praise her learning from the Spirit as superior to that of the schools, all the more so because it shone from a woman. The tension between monastic and nascent scholastic education adds a layer to what Barbara Newman calls the 'paradox of Hildegard's *docta ignorantia*'.[160]

Hildegard's works, particularly her exegesis and preaching, stand as remarkable among medieval women. Nonetheless, she and her oeuvre remain to a great extent the product of her cultural milieu. Evidence from German monasteries about the education of religious women no longer makes it possible to see Hildegard and her

[159] 'O ignis Spiritus Paracliti', *Symph*. 28, pp. 410–12 (p. 412).

[160] Newman, 'Hildegard of Bingen: Visions and Validation', p. 170.

works as isolated phenomena. Assumptions about her formation that take her self-portrayal as unlearned at face value ignore the method and content of monastic learning as well as Hildegard's lifelong education with her mentors and friends.

The *magistra* claimed authorization by Pope Eugene III and Bernard of Clairvaux. The language that Bernard employs in his letter to Hildegard appears elsewhere in his works to recognize the power and teaching of the Holy Spirit. The Spirit's exegetical illumination and the command to revitalize patristic exegesis carried forward from the 1141 vision into the *Expositiones euangeliorum*, which represent the product of monastic practices of exegesis, teaching, and preaching. Hildegard also preached outside her monastery, as evidenced in the *Vita Hildegardis* and in letters from clergymen. While no medieval account justifies the identification of four preaching 'tours', various sources attest to the *magistra*'s travels and preaching to other monastic communities and to cathedral audiences, presumably the chapters.[161] Moreover, the 'retrospective interpretation' of the visions took shape over a long period of time. That formulation would have included liturgical listening, reading, and the discussions that Hildegard entertained with others in her monastic network. The seer conveyed her interpretations in her many works, written, visual, and musical, in a tour de force of biblical exegesis, remarkable for its organic coherence.

---

[161] Hildegard did not claim the authority specifically to preach, but she apparently supported pastoral leadership for Benedictine monks. On the controversy over monks' preaching, see Van Engen, *Rupert of Deutz*, pp. 329–30. On Hildegard's views, see Mews, 'Hildegard and the Schools', p. 107; and *Sciuias*, II.17–21, pp. 190–94.

Chapter 2

HILDEGARD AND MONASTIC EXEGESIS

Incline the ear of your heart.[1]

The mere existence of a collection of gospel homilies authored by a twelfth-century woman raises immediate interest about the circumstances of their preaching, their content and the sources behind it, and the form and method of their composition. How did a woman produce such a remarkable work? In what setting did Hildegard convey her insights on Scripture? In what circumstances did she acquire knowledge of prior exegesis? How did she arrive at the unusual homiletic form she employed? This chapter and the following will address those questions. I shall first consider the monastic milieu as the locus for Hildegard's learning as well as teaching, preaching, and exegesis. An explanation of Hildegard's theology of exegesis follows. I then consider the senses of Scripture and the cases where Hildegard employs literal-historical interpretation. Finally, I look at the *Solutiones quaestionum XXXVIII* as an articulation of the *magistra*'s concept of exegesis.

[1] 'Inclina aurem cordis tui', Saint Benedict, *Regula*, ed. by R. Hanslik, CSEL, 75 (Vienna: Hoelder-Pichler-Tempsky, 1977), Prologue, p. 1 (Ps 44. 11). My use of 'ear of the heart' and 'eye of the mind' is inspired by Mary Carruthers, *The Book of Memory: A Study of Memory in Medieval Culture*, Cambridge Studies in Medieval Literature, 10 (Cambridge: Cambridge University Press, 1990), p. 27, where she emphasizes the 'eye of the mind' and observes that: 'There simply is no classical or Hebrew or medieval tradition regarding an "ear of the mind" equivalent to that of the "eye of the mind".' She notes the exception as the *Rule* of Benedict, but concludes that the image is 'not a general trope'. I argue that the practice of the 'ear of the heart' is extensive through monastic education, even if the use of the phrase may be limited. On the integration of audio and visual learning in monastic education, see Morgan Powell, 'The *Speculum virginum* and the Audio-Visual Poetics of Women's Religious Education', in *Listen Daughter*, ed. by Mews, pp. 111–35.

The Expositiones *and Monastic Life: The 'Ear of the Heart'*

How do Hildegard's *Expositiones* fit into monastic life? Monastic customs that called for explicating the *Rule* or another sacred text during chapter meetings each morning would have allowed for Hildegard to preach in chapter at the least. She probably expounded on the gospel reading during chapter meetings, when the male provost was absent — notably on the feast days for which Hildegard composed *Expositiones*. She may have preached on other days as well. When Volmar writes a letter that imagines the community's sorrow at losing the *magistra*'s voice and her 'new interpretation of Scripture', he speaks on behalf of the sisters, but he may mean that Hildegard delivered homilies at least sometimes in his hearing.[2] Certainly the letter implies that the community together listened to Hildegard interpret the Scriptures, whether in chapter or refectory readings.

Was Hildegard's homiletic role unique, or does any evidence point to other monastic women preaching? The customs at the double monastery of Admont allow for extrapolating what Hildegard would have done at Rupertsberg. Irimbert, Abbot of Admont (1172–76), recorded the practices for the superior of the women's community there: the *magistra* or her deputy (*vicaria*) presided over daily chapter meetings of the women. On feast days, when the abbot could not come to them, one of the nuns preached. Irimbert, who would have preached to the nuns through the window opening into their chapter house, remarks that literate nuns, 'marvelously trained in the knowledge of Scripture', were appointed (*dispositae*) to deliver exhortations.[3] Surely Hildegard took a more active role at Rupertsberg than she would have enjoyed in a double community such as Disibodenberg or Admont.

In the Benedictine milieu, sermons, informal and formal, were part of the monastic liturgy and routine. The community listened to patristic works which were read aloud during the nocturns of matins; public reading occurred in the refectory; devotional reading was integral to monastic discipline. Benedictine life holds at its centre the Scriptures and their interpretation through the spoken and written word as well as the 'lived exegesis' of the *Rule* and the Divine Office — the *opus Dei*. Hildegard herself wrote a commentary on the *Rule*, where she paraphrases its

---

[2] *Epistolarium*, II, 195, p. 443, lines 19–21.

[3] *Bibliotheca ascetica antiquo-nova*, ed. by Bernard Pez, 8 vols (Regensburg, 1725), VIII, 460: 'Capitulum suum inter se quotidie habent, Magistra uel ejus Vicaria praesidente. Et in festis diebus, cum Abbas ad eas non poterit uenire, sunt inter eas personae ad uerbum exhortationis faciendum dispositae. Valde quippe sunt litteratae, et in scientia sacrae scripturae mirabiliter exercitatae.' See Beach, 'Listening for the Voices', p. 188; and Borgehammar, 'Who Wrote the Admont Sermon Corpus?'.

directives for reading the Gospel after the nocturns on Sunday and other feast days, and she emphasizes the importance of committing the Scriptures to memory.[4] In accordance with the *Rule*, Hildegard's community would have heard patristic readings in the nocturns, followed by the gospel text itself.[5] The foundation for the *magistra*'s familiarity with the history of biblical interpretation, as for others in the religious life, remains the liturgy with the patristic readings for the night office.[6] Hildegard's aural reception of patristic texts began around age fifteen at the latest and continued all her life. The prodigious memory that Hildegard attributes herself in her letter to Guibert of Gembloux[7] would doubtless have allowed her to retain firmly the details that she heard.

Does the literary form of the *Expositiones* reflect monastic practice as well? Hildegard's progressive exegesis of the pericope clearly resembles the process of commenting on the *Rule*, as practised in Benedictine houses.[8] The verb *exponere* is employed for the process by which the abbot or abbess expounds a passage (*sententia*) of the *Rule* in chapter. Moreover, the *Rule* uses the term *expositiones* for the commentaries on the Scriptures that were written by the Fathers and read in the Divine Office.[9] Hildegard herself uses the term in her letters and in *Sciuias* to describe her biblical commentary. In so doing, she echoes the terminology of earlier Christian exegetes.[10]

---

[4] *De reg. Bened.*, pp. 67–97; *Expl. Rule*, pp. 24–25.

[5] Carlevaris calls attention to the importance of those readings in 'Ildegarda e la patristica', pp. 72–73.

[6] At Disibodenberg the cells of Hildegard and Jutta were situated so that they could hear the Divine Office. Guibert of Gembloux, *Epistolae*, II, 38, p. 373, lines 225–31: 'Tres [...] incluse [...] et preter fenestram admodum paruam, per quam aduentantibus certis horis colloquerentur et uictui necessaria inferrentur [...] in orationibus sacrisque meditationibus sedule Deo intendentes.' See Flanagan, *Hildegard of Bingen*, pp. 26–32; and on the archeological work at Disibodenberg, see E. J. Nikitsch, 'Wo lebte die heilige Hildegard wirklich? Neue Überlegungen zum ehemaligen Standort der Frauenklause auf dem Disibodenberg', in *Angesicht*, pp. 47–56.

[7] *Epistolarium*, II, 103R, pp. 261–62, lines 84–88; see p. 8, note 23.

[8] On sermons and chapter talks in Benedictine houses, see Leclercq, 'Recherches sur d'anciens sermons monastiques', p. 12; and *Love of Learning*, pp. 168–69.

[9] *Regula*, 9, 8, p. 61: 'Codices autem legantur in uigiliis diuinae auctoritatis, tam ueteris testamenti quam noui, sed et expositiones earum, quae a nominatis et orthodoxis catholicis Patribus factae sunt.' See also 'Die *Ecclesiastica Officia Cisterciensis ordinis*' des Cod. 1711 von Trient', ed. by B. Griesser, *Analecta Cisterciensia*, 12 (1956), 234–45, for uses of *exponere* in chapter talks.

[10] Hildegard uses *expositio* or *exponere* several times outside the *Expositiones*: *Epistolarium*, I, 1, p. 4, lines 17–20: 'interiorem intelligentiam expositionis Psalterii et Euangelii et aliorum uoluminum, que monstrantur mihi de hac uisione, que tangit pectus meum et animam sicut flamma comburens,

Furthermore, the word *expositio* denotes other commentaries on liturgical texts in the monastic tradition, such as the commentaries on sequences. The meaning of *expositio* as homily or commentary reflects the overall resemblance in form between medieval sermons (or homilies) and biblical commentaries; it sometimes proves difficult to differentiate the two.[11]

The sequential explanation of the gospel pericope exemplifies the genre that scholars of medieval sermons identify as the homily. Moreover, Johannes Trithemius readily used the term *homilias* to describe the texts when he noted the contents of the very large volume (*magnum volumen*) of Hildegard's works that he saw at Rupertsberg.[12] The differentiation of the homily from the sermon describes two basic methods of organization that medieval preachers followed: the progressive exegesis of a complete pericope, phrase by phrase; and the focus on certain phrases, words, or images to develop themes.[13] Terminology does not, however, reflect utter consistency in medieval usage. The word *expositio* was often used synonymously with *homilia* and *sermo*, which were equivalent in meaning by the twelfth century.[14] Still Hildegard's ear was filled with sequential commentary on a sacred text and with the practice of *lectio divina*. In the instances where Hildegard's citation of the Bible differs from the text of the Vulgate,[15] these differences indicate not only that

---

docens me hec profunda expositionis'. *Epistolarium*, I, 31R, p. 83, lines 7–11; *Sciuias*, p. 3, lines 10–18; *Sciuias*, p. 4, lines 30–35; *Sciuias*, pp. 5–6, lines 87–90; *Sciuias*, II.4, p. 164, lines 173–77. On the terminology of patristic exegetes, see Christine Mohrmann, '*Praedicare-tractare-sermo*', in *Études sur le latin des chrétiens*, 2 vols (Rome: Edizioni di storia e letteratura, 1961), II, 63–72.

[11] See Kienzle, 'Twelfth-Century Monastic Sermon', pp. 291–95. On twelfth-century biblical commentaries and their various titles, most of which were assigned by later editors, see Häring, 'Commentary and Hermeneutics'.

[12] *Chronicon monasterii Sponheimense*, ad annum 1179, II, 257: 'Inter caetera vero eius volumina, magnum in eodem loco volumen, et epistolas eius ad diversos, Homilias, vitas sanctorum et alia quae divinitus edocta edidit, continet.'

[13] See Kienzle, 'Introduction', in *The Sermon*, dir. by Kienzle, pp. 161–64. James E. Cross, 'Vernacular Sermons in Old English', in ibid., pp. 561–96 (p. 563). Thomas Hall, 'The Early Medieval Homily', in ibid., pp. 203–69 (pp. 205, 210), finds that defining the homily and its characteristics requires more effort than describing the sermon; nonetheless, 'homilies can be identified primarily through their use of one or more structural conventions and their systematic approach to scriptural exegesis'.

[14] See Mohrmann, '*Praedicare-tractare-sermo*'; and Jean Longère, *La Prédication médiévale* (Paris: Études augustiennes, 1983), p. 27.

[15] See the apparatus criticus for the *Expositiones*, where C. Muessig has noted major variants from the Vulgate. On *lectio divina* and monastic internalization of the Scriptures, see Leclercq, *Love of Learning*, pp. 73–76.

Hildegard knew the gospel pericopes by heart, but that she held in memory the Scriptures as cited in the liturgy, including the readings from patristic authors.

A homiliary was compiled for Benedictine usage by Paul the Deacon (d. 792), monk of Monte Cassino, at Charlemagne's request. The various other monastic homiliaries that were constituted represent modifications on the content of the standard homiliaries. Local monasteries supplemented the readings in accordance with regional devotion and interests, adding homilies on local saints in particular. Yet there remained a core of familiar patristic writers whose theology illuminated the events and readings of the liturgical year. Origen, Augustine, Jerome, Leo the Great, Gregory the Great, and Bede, among others, constituted the yearly diet for monastic rumination.[16]

While the liturgical books from Rupertsberg are not extant, scholars have investigated the liturgy at Disibodenberg and its connection to the adaptation of Cluniac customs at Hirsau.[17] Engelberg, Stiftsbibliothek, MS 103 reproduces the liturgy of Hirsau and probably comes from Disibodenberg itself.[18] Its readings include pericopes that Hildegard exegetes with related commentary from Gregory the Great, Bede, and others, which she inwardly digested and incorporated into her exegetical vision.[19] Moreover, the Hirsau lectionary contained some patristic material beyond

---

[16] On monastic homiliaries, see Hall, 'Early Medieval Homily', pp. 238–45; Réginald Grégoire, *Homéliaires liturgiques médiévaux: Analyse de manuscrits* (Spoleto: Centro italiano di studi sull'Alto Medioevo, 1980), pp. 423–86. To give one example here, Paul the Deacon included four of Origen's homilies: two on Luke (the Circumcision and Lk 2. 33–34) and two on Matthew (8. 1–2, 8. 23–25).

[17] On the Cluniac readings for the night office, see Raymond Étaix, 'Le Lectionnaire de l'office à Cluny', *Recherches augustiniennes*, 11 (1976), 91–159; C. Elvert, 'Die Nokturnenlesungen Klunys im 10–12 Jahrhundert', in *Corpus consuetudinum monasticarum*, 7.4, ed. by C. Hallinger (Siegburg: Schmitt, 1986), pp. 37–126.

[18] See Felix Heinzer, 'Der Hirsauer *Liber ordinarius*', *Revue Bénédictine*, 102 (1992), 309–47; E. Omlin, 'Das ältere Engelberger Osterspiel und der cod. 103 der Stiftsbibliothek Engelberg', in *Corolla heremitana: Festschrift zum 70. Geburtstag von Linus Birchler*, ed. by A. A. Schmid (Olten: Walter, 1964), pp. 101–26. See also Mews, 'Hildegard, the *Speculum virginum* and Religious Reform', p. 266. Another manuscript from Disibodenberg, Bern, Burgerbibliothek, MS 226, is described and termed 'The Only Surviving Witness', in Victoria Sweet, *Rooted in the Earth, Rooted in the Sky: Hildegard of Bingen and Premodern Medicine* (New York: Routledge, 2006), pp. 167–71.

[19] From the microfilm of Engelberg MS 103, Muessig and Kienzle have identified several gospel and patristic readings which correspond to the *Expositiones*. The microfilm is so faint that a proper study would require a visit to the original. Gospel and patristic readings which correspond to the *Expositiones* include Engelberg MS 103, fols 2ᵛ–3ʳ: Luke 21. 25–33, *Erunt signa*; fol. 3ʳ: Gregory

gospel commentary: Felix Heinzer points out an alternative reading for the Feast of the Conversion of Paul from the *Moralia in Iob* of Gregory I.[20]

The 'Eye of the Mind'

Homilies like Hildegard's were part of monastic written culture as well as oral practice. The *magistra* gained access to patristic and medieval authors through the 'eye of the mind'.[21] Until the eleventh century and the growth of cathedral schools, medieval biblical interpretation circulated primarily in monastic milieux. Monastic commentators heard, read, echoed, responded to, and extended patristic works as they developed the hermeneutical methods that grounded the scholastic exegesis of following centuries.

What other books besides homiliaries might Hildegard have known? It is possible that the *magistra* came to know the exegesis of patristic commentators through consultation or discussion of glossed books of the Bible. What scholars have observed in this regard about other twelfth-century monastic sermons may extend to Hildegard as well. Chrysogonus Waddell notes the patristic influence on language in Cistercian sermons, notably those of Bernard of Clairvaux:

> As often as not the biblical texts utilized by the Cistercians in their sermons were biblical texts drawn not directly from the Scriptures but from ecclesiastical writers and from glossed

---

the Great, *Homiliae in euangelia*, ed. by R. Étaix, CCSL, 141 (Turnhout: Brepols, 1999), I, pp. 5–6, lines 1–14; *Expos.* 53–56. Engelberg MS 103, fol. 14ʳ: John 2. 1–11, *Nuptiae factae sunt*; fol. 14ʳ⁻ᵛ: Bede the Venerable, *Homeliarum euangelii libri II*, ed. by D. Hurst, CCSL, 122 (Turnhout: Brepols, 1955), I, 14, p. 95, lines 5–21; *Expos.* 16–17. Engelberg MS 103, fols 21ᵛ–22ʳ: John 6. 1–14, *Abiit Ihesus*; fol. 22ʳ, Bede, *Homeliarum euangelii libri II*, II, 2, p. 193, lines 1–19; *Expos.* 3–4. Engelberg MS 103, fol. 50ʳ: Luke 5. 1–11, *Cum turbae irruerent in Ihesum*; Bede the Venerable, *In Lucae euangelium expositio*, ed. by D. Hurst, CCSL, 120 (Turnhout: Brepols, 1960), 2, 5, lines 540–600; *Expos.* 43–45. Engelberg MS 103, fol. 35ᵛ: John 3. 1–15, *Erat homo ex Phariseis*; Bede, *Homeliarum euangelii libri II*, II, 18, p. 311, lines 1–19; *Expos.* 34–36. Engelberg MS 103, fol. 51ᵛ: Luke 19. 41–47, *Cum appropinquaret*; fols 51ᵛ–52ʳ: Gregory the Great, *Homiliae in euangelia*, II, 39, pp. 380–81, lines 21–39; *Expos.* 46–48. Engelberg MS 103, fol. 52ʳ: Luke 18. 10–14, *Duo homines ascenderunt*; Ps.-Bede the Venerable, *Homiliae subditiae*, 10, *PL* 94: 289–90; *Expos.* 51–52.

[20] See Heinzer, 'Der Hirsauer *Liber ordinarius*', p. 316.

[21] Saint Benedict, *Regula*, 1, p. 1. See Leclercq, *Love of Learning*, pp. 73–74; Carruthers, *Book of Memory*, pp. 25–27; and on the *Speculum uirginum*, Powell, '*Speculum virginum* and the Audio-Visual Poetics'.

bibles. Consequently, the Scripture texts as they appear in so many sermons by Cistercian authors were surrounded with resonances of the patristic exegesis at large.[22]

For glossed books of the Bible, commentators and scribes from Hrabanus Maurus onward made their annotations from the recensions of their immediate predecessors instead of returning to the original patristic commentary. The scribe Otfrid of Weissenberg, although he had Jerome's commentary on Jeremiah at hand, derived his annotations from his teacher Hrabanus, who had rewritten and expanded Jerome's text. Whatever Hildegard gleaned through glossed biblical books would then stem from this Carolingian adaptation of patristic sources.

The complex transmission of glossed Bibles shows a map of historical development on which German-speaking monasteries occupy key points. Before the effort to produce a glossed version of the entire Bible in the late eleventh and early to mid-twelfth century at Laon and Paris, commentators glossed scriptural books, and monasteries exchanged exemplars for copying. Ninth-century manuscripts whose pages show planning for the copying of text and commentary together were written at Fulda, Weissenburg, and St Gall. The scriptorium at Tegernsee in southern Bavaria produced manuscripts for export; extant works include a glossed Psalter copied from a St Gall exemplar and a glossed copy of the Pauline and Catholic Epistles based on a Metz exemplar.[23]

Moreover, some evidence demonstrates the place of biblical commentary and glossed books of the Bible in the libraries of women's religious houses. Several examples appeared in the 2005 exhibition *Krone und Schleier*. The Evangeliary from Essen (Domschatz Essen, MS 1) bears interlinear and marginal glosses in Latin and Anglo-Saxon. Essen held a copy of Alcuin's commentary on John's Gospel, and Quedlinburg possessed Cassiodorus's *Exposition on the Psalms*. The female scribe Diemut of Wessobrun copied Gregory's *Homilies on Ezekiel*, and Lamspringe owned a collection of Augustine's homilies.[24] Analysis of the holdings of Admont, a double monastery with a double library, shows that the women's

---

[22] Chrysogonus Waddell, 'The Liturgical Dimensions of Twelfth-Century Cistercian Preaching', in *Medieval Monastic Preaching*, ed. by Carolyn A. Muessig (Leiden: Brill, 1998), pp. 335–49 (p. 348). Waddell notes that readings in Bernard's sermons that Jean Leclercq identified as coming from a pre-Vulgate Bible actually derive from patristic sources.

[23] Margaret Gibson, 'The Twelfth-Century Glossed Bible', in *Studia patristica*, XXIII, Papers Presented to the Tenth International Conference on Patristic Studies held in Oxford, 1987, ed. by Elizabeth A. Livingstone (Leuven: Peeters, 1989), pp. 232–44 (pp. 234–37, 244).

[24] *Krone und Schleier*: Domschatz Essen MS 1, cat. 93, pp. 233–34; Alcuin, cat. 97, p. 236; Quedlinburg, cat. 98, p. 236; Gregory, cat. 108, pp. 240–41; Augustine, cat. 109, p. 241.

library probably possessed a significant number of books beyond those required for liturgical use. Alison Beach's reconstruction of the contents of the women's library includes biblical commentaries and a collection of homilies that the monks borrowed from the nuns.[25] The library catalogue of Lippoldsberg, a female monastery, lists twenty-four volumes with biblical texts and/or commentary, including books of the Bible with the *Glossa ordinaria*, works of numerous patristic and Carolingian exegetes, and several contemporary commentators, notably Rupert of Deutz. The catalogue's opening rubric reads that Gunther (the spiritual director responsible for the expansion of the library) ordered, with the assistance of the prioress Margaret, that the books be copied and annotated from others in the vicinity.[26] Herrad of Hohenbourg must have participated in a 'network of book lending and borrowing', as Fiona Griffiths asserts, in order to compile the many sources she excerpted for the *Hortus deliciarum*.[27] Therefore, the exchange and copying of manuscripts in monastic networks and the extant manuscripts and catalogues of women's monasteries make it reasonable to presume that the scriptorium of Disibodenberg and perhaps that of Rupertsberg would have engaged in similar work of exchange and copying.[28]

Moreover, twelfth-century monastic thinkers participated in 'networking' and intellectual exchange; the exegetical and theological conversations that took place within monasteries extended outward to other communities. Exegetical conversations passed from the oral into the written.[29] The exegetical and theological

---

[25] Beach, *Women as Scribes*, pp. 79–84. See also Lutter, *Geschlect und Wissen*.

[26] 'Libros e vicino subscriptos tempore suo prefatus Guntherus mediante priore domna Margareta non solum scribi sed et hic annotari precepit.' *Catalogus Bibliothecae Lippoldesbergensis*, ed. by Wilhelm Arndt, MGH SS, 20 (Hannover, 1868), pp. 556–57 (p. 556). On Lippoldsberg, see Hotchin, 'Women's Reading and Monastic Reform in Twelfth-Century Germany', Appendix, pp. 178–89.

[27] Griffiths, *Garden of Delights*, pp. 75–81.

[28] Twelfth-century manuscripts produced at Rupertsberg include, for example, the *LDO*: Gent, University Library, MS 241, copied at Rupertsberg with provenance of Sts Eucharius and Matthias, Trier; Troyes, Bibliothèque municipale, MS 683, copied at Rupertsberg during the twelfth century and sent to Clairvaux; for the *Vite mer.*: Dendermonde, Benedictine Abbey, MS 9, copied at Rupertsberg *c.* 1175 and sent to Villers; for *Sciuias*: Vatican City, Biblioteca Vaticana, MS Pal. Lat. 311, produced before 1179 at Rupertsberg. See Albert Derolez, 'The Manuscript Transmission of Hildegard of Bingen's Writings: The State of the Problem', in *Context*, pp. 17–28, with list on p. 28. See also Laurence Moulinier, 'Abbesse et agronome: Hildegarde et le savoir botanique de son temps', in ibid., pp. 135–56 (p. 145).

[29] With respect to genre, the body of the letter may resemble the homily if one puts aside the conventions of the *ars dictaminis*. Both letter and homily treat questions about Scripture and

controversies that placed leading male figures such as Bernard of Clairvaux on centre stage also engaged the wider monastic community and women. Within Hildegard's epistolary corpus, various letters seek her response to complex questions that were being debated in the schools. She composed exegetical letters that reflect monastic discussion around the thorny problems of Scripture, which include discourses on Ezekiel 1 and associated texts, on Song of Songs 4. 6 and Psalm 103. 8, as well as opinions on theological controversy surrounding the Trinity.[30] Extant letters from Gerhoch of Reichersberg to the nuns at Admont and to an unnamed community of sisters (perhaps at Admont) reply to their request for his interpretation of Psalm 50 and of the significance of the centurion in Matthew 8. 5–13. Abelard's exegetical responses to Heloise are well known.[31] These demonstrate that women religious, like their male counterparts, showed eagerness for the exegetical wisdom of learned figures.[32] Still, the written request for women's opinions on scriptural questions seems to have been less common; certainly fewer records of it exist.

Nonetheless, communities of women engaged in the exchange of letters, which involved some level of training in the *ars dictaminis*, or art of composing letters. While the best-known letters from individual learned women in the twelfth century are those of Heloise, Hildegard, and Elisabeth of Schönau,[33] less renowned

include exhortations to the recipient or the audience. On letters, see Constable, *Letters and Letter Collections*; Kienzle, 'New Introduction', in *Letters of St. Bernard of Clairvaux*, trans. by James, pp. viii–xvii; Kienzle, 'Conclusion', in *The Sermon*, pp. 964–65.

[30] On Ezekiel 1, see *Epistolarium*, I, 84R, pp. 190–94. On Song of Songs 4. 6, see *Epistolarium*, III, 380, pp. 138–39. On Psalm 103. 8, see *Epistolarium*, III, 380, pp. 133–34. On the Trinity, see the correspondence on the Trinity with Odo of Soissons and with Eberhard of Bamberg. *Epistolarium*, I, 40, 40R, pp. 102–05; 30, 30R, pp. 83–88. McGinn discusses these in 'Hildegard of Bingen as Visionary and Exegete', pp. 333–34. Bartlett highlights the tension between cloister and schools in 'Commentary, Polemic and Prophecy'.

[31] *Letters of Peter Abelard: Beyond the Personal*, trans. by Jan M. Ziolkowski (Washington, DC: Catholic University of America Press, 2007), pp. 53–60, and Constant J. Mews, *Abelard and Heloise* (Oxford: Oxford University Press, 2005), pp. 200–01, on the *Problemata Heloissae*, exegetical questions posed by Heloise to Abelard, and his responses.

[32] Beach, 'Listening for the Voices', p. 192. Beach, 'Voices from a Distant Land: Fragments of a Twelfth-Century Nuns' Letter Collection', *Speculum*, 77 (2002), 34–54.

[33] See Constant J. Mews, *The Lost Love Letters of Heloise and Abelard: Perceptions of Dialogue in Twelfth-Century France*, trans. by Neville Chiavaroli and Constant J. Mews (New York: Palgrave, 2001); Mews, *Abelard and Heloise*, p. 65, on the practice of *ars dictaminis* before the proliferation of manuals in the twelfth century, and pp. 200–01. Elisabeth of Schönau, *The Complete Works*, trans. by Anne L. Clark, Classics of Western Spirituality (New York: Paulist

women composed and exchanged letters. Numerous religious women wrote to Hildegard for advice, whether individual superiors or communities seeking counsel.[34] Nineteen previously unknown letters from Admont evince at least a basic training in the *ars dictaminis* on the part of the nuns. Alison Beach also points out a letter from a sister at Lippoldsberg who requested books on the *ars dictaminis* from the Abbot of Reinhardsbrunn.[35] Current research on the documents from women's monasteries may reveal other evidence of their exchange of letters and their familiarity with the art of letter-writing.

Collaboration and Exchange of Books

Intellectual exchange took place viva voce as well, and Hildegard must have benefited from conversations with friends and secretaries.[36] Hildegard credits the steadfast assistance of Volmar in the prefaces to her visionary works. In addition, the seer mentions the 'noble girl' that scholars identify as Richardis, and she cites 'a certain girl' who assisted with the *Liber uitae meritorum* and the *Liber diuinorum operum*.[37]

Press, 2000), includes letters, notably at pp. 142–47, for a well-known letter to Hildegard, which is edited as two texts, *Epistolae* 202 and 203, in *Epistolarium*, I, pp. 455–58.

[34] Among numerous examples, see *Epistolarium*, II, 159, 174, pp. 355, 395–96; II, 250–51, pp. 529–32.

[35] Beach, 'Voices from a Distant Land', pp. 36–37 (p. 36, n. 13 on the letter from Lippoldsberg to Reinhardsbrunn), pp. 42–52. Beach (p. 37, n. 16) argues that the anonymous *magistra* of Admont was composing letters at night (*litteras composuit*), but the Latin *litteras* may denote writings of no specific genre rather than letters, generally *epistolas*. For background on religious women's letter-writing Beach cites Joan Ferrante's assertion that such writing was widespread: Joan Ferrante, *To the Glory of her Sex: Women's Roles in the Composition of Medieval Texts* (Bloomington: University of Indiana Press, 1997), p. 18. Beach also argues that some of this women's correspondence followed the norms of the *ars dictaminis*. This modifies, rightly in my opinion, the broad statement in *Medieval Women and the Epistolary Genre*, ed. by Karen Cherewatuk and Ulrike Wiethaus (Philadelphia: University of Pennsylvania Press, 1993), p. 8, that 'the majority of medieval women produced their letters outside' the 'male-dominated world of the *ars dictaminis*'.

[36] See J. Herwegen, 'Les Collaborateurs de sainte Hildegarde', *Revue Bénédictine*, 21 (1904), 192–203, 302–15, 381–403; and the discussion of the article and this topic by Derolez, 'Manuscript Transmission of Hildegard', p. 18.

[37] *Sciuias*, p. 5, lines 84–85: 'testimonio cuiusdam nobilis et bonorum puellae et hominis illius, quem [...] quaesieram et inueneram'; *Vite mer.*, p. 9, lines 26–28: 'Et ego testimonio hominis illius quem, ut in prioribus uisionibus prefata sum [...] et testimonio cuiusdam puelle mihi assistentis manus ad scribendum posui'; *LDO*, p. 46, lines 27–30: 'testificante homine illo, quem, uelut in

Richardis had died in 1152, before the writing of the last two works.[38] While Hildegard casts her female assistants as witnesses to her visions and as helpers, probably amanuenses, one need not eliminate the possibility that they discussed the visions and texts with their celebrated *magistra*.

A parallel from Admont may provide some insight on the working practices of nuns. The celebrated but anonymous *magistra* wrote late at night and dictated to a scribe. Her biographer notes that during periods of silence, the *magistra* dictated in Latin, not German; on other occasions when her sisters requested that she dictate verse or prose for them after compline, she wrote silently on wax tablets during the night and delivered her writings in the morning.[39] Perhaps Hildegard's female assistants assisted her composition in a similar manner.

When her *magister* and secretary Volmar died, Hildegard, profoundly shaken, recounts that sadness penetrated her soul and body when she was separated by death from the blessed man who had heard and discussed and corrected her work. She cried out to God for help: 'O my God, it pleased you when you gave me your servant as a helper for my visions. Now assist me as you see fit!'[40] Hildegard's nephew Wezelinus stepped in to assist his aunt with her writing: he diligently listened to (*audiuit*) and marked (*notauit*) all the words of the visions, and he consoled her by himself (*per seipsum*) and through other wise men (*per alios*

---

prioribus uisionibus meis prefata sum [. . .] testificante etiam eadem puella, cuius in superioribus uisionibus mentionem feci'.

[38] Dronke, 'Introduction', *LDO*, p. xxxvi, also points out that the 'certain girl' is not Richardis. He asserts that Volmar and the unnamed girls bear witness to the truth of Hildegard's visions. I suggest a broader role, that they might have discussed Hildegard's writings with her as her male secretaries did.

[39] Lutter, *Geschlecht und Wissen*, p. 228: 'Aliquando enim intempesta nocte litteras composuit et scribenti praedixit, silentii tamen observantiam retinens numquam aliqua theutonica verba protulit. Praeterea licet post completorium secundum regulam perpetuum haberet silentium, tamen cum rogaretur a parvulis, ut versus et prosas praediceret illis, sicut erat plena caritate et dilectione, accepit tabulas et scripsit eis reddendos in crastino versus et prosas.' See also Christina Lutter, 'Christ's Educated Brides: Literacy, Spirituality, and Gender in Twelfth-Century Admont', in *Manuscripts and Monastic Culture*, ed. by Beach, pp. 191–213 (pp. 202–07).

[40] Epilogue to the *LDO*, p. 463, lines 1–6, 13–15: 'In tempore illo, cum in uera uisione cum scriptura huius libri religioso uiro et obseruatione regule sancti Benedicti timorato michi assistente laborabam, tristicia animam et corpus meum perforauit, quoniam ab eodem felici uiro per conditionem mortis in hoc mundo orbata separabar'. 'Ipse enim in ministerium Dei omnia uerba uisionis huius in magno studio sine cessatione laboris audiuit et corrigendo disseruit'. 'O Deus meus, qui cum famulo tuo, quem michi ad istas uisiones adiutorem dedisti, ut tibi placuit fecisti, nunc ut te decet me adiuua!'

sapientes).[41] Wezelinus appointed Gottfried as provost of Rupertsberg from 1173 to 1176.[42] Testimonies to the provost's collaboration with Hildegard, such as those regarding Volmar or Guibert of Gembloux, are lacking. However, Gottfried authored the first book of the *Vita Hildegardis*.[43] Guibert of Gembloux, who stayed at Rupertsberg from 1177 to 1180, describes his exchange of ideas with Hildegard during the last year of her life:

> I am guided by her counsels [. . .] and daily refreshed by conversations with her. [. . .] nothing would please her more to see than [. . .] that I stay here [. . .] and undertake the spiritual service of herself and her daughters and examine the books she has written.[44]

Hildegard's correspondence documents the *magistra*'s exchange of ideas and books as well as visits from acquaintances with access to important libraries. Clerics from various places solicited and received copies of her works that were produced at Rupertsberg, and they journeyed there to seek her advice. It is reasonable to assume that they also discussed her works. Abbot Philip of Park travelled from the area of Louvain to talk to the seer face to face in the early 1170s, and a twelfth-century copy of *Sciuias* was produced at his monastery.[45] Abbot Gottfried of Salem wrote to Hildegard saying that he had read her visions; the provenance of an illuminated *Sciuias* manuscript from the twelfth century is in fact the Cistercian abbey of Salem, although the origin (place of production) of the manuscript is uncertain.[46] Another early manuscript of *Sciuias*, now missing, has a provenance of the Cistercian abbey

---

[41] *LDO*, p. 463, lines 23–30.

[42] *Epistolarium*, I, 10R, p. 25; *Letters*, I, pp. 46–47.

[43] *Epistolarium*, I, 10R, p. 25; *Letters*, I, pp. 46–47.

[44] Guibert of Gembloux, *Epistolae*, II, 38, pp. 367–68, lines 34–40: 'Consiliis eius dirigor, orationibus fulcior, nitor meritis, sustentor beneficiis, et cotidie recreor colloquiis. Nichil libentius ipsa ad presens, quantum ad exteriora spectat, uideret, quam ut in domo Domini, quam regit ipsa, omnibus diebus uite sue permanerem habitare, et ut interiorem curam ipsius et filiarum eius et considerandorum librorum quos scripsit, susciperem.' English translation: 'Letter to Bovo', in *Jutta and Hildegard*, trans. by Silvas, p. 100.

[45] Brussels, Royal Library, Codex 11568 (1492). See Derolez, 'Manuscript Transmission of Hildegard', pp. 26, 28; *Sciuias*, pp. xliv–xlv. *Epistolarium*, II, 179R, p. 408; *Letters*, II, 142.

[46] Heidelberg, Universitätsbibliothek, Cod. Sal. X, 16. See Derolez, 'Manuscript Transmission of Hildegard', pp. 26, 28; *Sciuias*, pp. xxxix–xliii. The editors, pp. xl–xli, cite a passage where G. of Salem writes: 'uidi et legi maxima sacramenta mysteriorum Dei, que per te in libro a te scripto Dominus scientiarum indignis hominibus aperiens reserauit' (Wiesbaden, Hessisches Landesbibliothek, Handschrift 2, fol. 349rb, *PL* 197: 285D). *Epistolarium*, II, 200, p. 453, lines 9–12; *Letters*, II, 175.

of Eberbach, whose Abbot Eberhard corresponded with Hildegard.[47] Arnold, Archbishop of Cologne, implored Hildegard to send a copy of *Sciuias*; presumably it was to be copied at Rupertsberg for him.[48] Guibert of Gembloux, before staying at Rupertsberg, made more than one attempt to seek the *magistra*'s opinion on matters of scriptural interpretation; her response comprises the *Solutiones quaestionum XXXVIII*, the text of which is preserved in the Riesenkodex written at Rupertsberg.[49] The monks at Villers received the *Liber uitae meritorum* as did the community at Gembloux, and both were hearing it read in the refectory.[50] Moreover, early manuscripts of both the *Liber uitae meritorum* and the *Liber diuinorum operum* have a provenance of the abbey of Sts Eucharius and Matthias near Trier.[51] Various letters document Hildegard's contacts with clergy in Trier.[52] Arnold, brother of Wezelinus and another nephew of the *magistra*, was elected Archbishop of Trier (1169–73). Arnold wrote to his aunt about kinship and friendship while he was in the presence of a mutual friend, Ludwig, Abbot of Sts Eucharius and Matthias; Arnold requested that his aunt send an account of an exorcism she had successfully performed at the request of himself and Ludwig.[53] In 1173, Hildegard wrote to Abbot Ludwig, informing him that after Volmar's death, she had not been able to finish the *Liber diuinorum operum*. She promises to send the finished product to him soon for correction. Another letter, which must have accompanied the manuscript, tells Ludwig that in reading her work, he has 'embarked on an

---

[47] Former Collection, F. W. E. Roth. Derolez, 'Manuscript Transmission of Hildegard', pp. 26, 28. *Epistolarium*, I, 82, pp. 184–85; *Letters*, I, 179.

[48] *Epistolarium*, I, 14, pp. 31–32; *Letters*, I, p. 52.

[49] The *Solutiones* are contained within the *Epistolae*, fols 328ra–434ra, Wiesbaden, Hessisches Landesbibliothek, Handschrift 2; *PL* 197: 1037–54. On the content, see Bartlett, 'Commentary, Polemic and Prophecy'; and on the genre, see Häring, 'Commentary and Hermeneutics', p. 177.

[50] Dendermonde, Benedictine Abbey, MS 9. Derolez, 'Manuscript Transmission of Hildegard', pp. 21, 28. *Vite mer.*, pp. xliv–xlvi; Guibert of Gembloux, *Epistolae*, I, 23, p. 253, lines 56–61; Hildegard, *Letters*, II, 108a, pp. 44–46, the text of which is not included in *Epistolarium* II. See also *Letters*, II, 107, p. 43, where the brothers of Villers acknowledged in 1176 that they received an unnamed work from the seer. See the discussion in Embach, *Die Schriften Hildegards von Bingen*, pp. 120–24.

[51] Trier, Library of the Seminary, MS 68; Gent, University Library, MS 241. See Derolez, 'Manuscript Transmission of Hildegard', pp. 20–21, 28. *Vite mer.*, pp. xlix–li; *LDO*, pp. lxxxvi–xcvii.

[52] See Holbach, 'Hildegard von Bingen und die kirchlichen Metropolen'.

[53] *Epistolarium*, I, 27, pp. 76–77; *Letters*, I, pp. 88–89.

adventure of the unicorn'. Hildegard bids him to guard the book, look over it, and correct it lovingly.[54] The epilogue to the *Liber diuinorum operum*, cited above, provides additional testimony to Ludwig's role. Like Wezelinus, Ludwig assisted Hildegard himself (*per seipsum*) and procured aid for her through other learned men (*per alios sapientes*).[55]

Through the words of the 'Living Light', Hildegard promises her collaborators — Volmar, Ludwig, Wezelinus, and the other learned men — a share of the reward for the labour of writing her visions. For added benefit to all her helpers, who must include some of the nuns mentioned above, the *magistra* specifies that when she heard these words, she was asking God to grant the reward of the heavenly Jerusalem to all who assisted her with her visions: that they would all rejoice without end.[56] That Hildegard discussed and received assistance with her visions indicates that the visions as we have them reflect the product of 'retrospective interpretation', that is, interpretation which takes shape over a long period of time.[57]

Hildegard's connection to Ludwig and Arnold in Trier probably enabled the exchange of the so-called *Hildegard-Gebetbuch* (*Prayerbook of Hildegard of Bingen*). Once erroneously thought to be an autograph, the *Gebetbuch* probably still has some connection to the saint; it was plausibly sent to her during the last year of her life by the monks at Sts Eucharius and Matthias near Trier. The iconographic plan of the *Gebetbuch* links prayers to illustrations of scriptural texts: the manuscript

---

[54] See Letters 214, 215, 215R, and 217, *Epistolarium*, III, pp. 471–78; *Letters*, III, pp. 194–99. According to Dronke and Derolez, the *magistra* sent what is now the Gent manuscript of the *LDO*, the oldest manuscript of the work. Ludwig would have corrected it and returned it to Hildegard for her final scrutiny. See Peter Dronke, *Women Writers of the Middle Ages: A Critical Study of Texts from Perpetua (d. 203) to Marguerite Porete (d. 1310)* (Cambridge: University of Cambridge Press, 1984), pp. 312–13. Derolez, *LDO*, pp. lxxxvi–xcvi, examines the Gent manuscript and identifies three correctors: Corrector 1 makes corrections as directed by Hildegard and introduces the commentary on the opening of Genesis; Corrector 2 corrects style and grammar; Corrector 3, perhaps Guibert of Gembloux, makes limited changes and always cancels the text he amends. See also Dronke, *Women Writers of the Middle Ages*, pp. 312–13.

[55] *LDO*, p. 464, lines 16–33.

[56] *LDO*, p. 464, lines 34–41: 'Ego autem de uiuente luce, quę me uisiones istas docuit, uocem sic dicentem audiui: istos qui simplicem hominem uisiones meas scribentem adiuuabant et consolabantur, participes mercedis laborum illius faciam. Et ego paupercula in eadem uisione docta dicebam: Domine mi, omnibus qui me in istis uisionibus, quas ab infantia mea infixisti, magno timore laborantem consolando adiuuabant, mercedem eternę claritatis in celesti Ierusalem dones, ita quod per te sine fine in te gaudeant.'

[57] See Emmerson, 'Representation of Antichrist', pp. 105–06.

opens with several Old Testament scenes that are important from the standpoint of Christian typological exegesis, but the majority of episodes derive from the Gospels and the life of Christ. The *Hildegard-Gebetbuch* and related manuscripts, such as the earlier Sélestat Prayerbook, present narrative image cycles with accompanying prayers that spur the viewer's devotional imagination. Some of the prayers in the *Gebetbuch* show corrections from masculine to feminine gendered forms, indicating that the book was probably transmitted from a male monastery to a female one.[58] The *Gebetbuch* testifies to the exchange of texts between monastic communities of men and women, a phenomenon that cannot be overlooked when assessing the contents of Hildegard's works.

Moreover, the user of the *Gebetbuch* called to mind the biblical texts, primarily gospel passages, as she looked upon the illustrations and read or recited the prayers.[59] The images provide a sort of 'visual exegesis' that continues in writing and oral performance through the reading and utterance of the prayers.[60] The pericope, absent from the pages in textual form except for allusions in the prayers, resides in the memory; the illustrations and the prayers prompt recollection of the text. In my view, the role that memory plays in the reader and viewer's use of the *Hildegard-Gebetbuch* bears comparison with the reception of the *Expositiones* by the nuns at Rupertsberg. Although the sisters at Rupertsberg listened to the pericopes with Hildegard's accompanying commentary, they needed to know the

[58] See Elisabeth Klemm, 'Das sogennante Gebetbuch der Hildegard von Bingen', in *Jahrbuch der Kunsthistorischen Sammlungen in Wien*, 74, n.s. 38 (Vienna: Verlag Anton Schroll, 1978), pp. 29–78; Elisabeth Klemm, 'Der Bilderzyklus im Hildegard-Gebetbuch', in *Hildegard-Gebetbuch: Faksimile-Ausgabe des Codex-latinus monacensis 935 der Bayerischen Staatsbubkiothek, Kommentarband* (Wiesbaden: Reichert, 1987), pp. 80–356 (pp. 283–89) on the provenance of the *Gebetbuch*. See also Jeffrey Hamburger (to whom I am grateful for introducing me to the *Gebetbuch*), 'Before the Book of Hours: The Development of the Illustrated Prayer Book in Germany', in *The Visual and the Visionary*, pp. 149–95. I am also grateful to Danielle Joyner for helpful observations and conversations on the *Gebetbuch*.

[59] See Hamburger, 'Before the Book of Hours', p. 166; Jeffrey Hamburger, 'Gebetbuch der Hildegard von Bingen', in *Krone und Schleier: Kunst aus Mittelalterlichen Frauenklöstern*, Kunst- und Ausstellungshalle der Bundesrepublik Deutschland, Bonn und dem Ruhrlandmuseum Essen (Munich: Hirmer; Bonn and Essen: Kunst- und Ausstellungshalle der Bundesrepublik Deutschland, Bonn und dem Ruhrlandmuseum Essen, 2005), cat. 200, pp. 311–12. On images and memory, see Carruthers, *Book of Memory*; and Cohen, *The Uta Codex*, p. 3, who asserts that scholarship on memory has not paid attention to 'how actual images may have functioned within [. . .] memory systems'.

[60] On visual exegesis, see Griffiths, *Garden of Delights*, pp. 239, 262, and works cited there.

gospel readings by heart in order to follow the *magistra*'s parallel running narra-tive.[61] From various perspectives then, Hildegard's *Expositiones* hold an early place in the development of a rich and varied tradition of biblical exegesis in women's communities.

The Expositores

Did Hildegard conceive of a lineage of biblical commentators? Did she speak of herself as an exegete in that line? The *magistra* refers to scriptural commentators as a group — the *expositores* or *doctores* — several times in the *Expositiones euan-geliorum*. In a homily on John 6. 1–14, Hildegard develops the theme of the transformation of Scripture and states that Jesus gave signs through the prophecies, the Gospels, and the *expositores*.[62] In another homily (on Matthew 2. 1–12), Hilde-gard explains that the gospel commentators gave instruction on how the sinner might repent and rise to salvation.[63] The *expositio* on Luke 19. 41–47a names the commentators: 'Gregorius, Ambrosius, Augustinus, Ieronimus, et alii similes'.[64]

---

[61] A later form of German manuscripts, the *evangelistaria*, included the gospel texts with trans-lations. The *plenaria* that came into use in the fourteenth century contained translations of Gospels and epistles for Sundays and feast days as well as glosses for the gospel texts. As the *plenaria* evolved, sermons were added. Finally, printed *plenaria* featured woodcuts that provided devotional images. Hans Jochen Schiewer, 'German Vernacular Sermons', in *The Sermon*, ed. by Kienzle, pp. 861–961 (p. 895).

[62] *Expo. Euang.*, 3, p. 198, lines 104–09: '*Illi ergo homines*, qui Christum in fide per baptismum et per multas alias uirtutes in ecclesia colunt, *cum uidissent*, in bona scientia, in bono intellectu ac in bono gustu dulcedinis uirtutem, *quod fecerat Iesus*, in humanitate, in passione ac in donis Spiritus Sancti, *signum*, per prophetiam et euangelium, uelut de expositoribus, *dicebant*, aperta uoce in laudibus credulitatis.'

[63] *Expo. Euang.*, 13, pp. 223–24, lines 20–25: '*Et congregans*, fraudulenter exquirendo, *omnes principes*, scilicet prophetas, *sacerdotum*, uidelicet euangelicorum, quia prophetia precessit, *et scribas populi*, id est expositores et doctores fidelium, *sciscitabatur ab eis*, per astutias suas, *ubi Christus nasceretur*, id est quomodo esse posset, ut peccator in penitentia resurgeret, quasi impossibile esset, ut peccator ad saluationem resurgeret.'

[64] *Expo. Euang.*, 47, p. 312, lines 13–14. *Expo. Euang.*, 3, p. 197, lines 81–83: '*Vt autem impleti sunt*, omnes in ecclesia cum ordinibus suis, *dixit discipulis suis* Iesus, qui capaces fuerunt sensu et intellectu, ut doctores ecclesiarum. *Collegerunt ergo*, id est doctores etiam instruxerunt diuinis preceptis eos qui in ecclesia simpliciter in pusillanimitate incedebant.' *Expo. Euang.*, 13, p. 224, line 27: '*At illi*, scilicet doctores ueritatis'; *Expo. Euang.*, 54, p. 323, lines 3–4: '*et stellis*, id est in sacerdotibus, doctoribus et spiritali populo'.

These doctors of the New Testament, following the revelation of the Gospels, transformed all of Scripture by spiritual interpretation into a coherent story of salvation through Christ.[65] In her other works, Hildegard speaks of *expositores* or *doctores* of Scripture but does not name or cite them directly.[66] In *Sciuias*, the *magistra* specifies three points or pointed edges coming together (*acumina incidentia*) on the pillar of God's word: the old law, the new grace, and the *expositores* of divine books.[67]

In contrast to her respect for patristic exegetes, the *magistra* criticized the lack of true inner knowledge of Scripture among contemporary teachers. She challenges them: 'But you, o masters and teachers of the people, why are you blind and mute in the inner knowledge of letters, which God has set forth for you?' In addition, she calls upon them to dispel the darkness of Saducees and heretics by teaching salvation history from God's creation onward.[68] In *Sciuias*, God's voice clarifies that Hildegard holds an important place in this picture; God laments that the seer's contemporaries paid scarce attention to the tomes of the doctors. In fact, that neglect of the *expositores* justifies God's decision to speak of new mysteries through the writings of Hildegard who would reveal secrets that had lain hidden in books.[69]

---

[65] *Expo. Euang.*, 47, pp. 312–13, lines 12–21: '*Quia uenient dies in te*, uidelicet alii in transmutatione et claritate, *et circumdabunt te*, doctores noui testamenti doctrina sua, ut Gregorius, Ambrosius, Augustinus, Ieronimus, et alii similes, *et coangustabunt te undique*, scilicet reuertendo in spiritalem significationem, *et ad terram prosternent te*, id est culturam tuam in sacrificio arietum et taurorum abstergent ab elatione, et ad humilitatem prosternent, *et filios tuos qui in te sunt*, scilicet carnales institutiones in spiritali intellectu ad humilitatem ducent. *Et non relinquent lapidem*, id est nullam litteram, nec iota unum, nec ullam culturam tuam, *super lapidem*, nisi mutetur.'

[66] A letter to Hildegard cites Gregory (*Regula pastoralis*, 3, 34, *PL* 77: 119A), but she does not take up the citation in her reply. *Epistolarium*, I, 50, p. 122, line 15: 'Ergo que scio uos apud Deum tanti esse meriti, quod ex Spiritus Sancti reuelatione cognoscere ualeatis quid expediat homini facere, propterea humilibus precibus exoro pietatem uestram, quatenus uelitis pro me Dominum consulere, si sibi placita sit conuersatio mea, ne me posthac sententia illa Gregoriana denotet, que dicit: Melius fuerat eis uiam ueritatis non cognouisse quam post cognitionem ab ea in deterius decidisse.'

[67] *Sciuias*, III.4, p. 394, lines 176–85: 'Quod autem eadem columna tres angulos habet ab imo usque ad summum quasi gladium acutos: hoc est quod circuiens et uolubilis in gratia fortitudo Verbi Dei, quam uetus testamentum praesignauit in nouo declarandam, manifestauit per Spiritum sanctum tria incidentia acumina, id est antiquam legem et nouam gratiam atque enucleationem fidelium doctorum.'

[68] *Expl. Symb.*, p. 127, lines 511–12: 'Vos autem, o magistri et doctores populi, quare caeci et muti estis in interiori scientia litterarum, quam Deus vobis proposuit'; 'The True Beginning of the Life of St. Rupert', in *Expl. Atha.*, p. 66.

[69] *Sciuias*, III.11, p. 586, lines 379–91.

In other words, Hildegard intended through God's revelation to revive and augment the teaching of her predecessors; furthermore, much as the *expositores*, she would teach the means to salvation. Hildegard's references to the *expositores*, and herself among them, point toward a deeper comprehension of her self-understanding as an exegete.

Spiritual Interpretation: Nec iota unum

Does Hildegard articulate a theology of exegesis? In the seer's explication of Luke 19. 41–47, the story of Jesus expelling the money changers from the temple, the Son of God incarnate coming at the fullness of time (*plenitudo temporis*) sheds tears of wisdom upon the old law, its writings, and its institutions. He proclaims that what lies hidden in the old law will be illuminated. The doctors of the New Testament — Gregory the Great, Ambrose, Augustine, and Jerome — will come with brilliance to change (*in transmutatione et claritate*) the old into the new, into the spiritual meaning (*in spiritalem significationem*). They will cleanse old ways of worship, namely animal sacrifices, from pride, and they will cast down carnal institutions, leading them to humility by means of spiritual understanding (*in spiritali intellectu*). No written word and no worship will remain without transformation.[70]

The Son of God speaking in the Gospel casts out avarice, idols, and other corruption. Through spiritual change and interpretation (*in spiritali transmutatione et interpretatione*), the edifice of revelation is that of truth, Hildegard explains. The locus of God is the building and the instruction (*edificatio*) that shows the truth. Jesus teaching daily in the temple (Lk 21. 47) represents the Son of God and the Gospels, the Word living and written. In the Church, the Word proceeds to spiritual understanding (*ad spiritalem intellectum*), and the new edifice or teaching (*edificatio*) appears (cf. 1 Cor 14. 3, 5, 12, 26), that is, the new interpretation of the old law (*in ista apparitione nouae edificationis et interpretationis antiquae legis*).[71]

---

[70] *Expo. Euang.*, 47, pp. 312–13, lines 12–19: '*Quia uenient dies in te* [...] *et coangustabunt te undique*, scilicet reuertendo in spiritalem significationem, *et ad terram prosternent te*, id est culturam tuam in sacrificio arietum et taurorum abstergent ab elatione et ad humilitatem prosternent, *et filios tuos qui in te sunt*, scilicet carnales institutiones in spiritali intellectu ad humilitatem ducent.' Hildegard praises the faithful and 'principal' teachers but does not name any in *Sciuias*, III.4.5, p. 394, line 185: 'enucleationem fidelium doctorum'; and 4.6, p. 394, lines 203–06: 'exquisita sapientia principalium magistrorum'.

[71] *Expo. Euang.*, 47, p. 313, lines 36–38. I have not located a precedent for the role that Hildegard assigns to the four doctors. Henri de Lubac examines the motif of the list of the doctors in

Thus Hildegard joins the Gospels, the new interpretation, the new Church, and the Son incarnate in her exposition and opposes them to the old interpretation and the temple. The new interpreters, the four principal doctors of the Latin Church, carry out the change: once the Word-human brings the Word-text, they endue it with the new spiritual meaning.

When Hildegard speaks of the spiritual interpretation of the old law, she designates a hermeneutic that is typological in its concept and method but tropological in its aims. Hildegard explains that spiritual interpretation illumined what was previously hidden; the old prefigured the new. In the old mode dwell avarice, pride, filth, and carnality, while the new ushers in truth, humility, purity, and spirituality. So profound a change occurs that not one word (*nec iota unum*) remains unchanged, an indication that, for Hildegard, every word of Scripture must be interpreted spiritually.[72]

The phrases *in transmutatione et claritate, in spiritalem significationem, in spiritali intellectu*, and *in spiritali transmutatione et interpretatione* bear comparison to the well-known passage in *Sciuias*, where the *magistra* describes her sudden understanding of the spiritual sense of the Scriptures, the exposition (*intellectum expositionis*) of the Psalter, the Gospels, and 'other catholic books from the volumes of the Old as well as the New Testaments'. A close look at Hildegard's statement in *Sciuias* that she did not master 'the interpretation of the words in the text, the division of syllables, the cases and tenses',[73] reveals more than the usual reading of this

---

Exegèse médiévale: Les quatre sens de l'Écriture, vol. I (Paris, 1959); English translation: *Medieval Exegesis*, vol. I, trans. by Mark Sebanc (Grand Rapids: Eerdmans; Edinburgh: T. and T. Clark, 1998), pp. 3–8.

[72] *Expo. Euang.*, 47, pp. 312–13, lines 18–21: 'carnales institutiones in spiritali intellectu ad humilitatem ducent. *Et non relinquent lapidem*, id est nullam litteram, nec iota unum, nec ullam culturam tuam, *super lapidem*, nisi mutetur'. The typological model of the Gospel replacing the old law dominates *Expo. Euang.* 49 on Mark 7. 31–37, one of Jesus's healing miracles. Jesus opening the ears and mouth of a deaf mute represents the opening of the Old Testament to the Gospel. *Expo. Euang.*, 49, lines 1–4: '*Exiens* Iesus, nascendo, *de finibus Tyri*, id est de genere Iudeorum, *uenit per Sidonem*, scilicet per prophetas, *ad mare Galileae*, uidelicet ad turbas populorum, qui in multis hac et illac uersabantur, *inter medios fines*, scilicet angeli et hominis, *Decapoleos*, uidelicet nouem ordines angelorum et decimus hominis.' For Origen, the *iota* contains this notion of the Word present in the Law: 'And "one iota or one title" is Jesus, the Word of God in the Law'. Origen, *Homilies on Luke*, trans. by Joseph T. Lienhard, Fathers of the Church, 94 (Washington, DC: Catholic University of America Press, 1996), Fragment 221, Luke 16. 17, p. 216.

[73] *Sciuias*, pp. 3–4, lines 24–33: 'Factum est in millesimo centesimo quadragesimo primo Filii Dei Iesu Christi incarnationis anno, cum quadraginta duorum annorum septemque mensium

text as a claim to sudden understanding of Scripture. The terms the *magistra* uses (*interpretationem uerborum textus eorum*) arguably refer to education in exegesis of scriptural texts, particularly the literal sense, inasmuch as it implies an explanation of grammar. Her statement may specifically distinguish spiritual understanding from exegetical training in the schools; the latter began with the literal: the grammatical workings of the text underlay the explanation of its historical meaning.[74]

Support for this distinction can be found in other writings from Hildegard's hand. In a letter to an unnamed teacher of biblical theology (*doctrina scripturarum pleniter imbutus*), Hildegard contrasts the two ways of knowing Scripture, much as she does in *Sciuias*. The *magistra* insists that she 'barely knows the grammar of the Scriptures' (*litteras scripturarum*) and that she receives her understanding without the aid of exterior senses. Her way of seeing in the true light (*in uero lumine*) grounds the hesitancy she expresses before she, a lowly woman who obeys the teachings of the masters, would give advice to male teachers (*magistris uirilis persone*). After these cautious but prudent protests, Hildegard proceeds to advise him, confident in her knowledge of inner meaning acquired through inner enlightenment.[75] In addition, the *magistra* describes her manner of knowing in the *Explanation of the Athanasian Creed*, the text of which she saw and heard in the inner knowledge of her soul (*in interiori scientia animae meae*).[76] Hildegard's letter to Bernard of Clairvaux affirms that she knew the 'inner meaning of the exposition (*interiorem intelligentiam expositionis*) of the Psalter, the Gospels, and other

---

essem, maximae coruscationis igneum lumen aperto caelo ueniens totum cerebrum meum transfudit et totum cor totumque pectus meum uelut flamma non tamen ardens sed calens ita inflammauit, ut sol rem aliquam calefacit super quam radios suos ponit. Et repente intellectum expositionis librorum, uidelicet psalterii, euangelii et aliorum catholicorum tam ueteris quam noui Testamenti uoluminum sapiebam, non autem interpretationem uerborum textus eorum nec diuisionem syllabarum nec cognitionem casuum aut temporum habebam.'

[74] See Bernard McGinn, 'The Originality of Eriugena's Spiritual Exegesis', in *Iohannes Scottus Eriugena: The Bible and Hermeneutics, Proceedings of the Ninth International Colloquium of the Society for the Promotion of Eriugenian Studies, Leuven and Louvain-la-Neuve, June 7–10, 1995*, ed. by Gerd Van Riel, Carlos Steel, and James McEvoy (Leuven: University Press, 1996), pp. 55–80 (p. 58), for a concise discussion of the literal sense. See also Lubac, *Medieval Exegesis*, vol. II, trans. by E. M. Macierowski (Grand Rapids: Eerdmans; Edinburgh: T. and T. Clark, 2000), pp. 41–50.

[75] *Epistolarium*, III, 280, p. 33, lines 6–10: 'Ego paupercula feminea forma, que doctrine magistrorum obedio et que uix litteras scripturarum cognosco, ualde formido ea, que in anima mea sine omni sensibilitate exteriorum sensuum meorum in uero lumine uideo, magistris uirilis persone dicere aut scribere.'

[76] *Expl. Symb.*, p. 129, line 567.

volumes'.[77] Bernard of Clairvaux himself extolled the superior worth of the inner meaning of the Scriptures,[78] and Hildegard falls clearly within this tradition of monastic exegesis. Finally, in the autobiographical narrative from the *Vita* (*c.* 1167), Hildegard speaks of carnal turning to spiritual: the 'soft raindrops' extinguished her corporal sensuality (*sensualitas corporis mei*) and turned her knowledge to another mode (*in alium modum*).[79] One thinks again of Bernard, in this instance his description of the impact of the Word on his soul, the inner renewal he felt from the presence of the Word and the depth of divine wisdom.[80] The *Expositiones* frequently develop the theme of converting the corporal and the sensual to the spiritual: textually, historically, and experientially. Exegesis, preaching, and

---

[77] *Sciuias*, p. 4, lines 30–33: 'Et repente intellectum expositionis librorum, uidelicet psalterii, euangelii et aliorum catholicorum tam ueteris quam noui Testamenti uoluminum sapiebam.' *Epistolarium*, I, 1, p. 4, lines 17–19: 'Scio enim in textu interiorem intelligentiam expositionis librorum, uidelicet psalterii, euangelii et aliorum uoluminum, que monstrantur mihi de hac uisione.' *V. Hild.*, II.2, p. 24, lines 88–90: 'In eadem uisione scripta prophetarum, euangeliorum, et aliorum sanctorum, et quorundam philosophorum, sine ulla humana doctrina intellexi, ac quedam ex illis exposui.' See Mews, 'Hildegard and the Schools', pp. 99–100.

[78] Bernard states that 'the law is spiritual, according to the Apostle's testimony, and was written for us, not only to please us with the appearance of its outer surface, but also to satisfy us with the taste of its inner meanings, as with a kernel of wheat' (Dt 32. 14). *Sermons for the Summer Season: Liturgical Sermons from Rogationtide and Pentecost*, trans. by B. Kienzle with contributions by J. Jarzembowski, Cistercian Fathers, 53 (Kalamazoo: Cistercian Publications, 1991), Fourth Sunday after Pentecost, 2–3, pp. 115–16; *SBOp*, V, p. 202, lines 18–20.

[79] *V. Hild.*, II.16, p. 43, lines 1–10. The phrase *in alium modum* brings to mind the designation that the Riesenkodex gives to Hildegard's allegories of Scripture, introducing alternate readings as simply *alio modo*. Hildegard also uses the phrase herself to introduce another way of reading the parable of the unjust steward and a second interpretation of John 1. 3 ('sine ipso factum est nihil'). *Expo. Euang.*, 2, p. 193, line 63: 'Vel alio modo, uillicus *iniquitatis* sacerdos intelligi potest.' *Expo. Euang.*, 9, p. 210, lines 16–18: 'Quamuis etiam alio modo intelligatur, ita quod sine filio nichil factum sit.'

[80] Bernard, *Sermo super Cantica*, 74, in *SBOp*, II, 239–44, at par. 6, p. 243, lines 9–27, and esp. lines 16–27: 'Ita igitur intrans ad me aliquoties Verbum sponsus, nullis umquam introitum suum indiciis innotescere fecit: non voce, non specie, non incessu. Nullis denique suis motibus compertum est mihi, nullis meis sensibus illapsum penetralibus meis: tantum ex motu cordis, sicut praefatus sum, intellexi praesentiam eius; et ex fuga vitiorum, carnaliumque compressione affectuum, adverti potentiam virtutis eius; et ex discussione sive redargutione occultorum meorum, admiratus sum profunditatem sapientiae eius; et ex quantulacumque emendatione morum meorum, expertus sum bonitatem mansuetudinis eius; et ex reformatione ac renovatione spiritus mentis meae, id est interioris hominis mei, percepi utcumque speciem decoris eius; et ex contuitu horum omnium simul, expavi multitudinem magnitudinis eius.'

teaching possess the power to transform the audience, to encounter the listener in an intermediary, 'liminal' space and move her to conversion.[81]

Origen

This broad notion of the spiritual interpretation of Scripture reveals the influence of Origen (*c.* 185–*c.* 254), who followed a method of Christian hermeneutics inspired by Clement of Alexandria (*c.* 150–215) and rooted in the works of Philo, the first-century philosopher who endeavoured to demonstrate that Platonic philosophy was in harmony with the inner or spiritual meaning of the Hebrew Scriptures. Origen discussed three senses of Scripture, which he distinguished as literal-historical; typological, pertaining to moral application; and spiritual, corresponding to the old covenant prefiguring the new. In *De principiis*, Origen relates the three senses respectively to the human body, soul, and spirit.[82] In Book Four of *De principiis*, he argues for the spiritual interpretation of Scripture and cites various passages that are impossible to interpret literally.[83] Hildegard's concept of spiritual interpretation draws on patristic and monastic exegesis that built upon Origen's notion of the spiritual sense of Scripture as that relating to the old covenant's prefiguring of the new, and more generally, as a higher level of interpretation, engaging the spirit or soul and enlightened by the Spirit, who authored the text. Origen

---

[81] On the concept of liminality and its application to the sermon, see Beverly Mayne Kienzle, 'Medieval Sermons and their Performance: Theory and Record', in *Preacher, Sermon and Audience in the Middle Ages*, ed. by C. A. Muessig (Leiden: Brill, 2002), pp. 89–124 (pp. 115–16); Cynthia L. Polecritti, *Preaching Peace in Renaissance Italy: Bernardino of Siena and his Audience* (Washington, DC: Catholic University of America Press, 2000), pp. 22–23.

[82] In Origen's influential *Commentary on the Song of Songs*, he connected the soul (not the spirit) to the spiritual sense. Among many studies of Origen and his impact on medieval exegesis, see McGinn, 'Spiritual Heritage of Origen in the West'; Beryl Smalley, *The Study of the Bible in the Middle Ages* (Oxford: Oxford University Press, 1952; repr. 1985), pp. 2–8, on Philo and Origen; Lubac, *Medieval Exegesis*, I, 142–72 and passim. See also Ronald Heine, 'Reading the Bible with Origen', in *The Bible in Greek Christian Antiquity*, ed. and trans. by Paul M. Blowers (Notre Dame: University of Notre Dame Press, 1997), pp. 131–48; Brian Daley, 'Origen's *De principiis*: A Guide to the Principles of Christian Scriptural Interpretation', in *Nova et Vetera: Patristic Studies in Honor of Thomas Patrick Halton*, ed. by John Petroccione (Washington, DC: Catholic University of America Press, 1998), pp. 3–21; and Robert D. Crouse, 'Origen in the Philosophical Tradition of the Latin West: St. Augustine and John Scotus Eriugena', in *Origeniana quinta*, ed. by Robert Daly (Leuven: Peeters, 1992), pp. 564–69.

[83] Origen, *De principiis*, ed. by P. Koetschau, *Origenes Werke*, vol. V, Die Griechischen Christlichen Schriftsteller der ersten Jahrhunderte, 22 (Leipzig: Hinrichs, 1913), 4.3.1, p. 324, lines 25–33.

states in *De principiis* that before Christ's coming, it was not possible to 'bring forward clear proofs of the divine inspiration of the old Scriptures'. This Christian appropriation of the Hebrew Scriptures resulted in a central role for salvation history in Christian exegesis, what Bernard McGinn calls the 'historical pole' of exegesis in comparison to the 'mystical pole'.[84] Both belong to spiritual exegesis, as Hildegard understood her exegetic endeavour. Scholars have debated whether Origen's references to non-literal exegesis constitute allegory or typology. He sometimes differentiates the two but also uses the terms synonymously.[85] The notion of spiritual exegesis encompasses both.

Certainly, Hildegard and her contemporary monastic neighbours knew some of Origen's writings in Latin translation. Peter Dronke's research on Hildegard's sources in the *Liber diuinorum operum* opened the way for charting the early exegete's influence on her. Dronke pointed to the presence in the library of St Maximin in Trier of a manuscript of Origen's *Homiliae in Genesim* (translated into Latin by Rufinus) along with other works that Hildegard might have known and consulted there.[86] A sampling of other libraries compiled by Stephen D'Evelyn shows that Sts Eucharius and Matthias at Trier, St Emmeram in Regensburg, Hirsau, and Michelsberg at Bamberg possessed a copy of the *Homiliae in Genesim*.[87] Sts Eucharius and Matthias at Trier also owned homilies on Matthew attributed to Origen, Hirsau possessed Origen's *In Matthaeum* and *De principiis*, and the Stadtarchiv of Cologne includes *In Matthaeum* and *De principiis* in addition to the *Homiliae in Genesim*.[88] I would add that Hildegard could have consulted a given book by Origen or another author through borrowing or gift giving.

[84] See McGinn, 'Originality of Eriugena's Spiritual Exegesis', pp. 57, 74, n. 8.

[85] Peter Martens, 'Revisiting the Allegory/Typology Distinction: The Case of Origen', *Journal of Early Christian Studies*, 16 (2008), 283–317.

[86] See *Catalogi Bibliothecarum Antiqui*, ed. by Gustav Becker (Bonn: Max Cohen, 1885; repr. Hildesheim: Olms, 1973), p. 179; Dronke, 'Platonic-Christian Allegories', p. 384, n. 11, pp. 391–93. Stephen D'Evelyn is completing a comprehensive study of the sources in the *Expositiones* and *Symphonia* and their presence in local library manuscripts to which Hildegard could have had access. I am grateful to him for the references here and in notes 87 and 88.

[87] Josef Montebaur, *Studien zur Geschichte der Bibliothek der Abtei St. Eucharius-Mathias zu Trier* (Freiburg: Herder, 1931), p. 147; Becker, *Catalogi Bibliothecarum Antiqui*, pp. 127, 219, 194.

[88] Montebaur, *Studien zur Geschichte der Bibliothek der Abtei St. Eucharius-Mathias zu Trier*, p. 147. There is some evidence of the presence of Origen's works in monastic establishments at Cologne. *Die Theologischen Handschriften des Stadtarchiv Köln*, ed. by Joachim Vennebusch, 5 vols (Cologne: Böhlau, 1976–80), II, 299; III, 200.

The *magistra* herself refers once to Origen (Orienus) in the *Expositiones* and echoes his exegesis at several points. In a homily on Luke 16. 19–31, the parable of Lazarus and the rich man, Hildegard discusses the wise and the proud. Where other exegetes state that prelates exemplify the sage and possibly proud,[89] the *magistra* compares the wise to Origen, explaining that the rich man represents 'those who extoll themselves unjustly in respect to their own wisdom'. Hildegard alludes here to the legend of Origen's fall.[90] She may also recall his interpretation of the rich man in the parable: a homily of Origen's on Ezekiel associates the rich man of the Lukan text and the Sodomite in Ezekiel with pride.[91]

Hildegard describes the process of exegesis in Origenian terms: *spiritalis significatio, spiritalis intellectus, spiritalis transmutatio* and *interpretatio*, as well as *aedificatio* for the process of interpretation.[92] Origen in the *Homiliae in Genesim* frequently uses the phrase *spiritalis intellectus*, employed by Hildegard, as well as *spiritalis sensus* and *spiritalis intelligentia*.[93] He describes his own commenting on

---

[89] See Gottfried of Admont, *Homiliae dominicales*, 59 (de praelatis et subditis), *PL* 174: 387. The *Homiliae dominicales* and *Homiliae in festa* are now considered to be the work of Irimbert of Admont, but they will be cited as they are ascribed in the *PL* edition, to Gottfried.

[90] *Expo. Euang.*, 37, p. 290, lines 36–37: '"et dives" illi qui in sapientia sua se injuste extollunt, ut Orienes, "et sepultus est"'. Carlevaris, 'Ildegarda e la patristica', p. 79, cites a similar spelling of Origen (Orienus) in Defensor Locogiacensis monachi, *Liber scintillarum*, ed. by Henri Rochais, CCSL, 117 (Turnhout: Brepols, 1957), p. 125. I am grateful to Bernard McGinn for pointing out the legend.

[91] Origen, *Homélies sur Ézéchiel*, ed. and trans. by Marcel Borret, SC, 352 (Paris: Cerf, 1989), pp. 314–16, on Ezekiel 16. 49, where Origen adduces the example of the rich man and Lazarus, read 'many days before', explaining himself this way: 'Sed si consideres hoc quod in praesenti scriptum est, et illud quod in Evangelio dicitur, videbis quia et illius maximum peccatum inter universa peccata superbia fuerit [...] in tantam superbiam elatus est despiciens paupertatem [...] talis autem est et dives, qui in Evangelio describitur, nulli dubium quin dives ille Sodomita sit. Quomodo autem Sodoma, et filiae Sodomorum superbae fuerunt, tales sunt arrogantes animae.' One passage in Origen, *Interpretationis Origenis in canticum canticorum*, *PL* 23: 1117–43 (col. 1127A), associates Dives, Salomon, and *sapientia* but without conclusions about pride. In contrast, Gregory the Great and others draw an opposition between Jews and Gentiles from the figures of Dives and Lazarus. See Stephen L. Wailes, *Medieval Allegories of Jesus's Parables* (Berkeley: University of California Press, 1987), pp. 245–60.

[92] *Expo. Euang.*, 47, pp. 312–13, lines 14–15, 19, 28–29, 31, 36, 37.

[93] A few examples of each follow from Origen, *Homélies sur la Genèse*, ed. by Henri de Lubac and Louis Doutreleau, SC, 7bis (Paris: Cerf, 1976): *spiritalis intellectus*: Homilies I.1.10, p. 52; VII.6.32, p. 210; VI.3.63, p. 192; XV.7.24, p. 370; *spiritalis sensus*: I.12.10, p. 54; VII.6.24, p. 208; XIII.3.17, p. 320; XIII.4.5, p. 326; *spiritalis intelligentia*: I.1.35, p. 26; II.1.106, p. 84; XI.1.2, p. 276. Ambrose also

the Scriptures as *expositio* and *expositiones*; the process of change from old to new as *mutatio*; and the purpose of teaching through spiritual interpretation of the Scriptures he calls *aedificatio*.[94] The general notion of *plenitudo temporis* appears in the Alexandrian's work, as does the image of *illuminatio* for Christ's action of ushering in the new interpretation.[95] Hildegard refers to *plenitudo temporis* and uses images of light in her *Expo. 47*.[96] Furthermore, Origen spells out clearly the notion of the human as the microcosm (*minor mundus*) of the universe and he describes the inner struggle of virtues and vices. These two key elements of Hildegard's thought derive, if only indirectly, from Origen.[97]

Several interpretations in the *Expositiones* stem from Origen's commentaries on Luke and Matthew; sections from both works were read in monastic homiliaries

---

uses *spiritalis intellectus* frequently, as in his *Expositio psalmi CXVIII*, ed. by M. Petschenig, CSEL, 62 (Vienna, 1913), 15.8, p. 334 and elsewhere. Bernard McGinn compares Hildegard's view of exegesis as *intelligentia spiritualis* and her place as 'visionary exegete' with that of Joachim of Fiore, Bonaventure, and Peter John Olivi. Joachim experienced a vision at Easter in the early 1180s, after which he perceived 'something of the fullness of [the book of Revelation] and of the entire harmony of the Old and New Testaments'. A second vision at Pentecost granted him insight into the Trinity. Joachim conceived of exegesis as *intelligentia spiritualis*, a view that Bonaventure and Olivi developed. McGinn, 'Hildegard of Bingen as Visionary and Exegete', p. 338. On Joachim of Fiore, see McGinn, *Presence of God*, II, 337–41. McGinn compares the Trinitarian iconography of Hildegard and Joachim in 'Theologians as Trinitarian Iconographers', in *The Mind's Eye: Art and Theological Argument in the Middle Ages*, ed. by Jeffrey F. Hamburger and Anne-Marie Bouché (Princeton: Princeton University Press, 2006), pp. 186–207.

[94] Origen calls his explanation *expositio* in *Homélies sur la Genèse*, II.6.12, 14, 25, 26, pp. 106, 108. He uses the notion of *mutatio* to describe interpretation according to the spiritual sense, occasioned by Christ's coming: 'Non enim Christus in iis nomina, sed intelligentiam commutavit. Commutat in eo.' *Homélies sur la Genèse*, XIII.3.73–74, p. 324. He refers to *aedificatio* in *Homélies sur la Genèse*, II.63.1–4, p. 88, asking what Noah's ark can contain of *spiritalis aedificationis*; and in *Homélies sur la Genèse*, II.6.84–86, p. 112: 'Et quamvis haec iam non morali sed naturali ratione discussa videantur, tamen quae ad praesens occurrere potuerunt, pro aedificatione tractavimus.'

[95] The concept of *plenitudo* appears in Origen, *Homélies sur la Genèse*, III.7.1–2, p. 140: 'Sed venio etiam ad Novum Testamentum, in quo est plenitudo omnium.' The notion of Christ's action of *illuminatio* is present in *Homélies sur la Genèse*, VII.6.18–24 and 29–31, p. 210; and *Homélies sur la Genèse*, XV.7.17–24, p. 370.

[96] *Expo. Euang.*, 47, p. 312, lines 1, 9; p. 313, lines 22–24.

[97] Origen explains the human as microcosm in *Homélies sur la Genèse*, I.11.31–36, pp. 52, 54: 'Cum ergo haec omnia fierent quae videntur iussu Dei per Verbum eius et praepararetur immensus iste visibilis mundus, simul autem et per allegoriae figuram ostenderetur quae essent quae exornare possent minorem mundum, id est hominem, tunc iam ipse homo creatur secundum ea quae in consequentibus declarantur.' On virtues and vices, see *Homélies sur la Genèse*, XII.3.10–22, p. 298.

in the Cluniac tradition. Moreover, the *magistra*'s first homily on Matthew 4. 1–11 reflects the opinion on Matthew 4. 8, which Origen expressed in *De principiis*. With regard to the third temptation, Hildegard explains that the mountain appeared spiritually and not physically, for no mountain on earth could be so high as to allow for seeing the entire earth. This explanation lies very near to Origen's on the same verse.[98] For another Matthean pericope, the parable of the laborers in the vineyard (Mt 20. 1–16), Hildegard's exegesis of the parable draws from the two broad strands of the tradition that interpret the hours of the workday either as the ages of the world or as the stages in an individual human life. Both these possibilities derive from Origen.[99] As far as the narrative details, Hildegard, like Origen and Paschasius Radbertus, interprets the five callings of the labourers as the five senses. Other exegetes, in keeping with one or the other dominant strand of interpretation, read the passage either in terms of the ages of the world or of human life, or in the context of good works or virtues related to faith and spiritual growth.[100] Hildegard's reading accords with her emphasis on the inner struggle.

One of Hildegard's readings of the parable of the prodigal son (Lk 15. 11–32) includes the association of the older brother in the story with the angels. Filled with jealousy because God through the incarnation gave so much heed to sinful humans, the celestial beings, which were created before humans, had no need for Christ's sacrifice.[101] Early interpretations of the parable among the Valentinians and in Gnostic circles cast the older son as the angels, whereas the younger son's demise corresponds to the fall of humankind, or of the soul into the material world.[102] Origen's *Homiliae in Genesim* constitute a possible source for Hildegard;

---

[98] Origen, *De principiis*, ed. by Koetschau, 4.3.1, p. 324, lines 25–33; Origen, *An Exhortation to Martyrdom, Prayer, First Principles, Book IV, Prologue to the Commentary on the Song of Songs, Homily XXVII on Numbers*, trans. by Rowan A. Greer, Classics of Western Spirituality (Mahwah: Paulist Press, 1979), *On First Principles*, p. 189. See McGinn, 'Spiritual Heritage of Origen in the West', p. 281, n. 85.

[99] See Wailes, *Medieval Allegories*, pp. 138–39.

[100] Dronke, 'Platonic-Christian Allegories', p. 384, n. 11, pp. 391–93, states that Origen and Hildegard are distinctive in interpreting the five callings of the labourers as the five senses. However, as Wailes, *Medieval Allegories*, p. 144, observes, Paschasius Radbertus also repeats this notion.

[101] *Expo. Euang.*, 27, p. 268, lines 66–67: '*Erat autem filius eius senior*, id est angeli qui ante hominem creati sunt, *in agro*, scilicet in celesti cultura'; lines 79–81: '*Indignatus est autem*, id est admiratus est stupendo, quomodo hec fieri possent, *et nolebat intrare*, quia passione Christi non indigent, nec gaudio quod, *super uno peccatore*, penitente fit.'

[102] François Bovon, *L'Évangile selon Saint Luc (15–19, 27)* (Geneva: Labor et Fides, 2001), pp. 50–51. See also Yves Tissot, 'Allégories patristiques de la parabole des deux fils (Lc 15, 11–32)',

there, the angels' anger targets Christ, not humanity, but in both cases, the incarnation underlies their ire. In connection with the notion of inheritance in Genesis 22. 17, Origen explains how the bad angels were jealous that Christ came and took sovereignty over what would have been theirs: 'And those angels who were holding each of the nations in power were stirred to anger.' Again he states: 'Christ [. . .] casting out those angels who were holding the nations in power and dominion, provoked them to anger.'[103] If this were indeed Hildegard's source, the notion of *hereditas*, which is crucial to the parable, and the clear notion of jealousy in both texts would have formed the associative bridge between the two.[104]

For the parable of the great supper (Lk 14. 16–24), Hildegard echoes some exegetical features that derive from Origen and are found in Augustine and Gregory the Great: namely the interpretation of the five pair of oxen (one invitee's excuse for not attending) as the five senses, and the general emphasis on bodily versus spiritual pleasures. Gregory the Great's Homily 36 appears in Paul the Deacon's collection and in the Cluniac lectionary.[105] In contrast, other exegetes

---

in *Exegesis: Problèmes de méthode et exercices de lecture (Gn 22 et Lc 15)*, ed. by François Bovon and Grégoire Rouiller, Bibliothèque théologique (Neuchâtel: Delachaux and Niestlé, 1975), pp. 243–72 (pp. 248–49); and Enrico Cattaneo, 'L'interpretazione di Lc 15, 11–32 nei Padri de la Chiesa', in *Interpretazione e invenzione: La Parabola del Figliolo prodigo tra interpretazioni scientifiche e invenzione artistiche*, ed. by Giuseppe Galli, Università degli studi di Macerta. Publicazioni della Facoltà di lettere e filosofia, 37 (Genova: Marietti, 1987), pp. 69–96 (pp. 90–92). Dronke, 'Platonic-Christian Allegories', pp. 394–95, notes the Gnostic orientation of Hildegard's interpretation of the parable.

[103] Genesis 22. 17: 'Hereditate capiet semen tuum ciuitates aduersariorum.' Origen, *Homélies sur la Genèse*, IX.3.1–23, p. 248: 'Unde et ad iracundiam excitati sunt angeli illi qui singulas quasque nationes sub potestate retinebant [. . .] Christus [. . .] depellens ipsos angelos potestate et dominatione quam habebant in nationibus, provocavit eos ad iracundiam.' On angels in Hildegard's thought, see Gunilla Iversen, '"O vos angeli": Hildegard's Lyrical and Visionary Texts on the Celestial Hierarchies in the Context of her Time', in *Angesicht*, pp. 87–114; Mary Ford-Grabowsky, 'Angels and Archetypes: A Jungian Approach to Saint Hildegard', *American Benedictine Review*, 41 (1990), 1–19; and Heinrich Schipperges, 'Die Engel im Weltbild Hildegards von Bingen', in *Verbum et Signum*, ed. by Hans Fromm and others, vol. II (Munich: Fink, 1975), pp. 99–117.

[104] Hildegard uses the word *hereditas* in her other homily on the parable, *Expo. Euang.*, 26, p. 262, lines 52–54: '*iam non sum dignus*, quia preuaricator sum, *uocari filius tuus*, ut in pristinam hereditatem me recipias'; p. 263, lines 71–72: '*Erat autem filius eius senior in agro*, scilicet qui bonam scientiam in cultura supernae hereditatis habet.'

[105] See Grégoire, *Homéliaires liturgiques médiévaux*, no. II, 38, p. 460; Étaix, 'Le Lectionnaire de l'office à Cluny', no. 147, p. 108.

such as Ambrose and Augustine focus on the three excuses together as refusals made by heathens, Jews, and heretics.[106]

In the *Vita Hildegardis*, the *magistra* alludes indirectly to Origen's homilies on Ezekiel. The seer recounts that she said to God: 'O, Lord God. All the ways in which you wound me I know are good, because all your works are good and holy, and because I have deserved all this from my infancy; and besides, I trust that you will not permit my soul to be tortured like this in the life that is to come.'[107] Furthermore, the biographer Theodoric cites Origen's praise for Deborah as a prophet, a statement recalling Origen's commentary on the Book of Judges, in order to strengthen his assertion that the gift of prophecy dwelled in Hildegard.[108]

Whether the *magistra* provided these references from her own reading or Theodoric supplied them from his, Origen's work evidently belonged to the literary culture they shared. Moreover, Hildegard's contemporary and correspondent, Elisabeth of Schönau, recounts that she asked the Virgin Mary whether Origen, 'that great doctor of the Church', had been saved or not. The Virgin replied that Origen's error did not derive from malice but from an excess of fervour for exegesis and of desire for scrutinizing divine secrets. Mary remembered the exegete with a special showing of light on her feast days and, according to a vision Elisabeth received from John the Evangelist, the Virgin herself would determine Origen's fate.[109]

Finally, Hildegard may draw the theology of her method itself from Origen's *De principiis*, where he writes about the Holy Spirit's aim 'to keep the logical order of the spiritual meaning'. If the Spirit found anywhere 'that what happened according to the narrative could be fitted to the spiritual meaning, He composed something woven out of both kinds into a single verbal account'. Even in the Gospels and Epistles, Origen writes, the Holy Spirit 'mingled not a few things by which the order of the narrative account is interrupted or cut up so that by the impossibility he might turn and call the mind of the reader to the examination of the inner meaning'. Origen explains that the Spirit intended always to hide the secret mean-

---

[106] Bovon, *L'Évangile selon saint Luc*, pp. 456–57; Wailes, *Medieval Allegories*, pp. 161–66.

[107] *V. Hild.*, II.8, p. 34; *Life*, in *Jutta and Hildegard*, trans. by Silvas, p. 170. Origen, *In Ezechiel, Hom.* 1, 1, ed. by W. A. Baehrens, *Origenes Werke*, vol. VII: *Homilien zum Hexateuch in Rufins Übersetzung* (Leipzig: J. C. Hinrichs, 1927), p. 319.

[108] *V. Hild.*, II.6, pp. 30–31; *Life*, in *Jutta and Hildegard*, trans. by Silvas, pp. 166–67. Origen, *In Liber Iudicum*, ed. by Baehrens, *Origenes Werke*, VII, p. 492, line 24 – p. 493, line 6.

[109] Elisabeth of Schönau, *Complete Works*, pp. 125–26; McGinn, 'Spiritual Heritage of Origen in the West', p. 263.

ing even more deeply.[110] Hildegard's commentary in the *Expositiones* cuts up the scriptural narrative to provide a spiritual meaning for each unit of the text. Through the power of the Spirit, the *magistra* aimed to reveal the depth of the secret meaning. To accomplish that, she mingled and wove various elements into single narratives as she interrupted the account of Scripture.

Hildegard could have had access to Origen's works, but she certainly could have become acquainted with his terms and ideas through any number of patristic and medieval Latin exegetes. Ambrose followed Origen's exegesis of Luke; Augustine drew from him for *De doctrina Christiana*, probably the most influential guide to hermeneutics for Western exegetes, which includes the theory of signification.[111] Jerome translated some of Origen's works;[112] Gregory the Great was influenced by Origen in his commentary on the Song of Songs.[113] Bede drew on Origen, as did the Carolingian exegetes, the scholars at Laon, and the twelfth-century Victorines and Cistercians.[114] John Scotus Eriugena composed a homily on John 1, read extensively in the liturgy, which was attributed falsely to Origen but also heavily

---

[110] Origen, *On First Principles*, 2.9, trans. by Greer, p. 188.

[111] The exegete prepares himself to interpret signs, natural and conventional, knowing that 'things are perceived more readily through similitudes'. Augustine of Hippo, *De doctrina Christiana*, ed. by J. Martin, CCSL, 32 (Turnhout: Brepols, 1962), 2. 6. 6, p. 37, lines 15–23: 'Nunc tamen nemo ambigit et per similitudines libentius quaeque cognosci et cum aliqua difficultate quaesita multo gratius inueniri [. . .] magnifice igitur et salubriter spiritus sanctus ita scripturas sanctas modificauit, ut locis apertioribus fami occurreret, obscurioribus autem fastidia detergeret.' See McGinn, 'Originality of Eriugena's Spiritual Exegesis', p. 75, n. 21; and on Augustine's interpretation of Scripture, *Augustine and the Bible*, ed. and trans. by Pamela Bright (Notre Dame: University of Notre Dame Press, 1999).

[112] For a brief discussion of the influence of Origen on these four fathers of the Latin Church, see Lubac, *Medieval Exegesis*, I, 150–59.

[113] R. A. Markus, *Gregory the Great and his World* (Cambridge: Cambridge University Press, 1997), pp. 46–47, nn. 59–60. Markus does not examine Gregory's sources in depth. Gregory's well-known letter to Leander of Seville, which prefaces the *Moralia in Iob*, describes biblical interpretation in terms that echo Origen's description of Noah's Ark: establishing the historical sense provides the foundation on which a stronghold of faith (*arcam fidei*) is constructed as a mental edifice (*fabricam mentis*), to which the moral sense can be applied like a coat of paint. Gregory the Great, *Moralia in Iob*, Ad Leandrum 3, 4; and Origen, *Homélies sur la Genèse*, II.1.1–10, p. 76. In the *Moralia*, Gregory uses the term *spiritalis intellectus*, which appears in Hildegard. Gregory, *Moralia in Iob*, 20.9, 28.18, and elsewhere.

[114] See McGinn, 'Spiritual Heritage of Origen in the West', p. 280. Paschasius Radbertus used Origen's commentary on Matthew. Dronke, 'Platonic-Christian Allegories', p. 384, n. 11, allows for this.

indebted to him.[115] Rupert of Deutz, Hildegard's near contemporary, shows some Origenist influence in his exegesis on the Song; and Bernard of Clairvaux was heavily indebted to the Alexandrian in his commentary on the Song.[116] As Beryl Smalley stated, 'To write a history of Origenist influence on the West would be tantamount to writing a history of western exegesis.'[117] E. Ann Matter's observation about Origen's influence on Bernard's sermons on the Song applies generally to Hildegard's exegesis as well: 'But it is Origen's sense of the drama of Christ and the soul that predominates in twelfth-century exegesis.'[118] Certainly, Hildegard belongs on the list of those who felt the strong influence of the Alexandrian exegete,[119] whether she consulted manuscripts of Origen's works directly, knew them through Office readings, or learned about them from others. I would add that Hildegard's method may have been influenced by her understanding of Origen's view of the Holy Spirit, working 'to keep the logical order of the spiritual meaning'. Moreover, Origen conceived of the Trinitarian authorship of Scripture,[120] a concept that may have influenced Hildegard's Trinitarian exegesis. I shall return to that in the context of Hildegard's theology of salvation history.

---

[115] See McGinn, 'Spiritual Heritage of Origen in the West'. On the reading of Eriugena in German nunneries during Hildegard's day, see Christel Meier, 'Eriugena im Nonnenkloster? Uberlegungen zum Verhältnis von Prophetentum und Werkgestalt in den figmenta prophetia Hildegards von Bingen', in *Eriugena redivivus: Frühmittelalterliche Studien* (Berlin: de Gruyter, 1985), pp. 466–97. Dronke, *LDO*, p. xii–xiv, xix, comments on Meier-Staubach's claims. On Eriugena and *intelligentia spiritalis*, see McGinn, 'Originality of Eriugena's Spiritual Exegesis'.

[116] E. Ann Matter traces Origen's influence on medieval commentators on the Song including Gregory, Rupert of Deutz, and Bernard of Clairvaux, in *The Voice of My Beloved: The Song of Songs in Western Medieval Christianity* (Philadelphia: University of Pennsylvania Press, 1990), pp. 20–48. See also McGinn, 'Spiritual Heritage of Origen in the West'. On Hildegard and Rupert, see Kathryn Kerby-Fulton, 'Prophet and Reformer: "Smoke in the Vineyard"', in *Voice*, pp. 70–90 (pp. 76–80).

[117] Smalley, *Study of the Bible*, pp. 1–2.

[118] Matter, *Voice of My Beloved*, p. 39.

[119] Lubac devotes a chapter to the reading of Origen's Latin works in *Medieval Exegesis*, I, 161–224.

[120] Peter Martens, 'Why Does Origen Refer to the Trinitarian Authorship of Scripture in Book 4 of Peri Archon?', *Vigiliae Christianae*, 60 (2006), 1–8.

The Senses of Scripture

If spiritual interpretation dominates Hildegard's exegesis, what role do the traditional senses of Scripture play in the *Expositiones*? What does Hildegard's use of the various scriptural senses say about her visionary understanding? John Cassian (*c.* 360–435) defines 'spiritualis scientia' as having three genres of interpretation: tropology, allegory, and anagogy, which contrast with the historical.[121] Henri de Lubac pointed out that there were 'basically only two senses of Scripture recognized everywhere in the ancient tradition: the one, which consists in the history or the letter; the other, which is more generally named spiritual, or allegorical, or mystical'.[122] This notion of one 'spiritual' approach, with three parts that contrast with the literal, weighs against the well-known pattern of expounding four senses of Scripture — historical-literal, allegorical, moral (tropological), and anagogical — best known from John Cassian's fourfold reading of Jerusalem (the historical city, the Church, the soul, the heavenly city).[123] Medieval exegetes did not follow the fourfold method rigorously, as E. Ann Matter demonstrates for interpretation of the Song of Songs. Honorius Augustodunensis's painstaking application of Cassianic interpretation contrasts with a more pervasive tendency towards fluidity and combination of interpretive modes.[124] For Hildegard as for her predecessors, the notion of 'spiritual understanding' encompasses both the frequent use of typology and tropology and the conviction that the hidden meaning of Scripture, revealed by spiritual interpretation, surpasses the literal or historical sense.

Hildegard follows no explicit threefold or fourfold pattern as she comments on the pericopes included in the *Expositiones*, yet there are subtle patterns at work which point beyond any sort of instantaneous interpretation of the texts.[125]

---

[121] John Cassian, *Collationes* 14.8, ed. by M. Petschenig, CSEL, 13 (Vienna, 1886), pp. 189–90: 'Theoretike uero in duas diuiditur partes, id est in historicam interpretationem et intelligentiam spiritualem [. . .]. Spiritualis autem scientiae genera sunt tria: tropologia, allegoria, anagoge'; discussed by McGinn, 'Originality of Eriugena's Spiritual Exegesis', pp. 59, 75, n. 17.

[122] Lubac, *Medieval Exegesis*, II, 25.

[123] See Lubac, *Medieval Exegesis*, I, 90–115, on the tendency of medieval exegetes to follow a trichotomy or a quadruple distinction.

[124] Matter, *Voice of My Beloved*, pp. 58–76.

[125] In the *LDO*, the *magistra* employs three levels of meaning for certain explanations: *littera*, *allegoria*, and *moralitas*, although the labels for the successive interpretations of Scripture were added later in the margins of the earliest manuscript. Citing *LDO*, II.17–47 on Genesis 1–2. 1, Peter Dronke, 'Platonic-Christian Allegories', pp. 386–87, makes a similar observation: 'whilst

Hildegard devotes one allegorical and one tropological reading to most of the pericopes in the collection. However, she treats John 1. 1–14 in one homily only; for three pericopes (Lk 5. 1–11, Lk 19. 41–47, Jn 3. 1–15), she presents three interpretations of the biblical text; and for Luke 21. 25–33, there are four different readings. Scholars explain Hildegard's method in different ways. Peter Dronke has described the pairs of *expositiones* as macrocosmic and microcosmic.[126] For the sets of *expositiones* that have more than two homilies, Joop van Banning has proposed a predominant mode of interpretation for each of the *expositiones*. He agrees that most of the pairs on one pericope offer allegorical and tropological readings. Up to six *expositiones* may fit into the category of literal-historical exegesis, according to van Banning: *Expo.* 5 on Matthew 1. 18–21; 9 on John 1. 1–14; 24 on Matthew 4. 1–11; 30 on John 10. 11–16; 47 on Luke 19. 41–47; 53 on Luke 21. 25–33. For the triple readings, he classifies Luke 5. 1–11 as allegorical, moral, and anagogical; Luke 19. 41–47 as literal, allegorical, and moral; and John 3. 1–15 as allegorical, moral, and anagogical. Finally, he argues that the four homilies on Luke 21. 25–33 follow the four senses of Scripture: literal-historical, allegorical, moral, and anagogical.[127] Nonetheless, van Banning also recognizes that Hildegard's interpretations in their 'grossen Linien' follow one mode but at the same time present some elements in a different mode and at times incongruently.[128]

The Literal Sense

How does a literal-historical reading from Hildegard differ from interpretations in that sense by her contemporaries or from the compendia in the *Glossa ordinaria*? A keen interest in the historical sense of Scripture becomes increasingly evident in the twelfth-century schools. This hermeneutical course became evident at the turn of the century when Anselm of Laon (d. 1117) undertook the glossing of the Gospels

---

Hildegard was clearly well aware of diverse exegetical methods, what is striking is how freely she proceeds in practice'. Derolez, *LDO*, p. xcv, observes that the terms *littera, allegoria, moralitas* 'do not occur in the text itself but were added afterwards in its margins'. Derolez also notes, p. xciii, that the commentary on Genesis, more systematic than that on John's Gospel, was introduced by Hand 1, or Corrector 1, whose changes to the text were done 'under the constant supervision and according to the directions of Hildegard'.

[126] Dronke, 'Platonic-Christian Allegories', pp. 383–84.

[127] Van Banning, 'Hildegard von Bingen als Theologin', pp. 260–67.

[128] Van Banning, 'Hildegard von Bingen als Theologin', p. 265.

(except Mark). As he selected commentary from available sources and added his own, he clearly demonstrated attention to the literal-historical sense. At mid-century, the scholars of the Abbey of St Victor in Paris continued to accentuate the literal-historical sense of Scripture, while retaining an interest in the monastic readings that valued allegory and typology. Hugh of St Victor in the *Didascalion*, a guide to exegesis inspired by Augustine, stressed the necessity of understanding the historical meaning of the text before proceeding to exegesis at other levels. For his *Adnotationes* on the Pentateuch, he consulted rabbinic scholars, and he composed a *chronicon* with chronological tables to aid with understanding events of biblical history.[129] This interest in the historical sense marked the influential work of Peter Comestor, whose *Historica scholastica* (*c.* 1170) exerted a strong influence on succeeding generations.[130]

Hildegard generally does not explain natural phenomena, the derivation of words, the nature of buildings, the history of names and biblical persons, or such elements of literal-historical exegesis that interested the schoolmasters of the day. Although keenly interested in science and healing, she does not probe nature with any scientific explanation. Similarly, as Charles Burnett observes, Hildegard's cosmology and astrology, albeit unusual, do not reflect the current scientific thought of her day.[131]

Hildegard's first homily for Christmas Eve (Mt 1. 18–21) represents perhaps the clearest case where the *magistra* explains the pericope on the literal-historical level. The principal figures, Joseph and Mary, represent nothing but themselves. The *magistra* gives the reasons why Mary had to have a husband.[132] Hildegard explains that, according to God's plan for man and woman, a woman with a child needs a provider. As a moral commentary, she adds that humility involves

[129] Hugh of St Victor, *Didascalion de studio legendi*, ed. by Charles Henry Buttimer, Catholic University of America Studies in Medieval and Renaissance Latin, 10 (Washington, DC: Catholic University Press, 1939). Guy Lobrichon, 'Une nouveauté: les gloses de la Bible', in *Le Moyen Âge et la Bible*, ed. by Pierre Riché and Guy Lobrichon, Bible de tous les temps, 4 (Paris: Beauchesne, 1984), pp. 95–114 (p. 106); Jean Châtillon, 'La Bible dans les écoles du XIIe siècle', in ibid., pp. 163–97 (pp. 181–82).

[130] Lobrichon, 'Une nouveauté', p. 106.

[131] See Châtillon, 'La Bible dans les écoles du XIIe siècle'; Charles Burnett, 'Hildegard of Bingen and the Science of the Stars', in *Context*, pp. 111–20. Neither does Hildegard inquire into the *quomodo* of miracles. Twelfth-century authors began to separate miracles from the natural order and thereby to investigate natural events. See Benedicta Ward, *Miracles and the Medieval Mind: Theory, Record, and Event, 1000–1215*, rev. edn (Philadelphia: University of Pennsylvania Press, 1987), pp. 7–8.

[132] *Expo. Euang.*, 5, pp. 203–04.

subjection, and pride could have snatched Mary if she had thought she had no need of a husband.[133] The *magistra* explains Joseph's character and his desire to leave Mary (Mt 1. 19) on the literal-historical level with no further comment: Joseph wanted to go away from Mary because of the rumour people circulated. Once he was gone, they would not know if he was dead or alive.[134] At one point in the homily, Hildegard recalls the joining of Adam and Eve, but she develops no allegorical narrative in this homily.[135]

The *expositio* on John 1 explains the text and constructs no parallel narrative. In this *expositio*, explanation of the theology of creation and incarnation obtains as the primary concern for Hildegard, as for other commentators.[136] The *magistra* remarks on the possibility of multiple interpretations of two controversial phrases in John 1, and she states her preference for one over the other.[137] The meaning of

---

[133] *Expo. Euang.*, 5, p. 203, lines 4–8: 'iustum est ut omnis femina, infantem habens, uirum procuratorem haberet [. . .] umilitas subsequitur in subiectione quoniam si Maria procuratorem non haberet, superbia facile subreperet, quasi uiro ad procurandum se non indigeret'. Jerome explains why Mary needs a husband and other exegetes follow suit. Jerome, *Aduersus Heluidium de Mariae uirginitate perpetua*, 4, PL 23: 193–216 (col. 187A–B); Jerome, *Commentariorum in Matheum Libri IV*, ed. by D. Hurst and M. Adriaen, CCSL, 77 (Turnhout: Brepols, 1969), 1, p. 10, lines 72–79; Bede, *Homeliarum euangelii libri II*, I, 5, p. 34, lines 61–68; and other sources cited in the apparatus fontium, *Expo. Euang.*, 5, p. 203. When Hildegard refers to a *uirum procuratorem*, she seems to echo Peter Chrysologus, *Collectio sermonum*, ed. by A. Oliuar, CCSL, 24, 24A, 24B (Turnhout: Brepols, 1975–82), 146 (p. 904, line 60: 'Procurator Ioseph sponsus').

[134] *Expo. Euang.*, 5, p. 204, lines 18–20: 'uolebat ab ea secedere propter rumorem populi, sic ut omnes ignorarent an uiueret an obisset'. There is no evident correspondence with the *Biblia latina cum glossa ordinaria*, facsimile reprint of the *Editio princeps*, Adolph Rusch of Strassburg 1480/81, intro. by Karlfried Froehlich and Margaret T. Gibson, 4 vols (Turnhout: Brepols, 1992), IV, 7, which focuses on explaining Mary's virginity.

[135] *Expo. Euang.*, 6, pp. 204–05. In contrast, the second treatment of the pericope constructs an allegory relating the betrothal of Mary and Joseph to the baptism of the faithful soul (Mary) and wisdom (Joseph). Van Banning, 'Hildegard von Bingen als Theologin', pp. 260–67, cites this second interpretation as an example of Hildegard's deliberate avoidance of the literal sense, even for the reading of a historical biblical story.

[136] Hildegard's homily on John 1 differs from the Johannine passage in the *Liber diuinorum operum* with its brilliant overlay of images. Dronke, 'Platonic-Christian Allegories', p. 388, suggests that the exposition be seen 'as a step towards the more majestic account of the prologue of John that Hildegard made into the culmination of Book I of the *LDO*. It may well be what she first set down regarding John's Prologue', the product of her 1163 vision. See also Barbara J. Newman, 'Commentary on the Johannine Prologue translated and introduced by Barbara Newman', *Theology Today*, 60 (2003), 16–33, on Book I of the *LDO*.

[137] Van Banning notes this also in 'Hildegard von Bingen als Theologin', p. 262.

nihil (Jn 1. 3b) proved crucial to the interpretation of Christian theology and occupied exegetes for centuries.[138] Hildegard deals with it extensively in her anti-heretical writings, and I shall examine it further in Chapter 6. This homily provides perhaps the only case in the *Expositiones* where the *magistra* discusses the meaning of a particular word or phrase for which an understanding of its literal significance proves essential for grasping the theological meaning.

The *magistra*'s first interpretation of Matthew 4. 1–11 stays close to a literal-historical sense of the passage. Hildegard explains that the Devil is a spirit without an aerial body; he does not change himself into any other form but remains as he is, showing himself as a very black shadow.[139] She clarifies further that the Devil, not Lucifer, tempted Adam. Divine power constrained him to hell, so that he could not carry out his wicked will. However, he can send out other evil spirits to deceive humans.[140]

In regard to the first temptation, changing stones into bread, Hildegard explains that the Devil did not tell Christ to make bread from nothing, but to change one created thing into another, which is contrary to God's righteousness.[141] To clarify what is against righteousness and what is not, Hildegard asserts that Jesus's miracle of changing water into wine was not contrary to nature: wine is liquid just like water, and, therefore, the water changed only in taste. If the stones had been

---

[138] *Expo. Euang.*, 9, p. 210, lines 13–19: '*Omnia*, uidelicet celum, terra et cetera quae in eis sunt, *per ipsum facta sunt*, in hoc quod Deus dixit *Fiat. Et sine ipso*, scilicet sine racionalitate, id est sine filio, *factum est nichil*, quod est contradictio. Deus angelum racionalem fecit; sed quod racionalitas Deum in angelo contradixit, ipse non fecit, sed fieri permisit. Quamuis etiam alio modo intelligatur, ita quod sine filio nichil factum sit.' See *Expo. Euang.*, 9, apparatus fontium, pp. 210–15.

[139] *Expo. Euang.*, 24, p. 253, lines 34–40: '*Et accedens temptator*, permissione Christi, quia ipsum uidit spiritalia et non carnalia operantem; et idcirco accessit ad eum, ut fuit spiritus, non aerium corpus sumens, nec aliquam aliam formam ullius creaturae se transfigurans, sed solum ut est, ita permanens, se in forma sua ut nigerrimam umbram ostendit: quia tantam uirtutem in Christo uidebat, quod se in aliam formam deceptuose transformare non audebat.'

[140] *Expo. Euang.*, 24, p. 253, lines 40–46: '*Et ideo temptator dicitur*, quia ille fuit qui Adam temptauit, non Lucifer; quoniam ille ex quo cecedit, de loco gehennalis perditionis motus non est, quia tanta fortitudo maliciae in illo est, si egredi permitteretur, quod etiam aerem in aliqua parte euerteret: unde per diuinam potentiam ita comprimitur, ne uoluntatem suam in nequicia sua exercere possit, sed tantum alios ad decipiendum homines emittit.'

[141] *Expo. Euang.*, 24, p. 254, lines 62–68: '*Et dixit: Dic solo uerbo, ut lapides isti*, quia ibi presentes erant, *panes fiant*. Non dixit ut de nichilo panes faceret, sed ut creaturam in alium modum mutaret, ut tanto ueracius cognosceret, si ipse Deus creatura esset. Et quod contrarium iustitiae Dei erat, fieri persuasit, quia aduersus iusticiam Dei esset, si creaturam aliquam in alium modum mutaret, ut diabolus semper fieri persuadet.'

made into bread, they would have lost their entire nature, as the loaves of bread would have also.[142]

With regard to the second temptation, Hildegard enters briefly into allegorical interpretation: the city to which the Devil led Christ in the second temptation prefigures the Church and the edifice of the virtues that was to be comprised in the Church. She then returns to the literal sense, when she explains that the Devil stirred up a whirlwind around Christ and placed him on the pinnacle, taunting him to throw himself down. She asserts that Christ was weightless, just as he was at his transfiguration and ascension.[143]

Concerning the third temptation, Hildegard explains on the literal level that the mountain appeared spiritually and not physically.[144] Finally, the arrival of the angels (Mt 4. 11) gives Hildegard a last opportunity to clarify that the temptations took place according to Christ's will, for the angels knew and worshipped him, and fulfilled his will.

While this summary highlights the elements of the homily that characterize the *magistra*'s exegesis as literal-historical,[145] Hildegard also looks back historically to the creation and develops a sort of reverse allegory that underscores her theology of

---

[142] *Expo. Euang.*, 24, p. 254, lines 68–73: 'Sed quod filius Dei aquam in uinum conuertit, hoc naturae contrarium non fuit, quia uinum sicut et aqua madidum est et fluit, ei ideo aqua saporem suum tantum mutauit; lapides autem si panes facti fuissent, omnino naturam suam perdidissent: sed et idcirco panes, quia primus et fortior cibus esurientium est.'

[143] *Expo. Euang.*, 24, p. 255, lines 85–103: '*Tunc assumpsit eum diabolus in sanctam ciuitatem*, ita scilicet quod diabolus, permissione Christi, quasi turbinem cum suggestione sua circa Christum fecerat, et hanc diabolus tetigit, et Christum secum ea leuitate sine pondere tulit, sicut etiam ipse Christus in monte transfiguratus est, et ut ad celos ascendit. [...] Sed diabolus, quia spiritus fuit, illa spiritaliter apparentia uidit, sciens illa quae ibi uidebat, ad Christum respicere, et artibus suis temptauit, si magnifica opera illa ullo modo in Christo per uanam gloriam impedire posset. Et turbinem illam, quam circa Christum sua suggestione ad temptandum eum excitauerat, ut predictum est, tetigit, et ita permissione ipsius, nullum pondus in eo sentiens, *statuit eum supra pinnaculum templi*, quod ibi apparere uidit, quod dum fecisset, et multum gaudens putaret, ut sicut Christus sibi in hoc consenserat, ita etiam in alio ei consensurum.'

[144] *Expo. Euang.*, 24, p. 256, lines 110–16: '*Iterum assumpsit eum*, permissione ipsius, *diabolus*, prefatam turbinem tangens, ut prius fecerat, *in montem excelsum ualde*, qui ibi etiam in deserto per uoluntatem Dei patris spiritaliter et non corporaliter in ipsis mirabilibus apparuit; ita ut ipse magnitudinem et celsitudinem miraculorum illorum pretenderet, quae per Christum in ecclesia futura erant, quia opera Dei et mirabilia eius super omnia magna et preclara apparent.' This explanation proves very near to Origen's on the same verse. Compare Origen, *De principiis*, 4.3.1, ed. by Koetschau, p. 324.25–33, signalled by McGinn, 'Spiritual Heritage of Origen in the West', p. 281, n. 85.

[145] See van Banning, 'Hildegard von Bingen als Theologin', pp. 262–63.

creation. The dominant mode of exegesis in this exposition remains literal-historical, even though the homily contains elements of an allegory of salvation history.

For *Expo.* 30 on John 10. 11–16, Hildegard focuses on the person of Christ. In her first exposition on this pericope, Hildegard interprets the shepherd as Christ, who feeds all. Creator and Redeemer of all creatures, he brought them to life and also gave up his life for his chosen.[146] The hired hand represents the Devil, who deceives the sheep, then flees from truth. The wolf designates rationality when it becomes wolfish in evil people and uses knowledge of good and evil boldly to contradict the Lord. Christ knows all the elect who remain with him and the creatures that have proceeded from him.[147] In his human nature, divinity knows him and he knows divinity.[148] Those who stray from faith have not yet touched Christ by good works but instead have contradicted him. Still they will hear him in true incarnation because they proceeded from him.[149] There will be one congregation in faith, as there is one God, blessed among all and above all.[150]

Van Banning considers Hildegard's interpretation in this homily as literal-historical with a focus on the incarnation.[151] I agree that the homily has an incarnational focus. However, I see a consistent allegory in that the biblical characters represent something other than themselves. The *magistra* arrives at history through the means of allegory in order to relate one of the principal events of salvation history: the incarnation. That use of allegory argues for considering this *expositio* among Hildegard's allegorical readings of Scripture.

---

[146] *Expo. Euang.*, 30, p. 274, lines 1–5: '*Ego*, uerbum patris, *sum pastor*, scilicet creator *bonus* creaturarum, quia omnes de me procedunt et ego eas omnes in plenitudine pasco. *Bonus pastor animam suam*, scilicet uitam, qua omnia suscitauit, *dat*, ponendo in corporali forma, *pro ouibus suis*, id est electis.'

[147] *Expo. Euang.*, 30, p. 275, lines 19–22: '*Ego*, qui omnia feci, *sum pastor bonus, et cognosco meas*, scilicet omnes electos qui in me manent et creaturas, quia de me processerunt, *et cognoscunt me meae*, quoniam omnes ad me aspiciunt postulando et gustando omnia necessaria.'

[148] *Expo. Euang.*, 30, p. 275, lines 22–25: '*Sicut nouit me* in humanitate *pater*, id est diuinitas, *et ego agnosco patrem*, scilicet diuinitatem, *et animam meam*, uidelicet uitam qua eas suscitaui, *pono* in humano corpore *pro ouibus meis*.'

[149] *Expo. Euang.*, 30, p. 275, lines 26–31: '*Et alias oues*, quae errant in fide et in multis uiciis, *habeo*, reseruatas ad penitentiam; *quae non sunt ex hoc ouili*, quia me bonis operibus nondum tetigerunt sed contradixerunt, *et illas oportet me adducere*, quoniam reseruati sunt ad uitam in qua illis clamabo, quia eas feci, *et uocem meam*, in uera incarnatione, *audient*, quia de me processerunt.'

[150] *Expo. Euang.*, 30, p. 275, lines 31–33: '*Et fiet unum ouile*, uidelicet una congregatio in fide, *et unus pastor*, scilicet Deus in omnibus et super omnia benedictus.'

[151] See van Banning, 'Hildegard von Bingen als Theologin', pp. 263–64.

In Hildegard's second homily on Luke 19. 41–47, Jesus represents no one but himself, an immediate indication that Hildegard is not developing an allegory in the homily. Nonetheless, elements of a typological reading of the pericope are evident. Hildegard situates her interpretation within the broad framework of transformation and transmutation, the Gospel replacing the Old Testament. The act of driving out the money changers (Lk 19. 45) represents the Gospel's expulsion of avarice, idols, and other 'filthy things'. The 'house of prayer' (Lk 19. 46) signifies the house of truth and edifice of revelation. Hildegard situates her explanation of the spiritual interpretation of Scripture in the context of the transformation of the Scriptures. Still her readings of the various elements of the passage are not allegorical and one may consider this homily as a nearly unambiguous example of literal-historical exegesis.[152]

Hildegard devotes four *expositiones* (53–56) to Luke 21. 25–33. The first of these is labeled *Littera* in the manuscript margin; the second *Allegoria*; the third and fourth are not identified by a specific mode of interpretation.[153] Those designations are made in a later hand.[154] Nonetheless, the first homily follows a literal interpretation of the Scripture rather closely. It also incorporates a cosmological dimension. Hildegard explains that the signs in the heavens (Lk 21. 25) indicate that humanity's evil deeds shake the elements of the cosmos. Humans in turn experience physical or natural consequences of their sin: the shaking wrought by heavenly bodies; aridity, the opposite of greenness (*uiriditas*); sadness instead of happiness. 'The air and water are affected,' Hildegard says, 'and the water extends to the sun, the moon and the stars, since those reflect from the water. And so those heavenly bodies shake humans violently with unaccustomed terror.'[155] Humans also provoke the anger of the angels.

---

[152] See van Banning, 'Hildegard von Bingen als Theologin', p. 264.

[153] *Expo. Euang.*, 53–56, pp. 321–29. Dronke, 'Platonic-Christian Allegories', pp. 386–87, suggests anagogical and moral designations for *Expos.* 55 and 56, while he also observes that they perhaps were seen as aspects of *Allegoria* and therefore not labelled as anything different. He does not mention the references to heresy and schism. Van Banning, 'Hildegard von Bingen als Theologin', pp. 264–65.

[154] See Derolez, *LDO*, p. xcv.

[155] *Expo. Euang.*, 53, p. 322, lines 9–15: 'Vnde cum homines mala opera faciunt, aer et aqua tanguntur; et aqua ea ad solem, lunam et ad stellas profert, quoniam haec de aqua lucent, et sic sydera ista inconsuetis terroribus homines secundum opera eorum concutiunt, *pre confusione*, quia aquae simul fuse sunt a Spiritu Sancto, *sonitus maris et fluctuum*, quoniam haec sonitum plangendo emittunt propter peruersa opera hominum.' See the discussion by Dronke, 'Problemata

While Hildegard does not construct a complete parallel narrative for this peri-cope, elements of allegory stand out. She interprets the heavenly bodies, sun, moon, and stars, as something other than themselves, and she envisions a community that encompasses the cosmos and extends back historically to time before the advent of Christ. The inter-relatedness and interaction of the cosmos, humankind, and the angels enhances the element of drama in the text. The signs announce Christ's coming in humanity and divinity. Greenness in the blossoming of trees and flowers signals redemption and reward for the righteous. The visible world will be trans-formed into a better and stable condition. Hildegard offers a visionary apocalyptic reading of the pericope, although she develops only a partial allegory. Van Banning considers it a literal-historical interpretation, and I agree, despite the presence of elements of the allegory of salvation history.[156]

One finds additional instances of Hildegard's use of the literal-historical sense in homilies where other modes of exegesis predominate. In a largely typological homily on Luke 2. 22–32, Hildegard first explains the purification rite on the literal level: 'a woman after childbirth was in silence until she brought the child to the temple'; but that leads to the allegory: 'so the Old Testament lay hidden until the New, when the Son of God was incarnated'.[157] While Hildegard remains largely consistent in her choice of the sense of Scripture she follows in her interpretations, she blends modes to a certain degree, as do other exegetes.

In summary, Hildegard employs a dominant pattern of literal-historical exegesis of Scripture in at most six of the *Expositiones*, as van Banning asserts. I see one of the six, on John 10. 11–16, as predominately allegorical. Van Banning's opinions do not differ greatly from mine, as he too notes that Hildegard disregards the historical sense even of historical biblical accounts such as the Christmas story. The fact that Hildegard employs some literal readings suggests that her range of exegesis developed over time, beyond the divine calefaction or 'soft raindrops' that she claims as her visionary and prophetic mode of understanding Scripture.

Hildegardiana', pp. 108–10, on the possible influence of Lucan and the Stoic notion of cosmic sympathy on Hildegard's thought.

[156] Van Banning, 'Hildegard von Bingen als Theologin', pp. 264–65.

[157] *Expo. Euang.*, 20, p. 47, lines 3–5: 'Quoniam ut mulier post partum in silentio est, usque dum infantem ad templum offerat, sic uetus testamentum in occulto latuit usque ad nouum, ubi filius Dei incarnatus est.' The *Glossa Ordinaria*, IV, 146, focuses on the circumcision, rather than the purification, but makes a general statement in line with typological interpretation: that while neither Joseph nor Mary needed circumcision or purification, they did so in order that 'we be freed from fear of the Law' (*ut nos solveremur a timore legis*).

Solutiones quaestionum XXXVIII

What do Hildegard's other works reveal about her use of the senses of Scripture? She employs threefold exegesis for some parts of the *Liber diuinorum operum*, which may stem from her familiarity with Gregory the Great, in particular his *Moralia in Iob*, where in the famous prefatory letter to Leander of Seville, he describes the exegetical process with imagery of building, establishing the literal sense as foundation, the 'typical' as structure, and the tropological as decoration.[158] Twelfth-century exegetes, including Hugh of St Victor and Abelard, practised a threefold exegesis; however, they differ from Hildegard and from Gregory in their emphasis on the literal understanding.[159] Gregory put his exegetical principles into practice in the *Forty Homilies on the Gospels*. In Homily 40, Gregory explains that the fruit of allegory is picked more sweetly when the truth of history solidly roots it. He also advises that he will explain the moral meaning of the text last, so that his listeners would better recall what they heard most recently.[160] Gregory strongly influenced monastic culture, and it should be no surprise that he would have inspired Hildegard's exegesis.

What patterns does Hildegard follow in the *Solutiones quaestionum XXXVIII* (1176), an exclusively exegetical work? The *Solutiones* open with a frame similar to many in the letter collection: the petitioner, in this case Guibert of Gembloux, requests a response from Hildegard to a particular question, praising the power of the Holy Spirit manifest in her. Guibert sent questions on behalf of the monks at

---

[158] Gregory the Great, *Moralia in Iob*, pp. 4–7 (p. 4 and p. 6): 'quisquis de Deo loquitur, curet necesse est, ut quicquid audientium mores instruit rimetur, et hunc rectum loquendi ordinem deputet, si cum opportunitas aedificationis exigit, ab eo se, quod loqui coeperat, utiliter deriuet. Sacri enim tractator eloquii morem fluminis debet imitari [...]. Sciendum uero est, quod quaedam historica expositione transcurrimus et per allegoriam quaedam typica inuestigatione perscrutamur, quaedam per sola allegoricae moralitatis instrumenta discutimus, nonnulla autem per cuncta simul sollicitius exquirentes tripliciter indagamus. Nam primum quidem fundamenta historiae ponimus; deinde per significationem typicam in arcem fidei fabricam mentis erigimus; ad extremum quoque per moralitatis gratiam, quasi superducto aedificum colore uestimus.' McGinn, 'Hildegard of Bingen as Visionary and Exegete', p. 348, also notes the similarity between Gregory's method and Hildegard's in the *Liber diuinorum operum*.

[159] *Letters of Peter Abelard*, p. 56.

[160] Gregory the Great, *Homeliae in euangelia*, II, 40, p. 394, lines 9–12: 'et quod uobis de moralitate historiae ualde est necessarium, hoc in expositionis nostrae ordine seruetur extremum, quia ea plerumque solent melius recoli que contingit postmodum audiri'. See Wailes, *Medieval Allegories*, p. 257.

Villers, who avidly desired the *magistra*'s solutions for various scriptural problems.[161] Hildegard's reply, unlike the *Expositiones*, opens with a vision — an allegory of Charity and the garden of virtues, whose noblest flower blooms in Christ. The *magistra* writes initially from a third person point of view, describing the garden; then she unfolds the allegory and uses the explanatory verbs *designat* (designates) and *significat* (signifies). The *magistra* then turns to the general audience of her allegory, nuns and monks who have renounced the world and belong among the angelic orders. She subsequently applies the allegory personally to Guibert in a series of exhortations, as she constructs layers of monastic spirituality from the undergirding virtue of humility to the rigorous daily practice of the *Rule* and the eschatological aim of dwelling in the heavenly Jerusalem.[162]

The replies to the thirty-eight questions follow upon the vision, explanation, and moral counsel. This structure places the work in the *solutiones* genre, a frequent vehicle for the thoughts of twelfth-century biblical scholars who grappled with Genesis and other passages of Scripture.[163] Thirty-two of the thirty-eight questions that Hildegard addresses in the *Solutiones* pertain directly to Scripture and touch on seventeen books of the Bible: Genesis, Exodus, Numbers, First and Fourth Kings (Second Samuel), Psalms, Wisdom, Ecclesiasticus, Job, Matthew, Luke, John, Acts, First and Second Corinthians, Ephesians, and Hebrews. Other questions relate to the *vitae* of Martin of Tours and Saint Nicholas. The *magistra* interprets the various biblical passages according to one of three senses of Scripture. The first six questions deal with the creation story in Genesis. Hildegard explains those perplexities in a literal-historical sense, without allegory. When the questions

---

[161] On the text, see Bartlett, 'Commentary, Polemic and Prophecy'; and on the genre, see also Häring, 'Commentary and Hermeneutics', p. 177; Châtillon, 'La Bible dans les écoles du XIIᵉ siècle', pp. 186–87. See McGinn, 'Hildegard of Bingen as Visionary and Exegete', pp. 333–34, and Bartlett, 'Commentary, Polemic and Prophecy', passim, on Hildegard's letters that respond to complex questions debated in the schools. The epistolary frame situates the *Solutiones* within the extensive corpus of monastic letters that were exchanged to probe exegetical or theological problems. See, for example, Kienzle and Shroff, 'Cistercians and Heresy'; Beverly Mayne Kienzle, 'The Works of Hugo Francigena: *Tractatus de conversione Pontii de Laracio et exordii Salvaniensis monasterii vera narratio; epistolae* (Dijon, Bibliothèque Municipale MS 611)', *Sacris erudiri*, 34 (1994), 287–317 (pp. 281–82, 303–11).

[162] *Solut.*, PL 197: 1039–40.

[163] See Smalley, *Study of the Bible*, pp. 66–82; Bartlett, 'Commentary, Polemic and Prophecy', p. 154; Häring, 'Commentary and Hermeneutics', p. 182.

move to texts that involve the patriarchs, she turns to typology.[164] Other questions seek clarification of biblical phrases like the 'tongues of angels' (*Quaest.* XIV on I Cor 13. 1), or ask Hildegard how to reconcile seemingly contradictory passages (*Quaest.* XII on III Kings 8 vs Hebrews 9).[165] The *magistra* resolves these problems without allegory, but as with the questions on Genesis, she steers clear of new scholastic approaches.[166] Still other questions address specific issues such as the nature of the fire in hell (*Quaest.* XXXIII).[167] Many questions phrase their inquiry with straightforward interrogative words, such as *quid est quod . . ., quomodo . . ., cur, quare,* and forms of *qualis*.[168] Certain questions lead Hildegard to a particular mode of interpretation, as when an allegorical explanation is sought for the length, width, height, and depth referred to in Ephesians 3. 18 (*Quaest.* XV).[169] In *Quaestio* XIX, Hildegard extracts both a moral and a physiological lesson from her explanation: the Devil sows discord and motivates sin from outside the body (I Cor 6. 18), from one human against another; but when desire boils up in the veins and marrow, the human incites and harms himself within his body.[170] This parallels the medical material in *Cause et cure*.[171]

---

[164] *Solut., Quaest.* I–VI, *PL* 197: 1040B–1042, on the creation story; *Quaest.* VII–X, *PL* 197: 1042C–1043D, on the patriarchs.

[165] *Solut., Quaest.* XII, *PL* 197: 1044B–C.

[166] Bartlett, 'Commentary, Polemic and Prophecy', pp. 161–64, describes this method as the 'rhetoric of prophecy'.

[167] *Solut., Quaest.* XXXIII, *PL* 197: 1051C–1052A.

[168] Examples of each follow: *Solut., Quaest.* I, 'Quomodo [. . .]', *PL* 197: 1040B; *Quaest.* II, 'Quid [. . .]', col. 1040D; *Quaest.* IV, 'Quo genere [. . .]', col. 1041C–D; *Quaest.* V, 'Quid est [. . .]', cols 1041D–1042A; *Quaest.* VI, 'Quales [. . .]', col. 1042B; *Quaest.* IX, 'Cur [. . .]', col. 1043C; *Quaest.* X, 'Quare [. . .]', cols 1043D–1044A. Other instances of the same words occur. This type of questioning reflects the attention to Genesis in the schools. It is interesting to compare the questions with the *joca monachorum*, the game-like questions and answers about Scripture that circulated widely in monastic circles. The latter tend to ask for recall of information, although they incorporate some interpretation, as in 'Qui est mortuus et non natus? Adam'. See Jacques Dubois, 'Comment les moines du Moyen Âge chantaient et goûtaient les Saintes Ecritures', in *Le Moyen Âge et la Bible*, ed. by Riché and Lobrichon, pp. 264–70. The questions posed in the *Solutiones* ask for interpretation, but not causal or scientific explanations.

[169] *Solut., Quaest.* XV, *PL* 197: 1045A–B.

[170] *Solut., Quaest.* XIX, *PL* 197: 1046B–C.

[171] On marrow and lust, see *Cause*, p. 105, line 26; p. 114, lines 11–14; p. 177, line 14; p. 179, lines 26–27; and others.

Two questions address pericopes that Hildegard exegetes in the *Expositiones*: Matthew 4. 11 (the ministry of the angels to Jesus in the wilderness) and Luke 16. 22–24 (the death and afterlife of the beggar Lazarus and the rich man). *Quaestio* XXI inquires what sort of ministry the angels provided to Christ in the wilderness. Hildegard sets the context for the question in the gospel passage when the Devil left Jesus after his failure to tempt him. She then answers that the angels' ministry was to sound forth praises, because humankind overcame the Devil's temptations through Christ.[172] This explanation corresponds in part to the interpretation she gives in one of the *Expositiones*, that the angels ministered to him 'in heavenly harmony and praise, because they will praise God endlessly'.[173] The two commentaries reveal a similar thought on the angels' praises, with the *quaestio* accenting the human's victory over sin.[174]

Quaestio XXXVI probes details in the parable of Lazarus and the rich man, asking about the significance of the bosom of Abraham, the finger of Lazarus, and the tongue of the rich man (Lk 16. 22–24). Hildegard responds with a moral allegory different from her interpretations in the two *expositiones* on the passage (37, 38). In the *Solutiones*, she explains the bosom of Abraham allegorically as the obedience showed to God, the finger of Lazarus as the ministry of obedience, and the rich man's tongue as self-will.[175] In the *Expositiones*, Abraham's bosom represents in one text the comprehension and joyous embrace of the Gospels and prophets for all who fulfill them in deed (*Expo. Euang.* 37), and in the second (*Expo. Euang.* 38), the appetite for hope. Lazarus's finger denotes in one homily (*Expo. Euang.* 37) the smallest part of a deed dipped in wisdom, and in the other (*Expo. Euang.* 38), the tiniest matter (*causae*) of one moaning for God. The rich man's tongue stands for his excessive speech (*Expo. Euang.* 37) and then (*Expo. Euang.* 38) for the works that he performed with the tongue. The latter reading in the homily approaches Hildegard's exegesis in the *Solutiones*, where the wealthy man designates pleasure that exudes in self-will.[176] However, neither of the *quaestiones* on these gospel

---

[172] *Solut., Quaest.* XXI, *PL* 197: 1046D–1047A.

[173] *Expo. Euang.*, 25, p. 260, lines 80–82.

[174] *Glossa Ordinaria*, IV, 15, reads that 'the retinue of angels teaches the glorious reward after our struggle' ('sicut in hoc agone militia nostra prestruitur, ita in obsequio angelorum gloriosa remuneratio docetur').

[175] *Solut., Quaest.* XXXVI, *PL* 197: 1052C–D.

[176] *Expo. Euang.*, 38, p. 293, lines 1–5: '*Homo quidam*, scilicet uoluptas in homine, *erat diues* ualde in uicissitudine pinguedinis propriae uoluntatis, *et induebatur*, id est iniit, *purpura*, scilicet gustum peccati, *et bisso*, uidelicet deliciis, *et epulabatur*, multiplicat cottidie unumquodque uicium, *splendide*, ante faciem cordis sui.'

passages repeats verbatim what Hildegard states in the *Expositiones*.[177] Instead she provides different and primarily tropological readings.

The range of interpretation evident in the *Solutiones* further testifies to the depth of Hildegard's exegetical knowledge and at the same time to her preference for moral interpretation. Hildegard describes her tropological method in her response to *Quaestio* XXXV, on parables and why Jesus used them. The *magistra* replies that Jesus set forth parables to demonstrate that virtues can vanquish the spiritual vices.[178] Parables prove necessary, because the serpent caused humans to lose their spiritual vision. Consequently, the divine mysteries are not to be seen except as a person sees his face in a mirror: 'Those conceived in sin cannot grasp words of life other than in parables.'[179] The *magistra* echoes the merit and even the necessity of teaching by parables in Letters 268 and 389. 'God,' she states, 'set parables and metaphors before humankind, through which, usually, they are taught the way to salvation better than through the naked words themselves.'

Explaining the motif of new wine and old wine skins, Hildegard explains that the best wine in the skins signifies the sweetest doctrine, which Jesus taught people by means of parables. These passages from the *Solutiones* and the *Letters* recall both Augustine's observation on the necessity of similitudes and Otloh of St Emmeram's teaching on parables.[180] Furthermore, they explain the value and the method of tropological interpretation that Hildegard implemented in the *Expositiones*: she constructed parables of virtue and vice for the benefit of her community and created mirrors for biblical texts in order to elucidate their mysteries. This brief

---

[177] *Glossa Ordinaria*, IV, 139: 'Sinus Abrahae est requies beatorum pauperum [. . .]'; 2. 'Sinus Abrahae requies est patris in quae recumbunt venientes ab oriente et occidente cum Abraham, Ysaac, et Iacob.' For the finger, the *Glossa* explains that 'he who refuses to give crumbs to Lazarus desired to have a drop of water on his finger, and who gave not even the least in life sought the least in death'.

[178] *Solut., Quaest.* XXXV, *PL* 197: 1052.

[179] On the loss of spiritual vision, see *Solut., Quaest.* III, VI, VIII, *PL* 197: 1041, 1043.

[180] *Epistolarium*, III, 389, p. 162, lines 326–33: 'Botrorum autem optimum uinum suam dulcissimam doctrinam significat, qua homines in parabolis docebat, quid diuina mysteria generi per consilium serpentis obnubilato uidenda non sunt, nisi ut facies hominis in speculo, in quo tamen non est, resplendet. Quomodo enim posset uita mortali homine uideri? Ipse enim obscura uerba hominibus locutus est, scilicet parabolas, quia in peccatis concepti uerba uitae aliter capere non possunt.' *Letters*, III, 389, p. 190; *Letters*, III, 268, pp. 63–64. Newman, *Sister of Wisdom*, pp. 79–85, signals Hildegard's use of parables, as personification of virtues, notably in her Letters 93, 23, 135, and 144; and the taste for personification of virtues in certain writings of Bernard of Clairvaux, Hugh of St Victor, and Rupert of Deutz.

look at the *Solutiones* widens our perspective on Hildegard's range of exegetical knowledge and provides further evidence for her use of the literal, allegorical, and tropological senses of Scripture. Moreover, she articulates clearly her preference for moral exegesis and for teaching with parables.

Conclusion

Hildegard gained access to the exegesis of her predecessors through the 'ear of the heart' and the 'eye of the mind'. The patristic biblical commentary that she heard in the monastic liturgy grounded Hildegard's exegesis. Moreover, she engaged in intellectual dialogue through conversations and the exchange of written texts. A survey of Hildegard's scriptural knowledge, evidenced throughout her writings, reveals the amazing breadth of her exegesis and her use of interpretation in various senses of Scripture. Nonetheless, the broad concept of spiritual interpretation applies most often to her approach. Hildegard, like other twelfth-century monastic writers, viewed both the Bible and the world as a composite of signs that acquired their real meaning only through spiritual interpretation. The elements, creatures of nature, colours, numbers, names, all revealed spiritual realities. This pervasive use of allegory reflects what Marie-Dominique Chenu called 'the symbolist mentality' and defined as a 'conviction that all natural or historical reality possessed a signification which transcended its crude reality and which a certain symbolic dimension of that reality would reveal to man's mind'.[181]

Gregory the Great described the mystery of Scripture with the image of a river, at once shallow and deep enough for an elephant to swim and a lamb to walk.[182] By the twelfth century, the journey along the exegetical river, like Hildegard's preaching peregrinations, involved many places where her boat might have put to shore. The identification of specific stopping places remains problematic, but the history of the *magistra*'s exegetical journey begins with Origen and the notion of spiritual exegesis that Hildegard inherited from him.

Clearly, Hildegard learned from many sources and added to her knowledge as the years passed; she explored new problems of interpretation such as the answers

---

[181] Marie-Dominique Chenu, *Nature, Man, and Society in the Twelfth Century: Essays on New Theological Perspectives in the Latin West*, ed. and trans. by Jerome Taylor and Lester K. Little (Chicago: University of Chicago Press, 1968), pp. 99–145.

[182] Gregory the Great, *Moralia in Iob*, p. 6, lines 177–78: 'Quasi quidam quippe est fluuius, ut ita dixerim, planus et altus, in quo et agnus ambulet, et elephas natet.'

in the *Solutiones* and the relationship between Genesis 1 and John 1. The accumulation of knowledge through the 'ear of the heart' and the 'eye of the mind' grounded the learned ingredient of her dazzling exegesis and led beyond the initial enlightenment she described in the visions to a continuing education that I shall probe in the next chapter. How did Hildegard's works attain a level of sophistication in learning that prompted the dismissal of her works by Johannes Trithemius as too brilliant to represent the product of a woman?[183]

---

[183] Johannes Trithemius, *Chronicon monasterii Sponheimense*, in *Opera historica*, II, ab annum 1179, p. 257, lines 12–21.

HILDEGARD'S METHOD OF EXEGESIS

I put a moat and a wall around them with the words of the Sacred Scriptures, regular discipline, and good habits.[1]

Hildegard of Bingen constructed moral fortifications, a moat and a wall, for her sisters with the exegesis of the *Expositiones euangeliorum*. Her exegesis, teaching, and preaching constitute an inseparable triad. As Beryl Smalley stated, 'Exegesis is teaching and preaching. Teaching and preaching is exegesis. This was the strongest impression left by St Gregory on medieval Bible study.'[2] Hildegard of Bingen inherited this view; moreover, it lay deeply grounded in Benedictine spirituality and the concept of a superior's accountability for the salvation of souls in his or her charge.[3] The responsibilities for teaching weighed heavily on Hildegard, and her correspondence with abbesses and abbots demonstrates her strong feeling that a superior should inspire her sisters to desire to hear her words. [4]

Yet the written record of Hildegard's homilies, the exegesis of a twelfth-century woman, raises many questions about these exceptional texts. In the previous chapter, I dealt with the circumstances for the *magistra*'s teaching and preaching.

---

[1] *V. Hild.*, II.12, p. 37, lines 29–32: 'At ego per ostensionem Dei eis hoc innotui ipsasque uerbis sanctarum scripturarum et regulari disciplina bonaque conuersatione circumfodi et muniui'; *Life of Hildegard*, p. 60. Silvas, *Jutta and Hildegard*, p. 174, translates the passage as 'I fenced them about and armed them [. . .]', which overlooks the notion of digging (*circumfodere*).

[2] Smalley, *Study of the Bible*, p. 35.

[3] Saint Benedict, *Regula*, 2.6, pp. 21–29.

[4] See Van Engen, 'Abbess'. Hildegard wrote that a certain abbess was bearing her burden well, because her sheep wanted to hear God's admonishment through her teaching: *Epistolarium*, II, 150R, p. 339, lines 2–4.

She learned from the 'ear of the heart' and the 'eye of the mind', but how did she know how to interpret the Scriptures in more than one mode? How did she come to put her exegesis into the written form it takes? Even though the genre of the homily was familiar to her, how did she construct an exegetical commentary without an education in the schools to train her? What was her education like? What model might she have followed for her homilies? Are there contemporaneous homilies with which to compare the *Expositiones*, and do they reveal any similarities in form or theme to Hildegard's exegesis? This chapter undertakes a careful philological and comparative examination of Hildegard's method in order to explore how the *Expositiones* appear 'very obscure' but at the same time evidence remarkable creativity.

Hildegard's Education

The sequential explanation of a biblical passage belongs squarely to monastic literature, but how would Hildegard have learned how to implement the technique? When Jutta instructed the young girl on 'the Psalms of David, and showed her how to make a joyful sound on the ten-stringed psaltery',[5] what exactly was she teaching and how? Was she preparing her in any way for exegesis? Is there any evidence that the syntactical features of Hildegard's glossing reflect her education in the monastery?

Jutta and Hildegard could hear from their enclosure the monks' recitation of the Divine Office, a constant lesson in the Scriptures and other sacred texts.[6] At some point Volmar, whom Hildegard called her *magister*, began to supplement her education. In the *Vita Hildegardis*, the *magistra* spells out how she revealed her visions to Volmar and began to write them:

> I made these things known to a certain monk who was my teacher. He was a person of good observance and sincere intention and averse to prying into others' conduct the way many do. Hence, he listened willingly to these happenings. He was astounded, and he enjoined me to write them down secretly until he could ascertain what and whence they

---

[5] *V. Hild.*, I.1, p. 6, lines 19–20: 'et carminibus tantum Dauiticis instruens in psalterio dechacordo iubilare premonstrabat'; *Life of Hildegard*, p. 26.

[6] Guibert of Gembloux, *Epistolae*, II, 38, p. 373, lines 225–31. See also Flanagan, *Hildegard of Bingen*, pp. 26–32. On the archeological work at Disibodenberg, see Nikitsch, 'Wo lebte die heilige Hildegard wirklich?'.

came. Once he understood they were from God, he informed his abbot and with great desire he worked on these things with me.[7]

The following process emerges from these remarks. Between the occurrence of the visions and their first writing, a conversation about their content occurred. After Volmar read what Hildegard wrote and discussed it with the abbot, he collaborated with her. Hildegard does not elaborate on the nature of that collaboration. Volmar must have at least confirmed that his pupil understood the sacred writings; his partnership would then have helped in elaborating the meaning of the visions. Unfortunately, the substance of Volmar's tutoring sessions cannot be retrieved, nor can the full contents of the Disibodenberg or Rupertsberg library. Manuscripts and library catalogues from other religious houses in the Hirsau network provide parallel evidence for their resources and learning in patristic authors, contemporary writers, and the liberal arts.

What of Jutta's instruction of Hildegard in the Psalms? Adalbert, prior of St Disibod, wrote to the seer in 1150–55 and asserted: 'We know how you were brought up among us, and how you were taught, and how you lived, that you pursued none other than woman's work, that you were imbued with no books other than the simple Psalter.'[8] The 'heavenly dew' that Adalbert esteemed proves to be complex. Learning the Psalms provided at least basic instruction in Latin. The program for education in the monastery began with the Psalms, hymns, and canticles and advanced to the *Rule of Benedict*, Scripture, and patristic authors. The Psalter was glossed for education in the monastery, and glosses on the Psalms, like those on hymns, included lexical and theological instruction and incorporated pedagogical pointers. Oblates were probably taught the Psalms, hymns, and canticles while they were learning to read and before they studied grammar with any intensity.[9] The glossed Psalter held such importance that the twelfth-century

---

[7] *V. Hild.*, I.3, p. 8, lines 9–10: 'cuidam monacho quem sibi magistrum preposuerat'; II.2, p. 24, lines 81–82: 'cuidam monacho magistro meo'. *Life of Hildegard*, p. 28, p. 45.

[8] *Epistolarium*, I, 78, p. 175, lines 10–15: 'Scimus enim quomodo apud nos educata, quomodo docta, quomodo conuersata estis; quia non alio quam muliebri operi institis, non aliis codicibus quam simplici Psalterio imbuta estis [. . .] sed diuina pietas celesti rore, ut uoluit uos imbuit et magnitudinem secretorum suorum uobis aperuit.' The *Acta inquisitionis*, p. 119, echo this view: 'et eadem per spiritus sancti reuelationem, quae praeter psalterium litteras non didicerat, multos libros composuerit, quos dignum est in notitiam ecclesiae Romanae deduci'.

[9] I am indebted to Susan Boynton and her works: 'The Didactic Function and Context of Eleventh-Century Glossed Hymnaries', in *Der lateinische Hymnus im Mittelalter: Überlieferung-Ästhetik-Ausstrahlung*, ed. by Andreas Haug, Monumenta Monodica Medii Aevi, Subsidia, 4

Abbot of Cluny, Peter the Venerable, praised a pious monk for 'always carrying a glossed psalter' and 'turning his eye immediately to the glosses if he found anything he didn't understand'.[10] Glosses on the Psalms and on hymns deepened the understanding of the texts and enhanced their performance.[11] Most of the manuscripts examined thus far that elucidate this type of instruction come from male monasteries. However, the process that emerges from their analysis would match Hildegard's description of her education. Moreover, some glossed manuscripts may provide clues on Hildegard's apparently novel exegetical method.[12]

Clearly Hildegard had reached a level of Latin literacy that allowed her to compose her own works in simple Latin. From his work on literacy in English nunneries, David Bell distinguishes four levels of Latin literacy: reading a text without comprehending it; reading and comprehending common liturgical texts; reading and comprehending less common liturgical texts or texts not from the liturgy; composing and writing one's own text, as Hildegard did. Bell's findings confirm that liturgical texts, notably the Psalter and the primer (the Office of the Virgin supplemented by the penitential Psalms, gradual Psalms, a litany, and the Office of the Dead), constituted the basic textbooks for teaching and learning Latin.[13]

(Kassel: Bärenreiter, 2004), pp. 301–29 (p. 307, n. 32), on the Murbach statutes of 816; 'Training for the Liturgy as a Form of Monastic Education', in *Medieval Monastic Education*, ed. by Ferzoco and Muessig, pp. 7–20 (pp. 14–15); 'Latin Glosses on the Office Hymns in Eleventh-Century Continental Hymnaries', *Journal of Medieval Latin*, 11 (2001), 1–26; 'Orality, Literacy, and the Early Notation of the Office Hymns', *Journal of the American Musicological Society*, 56 (2003), 99–167; *Shaping a Monastic Identity: Liturgy and History at the Imperial Abbey of Farfa, 1000–1125* (Ithaca: Cornell University Press, 2006).

[10] Petrus Venerabilis, *De miraculis*, I.xx, lines 48–55, CCCM, 83 (Turnhout: Brepols, 1988), p. 60; cited by Boynton, 'Didactic Function and Context of Eleventh-Century Glossed Hymnaries', p. 301.

[11] Latin hymn glosses probably developed to meet the need to teach the expanded repertoire of hymns that was compiled in the ninth century. Boynton, 'Didactic Function and Context of Eleventh-Century Glossed Hymnaries', pp. 302–05.

[12] I am grateful to Erika Kihlman, *'Expositiones sequentiarum': Medieval Sequence Commentaries and Prologues. Editions with Introductions*, Acta Universitatis Stockholmiensis, Studia Latina Stockholmiensia, 53 (Stockholm: Stockholm University, 2006). The first currently known example of a sequence commentary, Alan of Lille's *Expositio prosae de angelis*, dates from approximately the late twelfth century.

[13] David Bell, *What Nuns Read: Books and Libraries in Medieval English Nunneries*, Cistercian Studies, 158 (Kalamazoo: Cistercian Publications, 1995), pp. 57–67.

The *Vita Hildegardis* indicates that Volmar ('one faithful man alone') 'arranged the *magistra*'s words according to the rules of the grammatical art — cases, tenses, kinds — which she did not know', without presuming to add or take away from their meaning.[14] In other words, Volmar corrected Hildegard's grammar. Guibert of Gembloux comments in similar terms on Hildegard's lack of grammatical savvy at the same time that he compares her to St Martin for her quick wit and praises her brilliant theological insight and understanding of the Scriptures.[15]

While Hildegard's written Latin does not evidence the grammatical sophistication of her school-educated male secretaries, she clearly possessed a high level of Latin literacy. Moreover, Peter Dronke observes that 'she writes a Latin that is as forceful and colourful, and at times subtle and brilliant, as any in the twelfth century'.[16] Whether or not one assesses Hildegard's Latinity as highly as Dronke, his view cautions against underestimating the *magistra*'s Latin. Moreover, it is reasonable to assume that Hildegard's ability to comprehend Latin texts through reading or listening surpassed her capacity in writing. She built upon a basic education and literacy that should not be undervalued because of its monastic context, her gender, or her protestations of unlearnedness.

Glossa Hildegardiana

Medieval Glosses

Does Hildegard's method of exegesis reflect the way in which she was taught? To begin to answer that question, it is necessary to look briefly at medieval glosses. A gloss in its simplest form provides a synonym. Isidore of Seville, echoed by Hugh of St Victor, identified a gloss as one word that defines a concept, as in the example *contitescere est tacere* (to become silent is to stop talking). Carolingian scholars such as Haymo of Auxerre and John Scotus Eriugena produced glossaries that gave interpretations of difficult scriptural words.[17] William of Conches extended the

---

[14] *V. Hild.*, II.1, pp. 20–21, lines 27–30: 'uno solo fideli uiro symmista contenta, qui ad euidentiam grammatice artis, quam ipsa nesciebat, casus, tempora et genera quidem disponere, sed ad sensum uel intellectum eorum nichil omnino addere presumebat uel demere'; *Life of Hildegard*, p. 42.

[15] Guibert of Gembloux, *Epistolae*, I, 18, p. 231, lines 215–23.

[16] Dronke, *Women Writers of the Middle Ages*, p. 200.

[17] Lobrichon, 'Une nouveauté', p. 96, n. 2; John Contreni, 'The Biblical Glosses of Haimo of Auxerre and John Scottus Eriugena', *Speculum*, 51 (1976), 411–34.

definition of gloss: commentary consisted of the *sententia* or general idea of the text, while the gloss included the commentary plus the explanation of the literal meaning of the words. That definition reveals his awareness of the category of glossed books, which were becoming more numerous around 1100 and appearing in library catalogues with that terminology.[18]

Gernot Wieland defines a gloss as 'anything on a page which is not text proper, but which is intended to comment on the text'.[19] Glossed hymns and sequences, as well as glossed books of the Bible, include interlinear and marginal glosses. For biblical glosses, the interlinear notations generally provide an explanation of vocabulary or set forth a simple historical or allegorical interpretation. Marginal glosses develop lengthier commentary and import passages from patristic expositions.[20] Hildegard's near contemporary, the learned canoness Herrad of Hohenbourg, made extensive use of both Latin and German glosses in her *Hortus deliciarum*; her glosses are primarily interlinear but also marginal.[21]

It may have been in glossed hymnaries that Hildegard found monastic models for paraphrase and theological commentary.[22] Susan Boynton has identified various types of paraphrase glosses, from simple ones that reorder the wording of hymns to more complex and interpretative glosses that signal theological elements of the strophe.[23] Boynton and Martina Pantarotto's study of an eleventh-century breviary from the women's community at Santa Giula (Brescia) analyses glosses

---

[18] Lobrichon, 'Une nouveauté', pp. 96–97.

[19] See Gernot Rudolf Wieland, *The Latin Glosses on Arator and Prudentius in Cambridge University Library, MS Gg.5.35* (Toronto: Pontifical Institute of Mediaeval Studies, 1983), p. 7. On biblical glosses, see also Gibson, 'Twelfth-Century Glossed Bible', pp. 232–33; Lobrichon, 'Une nouveauté', pp. 96–98; Laura Light, *The Bible in the Twelfth Century: An Exhibition of Manuscripts at the Houghton Library* (Cambridge, MA: Harvard College Library, 1988), pp. 79–101, with reproductions of manuscripts.

[20] Gibson, 'Twelfth-Century Glossed Bible', pp. 232–33.

[21] Modern scholars who define medieval glosses generally adopt the later, broader definition of William of Conches. See Griffiths, *Garden of Delights*, pp. 341–55, and her analysis of recent scholarship on glosses and its relevance to Herrad's work. Herrad was acquainted with the eleventh-century *Summarium Heinrici* and its Latin-German glosses, as was Hildegard, notably for the association of *uiriditas, uirga*, and *uirgo*. See *Summarium Heinrici, Band 1. Textkritische Ausgabe der ersten Fassung: Buch 1–X*, ed. by Reiner Hildebrandt (Berlin: de Gruyter, 1974), pp. 89–110. I am grateful to Audrey Pitts for her work on the *Summarium* and the *Expositiones*.

[22] Boynton, 'Didactic Function and Context of Eleventh-Century Glossed Hymnaries', pp. 302–05; Boynton, 'Training for the Liturgy', pp. 14–15.

[23] Boynton, 'Latin Glosses on the Office Hymns', pp. 7–8.

that range from several categories of lexical and grammatical glossing to allegorical and theological commentary. They also include marginal glosses with paraphrases that expound the meaning of the hymn.[24] Hildegard may have assimilated such a method of glossing from her education and developed it in her own way.

Sequence commentaries from a later period contain examples of prose paraphrases of sequence texts written in what Erika Kihlman calls a 'flowing' technique: 'the commentary text seems to flow in and out of the sequence text'. However, the first currently known example of a sequence commentary dates from the end of the twelfth century, and the texts that Kihlman edits date from the late thirteenth century onward. The sequence commentaries illustrate a later development in glossing that shows striking similarities to Hildegard's method of paraphrase.[25] However, as far as I know, neither the eleventh-century hymn glosses nor the later examples from sequence commentaries constitute a separable narrative in a particular mode of interpretation.

Hildegard's Method of Glossing

The techniques of glossing provide a first step for describing Hildegard's method in the *Expositiones*. In contrast to the standard practice of placing glosses outside the text, Hildegard keeps her glosses in parallel with the scriptural passage: she constructs a continuous narrative out of comments that I describe as intratextual glosses. The dual narratives prove baffling at times, doubtless what led the first editor of the *Expositiones* to change the manuscript reading in some places.[26] Careful study of examples from the *Expositiones*, other commentators, and the *Glossa ordinaria* itself will clarify Hildegard's technique. Comparison with the *Glossa ordinaria* must be assessed cautiously. The *Glossa* is best represented by the *editio princeps* from the late fifteenth century, a leap forward of over three centuries. However, the *Glossa* largely consists of a digest of patristic thought and constitutes a standard that was used from the mid-twelfth century onward and that was not confined to the schools. The substance of the *Glossa* remained rather stable and provides a useful standard for comparison when editions of glossed books from

---

[24] Susan Boynton, 'Ricerche sul breviario di Santa Giulia (Brescia, Biblioteca Queriniana, ms H VI 21)' (co-authored with Martina Pantarotto), *Studi medievali*, 42 (2001), 301–18.

[25] See Kihlman, '*Expositiones sequentiarum*', p. 20, and examples of paraphrase, pp. 77, 89, and others.

[26] *Expo. Euang.*, ed. by Kienzle and Muessig, p. 159.

specific times and places are lacking. The prospect of localizing any particular commentary from the *Glossa ordinaria* as to its author, place, and time requires extensive manuscript research beyond the scope of this volume.[27]

Each of the fifty-eight *Expositiones euangeliorum* comments on the biblical passage progressively. After each passage, the *magistra* added her explanations, as in this continuous commentary on Matthew 2. 7:

> *Tunc Herodes*, diabolus, *clam*, scilicet in astutia sua, *uocatis magis*, inquisitoribus creaturarum, *diligenter didicit ab eis*, requirendo *tempus*, uidelicet gustum intellectus, *stellae*, id est donorum Dei, *quae apparuit eis*, scilicet qui eis ostensus est.[28]

> [*Then Herod*, the Devil, *secretly*, namely in his craftiness, *having called together the kings*, the questioners of the creatures, *learned diligently from them*, seeking *the time*, clearly the appetite for understanding, *of the star*, that is, for God's gifts, *which appeared to them*, namely which was shown to them.]

A literal translation of the verse and commentary shows the running, sequential form of Hildegard's interpretation. However, since English does not show gender agreement as Latin does, the links between relative pronouns and antecedents are not obvious, as for *stellae* (of the star) and *quae* (which), and *gustum intellectus* (the appetite for understanding) and *qui* (which). Hildegard's audience would retain the gender and number of the Latin words and make connections that English does not permit. Moreover, the sisters would know the Scripture by heart and thus be able to process both channels of text.

For modern readers, the *magistra*'s word by word commentary may seem somewhat disjointed. Latin allows for a connectedness that lacks in English translation. Recall that even the learned Trithemius called the texts 'very obscure and unintelligible, except to the devout and learned'. Yet Hildegard's commentaries frequently stand as a narrative with overall if not complete coherence. The flow of her interpretive text incorporates certain words from the scriptural passage but passes over or substitutes for others. Much as a simultaneous translator retains one language and produces a translation in another, Hildegard held the language of Scripture in mind and produced her interpretation. Another look at the *magistra*'s commentary on Matthew 2. 7 will illustrate this:

> *Tunc Herodes*, diabolus, *clam*, scilicet in astutia sua, *uocatis magis*, inquisitoribus creaturarum, *diligenter didicit ab eis*, requirendo, uidelicet gustum intellectus, *stellae*, id est donorum Dei, *quae apparuit eis*, scilicet qui eis ostensus est.

---

[27] See examples traced by Gibson in 'Twelfth-Century Glossed Bible', pp. 237–40.

[28] *Expo. Euang.*, 12, p. 221, lines 45–48.

When one focuses on the flow of the interpretation, certain elements of the scriptural text prove necessary to produce a coherent second text, while others do not. The scriptural words *tunc* and *vocatis* and the phrase *diligenter didicit ab eis* ground the construction of an alternate statement and reading of the text:

> *Tunc* [...] diabolus [...] in astutia sua, *uocatis* [...] inquisitoribus creaturarum, *diligenter didicit ab eis*, requirendo [...] gustum intellectus, [...] id est donorum Dei, [...] qui eis ostensus est.

> [*Then* the Devil in his craftiness *called* the questioners of the creatures and *learned diligently from them*, seeking the appetite for understanding — that is, for God's gifts — which was shown to them.]

Hildegard's consistent use of these separable streams of thought indicates that her sisters were accustomed to listening in such a way that they understood both texts simultaneously. Assuming that the nuns knew the Scriptures by heart, as Hildegard recommends in her commentary on the *Rule*, they could more easily direct their attention to the non-scriptural commentary, the second narrative, and not be confused by what elements belonged to which narrative.[29]

Occasionally Hildegard employs the simplest sort of gloss, as Isidore and Hugh of St Victor defined it: a word that provides a synonym. One may consider these glosses as examples of literal exegesis, where Hildegard clarifies the meaning of words or phrases. A clear instance occurs in both homilies on Mark 16. 1–7, where the *magistra* defines the word *reuolutum* (rolled back) with the phrase *id est ablatum* (that is, removed).[30] In two other cases, the gloss for a phrase in one homily seems lexical while in the other homily, it does not. In *Expositio* 11 on Matthew 2. 13–18, she explains *Qui consurgens* (And standing up) in verse 14 as *se erigendo* (raising himself up).[31] In the previous homily (10), Hildegard adds an adverbial prepositional phrase to *Qui consurgens*; the phrase follows the line of her interpretation: *de tenebrosa natura ad rectitudinem* (from dark/shadowy nature to uprightness).[32] In *Expositio* 11, the *magistra* glosses *ululatus multus* (much wailing)

---

[29] *De reg. Bened.*, pp. 73–74. *Expl. Rule*, pp. 24–25. I am grateful to Carolyn Muessig for suggesting the phrase 'separable streams' to describe the simultaneous narratives.

[30] *Expo. Euang.*, 28, p. 270, line 28; *Expo. Euang.*, 29, p. 273, lines 15–16. *Glossa Ordinaria*, IV, 135, provides no lexical gloss but interprets the stone as original sin (interlinear) and the old law, which was written on stone (marginal).

[31] *Expo. Euang.*, 11, p. 217, line 11.

[32] *Expo. Euang.*, 10, p. 215, line 12. *Glossa Ordinaria*, IV, 9, states that Joseph represents preachers who brought faith to the gentiles (*gentes*).

with *uidelicet tristicia* (clearly sadness), again a lexical gloss, whereas the reading in *Expositio* 10 for *ululatus multus* gives *scilicet calumpnia* (namely calumny) in accordance with the typological theme of leaving the plots of the Devil and the darkness of the old law behind.[33]

Hildegard's glosses at times provide definitions and clarify terms. For Matthew 2. 17, 'Then what was said through Jeremiah was fulfilled', Hildegard explains that *quod dictum est* (what was said) means that which God uttered through the exhortation of the Holy Spirit. She adds that no one could stand who wants to stand on his own, but the one whom God sustains will stand because God is that one's staff (*baculus*).[34] Clearly the *magistra* would have had not only Jeremiah in mind, but her own status as prophetic writer and exegete who claimed the Spirit's inspiration. In contrast, for Matthew 1. 18–21, Hildegard explains prophecy with respect to Joseph's dream: the angel appeared to him in a dream and not while he was awake, because he did not have the gift of prophecy.[35] Hildegard makes it very clear in her visionary works that she received her own visions while fully awake. In these two instances, the *magistra*'s commentaries constitute explanatory discourse that belongs to the mode of historical-literal interpretation but subtly underscores her prophetic gift.

In other instances, Hildegard speaks from the perspective of a commentator who knows the exegetical and theological controversies around a particular verse of Scripture. For her exegesis of two contested phrases in John 1 (verses 3 and 4), the *magistra* expounds two interpretations but makes it clear which she prefers. For 'sine ipso factum est nihil' (without him nothing was made, verse 3), Hildegard explains that *nihil* means contradiction, but she allows for another understanding

---

[33] *Expo. Euang.*, 11, p. 219, line 42; *Expo. Euang.*, 10, p. 216, line 38. *Glossa Ordinaria*, IV, 10, situates the passage in the history of Israel, then provides an allegorical interpretation of Rachel as a figure for the Church.

[34] *Expo. Euang.*, 11, p. 218, lines 35–39: '*Tunc adimpletum est quod dictum est per Ieremiam prophetam dicentem*, scilicet quod a Deo dictum est in exhortatione Spiritus Sancti, quia nullus stare possit qui per se stare uult, sed ille stabit quem Deus sustentat, quoniam ipse baculus illius est.' The *Glossa* does not define prophecy here (*Glossa Ordinaria*, IV, 10), but for Matthew 1. 18–21, *Glossa Ordinaria*, IV, 7, gives a definition of prophecy: 'Prophetia signum est praescientiae Dei.'

[35] *Expo. Euang.*, 5, p. 204, lines 21–23: '*Haec autem eo cogitante, ecce angelus Domini in somnis ei apparuit*, quia in his dubitauit; angelus ei in somnis et non uigilanti apparuit; et quoniam etiam spiritum prophetiae non habuit.' Lobrichon, 'Une nouveauté', p. 112, remarks on the changes in the gloss on Matthew as clerics became concerned with guarding their authority over the Word.

of the phrase: without the Son, *nihil* was made.[36] When Hildegard turns to verse 4, 'quod factum est in ipso' (what was made in him), she comments that 'what was made' *in ipso* was made in the Son of God incarnated or in rationality. That 'was life' (*uita erat*). Another reading of the same phrase means that all things which were made have life in God.[37] Hildegard prefers the first interpretation, that life is the incarnation of God's son.

Hildegard again interjects the perspective of a commentator who takes a position vis-à-vis others when she interprets Matthew 2. 1–12. With respect to Herod's wily questions about the infant's whereabouts, the *magistra* observes that some commentators and teachers ask how it is possible that a sinner may rise up and be saved: 'How could it be that a sinner would arise by penance, as if (*quasi*) it were impossible for a sinner to rise up to salvation?'[38] She downgrades this opinion with the conditional phrase introduced by *quasi* and by associating the question with Herod. Teachers of the truth (*doctores ueritatis*), on the other hand,

---

[36] *Expo. Euang.*, 9, p. 210, lines 14–22: '*Et sine ipso*, scilicet sine racionalitate, id est sine filio, *factum est nichil* quod est contradictio. Deus angelum racionalem fecit; sed quod racionalitas Deum in angelo contradixit, ipse non fecit sed fieri permisit. Quamuis etiam alio modo intelligatur, ita quod sine filio nichil factum sit. Deus deleri non potest. Sed quod ipsum deleri uoluit, nichil erat, quia hoc fieri non potuit. Angelus enim id quod est nichil inuenit, quem homo postea subsecutus, idem per inobedientiam fecit.' Augustine, *In Iohannis euangelium tractatus CXXIV*, ed. by R. Willems, CCSL, 36 (Turnhout: Brepols, 1954), I, 13, p. 7, lines 3–11; Haymo of Auxerre, *Homiliae de tempore*, I, 5, *PL* 118: 57; Heiric of Auxerre, *Homiliae per circulum anni*, ed. by R. Quadri, CCCM, 116, 116A, 116B (Turnhout: Brepols, 1992–94), I, 11, p. 95, lines 148–56; p. 95, lines 149–53 (*negationem*). The *Glossa Ordinaria*, interlinear, IV, 224, reads: 'nulla res subsistens sine ipso est facta'; the marginal gloss has entries from Origen, Augustine, John Chrysostom, and Hilary.

[37] *Expo. Euang.*, 9, pp. 210–11, lines 23–28: '*Quod factum est in ipso*, id est in uerbo, scilicet in racionalitate, uidelicet in filio Dei, qui erat homo incarnatus, *uita erat*, quia filius Dei homo talis erat quod nichil ipsum nec tetigit, nec intrauit, sicut in angelum et in hominem fecit; quamuis etiam *quod factum est* aliter intelligi possit, quia omnia quae facta sunt in Deo uitam habent. *Et uita*, id est incarnatio filii Dei.' In her commentary on the Athanasian Creed, Hildegard includes both interpretations of verse 4: that *nihil* could not pertain to God, and that all things have life in God; but she does not overtly differentiate the two as in the *Expositiones. Expl. Symb.*, p. 118, lines 250–60. John Scotus, *Homélie sur le prologue de Jean*, ed. by E. Jeauneau, SC, 151 (Paris: Cerf, 1969), pp. 242, 244; Heiric, *Homiliae*, I, 10, lines 92–109, p. 84; I, 11, pp. 96–97, lines 167–199, at p. 96, lines 177–78. The *Glossa Ordinaria*, IV, 224, reads (interlinear): 'haec vita, id est sapientia Dei'; the marginal gloss cites Augustine only for this.

[38] *Expo. Euang.*, 13, pp. 223–24, lines 23–25: '*sciscitabatur ab eis* per astutias suas *ubi Christus nasceretur*, id est quomodo esse posset, ut peccator in penitentia resurgeret, quasi impossibile esset, ut peccator ad saluationem resurgeret'. *Glossa Ordinaria*, IV, 8, reads: 'Alleg: Stella est illuminatio fidei quae ad Christum ducit'.

reply that this takes place in penitence when the sinner out of humility confesses his sins.[39] The *magistra* goes on to extol the power of repentance: when accompanied by confession and the practice of virtues, such repentance crushes the Devil in the abyss.[40] Thus Hildegard demonstrates an awareness of differing views about penitence and absolution, a pressing theme in twelfth-century theological debates.[41]

In both homilies on the parable of the prodigal son,[42] Hildegard steps aside briefly from her parallel narrative to explain an apparent discrepancy in the biblical story: the son mentions the hired servants when he rehearses his repentance speech (Lk 15. 19) but omits them when he actually addresses his father (Lk 15. 21). According to Hildegard, the son does not speak about the hired servants, as he did when planning his confession of sin, because he looks only for God's grace. Once he receives grace, the son may apply himself to practising good works as the hired servants had been doing all along.[43] In this reading, the hired labourers represent those who have fulfilled God's will with their blood and toil,[44] whereas in the second homily, the workers designate those who have earned eternal life. Hildegard states that the son omits them because he awaits no reward from his past deeds. He places himself in God's grace.[45] In both readings, then, Hildegard departs from the narrative to explain a missing element; commentators before her, notably Augustine, did likewise.[46]

For the most part, however, Hildegard systematically utilizes glossing to facilitate her allegorical or tropological interpretations. In *Expositio* 2 on Luke 16. 1–9,

---

[39] *Expo. Euang.*, 13, p. 224, lines 27–29: '*At illi*, scilicet doctores ueritatis, *dixerunt ei* respondendo: *In Bethlehem* Iuda, id est in penitentia quae nouit peccatum in humilitate confitendo.'

[40] *Expo. Euang.*, 13, p. 224, line 335. *Sciuias*, II.7.25, p. 324, lines 588–91, 596–98; *LDO*, I.1, p. 47.

[41] See Paul Anciaux, *La Théologie du sacrement de pénitence au douzième siècle*, Universitas Catholica Lovaniensis, Dissertationes ad gradum magistri in Facultate Theologica vel in Facultate Iuris Canonici consequendum conscriptae, Series II, 41 (Louvain: Nauwelaerts, 1949). Hildegard seems to target identifiable teachers and commentators, but it is not clear who they are.

[42] *Expo. Euang.*, 26 and 27, pp. 260–69.

[43] *Expo. Euang.*, 26, p. 262, lines 54–55: 'Hic autem de mercennariis non dicit, sed tantum gratiam Dei expectat.'

[44] *Expo. Euang.*, 26, p. 262, lines 41–43.

[45] *Expo. Euang.*, 27, p. 267, lines 49–50: 'Sed de mercennariis silet quia de transacto opere suo nullam mercedem sperat, se tantum in gratiam Dei ponens.'

[46] Augustine raises the discrepancy in his *Quaestionum euangeliorum*, ed. by A. Mutzenbecher, CCSL, 44B (Turnhout: Brepols, 1980), 2, 33, 3, p. 77, lines 87–90. See additional sources in the apparatus fontium, *Expo. Euang.*, 27, p. 267, and *Glossa Ordinaria*, IV, 136.

she glosses the phrase in Luke 16. 8, 'filii huius saeculi' (children of this world), tropologically as 'id est peccatores in seculo conuersantes' (that is sinners dwelling in the world).[47] At times her glosses blend non-literal and literal interpretation. Hildegard explains the phrase in Luke 16. 9, 'de mammone iniquitatis' (from the mammon of iniquity), allegorically as 'de pullulatione iniquitatis' (sprouting up of iniquity), and then clarifies the meaning of *iniquitatis* with the phrase 'id est viciorum' (that is of vices).[48] The second gloss defining *iniquitatis* comes close to providing a synonym but it also extends to the tropological interpretation of virtue and vice that Hildegard develops for this pericope.

Hildegard adds and employs many words or phrases without an introductory phrase such as *id est* in order to extend the meaning of the biblical text in accordance with her allegory.[49] In some instances, Hildegard changes the subject and indirect object in the scriptural text by adding the words of her commentary. For Luke 16. 7, the master in the parable speaks to the debtor: *Ait illi* (said to him). No explicit subject or indirect object appears in the scriptural text. Hildegard adds *creaturae* to the indirect object and supplies Adam as the subject, reading: 'Ait illi creaturae Adam' (Adam said to the creation).[50] Her commentary often adds a noun following a demonstrative pronoun, thus assigning the pronoun an adjectival function. For Luke 16. 26, the *magistra* adds *predictis causis* to the scriptural *Et in his omnibus* to read: 'Et in his omnibus predictis causis' (and in all these aforesaid matters), so that the pronoun *his* (these) then functions as an adjective modifying *causis* (matters).[51] Similarly Hildegard adds nouns or pronouns in the genitive to create partitive constructions. For John 6. 7, '*ut unusquisque* illorum *modicum quid* temperamenti *accipiat*' (*so that each one* of them *for the measure* of temperament *that he may receive*), the partitive genitives *illorum* (of them) and *temperamenti* (of temperament) can be read without interruption within the biblical text.[52]

Hildegard frequently supplements the scriptural text with adverbial phrases or gerunds in the ablative to construct her interpretation. For John 6. 5, 'Cum

---

[47] *Expo. Euang.*, 2, p. 193, lines 68–69. *Glossa Ordinaria*, IV, 138, reads: 'Filii huius seculi, id est tenebrarum.'

[48] *Expo. Euang.*, 2, p. 194, lines 79–80. *Glossa Ordinaria*, IV, 138, explains that mammon, a Syrian word in origin, means the richness of iniquity: 'Mammona lingua syrorum: divitiae iniquitatis, quia de iniquitate collectae sunt.'

[49] The following examples are taken from Kienzle and Muessig, 'Introduction', *Expo. Euang.*, pp. 174–77.

[50] *Expo. Euang.*, 1, p. 189, line 58.

[51] *Expo. Euang.*, 37, p. 291, line 65. The *Glossa Ordinaria*, IV, 139, has no note for this.

[52] *Expo. Euang.*, 4, p. 200, lines 35–36.

subleuasset ergo in laude felicitatis oculos' (When he had raised his eyes, therefore, in praise of blessedness), the adverbial phrase modifies the verb in the scriptural text, *subleuasset* (had raised).[53] When the *magistra* adds a gerund in the ablative, it sometimes extends the meaning of the verb, like a synonymous aorist, following the usage of the Vulgate. For Matthew 2. 5, Hildegard adds *respondendo* (responding) to *Dixerunt ei* (They said to him) in order to read: 'Dixerunt ei respondendo' (They said to him responding).[54] At times the meaning of the gerund that the *magistra* adds differs considerably from the scriptural verb, as with Luke 2. 5: 'ut profiteretur, enarrando, cum Maria, id est cum caritate' (that he set forth, by relating, with Mary, that is with charity). The meaning of *enarrare* (to relate or tell) remains consistent with the moral allegory of virtue and vice that Hildegard constructs from Joseph and Mary's journey to Bethlehem, but it is not synonymous with the idea of journeying (*proficiscor*).[55]

In some instances, Hildegard adduces biblical phrases or sentences which are not part of the homily's pericope. These constitute another form of Hildegardian commentary in that she uses biblical citations to indicate her gloss on the gospel text in question. For example, in a homily on Luke 16. 1–9, she intercalates a quote from Genesis 5. 3, 'ad imaginem et similitudinem', in 'Homo quidam erat diues' (Lk 16. 2) to indicate her interpretation: '*Homo quidam*, scilicet ille qui hominem *ad imaginem et similitudinem* fecit, *erat diues*' (*A certain man*, namely the one who made the human *in his image and likeness, was rich*).[56]

Hildegard's commentary uses various syntactical structures or glosses to construct her interpretations of the text. Moreover, she consistently deals with units of Scripture in sequence. The *magistra* treats the whole of each verse, either word by word or phrase by phrase. A comparison of the *magistra*'s exegesis on the Lukan Christmas story with that of her predecessors will sharpen the analysis of the *Glossa Hildegardiana*.

Hildegard interprets each unit of Luke 2. 1: the edict, Caesar Augustus, the act of enrolling, and the entire earth.

Exiit edictum, id est antiquum consilium, *a Cesare Augusto*, scilicet a superno patre, *ut describeretur*, id est ut procederet, *uniuersus orbis*, uidelicet omnis creatura.

---

[53] *Expo. Euang.*, 4, p. 199, line 20.

[54] *Expo. Euang.*, 13, p. 224, line 27.

[55] *Expo. Euang.*, 8, p. 208, lines 12–13.

[56] See *Expo. Euang.*, 2, p. 191, lines 3–4.

The edict represents God's ancient plan; Caesar Augustus designates the heavenly Father; the enrollment refers to the act of going forth; and the entire earth symbolizes all creation. The second homily on the same pericope follows a similar procedure:

> *Exiit edictum*, scilicet quoddam constitutum, *a Cesare Augusto*, id est a propria uoluntate, *ut describeretur*, scilicet dilataretur, *uniuersus orbis*, uidelicet per totum corpus.

Here the edict refers to what has been appointed by the will, signified by Caesar Augustus. The entire earth represents the whole body, the site for the extension of what the will has appointed. The act of enrolling signifies that extension.

The words or phrases *scilicet, id est, uidelicet* mark and set apart each unit of commentary. The connecting word or phrase also directs the interpretation to the allegorical or tropological level of Hildegard's parallel or second narrative. The first interpretation pertains to the creation, the beginnings of salvation history; the second develops an allegory of the soul, where the will extends through the body.[57] The gospel text itself occupies the middle ground, the history of incarnation posed between the creation and the struggle of the soul in the world. The whole, which may seem a clumsy ramble through the text, skilfully engages the creation, incarnation, and the soul's battle in the world.

How do Hildegard's narratives compare to the commentaries of Gregory the Great and others? With respect to the form, most expositors process larger clusters of words, discussing one phrase or group of phrases at a time, then moving on to the next, developing little if any connection to the preceding discussion.[58] As E. Ann Matter observes about Gregory's commentary on the Song of Songs, 'Taking two or three lines of text at a time, Gregory expands a series of running narratives in different modes of interpretation, which are related but never congruent.'[59] Likewise, Anne-Marie Bouché remarks that Gregory's method shows 'internal coherence within each of his hermeneutic categories' although 'the various interpretations of each passage are widely separated and dispersed among the three sections'.[60] In contrast, Hildegard constructs a running narrative that adheres

---

[57] Dronke, 'Platonic-Christian Allegories', p. 385, classifies the two readings as 'primarily cosmological' and 'primarily psychological', but he notes that Hildegard's reading moves from allegory to tropology within the homily.

[58] See Hall, 'Early Medieval Homily', pp. 205–06, and the sample text, pp. 248–64.

[59] Matter, *Voice of My Beloved*, pp. 94–95.

[60] Anne-Marie Bouché, 'The Spirit in the World: The Virtues of the Floreffe Bible Frontispiece: British Library, Add. Ms. 17738, fols 3ᵛ–4ʳ', in *Virtue and Vice: The Personifications in the*

to one principal mode of interpretation, even if she sometimes blends modes within the same narrative. When Hildegard embarks on a markedly different hermeneutical pattern, she begins a new homily.

Ambrose and Bede, the principal Western commentators on Luke, cite the whole of the verse in their commentaries as Gregory does, and they then explain it from multiple perspectives. Bede's homily on Luke 2. 1–4 opens with a direct address to his audience, followed by a summary of the content of verses 1–3 as he develops his theme. He does not comment on the pericope unit by unit until verse 4, 'Ascendit autem et Ioseph' (and Joseph went up), whereupon he cites the entire verse and then stands back to explain: 'Divinitus constat esse procuratum' (It is apparent that it was divinely arranged).[61] Gregory the Great's commentary in Homily 8 proceeds sequentially through the passage, but in contrast to Ambrose and Bede, he comments on clusters of the text a few lines at a time.[62]

The *Glossa ordinaria* pastes together the material of these three exegetes.[63] The interlinear gloss explains the purpose clause in Luke 2. 1, 'ut describeretur uniuersus orbis' (that the whole world be enrolled), on a historical-literal level, rewording it to state that the edict required the entire globe of the earth to set out for the census.[64] The marginal gloss first provides further historical material, which is excerpted from Bede's commentary on Luke as it discusses the *pax Augustana* and the various reasons why Christ wanted to be born during an era of peace. The second entry for the verse explains on the level of allegory that Christ's coming at a time of census indicates his advent in the flesh, so that he would list those who were chosen for eternity. This echoes Gregory the Great nearly verbatim.[65] Next the gloss again borrows from Bede, without naming him, to connect the name Augustus to the verb *augere* (to increase); the enrollment refers not to money but to the

---

Index of Christian Art, ed. by Colum Hourihane (Princeton: Princeton University Press, 2000), pp. 42–65 (p. 51).

[61] Bede, *Homeliarum euangelii libri II*, VI, pp. 37–38, 39. See also Ambrose of Milan, *Expositio euangelii secundum Lucam*, ed. by M. Adriaen, CCSL, 14 (Turnhout: Brepols, 1957), II. 36, 38, pp. 46–47.

[62] Gregory the Great, *Homiliae in euangelia*, I, 8, pp. 53–56.

[63] Dronke, 'Platonic-Christian Allegories', p. 384, n. 12, concludes that he sees 'no positive indication that Hildegard knew or used the *Glossa ordinaria* itself'. He does not pursue comparisons with it.

[64] *Glossa Ordinaria*, IV, 145.

[65] *Glossa Ordinaria*, IV, 145. Gregory the Great, *Homiliae in euangelia*, I, 8, p. 54, lines 4–6; Bede, *In Lucae euangelium*, 1, 2, p. 48, lines 1163–65.

offering of faith;[66] the worldly enrollment is displayed but the spiritual is fulfilled. A typological note follows: once the old enrollment of the synagogue was abolished, the new census of the Church was prepared. This repeats Ambrose nearly word for word.[67] However, an adjoining clause that refers to the designation of faith, not of coinage, picks up Bede again.[68] Two additional glosses add historical material: the census of the whole world indicates the very peaceful and quiet state of the kingdom; and the census was conducted so that the King would know the number of people and the size of the kingdom, because Judea was a dependency (*stipendiaria*) of the Romans.[69] For the remainder of the passage, the *Glossa* retains its historical focus but provides a few readings on another level. For *locus in diuersio*, it first explains that *diuersorium* means 'a house between two walls having two doors', then gives an allegorical interpretation of the same word as 'the Church between paradise and the world'.[70]

In contrast, Hildegard explains *locus in diuersio* first in the context of the description of humankind before the Fall, when the human did not yet have a 'secret place' for the evil he would begin, and second, in her tropological reading of virtue and vice: the manger represents Humility and has no place for Vanity.[71] Several tropological comments do appear in the *Glossa*: the wrapping of the infant represents the binding of the hands and feet to direct them towards good works and point them on the path of peace.[72] Hildegard holds to her allegory of virtues and vices: the cloths first designate upright desires, which cover Good Intention (the infant); and second, the wrapping stands for the embracing of the infant, who represents Humility.[73] The *magistra*'s interpretation for this verse reveals little

---

[66] *Glossa Ordinaria*, IV, 145. Bede, *In Lucae euangelium*, 1, 2, p. 52, line 1313.

[67] *Glossa Ordinaria*, IV, 145. Ambrose of Milan, *Expositio euangelii secundum Lucam*, p. 46, lines 498–501.

[68] *Glossa Ordinaria*, IV, 145. Bede, *In Lucae euangelium*, 1, 2, p. 52, line 1313.

[69] *Glossa Ordinaria*, IV, 145. Bede, *Homeliarum euangelii libri II*, VI, pp. 37–38.

[70] *Glossa Ordinaria*, IV, 145.

[71] *Expo. Euang.*, 7, p. 206, lines 27–28: '*quia non erat eis locus in diuersorio*, scilicet quoniam nondum habebat secretum locum incepti mali'. *Expo. Euang.*, 8, p. 208, lines 20–21: '*quia non erat eis locus in diuersorio*, quia nullum locum uanitatis habet'.

[72] *Glossa Ordinaria*, IV, 145.

[73] *Expo. Euang.*, 7, p. 207, lines 45–46: 'scilicet bonam intentionem, *pannis inuolutum*, id est in rectis desideriis'; *Expo. Euang.*, 8, p. 208, line 19: '*et pannis eum inuoluit*, id est in amplexibus eum habet'. A gloss for verse 15 labelled *Mor.* (*moraliter*) explains the word *transeamus* as leaving sin and crossing over to contemplation of heaven. Hildegard does not comment on that verse, but the

correspondence in form or content to the digest of the opinions of patristic expositors that was transmitted in the *Glossa*.

Nonetheless, a few hints for Hildegard's themes may stem from patristic precedents. Ambrose associates the census with the formation of the new Church; in so
doing he refers to *census animorum* (enrollment of souls) for Luke 2. 1, and *professio
mentium* (profession of minds) for Luke 2. 2. Moreover, Ambrose asks where Christ
might be born if not in the heart. That may have provided a point of departure for
Hildegard to develop her second reading that implicates the soul. Bede also gives
brief attention to the soul, and builds on Ambrose by comparing the conception of
Christ in the virgin's womb and in the souls of believers.[74] Features from Gregory
the Great's Homily 8 on the Gospels, the reading in Paul the Deacon's homiliary,
and the Cluny lectionary appear in each of Hildegard's homilies.[75] Gregory considers
the census (Lk 2. 1) a clear indicator of the incarnation, whereas Hildegard in her
first reading links the incarnation with the creation, which took place through the
Word of the Father, the head of all formation before he was incarnate.[76] This accent
on the creation leads the *magistra* to imagine the time before the Fall; she extends
the story back to the beginning of salvation history. Gregory introduces the notion
of discord between the angels and humankind: once humanity was redeemed, the
angels recognized humans as fellow citizens. Bede echoes this theme in his commentary. Hildegard pushes her chronological frame back to the time before the
discord, that is before the Fall, and thus provides a wider sweep of history.

Hildegard's allegory of the soul in her second homily on the pericope may find
inspiration in the same Gregorian text.[77] The great Bishop's Homily 8 exhorts each

---

notion of *transitus* echoes Gregory the Great, *Homiliae in euangelia*, II, 21, p. 176, lines 87–88;
p. 179, lines 161–62.

[74] Ambrose of Milan, *Expositio euangelii secundum Lucam*, 2, 36, 38, pp. 46–47, lines 498,
525–27; Bede, *In Lucae euangelium*, I, ii, p. 48, lines 1163–65: 'Quotidie in utero virginali, hoc est
in animo credentium per fidem concipitur, per baptisma gignitur.'

[75] Gregory the Great, *Homiliae in euangelia*, I, 8. Paul the Deacon has the same Gregorian
homily, as does the Cluny lectionary, which also includes Bede, *Homeliarum euangelii libri II*, I, 6.
See Grégoire, *Homéliaires liturgiques médiévaux*, no. 24, p. 434; Étaix, 'Le Lectionnaire de l'office
à Cluny', no. 22, p. 97; no. 32, p. 98.

[76] *Expo. Euang.*, 7, pp. 205–06, lines 5–10: '*Haec descriptio prima*, id est creatio, *facta est a
preside Siriae, Cirino*, scilicet per uerbum patris, quod erat caput omnis formationis, et quod etiam
incarnandum erat. *Et ibant omnes*, scilicet unaqueque creatura, *ut profiterentur singuli in suam
ciuitatem*, uidelicet ut perficerent inicium suum secundum naturam suam, ut eis in officio suo
constitutum erat, id est eundo, natando uolando.'

[77] *Expo. Euang.*, 8, pp. 207–09.

person to defend God's honour against vices: lust, foul thinking, malice, envy, pride, and ambition.[78] Hildegard's second homily on Luke 2. 1–14 includes the notion of virtues and vices, specifically vanity, going out to contend with one another. However, she focuses on the primary monastic virtues of charity, humility, and obedience. In Hildegard's tropological narrative, Good Desire (Joseph) comes up from the culture of customary behaviour (Galilee) and human reason (Nazareth); Good Desire enters the hidden path of the knowledge of God (the city of David) and of salvation of the soul (Bethlehem). It (Good Desire) knows good and evil (David) and it has joined with Charity (Mary and her pregnancy) to produce other virtues.[79]

Hildegard to some measure completes Gregory the Great's picture, as she extends the standard liturgical homily for this feast by offering advice on how to implement Gregory's exhortation to combat the vices. Therefore, the *magistra* likely developed her interpretation from Gregory's Homily 8, a source that she learned at the least aurally if not through individual reading. She devised an interpretation that responded directly and simply to what her sisters heard read, and she did so in order to provide further and practical moral food for thought.

The *magistra*'s homilies on the parable of the prodigal son (Lk 15. 11–32)[80] provide further illustrations of the ways in which she constructs an interpretation that stems from and runs in parallel to the biblical text. In Homily 26, Hildegard again comments on each element of the first verse and begins a moral allegory by commenting on each element of Luke 15. 11:

---

[78] On the incarnation, see Gregory the Great, *Homiliae in euangelia*, I, 8, p. 54, lines 12–15. On the angels, see Gregory the Great, *Homiliae in euangelia*, I, 8, pp. 55–56, lines 35–52; Bede, *In Lucae euangelium*, I, 2, p. 51, lines 1273–76. On the vices, see Gregory the Great, *Homiliae in euangelia*, I, 8, p. 56, lines 61–64: 'Vindicemus moribus dignitatem nostram, nulla nos luxuria inquinet, nulla turpis cogitatio accuset, non malitia mentem mordeat, non inuidiae rubigo consumat, non elatio inflet, non ambitio per terrena oblectamenta dilaniet.'

[79] *Expo. Euang.*, 8, p. 208, lines 7–14: '*Ascendit autem*, sursum, *et Ioseph*, id est bonum desiderium, *a Galilea*, scilicet a consuetudine, *de ciuitate Nazareth*, id est a cultura quam in racionalitate habet, *in Iudeam*, in *ciuitatem Dauid*, uidelicet in artam uiam agnitionis Dei, *quae uocatur Bethlehem*, id est saluatio animae; *eo quod esset de domo*, scilicet de creatura, *et familia Dauid*, sciens bonum et malum, *ut profiteretur*, enarrando, *cum Maria*, id est cum caritate, *desponsata sibi*, scilicet coniuncta, *uxore pregnante*, parere uirtutes.' This allegory will be discussed below in the context of virtues and vices.

[80] *Expo. Euang.*, 26 and 27. Hildegard's reading generally reflects the penitential interpretation of the parable, with no indication of the Jew-Gentile typology. See Wailes, *Medieval Allegories*, pp. 238–45. On the three strands of patristic interpretation for the parable, 'ethical', 'ethnic', and 'penitential', see Bovon, *L'Évangile selon saint Luc*, pp. 50–59.

Homo quidam, ad cuius *imaginem et similitudinem* homo creatus est, *habuit duos filios*, cum homini dat scientiam boni et mali.[81]

[*A certain man, in whose image and likeness* the human was created, *had two sons*, when he gave the human knowledge of good and evil.]

The *magistra*'s hermeneutic at once incorporates traditional elements and extends or transforms them. The man or father in the parable generally represents God, but Hildegard highlights God as Creator. In contrast, the *Glossa ordinaria*, in its digest of the views of various commentators, explains in an interlinear note at the outset: 'This parable is taken generally as about the Jew and the Gentile; but it can be taken as about the penitent and righteous, or the righteous for himself.' The *Glossa* introduces the concept of creation when it states that the human exercised free will when he left the Creator. However, the reference to the Creator stops there; no allegory such as Hildegard's ensues.[82]

In the *magistra*'s text, the biblical and interpretive narratives proceed simultaneously: the human being, after receiving the knowledge of good and evil, goes astray. The commentary for Luke 15. 15 illustrates her tropological interpretation:

Et abiit, a Deo recedendo, *et adhesit uni ciuium regionis illius*, cum se coniunxit maliciae, quae in mente illius sedem sibi fecerat; *et misit illum in uillam suam*, scilicet in culturam uiciorum, in qua ipsa residebat, *ut pasceret porcos*, ut uiciis nutriret nequitiam.[83]

[*And he went away*, withdrawing from God, *and joined himself to a citizen of that region*, when he united himself to Malice, which had made a place for itself in his mind; *and he sent him to his farm*, namely to the cultivation of vices, in which he resided, *in order to feed the pigs*, in order to nourish wickedness with vices.]

In Hildegard's reading, the younger son travels away and joins a resident of another region, just as the soul meets up with malice, cultivates vices, and lives off wickedness. In contrast, the *Glossa* pauses to explain the unclean nature of pigs, an example of its emphasis on the literal-historical sense; it then indicates that the son became a servant of the Devil.[84]

With regard to the elder brother's response and jealousy over the banquet (Lk 15. 25), Hildegard expands his voice, as I shall discuss shortly, while Ambrose, Augustine, Bede, and others direct their attention to explaining the goat that will be consumed at the banquet. Ambrose remarks on the older brother's involvement

---

[81] *Expo. Euang.*, 26, p. 260, lines 1–3.

[82] *Glossa Ordinaria*, IV, 195.

[83] *Expo. Euang.*, 26, p. 261, lines 21–24.

[84] *Glossa Ordinaria*, IV, 196.

with earthly work and his envy over the kid (goat), which Ambrose associates with Antichrist and contrasts with the innocent lamb. Augustine in turn objects to the identification of the kid with Antichrist. Bede echoes Ambrose on the older brother's preoccupation with earthly matters, but, in line with Augustine, he dismisses the interpretation of the kid as Antichrist and views the animal as a figure of the sinner, following a 'penitential' line of interpretation.[85] Like Ambrose, Bede addresses questions to his reader, but retains the third person voice for most of his commentary on the passage. In the Pseudo-Bedan homilies, which drew heavily on Bede's commentary on Luke and circulated under Bede's name,[86] the exegete comments at length in the third person, to explain the brother's words: 'Quaeritur quomodo ille populus nunquam mandatum Dei praeterisse dicatur' (He asks how the people may be said to have never transgressed God's command). He then dismisses any notion that the kid represents Antichrist: 'Peccator profecto haedi nomine significari solet, sed absit ut Antichristum intelligam'[87] (In fact, the sinner usually is designated under the name 'goat'; far be it from me to understand [the goat] as Antichrist).

The *Glossa* explains the older brother's reaction as the anger of the Jews against Jesus for feasting with Gentiles. It attributes to Jerome the statement that the brother followed the righteousness of the law and not the righteousness of God. The marginal glosses enumerate the typological readings and then shift to the penitential line of interpretation. The notion of envy enters with two examples: the sons of Zebedee, and the angels' jealousy at the implication that the world, including the heavens, would belong to Christ.[88] The jealous angels figure in Hildegard's other homily on the parable.[89] As for the hotly debated kid, the *Glossa* identifies

---

[85] Ambrose of Milan, *Expositio euangelii secundum Lucam*, 239, pp. 293–94, lines 2615–17; Augustine, *Quaestionum euangeliorum*, 2, 33, 3, p. 78; Bede, *In Lucae euangelium*, IV. 15, pp. 293–94, lines 2530–50.

[86] Pseudo-Bede, *Homiliae subdititiae*, PL 94: 267–516. See the Appendix to Bede, *Homeliarum euangelii libri II*, pp. 382–84. Their attribution is not certain, but Jean Leclercq, 'Recherches sur d'anciens sermons monastiques', p. 2, identified them with the works of Haymo of Auxerre.

[87] Ps.-Bede, *Homiliae subditiae*, PL 94: 379A–B.

[88] The *Glossa* cites the apostles' indignation at the request of the mother of the sons of Zebedee. Mark 10.35–45 concerns the jealousy between James and John, sons of Zebedee, over who was the greatest. *Glossa Ordinaria*, IV, 197.

[89] *Expo. Euang.*, 27, p. 268, lines 66–67: '*Erat autem filius eius senior*, id est angeli qui ante hominem creati sunt, *in agro*, scilicet in celesti cultura'; p. 268, lines 79–84: '*Indignatus est autem*, id est admiratus est stupendo quomodo hec fieri possent, *et nolebat intrare*, quia passione Christi non indigent, nec gaudio quod *super uno peccatore* penitente fit. *Pater ergo illius egressus*, in ostensione

the animal as Antichrist, to be immolated at the end of time.[90] All the commentators guard a distance from the text that contrasts markedly with Hildegard's manner of speaking from within and in parallel to the narrative.

Does any monastic commentator follow a method of exegesis that resembles the *magistra*'s tropological story-telling? Bernard of Clairvaux spins a moral tale that weaves phrases from the Lukan pericope into one of his *Parabolae*, a collection of texts that resemble lengthy *exempla*, the short illustrative anecdotes that medieval preachers employed to illustrate and lighten their sermons. Unlike the *exempla*, however, the *Parabolae* of Bernard stand on their own as independent narratives.[91] They were probably delivered in the vernacular but taken down and preserved in Latin. The *Parabolae* have been considered close in form to their oral delivery, as have the *Sententiae*, short outline-like compositions that were jotted down before or after sermons. They reflect the form and substance of the abbot's chapter talks.[92]

---

uoluntatis misericordiae suae, *cepit rogare illum*, ubi angelos misit in salutem populi per admonitionem Spiritus Sancti in reedificatione ecclesiae, cum angeli ad necessitates hominum mittuntur.'

[90] *Glossa Ordinaria*, IV, 197.

[91] The *exemplum* represents a genre associated with and encompassed by the sermon. On the medieval *exemplum*, see Claude Brémond, Jacques Le Goff, and Jean-Claude Schmitt, *L'Exemplum*, Typologie des Sources du Moyen Âge Occidental, 40 (Turnhout: Brepols, 1982), esp. p. 37; Jacques Berlioz and Marie-Anne Polo de Beaulieu, *Les Exempla médiévaux: Introduction à la recherche, suivie des tables critiques de l'Index exemplorum de F.-C. Tubach*, Classiques de la littérature orale (Carcassonne: GARAE/Hesiode, 1992). Nicole Bériou, 'Les Sermons latins après 1200', in *The Sermon*, dir. by Kienzle, pp. 363–447 (p. 372), observes: 'Quant à l'*exemplum*, dont l'efficacité persuasive est indéniable, il n'est jamais une partie constitutive de la structure du sermon. La meilleure preuve en est qu'il peut être introduit ou omis à volonté, comme on l'observe souvent dans les versions différentes d'un même sermon.' On genres with an independent function and those with a dependent function, see Hans-Robert Jauss, 'Littérature médiévale et théorie des genres', *Poétique*, 2 (1970), 79–101 (p. 83).

[92] Kienzle, 'Twelfth-Century Monastic Sermon', p. 277. Bernard of Clairvaux's editors define *sententiae* in the following manner: 'quae sive compendia sunt sive schemata orationum quas ipse habuit que edidit', *SBOp*, VI.2, *Ad lectorem* (no page number). The *sententiae* frequently have a simple, numerical structure; the shortest *sententiae* constitute a list of the sermon's main points, with numbering to aid the preacher and the listener. On the *sententiae*, see Leclercq, *Love of Learning*, pp. 169–70; and Christopher Holdsworth's suggestion that the *Parabolae* and *Sententiae* are 'the unrevised notes taken by some of [Bernard's] listeners': 'Were the Sermons of St Bernard on the Song of Songs ever Preached?', in *Medieval Monastic Preaching*, ed. by Muessig, pp. 295–318 (p. 316). However, I think it just as likely that the *Sententiae* represent the sort of outline Bernard might have used as an aide-mémoire, composed before preaching, which Holdsworth, p. 315, also allows in Bernard's preparation for preaching. Kienzle, 'Twelfth-Century Monastic Sermon', pp. 291–95.

Bernard's *Parabola* I narrates, with only a few direct allusions to Scripture, the story of a wealthy and powerful king (God), who created the human being, granted him free will, and forbade him to eat from the tree of the knowledge of good and evil. The human in the tale, who at first resembles his first ancestor, disobeyed, but he thereafter took a course that varies from Adam's in Genesis: he fled and began to wander through fields of vices. Bernard turns banishment from the Garden, as in Genesis 3, into the deliberate violation of monastic stability. The ancient enemy and a host of vices vie for the human against an army of virtues. Bernard enlivens the tale by giving voice to the personifications of Hope, Prudence, Fortitude, Wisdom, and Charity.[93] The *parabola* provides insight on monastic taste for stories that might have entertained converted knights who had left behind feudal pursuits.[94]

In contrast, Hildegard's narratives remain focused on inner conflict and do not resort to the language and conventions of epic poetry that Bernard employs. Moreover, she follows the scriptural text faithfully and sequentially. Still the *Parabolae* stand as an important contemporary witness to the taste for scripture-based storytelling in twelfth-century monastic circles.[95] Finally, the telling of *parabolae* based on gospel stories bears comparison to the taste for narrative that scholars have signalled in medieval commentaries on the Song of Songs.[96]

---

[93] *Parabolae*, *SBOp*, VI.2, 261–303 (pp. 261–67).

[94] Otfrid of Weissenburg's *Evangelienbuch* constitutes a precedent for the genre. Otfrid, a biblical scholar, directed Old High German verse renderings of biblical narratives to a late tenth-century courtly audience. See discussion of the *Evangelienbuch* and reproduction of a page in Margaret T. Gibson, *The Bible in the Latin West* (Notre Dame: University of Notre Dame Press, 1993), pp. 8, 40–41.

[95] Similar to Bernard's *Parabolae* and *Sententiae* are other collections of short monastic texts such as Odo of Cambrai's *Homilia de uillico iniquitatis* on the parable of the unjust steward (*PL* 160: 1131–50), a copy of which was held at St Eucharius at Trier (Montebaur, *Studien zur Geschichte der Bibliothek der Abtei St. Eucharius-Mathias zu Trier*, p. 141), and the *sententiola* or *dicta* of Anselm of Canterbury, talks recorded by Alexander, monk of Christ Church, Canterbury. Alexander explains that Anselm spoke these various things *in commune* and that he, Alexander, took them down in various places. Others, which were borrowed or stolen, became lost. *Memorials of St. Anselm*, ed. by R. Southern and F. S. Schmitt, Auctores Britannici Medii Aevi, 1 (London: Oxford University Press 1969), p. 107. Jean Leclercq discusses monastic literary genres in *Love of Learning*, pp. 153–90, and the informal *sententiae* and related texts, pp. 168–70.

[96] See Matter, *Voice of My Beloved*, pp. 55–58, who connects to medieval commentaries on the Song Tzvetan Todorov's analysis of the Quest of the Holy Grail and his concept of '"quest for narrative", the desire to turn an elliptical series of poems into a coherent story of God's love'.

Vox Dramatis Personae

What else proves distinctive about Hildegard's exegesis? A careful reading reveals that she speaks in at least three modes in her homilies. How would we characterize them? Her voice as commentator, *uox expositricis*, at times follows the tone but not the content of patristic models. Her narrative voice, *uox narrativa*, tells a moral story. A third mode of discourse becomes evident when she gives biblical characters a voice that extends beyond the scriptural text. She assumes the *uox dramatis personae*, extending with her own words what a biblical character says in the scriptural text.

What characters does Hildegard assume? She develops the voice of the older brother in the parable of the prodigal son, retaining the brother's voice (Lk 15.25) in the first person of the biblical text and extending it in accordance with her allegory. The brother protests that he has tried to live moderately and in conformity with the father's rules:

> *At ille respondens*, in cogitationibus suis, *dixit patri suo*, Deo: *Ecce tot annis*, id est in mensuris et moderationibus, *seruio tibi*, in bonis, *et nunquam mandatum tuum preteriui*, illud negando, ut frater meus; *et nunquam dedisti michi hedum*, scilicet non permisit, *ut*, in parte peccatorum, *cum amicis meis*, uidelicet cum uirtutibus, *epularer*, id est tantum rumorem de bonis actibus meis haberem, ut iste frater meus de conuersione sua.[97]

> [And *responding*, in his pondering, *he said to his father*, God: *Behold for so many years* in measure and moderation, *I have served you* in good things and *I never transgressed against your commandment* by denying it as my brother did; and *you never gave me a kid*, namely it was not allowed *that I might feast*, on the part of sinners *with my friends*, that is with the virtues; in other words, that I might have as great a report about my good actions as this brother of mine about his conversion.]

The sequential commentary interprets the older brother's words for the principal units of the text: the thoughts, the moderate and good behaviour, the fact of never breaking God's command, the goat as a sacrifice not allowed. Then, for the word *epularer* (that I might feast), the *magistra* expands the older son's thoughts beyond the scriptural text to have the brother develop a comparison between himself and his younger brother: 'You did not allow me to have as great a report about my good actions as my brother about his conversion.' The contrasting treatment for the two siblings occupies the foreground for Hildegard, and the goat fades into the background. The *magistra* simultaneously extends the parable, by giving the older brother more to say, and enhances the interpretation she provides her community for its life under the *Rule*.

---

[97] *Expo. Euang.*, 26, p. 264, lines 90–97.

In a bolder move, Hildegard takes on God's voice in *Expositio* 11 on Matthew 2. 13 –18, when she comments on God's statement through the prophet Hosea (11. 1): 'I have called my son out of Egypt.' Hildegard constructs the voice of God speaking about an individual soul: 'I will lead out the soul of the one who believes in me and he will not die to eternity, because I am life in which darkness is never found. For to the one who looks upon me from his sins, I will give life, as I made Adam, whom I created from clay.'[98] Hildegard has God speak as the Creator, who fashioned Adam, and the Redeemer, who gives life to the repentant. At the same time, she adeptly constructs a tropological interpretation that focuses on the soul.[99]

In a striking interpretive move, Hildegard has the voices of God, Adam, and Jesus emerge from the text in her commentary on the parable of the unjust steward (Lk 16. 1–9). The *magistra* adduces God's commands from Genesis and mixes them with words she herself fashions for God. The rich man's summoning of the steward (Lk 16. 2) represents Adam's transgression of the divine command when God called out, 'Where are you?' (Gn 3. 9). Hildegard adduces another verse from Genesis, 3. 11, to continue God's speech and her parallel between the two biblical passages: 'Who told you that you were naked if you have not eaten of the tree of which I commanded you not to eat?'[100] The *magistra*'s commentary retains the direct speech of both the master's demand that the steward make an account of his stewardship and his order that he no longer serve as a steward. She has God say to Adam: 'You will be judged in accordance with your works and you will lose the land of the living. You are not able to excuse yourself, since you have performed evil.' Hildegard continues God's speech with citations from Genesis 3. 17–19, but she completes it with her own words uttered in God's voice:

> *Cursed is the ground by your deed. In toil you shall* eat of it *all the days of your life* (Gn 3. 17); *thorns and thistles it shall bring forth to you, and you will eat the plants of the earth* (Gn 3. 18). *In the sweat of your face, you shall eat* your *bread* (Gn 3. 19), because you began the first work, evil and bitter.[101]

---

[98] *Expo. Euang.*, 11, p. 218, lines 17–21: 'educam animam illius qui in me credit, et non morietur in eternum, quia ego sum uita in qua nunquam tenebrae inuentae sunt. Qui enim ad me de peccatis suis aspicit, illi dabo uitam, ut Adae feci, quem de limo formaui'.

[99] *Glossa Ordinaria*, IV, 9, shows no trace of this.

[100] *Expo. Euang.*, 1, p. 187, lines 10–13: '*Et uocauit illum*, ubi dixit: *Vbi es*, quando diuinum preceptum transgressus est. *Et ait illi: Quid hoc audio de te*, ubi iterum dixit: *Quis enim indicauit tibi quod nudus esses, nisi quod de* ligno, de quo preceperam tibi ne comederes, comedisti?'

[101] *Expo. Euang.*, 1, p. 188, lines 16–20: 'Et ideo *maledicta terra in opere tuo. In laboribus comedes ex ea cunctis diebus uitae tuae. Spinas et tribulos germinabit tibi, et comedes herbas terrae. In sudore uultus tui uesceris pane* tuo, quoniam tu etiam malum et amarum opus primum incepisti.'

The last clause, 'because you began [...]', represents the *magistra*'s addition to the biblical texts she cites. Hence she expresses the mind and voice of God for her audience. She completes her retelling of the narrative with a brief statement in the third person, echoing Genesis 3. 21, 'And God made' for them 'garments of skins', and Genesis 3. 24, 'he drove out' Adam.[102] The Gospel becomes for Hildegard the springboard for retelling and elaborating on the story of Genesis 3.

Hildegard continues her reverse allegory or typology as she turns the steward's inner monologue in the parable (Lk 16. 3–4) into Adam's conversation with his conscience after he left paradise. She retains the use of the first person from the parable as she has Adam ask himself: '*What shall I do since* God *is taking away* that honour which was given to me while in innocence in paradise, expelling me because I broke his command?' The latter question consists almost entirely of words that Hildegard provides for Adam. The *magistra* continues his monologue as she imagines Adam's lament on the loss of his dominion over the creation:

> I am not able to make creatures subject to me in obedience, as they were subject to me in paradise, although I will not be able to forget that honour given to me, and I will supplicate the creatures subjected to me with mourning and wailing. In my soul *I know what I will do* when I lose the honour that I had in paradise. Let these creatures which were first subjected to me *accept me* in their dwelling places, so that we may live and dwell together at the same time on earth.[103]

The speech is entirely extra-scriptural and represents the *magistra*'s projection of Adam's voice. Obedience and its centrality to the proper ordering of created beings undergirds the speech of Adam and teaches a lesson crucial to monastic spirituality. Hildegard's insistence on obedience may also reflect her reaction against Richardis's departure. The *magistra*'s creative interpretation becomes even clearer when we compare it to the *Glossa ordinaria*, where the interlinear comment for the

---

[102] *Expo. Euang.*, 1, p. 188, lines 20–21: 'Et fecit eis *tunicas pellicias. Eiecitque Adam.*'

[103] *Expo. Euang.*, 1, p. 188, lines 24–36: '*Quid faciam, quia dominus meus*, scilicet Deus, *aufert a me uillicationem*, id est honorem illum qui michi in paradiso datus est in innocentia, expellens me, quia preceptum eius transgressus sum? *Fodere non ualeo*, id est non possum facere ut deinceps creaturas ita michi cum obedientia subiciam, ut in paradiso michi subiectae fuerunt, quamuis non ualeam obliuisci honoris illius qui michi in ipso datus est; *mendicare erubesco*, ita ut subiectis michi creaturis luctu et eiulatu supplicem. *Scio* in sensibilitate animae meae *quid faciam, ut cum amotus fuero a uillicatione*, scilicet cum perdidero honorem quem in paradiso habebam, *recipiant me* hae creaturae quae michi prius subiectae fuerunt *in domos suas*, scilicet in cohabitationes ipsarum, ut simul in terra uiuamus et commoremur.'

steward's monologue reveals the common eschatological thinking on this passage: He asks, 'What should I do to avoid punishments?' (of hell).[104]

The *magistra* also assumes Christ's voice in explicating the same parable. She summarizes rapidly the story of salvation history, incorporating the association of the steward with Adam, and she then moves to an exhortation.[105] Hildegard uses Luke 16. 9, which follows directly upon the parable, as a springboard to bring her story to an exhortation. The verse begins with 'Et ego vos dico' (And I tell you) as Christ begins to exhort his listeners. The seer expands the 'ego', the voice of Christ, and has him urge humankind to make friends of good angels and humans in righteousness and truth, to do good works, and to turn away from sin, so that God may receive them in heaven and they may regain the inheritance that Adam lost:

> *And I* Christ *say to you* human beings: *Make friends for yourselves* of good angels and humans, in righteousness and truth, so that they esteem you in good works and so that they may receive you with good report and praise for reward before God, when you no longer possess *the mammon of iniquity*, namely of sin and depravity, and clearly when the bodily strength in you has *failed* and you ought to pass from this world. You have led them from faithlessness to faith and from sin to righteousness; and this *in the eternal tabernacle*; clearly, they will meet you with the heavenly reward and *will receive you* into the heavenly and unfailing fatherland which you lost in Adam.[106]

Hildegard seems to employ Jesus's persona here to exhort, much as she voices the utterances of God when she reveals her visions. Certainly, her exhortation in Jesus's voice moves into the genre of preaching, the *uox praedicatricis*. Hildegard takes on Christ's authoritative persona to engage in the evident rhetoric of homiletics.

Are there precedents for Hildegard's allegory? Some parallels in Western exegesis may lead Hildegard to link the parable and Genesis, a connection she also makes in two of her letters and the *Liber diuinorum operum*.[107] A few authors associate the villa and creation, entrusted to the human, but they do not develop a full allegory

---

[104] *Glossa Ordinaria*, IV, 197.

[105] *Expo. Euang.*, 1, pp. 188–90, lines 37–87.

[106] *Expo. Euang.*, 1, p. 190, lines 88–98: '*Et ego*, scilicet Christus, *uobis* hominibus *dico: Facite uobis amicos*, angelos bonos et homines, in iusticia et ueritate, ita ut uos in bonis operibus diligant, et hoc *de mammone iniquitatis*, scilicet de opere prauitatis et peccati, *ut cum defeceritis*, uidelicet cum corporales uires ita in uobis defecerint ut de hoc mundo transire debeatis, *recipiant uos* cum bono rumore et laude remunerationis ante Deum, quos in hoc seculo de infidelitate ad fidem et de peccato ad iusticiam adduxistis, et hoc *in eterna tabernacula*, scilicet ut ipsi cum superna mercede uobis occurant et uos recipiant in celestem et in indeficientem patriam quam in Adam perdidistis.'

[107] *Epistolarium*, II, 113R, p. 282, lines 76–81; *Epistolarium*, II, 177R, p. 403, lines 4–6; *LDO*, I.4.40, pp. 175–76, lines 13–16.

of creation.[108] Hildegard echoes a well-known letter of Jerome when she connects the villa owner to God and she links the number 50 to the five senses.[109] However, patristic exegesis of this parable tended to focus on almsgiving. The *Glossa ordinaria* explains that on an allegorical level, the steward represents one to whom God entrusts money for the poor.[110] Moreover, Hildegard's predecessors often linked the steward with the Jews. Hildegard does not incorporate the standard exegesis of the steward as the Jews into her homilies, even though one of her letters draws on that.[111]

Hildegard's exegesis of the parable demonstrates that the seer seizes an exegetical opportunity to retell the story of Adam's disobedience and God's reproach. In her portrayal, a self-reflective Adam resolves to set creation in order. Moreover, he and the creatures that observe God's plan exemplify the relationships that hold in a paradigm for proper authority in the monastery. Hildegard directs the theology of history to inform contemporary monastic life. The various voices in the commentary on the parable of the unjust steward demonstrate that Hildegard herself may have staged a one-actress drama. She assumes God's voice with borrowings from Scripture and additional words of her own. Christ's voice contains scriptural echoes but consists mainly of Hildegard's own exhortations in his name. She adapts Adam's voice more freely, perhaps because he is the one human *dramatis persona*.

The *magistra*'s assumption of God's voice in the *Expositiones* parallels to some degree her relaying of God's speech in her visionary works. Certainly, however, the *magistra* does not preface the *Expositiones* as a whole, or any single homily, with the voice of 'The One Enthroned'. The absence of a claim to visionary experience may indicate that her authority needed no bolstering when she spoke in the secure

---

[108] Peter Chrysologus, *Collectio sermonum*, 125, p. 767, lines 25–27; Haymo of Auxerre, *Homiliae de tempore*, 121, *PL* 118: 647; Heiric of Auxerre, *Homiliae*, pars aestiua, II, 28, p. 263, line 214.

[109] Ps.-Theophilus, *Commentarius in quattuor euangelia*, ed. by A. Hamman and L. Guillaumin (Paris, 1966), *PLS* 3: 1282–1329 (cols 1321–22); Jerome, *Ad Algasiam Liber quaestionum undecim*, in *Epistulae*, ed. by I. Hilberg, CSEL 54, 55, 56 (Vienna, 1910–18), Epist. 121, vol. 56, 6, p. 25, lines 1–2; Heiric of Auxerre, *Homiliae*, pars aestiua, II, 28, p. 258, line 34; p. 263, lines 208–10; Ps.-Hrabanus Maurus, *Allegoriae in uniuersam sacram Scripturam*, *PL* 112: 911; Ps.-Anselm of Canterbury, *Homiliae et exhortationes*, 12, *PL* 158: 655; Odo of Cambrai, *Homilia de uillico iniquitatis*, *PL* 160: 1134.

[110] *Glossa Ordinaria*, IV, 197, marginal gloss. See Wailes, *Medieval Allegories*, pp. 247–49.

[111] *Epistolarium*, III, 113R, p. 82, lines 76–81: 'Villicus etiam iste synagoga est.' See Wailes, *Medieval Allegories*, pp. 245–53.

context or 'framing' that Rupertsberg provided. There she taught and preached to her sisters in an environment where she insisted on choosing the male provost who provided not only the sacraments but also intellectual support for the exegesis that she was divinely commanded to carry out.[112] The *Expositiones* emanate from that milieu; although lacking a visionary preface, they reveal intercalations of divine voice. Arguably Hildegard's appropriation of God's persona within biblical commentary enhanced the authority of her interpretation, much as her assumption of Jesus's voice strengthened her parenetic exhortation.

The Expositiones *and the Admont Homilies*

Hildegard's exegetical storytelling seems unmatched, except perhaps for the *Parabolae* of Bernard of Clairvaux. One further collection of texts must be examined, however: the homilies from Admont, nearly contemporaneous with the *Expositiones*. Both collections come from monasteries connected to the Hirsau reform movement. Numerous homilies from the two collections comment on the same pericopes.[113] In addition, my study of parallel passages for Hildegard's exegesis reveals numerous points of comparison with the Admont homilies.[114] In many cases, those involve interpretations that focus on the soul. Scholars investigating the Admont texts signal the importance of moral interpretation, as well as the role of salvation history with a threefold Augustinian scheme in the commentaries on Ruth, much like what I have demonstrated in the *Expositiones*. Furthermore, they point to the Marian emphasis of some texts and, more strikingly, the illustrations that represent female figures and seem intended for the women's community.[115]

---

[112] *Sciuias*, III.11, p. 586, lines 379–91.

[113] Common pericopes include Matthew 1. 18–21, Matthew 2. 1–12, Matthew 4. 1–11, Matthew 8. 1–13, Mark 7. 31–37, Mark 16. 1–7, Mark 16. 14–20, Luke 1. 57–68, Luke 2. 22–32, Luke 2. 42–52, Luke 5. 1–11, Luke 14. 16–21, Luke 15. 11–32, Luke 16. 19–31, Luke 18. 10–14, Luke 19. 41–47, Luke 16. 1–9, Luke 21. 25–33, John 2. 1–11, John 3. 1–15, John 6. 1–14, John 10. 11–16.

[114] See the index fontium for the *Expo. Euang.*, pp. 580–82.

[115] See Ulrich Faust, 'Gottfried von Admont', *Studien und Mitteilungen zur Geschichte des Benediktinerordens und seiner Zweige*, 75 (1964), 273–359; Alison I. Beach, 'The Multiform Grace of the Holy Spirit: Salvation History and the Book of Ruth at Twelfth-Century Admont', in *Manuscripts and Monastic Culture*, ed. by Beach, pp. 125–37; Stefanie Seeberg, 'Illustrations in the Manuscripts of the Admont Nuns from the Second Half of the Twelfth Century: Reflections on their Function', in ibid., pp. 99–121; Johannes Beumer, 'Der mariologische Gehalt der Predigten

Irimbert should be considered the author of the Admont sermon corpus, previously ascribed to Gottfried, Irimbert's older brother and the Abbot of Admont
from 1137 to 1165. However, the nuns at Admont played some role in preaching
and exegesis at the double monastery. Evidence points to interaction between Irimbert and the nuns in the four extant manuscripts of the Abbot's commentaries on
Ruth, and sermon manuscripts were owned by the nuns' library.[116] The definitive
edition of the Admont texts is not yet available. Still, some comparisons with the
Expositiones can be pursued. I shall focus on the form of the texts as it relates to the
authorial voice and to some extent, the audience.

Comparisons in Method and Structure

How do the *Expositiones* and the Admont homilies on the same pericopes compare
with respect to form? The Admont texts often reveal a consistent structure: an
introduction with reflection on the task of preaching; the signalling of a connection between the Gospel and the other daily readings; the announced interpretation of the pericope in more than one sense; and the conclusion of the homily
with a sequence of exhortation, prayer, and doxology. One homily (on Lk 16. 1–9)
states at the outset that it intends to seek out the hidden, inner meaning of the
pericope.[117] Another (on Jn 10. 11–16) contrasts the outward hearing (*exterior
auditus*) of the words of the Gospel and the fruit of spiritual understanding
(*intelligentiae spiritalis fructus*).[118] The introduction to another homily (on Mk
7. 31–37) points out how the Gospel corresponds to the other reading of the day,
II Corinthians 3. 5–8, and how the Gospel, the reading, and the prayer prove harmonious.[119] Homily 59 refers to the daily excellence of the Mass (*hodierna missae
excellentia*) and the praises of song; it concludes with a direct exhortation to the

---

Gottfrieds von Admont', *Scholastik*, 35 (1960), 43–49; Ingrid Roitner, 'Das Admonter Frauenkloster im zwölften Jahrhundert: Ein Musterkloster des *Ordo Hirsaugiensis*', *Studien und
Mitteilungen zur Geschichte des Benediktinerordens und seiner Zweige*, 15 (2005), 199–289.

[116] The entire corpus is not yet available in a modern edition. See Beach, 'Listening for the
Voices', pp. 188–89. Borgehammar, 'Who Wrote the Admont Sermon Corpus?', p. 50, notes the
predominance of moral exegesis and a male audience; at p. 50 he also signals that there are feminine
forms in some texts.

[117] Gottfried of Admont, *Homiliae dominicales*, 75, *PL* 174: 530A.

[118] Gottfried of Admont, *Homiliae dominicales*, 47, *PL* 174: 318C–D.

[119] Gottfried of Admont, *Homiliae dominicales*, 79, *PL* 174: 555D–557B.

brothers and a doxology.[120] Homily 31 also concludes with an exhortation and a doxology.[121] The evident liturgical and Eucharistic structure of these Admont homilies places them directly in the tradition of male monastic preaching. In contrast, the involvement of the Admont sisters in production and use of the manuscripts becomes evident from textual markers that relate to the Divine Office.[122]

Given these differences in structure and authorial voice, what differences or similarities in exegetical method do we detect in the *Expositiones* and the Admont texts? The Admont homilies generally comment on the text by explaining each verse or unit sequentially, at times offering multiple interpretations for one verse, at other times pursuing one mode of commentary through the whole pericope and then resuming it with a second or third level of interpretation.[123] Homily 31 marks the transition from one sense of Scripture to the other in a very straightforward manner, stating: 'After going through these matters briefly according to the allegorical sense, let us turn the eye of the mind towards ourselves and let us see what this parable teaches us on the moral level.'[124] Homily 25 (on Mt 4. 1–11) signals the interpretations on three levels: allegorical, literal, and moral, stating, 'First let us see, according to the allegorical sense how our Lord Jesus Christ was led into the desert and tempted', and later: 'Having offered these things briefly according to the literal sense, let us now enter into the moral sense.'[125] These evident structural and interpretive divisions differ greatly from Hildegard's running commentary in the *Expositiones*. As Stephen Wailes observes about the Admont homily on Luke 14. 16–21, 'The result is not an allegory of the parable, but allegories of the individual verses.'[126]

Hildegard's allusions to patristic expositors are indirect: she does not refer to them by name or quote directly from their works. Do the Admont homilies acknowledge exegetical precedents? In some instances, the Admont author

---

[120] Gottfried of Admont, *Homiliae dominicales*, 59, *PL* 174: 399B, 401B.

[121] Gottfried of Admont, *Homiliae dominicales*, 31, *PL* 174: 207C–208A.

[122] Seeberg, 'Illustrations in the Manuscripts of the Admont Nuns', p. 118.

[123] See Gottfried of Admont, *Homiliae dominicales*, 25, on Matthew 4. 1–11, *PL* 174: 165D, 170C.

[124] Gottfried of Admont, *Homiliae dominicales*, 31, *PL* 174: 204A: 'His secundum sensum allegoricum breviter transcursis, ad nosmetipsos oculum mentis convertamus, et quid nobis parabola haec moraliter insinuet, videamus.'

[125] Gottfried of Admont, *Homiliae dominicales*, 25, *PL* 174: 165D, 170C.

[126] Wailes, *Medieval Allegories*, p. 160.

acknowledges Gregory the Great by name and cites from one of the *Forty Homilies on the Gospels*, directly or in a paraphrase.[127] The Admont homilist makes a protest of humility in the face of the great Bishop's exegesis; he adds that Gregory wrote for a mixed audience, while he will edify those in monasteries.[128] Such a clear authorial statement of debt to a source and to the intent and audience of the homily does not occur in the *Expositiones* of Hildegard.

Content of the Expositiones *and the Admont Homilies*

A full treatment of authorial voice as it relates to the content and themes of the Admont homilies and the *Expositiones* would require another chapter, or perhaps a volume, even if we looked only at the homilies that comment on the same pericopes. Yet leaving the question unexplored is not satisfactory in the face of such intriguing material. I shall begin to chart the territory by exploring three sets of homilies with a similar thematic and tropological focus on penitence.

John 3. 1–15

Both Hildegard and Irimbert accent this penitential theme in their readings of the story of Nicodemus and the complex questions he poses to Jesus (Jn 3. 1–15). Hildegard's third *expositio* on the pericope constructs an allegory of the individual sinner that parallels to some degree the reading of Irimbert, who devotes a portion

---

[127] See Gottfried of Admont, *Homiliae in festa totius anni*, 14, *PL* 174: 682 and Gregory the Great, *Homiliae in euangelia*, I, 10, p. 70, lines 114–23, pp. 70–71, lines 123–33; Gottfried of Admont, *Homiliae dominicales*, 47, *PL* 174: 319D: '*Dimittit* autem *oves*, sicut ait beatus Gregorius, "non mutando locum, sed subtrahendo solatium", *fugit* autem, "quia se sub" suae perversitatis et inutilitatis "silentio abscondit".' Gregory the Great, *Homiliae in euangelia*, I, 14, p. 98, lines 40–42. Gottfried of Admont, *Homiliae dominicales*, 48, *PL* 174: 324B; Gregory the Great, *Homiliae in euangelia*, I, 14, p. 98, lines 45–46.

[128] Gottfried of Admont, *Homiliae dominicales*, 61, *PL* 174: 416A–B: 'Praesumptionis argui timemus, quod super verba et sententias sanctorum expositorum, et praecipue beati Gregorii, qui excellenter exposuit parabolam istam, aliquid dicere vel exponere audemus. [...] Quamvis enim ad intellectum et sapientiam beati Gregorii nos, qui insipientes et imperiti sumus, nequaquam attingere possimus, tam quia in expositione hujus parabolae non spiritalibus sed saecularibus hominibus pro loco et tempore tunc loquebatur, nihil in hoc honori et gloriae ipsius subtrahere nos credimus, si spiritalibus spiritalia comparantes, ad aedificationem eorum qui in monasteriis sunt, ea, quae Deus donaverit, dicere humilitas nostra attentaverit.'

of his Homily 58 to a moral interpretation that deals with compunction and meditation.[129] Irimbert dwells on penitence, referring to *penitentia, compunctio*, and the goal of contemplating the invisible in heaven.[130] As in other homilies, he first interprets the text according to a typological allegory. He then calls for turning the eye of the heart (*oculum cordis*) inward and signals clearly his transition to the moral sense.[131] He discusses three steps to salvation: the inspiration of good will, rebirth by abstaining from vices and carnal desires, and finally, the compunction of a humble heart. After summarizing these three, he adds a fourth: meditation on heavenly matters.[132]

Hildegard's emphasis lies on the journey from sin through penance, specifically compunction, as shown through tears and confession. The rejection of vices and of aridity — the opposite of *uiriditas* and new birth in Hildegard's thought — constitutes part of the process of repentance and conversion to new life. The theme emerges clearly from the choice of words in the homily: the *magistra* employs the word *penitentia* eleven times and the substantive *penitentes* and the verb *penitet* once each, thirteen references in a homily forty-six lines or 621 words in length.[133] If all the words in the same semantic field were included, that is words such as *compunctio, gemitus*, and *suspiria* that relate to the theme, the number would more or less triple. Both Hildegard and Irimbert take their audience through the process of penitence and end with an evocation of eternal life that begins with contemplation in the present: for Hildegard 'the contemplation of the invisible in heaven', and for Irimbert, 'the sweetness of intimate contemplation that will be fulfilled in the future without end'.[134]

---

[129] *Expo. Euang.*, 36, pp. 286–88; Gottfried of Admont, *Homiliae dominicales*, 58, *PL* 174: 379C–386C.

[130] On penitence, see Gottfried of Admont, *Homiliae dominicales*, 58, *PL* 174: 379D; on compunction, see *PL* 174: 383D–385A; on contemplation, see *PL* 174: 381D, 385A–386B.

[131] Gottfried of Admont, *Homiliae dominicales*, 58, *PL* 174: 380D–381A: 'Jam lectionem evangelicam breviter ad allegoria praenotavimus. Nunc ad nosmetipsos oculum cordis reducentes moralem in ea sensum discamus.'

[132] Gottfried of Admont, *Homiliae dominicales*, 58, *PL* 174: 382B–383CD, 385A–B, 385A–B (contemplation).

[133] *Expo. Euang.*, 36, pp. 286–88, lines 5, 25–26 (twice), 28 (verb *penitet*), 30, 35, 39–40, 55, 64, 65 (*penitentes*), 67 (twice).

[134] *Expo. Euang.*, 36, pp. 287–88, lines 52–58: '*Et nemo ascendit in celum*, ut celestia desideret, *nisi qui de celo descendit*, per suspiria cordis ostendens quod absconsum et occultum erat in corde suo, *filius hominis*, scilicet in hoc se hominem per penitentiam demonstrans, *qui est in celo*, quia gemitus primum in occulto cordis incipit et tandem homines ad inuisibilem contemplationem,

The *Rule of Benedict* underlies the theme and vocabulary of the texts for the language of sighs and tears, the insistence on penitence, and the goal of contemplation.[135] Nonetheless, the homilies of Haymo and Heiric of Auxerre, who insist on the theme of penitence, may represent another stop visited by Hildegard and Irimbert on their exegetical journeys. Moreover, John 3. 1–15 was the gospel reading for the liturgy of Holy Cross Day, and preaching on the feast of the cross emphasized penitence for centuries.[136] Nonetheless, no evidence of the growing emphasis on the passion surfaces in these homilies from Rupertsberg and Admont.

Matthew 2. 1–12

Homilies on Matthew 2. 1–12 call upon a common Gregorian source but construct their interpretation in different ways. Hildegard's second interpretation of Matthew 2. 1–12 (*Expo.* 13) relates closely to her preceding tropological reading of Matthew 2. 13–18 (*Expo.* 11).[137] The two pericopes together narrate the events from Jesus's birth to the flight into Egypt and the massacre of the innocents. The child Jesus plays the central role in both pericopes; the motif of innocence extends from the *puer* Jesus (Mt 2. 8–9, 11, 13–14), who is protected by Mary and Joseph, to all male infants (*omnes pueros*) who were slaughtered in Herod's wrath.[138]

Central to Hildegard's text is the theme of penitence: the human action necessary for the process of redemption to occur. Jesus's birth in Bethlehem (Mt 2. 1) represents the birth of Christ in the penitence of the sinner (*homo peccator*) who confesses his sins amidst the Devil's temptations. The Magi (Mt 2. 1 and

---

quae in celo est, perducit.' Gottfried of Admont, *Homiliae dominicales*, 58, *PL* 174: 386B–C: 'sed vitam eternam habere in praesenti inchoat per intimae contemplationis dulcedinem, quam in futuro sine fine per incommutabilem habebit plenitudinem'.

[135] See *Expo. Euang.*, 36, p. 286, line 22, and Saint Benedict, *Regula*, 4, 57–58, p. 35.

[136] Étaix, 'Le Lectionnaire de l'office à Cluny', no. 251, p. 116; no. 121, p. 106. See Haymo of Auxerre, *Homiliae de tempore*, 108, *PL* 118: 580–81; Heiric of Auxerre, *Homiliae*, 2, pars aestiua 2, 16, pp. 137, lines 24–27. Beverly Mayne Kienzle, 'The Clash between Catholics and Cathars over Veneration of the Cross', in *Iconoclasm and Iconoclash: Struggle for Religious Identity*, ed. by W. van Asselt and others, Jewish and Christian Perspectives Series, 14 (Leiden: Brill, 2007), pp. 263–79.

[137] On Matthew 2. 1–12: *Expo. Euang.*, 12, 13, pp. 219–25; on Matthew 2. 13–18: *Expo. Euang.*, 10, 11, pp. 215–19.

[138] *Expo. Euang.*, 13, pp. 224–25, lines 46, 52, 56. Gottfried of Admont, *Homiliae in festa*, 14, *PL* 174: 681.

others) signify knowledge of God, when the human turns to God from the garden of God's grace, spiritual joy, and the vision of peace.[139]

Admont Homily 14 on this pericope also focuses on penitence, as does Gregory the Great's Homily 10, doubtless the inspiration for both twelfth-century collections.[140] The Admont author develops an allegory of the soul, similar to Hildegard's focus on *homo peccator* in *Expositio* 13. Unlike Hildegard, the Admont homily follows a Marian interpretation: Mary represents at once the faithful bride and the soul.[141] Hildegard and the Admont text refer several times to the theme of the Devil's temptations.[142] Both interpret the *puer* Jesus and the *pueros*, the many victims, as innocence.[143] The gifts of the Magi represent specific virtues for both exegetes, as for Gregory the Great.

The Admont author confirms Gregory's influence with a direct reference, 'ut beatus Gregorius dicit' (as blessed Gregory says), and a paraphrase very close to the explanation of the gifts in Gregory's Homily 10. The first gift, gold (*aurum*), signifies wisdom (*sapientia*) for Gregory and the gleam of heavenly wisdom (*coelestis sapientiae nitor*) in the Admont text; incense (*thus*) designates the power of prayer (*uirtus orationis*) in both homilies, and likewise, myrrh stands for mortification of the flesh (*carnis mortificatio*) in both texts.[144] Hildegard follows the

---

[139] *Expo. Euang.*, 13, p. 223, lines 1–3, 5–8: '*Cum natus esset* in gemitibus et lacrimis *Iesus*, qui saluator mundi est, *in Bethlehem*, id est in penitentia hominis, *Iudae*, qui peccata sua confitetur'; '*ecce magi*, id est cognitio Dei, ubi homo ad Deum conuertitur, *ab oriente*, uidelicet ab ortu gratiae Dei, *uenerunt* in spiritali gaudio *Iherosolimam*, scilicet in uisionem pacis, quia Deus penitentem hominem suscipit'.

[140] Gottfried of Admont, *Homiliae in festa*, 14, *PL* 174: 677C–683C. Gregory the Great, *Homiliae in euangelia*, I, 10, pp. 70–71, lines 123–33. The homiliary of Paul the Deacon contains Gregory the Great's Homily 10 for Matthew 2. 1–12, and Bede's Homily 1.10 for Matthew 2. 13–18. See Grégoire, *Homéliaires liturgiques médiévaux*, no. 36, p. 437; Étaix, 'Le Lectionnaire de l'office à Cluny', no. 31, p. 98. On Matthew 2. 1–12, Grégoire, *Homéliaires liturgiques médiévaux*, no. 48, p. 439; Étaix, 'Le Lectionnaire de l'office à Cluny', no. 41, p. 99.

[141] Gottfried of Admont, *Homiliae in festa*, 14, *PL* 174: 681C: 'Mater Jesu eadem est quae et sponsa fidelis, revera quaelibet anima.'

[142] *Expo. Euang.*, 13, pp. 223–25, lines 4, 15–16, 51, 70–71. Gottfried of Admont, *Homiliae in festa*, 14, *PL* 174: 677D–683C.

[143] *Expo. Euang.*, 12, pp. 221–22, lines 53, 64, 69; *Expo. Euang.*, 13, pp. 224–25, lines 46, 52, 56. Gottfried of Admont, *Homiliae in festa*, 14, *PL* 174: 681A.

[144] Gregory the Great, *Homiliae in euangelia*, I, 10, p. 70, lines 114–23, pp. 70–71, lines 123–33; Gottfried of Admont, *Homiliae in festa*, 14, *PL* 174: 682. On the virtues, see additional sources in the apparatus fontium, *Expo. Euang.*, 13, pp. 223–25.

content of the Gregorian source; however, she does not cite it as the Admont author does, but gives a brief explanation of each gift: gold indicates the human beginning to know God; incense signifies the revealing of sins in confession; myrrh represents the subjection of the whole self in restraint.[145] Hence both Hildegard and the Admont homily show the influence of the Gregorian source and its accent on penitence, but they use it differently.[146]

Hildegard and the Admont homily modify their Gregorian source when they introduce the concept of Jesus's birth in the human heart,[147] a motif that runs through patristic literature. Origen, in a homily on Exodus, associates the Word-Child, the heart of the soul, and grace. Ambrose in a letter interprets Bethlehem, house of bread, as the soul that receives the bread from heaven, and in *De uirginitate* reads Mary as the soul that spiritually gives birth to Christ. Bede develops the Augustinian notion of giving birth to good works. Twelfth-century theologians Hugh of St Victor, Bernard, and Guerric of Igny all bring this Ambrosian-Augustinian theme to its high point with Mary as the moral model of the soul.[148] Hildegard does not pick up the Marian theme here, and the Admont author stays closer to the tradition in that respect.

Mark 7. 31–37

The *Expositiones* and the Admont homilies both develop tropological commentaries on Mark 7. 31–37, a text that often receives a typological interpretation,

---

[145] *Expo. Euang.*, 13, p. 225, lines 66–68: '*aurum*, quod homo incipit Deum cognoscere, *thus*, quod peccata sua in confessione aperit, *et mirram*, quod se totum in constrictione prosternit'.

[146] Gregory the Great, *Homiliae in euangelia*, I, 10, pp. 70–71, lines 123–33 on the three gifts and penitence; p. 71, lines 136–38 on the interpretation of *regio* as paradise.

[147] *Expo. Euang.*, 13, p. 223, lines 1–3: '*Cum natus esset* in gemitibus et lacrimis *Iesus*, qui saluator mundi est, *in Bethlehem*, id est in penitentia hominis, *Iudae*, qui peccata sua confitetur.' Gottfried of Admont, *Homiliae in festa*, 14, *PL* 174: 677C: 'Dominus et Salvator noster [. . .] qualiter adhuc in electorum nascatur cordibus [. . .] evangelista describit.' Gregory the Great, *Homiliae in euangelia*, I, 10, pp. 66–67, lines 20–47. Gregory juxtaposes the birth of the Lord with the Jews' hardness of heart in the face of prophecy and miracles, but Hildegard and the Admont homily do not include that anti-Jewish theme for this pericope.

[148] For the history of this theme, prominent in the later works of Meister Eckhart, see (Karl) Hugo Rahner, 'Die Gottesburt: die Lehre der Kirchenväter der Geburt Christi im Herzen des Glaübigen', *Zeitschrift für Katholische Theologie*, 59 (1935), 333–418. The notion of penitence does not figure in the texts cited by Rahner. Neither do they mention Zacchaeus, subject of Hildegardian homilies 57–58 on penitence.

where Jesus opening the deaf mute's ears and mouth represents the Old Testament opening to the Gospel. However, within the typological strand of commentary, Bede interprets Jesus's action of placing his fingers in the man's ears as opening the heart to the gifts of the Holy Spirit. That reading carries through numerous commentaries and provides a common starting point for Hildegard and the Admont homilies to pursue their moral interpretation.[149] In Hildegard's second homily on this pericope, a tropological allegory of the faithful soul, the human descends into sin and does not heed God's commands, so God leaves him. Yet God's charity opens the sinner's ears through the gifts of the Holy Spirit; by means of confession, the sinner, issuing sighs of repentance, is led back to God.[150]

Admont Homily 79 also accents the moral interpretation of the passage and interprets the deaf mute as the sinful human. The homilist begins by enumerating seven gifts of the Holy Spirit; he then explains the harmony of Gospel, reading, and prayer.[151] This type of reflection, linking the Gospel to the surrounding liturgy, does not appear in the *Expositiones*. After the liturgical introduction, the Admont homily takes up the gospel text again and explains it tropologically.[152] The interpretation of Tyre as anguish (*angustia*) provides the point of departure for discourse on the human condition of sin and the occasion to traverse the sea (of Galilee, Mk 7. 31) by penitence. Hildegard reads Tyre more generally as human sins.[153] The Admont homily builds from the Latin *ingemuit* (groaned), the verb for Jesus's command for the man to open his ears and mouth, and reflects on the word *gemitus* (groaning, moaning, or wailing) and human actions. Hildegard introduces

---

[149] See *Expo. Euang.*, 49, p. 316, lines 12–16; *Expo. Euang.*, 50, p. 317, lines 16–18. Gottfried of Admont, *Homiliae dominicales*, 79, *PL* 174: 555–61. Bede, *In Marci evangelium expositio*, II, vii, p. 525, lines 1445–47; Bede, *Homeliarum euangelii libri II*, II, 6, p. 221, lines 43–44; and other sources cited in the apparatus fontium, *Expo. Euang.*, 49–50, pp. 315–18. The *Glossa Ordinaria*, IV, 108–09 (p. 108, marg.), gives the reading of Bede on the gifts of the Holy Spirit.

[150] *Expo. Euang.*, 50, pp. 317–18. Gottfried of Admont, *Homiliae dominicales*, 79, *PL* 174: 555–61. For the homiliary of Paul the Deacon and the Cluny lectionary, Bede (2.6), see Grégoire, *Homéliaires liturgiques médiévaux*, no. II, 69, p. 465; Bede, commentary: Étaix, 'Le Lectionnaire de l'office à Cluny', no. 157, p. 109.

[151] Gottfried of Admont, *Homiliae dominicales*, 79, *PL* 174: 555D–557B.

[152] Gottfried of Admont, *Homiliae dominicales*, 79, *PL* 174: 559C.

[153] *Expo. Euang.*, 50, p. 317, lines 1–2: '*Exiens Iesus, scilicet Deus, de finibus Tyri*, id est de peccatis hominum, quia cum homo ad peccata declinat.'

a similar comment on the sounds of repentance, but she derives it from the cries of the man himself: his prayers and sighs when he beseeches Jesus for healing.[154]

What do these sets of homilies on Mark 7. 31–37 reveal about the approach and emphasis of their authors? Both authors tend to tropological interpretation, but the Admont homilies change very evidently from one sense of Scripture to another. Hildegard's continuous narrative differs clearly from the obvious linear division of the Admont homilies.

Mark 16. 1–7, Luke 2. 22–32, and the Gender of the Audience

To this point, some differences we have signalled in authorial voice or exegetical approach probably relate to the gender of the author, that is the level and sort of education each received and their role in the liturgy. Are there any such differences that may relate to the gender of the audience? A brief look at homilies on Mark 16. 1–7 and Luke 2. 22–32 provides a preliminary look at factors that may shed light on the audience's gender.[155]

Mark 16. 1–7

Hildegard's first Easter homily begins with a typological interpretation of the Old and New Testaments, which she applies to women in the religious life: the old law, according to the *magistra*, taught carnal union (*carnalem copulam*), as in Genesis 1. 28, 'Increase and multiply and fill the earth', whereas the new law advocates abstinence and chastity through the exhortation of the Holy Spirit.[156] The second homily recounts an allegorical drama that initiates with the problem of choosing between good and evil and then sets in motion a struggle between virtues and

---

[154] Gottfried of Admont, *Homiliae dominicales*, 79, PL 174: 562A. *Expo. Euang.* 50, p. 317, line 11: '*et deprecabantur eum*, per orationes et suspiria'.

[155] Additional elements of the Admont homily that differ from Hildegard include the opening digression, in this case on the lion, symbol of Mark the evangelist, and the closing doxology. The homilist refers to the preceding liturgical season of Lent, and he assigns a threefold significance to the ointments necessary for attaining salvation. Gottfried of Admont, *Homiliae in festa*, PL 174: 795D (on the lion); 801B (doxology); 799A (on Lent); 796C–798C (on the ointments for Christ's feet, hands, and head).

[156] *Expo. Euang.*, 28, p. 270, lines 18–26.

vices.[157] Hildegard's contemporaries at Admont also read the passage as a tropological allegory of the soul and the virtues.[158]

Both Hildegard's *Expositiones* and the Admont homily follow Gregorian cues in their tropological interpretation and in certain details.[159] The identification of Mary Magdalene as *peccatrix penitens* in both of Hildegard's *Expositiones* and Admont Homily 35 derives from Gregory, whose famous fusion of the three Marys became the standard for medieval exegetes.[160] Additionally, the *magistra's* two homilies and the Admont text develop another element of Gregory the Great's Homily 21 for Easter, the significance of Galilee (Mk 16. 7) as *transmigratio*.[161] Gregory builds on the interpretation of the ointment's scents (Mk 16. 1) as virtues and thereby joins the concepts of *transmigratio* and moral struggle.[162] The

[157] *Expo. Euang.*, 28, 29, pp. 269–74. Jaehyun Kim compares Hildegard's exegesis to that of Gregory the Great in 'Hildegard of Bingen's Gospel Homilies and her Exegesis of Mark 16. 1–7', unpublished paper, International Congress of Medieval Studies, Kalamazoo, Michigan, May 1999.

[158] Gottfried of Admont, *Homiliae in festa*, 35, *PL* 174: 796B.

[159] Gregory the Great's Homily 21 was included in the homiliary of Paul the Deacon and the Cluny lectionary. Gregory the Great, *Homiliae in euangelia*, II, 21, pp. 173–79. Grégoire, *Homéliaires liturgiques médiévaux*, no. II, 5, p. 454; Étaix, 'Le Lectionnaire de l'office à Cluny', no. 87, p. 103.

[160] *Expo. Euang.*, 28, p. 269, lines 1–2; *Expo. Euang.*, 29, p. 272, lines 1–3. Gottfried of Admont, *Homiliae in festa*, 35, *PL* 174: 796. See Gregory the Great, *Homiliae in Hiezechihelem prophetam*, ed. by M. Adriaen, CCSL, 142 (Turnhout: Brepols, 1971), II, 8, 21, lines 589–92: 'In hoc fonte misericordiae lota est Maria Magdalene, quae prius famosa peccatrix, postmodum lavit maculas lacrimis, detersit maculas corrigendo mores.' Gregory the Great, *Homiliae in euangelia*, II, 25, pp. 215–16, lines 285–314. See Haymo of Auxerre, *Homiliae de tempore*, 70, *PL* 118: 446; Ambrosius Autpertus, *Expositionis in Apocalypsin libri I–V, libri VI–X*, ed. by R. Weber, CCCM, 27, 27A (Turnhout: Brepols, 1975), I, 5c, p. 48; II, 3, 4, p. 164; Leo the Great, *De Conflictu vitiorum atque virtutum libellus*, *PL* 143: 568–69; Ps.-Petrus Damianus, *Sermo* 29, *PL* 144: 660. Hildegard does not dwell on Magdalene, however, here or in other writings. The *Glossa Ordinaria*, IV, 135, marg., is concerned with explaining the timing of the events and not the symbolism of the three women. However, it offers a moral interpretation related to the scent of virtue.

[161] *Expo. Euang.*, 28, p. 272, lines 58–59; *Expo. Euang.*, 29, p. 273, lines 37–38; Gottfried of Admont, *Homiliae in festa*, 35, *PL* 174: 801A; Gregory the Great, *Homiliae in euangelia*, II, 21, p. 176, lines 87–88; p. 179, lines 161–62; Bede, *In Marci euangelium*, 4, 16, 3–7, pp. 641–42, lines 1819–27; additional sources in the apparatus fontium, *Expo. Euang.*, 28, 29, pp. 272–73; *Glossa Ordinaria*, IV, 136, marg.: 'Galylea namque transmigratio facta interpretatur.'

[162] On the virtues, see Gregory the Great, *Homiliae in euangelia*, II, 21, p. 174, line 28; p. 177, lines 92–93; p. 179, line 161; Bede, *In Marci evangelium*, IV, xvi, 3–7, p. 642, lines 1824–25; Heiric of Auxerre, *Homiliae*, pars aestiua, II, 1, p. 5, lines 74–75: 'sancta mulieres animas figurant

Gregorian reading of the ointment and the thematic emphasis on the journey from vice to virtue, from the death of sin to eternal life, echoes in Hildegard's *Expositio* 28 and the Admont homily.[163]

Gregory the Great concludes his Homily 21 with an exhortation to move from vice to virtue. Hildegard in *Expo.* 28 explains how the soul, with the aid of the virtues, benefits from grace to do good works,[164] while her second homily discusses how the grace of God with the aid of the virtues, notably desire for heaven, assists in the removal of carnal desires, signified by the hardness of the stone (Mk 16. 3–4).[165] The Admont homilist concludes the text with a return to the theme of *transmigratio* and an exhortation for sinners to put aside fear and undertake the journey from vice to virtue, death to life.

Both Hildegard's *Expositio* 28 and Admont Homily 35 differ somewhat from Gregory the Great's interpretation of the angel's white stole as soothing whiteness (*blandimentum candoris*); they read the stole as innocence. Hildegard further interprets the whiteness as a sign of virginity.[166] This constitutes one of several references she makes in the same text to virginity, virgins, and chastity.[167] The thematic insistence on virginity suggests that the *magistra* of Rupertsberg addresses an audience of religious women, whereas the Admont homily refers to desires of the flesh and worldly intentions but not to virginity.[168] Hildegard and the Admont author both seem to have taken Gregory as their point of departure and adapted his moral advice for their audiences.

---

spiritalium virtutum pignoribus referta'; p. 15, line 409; Gottfried of Admont, *Homiliae in festa*, 35, *PL* 174: 797; and additional sources in the apparatus fontium, *Expo. Euang.*, 28, 29, pp. 269–73. On *transmigratio*, see Gregory the Great, *Homiliae in euangelia*, II, 21, p. 176, lines 87–88; p. 179, lines 161–62; Bede, *In Marci evangelium*, IV, xvi, 3–7, pp. 641–42, lines 1819–27; Gottfried of Admont, *Homiliae in festa*, 35, *PL* 174: 797; and additional sources in the apparatus fontium, *Expo. Euang.*, 28, 29, pp. 269–73. The *Glossa Ordinaria*, IV, 135–36, relies heavily on Bede.

[163] *Expo. Euang.*, 28, p. 270, lines 5–6, 9; *Expo. Euang.*, 29, p. 272, lines 5–6; Gottfried of Admont, *Homiliae in festa*, 35, *PL* 174: 797C, 801A.

[164] *Expo. Euang.*, 28, pp. 273–74, lines 28–40.

[165] *Glossa Ordinaria*, IV, 135. See note 30 above.

[166] *Expo. Euang.*, 28, p. 271, lines 42–43: 'stola, scilicet prima ueste innocentiae, *candida* in candore uirginitatis'; Gottfried of Admont, *Homiliae in festa*, 35, *PL* 174: 799D; Gregory the Great, *Homiliae in euangelia*, II, 21, p. 175, lines 51–52.

[167] *Expo. Euang.*, 28, pp. 271–72, lines 19–20, 24, 33–34, 35, 38, 42–43.

[168] Gottfried of Admont, *Homiliae in festa*, *PL* 174: 797C.

Luke 2. 22–32

Hildegard's two interpretations of Luke 2. 22–32 differ broadly from the Admont homily, and the contrast again points to the possible difference in gender of the audiences.[169] Hildegard offers two readings for the feast of the Purification: the first situates the passage in salvation history and the second reworks it as an allegory of the soul. Neither delves into the liturgical details about candles or wax that often appear in Purification sermons and that correspond to the blessing of candles and the rejoicing in light that gives the feast the name of Candlemas in some traditions.[170] The typological framework that the *magistra* follows in the first homily, where the purification of Mary represents the transformation of the old law into the new, appears in Bede.[171] Hildegard's second exposition on the pericope holds up the virginal life as the ideal for her community of nuns but does not enter into the historical theological controversy over Mary's virginity, as do her predecessors Bede and Haymo of Auxerre.[172]

The Admont preacher indicates at the outset of the text that the notion of purification applies to each and every soul every day,[173] but the perspective moves

---

[169] *Expo. Euang.*, 20–22, pp. 241–45. Gottfried of Admont, *Homiliae in festa*, 20, *PL* 174: 708B–713D.

[170] See Beverly Mayne Kienzle, 'Mary Speaks Against Heresy: An Unedited Sermon of Hélinand of Froidmont for the Purification, Paris, B.N. MS. Lat. 14591', *Sacris Erudiri*, 32 (1991), 291–308. *Glossa Ordinaria*, IV, 146, focuses on the circumcision, rather than the purification, but makes a general statement in line with typological interpretation: that while neither Joseph nor Mary needed circumcision or purification, they did so in order that 'we be freed from fear of the Law' ('ut nos solveremur a timore legis').

[171] Bede, Homily 1.18, was the selection in the Cluny lectionary, while Paul the Deacon's homiliary included a Nativity sermon by Augustine: Sermo 370, 2, *PL* 39: 1657–58; Grégoire, *Homéliaires liturgiques médiévaux*, no. 65, p. 442. Eligius Dekkers, *Clavis patrum latinorum*, 3rd edn, CCSL (Turnhout: Brepols, 1995), Aug. 285, p. 122, identifies sermons 370–73 as genuine. Bede, 1.18 (vv. 22–35), not in Grégoire, *Homéliaires liturgiques médiévaux*, but in Étaix, 'Le Lectionnaire de l'office à Cluny', no. 2, 29, p. 114. Bede, *In Lucae euangelium*, I, ii, pp. 61–62, lines 1673–80 (de antiqua lege); cf. *Homeliarum euangelii libri II*, I, 18, p. 129, lines 29–35. See also Ambrosius Autpertus, *Sermo in purificatione sanctae Mariae*, ed. by R. Weber, CCCM, 27B (Turnhout: Brepols, 1979), 3, pp. 986–87, lines 10–30.

[172] Bede, *In Lucae evangelium*, I, ii, p. 62, lines 1690–96 (de virginitate); Haymo of Auxerre, *Homiliae de tempore*, 14, *PL* 118: 100.

[173] Gottfried of Admont, *Homiliae in festa*, 20, *PL* 174: 708C: 'Igitur per dies purgationis Jesu omne tempus labentis saeculi potest accipi, in quo unaquaeque anima necesse habet quotidie purgari.'

beyond the individual person. The homily asserts that Christ is purified through the purification of the members of his body in the Church, and it discusses the attainment of eternal life for the elect within the Church. The choice of meanings for the avian offerings in the scriptural narrative demonstrates the line of interpretation: the pair of turtledoves (*par turturum*), which for Hildegard signifies innocence and chastity, as in Bede, represents for the Admont author those leading the contemplative life. The two young pigeons (*duos pullos columbarum*) designate good works for Hildegard and in the Admont text stand for those in the active life.[174] For the Admont author, the two young pigeons evoke the one perfect *columba*, or dove, of Song 6. 9 that designates the Church. Although the dove is 'perfect', the 'only one of her mother', and 'the chosen one of her genitrix', various types of doves, namely styles of Christian life, are found within her.[175]

The Admont text, nonetheless, joins Hildegard's in the accent on the religious life. Both the twelfth-century texts may draw on Augustine's Sermon 370, the reading in Paul the Deacon's homiliary, which praises virginity and the life of continence. The great Bishop also observes grounds for rejoicing among widows like Anna and married women such as Elizabeth, who foretold the Lord's birth.[176] The Admont homily's inclusion of participants in the active life may reflect this Augustinian perspective to some degree. In contrast to the Admont text, Hildegard incorporates the themes of chastity and innocence from the Bedan homily and centres her interpretation on an individual rather than an ecclesial reading of the pericope. Hildegard's homily seems to address the particular concern of a female audience whereas the Admont author takes a more ecclesiological view that would interest male clergy.

What preliminary conclusions may be drawn from the brief look at the two collections? Clearly the *Expositiones* and the Admont homilies share a taste for tropological interpretation and the drama of the soul. Such similarities in the

---

[174] *Expo. Euang.*, 21, pp. 243–44, lines 15–17: '*par turturum*, id est innocentiam et castitatem, *aut duos pullos columbarum*, scilicet sancta opera, se ita martirizantes in conflictu uiciorum'.

[175] Gottfried of Admont, *Homiliae in festa*, 20, *PL* 174: 709C–710C: 'Licet ergo tota simul Ecclesia *una* sit *columba perfecta, una matris suae, electa genetrici suae*, diversae tamen columbae inveniuntur, quae ex diverso religionis habitu ad unam fidei concordiam colliguntur.' The Admont homily also discusses three laws.

[176] Augustine of Hippo, Sermo 370, *De nativitate Domini, PL* 39: 1657: 'Numquid enim solae virgines ad regnum coelorum perveniunt? Perveniunt et viduae.' See also Ps.-Anselm of Canterbury, *Homiliae et exhortationes*, 6, *PL* 158: 624B.

emphasis on tropology embrace both male and female listeners.[177] The method for conveying the moral sense differs substantially, however, even when specific elements of the interpretation coincide and draw on patristic commentators, chiefly Gregory the Great. Certain differences in theme and structure probably pertain to male authorship, as when the homiletic voice from Admont frames the readings within the liturgy. Different thematic focuses, such as clerical responsibility on the one hand and virginity on the other, may reflect the gender and concerns of the audience. However, the Admont homilies, as their scholars emphasize, addressed both men and women simultaneously. Only a few of the *Expositiones* indicate that Hildegard may have been speaking to a mixed audience, the community she had left at Disibodenberg. Rich material remains for further comparison of the *Expositiones* with the Admont homilies and awaits the definitive edition of the latter. Thus far, nowhere in the Admont homilies have I found the sort of consistent dramatic narrative exegesis that Hildegard constructs throughout the *Expositiones*. Indeed, this comparison of the Admont homilies and the *Expositiones* provides further evidence that Hildegard stands out from her contemporaries in her creativity and ability to innovate even in the traditional realm of exegesis.

Conclusion: Vox Hildegardis

The *magistra* implemented her responsibility for her nuns' salvation through the interpretation of Scripture in the *Expositiones euangeliorum*. Medieval monastic life, liturgy, and literature provide the context for the *magistra*'s method of sequential commentary and the genre of the homily. Hildegard uses a variety of intratextual glosses to construct a continuous narrative that I call the *Glossa Hildegardiana*. Her commentary displays narrative coherency and characteristics of drama. Furthermore, the *magistra*'s exegesis develops the voice of biblical characters, the *uox dramatis personae*: she extends their voices with her own words to create the *Vox Hildegardis*, and she at times adopts their voices to exhort in a *uox praedicatricis*. The combined impact of these techniques produces what I term Hildegard's dramatic narrative exegesis.

Hildegard's *Expositiones* clearly belong to monastic homiletic and exegetical traditions, but they nonetheless differ from many, if not most, extant monastic sermons in several respects: the deliberately progressive, almost word-by-word exegesis; the construction of a coherent narrative in the commentary; and the

---

[177] Lutter, 'Christ's Educated Brides'.

frequent extension of the voice of the biblical characters. The story that unfolds in Hildegard's narrative often reflects the structure of the biblical text itself, seeming like a parable based on a parable. Patristic and medieval exegetes understood that the proper interpretation of *parabolae* (parables) and *similitudines* (metaphors or similes) conveyed truth. Interpreters differed in what aspect of Christian teaching they emphasized. More commonly, a patristic or medieval exegete would point out that some elements of the parable refer to the creation or alternately to the soul but would not develop a reading that followed either of those allegories thoroughly as Hildegard's dramatic narratives do.

Moreover, the blending of the *magistra*'s voice with that of the gospel text, and at times with another passage of Scripture such as Genesis, creates a multi-level drama in which she engages as commentator and which contrasts significantly with the distance that most commentators take from the scriptural text. The hierarchy of commentary and Scripture, evident in the scripts and layout of glossed Bibles where comments are compressed into the margins or between the lines, disappears when all voices proceed simultaneously and occupy the same space on the page.[178] Arguably, the simultaneity also allows the commentator's voice the opportunity to take the primary role, and Hildegard at times seizes it.

The designation of dramatic narrative also helps to capture the performative nature of the *Expositiones*. Hildegard re-creates the biblical story for her sisters. The meaning of the scriptural text is intact, not altered, but the richness of possible meanings comes to life in a new performance of the story. The character of drama and performance is crucial to the retelling: the dramatic vision of Hildegard shapes her account of the biblical story. The *Expositiones*, particularly those that represent the struggle of the faithful soul, have the potential for transformation to and from drama, and to and from visionary accounts, just as they aim to transform the souls of the audience.[179] The story unfolds like the acts of a drama voiced and performed by Hildegard herself as *magistra*, narrator, and interpreter. Whether or not the *magistra* was cognizant of her innovation, she certainly expressed a keen awareness of the impact of her voice on her sisters. Writing the *Explanatio Symboli Sancti*

---

[178] I am grateful to Jess Michalik for this idea that the single text with 'distinct strands' differs from the hierarchial importance given to the principal scriptural text in most biblical commentary.

[179] Fassler, 'Composer and Dramatist', p. 157, observes that Hildegard translated 'freely from theological writing to drama, to songs, to visual arts'. Barbara J. Newman, 'Poet: Where the Living Majesty Utters Mysteries', in *Voice*, pp. 176–92 (p. 177), also notes that the union of 'soul and body, song and speech, God and humanity, underlies all of Hildegard's teaching'; and Caviness, 'Artist', pp. 110–15, makes a similar observation about Hildegard's art.

Athanasii, she looks ahead to her death and hopes that her voice, which 'resounded in charity', will never be forgotten.[180] Margot Fassler argues that Hildegard, as religious superior of her community, would have intoned her own elaborate liturgical responsories and thus asserted her leadership in liturgy as another dimension of her theological teaching.[181] The range of her voice in liturgical performance directed her sisters and resounded among them in multiple modes. In liturgical song, the voice modulation and intonation that characterize drama add to the dramatic quality of the performance. Likewise, the liturgical speech of Hildegard's commentary on the *Expositiones* must have included such changes in modulation and intonation. Dramatic elements of the extant texts lead us to imagine the *magistra*'s performance before the audience of her sisters, even though ultimately it remains irretrievable.

Applying the contemporary notion of 'framing' from performance theory to the delivery of the *Expositiones* may assist a modern reader to grasp a distant environment and the continuous commentary of Hildegard's homilies. The frame for the *Expositiones* would involve liturgical practice, its language and symbols, the accustomed space for performing the *Expositiones* — probably the chapter house at Rupertsberg — and the audience of Hildegard's sisters.[182] Upon imagining the performance behind the texts, the potentially confusing commentary may come alive. One needs to perform the texts in some sense, to read them aloud and attempt to imagine Hildegard uttering them in the monastic setting, in order to appreciate them.

In Hildegard's exegetical method, a blend of literary modes springs from the structure and images of the scriptural texts and constitutes both a harmonious voice, *uox symphonialis*, to borrow Hildegard's own term for the sweetness of the human spirit, and a consonant view or *symphonia* of Christian history intended to praise God and anticipate the sight of heaven.[183] Foremost in her homilies,

---

[180] *Expl. Symb.*, 46–49, pp. 110–11: 'Spiritus sanctus uobis dona suadet, quia post finem meum, uocem meam amodo non audietis. Sed uox mea nunquam ducatur inter uos in obliuionem, quae frequenter inter uos in charitate sonuit.'

[181] Fassler, 'Composer and Dramatist', pp. 153–55.

[182] Mary Suydam applies Manfred Pfister's definition of drama and Gregory Bateson's concept of 'framing' in 'Background: An Introduction to Performance Studies', in *Performance and Transformation: New Approaches to Late Medieval Spirituality*, ed. by Mary A. Suydam and Joanna E. Zeigler (New York: St Martin's Press, 1999), pp. 1–26. See Kienzle, 'Medieval Sermons and their Performance', pp. 90–93.

[183] In *Solut.*, *PL* 197: 1049, Hildegard states: 'De torrente itinere superioris aetheris, per quem firmamentum evolvitur, sonus elementorum jucundus et gloriosus existit, ut etiam symphonialis

however, stands the moral concern to equip her audience on how to internalize the Scriptures and live the monastic life. The tropological character of her interpretation finds longstanding roots in the exegesis of Gregory the Great and its impact in monastic circles.[184] The notion of Christian life as an ongoing struggle is a key feature of Hildegard's moral thought.[185] Its roots delve deeply into monastic spirituality and literature. Hildegard's method complements her vision of the human condition: elements of narrative and drama mesh with the thematic focus on salvation history, itself a drama and narrative of humankind from its origins.

vox spiritus hominis, dulcis est in vita sua.' See also *Epistolarium*, I, 23, p. 65, line 141, where Hildegard describes the soul as *symphonialis*. In *Expo. Euang.*, 26, p. 263, line 75, Hildegard glosses *symphonia* as 'gaudium supernae uisionis', and in *Expo. Euang.*, 27, p. 268, line 70, as 'rumorem bonae laudis'. Dronke, 'Platonic-Christian Allegories', p. 383, compares Hildegard's use of metaphor in the *Symphonia* and the *Expositiones*, observing that all the metaphors in a given homily are interdependent.

[184] Hildegard's moral exegesis constitutes a modification to Henri de Lubac's assertion that Bernard of Clairvaux introduced a taste for the moral sense that characterized the Cistercian approach to Scripture (as opposed to the Benedictine). Lubac, *Medieval Exegesis*, II, 143–53. See the discussion by Chrysogonus Waddell, 'Liturgical Dimension of Twelfth-Century Cistercian Preaching', p. 347, of the Cistercian concern for 'interiorization' of the text.

[185] In 'Poet', p. 190, Newman discusses the 'dialectical nature' of Hildegard's moral thought. Newman discusses the moral allegory in Hildegard's letters on pp. 79–82 of *Sister of Wisdom*.

THE THEOLOGY AND DRAMA
OF SALVATION HISTORY

Now then, direct them and show them by a true admonition that, in the beginning, God created heaven and earth and the rest of creatures, and for the sake of humankind God placed the human being in the pleasant place of paradise and gave him a command that was violated.[1]

Hildegard calls upon her contemporaries to break through the darkness of heretical beliefs and teach the account of salvation from God's creation onward. Does the *magistra* herself teach the history of salvation in the *Expositiones euangeliorum*? Indeed, I will argue that the depiction of salvation history lies at the core of Hildegard's thought in the *Expositiones*. But what concept of history do the homilies reveal? Does Hildegard's theology of history reflect the thought of her predecessors or her contemporaries? What structure does she employ for the narrative of history and what theology underlies it? How does the treatment of salvation history in the *Expositiones* compare to her other works? To open the way for answering these questions, this chapter first looks to the theology of history in the works of Augustine and its impact on Hildegard and her contemporaries. I then explore the *magistra*'s largely threefold division of history to determine if her exegesis reveals a Trinitarian framework. Finally, I consider whether the emphasis on salvation history in the *Expositiones* provides a nexus for thematic consistency in Hildegard's works.

---

[1] *Expl. Symb.*, p. 128, lines 545–49: 'Nunc regite eos, per ueram admonitionem ipsis ostendentes, quod Deus in principio propter hominem celum et terram et reliquas creaturas creauit, et quod hominem in uoluptuosum locum paradysi posuit, eique preceptum quod preuaricatus est, dedit.' *Expl. Atha.*, pp. 68–69.

The Augustinian Heritage

To what extent does Hildegard draw on patristic theology of history? Augustine of Hippo's divisions of history dominated Western thinking; six historical ages mirrored the six working days of creation and corresponded to interventions of God: the first extended from Adam to Noah; the second from Noah to Abraham; the third from Abraham to David; the fourth from David to the Babylonian captivity; the fifth from the captivity to the coming of Christ; the sixth spanned time from the incarnation until the end of the world.[2] Christian thinkers at once show difficulty and creativity in defining the sixth age and in determining how to represent the seventh day, when God rested from labour. Hugh of St Victor, developing Augustine's thought, correlated the days to stages of redemption, with the seventh day corresponding to eternal blessedness.[3]

Augustine also introduced the notion that the six divisions marked the phases of human life. Likewise, Honorius Augustodunensis spelled out the stages of human existence in his *De imagine mundi*: infancy, childhood, adolescence, youth, old age, and extreme old age. Abelard, too, followed the coordination of the days of creation with the ages of history and human life.[4] This pattern of correspondence underlay the connection between the human as microcosm and the history of the universe as macrocosm, which Honorius represented in the *Elucidarium*, the most influential of his twenty-two works.[5] The representation of the human as

---

[2] On this theme, see Hildegard L. C. Tristram, *Sex aetates mundi: Die Weltzeitalter bei dem Angelsachsen und den Iren: Untersuchungen und Texte*, Anglistische Forschungen, 165 (Heidelberg: Winter, 1985); J. A. Burrow, *The Ages of Man: A Study in Medieval Writing and Thought* (Oxford: Clarendon Press, 1988); Robert A. Markus, 'History', and John M. Quinn, 'Time', in *Augustine Through the Ages: An Encyclopedia*, ed. by Allan D. Fitzgerald (Grand Rapids: Eerdmans, 1999), pp. 432–43, 837. Works discussed include Augustine's *De ciuitate Dei, De Genesi ad litteram*, and *Contra Faustum*.

[3] Chenu, *Nature, Man and Society*, pp. 180–82. Richard of St Victor introduced the notion of successions: patriarchs, judges, kings, priests. See also Lubac, *Medieval Exegesis*, II, 41–69, on patristic and medieval concepts of history and historical interpretation. On Abelard and the days of creation, see *Letters of Peter Abelard*, pp. 53–60.

[4] On Honorius and his works including *De imagine mundi*, see Valerie I. J. Flint, 'The Chronology of the Works of Honorius of Autun', *Revue Bénédictine*, 82 (1972), 215–42; Flint, 'The Place and Purpose of the Works of Honorius of Autun', *Revue Bénédictine*, 87 (1977), 97–127. *Letters of Peter Abelard*, pp. 53–60.

[5] A theological summa in dialogue form, the *Elucidarium* survives in over three hundred manuscripts. See Chenu, *Nature, Man and Society*, pp. 179–81. On Honorius's influence on Herrad, see Griffiths, *Garden of Delights*, pp. 109–12. The chronicler Lambert of St Omer also describes the

microcosm pertains not only to the theology of history but also to Hildegard's writings on the struggles of the soul.

Patterns of historical division simpler than that of the six ages also occur in Augustine's works and highlight the incarnation. In the *Enchiridion*, Augustine spoke broadly of a threefold division of time *ante legem, sub lege*, and *sub gratia*.[6] At times Augustine reduced those three ages to two broad periods: one looking to Christ's coming and the other following his advent. The great Bishop also viewed history as a drama of salvation: the creation and Fall constitute the opening scene; the redemption of fallen humanity occupies the middle act; the final act comes with reward and punishment on the last day. Finally, Augustine compared the history of humankind and the life of the individual sinner.[7] The threefold division and the notion of history as drama prove influential for Hildegard's concept of time.

Theologians of history who wrote around the same period as Hildegard include Anselm of Havelberg (*c.* 1095–1155), Gerhoch of Reichersberg (d. 1169), and Otto of Freising (1111/14–58).[8] In Anselm's relatively optimistic view, the Church would continuously pass through stages of renewal and the canons (not monks) would play the primary role in renewing the Church in the modern age, the *aetas moderna* which Anselm placed within the age *sub gratia*.[9] Gerhoch of Reichersberg and Otto of Freising took sharply opposing sides in the conflicts

---

macro- and microcosm in the *Liber floridus*, an illustrated encyclopedia. On Lambert of St Omer, see *The Autograph Manuscript of the 'Liber floridus': A Key to the Encyclopedia of Lambert of Saint-Omer*, ed. by Albert Derolez, Corpus Christianorum Autographa Medii Aevi, 4 (Turnhout: Brepols, 1998); and *Liber floridus Colloquium: Papers Read at the International Meeting Held in the University Library, Ghent, on 3–5 September 1967*, ed. by Albert Derolez (Gent: Story–Scientia, 1973). Both Honorius and Lambert display with Hildegard a type of 'visual thinking', as Caviness, 'Artist', p. 124, terms it, 'such that their texts virtually require images'.

[6] Chenu, *Nature, Man and Society*, p. 182.

[7] See Quinn, 'Time', p. 837.

[8] These churchmen, along with Rupert of Deutz and Hildegard, have been grouped loosely as part of a school of German Symbolism, whose writers extend the typological reading of the Old Testament (as a prefiguration of the New) into a symbolic reading of Scripture that could predict future events. On *Symbolismus*, see Van Engen, *Rupert of Deutz*, p. 9; Kerby-Fulton, 'Prophet and Reformer', p. 76; Chenu, *Nature, Man and Society*, p. 192, in disagreement with J. Spörl, who grouped Honorius Augustodunensis, Hugh of St Victor, and Hildegard, explaining their symbolic interpretation of history by their Germanic temperament.

[9] Chenu, *Nature, Man and Society*, pp. 174, 183–84. Anselm, a Premonstratensian who was named Bishop of Havelberg and Archbishop of Ravenna (1155), traveled to Constantinople to argue for the primacy of Rome.

between the papacy and the Empire. At Reichersberg, a monastery in present-day Austria, Gerhoch maintained strong reformist views in spite of considerable opposition. His works evoke apocalyptic fury in order to urge contemporary reform.[10] In contrast, Otto of Freising, half-brother of Emperor Conrad III and uncle of Frederick I, viewed Christian history through imperial eyes. The eight books of Otto's *Chronicle*, inspired by and modeled on Augustine's *City of God*, view history as a conflict between the 'City of God' and the 'City of the Devil'.[11] Otto seized upon the Augustinian theme that the Roman Empire prepared the way for Christ's birth; accordingly, he identified the Holy Roman Empire as the inheritor of Christian destiny.[12] Hildegard does not espouse Otto's political theology of empire; while she shares his Germanocentric outlook on contemporary conflicts, she extends her visionary gaze far beyond the events of her world.

While Gerhoch of Reichersberg and Otto of Freising belonged to a cultural milieu close to Hildegard's, the widely influential works of Honorius Augustodunensis and Rupert of Deutz more likely exerted an influence on the *magistra* as well as on Herrad of Hohenbourg.[13] Honorius's *Elucidarium* contains three parts: the first deals with the threefold division of time into creation, incarnation, and redemption; the second focuses on the Church in the world; the third evokes the end times.[14] From the Augustinian frameworks, Rupert of Deutz applied the

[10] Gerhoh of Reichersberg, *Libelli selecti*, ed. by Ernst Sackur, in *Libelli de lite imperatorum et pontificum*, MGH Libelli, 3 (Hannover, 1897), pp. 131–525. Chenu, *Nature, Man and Society*, pp. 198, 321. Gerhoch supported Alexander III in the disputed election of 1159 and incurred the hatred of the Hohenstaufen supporters. The monastery of Reichersberg suffered attacks; Conrad I, the Archbishop of Salzburg, was banished; and Gerhoch was forced to flee into exile. Gerhoch denounced Peter Lombard, Abelard, and Gilbert of la Porrée; even Alexander III appealed to him to keep silent. On Gerhoch and Otto of Freising, see Constant J. Mews, 'Accusations of Heresy and Error in the Twelfth-Century Schools: The Witness of Gerhoh of Reichersberg and Otto of Freising', in *Heresy in Transition: Transforming Ideas of Heresy in Medieval and Early Modern Europe*, ed. by Ian Hunter, John Christian Laursen, and Cary J. Nederman (Aldershot: Ashgate, 2005), pp. 43–57.

[11] Otto of Freising, *Chronicon seu rerum ab initio mundi ad sua usque tempora 1146 libri VIII, sive Historia de duabus civitatibus*, ed. by Adolf Hofmeister, MGH SS, 20 (Hannover, 1868), pp. 115–301. Seven books span the period from the creation to 1146; the eighth book treats the end times and the beginning of the divine state.

[12] Chenu, *Nature, Man and Society*, pp. 185, 194–96.

[13] See Griffiths, *Garden of Delights*, pp. 64–72.

[14] See the works of V. Flint cited in note 4 above. Honorius worked in the circle of Anselm of Canterbury, then moved to Regensberg, and later to the Benedictine monastery of Lambach.

numerical theology of the ages to the Divine Office and the liturgical year in *De diuinis officiis*. For example, Rupert associated the seven Sundays forward from Septuagesima (the seventh Sunday before Easter) with the seven ages of the world, and he connected the days of Holy Week to the seven days of creation. Likewise, the octave of Easter represented the new life that is described in the beatitudes and rendered possible by the seven gifts of the Spirit.[15]

In *De sancta trinitate et operibus eius* (composed 1112–16), Rupert endeavoured to understand the Trinity (*tripartum Trinitatis opus*) through discernment of the works particular to Father, Son, and Holy Spirit: the Father's work — creation — was revealed in the seven days; the Son's — redemption — was shown in the seven ages; and the Spirit's — renovation — was demonstrated through the seven gifts of the Spirit. Another triad, three ages, marks the Spirit's work in history: creation to the Fall; the Fall to the passion of Christ; the resurrection to the end of time and the general resurrection. The three ages belong respectively to Father, Son, and Holy Spirit.[16] Truth, contained in Scripture, manifested itself over the course of salvation history, and exegesis of Scripture provided the path to understanding truth. Rupert moved systematically through Scripture and tackled problems that had perplexed Christian exegetes since Augustine. Questions provoked by Genesis, such as the nature of the waters above the firmament and the state of Enoch and Elijah while waiting in paradise after their ascent, stem from the early twelfth century's interest in creation and fondness for commentary on Genesis.[17] Hildegard addresses some of the same problems in the *Solutiones*.[18]

The dominance of allegory in the theology of history strikes the eye in illustrated manuscripts from Hildegard's era, notably the *Hildegard-Gebetbuch* and its predecessor, the Sélestat *liber precum* (c. 1150).[19] The so-called *Prayerbook of Hildegard of Bingen*, which places the life of Christ in the perspective of salvation

---

[15] Van Engen, *Rupert of Deutz*, pp. 59–63.

[16] The Prologue to Rupert of Deutz, *De sancta trinitate et operibus eius*, ed. by R. Haacke, CCCM, 21–24 (Turnhout: Brepols, 1971–72), 21, pp. 125–27, summarizes succinctly Rupert's view of history.

[17] Van Engen, *Rupert of Deutz*, pp. 85–86; *Letters of Peter Abelard*, p. 55.

[18] *Solut.*, Quaest. II, *PL* 197: 1040D–1041A, on waters 'sub firmamento' and 'super firmamentum'. *Quaest.* XXIX, *PL* 197: 1050B, treats the needs of Enoch and Elijah in paradise and explains God ordered things such that they had no bodily needs.

[19] Sélestat, Bibliothèque humaniste, MS 104, Hamburger, 'Before the Book of Hours', pp. 151–52, identifies the Sélestat *liber precum* as 'an early, perhaps the earliest surviving example of a prayer book of German origin with an extensive cycle of narrative illustrations'. References indicate that it was made for a house of Benedictine women.

history, depicts more than seventy scenes from salvation history beginning with the creation and extending to the second coming.[20] Nearly all the miniatures, placed on the verso (left) face prayers on the recto (right), balancing text and image equally.[21] The *Prayerbook* provides contemporary visual parallels for ten gospel pericopes that Hildegard expounded in the *Expositiones*: Luke 2. 1–14, the nativity and the announcement to the shepherds;[22] Matthew 2. 1–12, the visit of the wise men;[23] Luke 2. 22–39, the presentation in the temple;[24] Matthew 2. 13–15, the flight into Egypt;[25] Luke 2. 41–51, Jesus at age twelve in the temple;[26] Matthew 4. 1–7 and 8–11, the temptation of Christ;[27] John 2. 1–11, the marriage at Cana;[28] John 6. 1–14, the feeding of the five thousand;[29] Mark 7. 31–37, the healing of the deaf mute;[30] and Mark 16. 19, the ascension.[31] In addition, the *Prayerbook*

---

[20] Gerard Achten underscores the salvation-historical perspective of the *Gebetbuch* and identifies its placing of the entire earthly life of Christ in that perspective as the original feature of the work. 'Die Gebete des Hildegard-Gebetbuches', in *Gebetbuch*, pp. 15–70 (p. 20): 'Das Gebetbuch stellt unter Verarbeitung der theologischen Erkenntnisse der Zeit das gesamte irdische Leben Christi in eine heilsgeschichtliche Perspektive. Darin liegt die Originalität des Werkes.'

[21] Hamburger, 'Before the Book of Hours', p. 166, nn. 35–38, identifies five additional manuscripts of this sort of prayer book, thus a total of seven.

[22] *Expo. Euang.*, 7 and 8 on Luke 2. 1–14; fols 13ʳ, 14ʳ; Klemm, 'Der Bilderzyklus im Hildegard-Gebetbuch', pp. 134–39, 139–41. Note that the *Prayerbook* devotes two scenes to this.

[23] *Expo. Euang.*, 12 and 13 on Matthew 2. 1–12; fol. 15ʳ; Klemm, 'Der Bilderzyklus im Hildegard-Gebetbuch', pp. 141–44.

[24] *Expo. Euang.*, 20 and 21 on Luke 2. 22–32; fol. 16ʳ; Klemm, 'Der Bilderzyklus im Hildegard-Gebetbuch', pp. 144–46.

[25] *Expo. Euang.*, 10 and 11 on Matthew 2. 13–18; fol. 17ʳ; Klemm, 'Der Bilderzyklus im Hildegard-Gebetbuch', pp. 146–48.

[26] *Expo. Euang.*, 14 and 15 on Luke 2. 42–52; fol. 19ʳ; Klemm, 'Der Bilderzyklus im Hildegard-Gebetbuch', pp. 148–50.

[27] *Expo. Euang.*, 24 and 25 on Matthew 4. 1–11; fols 20ʳ, 21ʳ; Klemm, 'Der Bilderzyklus im Hildegard-Gebetbuch', pp. 153–56. Note that the temptations are divided into two scenes.

[28] *Expo. Euang.*, 16 and 17 on John 2. 1–11; fol. 22ʳ; Klemm, 'Der Bilderzyklus im Hildegard-Gebetbuch', pp. 156–58.

[29] *Expo. Euang.*, 3 and 4 on John 6. 1–14; fol. 24ʳ; Klemm, 'Der Bilderzyklus im Hildegard-Gebetbuch', pp. 160–64.

[30] *Expo. Euang.*, 49 and 50 on Mark 7. 31–37; fol. 30ʳ; Klemm, 'Der Bilderzyklus im Hildegard-Gebetbuch', pp. 172–74.

[31] *Expo. Euang.*, 32 and 33 on Mark 16. 14–20; fol. 69ʳ; Klemm, 'Der Bilderzyklus im Hildegard-Gebetbuch', pp. 255–58.

illustrates texts from the Old Testament that Hildegard often adduces as part of her exegesis: Genesis 1. 1–31;[32] the Fall;[33] the expulsion;[34] the offering of Abraham;[35] and the burning bush.[36] Various scenes in the *Prayerbook* represent additional miracles of Christ and the passion,[37] but those scriptural passages do not occupy Hildegard's attention in the *Expositiones*. The *Gebetbuch* offers significant parallels for the theology of history in Hildegard's era, as it was expressed visually and in the performative texts of the prayers.

Nearly contemporary with Hildegard's writings, the *Hortus deliciarum* constitutes a compilation of texts and images that Herrad, in Fiona Griffiths's words, wove 'together into a coherent and carefully structured presentation of salvation history'. Unlike Hildegard, with her subtle and at first glance imperceptible use of patristic and medieval authors, Herrad compiled more than eleven hundred excerpts from her predecessors and contemporaries, identified most of them, and described them as the 'diverse flowers of sacred Scripture and philosophical writings'. Herrad clearly relied on the works of Honorius Augustodunensis, but she adapted them to her own purposes.[38]

What parallels from Hildegard's predecessors and contemporaries prove fruitful to the analysis of the *magistra*'s paradigm of history in the *Expositiones*? She does use terminology that derives from Augustinian thought, when she refers to time *ante legem*, to *uetera lex* and *noua lex*, and she speaks of Christ's extension or effusion of *gratia*.[39] Generally, Hildegard distinguishes three eras of history. She

---

[32] Fol. 1ʳ; Klemm, 'Der Bilderzyklus im Hildegard-Gebetbuch', pp. 100–09.

[33] Fol. 4ʳ; Klemm, 'Der Bilderzyklus im Hildegard-Gebetbuch', pp. 114–16.

[34] Fol. 6ʳ; Klemm, 'Der Bilderzyklus im Hildegard-Gebetbuch', pp. 118–19.

[35] Fol. 8ʳ; Klemm, 'Der Bilderzyklus im Hildegard-Gebetbuch', pp. 122–24.

[36] Fol. 9ʳ; Klemm, 'Der Bilderzyklus im Hildegard-Gebetbuch', pp. 125–27.

[37] These are described by Klemm, 'Der Bilderzyklus im Hildegard-Gebetbuch', pp. 219–40.

[38] Herrad cast herself as author in her prologue and does not identify the sources there, but she does label the excerpts with headings that give the titles and / or names of the authors, such as *Ex sententiis Petri Lombardi*, or *Rupertus*. See Griffiths, *Garden of Delights*, pp. 64–72, on the influence of Honorius and Rupert.

[39] References to time *ante legem* occur in *Expo. Euang.*, 41, p. 301, lines 1–2: '*Elisabeth*, id est Abel, Noe et Enoch, et aliorum iustorum qui ante legem erant'; line 18: '*Et respondens mater eius, uetus iusticia quae ante legem erat*'; lines 21–22: '*Et dixerunt in ueteri lege ad illam*, scilicet ad illos qui ante legem fuerunt'. Hildegard speaks of the *noua lex* in *Expo. Euang.*, 41, p. 302, lines 41–44: '*Et posuerunt omnes*, nouos sensus et intellectus in noua lege, *qui* audierunt bona intentione, *in corde suo dicentes*, scilicet in bonis desideriis. *Quis putas puer iste erit* in noua lege, quia non est de mundo?' On *gratia*, see *Expo. Euang.*, 58, p. 331, lines 1–2: '*Egressus Iesus*, scilicet filius Dei, uenit in

arguably combines the Augustinian *ante legem* and *sub lege*, or the first five of six ages, into one period reaching from the creation to the incarnation. The second era evident in the *Expositiones*, one that begins at the incarnation and includes the present, recalls but does not equate to the Augustinian time *sub gratia*. The latter corresponds to the sixth age as delineated by Augustine and extends from the incarnation until the end of time. When Hildegard divides the present into a distinct third age, she joins other twelfth-century thinkers who carve out a space in the Augustinian *sub gratia* in order to focus on their contemporary audience. Hildegard accents the present, where the drama of the individual sinner unfolds.[40] The last days stand apart as an era yet to come, rather than a distant or not so distant extension of present time. Moreover, the notion of the world's current decrepitude influenced Hildegard's description of the slackening and wavering of righteousness at the time when she was born.[41]

After considering the thought of the *magistra*'s predecessors and near contemporaries, I suggest that, after Augustine, the most influential concept for Hildegard's thought and exegesis on the theology of history proves to be Rupert of Deutz's threefold, Trinitarian division of history. That will be further evident when we examine the *magistra*'s exegesis of Luke 19. 41–47: she composes three homilies and highlights the work of the Creator in the first, the Redeemer in the second, and the Spirit in the third. Moreover, Rupert extended into the present the third age of the Holy Spirit, comparable to Augustine's period *sub gratia*.[42] Hildegard too saw the Spirit at work through grace in current time, and her view of the Holy Spirit as the guiding force behind history probably owes much to Rupert.[43]

---

admonitione Spiritus Sancti, *perambulabat*, scilicet gratia sua perfudit'; p. 332, lines 21–24: '*Et cum uenisset*, filius Dei, *ad locum*, id est cum uidisset conuersationem illius malam esse, *suspiciens* gratia sua *Iesus* Christus *uidit illum*, ita ut per misericordiam suam illum nollet derelinquere'; *Expo. Euang.*, 3, pp. 194–95, lines 8–11: 'et alia multa miracula *quae* Christus *faciebat* per discipulos suos et alios fideles *super his qui infirmabantur*, ubi desuper gratiam suam misit ad istos qui prius infirmi in fide erant, ita quod postea in baptismo sanati sunt'.

[40] Compare Irimbert's homilies on Ruth. See Beach, 'Multiform Grace of the Holy Spirit'.

[41] *V. Hild.*, II.2, p. 22, lines 41–44; *Life of Hildegard*, pp. 43–44.

[42] Van Engen, *Rupert of Deutz*, pp. 90–93, on *De sancta Trinitate*, asserts that Rupert's work, leaving aside polemical writings on the *filioque* clause, was the first 'separate treatment of the Holy Spirit in the West', and that it marked a new piety focused on the work of the Spirit in Christian life. In Rupert's view, monks followed in the line of the apostles and occupied their place during the present age.

[43] Arduini, *Rupert von Deutz*, pp. 247, 308–22, 422, asserts the influence of Rupert's exegesis on Gerhoch of Reichersberg and Hildegard, in particular the visionary, prophetic origin of his

Salvation History and the Trinity in the Expositiones

How do the *Expositiones* frame and divide salvation history with a Trinitarian emphasis? Most of the homilies belong to sets that expound dual interpretations of the scriptural text: the first reading elaborates a lesson on salvation history and the second teaches a moral lesson, as for the parable of the labourers in the vineyard (Mt 20. 1–16), where Hildegard devotes one homily to the creation story and another to the soul.[44] However, for this pericope and others, the biblical text constitutes one of three parts of Hildegard's narrative; the two sets of commentary frame the biblical text in such a way that a threefold, Trinitarian view emerges: the Gospel corresponds to the time of the incarnation, while the first interpretation looks back in history, as to the creation, and the second provides moral lessons for the present. In that way, Hildegard's method itself bespeaks Trinitarian theology.[45]

A triad of homilies on Luke 19. 41–47, the story of Jesus expelling the money changers, shows Hildegard setting forth a decidedly Trinitarian interpretation of the gospel text.[46] The first *expositio* offers a panorama of salvation history from the moment of creation to the time of Christ's teaching; the second focuses on the incarnation, and the third on the individual sinner. The person of Jesus represents in turn the Creator, the Redeemer, and the Holy Spirit. Hildegard highlights the creation and fall of humankind as she gives a voice to the lamenting Creator who made the human in his own image and likeness. As Jesus wept (Lk 19. 41), God

---

scriptural understanding. Christel Meier asserts that Eriugena's Trinitarian thought, as well as his concept of the *propheta theologus*, influenced each of Hildegard's visionary works and the structure of the trilogy. See also Christel Meier, 'Scientia divinorum operum: Zu Hildegards von Bingen visionär-künstlerischer Rezeption Eriugenas', in *Eriugena redivivus: Zur Wirkungsgeschichte seines Denkens im Mittelalter und in Übergang zur Neuzeit: Vorträge des V. Internationalen Eriugena-Colloquiums, Werner-Reimers-Stiftung Bad Homburg, 26.–30. August 1985*, ed. by W. Beierwaltes (Heidelberg: Carl Winter Universitätsverlag, 1987), pp. 89–141.

[44] *Expo. Euang.*, 22, 23, pp. 245–51.

[45] For another example of the multi-temporal mode of Hildegard's thinking, see *Expo. Euang.*, 27, p. 266, lines 42–43, on the parable of the prodigal son, Luke 15. 11–32, where the phrase *cecedit super collum eius* ('he embraced him'; lit: he fell upon his neck, Lk 15. 20) prompts her to adduce simultaneous examples from the history of the patriarchs and from the New Testament: the embrace of Jacob and Esau as well as others (Gn 33. 4 and others) enters into the parallel she draws between the father of the parable's greeting to his son and Gabriel's salutation of Mary at the annunciation. Through the phenomenon of reminiscence, the gospel text brings to Hildegard's mind both an earlier gospel passage and similar scenes of greeting from the Old Testament. I am grateful to Kyle Highful for identifying this echo of Jacob and Esau in the homily.

[46] *Expo. Euang.*, 46–48, pp. 311–15.

weeps when he expresses foreknowledge of human death and trangression of his command in Genesis 2. 16–17: 'From every tree of paradise you may eat'.[47] The human, driven into exile and alienated from God, experiences night, death, and hardships 'like a strong wind'. Hildegard interprets Jesus's act of driving out the money changers (Lk 19. 45) as an event that alters the course of history: God made the human being a temple and drove out unbelief and illicit desires. The 'house of prayer' (Lk 19. 46) signifies the chastity and holiness that should exist in the human, while the 'den of robbers' (Lk 19. 46) denotes the fraud and falsehood fabricated by the Devil.[48]

The second homily, crucial for understanding Hildegard's views on exegesis, has an incarnational focus: the *magistra* explains Jesus's transformation of the law and the understanding of the Scriptures. Hildegard depicts Christ weeping over the edifice of the old law,[49] which contrasts with the edifice of revelation and truth.[50] The *magistra* explains that Jesus and subsequently the 'doctors of the New Testament' changed the old into the new spiritual meaning.[51] Hildegard reads the act of driving out the money changers (Lk 19. 45) as the Gospel's expulsion of avarice, idols, and other 'filthy things'.[52] Thus she situates the spiritual interpretation of

---

[47] *Expo. Euang.*, 46, p. 311, lines 1–7: 'Cum appropinquaret Iesus, id est Deus, Ierusalem, scilicet ad creationem illam, ut creaturas creare uellet, *uidens ciuitatem*, uidelicet hominem, *fleuit super illam*, ubi intima dilectione hominem ad imaginem et similitudinem suam fecit, *dicens: Quia si cognouisses et tu*, quae ego scio, precaueres tibi mortem, quia si aliud quam me quesieris, peribis, cum dixit: *Ex omni ligno paradysi comede, de ligno autem scientiae boni et mali ne comedas.*'

[48] *Expo. Euang.*, 46, pp. 311–12, lines 25–29: '*domus mea*, scilicet homo, *domus orationis est*, quia in eo castitas et sanctitas esse deberent. *Vos autem*, qui peruersi estis, *fecistis illam speluncam latronum*, quoniam fraus et mendacium a diabolo factum est'.

[49] *Expo. Euang.*, 47, p. 312, lines 2–6: 'Iesus [. . .] *uidens ciuitatem*, uidelicet omnem edifica- tionem ueteris legis ab Abel usque ad se, *fleuit*, ita ut educeret fontem sapientiae, *super illam*, scilicet super omnes litteras et institutiones eius.'

[50] *Expo. Euang.*, 47, p. 313, lines 28–38: '*Scriptum est*, in spiritali transmutatione et interpreta- tione, *quia domus mea*, id est edificatio reuelationis, *domus orationis est*, scilicet ueritatis, quia nec celum, nec terra alium Deum preter me ostendunt, sed edificatio mea in qua me inuenietis, ostendit uobis ueritatem. [. . .] *Et erat docens cottidie in templo*; quia ipse filius Dei in ista apparitione nouae edificationis et interpretationis antiquae legis ad spiritalem intellectum procedit usque in finem in ecclesia.'

[51] *Expo. Euang.*, 47, p. 312, lines 13–16: 'doctores noui testamenti doctrina sua, ut Gregorius, Ambrosius, Augustinus, Ieronimus, et alii similes, *et coangustabunt te undique*, scilicet reuertendo in spiritalem significationem'.

[52] *Expo. Euang.*, 47, p. 313, lines 26–27: 'idola et alias spurcicias, quas homines pro Deo habebant'.

Scripture in the broad context of the transformation of word, worship, and carnality. The old and new buildings correspond to the transformation of the old writings and understanding into the new spiritual meaning of Scripture. The building of the new edifice requires the transmutation of the old stones into new.[53] The cleansing process of penitence evokes a sort of deconstruction of sin, with no stone remaining in place.[54]

Homily three focuses on the individual sinner and the drama of her conversion from sin to righteousness, from vices to virtues, from the thieves' den to the temple (Lk 19. 47), where angels and saints openly and joyously praise the repentant sinner. Hildegard casts Jesus weeping (Lk 19. 41) as the Holy Spirit lamenting that the human does not see dangers. The Spirit speaks with imagery that stems from patristic sources and from the everyday world of the Rhineland: 'If only you had recognized the dangers', the Spirit exclaims to the human, 'you would press yourself like a wine press, and like a mill, you would turn yourself here and there.'[55] The metaphors of the wine press and the mill operate on more than one level of association: the biblical and patristic image with its rich symbolism pointed to the

---

[53] *Expo. Euang.*, 47, p. 313, lines 19–21: '*Et non relinquent lapidem*, id est nullam litteram, nec iota unum, nec ullam culturam tuam, *super lapidem*, nisi mutetur.'

[54] *Expo. Euang.*, 48, p. 314, lines 18–20: '*Et non relinquent lapidem super lapidem*, quia penitentia ita penetrabit te, ut nullum uicium, nec ullam spurciciam dimittet, quin omnia a te abstergat.' In the *Expositiones* and 'O uos felices radices', Hildegard describes Christ as a whetstone that files away sin. See *Expo. Euang.*, 35, pp. 384–85, lines 48–50: '*Tu es magister*, id est faber, qui omnia limas, *in Israel*, quae limanda sunt, et *haec ignoras*, quia quid est quod limas, nisi quod nescis?' *Symph.* 32, p. 418, lines 1–9: 'O uos felices radices [...] et o tu ruminans ignea uox, | precurrens limantem lapidem | subuertentem abyssum'. The letters employ the cornerstone image: *Epistolarium*, I, 25R, p. 71, lines 1–2: 'O tu persona [...] statum tuum nunc uideo uelut duos parietes quasi angulari lapide coniunctos'; *Epistolarium*, I, 40R, p. 105, line 43: 'ut etiam uiuus lapis sis in lapide angulari'. On the whetstone image in 'O uos felices radices', see Peter Dronke, 'Hildegard's Inventions: Aspects of her Language and Imagery', in *Umfeld*, pp. 299–320 (pp. 311–12).

[55] *Expo. Euang.*, 48, p. 314, lines 7–8: 'ut torcular te comprimeres, et ut molendinum te hac et illac uerteres'. Both images appear in patristic texts and in Hildegard's other works. For a few examples of *torcular*, see *Epistolarium*, I, 77R, p. 179, lines 77–79; *Sciuias*, I.3, p. 59, lines 627–28; *Sciuias*, I.4, p. 62, lines 99–100; *Sciuias*, III.8, p. 497, lines 674–76; Augustine of Hippo, *Enarrationes in psalmos*, ed. by E. Dekkers and J. Fraipont, CCSL, 38–40 (Turnhout: Brepols, 1956), Ps. LV, 4, p. 680, lines 44–45; Rupert of Deutz, *De sancta trinitate*, 23, In Libros regum, II, p. 1250, lines 442–43; and additional sources in the apparatus criticus, *Expo. Euang.*, 48, p. 314. For *molendinum*, see *Epistolarium*, I, 25R, p. 72, lines 46–48; Augustine, *Enarrationes in psalmos*, Ps. 36, sermo 1, 2, line 25: 'et molendinum puto dictum mundum istum; quia rota quadam temporum uoluitur, et amatores suos conterit'; and other examples in the apparatus criticus, *Expo. Euang.*, 48, p. 314.

visual and concrete presence of the numerous vineyards and the mill owned by the Rupertsberg community.[56]

The *magistra* states that the 'reddening light' of repentance will descend on the human, a patristic image that she employs in *Sciuias*.[57] This light surrounding the human produces tears of weeping and sighs, frequent markers of repentance in Hildegard's writings and an echo of the *Rule of Benedict*.[58] Made strong in faith, the heart was formerly a brothel because of the Devil's temptation.[59] The seer underscores the antithesis between the prideful and the faithful heart with sexual metaphors of the brothel and of the lustful who associate with harlots. Jesus chasing the money changers from the temple (Lk 19. 45) represents casting out pride from the heart of those who draw lust to themselves with harlots, and the den of thieves (Lk 19. 47) represents the heart that, under the sway of the Devil, was formerly a brothel.[60] This strong imagery colours the sin of pride with connotations of sexual wantonness. One can imagine that Hildegard's lament for dangers not foreseen reflects tension in her monastery and perhaps her anguish at Richardis's departure, for the *magistra* likewise decries the attraction of pride in other texts related to her friend's election as abbess at Bassum.

---

[56] *Jutta and Hildegard*, trans. by Silvas, pp. 238, 241, on donations to Rupertsberg. Hildegard mentions the wine press in *V. Rup.*, *PL* 197: 1089B.

[57] *Expo. Euang.*, 48, p. 314, lines 13–14; *Sciuias*, II.1, p. 118, lines 285–86, *Scivias* (Eng.), p. 154; *Sciuias*, II.2, p. 124, lines 13–20, *Scivias* (Eng.), p. 161; *Sciuias*, II.3, p. 135, lines 79–82, *Scivias* (Eng.), p. 169. The image appears in Ambrose and Jerome: Ambrose of Milan, *De Noe*, ed. by C. Schenkl, CSEL, 32.1 (Vienna, 1897), 27, 103, p. 484, line 11: 'diuersi tamquam radiorum solis nunc rutilantium'; Jerome, *Commentarii in Ezechielem libri XIV*, ed. by F. Glorie, CCSL, 75 (Turnhout: Brepols, 1964), I, i, p. 13, line 266: 'scintillas rutilantes'.

[58] Saint Benedict, *Regula*, 4, 57–58, p. 35: 'Mala sua praeterita cum lacrymis vel gemitu quotidie in oratione Deo confiteri, de ipsis malis de caetero emendare.' See also *Expo. Euang.*, 13, p. 223, line 1: 'in gemitibus et lacrimis'.

[59] *Expo. Euang.*, 46, pp. 311–12, lines 25–29: '*Scriptum est* in uera demonstratione, *quia domus mea*, scilicet homo, *domus orationis est*, quia in eo castitas et sanctitas esse deberent. *Vos autem*, qui peruersi estis, *fecistis illam speluncam latronum*, quoniam fraus et mendacium a diabolo factum est.'

[60] *Expo. Euang.*, 48, p. 315, lines 23–32: '*Et ingressus in templum*, ita ut admonitio Spiritus Sancti ingrediatur in cor hominis, *cepit eicere uendentes in illo*, scilicet fugat superbiam a corde hominis illius, *et ementes*, uidelicet illos qui libidinem per scorta sibi adtraxerunt, *dicens illis*: *Scriptum est*, id est firmatum est, *quia domus mea*, cor hominis, *domus orationis est*, uidelicet cultura angelorum et exemplum sanctorum hic erit. *Vos autem*, in iniquitate uestra, *fecistis illam speluncam latronum*, quia olim lupanar fuit in suggestione diaboli. *Et erat docens cottidie in templo*, ita ut aperte facta sit laus angelorum et gaudium populorum in homine illo.'

Does Hildegard's reading of this pericope show any debt to her predecessors? She concurs in some respects with earlier exegesis, particularly the reading of Gregory the Great, who includes a moral interpretation touching on the theme of conversion.[61] Bede follows and develops this, but neither Gregory nor Bede relates the passage to the creation or to the spiritual interpretation of Scripture, as Hildegard does. Furthermore, to my knowledge, no earlier writer including Ambrose develops a threefold, Trinitarian interpretation of the pericope.[62] The *magistra* clearly, and I assume purposefully, shapes her reading to demonstrate the working of the Trinity in salvation history.

Hildegard devotes three homilies to two other pericopes: Luke 5. 1–11, the miraculous catch, and John 3. 1–15, the story of Nicodemus.[63] A Trinitarian theological and exegetical frame becomes especially clear in the homilies on Luke 5. 1–11.[64] In the first homily in the set, Hildegard views salvation history briefly: beginning with creation, she describes the human's endowment with the knowledge of good and evil, the Fall, and Christ's coming to open the path to good works and the heavenly Jerusalem. For the second homily, the *magistra* starts from the incarnation and treats the turning from the old law to the new in the Gospel, when humankind accepts belief in Christ's dual nature and subjects itself to God's commands. In the third homily, Hildegard dramatizes the virtues' role in conversion and victory over the Devil.

The *magistra* interprets key elements in this biblical narrative consistently and tersely. The crowds (Lk 5. 1) in the three homilies represent respectively the substance of created beings, the Scriptures, and the virtues.[65] Correspondingly, the character of Jesus stands for God the Creator, God incarnate, and the virtue of fortitude.[66] The two boats (Lk 5. 2) designate in the first homily the elements and

---

[61] Gregory the Great, *Homiliae in euangelia*, II, 39, which figures in the lectionary of Cluny. Étaix, 'Le Lectionnaire de l'office à Cluny', no. 155, p. 109.

[62] See Ambrose, *Expositio euangelii secundum Lucam*, IX.16–18, p. 337; Gregory the Great, *Homiliae in euangelia*, II, 39, pp. 383–85; Bede, *In Lucae euangelium*, lib. 5, p. 349; and Gottfried of Admont, *Homiliae dominicales*, 76, *PL* 174: 542–49.

[63] *Expo. Euang.*, 43–45 (Lk 5. 1–11), pp. 305–10; 34–36 (Jn 3. 1–15), pp. 283–92.

[64] See Beverly Mayne Kienzle, 'Hildegard of Bingen's Exegesis of Luke', in *Early Christian Voices in Texts, Traditions, and Symbols: Essays in Honor of François Bovon*, ed. by David H. Warren, Ann Graham Brock, and David W. Pao (Boston: Brill, 2003), pp. 227–38.

[65] *Expo. Euang.*, 43, p. 305, line 1; *Expo. Euang.*, 44, p. 307, line 1; *Expo. Euang.*, 45, p. 309, line 1.

[66] *Expo. Euang.*, 43, p. 305, line 2; *Expo. Euang.*, 44, p. 307, lines 1–2; *Expo. Euang.*, 45, p. 309, line 2.

other created things, in the second, the dual nature of Christ, and in the third, conversion and salvation.[67] Simon Peter (Lk 5. 3 and others) denotes the human being at creation, the incarnated Son, and finally, the righteous.[68] Lowering the nets (Lk 5. 4–6) first indicates the human's transgression of divine commandments in paradise, then Jesus's converting his disciples to the Gospel, and third, the righteous human's recourse to the virtues for assistance.[69] Hildegard's parallel narratives end on a positive note in all three homilies. Following Jesus means in the first homily following the Gospel; in the second case, it indicates that believers subject themselves to God's commands; in the third, sadness turns into joy for the righteous, who persevere in fortitude with God.[70]

Does Hildegard's reading follow the exegetical tradition for this pericope? In fact, her interpretations of the miraculous catch depart from the ecclesiological readings of Ambrose, Gregory the Great, Bede, and other exegetes; in that strand, the boat represents the Church and Peter designates its obedient leader, the fishermen stand for doctors of the Church or preachers, and their nets signify the *apostolica instrumenta*, especially the subtle preaching that hauls in sinners to Christ.[71] The liturgical reading of Bede's commentary on Luke disseminated that model widely.[72] The *magistra*'s contemporary Irimbert of Admont offers a moral interpretation: the two boats stand for the inner and outer human being, and the boats' coming ashore signifies the sinners' conversion.[73] However, the Admont

---

[67] *Expo. Euang.*, 43, p. 305, line 6; *Expo. Euang.*, 44, p. 307, lines 6–7; *Expo. Euang.*, 45, p. 309, line 5.

[68] *Expo. Euang.*, 43, p. 305, line 11; *Expo. Euang.*, 44, p. 307, line 13; *Expo. Euang.*, 45, p. 309, line 11.

[69] *Expo. Euang.*, 43, p. 305, lines 18–19; *Expo. Euang.*, 44, p. 307, lines 20–22; *Expo. Euang.*, 45, p. 309, lines 17–18.

[70] *Expo. Euang.*, 43, p. 306, lines 57–58; *Expo. Euang.*, 44, p. 308, line 58; *Expo. Euang.*, 45, p. 310, lines 51–52.

[71] Ambrose, *Expositio euangelii secundum Lucam*, 68–72, pp. 131–33; Gregory the Great, *Homiliae in euangelia*, II, 24, p. 199, lines 62–75; Bede, *In Lucae euangelium*, 2, 5, pp. 113–14; Heiric of Auxerre, *Homiliae*, pars aestiua, II. 21, pp. 193–94, lines 77–116. *Glossa Ordinaria*, IV, 156–57, follows the same vein and cites Bede frequently.

[72] Bede, *In Lucae euangelium*, 2.5 is the reading in Paul the Deacon and the Cluny lectionary. See Grégoire, *Homéliaires liturgiques médiévaux*, no. II, 57, p. 463; and Étaix, 'Le Lectionnaire de l'office à Cluny', no. 150, p. 108.

[73] Gottfried of Admont, *Homiliae dominicales*, 66, *PL* 174: 463A–B, builds a portion of its commentary on this pericope from an allegory of the days of creation, but does not resemble

homily applies Peter's act of throwing himself at Jesus's knees in confession of sin (Lk 5. 8) to a lesson on the proper conduct between prelates and their subordinates.[74] For the same verse, Hildegard continues her allegory of conversion and sees Peter as the righteous, who cast themselves before God and acknowledge their sin.[75] Hildegard does not adopt such a hermeneutical framework, which particularly suited a male clerical audience, in any of her three *expositiones* on Luke 5. 1–11. Instead she emphasizes the workings of the Trinity in salvation history.

Are there parallels for Hildegard's exegetical interpretation of the Trinity in her other works? She expresses her theology of the Trinity in the text and illustrations of *Sciuias* and the *Liber diuinorum operum*. Four visions in *Sciuias* and two in the *Liber diuinorum operum* concern the Trinity. Bernard McGinn discusses three images that accompany those visions. Two Trinitarian illustrations of *Sciuias* comprise the pillar with three edges that designate the three persons of the Trinity and the sapphire-coloured Christ who stands with two circles that represent God and the Holy Spirit. In the *Liber diuinorum operum*, one illustration depicts divine love as a human figure holding a lamb and having two heads, one that extends from the other, and two pair of wings. McGinn explains that Hildegard's iconography reveals that she was fascinated with 'the economic Trinity, that is, the Trinity revealed in history', but she had 'little interest in the inner life of the Trinity'. The concern with Trinitarian mysticism becomes evident in the later Middle Ages. Hildegard, like her contemporary Joachim of Fiore, who made an elaborate drawing of the 'ten-stringed psaltery' to represent the Trinity, 'was more concerned with showing the action of the triune God in the history of salvation than in trying to manifest how humans during this life can share in the hidden inner life of the Father, Son, and Holy Spirit'.[76] McGinn's analysis of the *magistra*'s iconographic emphasis on the workings of the Trinity in history reinforces what I observe about the homilies and their textual representation of the intervention of the three persons of the Trinity in history.

Hildegard's analysis in form or content. The Admont author departs from the liturgical timing of the homily, the fifth Sunday of Pentecost, to discuss the first five days of God's creative work.

[74] Gottfried of Admont, *Homiliae dominicales*, 66, *PL* 174: 466A. See also Homily 67, on II Kings 7, *PL* 174: 467D–468A, 470B, on the responsibility of priests and prelates.

[75] *Expo. Euang.*, 45, p. 310, lines 35–38: '*Quod cum uideret Simon Petrus*, scilicet iusti, *procidit ad genua Iesu, dicens*, cum se prosternunt ad Deum: *Exi a me*, quia non sumus digni cum Deo esse, *quia peccator sum, Domine*, quoniam in tam magna contaminatione sumus.'

[76] McGinn, 'Theologians as Trinitarian Iconographers', pp. 187–95.

From Creation to Antichrist: Matthew 4. 1–11

Hildegard more often offers pairs of interpretations rather than triads. Do those dual *expositiones* still reflect her Trinitarian view of history? To begin answering that question, I look first to an *expositio* on Matthew 4. 1–11, where Hildegard covers the entire span of salvation history. Given the complexity of the biblical narrative and the story of its reception, I shall consider possible debts to earlier exegesis as the pericope unfolds. The homily on Matthew 4. 1–11 stretches ambitiously from the creation to the last days and the coming of Antichrist. Hildegard explains that Jesus going into the wilderness (Mt 4. 1) signifies the Word of the Father being led by the Holy Spirit into the substance of created beings, even before they were differentiated by species and function.[77] The emphasis in this context on Christ's role at the creation may seem distinctive, and in fact, it has little exegetical precedent.[78] In contrast, when the *magistra* asserts that the Holy Spirit led Christ to fast in the wilderness so that he could manifest his divinity, she follows Gregory the Great and other commentators. Hildegard emphasizes, as does Gregory, that the temptation of Christ could occur only outwardly, through hearing, and not inwardly.[79]

The forty days of the fast (Mt 4. 2) indicate that after Adam's expulsion, his children up to Noah did not fully honour God. The forty nights (Mt 4. 2) signify

---

[77] *Expo. Euang.*, 24, p. 254, lines 74–79: '*Qui respondens dixit: Scriptum est: Non in solo pane uiuit homo*, panem comedens, *sed in omni uerbo*, Dei, quod ego sum, *quod procedit de ore Dei*, id est cum ceteris etiam creaturis, quae per uerbum Dei creatae sunt, cum dixit Deus: Fiat lux, et *fiant luminaria*, et reliquae creaturae, quia cum eis et cum elementis homo uiuit.' *Expo. Euang.*, 25, p. 257, lines 1–6: '*Ductus est Iesus*, scilicet uerbum patris, per quod omnia creata sunt, *in desertum*, id est materiam creaturarum, ante quam creaturae per species distinctae essent, et ante quam quicquam operarentur: *a Spiritu*, uidelicet a Spiritu Sancto qui omnia uiuificat, quoniam pater est aeternitas, filius per quem omnia creantur, Spiritus Sanctus per quem omnia uiuificantur.' See also *Expo. Euang.*, 24, p. 252, line 11.

[78] Heiric of Auxerre cites Genesis 1. 3, 'Fiat lux', in connection with Jesus's response to the first temptation; *Homiliae*, pars hiemalis, I, 28, p. 232, lines 146–47. Compare other sources in the apparatus fontium, *Expo. Euang.*, 24, p. 254.

[79] *Expo. Euang.*, 24, p. 252, lines 7–8: '*ut temptaretur a diabolo*, solo scilicet auditu diabolo ad eum loquente, non alio modo'. Gregory the Great, *Homiliae in euangelia*, I, 16, p. 111, lines 28–29: 'temptatio foris non intus fuit'. Paul the Deacon has Gregory I, 16, as does the Cluny lectionary. See Grégoire, *Homéliaires liturgiques médiévaux*, no. 76, p. 444; Étaix, 'Le Lectionnaire de l'office à Cluny', no. 65, p. 101. See additional sources in apparatus fontium, *Expo. Euang.*, 24, p. 252; and *Glossa Ordinaria*, IV, marg., p. 13: 'Ut tentaretur: Non tentatur a dyabolo, nisi qui ad desertum exierit id est bono studere ceperit.'

nights of sin, much like the seer's depiction of night in the illumination for *Sciuias* II.1: Adam's fall.[80] In this homily, Adam's children, sullied by the four elements, had not yet observed the Ten Commandments.[81] The *magistra* borrows the numerology and the Christ-Adam parallel from Gregory the Great and other exegetes. Within the compass of the four elements, from Adam's fall all the way to Noah, the Devil accomplished all his evils in humankind before the flood.[82] With the flood, God purged the earth of those sullied creatures, and afterwards, God restored humankind. Righteousness returned, but the Devil began to threaten that righteousness with idols and phantasms.[83]

The three temptations in Hildegard's interpretation correspond to errors promulgated in three phases of history: idol worship, false beliefs, and deceptions of the Devil. She eschews the trio of vices that most exegetes adduce — gluttony, vainglory, and avarice — and limits herself to explaining temptation number two as vainglory.[84] Hildegard renders the first temptation (Mt 4. 3) as the Devil telling Christ to work by his own command as God did, when 'He commanded and they were made'.[85] The Devil explains that he brought about the making of many idols,

---

[80] *Sciuias*, II.1, pp. 110–12, esp. lines 60–61; p. 117, lines 254–58.

[81] *Expo. Euang.*, 25, p. 257, lines 12–14: 'quia etiam in quatuor elementis uelut in noctibus peccatorum sordebant, cum nondum decem precepta legis perceperant'. Gregory the Great, *Homiliae in euangelia*, I, 16, p. 113, lines 90–96. See additional sources in apparatus fontium, *Expo. Euang.*, 25, p. 257. *Glossa Ordinaria*, IV, 113, marginal glosses, includes four parts of the world, ten precepts of the law; decalogue, four Gospels.

[82] *Expo. Euang.*, 25, p. 257, lines 10–20. The compass recalls the explanatory text of *Sciuias*, III.2, which enumerates Adam, Noah, Abraham, and Moses: *Sciuias*, III.2.7, pp. 354–55, lines 215–37.

[83] *Expo. Euang.*, 25, pp. 257–58, lines 20–23: '*Et accedens* per multas uanitates *temptator*, scilicet diabolus, ad homines, quia cum iusticiam post diluuium apparere uideret, idola et multa fantasmata aduersum eandem iustitiam facere cepit.'

[84] *Expo. Euang.*, 24, p. 255, lines 94–98: 'Sed diabolus, quia spiritus fuit, illa spiritaliter apparentia uidit, sciens illa quae ibi uidebat, ad Christum respicere, et artibus suis temptauit, si magnifica opera illa ullo modo in Christo per uanam gloriam impedire posset.' See additional sources in apparatus fontium, *Expo. Euang.*, 24, p. 255. *Glossa Ordinaria*, IV, 13–14, interlinear glosses note *gula*, *vanagloria*, and *avaricia*; marginal signals *gula*, *avaricia*, and *superbia*. On specific sins, see Richard Newhauser, *The Treatise on Vices and Virtues in Latin and the Vernacular*, Typologie des Sources du Moyen Âge Occidental, 68 (Turnhout: Brepols, 1993); Morton Bloomfield, *The Seven Deadly Sins: An Introduction to the History of a Religious Concept, with Special Reference to Medieval English Literature* (East Lansing: Michigan State College Press, 1952); and Donald Howard, *The Three Temptations: Medieval Man in Search of the World* (Princeton: Princeton University Press, 1966).

[85] Ps 32. 9: 'quoniam ipse dixit et facta sunt, ipse mandauit et creata sunt'.

and he tells Jesus to make other rituals, so that he will be worshipped like God.[86] In Hildegard's view, the Devil wanted to ridicule God.[87] Hildegard lends Jesus a reply that underscores her theology of the creation and disputes the beliefs of the Cathars: God created all visible things and the Creator is known through the creation.[88]

Hildegard interprets the holy city in the second temptation (Mt 4. 5) as the Jewish people, who received the law.[89] The *magistra* casts the Jews in an implicit alliance with the Devil here, asserting that the Devil set many traps for Jesus on earth through the Jewish people. This anti-Jewish reading may derive from Gregory, who questions whether Pilate, Jesus's Jewish persecutors, or the soldiers who crucified Christ were not members of the Devil (*diaboli membra*), a reading that establishes a rhetorical and theological counter-model to the members of Christ's body.[90] Hildegard's explicit association of the Devil and the Jews occurs nowhere else in the *Expositiones*. In fact, the *magistra* generally eschews the many typological characterizations of the Jews where the exegetical tradition opposes them to the Gentiles.[91] I signal those homilies as a topic for further research, as their full study would require a thorough investigation of the tradition and of the same pericopes in the *magistra*'s other works.

For the third temptation, Hildegard interprets the high mountain (Mt 4. 8) as a mountain of error, whose height extends to the edge of the windstorm in

[86] *Expo. Euang.*, 25, pp. 257–58, lines 20–23. See Rupert of Deutz, *De sancta trinitate*, 23, *In Euangelistas*, p. 1796, lines 556–58: 'pagani [. . .] diabolum in simulacris adoraverunt'. In *Expo. Euang.*, 24, p. 254, lines 68–73, Hildegard alludes to the miracle at Cana: 'Sed quod filius Dei aquam in uinum conuertit, hoc naturae contrarium non fuit, quia uinum sicut et aqua madidum est et fluit, ei ideo aqua saporem suum tantum mutauit; lapides autem si panes facti fuissent, omnino naturam suam perdidissent: sed et idcirco panes, quia primus et fortior cibus esurientium est.' See additional sources in the apparatus fontium, *Expo. Euang.*, 24, p. 254.

[87] *Expo. Euang.*, 25, p. 258, line 30: 'Et hoc Deum deridendo dixit.'

[88] *Expo. Euang.*, 25, p. 258, lines 34–36: 'per creaturam creator cognoscitur et quod summus eam creauerit intelligitur [. . .] haec uisibilia a Deo creata esse'.

[89] *Expo. Euang.*, 25, p. 258, lines 40–43: '*Tunc assumpsit eum diabolus in sanctam ciuitatem*, scilicet in iudaicum populum, cui sanctitas legis data fuit, quia cum Christus incarnatus esset et cum iam uerba predicationis suae emitteret, diabolus multas insidias per iudaicum populum ei posuit.'

[90] Gregory the Great, *Homiliae in euangelia*, I, 16, p. 110, lines 12–14.

[91] *Expositiones* that eschew the ethnic interpretive model include Matthew 8. 1–3, healing the leper and the centurion's servant; Luke 15. 11–32, the prodigal son; Luke 16. 19–31, Lazarus and the rich man; Luke 14. 16–21, the great banquet; Luke 18. 10–14, the pharisee and the publican; Luke 16. 1–9, the unjust steward. The boy in John 6. 1–14, the story of the loaves and fishes, provides another example of a figure Hildegard does not interpret as the Jews.

Antichrist. The Devil shows Christ the false deceptions he will use to assail the faithful in the last days. Hildegard asserts that most of humanity from everywhere on earth will turn towards Antichrist and worship him.[92] The Devil tells Christ and the faithful who are members of his body that, if they desert the worship of the Christians, some human beings will worship them as God. The Church, already dejected, will not be able to hold up further. Jesus's command, 'Be gone, Satan!' (Mt 4. 10), prefigures striking down the Antichrist in the last days. Then, Hildegard asserts, the Devil will no longer have any power, and the angels will praise God without end (Mt 4. 11).[93]

While Hildegard follows the lead of patristic exegetes on some points, such as the parallel between Christ and Adam,[94] her emphasis lies on portraying the sweep of salvation history as the setting for this episode in Christ's life. Moreover, Hildegard's accent on creation and on the role of Christ at the creation connects tightly to her lengthy moral advice: she equips her nuns to recognize and combat the Devil, who can send evil spirits out from hell to deceive humans.[95] Gregory's *Moralia in Iob* and earlier sources presuppose the tension that lies in the confrontation between Christ and Satan, who sought to ascertain Christ's nature by tempting him to perform miracles. However, Gregory does not dwell on the means to recognize or avoid the Devil.[96] For Hildegard, Satan not only tempts Christ but

---

[92] *Expo. Euang.*, 25, p. 259, lines 59–65: '*Iterum*, post hanc temptationem, *assumpsit eum*, scilicet Christum in fidelibus membris suis, *in montem excelsum ualde*, id est in montem erroris, qui altitudinem suam usque ad labrum uenti extendet in antichristo, *et ostendit ei* per fallaces deceptiones in quibus fideles homines in nouissimo tempore impugnabit, *omnia regna mundi*, quia de omnibus regnis terrarum maxima pars hominum ad antichristum declinabit.'

[93] *Expo. Euang.*, 25, p. 260, lines 79–82: '*Tunc reliquit eum diabolus*, ita quod nullam potestatem contra Deum ultra eleuabit; *et ecce angeli accesserunt* in plenitudine et perfectione caritatis *et ministrabant ei* in celesti armonia et laude, quoniam sine fine Deum laudabunt.'

[94] The parallel appears more clearly in *Expo. Euang.*, 24, p. 253, lines 24–27: 'Et ante quam temptaretur, ieiunauit, ut uirtus diuinitatis in ipso uideretur et ut per hoc diabolus ad temptandum eum incitaretur, dum cogitaret quis homo ille esset qui tantam fortitudinem in se haberet, quasi diceret: Quid? Ille alius Adam esset?'

[95] *Expo. Euang.*, 24, p. 253, lines 40–46: 'Et ideo temptator dicitur, quia ille fuit qui Adam temptauit, non Lucifer; quoniam ille ex quo cecidit, de loco gehennalis perditionis motus non est, quia tanta fortitudo maliciae in illo est, si egredi permitteretur, quod etiam aerem in aliqua parte euerteret: unde per diuinam potentiam ita comprimitur, ne uoluntatem suam in nequicia sua exercere possit, sed tantum alios ad decipiendum homines emittit.'

[96] Gregory the Great, *Moralia in Iob*, XXXIII, 8, p. 1687, line 52: 'Qui cum deum incarnatum esse dubitaret, hoc expetitis miraculis uoluit temptando cognoscere.' See additional sources in the apparatus fontium, *Expo. Euang.*, 24, p. 253.

also, through his heretical followers, challenges the foundation of the world.[97] The *magistra* heightens the dynamic interplay of the tempter and Christ, and in so doing, she evokes the struggle of humankind throughout history, setting her sisters' preparation for the rigours of Lent in a broad historical context.

Does the *Hildegard-Gebetbuch* offer a significant parallel witness for the exegesis of this pericope? It devotes three scenes and two prayers to the temptations passage; illustrations for the first and second temptations fill one page, while the third temptation occupies the other. The prayer for the first two scenes evokes the exegetical theme that Hildegard nearly eschewed, the link between the three temptations and the three vices of gluttony, vainglory, and avarice.[98] The second prayer beseeches the Lord's aid so that the supplicant may follow God's will and avoid the Devil's temptations and the pains of Hell.[99] The moral message of the gospel passage predominates for the prayers in the *Gebetbuch* as for the *magistra*'s homily. Beyond that, no textual or visual correspondence with Hildegard's reading of the passage is evident.[100] However, both the *Prayerbook* and Hildegard's *Expositiones* seem to develop a longer than usual commentary, written or visual, in order to equip the audience against the Devil. They demonstrate the prevalence of tropological

---

[97] *Expo. Euang.*, 25, p. 258, lines 31–39: '*Qui respondens dixit*, uidelicet uerbum patris: *Scriptum est*, in ueraci scriptura: *Non in solo pane*, id est non in illa sola creatura, qua homo frequenter utitur, uel quae ei subiecta ministrat, quia per creaturam creator cognoscitur, et quod summus eam creauerit intelligitur, *uiuet homo*, ita ut hoc sibi ad salutem sufficiat, quod haec uisibilia a Deo creata esse credat, *sed in omni uerbo*, quod non potest carnalibus oculis uidere, nec manibus palpare, nec sensu capere, *quod procedit*, inuisibiliter, *de ore Dei*, natum ineffabiliter, ita ut ipsum filium Dei et filium hominis ueraciter credant.'

[98] *Gebetbuch*, fols 20^v–21^r.

[99] *Gebetbuch*, fols 21^v–22^r.

[100] The *Drogo Sacramentary*, *c.* 850, fits three scenes into one initial of a prayer. See Mayr-Harting, *Ottonian Book Illumination*, I, 80. Hamburger discusses the three temptations in the Sélestat *liber precum* and the ceiling panel at St Martin in Zillis (*c.* 1130) in 'Before the Book of Hours', pp. 164–65. See Griffiths, *Garden of Delights*, pp. 202–03, on Herrad of Hohenbourg's depiction of the scene in the *Hortus deliciarum*. On the importance of the Lenten theme of the temptations, see Emile Mâle, *The Gothic Image: Religious Art in France of the Thirteenth Century* (New York: Harper and Row, 1958), p. 181. More recent studies include Lucy A. Adams, 'The Temptations of Christ: The Iconography of a Twelfth-Century Capital in the Metropolitan Museum of Art', *Gesta*, 28 (1989), 130–35, who notes the popularity of the theme in twelfth-century art; and Charles T. Little, '*Membra Disiecta*: More Early Stained Glass from Troyes Cathedral', *Gesta*, 20 (1981), 119–27 (pp. 119–21). J. Squilbeck surveys the theme in 'La Tentation du Christ au désert et le Belliger Insignis', *Bulletin des Musées Royaux d'Art et d'Histoire*, 39 (1967), 117–52. I am grateful to J. Hamburger for these references.

interpretation in twelfth-century monastic communities, and they reflect the centrality of the temptations theme in Christian art.

Act One: Creation to Incarnation

The *expositio* just studied covers the entire span of salvation history. Do others focus on one era or another? In fact, certain homilies extend from the creation of humankind and other creatures up to the incarnation, expounding, as it were, the first act of salvation history. Do these homilies reveal Hildegard's theology of creation and the natural world? *Expositiones* on Luke 14. 16–24 and Matthew 20. 1–16 clearly lay out the *officia* or responsibilities and proper place of various creatures and demonstrate Hildegard's keen interest in the natural world as well as her concept of the divinely appointed role and function of all creatures. When Volmar praises Hildegard's 'new and unheard of sermons', he mentions her explanations of 'the nature of diverse creatures'. Moreover, the *Vita Hildegardis* explains that the *magistra* 'made known certain matters regarding human nature and of the elements and of various creatures, and how human beings could be aided by them'.[101] I suggest that Volmar's letter and the *Vita Hildegardis* refer not only to the *magistra*'s scientific works but also to her exegesis when she relates parables to the creation story.

In the first homily we study, on the parable of the great banquet (Lk 14. 16–24), how does Hildegard leap from the banquet to the creation? The *magistra* interprets the householder (Lk 14. 16) as Adam, the first created and the one charged with responsibility over other creatures.[102] As the host orders the servant to bring in guests to the banquet (Lk 14. 17), so Adam reacts to the disobedience of his children and commands them to join him in the work of cultivation and to show fruitful obedience to him.[103] The people who make excuses for not attending the

---

[101] *Epistolarium*, II, 195, p. 443. *V. Hild.*, II.1, p. 20: 'et quedam de natura hominis ac elementorum diuersarumque creaturarum, et quomodo homini ex his sucurrendum sit'; *Life of Hildegard*, p. 41.

[102] *Expo. Euang.*, 39, p. 296, lines 1–4: '*Homo quidam*, scilicet Adam, *fecit*, id est lucratus est, *cenam magnam*, uidelicet hunc caducum mundum quandoque finiendum, quod cena designat, *et uocauit multos*, scilicet illos qui de se nascituri erant.'

[103] *Expo. Euang.*, 39, p. 296, lines 4–13: '*Et misit* admonendo *seruum suum*, id est creaturam, quae ei in seruitute subiecta fuit, *hora cenae*, scilicet in tempore mundi, *dicere* ostendendo, *inuitatis*, scilicet humano generi, quod ad culturam mundi inuitatum erat, *ut uenirent*, per ostensionem suam in studio, desiderio, et uoluntate, sicut et ipse laborando, plantando, tangendo, omniaque cum

banquet (Lk 14. 18–20) represent humans who disobey God and do not remain in the state in which they were created.[104] Hildegard allegorizes the host's order to compel people to come in (Lk 14. 23) as Adam's instruction for creation to enter every sphere of human activity and order the earth to open and bring forth plants with greenness (*uiriditas*). Consequently, it will flower and bear fruit and strong juices, namely wine.[105] The *magistra* interjects the horticultural perspective that the vine is more a plant than a tree: 'uitis magis est herba quam arbor'.[106] From this fruitfulness, earth will be filled with understanding.[107] Consequently, Hildegard paints a sort of garden where the creatures obey Adam and busy themselves toiling and planting to produce the fruit of greenness and benefit for all. Surely this image projects a view not only of the pre-lapsarian garden but also of an orderly monastery untroubled by disobedience.[108] Obedience to Adam, as to a religious superior,

---

uiriditate et utilitate fructuum obedientiam ei exhibebant, quoniam ipse primus fuit cui Deus ea subiecerat: *quia iam parata sunt omnia* quae uobis necessaria sunt, in nobis inuenitis; et ideo nobiscum in obedientia estote, sicut et nos creatori nostro obedimus.'

[104] *Expo. Euang.*, 39, p. 296, lines 14–16: '*Et ceperunt* in inceptione operis *simul omnes* homines *excusare* de obedientia, ne ita in statu suo Deo ut creati erant, obedirent, sicut aliae creaturae in statu suo permanent.'

[105] *Expo. Euang.*, 39, p. 298, lines 57–64: '*Et ait dominus*, scilicet Adam, *seruo*, id est creaturae: *Exi* cum seruitute *in uias*, id est in omnem circuitum et ambitum operum hominum, *et* plateas, scilicet in inflexionem herbarum, *et compelle intrare*, scilicet constringe terram se aperire, ut germinet in omnibus, uiriditate et fructu, ac etiam ui fortissimi suci, scilicet uini, quia uitis magis est herba quam arbor, et ut herba in terra plantatur, et nutritur, *ut impleatur*, id est ut plena sit *domus mea*, scilicet uenter totius comprehensionis quam in mundo comprehendo.'

[106] *Expo. Euang.*, 39, p. 298, lines 57–64. Hildegard does not state the same explicitly in *Cause*, 53–55, pp. 55–57, where she compares trees (*arbores*), grain (*frumentum*), vines (*uinum*), and grasses/herbs (*herbe*) sequentially according to the region of their growth. In *Cause*, 317, p. 190, she compares *uinum* and *frumentum*: 'Terra autem, que in frumento fertilis est, si uinum gignit, hoc infirmis hominibus ad bibendum sanabilius est quam uinum, quod in fructifera terra nascitur, scilicet que modicum frumenti gignit, etiam si istud pretiosior illo est. Vinum enim sanat et letificat hominem bono calore et magna uirtute sua.'

[107] The *magistra* reads the command in Luke 14. 21–24 the same way in *LDO*, II.1.30, p. 301, lines 25–27.

[108] *Expo. Euang.*, 39, p. 296, lines 4–11: '*Et misit*, admonendo, *seruum suum*, id est creaturam, quae ei in seruitute subiecta fuit, *hora cenae*, scilicet in tempore mundi, *dicere*, ostendendo, *inuitatis*, scilicet humano generi, quod ad culturam mundi inuitatum erat, *ut uenirent*, per ostensionem suam in studio, desiderio, et uoluntate, sicut et ipse laborando, plantando, tangendo, omniaque cum uiriditate et utilitate fructuum, obedientiam ei exhibebant, quoniam ipse primus fuit, cui Deus ea subiecerat.'

goes hand in hand with obedience to God.[109] Proper work carried out in obedience to the superior benefits all.

Is there any precedent for Hildegard's interpretation? The link that she develops between the parable and the creation story does appear in Tertullian, who refers to the creation or to Adam in his explanations of the pericope. Gregory the Great alludes briefly to the human's loss of spiritual delights after his sin in paradise, but he identifies the hour of the banquet as the end of time, not the beginning.[110] Moreover, the exegetical tradition emphasizes the heavenly banquet and designates the servant as the sending of preachers and not as Adam.[111] Ambrose, Augustine, and others focus on the three excuses together as refusals made by heathens, Jews, and heretics. Augustine grounds the tendency to read the householder's order to 'compel them to enter' as a justification for using force — a topic current in Hildegard's day but far from her interpretation of the text in this homily.[112] Moreover, exegetical features in Origen, Augustine, and Gregory the Great convey an emphasis on bodily versus spiritual pleasures, which Hildegard develops into a separate interpretation.[113]

Do Hildegard's other writings reflect this pre-lapsarian garden? *Sciuias* II.1 offers a compelling parallel for the *magistra*'s representation of Adam as the steward of other creatures. She designs a rich visual representation of creation, Adam's place in it, and his prefigurement of Christ. The upper area of the illustration shows the sphere of the Trinity and Adam sniffing the flower of obedience. In the central area, shining stars represent the prophets, as they do in some *expositiones*, and six medallions enclose the works fashioned on the six days of creation. The

---

[109] *Expo. Euang.*, 39, p. 296, lines 11–13: '*quia iam parata sunt omnia* quae uobis necessaria sunt, in nobis inuenitis; et ideo nobiscum in obedientia estote, sicut et nos creatori nostro obedimus'.

[110] Tertullian, *Aduersus Marcionem*, ed. by E. Kroymann, CCSL, 1 (Turnhout: Brepols, 1954), IV, 31, 2, p. 629, lines 28–31; Gregory the Great, *Homiliae in euangelia*, II, 26, p. 33, line 40.

[111] *Glossa Ordinaria*, IV, 93 (interlinear and marginal); Wailes, *Medieval Allegories*, pp. 161–66. Wailes, p. 166, notes that the Admont homily provides 'not an allegory of the parable, but allegories of the individual verses'.

[112] See François Bovon, *L'Evangile selon saint Luc (9,51–14,35)* (Geneva: Labor et Fides, 1996), pp. 456–60. On the related use of the 'Parable of the tares' (Mt 13. 24–30, 36–52) by Augustine of Hippo against the Donatists, see Wailes, *Medieval Allegories*, pp. 161–66, and Ulrich Luz, *Das Evangelium nach Matthäus 2, Mt 8–17* (Zürich: Benziger; Neukirchen-Vluyn: Neukirchener Verlag: 1985), pp. 343–48; and Kienzle, *Cistercians, Heresy and Crusade*, p. 166.

[113] Gregory the Great's Homily 36 appears in Paul the Deacon's collection and in the Cluniac lectionary. See Grégoire, *Homéliaires liturgiques médiévaux*, no. II, 38, p. 460; Étaix, 'Le Lectionnaire de l'office à Cluny', no. 147, p. 108.

night of fallen world surrounds them. In the lower portion of the scene, the old Adam descends and Christ rises to redeem him.[114] In accord with Hildegard's use of Augustinian categories of time, one may consider the two upper areas of the image as time *ante legem,* while the lower looks to time *sub gratia.*

How does Hildegard develop her theology of creation and the created order in her exegesis of Matthew 20. 1–16, the parable of the householder (or the labourers in the vineyard)? Hildegard takes a striking approach to the parable, when she correlates the stages of the gospel narrative with the days of creation.[115] From the householder's morning entrance into his vineyard (Mt 20. 1) to the payment of the workers 'from the first up to the last' (Mt 20. 8), the *magistra* adduces passages from the creation account in Genesis and sets them in parallel to the events and days of the gospel narrative. Her commentary explains the duties of the creatures and the singular status of the human set forth in Genesis.

Hildegard reads the householder going into the vineyard as God, Creator and Son, when he created heaven and earth, saying 'Let there be light' (Gn 1. 3), and leading diverse creatures into the world on the first day.[116] She interprets the agreement with the labourers to signify God's work on the second day, when he divided waters from waters (Gn 1. 6–7); he 'agreed' with the creatures existing then that for each day they were going to fill, they would work in the world.[117] She relates the third hour in the parable to the third day, when God said: 'Let the waters which are under heaven gather into one place, and let the dry land appear' (Gn 1. 9). Hildegard explains that when creatures still were not working, God said to

---

[114] *Sciuias,* II.1.1–17, pp. 110–23, *Scivias* (Eng.), pp. 149–57. Newman, *Sister of Wisdom,* pp. 167–71, discusses the imagery of text and image for this illustration.

[115] *Expo. Euang.,* 22, pp. 245–49. See Dronke, 'Platonic-Christian Allegories', p. 391: Hildegard turns the parable 'into a new kind of *figura*: what she sees fulfilled here in the New Testament narrative is nothing less than the opening of the Old Testament — the work of the six days. The time measurements — the hours of the vintner's day — do not harmonize readily with those that feature in Genesis; yet Hildegard achieves a *tour de force* of recounting two disparate narratives simultaneously'.

[116] *Expo. Euang.,* 22, p. 245, lines 1–5: '*Simile est regnum celorum,* scilicet secretorum, *homini patrifamilias,* uidelicet illi qui Deus et homo est, *qui exiit primo mane,* quando celum et terram creauit, et quando *Fiat lux* dixit, *conducere,* in prima die, *operarios,* id est diuersas creaturas, *in uineam suam,* uidelicet in mundum.'

[117] *Expo. Euang.,* 22, pp. 245–46, lines 6–10: '*Conuentione autem facta,* in secunda die, quando diuisit *aquas ab aquis, cum operariis,* id est creaturis quae tunc erant; *ex denario diurno,* scilicet ex officio suo, quod per singulos dies impleturae erant, *misit eos in uineam suam,* id est ut operarentur in mundo.'

them: 'Let the earth bring forth vegetation', etc.; and he promised to give them whatever would be fair for their service, according to the nature of their creation.[118] In the *magistra*'s reading, God's going out at the sixth and the ninth hours indicates the creative work of the fourth day, when God said 'Let there be lights in the firmament of heaven' (Gn 1. 14–15), and the fifth day, when he commanded 'Let the waters bring forth swarms of living creatures' (Gn 1. 20).[119] She relates the eleventh hour in the gospel text to the sixth day when God created humankind in his image and likeness (Gn 1. 26–27). The other creatures were ready for work, but had told God that they had no one to guide them.[120] In Hildegard's allegory, evening and the call to the workers in the parable correspond to the seventh day, when God completed his work (Gn 2. 2). As the householder spoke to the steward, God instructed Adam to call the various creatures and enjoin on them the services they were to render. However, in Adam's transgression, they went with him into the whirlwind (*in turbinem*).[121] Hildegard explains that the act of paying the workers 'beginning from the last up to the first' commences with the beasts and cattle, which were created with humankind and made after other creatures, and then moves to those that were created first. She clarifies her interpretation further, when she speaks to Adam in God's voice: 'Assign duties first, according to their nature, to those that are more like you and dwell with you on earth and also were created with you; and then show their duties to those which at first preceded in creation and which are unlike you in their nature.'[122]

Hildegard interprets the awarding of one denarius to those who came at the eleventh hour (Mt 20. 9) to mean that those who were created with humankind on the sixth day received particular duties according to their nature. Wild creatures were placed in the forest and domestic ones in the inhabited countryside. The labourers who come first (Mt 20. 10) stand for those who were created first, such as birds. Since the birds could both fly in the air and walk on earth, they thought they would have greater potential than would the herds. However, each was assigned one duty according to their nature: birds the duty of flying and fish of

---

[118] *Expo. Euang.*, 22, p. 246, lines 11–18.

[119] *Expo. Euang.*, 22, p. 246, lines 19–23.

[120] *Expo. Euang.*, 22, p. 246, lines 24–32.

[121] *Expo. Euang.*, 22, p. 247, lines 33–42.

[122] *Expo. Euang.*, 22, p. 247, lines 45–49: 'Quasi diceret: Illis quae tibi magis assimilantur, et tecum in terra conuersantur, et quae etiam tecum creata sunt, officia sua secundum naturam suam primum impone, et tunc illis quae primum in creatione processerunt, et quae in natura sua tibi dissimiliora sunt, officia sua ostende.'

swimming, just as the one duty of walking on land was assigned to beasts. In the *magistra*'s reading, the labourers' grumbling against the householder (Mt 20. 11–12) represents the creatures' complaint against the Creator: they had carried various burdens since before the others were created. Hildegard has the Creator respond directly, with words from the Scripture and her additions, that he had assigned their duties justly and that they had agreed to the duties that he enjoined on them. He gave the potential to carry out their duties to the creatures that tread upon the earth as well as to those that fly in the air and were created earlier.[123] Further, he questions them: 'Is it not permitted that I who am the Creator do what I will in creation? Is your knowledge not foolish when you want more than is suitable for you, since I have created you well and beautifully?'[124]

Hildegard applies Jesus's teaching about the first and the last to the order of created creatures. The creatures that were fashioned later, such as the herds, will work first, because herds first began to walk with and dwell with humankind. Moreover, because of their meat, pelts, and service, they are more useful to human beings than birds are. Those that came forth earlier in creation will fulfill their duties last, because birds are not as useful for humans as herds. The notion that 'many are called, but few are chosen' (Mt 20. 16), means that many and diverse creatures are called to fulfill their appointed duties; but the human being alone is chosen by God to be made in God's image and likeness (Gn 1. 26–27) and is predestined for heavenly things.[125]

Are there any parallels for the *magistra*'s creative exegesis? The two major strands of interpretation, both derived from Origen, either read the hours of the workday as the ages of the world or focus on the individual.[126] A few elements in

---

[123] *Expo. Euang.*, 22, p. 248, lines 75–85: '*Amice*, iussionem meam perficiendo, *non facio tibi iniuriam*, sed do tibi officium tuum, secundum iustum modum, ne mensuram tuam transcendas, plus ascendendo uel descendendo quam tibi datum sit, non autem secundum quod posses. *Nonne ex denario*, scilicet ex officio illo quod tibi iniunxi, in hoc quod dixi *fiat, conuenisti mecum*, ut iussionem meam impleres? *Tolle*, officium, *quod tuum est*, in natura tua, *et uade*, illud implendo. *Volo autem et huic nouissimo*, scilicet quae postea creata est, et quae super terram uadit, *dare*, possibilitatem ut officium suum impleat, *sicut et tibi*, quae prius creata es, et in aere uolas.'

[124] *Expo. Euang.*, 22, p. 248, lines 85–89: 'An *non licet michi*, qui creator sum, *quod uolo facere*, in ipsa creatura, ita ut ipsa rebellis dicat: Cur me fecisti sic? *An oculus tuus*, scilicet scientia tua, *nequam*, id est stulta, *est*, cum plus uelis quam tibi conueniat, *quia ego bonus sum*, qui te bene et pulcre creaui?'

[125] *Expo. Euang.*, 22, pp. 248–49, lines 90–102.

[126] See Wailes, *Medieval Allegories*, pp. 138–39.

Hildegard's narrative have precedents: Gregory the Great and others read the vine-yard owner as the Creator;[127] Origen and Paschasius Radbertus interpret the work-ers as the five senses;[128] Paschasius reads the steward as Adam.[129] The labourers' varying times and excuses furnish material that some exegetes develop into an opposition between Jews and Gentiles,[130] a thematic that Hildegard does not pursue here or elsewhere. Distinctly from other commentators, Hildegard focuses on Adam, his dominance over the rest of creation, and the role of the various crea-tures. Her emphasis on the creation shows some affinities with contemporary schoolmen and the keen interest in hexameral commentary, culminating with Peter Comestor's *Historia scholastica*.[131] However, the seer develops her teaching not from Genesis as her base text but from the Gospel, thus using a striking reverse or anti-typology.[132] Christ, one in being with the Creator, provides through the gospel words the framework for both stories, the parable and Hildegard's allegory. The advance from Adam to Christ dominates the composition of the *expositio* as it does the illumination of *Sciuias* II.1; Hildegard superimposes one biblical narra-tive on the other, much as she structures the layers of the illumination.[133]

Act Two: Christ, Creator, and Son Incarnate

How does Hildegard represent Christ beyond the time of the creation? Do the *Expositiones* depict a second act in salvation history, the time *sub gratia* where the shining new Adam redeems humanity? Christ, at once Creator and Redeemer,

---

[127] Gregory the Great, *Homiliae in euangelia*, I, 19, p. 143, lines 5–7; Paschasius Radbertus, *Expositio in Matheo Libri XII*, ed. by B. Paulus, CCCM, 56, 56A, 56B (Turnhout: Brepols, 1984), X, p. 975, lines 1472–75. For other examples, see the apparatus criticus, *Expo. Euang.*, 22, p. 247.

[128] Origen, *Commentarius in Matthaeum*, ed. by E. Klostermann, and E. Benz, *Origenes Werke*, vols X.1, XI, Die Griechischen Christlichen Schriftsteller der ersten Jahrhunderte, 40, 41.1 (Berlin: Akademie-Verlag, 1935; Leipzig: J. C. Hinrichs, 1941), XVI, 35, p. 452, lines 15–20; Paschasius Radbertus, *Expositio in Matheo*, IX, pp. 979–80, lines 1588–1619.

[129] Paschasius Radbertus, *Expositio in Matheo*, IX, p. 980, lines 1623–25.

[130] Wailes, *Medieval Allegories*, pp. 139–42.

[131] See Van Engen, *Rupert of Deutz*, pp. 82–86; Smalley, *Study of the Bible*, pp. 66–82; *Letters of Peter Abelard*, pp. 53–60; Bartlett, 'Commentary, Polemic and Prophecy', p. 154; Häring, 'Com-mentary and Hermeneutics', p. 182.

[132] A near parallel lies in Rupert of Deutz's claim to find events of the Old Testament predicted in the Book of Revelation. See Van Engen, *Rupert of Deutz*, p. 279.

[133] *Sciuias*, II.1.1–17, pp. 110–23.

remains ever present thematically in the *Expositiones*; however, in terms of the 'economy of the work', in only a few homilies does he occupy the most textual space. In Hildegard's exegesis of John 10. 11–16, the shepherd who feeds all (Jn 10. 11) represents the Creator, who brought the creatures to life, and the Redeemer, who gave up his life for his chosen.[134] Christ (the shepherd) knows all the elect who remain with him and the creatures that have proceeded from him; they look to him demanding and tasting all that is necessary.[135] As the shepherd knows the sheep and the sheep know the shepherd (Jn 10. 14), Christ in his human nature knows divinity and divinity knows him. As the shepherd gives his life for the sheep (Jn 10. 15), so Christ places in a human body the life with which he gave life to the chosen.[136] Hildegard's allegory centres on the redemptive role of Christ at the same time that she underscores his role as Creator.

Does Hildegard's exegesis of John 10. 11–16 display any features distinct from the tradition? She follows the identification of the good shepherd with God in Christ, well-established from Augustine onward.[137] Her interpretation of the sheep as the elect finds precedent in Gregory the Great, as does her reading of the hired hand as the Devil.[138] The seer's reading differs decisively from that of an Admont homily, which emphasizes ecclesiastical leadership, hails the apostles Peter and Paul,

---

[134] *Expo. Euang.*, 30, p. 274, lines 1–5: '*Ego*, uerbum patris, *sum pastor*, scilicet creator *bonus* creaturarum, quia omnes de me procedunt et ego eas omnes in plenitudine pasco. *Bonus pastor animam suam*, scilicet uitam, qua omnia suscitauit, *dat*, ponendo in corporali forma, *pro ouibus suis*, id est electis.'

[135] *Expo. Euang.*, 30, p. 275, lines 19–22: '*Ego*, qui omnia feci, *sum pastor bonus, et cognosco meas*, scilicet omnes electos qui in me manent et creaturas, quia de me processerunt, *et cognoscunt me meae*, quoniam omnes ad me aspiciunt postulando et gustando omnia necessaria.'

[136] *Expo. Euang.*, 30, p. 275, lines 22–25: '*Sicut nouit me* in humanitate *pater*, id est diuinitas, *et ego agnosco patrem*, scilicet diuinitatem, *et animam meam*, uidelicet uitam qua eas suscitaui, *pono* in humano corpore *pro ouibus meis*.'

[137] Augustine, Sermo 137, *PL* 38: 764; Augustine, Sermo 214, *PL* 39: 2143; Augustine, *In Iohannis euangelium*, XLVI, 3, p. 399, lines 13–14. For additional references, see the apparatus criticus, *Expo. Euang.*, 30, pp. 274–75. *Glossa Ordinaria*, IV, 249, marginal, explains the shepherd, wolf, and hired hand in its commentary on John 10. 1–10.

[138] *Expo. Euang.*, 30, p. 274, lines 4–7: '*pro ouibus suis*, id est electis. *Mercennarius*, uidelicet diabolus, qui post ruinam se ouibus in fallacia coniunxit'. Gregory the Great, *Homiliae in euangelia*, I, 15, p. 100, lines 112–13 (*pascua electorum*); on the Devil, see Gregory the Great, *Homiliae in euangelia*, I, 15, p. 98, line 51. Gottfried of Admont, *Homiliae dominicales*, 47, *PL* 174: 318; Rupert of Deutz, *Commentaria in Euangelium Sancti Iohannis*, ed. by R. Haacke, CCCM, 9 (Turnhout: Brepols, 1969), IX, p. 522, lines 1910–12. See other sources in the apparatus fontium, *Expo. Euang.*, 30, p. 274.

and holds up Peter as the first pastor of the Church. Moreover, the Admont text signals the threefold nourishment that the pastor should provide: preaching, good works, and prayer.[139] The relationship Hildegard emphasizes is that between Christ and all faithful creation; she does not mention prelates at all for this pericope.

While Christ, one in being with the Creator, figures prominently in Hildegard's creation-focused allegories, she places the human Christ at the centre of a homily on John 6. 1–14, the story of the miracle of the loaves and fishes. The sea of Galilee (Jn 6. 1) represents the passion — the anguish and tribulation that Christ suffered in this world. The other side of the sea of Tiberias (Jn 6. 1) refers to heaven, the region which humankind aspires to reach because Jesus rose from the dead.[140] The homily turns quickly to tropological and typological commentary, however. As the crowd followed him and saw the wonders he worked (Jn 6. 2), so believers of one heart and mind follow Christ's footsteps in faith, aided by visible signs such as the Holy Spirit's descent in tongues of fire and the miracles the disciples performed.[141] Christ remains near, both through the sacraments of the Eucharist and confession and through the ardour of faith that brings about good works.[142] When the *magistra* interprets Jesus's question to Philip, as to where they might buy bread (Jn 6. 5), she explains that Jesus looked at the commands of the old law and asked where from it the righteous would draw an example of belief and holiness. He examined carefully its significations and miracles to see what he could derive from them for the salvation of believers.[143]

---

[139] Gottfried of Admont, *Homiliae dominicales*, 48, *PL* 174: 323B–D, 326A–C on the reading for the day (II Pt 2. 25) and the role of the bishop; 323CD on the 'trinam pastionem, praedicationem, operationem, orationem'. The citation to Gregory's homily is found at col. 324B. Gregory the Great, *Homiliae in euangelia*, I, 14, p. 98, lines 45–46.

[140] *Expo. Euang.*, 3, p. 194, lines 1–4: '*Abiit Iesus trans mare Galileae*, id est in passione sua per angustiam et tribulationem mundi istius, *quod est Tyberiadis*, scilicet iustae et summae regionis, ad quam omne genus humanum inclinatur et ad quam se tendebat, cum a mortuis resurrexisset.'

[141] *Expo. Euang.*, 3, pp. 194–95, lines 4–11: '*Et sequebatur eum*, scilicet uestigia ipsius, maxima *multitudo credentium* quibus *erat cor unum et anima una, quia uidebant*, et in fide ac uisu oculorum, *signa*, ubi Spiritus Sanctus in igneis linguis super credentes descendit, et alia multa miracula *quae* Christus *faciebat* per discipulos suos et alios fideles *super his qui infirmabantur*, ubi desuper gratiam suam misit ad istos qui prius infirmi in fide erant, ita quod postea in baptismo sanati sunt.'

[142] *Expo. Euang.*, 3, p. 195, lines 17–21: '*Erat autem proximum*, id est in assidua frequentatione propinquitatis, *Pascha*, scilicet communio corporis et sanguinis Christi, innocentis agni, *dies festus Iudeorum*, id est incipiens et lucens, bonus et magnus ac preclarus ardor fidei ac bonorum operum in cordibus credentium et peccata sua confitentium.'

[143] *Expo. Euang.*, 3, p. 195, lines 25–31: '*dicit* per inspirationem suam *ad Philippum*, scilicet ad simplicia legalia precepta ueteris legis: *Vnde*, id est de quibus legalibus factis uel preceptis

Various persons and elements of the gospel story illustrate righteous behavior. The two fish (Jn 6. 9) represent the dual nature of Christ, God and man.[144] Hildegard interprets Jesus's instruction to make the people lie down (Jn 6. 10) as a command to order an upright peace in the Church. Jesus's gesture of taking the loaves (Jn 6. 11) corresponds to his drawing the righteous and holy into his grace through the commandments of the law.[145] Distributing loaves (Jn 6. 11) stands for showing the gifts of grace, while handing out the fish refers to monks and virgins who stand as the greatest example of contempt for the world.[146]

Such intratextual references signal that Hildegard directs this homily to men and women in the monastic life; she perhaps intended it for the community at Disibodenberg.[147] Her conclusion applies even more broadly: Those who worship Christ in the Church through baptism and many other virtues see with knowledge, understanding, and appetite for sweetness the virtue that Jesus demonstrated in his humanity and passion, and in the gifts of the Holy Spirit. He gave a sign through the prophecies, the Gospels, and the *expositores*.[148] They acclaim the belief that he

---

antiquorum sacrificiorum, *ememus*, scilicet prouocabimus aut ostendemus, *panes*, uidelicet iustos et sanctos homines in operibus suis, *ut manducent hi* de quibus exemplum credulitatis et sanctitatis trahant?'

[144] *Expo. Euang.*, 3, p. 196, lines 53–56: '*et duos pisces*, uidelicet qui Christum uerum Deum et hominem in pura et perspicaci conuersatione spiritalis uitae imitantur, ut monachi et uirgines seculo perfecte renuntiantes'.

[145] *Expo. Euang.*, 3, p. 197, lines 62–64, 71–72: '*Facite homines discumbere*, id est ordinate credentibus rectam et bonam quietem in preceptis meis in ecclesia. [. . .] *Accepit ergo panes Iesus*, scilicet cum iustos et sanctos homines in uirtutibus per legalia precepta ad gratiam suam contraxit.'

[146] *Expo. Euang.*, 3, p. 197, lines 74–80: '*distribuit discumbentibus*, cum eos in exemplum credentibus dedit et proposuit, ubi se in humilitate pro Christi nomine quasi ad terram prostrauerunt. *Similiter* in inspiratione sua, *et ex piscibus*, scilicet illorum qui angelicum ordinem, ut monachi et uirgines, adierunt, qui uelut maximum exemplum contemptus mundi fidelibus sunt, *quantum uolebant*, uidelicet quantum querit desiderium ecclesiae in sancta conuersatione.'

[147] See *Epistolarium*, I, 77, 77R, pp. 166–75.

[148] *Expo. Euang.*, 3, p. 198, lines 90–109: '*Collegerunt ergo*, id est doctores etiam instruxerunt diuinis preceptis eos qui in ecclesia simpliciter in pusillanimitate incedebant nec se ad altiora tollere audebant, ut quidam seculares qui simpliciter uiuunt, *et impleuerunt duodecim chophinos fragmentorum*, ita quod perfecerunt predicatores et uerba apostolorum, cum tam simplices quam pusillanimes, quasi fragmenta, etiam ad fidem illam perduxerunt quam apostoli docuerant [. . .]. *Illi ergo homines*, qui Christum in fide per baptismum et per multas alias uirtutes in ecclesia colunt, *cum uidissent* in bona scientia, in bono intellectu ac in bono gustu dulcedinis uirtutum, *quod fecerat Iesus* in humanitate, in passione ac in donis Spiritus Sancti, *signum* per prophetiam et euangelium, uelut de expositoribus, *dicebant* aperta uoce in laudibus credulitatis.'

completed all the prophets in himself by his miracles in the fullness of time, so that he not only fulfilled all his works, foretold long ago, but he will prepare them up until the last day, when the world will have completed its course.[149]

How does Hildegard's exegesis of John 6. 1–14 compare to that of other interpreters? Exegetes allegorized the number of characters and elements in the pericope,[150] and features of Hildegard's reading correspond roughly to the exegetical tradition evident from Bede onward. The sea represents the tribulations of this world;[151] the number of loaves designates the five senses;[152] the bread's coarseness points to the harshness of life;[153] the disciples who fill the baskets stand for the doctors and preachers who lead people to faith.[154] Moreover, the *magistra*'s christological focus concurs in some aspects with Rupert of Deutz's commentary on John, where he reads various details in a christological pattern.[155] The *Hildegard-Gebetbuch* echoes the typological accent of Hildegard's homily. The *Gebetbuch* illustrates this pericope (fol. 24ᵛ) with Jesus on the left of the scene receiving the two fish and five loaves while the crowd sits below. The prayer (fol. 25ʳ) addresses Christ as the cornerstone, who distributes the five loaves and the two fish. In line

---

[149] *Expo. Euang.*, 3, p. 198, lines 109–14: '*Quia hic est uere propheta*, qui omnes prophetas in semetipso compleuit, *qui uenturus est*, proficiendo in miraculis suis in plenitudine temporis, *in mundum*, ut omnia opera ipsius, quae ante multa tempora predicta sunt futura, implerentur, quae patrabit usque ad nouissimum diem, cum mundus in cursu suo complebitur.'

[150] The homiliaries of Paul the Deacon and the Cluny lectionary include a homily from Bede. See Grégoire, *Homéliaires liturgiques médiévaux*, no. 60, p. 441; Étaix, 'Le Lectionnaire de l'office à Cluny', no. 53, p. 100.

[151] Bede, *Homeliarum euangelii libri II*, II, 2, p. 194, lines 35–38. See other sources in the apparatus fontium, *Expo. Euang.*, 3, p. 198.

[152] Bede, *Homeliarum euangelii libri II*, II, 2, p. 197, lines 157–59; Gottfried of Admont, *Homiliae dominicales*, 35, *PL* 174: 240, gives two readings, including the interpretation of Augustine, who sees the five as the five books of Moses. See other sources in the apparatus fontium, *Expo. Euang.*, 3, p. 198.

[153] Bede, *Homeliarum euangelii libri II*, II, 2, p. 196, lines 116–18; Gottfried of Admont, *Homiliae dominicales*, 35, PL 174: 240. See other sources in the apparatus fontium, *Expo. Euang.*, 3, p. 198.

[154] Bede, *Homeliarum euangelii libri II*, II, 2, p. 198, lines 187–99; Rupert of Deutz, *Commentaria in Euangelium Sancti Iohannis*, VI, p. 311, lines 431–35. See other sources in the apparatus fontium, *Expo. Euang.*, 3, p. 198.

[155] Rupert of Deutz, *Commentaria in Euangelium Sancti Iohannis*, VI, p. 302, lines 96–99; (on footsteps) VI, p. 304, lines 179–81; (on the Holy Spirit) VI, p. 303, lines 119–22; (on baptism) VI, p. 302, lines 102–06; (on the innocence of the lamb) VI, p. 304, lines 162–63.

with a standard interpretation of the passage, the loaves signify the books of Moses and the fish represent the Old Testament and the Gospels.[156] The prayer also beseeches Christ to open the *medullam grani* (the kernel of wheat), that is, to give spiritual understanding and to refresh the soul.[157] Hence, the *Gebetbuch* teaches exegesis through the performance of prayer and furthermore echoes a key Hildegardian theme — the spiritual understanding of Scripture that runs parallel to the transformation of history.

While Hildegard's homily shares a similar thematic emphasis with the *Hildegard-Gebetbuch* for this pericope, overall the *Gebetbuch* shows itself more in line with the tendency in twelfth-century spirituality to accent the sufferings of the human Christ. It devotes several scenes to the passion.[158] Indeed, Rupert of Deutz also reveals a greater overall emphasis on the passion in his exegesis, beginning with his initial illuminating vision, than Hildegard does in the *Expositiones*. While the *magistra* opens her *expositio* with an accent on the human nature of Christ and his actions in the world, she nonetheless develops a typological message. Moreover, not as many *expositiones* focus directly on Christ as they do on the creation or on the soul's struggle. Yet he is never completely absent from the homilies: Creator, Redeemer, sender of the Holy Spirit, Christ plays a role in all the acts of history.

How does Christ's role in the *Expositiones* compare to that in the *magistra*'s other works? Hildegard's theology of Christ as Creator as well as Redeemer resounds in two antiphons from the *Symphonia*. 'O pastor animarum' calls upon Christ as shepherd of souls and Creator, the first voice (*prima uox*) that uttered the command of creation:

> O shepherd of souls, o first voice through which we were all created, may it now please you to find it worthy to free us from our miseries and illnesses.[159]

[156] On the five loaves as the five books of Moses, see the sources in the apparatus fontium, *Expo. Euang.*, 3, p. 198, including Rupert of Deutz, *Commentaria in Euangelium Sancti Iohannis*, VI, p. 307, lines 275–77; Gottfried of Admont, *Homiliae dominicales*, 35, *PL* 174: 240, who gives two readings.

[157] *Glossa Ordinaria*, IV, 238, marginal, refers to the *medulla* of the coarse bread and the spiritual sense.

[158] The *Gebetbuch* depicts the events of Holy Week from Jesus's entrance into Jerusalem (fols 49ᵛ, 50ʳ) to Jesus's death and burial (fols 62ᵛ, 63ʳ).

[159] 'O pastor animarum', *Symph.*, 4, p. 377, lines 1–7. 'O pastor animarum | et o prima vox | per quam omnes creati sumus, | nunc tibi, tibi placeat | ut digneris | nos liberare de miseriis | et languoribus nostris.' For examples of the image of the Good Shepherd in Hildegard's works, see *Sciuias*, II.1 (p. 111, 89 and others); *Epistolarium*, I, 61R (p. 143, lines 1–2); *LDO*, III.5.20 (p. 439, lines 2–3, 5).

Speaking for humankind, Hildegard beseeches the shepherd of souls for deliverance from misery and illness. 'O cruor sanguinis' also evokes the word that sounded forth at creation. The sound of creation folds into the lament of the elements when the Creator's blood was shed.

> O flow of blood, that sounded forth on high, when all the elements folded themselves into a voice of lament with trembling because the blood of their Creator touched them.[160]

The antiphon ends much like the first with an appeal to heal humankind of its sickness: 'ungue nos | de languoribus nostris' (anoint us, [heal us] from our illnesses). In both pieces as in the homilies just discussed, Hildegard addresses Christ, at once Creator and Redeemer.

In *Sciuias*, Hildegard places Christ at the centre of the process of building salvation. The virtues stand around the figure of Christ seated on a mountain, as he was on the cornerstone (*Sciuias*, III.2), and they occupy other places in the grand edifice of salvation.[161] Particular virtues do evoke the human nature of the Saviour. In one scene, where the virtues occupy the centre of a building, Longing stands to the side and regards a crucifix; in another, Hope gazes upon a crucifix, while several virtues ascend and descend a ladder resting on the pillar of the Saviour's humanity.[162] Even so, the contemplation of the crucifix and of Christ's suffering remains a peripheral theme in these visions from *Sciuias*, as it does in the *Expositiones*. Hildegard's Christology further reveals itself in the *Liber diuinorum operum* and in other works that I will discuss in the context of her anti-heretical writings.

Act Three: The Soul and the Virtues

How do the *Expositiones* move into the third act of Hildegard's drama of salvation history? How does she exegete and preach in such a way as to enlighten the journey that she, her nuns, and other Christians strived to travel? If God and Christ oversee the first act, and his life, death, and resurrection occupy the second act, does the third person of the Trinity dominate the third? Indeed, once Christ made the journey, the Holy Spirit intervenes particularly in this third era, and the Spirit's

---

[160] 'O cruor sanguinis', *Symph.*, 5, p. 378, lines 1–8. 'O cruor sanguinis | qui in alto sonuisti, | cum omnia elementa | se implicuerunt | in lamentabilem vocem | cum tremore, | quia sanguis Creatoris sui | illa tetigit.' My translation, very close to *Symphonia*, ed. and trans. by Newman, p. 103.

[161] *Sciuias*, III.2, pp. 349–70, III.3, pp. 371–88; *Scivias* (Eng.) pp. 325–39, 343–54.

[162] *Sciuias*, III.3.13, pp. 371–88 at p. 387 (*Gemitus*); *Scivias* (Eng.), pp. 353–54. *Sciuias*, III.8.23, pp. 478–514 at p. 510 (*Spes*); *Scivias* (Eng.), p. 445.

inspiration guides all of history. Christ sent the Spirit at Pentecost, and the Spirit in turn sends the virtues to aid humankind in walking a righteous path and avoiding vice. The *expositiones* that interpret the gospel readings in terms of the soul's struggle to maintain the course present striking similarities with the *Ordo uirtutum* and prove so numerous that they require a separate chapter. The analysis of one homily suffices here to illustrate the Trinitarian accent in Hildegard's exegetical narratives of the struggle between virtue and vice.[163]

An exposition on the wedding at Cana (Jn 2. 1–11) presents a moral allegory of virtues and vices. The wedding (Jn 2. 1) signifies the new offspring born when the human recognizes and corrects his sin.[164] The short supply of wine (Jn 2. 3) represents the virtue of perfection, deficient while the human is in the flesh.[165] The steward (Jn 2. 5) stands for the virtues that aid the human to fulfill the divine commands, bringing the gifts of the Holy Spirit (the water in the gospel story, Jn 2. 7) to all the people on the journey to perfection.[166] The miracle at Cana signifies the transformation of sins on the part of humans who evidence a 'new man' by praising God and following his footsteps by means of penitence.[167]

Does Hildegard's exegesis in this homily reveal any patristic precedents? Bede's Homily 14, the selection in Paul the Deacon's homiliary, seems to have had little

---

[163] Hildegard also depicts the conflict of vices and virtues in her fourth homily on Luke 21. 25–33. *Expo. Euang.*, 56, pp. 327–29.

[164] *Expo. Euang.*, 17, pp. 233–34, lines 1–6: '*Nuptiae factae sunt* in gaudio nouae sobolis, quando homo seipsum recognoscit et corripit: *in Chana*, scilicet ut mala sua zelando diiudicet, *Galileae*, et peccata sua transiendo dimittit, *et erat mater*, id est bonum exemplum genitricis Dei, *Iesu*, saluatoris, *ibi*, in gaudio nouae sobolis.'

[165] *Expo. Euang.*, 17, p. 234, lines 10–12: '*Et deficiente* in homine *uino*, id est uirtute perfectionis, *dicit* in requirendo *mater*, scilicet bona exempla, *Iesu ad eum: Vinum*, id est uirtutem perfectionis, *non habent*, nisi tu Deus dederis eis.'

[166] *Expo. Euang.*, 17, p. 235, lines 34–39: '*Vt autem gustauit*, id est intellexit, *architriclinus*, omnis populus, *aquam*, bonum iter in homine, *uinum factam*, scilicet bono opere completum, *et non sciebat*, uidelicet non intelligebat, *unde esset*, id est de quibus donis Dei; *ministri autem*, scilicet uirtutes, *sciebant qui hauserant*, id est qui ministrant et deferunt *aquam* in bono itinere, dona Spiritus Sancti.'

[167] *Expo. Euang.*, 17, p. 235, lines 50–55: '*Hoc fecit inicium signorum*, quod homo conpungitur, *Iesus in Chana*, ubi homo per diuinam inspirationem seipsum diiudicat, *Galileae*, peccata sua in penitentia transiens, *et manifestauit* in nouo homine *gloriam suam*, quia *uenit peccatores saluos facere. Et crediderunt in eum*, laudantes ipsum, *discipuli eius*, scilicet qui uestigia eius in penitentia secuti sunt.'

impact on her.[168] Possible echoes of Gaudentius of Brescia sound in the *magistra*'s reading of the six jugs as the five senses plus the will. The six jugs are more commonly read as the six ages of the world. Gaudentius interprets the six jugs as six human senses ('uisus oculorum, auditus aurium, odoratus narium, loquela oris, attrectatio manuum, incessus pedum'), hard as stone, dead, and motionless, before humans believed in the resurrection.[169] Irimbert of Admont's allegorical interpretation of the wedding as the union of God and the faithful soul proves the closest to Hildegard's reading. Irimbert sees the stone water jugs as representative of solidity or of the human's hardness of heart. He includes the senses in his reading, but he sees them as represented by the servants and not the jugs.[170] For Hildegard in contrast, the servants stand for the virtues. Accordingly, none of these interpretations develops an allegory of virtue and vice as Hildegard does.

The *Hildegard-Gebetbuch* (fol. 22ᵛ) provides another parallel witness to the depiction of the miracle at Cana. Jesus and Mary stand behind the banquet table on the left of the scene with a woman guest and the steward on the right. Six brightly coloured jugs sit in the foreground, in front of the banquet table. A servant fills them with water from a smaller vessel. The prayer (fol. 23ʳ) opens with imagery of the heavenly bridegroom who took humanity as his bride and deigned to attend a human wedding in order to display holy mysteries by performance of a miracle. The moral import of the prayer corresponds to the thematic focus of Hildegard's homily: a moral allegory of virtues and vices in which the wedding signifies the new offspring born when the human recognizes and corrects his sin, and the miracle at Cana represents the transformation of sins through penitence. Subsequently, the prayer employs the salvation-historical motif of Hildegard's first homily: changing water into wine signifies transforming the old law into the sweetness of the Gospel.[171]

---

[168] Bede, *Homeliarum euangelii libri II*, I, 14: Grégoire, *Homéliaires liturgiques médiévaux*, no. 60, p. 441; Étaix, 'Le Lectionnaire de l'office à Cluny', no. 53, p. 100.

[169] Gaudentius of Brescia, *Tractatus XXI*, ed. by A. Glück, CSEL, 68 (Vienna: Hoelder-Pichler-Tempsky, 1936), IX, p. 83, lines 238–41. See the other sources in the apparatus fontium, *Expo. Euang.*, 16, 17, pp. 232, 234. In contrast, Caesarius interprets the jugs as the six ages of history or of human life, and he indicates that the jugs are filled with prophecy and the mysteries of the Old Testament. Caesarius of Arles, *Sermones*, ed. by G. Morin, CCSL, 103–04 (Turnhout: Brepols, 1953), II, 169, 10, p. 692. *Glossa Ordinaria*, IV, 228, marginal, discusses the six ages.

[170] Gottfried of Admont, *Homiliae dominicales*, 16, *PL* 174: 109–11.

[171] *Expo. Euang.*, 16, p. 232, lines 34–43: '*Dicit* inspiratione sua *eis Iesus: Implete ydrias*, id est uetus et nouum testamentum, *aqua* sapientiae, ut homo Deum cognoscat. *Et impleuerunt eas* diuersa scientia *usque ad summum*: quia cum homo in circumcisione et in lege nichil amplius

That transformation allowed the remission of sin. The supplicant beseeches Christ for inner change: turning vices to virtues, performing true penitence and good works. Hildegard devotes one homily to each mode of interpretation, whereas the prayer incorporates both the typological and the moral readings of the pericope.

Epilogue: Satan, Antichrist, and the Heavenly Jerusalem

Does Hildegard devote attention in the *Expositiones* to the end times as she does in *Sciuias* and the *Liber diuinorum operum*? Does she offer a glimpse of the heavenly Jerusalem, as she does in the *Symphonia*? The victory of virtue over vice requires the defeat of the Devil, depicted in *Sciuias* as a sort of black and hairy worm, chained at the neck, hands, and feet and lying in an abyss. A shining multitude descends from a great luminous mountain and crushes him underfoot.[172] In that passage Hildegard uses the verb *conculco* for stomping on Satan. Similarly, in the *Liber diuinorum operum*, I.1, the figure of the Trinity stomps triumphantly on the Devil, while the serpent wrapped around the Tempter holds his right ear by the teeth.[173]

Two *Expositiones* envision the end times and introduce Antichrist. In a homily on Matthew 4. 1–11, the Tempter shows Christ the false deceptions he will use to assail the faithful in the last days, promising that they will have human beings who worship them as God, if they desert the worship of the Christians. Hildegard warns that most of humanity from everywhere on earth will turn towards Antichrist and worship him. The Church, already dejected, will not be able to hold up further.[174]

---

operari potuit, tunc clamabant: *Vtinam dirumperes celum, et descenderes*, desiderantes ut uerbum patris incarnaretur! *Et dicit eis Iesus* in admonitione sua: *Haurite nunc*, in me quod in uobis non habetis, *et ferte* demonstrantes *architriclino*, id est ueteri testamento, quia cum homo incipit Deum cognoscere, postea bonum operatur, et deinde Deum in lege amplectitur.'

[172] *Sciuias*, II.7.25, p. 324, lines 588–91, 596–98: 'Quod ueri cultores Dei qui toto annisu terrena conculcant antiquum serpentem forti contritione deiciunt [. . .]. Sed quod uides quod magna multitudo hominum in multa claritate fulgentium uenit, que predictum uermen fortiter ubique conculcans acriter eum cruciat [. . .] fidele agmen credentium [. . .] uirgines, martyres et ceteri huiusmodi cultores Dei, qui totu annisu terrena conculcant et celestia desiderant.' *Scivias* (Eng.), p. 303.

[173] *LDO*, I.1, p. 47, line 20: 'et serpentem quendam pedibus suis conculcabat'.

[174] *Expo. Euang.*, 25, p. 259, lines 62–72: '*et ostendit ei* per fallaces deceptiones in quibus fideles homines in nouissimo tempore impugnabit, *omnia regna mundi*, quia de omnibus regnis terrarum maxima pars hominum ad antichristum declinabit, *et gloriam eorum*, scilicet culturam illam quam tunc decepti inibunt, *et dixit* per deceptiones suas *illi*, scilicet Christo, uidelicet fidelibus Christi qui

Jesus's command, 'Be gone, Satan!' (Mt 4. 10), prefigures striking down the Antichrist in the last days. The Devil will no longer have any power, and the angels will praise God without end.[175] The high mountain (Mt 4. 8–9) reaches to the edge of the windstorm in Antichrist. The mountain of *Sciuias*, III.11.27 echoes that image, doubtless drawn from *De Antichristo*, the widely diffused tenth-century treatise by Adso of Montier-en-Der.[176] Hildegard echoes Adso again in a homily on Luke 21. 25–33,[177] where the signs (Lk 21. 25) point to the coming of Antichrist's heretical ministers.[178]

Moreover, Hildegard introduces the theme of stomping on the Devil in the *Expositiones*, as she does in *Sciuias*. In one instance, she refers to crushing the Devil, with the verb *contero, -ere*. In a homily on Matthew 2. 1–12, where Herod represents the Devil, she teaches that 'penitence crushes the Devil in the abyss', a correspondence to the portrayal of the virtuous trampling the Devil underfoot in *Sciuias*.[179] Elsewhere in the *Expositiones*, Hildegard refers to the virtues themselves

---

membra ipsius sunt: *Haec omnia* quae uides, homines scilicet qui me ut Deum colunt, te deserentes, *tibi dabo*, ita ut tu mecum ab eis colaris, *si cadens*, scilicet si culturam christianorum deseris, quia ecclesia iam deiecta ultra stare non poterit, *adoraueris me*, quoniam iam nullus te adorat, cum ad me conuersi te dereliquerint.'

[175] *Expo. Euang.*, 25, p. 259, lines 73–76: '*Tunc dixit ei*, scilicet diabolo, *Iesus* in nouissimo tempore, in zelo suo, ubi antichristus occidetur confusus: *Vade* in locum quem promeruisti, uidelicet dampnationis tuae, *Sathanas*, qui deorsum cecidisti.'

[176] *Expo. Euang.*, 25, p. 259, lines 59–62: '*Iterum*, post hanc temptationem, *assumpsit eum*, scilicet Christum in fidelibus membris suis, *in montem excelsum ualde*, id est in montem erroris, qui altitudinem suam usque ad labrum uenti extendet in antichristo.' *Sciuias*, III.11.27, line 553: 'usque ad labrum uenti procedit'; *Scivias* (Eng.), p. 502. Adso Dervensis, *De ortu et tempore Antichristi*, CCCM, 45 (Turnhout: Brepols, 1976), p. 24, lines 68–71. See also Richard Emmerson, 'Antichrist as Anti-Saint: The Significance of Abbot Adso's Libellus de Antichristo', *American Benedictine Review*, 30 (1979), 175–90.

[177] Adso, *De ortu et tempore Antichristi*, p. 22, lines 9–16.

[178] *Expo. Euang.*, 54, pp. 323–24, lines 1–12: '*Erunt signa*, id est portenta, *in sole*, scilicet in Christo, ita ut errantes humanitati saluatoris resistant, *et luna*, uidelicet in ecclesia, cum heretici ecclesiam impugnare conabuntur [...] id est antichristi, qui multas tempestates errorum educet, *et fluctuum*, scilicet hereticorum ministrorum ipsius, qui per uniuersum orbem mendaciis et deceptionibus suis discurrent.'

[179] *Expo. Euang.*, 13, p. 224, lines 34–35: '*Ex te enim exiet*, quia penitentia diabolum in abysso conterit.' A possible echo of this motif of trampling the Devil occurs when Hildegard interprets the shoes given the prodigal son as instruments for renouncing the Devil: *Expo. Euang.*, 26, p. 263, lines 59–61: '*et date anulum in manu eius*, scilicet comprehensionem bonorum operum, *et calciamenta*, per quae diabolo abrenuntiet'. *Sciuias*, II.7.25, p. 324, lines 588–91, 596–98: 'Quod ueri cultores

conquering the Devil as they thoroughly sift out (*excribro*) vices, so that the vices can no longer raise themselves up and the Devil can no longer rage.[180] Despite these allusions to Antichrist and Satan in the *Expositiones*, the figure of Antichrist in the *Expositiones* occupies less textual ground than in the visionary works. He lurks as a distant threat in the homilies but lacks the vivid portrayal and association with Ecclesia that occurs in *Sciuias*.[181] The introduction of Antichrist and apocalyptic themes in *Sciuias* bolsters the sense of crisis that Hildegard creates there to frame the need for the intervention of her prophetic and exegetical voice. The feeling of crisis and the need for self-justification do not play the same role in homilies intended for her sisters.

How do the *Expositiones* depict the reward for those who succeed in trampling the Tempter and defeating Antichrist? In monastic spirituality, the heavenly Jerusalem represents the object of contemplation and the destination in the afterlife, to be attained by living in accordance with *Rule*.[182] In the *Expositiones*, as in the *Symphonia* and the *Ordo uirtutum*, Hildegard evokes the eternal city with traditional monastic imagery, retaining the exegesis of the heavenly Jerusalem as the vision of peace and salvation, the final resting place for those who perform good works in this life.[183] The *magistra* refers to the edifice of revelation and to

---

Dei qui toto annisu terrena conculcant antiquum serpentem forti contritione deiciunt [...] Sed quod uides quod magna multitudo hominum in multa claritate fulgentium uenit, que predictum uermen fortiter ubique conculcans acriter eum cruciat [...] fidele agmen credentium [...] uirgines, martyres et ceteri huiusmodi cultores Dei, qui totu annisu terrena conculcant et celestia desiderant'; *Scivias* (Eng.), p. 303.

[180] *Expo. Euang.*, 55, p. 327, lines 49–55: '*Amen dico uobis*, omnibus, *non preteribit* de tenebris ad lucem, de caducis ad eterna, *generatio haec*, scilicet homines, *donec omnia fiant*, prelia ista, quae predixit in uirtutibus et in uiciis, scilicet usque dum omnia uicia per uirtutes ita excribrentur et perscrutentur, ut se plus erigere non ualeant, et ut etiam diabolus per uirtutes ita superetur, quod nichil amplius insanire possit.'

[181] See Emmerson, 'Representation of Antichrist'.

[182] A study of this material appears in Beverly Mayne Kienzle, 'Constructing Heaven in Hildegard of Bingen's *Expositiones evangeliorum*', in *Envisaging Heaven in the Middle Ages*, ed. by Ad Putter and C. A. Muessig, Routledge Studies in Medieval Religion and Culture (London: Routledge, 2006), pp. 34–43.

[183] *Expo. Euang.*, 14, p. 226, lines 10–21: '*remansit puer Iesus in Iherusalem*, quia ipse incarnatus operatus est in redemptione [...]. *Et non inuenientes*, eum in ulla similitudine illis similem esse, *regressi sunt in Ierusalem*, scilicet redemptionem pacis, *requirentes eum*, scrutando quid in illo appareret in philosophis et sapientibus.' *Expo. Euang.*, 20, p. 241, lines 7–10: '*Sicut scriptum est in lege Domini*, uoluntas eius, *tulerunt*, scilicet sanctitas quae in antiqua lege fuit, *Iesum*, id est

inspiration, secrets, and musical harmony emanating from heaven or dwelling there.[184] Ultimately, heaven for Hildegard is the realm of hidden mysteries, the source of divine inspiration.

Conclusion: Salvation History in the Hildegardian Corpus

How does the three-act drama of salvation history in the *Expositiones* compare to the framework for history in Hildegard's other works? The *magistra* employs varying schemes in her visionary works. In *Sciuias*, Hildegard defines the number of ages in nearly Augustinian terms, according to the six working days of creation. In her view, however, the sixth day has finished and the world has been placed in the seventh day.[185] In the same work, the *magistra* defines the five ages of the world, each represented by an animal: the fiery dog, the yellow lion, the pale horse, the black pig, and the grey wolf. She repeats the fivefold scheme with more precision in the *Liber diuinorum operum* and makes deliberate cross-references to her previous work, as when she explains: 'This is the age of the wolf trampling and devouring all

---

saluatorem, *in Iherusalem*, uidelicet ad uisionem pacis nostra.' *Expo. Euang.*, 21, p. 243, lines 5–7; p. 244, lines 18–19: '*tulerunt*, qui uirginitatem uouent bono exemplo, Iesum, id est uirginitatem, *in Iherusalem*, scilicet ad uisionem uerae pacis et salutis [. . .]. *Et ecce homo*, qui in uirginitate talis esse debet, *erat in Ierusalem*, scilicet in uisione salutis, *cui nomen Symeon.*' *Expo. Euang.*, 43, p. 306, lines 51–53: '*Ex hoc iam eris homines capiens*, ita ut propter bona opera quae facturus eris, in comprehensionem celestis Ierusalem uerteris.' 'O Ierusalem', *Symph.*, 49, pp. 436–39; *Ordo*, p. 520, line 335: 'qui nunc lucent in superna bonitate!'

[184] *Expo. Euang.*, 47, p. 313, lines 28–38: '*Scriptum est*, in spiritali transmutatione et interpretatione, *quia domus mea*, id est edificatio reuelationis, *domus orationis est*, scilicet ueritatis, quia nec celum, nec terra alium Deum preter me ostendunt, sed edificatio mea in qua me inuenietis, ostendit uobis ueritatem. [. . .] *erat docens cottidie in templo*; quia ipse filius Dei in ista apparitione nouae edificationis et interpretationis antiquae legis ad spiritalem intellectum procedit usque in finem in ecclesia'; *Expo. Euang.*, 48, p. 314, lines 1–3: 'Cum appropinquaret, inclinando se, Iesus, id est admonitio Spiritus Sancti, Ierusalem, scilicet ad hominem plenum uiciis et spurciciis, *uidens ciuitatem*, uidelicet edificationem saluationis.'

[185] *Sciuias*, III.11, p. 558, lines 446–51: 'Vt enim praedictum est, in sex diebus perfecit Deus opera sua. Quinque dies quinque numeri saeculi sunt; in sexto noua miracula in terris propalata sunt, uelut in sexta die primus homo formatus est. Sed nunc sextus numerus finitus est usque ad septimum numerum, in quo nunc cursus mundi uelut in septima die requiei positus est'; *Scivias* (Eng.), pp. 498–99. See Kathryn Kerby-Fulton, *Reformist Apocalypticism and Piers Plowman* (Cambridge: Cambridge University Press, 1990) on the Hildegardian ages, pp. 8, 45–46. Kerby-Fulton asserts that for Hildegard and other medieval Christians, the present corresponded to the seventh age, and the Augustinian sixth age was over.

things, which is described in the book *Sciuias*.'[186] In contrast to the five ages of the world, the *magistra* refers in the *Vita Hildegardis* to the five tones of righteousness (*toni iusticie*), signs of redemption sent by God that sound (*intonant*) for humankind: the sacrifice of Abel, the ark of Noah, the gift of the law to Moses, the incarnation, and the completion of time at the second coming.[187] The musical imagery of righteousness contrasts sharply with the harsh evocation of the five ages.

Building imagery is key to *Sciuias* as well: Hildegard envisions the edifice of salvation with God in Christ sitting on his throne, on the corner of a building, which rests on top of the mountain of faith.[188] The voice of the One enthroned guides us around the edifice from the creation of Adam in the south to Noah in the east, to Abraham and Moses in the north, and the Trinity in the west, although

[186] *Sciuias*, III.11, pp. 578–80; *Scivias* (Eng.), pp. 494–95; *LDO*, III.10.33, p. 457, lines 42–44: 'tempus hoc omnia conculcans omniaque deuorans lupus, qui in libro Sciuias describitur'; III.10.15, p. 432, lines 1–2: 'Dies autem istos, qui iniusticia torpent, ut prefatum est, canis igneus sed non ardens in libro Sciuias designat'; III.10.17, p. 436, lines 1–2: 'inter hec omnia, uelut leo in libro Sciuias notatus otendit'; III.10.21, p. 441, lines 8–9: 'inter omnia hec, quemadmodum equus in libro Sciuias demonstrat'; III.10.26, p. 447, lines 26–27: 'quod et porcus in libro Sciuias descriptus manifestat'.

[187] *V. Hild.*, II.2, pp. 21–22; *Life of Hildegard*, pp. 42–43.

[188] Hildegard explains that the building lies at an oblique angle; Christ as *lapis angularis* sits on the angle: *Sciuias*, III.2.5, p. 353, lines 184–92: 'Quod autem idem aedificum aliquantulum est in obliquum positum: hoc est quod homo qui opus Dei est non potest prae fragilitate sua incedere firmiter sine peccato et audaciter sine timore fragilis carnis diabolum superando, sed eum oportet illum humiliter deuitare et insidias eius sapienter fugere ne peccet, atque se fideliter coiungere bonis operibus et sic constare in Filio Dei, qui quasi in angulo sedens lapis angularis est, ita etiam opus electum coniungens in homine'; *Scivias* (Eng.), p. 327. This recalls Matthew 21. 42; I Peter 2. 7, Ephesians 2. 14, 20, Daniel 2. 34–35 ('abscisus est lapis sine manibus'), and the hymn *Urbs Jerusalem beata*, *Analecta Hymnica Medii Aevi*, ed. by G. M. Dreves and C. Blume, 58 vols (Leipzig: Fues Verlag (R. Reisland), 1866–1922), II (1888), 1, no. 93. str. 6: 'Angularis fundamentum Christus lapis missus est.' The *magistra* alludes to the Daniel verses in *Epistolarim*, I, 6, p. 14, lines 6–10: 'Et ecce mons magnus et excelsus, et ualde elegans et expolitis lapidibus factus contra orientem apparuit, supra quem quoddam magnum edificium stabat, de lignis et de lapidibus communis edificationis factum.' Her biographer cites them in the *V. Hild.*, III.16, p. 54, lines 32–35, to describe her prophetic gifts. See also Rupert of Deutz, *Commentaria in Euangelium Sancti Iohannis*, I, p. 32, lines 892–95: 'Quia uidelicet eodem sensu hoc dictum est: me oportet minui illum autem crescere uel illud quod in figura eius dixit daniel de lapide qui abscisus de monte sine manibus statuam comminuerat.' Rupert of Deutz, *De sancta trinitate*, 16, *In Numeros*, 1, p. 956, line 1658: 'Sic daniel in babylonia somnia nabuchodonosor prius audiuit et ipse sua uidit ac deinde reuelante dei spiritu coniciendo non in incertum de rebus futuris prophetauit'. See also Caesarius of Arles, *Sermones*, II, 169, 3, p. 693. See G. Ladner, 'The Symbolism of the Biblical Corner Stone in the Medieval West', *Mediaeval Studies*, 4 (1942), 43–60.

those figures do not appear in the illustration.[189] Their presence in the text calls to mind the Augustinian ages culminating in the incarnation, and it connects to *Expositiones* on the same theme. A similar envisioning of history as a great city appears in the *Liber diuinorum operum*, further evidence of the connection Hildegard herself makes between the two visionary works. The *Liber diuinorum operum* opens with the vision of a city representing divine providence: 'For you see, as it were, the squared form of a great city, which designates the stable and firm work of divine providence (*predestinationis*).'[190] Each subsequent vision elaborates on one area within the great city until Hildegard reaches the end of time with the tenth vision.[191] Material for exploring intertextuality and 'intervisuality' abounds.[192]

Compositions from the *Symphonia* also relate to the theology of history. Antiphons for the Virgin, 'Cum erubuerint' and 'Hodie aperuit', encompass all of salvation history from perdition to redemption by presenting Mary as the counterpart of Eve, a topos of medieval theology that Hildegard's music underscores.[193] Melismas — phrases of music sung on a single vowel sound — highlight the structure and meaning of the words and underscore the antithesis between Eve and Mary. In 'Cum erubuerint', the melismas accentuate the movement from the shame of the Fall to redemption that Mary's voice made possible when she uttered her acceptance of Gabriel's message.[194] For 'Hodie aperuit', the contrast between the Fall and Mary's role in redemption is highlighted by the melismas and images of opening and closing, the destruction of the serpent, and the blossoming of the virginal flower.[195]

---

[189] *Sciuias*, III.3.2, 4–7, 14, pp. 349, 352–54, 360; *Scivias* (Eng.), pp. 325–39.

[190] *LDO*, III.1.2, p. 346, lines 5–7: 'Vides enim quasi cuiusdam magnę ciuitatis instrumentum quadratum, quod designat diuinę predestinationis opus stabile et firmum.'

[191] *LDO*, III.2–5, pp. 353–417.

[192] On intervisuality in Hildegard, see Caviness, 'Artist', p. 119.

[193] 'Cum erubuerint', *Symph.*, 14, p. 389; 'Hodie aperuit', *Symph.*, 11, p. 386; 'Cum processit factura', *Symph.*, 13, p. 388; 'O quam magnum miraculum,' *Symph.*, 16, p. 391, lines 28–31.

[194] Marianne Pfau, 'Music and Text in Hildegard's Antiphons', in *Symphonia*, ed. by Newman, pp. 89–93, explains that 'Cum erubuerint' reveals three melismas and three major units of syntax (*Cum [. . .] casus, tunc [. . .] uoce, hoc [. . .] casu*). The first melisma has fourteen notes, the second sixteen, and the third is expanded to forty-eight. The extensive range of the third moves from low pitch up to high e, and descends again on -*su*.

[195] Pfau, 'Music and Text in Hildegard's Antiphons', pp. 89–93, explains that 'Hodie aperuit' features melismas in lines 1–4, while line 5, which talks about the serpent, has none and descends. Line 6 moves upward at the dawning, and lines 7–8 have lengthy melismas, with the melisma on *flos* in line 7 surging upward. See also Dronke, 'Hildegard's Inventions', pp. 312–13.

Melismas in medieval chant represent an example of wordless singing or neumatizing. Wordless phrases express the joyous mysteries of the faith. Amalarius of Metz (*c.* 775–850) wrote that melismatic singing brought about a type of rejoicing that needs no words. Notker Balbulus, ninth-century monk of St Gall, advocated this type of singing for the sequence. However, according to Lori Kruckenberg, wordless singing found disfavour and for the most part had gone out of style by the end of the tenth century in Germany.[196] The *magistra's* continuing use of melismas constitutes a curious case: on the one hand, a traditional or conservative tendency to guard melismatic singing, and on the other, a pattern of innovation and eccentricity. This unusual pattern in Hildegard's music mirrors the simultaneous innovation and preservation of tradition in her exegesis and theology of salvation history.

Hildegard's theology and representation of salvation history found its roots in Augustine's theology of history, which had an impact on the writings of her near contemporaries. Visual witnesses, notably the so-called *Hildegard-Gebetbuch*, testify to the prevalence of the theme. Hildegard's exegesis demonstrates a pattern that connects the gospel texts to the whole or part of salvation history, the two periods before and after the incarnation, and a third act representing the soul's inner struggle as it lives out the promise of the Word with the aid of the Holy Spirit. Various homilies deal with one of the three acts of salvation history. Some homilies, such as one on Matthew 4. 1–11, view the course of history in one text. Others focus on the role of Christ as Creator and Redeemer; still more deal with the work of the Spirit in contemporary time, when the allegorical faithful soul and Hildegard's Benedictine sisters struggled in the religious life. A few *expositiones* evoke the end times and the vision of the heavenly Jerusalem. Her emphasis generally remains incarnational; salvation history leads to redemption of the Church, the world, and the individual sinner through Christ. The theology of history permeates the *Expositiones* as well as Hildegard's other works.

---

[196] I am grateful to Lori Kruckenberg's research as presented in the paper, 'Liturgical Music for St. John the Evangelist with Special Emphasis on the Sequence', in *Leaves from Paradise*, ed. by Hamburger, pp. 133–60. For the works of Amalarius, see *Amalarii episcopi Opera liturgica omnia*, ed. by Jean-Michel Hanssens, 3 vols (Vatican City: Biblioteca apostolica vaticana, 1948–50). Kruckenberg cites the following passage from III, 56: 'Quando veneris, cantor, ad intellectum, celebra neuma, id est fige gradum in stantibus et manentibus rebus. Quid hoc vult? Vult nempe te docere, se aliquando veneris ad intellectum in quo conspicitur divinitas et aeternitas, ut desiderio mentis preceris, morans in eo. Si enim intellexeris illa, ibi te delectabit morari, in his quae iubilabis, id est laetaberis sine verbis transitoriis.'

Perhaps most striking in their exegetical innovation are the *Expositiones* that exemplify Hildegard's Trinitarian interpretation and those that draw the creation story out of the text of the Gospel. The three homilies on Luke 19. 41–47 reveal a clearly Trinitarian inspiration that departs significantly from any previous exegesis of the pericope and therefore demonstrates remarkable theological and exegetical innovation. The trio of *expositiones* on Luke 5. 1–11 also develops a Trinitarian interpretation that goes far beyond the norm in its innovation: each person of the Trinity plays a role, and the virtues emanate from the Spirit to assist humans after Christ's redeeming work. While Hildegard may have found some hints in prior exegesis for her readings of Luke 14. 16–24 and Matthew 20. 1–16, her innovative readings create narratives on key themes of Genesis. For the Lukan parable, Hildegard paints a sort of pre-lapsarian garden which figures an orderly monastery untroubled by disobedience. For the Matthean text, the seer develops her teaching not from Genesis as the base text, but from the Gospel, thus using a striking reverse or anti-typology. Christ, one in being with the Creator, provides through the gospel words the framework for both stories, the parable and Hildegard's allegory.

The theology of history so dominates the content of the *Expositiones* that the homilies deserve recognition as a major work on salvation history. The thematic and methodological parallels between the *Expositiones* and Hildegard's other compositions demonstrate how the vision of salvation history provides a nexus for thematic consistency in the *magistra*'s entire opus. In her written, visual, and musical works, Hildegard represented salvation history, extending from the individual soul to the cosmos and encompassing the whole of Christian history from creation to the end of time. She wove together the narratives of salvation history and the struggles of the individual sinner to constitute a sort of drama, like the itinerary of the soul in the *Ordo uirtutum*, inspired and guided by the Holy Spirit, and like the personal journey that she and her sisters undertook in the religious life. In her theology of history, Hildegard retains the foundation of twelfth-century monastic thought and its Augustinian sources at the same time that she constructs an edifice of collective and personalized instruction about the history of salvation, which she described as 'a moat', and 'wall around her sisters' intended to fortify them against evil.

THE *EXPOSITIONES* AND THE *ORDO UIRTUTUM*

Good Desire dwelled with Charity so that the splendour of good works would shine forth. Charity gave birth to Obedience, the first virtue, embraced the child and placed him in Humility, because there was no room in Vanity.[1]

Hildegard's interpretation of the holy family (Lk 2. 1–14) as the virtues of Charity (Mary), Good Desire (Joseph), and Obedience (Jesus) exemplifies her dramatic telling of scriptural allegories in the *Expositiones* and leads us to search for parallels with her morality play, the *Ordo uirtutum*. Does Hildegard transform other biblical figures into personified virtues, and if so, do those virtues play roles comparable to their parts in the *Ordo*? The *Ordo* represents the soul's struggle with the Devil, its penitence, and its restoration with the aid of the rescuing virtues. To what extent does Hildegard develop a drama from the elements of the scriptural narrative? Do the *Expositiones* reveal themes or plot lines similar to the *Ordo*? What models would Hildegard have for representing the soul's struggle in dramatic form, or as a struggle between virtue and vice? In fact, she drew on liturgical and didactic precedents in monastic drama and on a rich tradition of literary and visual representations of virtues and vices. This chapter surveys those precedents and then explores the *Expositiones* and the *Ordo uirtutum* to identify comparable features that shed light on Hildegard's exegesis and preaching: semantic parallels; techniques of *allegoresis*; correspondences in theme, structure, and plot; and characters either common to both works or notably missing from either.

[1] *Expo. Euang.*, 8, p. 208, lines 15–21: '*Factum est autem cum essent ibi*, uidelicet cum bonum desiderium cum caritate sic uersatur, *impleti sunt dies ut pareret*, scilicet ut splendor bonorum operum appareret. *Et peperit*, producendo, *filium suum primogenitum*, scilicet obedientiam, primam uirtutem, *et pannis eum inuoluit*, id est in amplexibus eum habet; *et reclinauit eum in presepio*, ponens in humilitate, *quia non erat eis locus in diuersorio*, quia nullum locum uanitatis habet.'

The Drama of the Soul and the Virtues and Vices

Drama animates all liturgical celebration, and the earliest medieval plays grew from the Easter liturgy. Resurrection plays count among the first liturgical dramas that were staged in medieval monasteries, and extensive evidence points to their performance in Germany. A liturgical drama from Hildegard's immediate environment remains: Engelberg, Stiftsbibliothek, MS 103, a *Liber ordinarius* identified with the Hirsau usages and probably with Disibodenberg, contains an Easter play.[2] Does the staging of plays suggest any link between liturgical drama, exegesis, and preaching? It seems that boundaries between the genres were indeed fluid. Monastic plays performed at Epiphany or the Feast of the Innocents elucidate this fluidity. Susan Boynton suggests that Rachel's lament in texts from Fleury and Freising may be described as a 'dramatized sermon' with an exegetical plan on three levels: typological, allegorical, and tropological.[3] Did women's communities participate in liturgical plays? More than twenty texts of the *Visitatio sepulcri* from women's monasteries are extant, and in them, women played the roles of women. These, including manuscripts from Andernach, Essen, Gandersheim, and Gernrode, date from the thirteenth century onwards, but may reflect earlier practices.[4] Liturgical drama, therefore, developed as performative exegesis in male and female monastic communities. How else might Hildegard have related drama to preaching and exegesis?

Drama such as the Fleury plays described above served as a teaching medium.[5] Moreover, convent drama extended beyond the Office. The learned canoness

---

[2] See Omlin, 'Das ältere Engelberger Osterspiel und der cod. 103 der Stiftsbibliothek Engelberg'; and Heinzer, 'Der Hirsauer *Liber ordinarius*'. See also Mews, 'Hildegard, the *Speculum virginum* and Religious Reform', p. 266.

[3] Susan Boynton, 'From the Lament of Rachel to the Lament of Mary: A Transformation in the History of Drama and Spirituality', in *Signs of Change: Transformations of Christian Traditions and their Representation in the Arts, 1000–2000*, ed. by Nils Holger Petersen, Claus Clüver, and Nicolas Bell, Studies in Comparative Literature, 43 (Amsterdam: Rodopi, 2004), pp. 319–40 (p. 326). Boynton compares the lament of Rachel in plays for the Epiphany or the Feast of the Innocents to the *planctus Mariae* in two passion plays.

[4] Among many sources on medieval liturgical drama, see Dunbar H. Ogden, *The Staging of Drama in the Medieval Church* (Newark: University of Delaware Press, 2002), especially the discussions of the *Visitatio sepulcri* in German monasteries, pp. 39–66, 117–19, and pp. 143–53 on the role of women in drama from women's religious houses.

[5] Julia Bolton Holloway, 'The Monastic Context of Hildegard's *Ordo virtutum*', in *The Ordo virtutum of Hildegard of Bingen: Critical Studies*, ed. by A. E. Davidson (Kalamazoo: Medieval Institute Publications, 1992), pp. 63–77 (p. 67), observes that defiance to the obedience mandated by the *Rule* played out in the Office itself and gives the example of the Office for St Scholastica.

Hrotsvitha (*c.* 935–*c.* 975) composed plays for her sisters at the imperial convent of Gandersheim, where the nun Adelheid assumed the post of abbess after leaving Rupertsberg in 1151. One of Hrotsvitha's plays, entitled *Sapientia*, includes female characters that bear the names of virtues: Sapientia, the mother, and her daughters Fides, Spes, and Karitas. However, Hrotsvitha does not cast them as personifications but as historical women.[6] While there is no evidence for a direct influence of Hrotsvitha on Hildegard, I would argue nonetheless that the possibility of influence should not be ruled out. The writings of the erudite canoness demonstrate the taste for drama in a foundation for learned women connected to the Ottonian court, a community with which Hildegard maintained contact through Adelheid. Furthermore, Hrotsvitha wrote expressly in praise of the chastity of virgins, a theme of Hildegard's works.[7]

The mundus minor

Do these moral dramas have counterparts in the visual arts and in other literature? The twelfth-century accords a striking attention to inward-looking spirituality, often depicted as a struggle within the soul. This interior focus found roots in such major writers as Origen, Evagrius Ponticus, Prudentius, and Gregory the Great. Origen describes a conflict between virtues and vices within the individual soul, which he describes as a microcosm or *mundus minor*, following the parallel between microcosm and macrocosm that was diffused through the *Timaeus* of Plato.[8]

---

[6] See Peter Dronke, *Poetic Individuality in the Middle Ages: New Departures in Poetry 1000–1150*, 2nd edn (London: Westfield College, University of London Committee for Medieval Studies, 1986), p. 169, n. 2; Dronke, *Women Writers of the Middle Ages*, pp. 55–83, where he challenges the notions that Hrotsvitha's plays were either naïve or not intended for performance. Dronke highlights Hrotsvitha's skillful use of Terence and Vergil to both instruct and amuse her audience. See *Hrotsvit of Gandersheim: A Florilegium of her Works*, trans. by Katharina Wilson (Woodbridge: Brewer, 1998). *Hrotsvit: opera omnia*, ed. by Walter Berschin, Bibliotheca scriptorum graecorum et romanorum Teubneriana (Munich: Saur, 2001).

[7] Pamela Sheingorn, 'The Virtues of Hildegard's *Ordo virtutum*; or, It *Was* a Woman's World', in *Ordo virtutum of Hildegard of Bingen*, ed. by Davidson, pp. 52–57, proposes that the consecration of virgins may be the occasion for the *Ordo*'s composition. See also Fassler, 'Composer and Dramatist', pp. 150–53, on the function of the *Ordo*.

[8] On twelfth-century interest in the *Timaeus*, see Chenu, *Nature, Man and Society*, pp. 30–32. Origen explains the human as microcosm in *Homélies sur la Genèse*, I.11, pp. 52–54, lines 31–36: 'Cum ergo haec omnia fierent quae uidentur iussu Dei per Verbum eius et praepararetur immensus

Many representations of the theme derived directly from the commentary of Chalcidius on the *Timaeus*. The latter as well as John Scotus Eriugena's reflections on continuity between humankind and the cosmos sparked great interest and further commentary in the early twelfth-century schools, particularly at Chartres. Bernard Silvester composed the influential *De mundi universitate*, which describes the universe as macrocosm and the human as microcosm.[9]

In addition, writings from monastic *milieux*, such as the *Elucidarium* of Honorius Augustodunensis, depict the theme of microcosm and macrocosm. Honorius includes a diagram of the human as microcosm, and manuscripts of the encyclopedic *Liber floridus* of Lambert of St Omer, composed between 1090 and 1120, include drawings of microcosm and macrocosm.[10] Hildegard's sources doubtless derive from the monastic tradition more than from twelfth-century schools and the interest in the philosophy of nature.[11] What Laurence Moulinier concludes from the scrutiny of botanical knowledge in the work of Hildegard and Bernard Silvester provides a useful parallel here. Moulinier observes that both authors link

iste uisibilis mundus, simul autem et per allegoriae figuram ostenderetur quae essent quae exornare possent minorem mundum, id est hominem, tunc iam ipse homo creatur secundum ea quae in consequentibus declarantur'. See also *Homélies sur l'Exode*, ed. and trans. by Marcel Borret, SC, 321 (Paris: Cerf, 1985), 13.3, p. 274, line 25. *Homélies sur la Genèse*, XII.3, p. 298, lines 10–22: 'Ego puto quod de singulis nobis hoc dici potest quia duae gentes et duo populi sint intra nos. Nam et uirtutum populus intra nos est et uitiorum nihilominus populus intra nos est'; and XII.3, p. 298, lines 23–29.

[9] On Alan of Lille, see Newman, *God and the Goddesses*, pp. 51–89; and Dronke, *Dante and Medieval Latin Traditions* (Cambridge: Cambridge University Press, 1986), pp. 8–13, who asserts that Alan saw himself as prophet and poet. See also Ernst R. Curtius, *European Literature and the Latin Middle Ages*, Bollingen Series, 36 (Princeton: Princeton University Press, 1973), pp. 117–22.

[10] Herrad of Hohenbourg probably followed Honorius's model for the illustration of microcosm and macrocosm in the *Hortus deliciarum*. See Griffiths, *Garden of Delights*, pp. 64–67; Caviness, 'Artist', p. 124; Chenu, *Nature, Man and Society*, pp. 18–48, 181; Van Engen, *Rupert of Deutz*, pp. 85–86.

[11] Hildegard refers to Philosophy in one parable; in the *V. Hild.*, she asserts that she came to understand the writings of the philosophers along with other texts. See *Epistolarium*, I, 80R, pp. 181–82 (p. 181), lines 16–21, 27–30; *V. Hild.*, II.2, p. 24. See Burnett, 'Hildegard of Bingen and the Science of the Stars', pp. 111–15, on Hildegard's view of the universe. Stephen D'Evelyn, 'The Figure of Eve in the Lyrics of Hildegard of Bingen', unpublished conference paper, points out Chalcidian vocabulary in Hildegard's 'O Splendissima gemma': *Symph.*, 10, p. 385, line 8: 'primam materiam'; line 15: 'prima materia'. The same phrase occurs in the *Solut.*, PL 197: 1040, when Hildegard discusses the six days and works of creation: 'Post creationem etiam primae materiae nulla mora fuit'. See also Newman, *Sister of Wisdom*, pp. 83–87.

tightly the themes of *natura rerum* and *natura corporis*, but for Hildegard the 'theological design is by far more present'. One finds a 'true theology of creation from which plants are not excepted'.[12]

Virtues and Vices

Monastic thought provided Hildegard with a rich literature on virtues and vices. Evagrius Ponticus (*c.* 345–*c.* 399) delineated an octad of evil thoughts that the monk must combat. His octad reached Latin culture through the works of John Cassian and Martin of Braga (*c.* 520–*c.* 580), whose work supplemented Evagrius's lessons with Seneca's teaching on the virtues. Gregory the Great (*c.* 540–*c.* 604) derived a list of seven principal vices from the root of pride in the *Moralia in Iob*. Inspired by the *Moralia*, monastic exegetes developed treatises discussing the virtues and vices and wove them into sermons.[13] During the Ottonian period, the *Moralia* received a respect approaching that given the Bible. The scriptorium at St Maximin in Trier, a monastery with which Hildegard maintained contact, produced a masterpiece copy of the *Moralia*, in two pandects with thirty-five initials. John of Gorze, the tenth-century reformer, reportedly memorized nearly the whole of the *Moralia* in order to cite it as often as possible in sermons and prayers.[14] Otloh of St Emmeram, in *De institutione clericorum*, provided instruction on which virtues would prove effective against key vices; and in the *Liber uisionum*, he echoes Gregory's *Dialogues* on the moral value of telling miracle stories.[15]

[12] Moulinier, 'Abbesse et agronome', p. 141: 'l'arrière-plan théologique est beaucoup plus présent [...] en d'autres termes une véritable théologie de la Création à laquelle les plantes ne font pas exception'. For other discussions on the influence of classical texts on Hildegard's cosmology, see Burnett, 'Hildegard of Bingen and the Science of the Stars', p. 101, n. 1, who argues that Hans Liebeschütz modified his claim for parallels between Hildegard's cosmology and Eastern sources in *Das allegorische Weltbild der heiligen Hildegard von Bingen* (Leipzig, 1930; repr. with Nachwort, Darmstadt: Wissenschaftliche Buchgesellschaft, 1964), pp. 82–84.

[13] On the treatises, see Newhauser, *Treatise on Vices and Virtues*, pp. 99–114. See also Liebeschütz, *Das allegorische Weltbild*, pp. 37–38.

[14] Mayr-Harting, *Ottonian Book Illumination*, pp. 118, 209. On Gregory's influence in exegesis, see Lubac, *Medieval Exegesis*, II, 117–25.

[15] The *Moralia*'s impact on illustrated manuscripts continued into the twelfth century, as evidenced by the frontispiece of the Floreffe Bible, which portrays Ezekiel and St John. See Bouché, 'Spirit in the World'.

In addition to these monastic compositions on moral training for the religious life, literature and art on the virtues and vices show the profound influence of the *Psychomachia* of Prudentius (*c.* 348–*c.* 405). The *Psychomachia* drew on classical precedents but provided a markedly Christian allegory that introduced into western culture the theme of the battle between personified figures of virtue and vice. Female warriors engage in an epic battle to defend the Christian faith against attacks.[16] Illustrated manuscripts of the *Psychomachia* had an impact on the developing iconography and literature of virtues and vices, including several works nearly contemporaneous with Hildegard's writings: the *Speculum uirginum*, the *Liber de fructu carnis et spiritus*, and the *Hortus deliciarum*.[17] Both the *Speculum uirginum* and the *Liber de fructu carnis et spiritus* may belong to a Hirsau milieu, since they have been attributed to Conrad of Hirsau.[18] Both employ the schematic layout of the tree for virtues and vices.[19] Herrad of Hohenbourg devotes five consecutive folios to a psychomachia cycle.[20] Finally, the *Hildegard-Gebetbuch* devotes eight folios to depictions of the beatitudes (Mt 5. 3–10). Two sets of figures, the virtuous and blessed (both male and female pairs), stand in the upper half of each page, while the corresponding vices, the cursed, are embodied in two men who occupy the lower half.[21] The Hand of God projects from the top into the upper half of the page.[22]

---

[16] Adolf Katzenellenbogen, *Allegories of the Virtues and Vices in Medieval Art* (Toronto: University of Toronto Press and Medieval Academy of America, MART repr. 1989), p. 54. S. Georgia Nugent, 'Virtus or Virago? The Female Personifications of Prudentius's *Psychomachia*', in *Virtue and Vice*, ed. by Hourihane, pp. 13–28; Joanne S. Norman, *Metamorphoses of an Allegory* (New York: Lang, 1988), pp. 88–99; Richard Stettiner, 'Die Illustrierten Prudentiushandschriften', in *Die Illustrierten Prudentiushandschriften* (Berlin: Preuss, 1895); Curtius, *European Literature*, pp. 38–39, on Martianus Capella.

[17] Katzenellenbogen, *Allegories of the Virtues and Vices*, pp. 1–13, 16, also points out a section of the Gospel Book of Henry the Lion.

[18] See Jutta Seyfarth, 'The *Speculum virginum*: The Testimony of the Manuscripts', in *Listen Daughter*, ed. by Mews, pp. 41–57.

[19] Bloomfield, *Seven Deadly Sins*, pp. 160–61. Mews, 'Hildegard, the *Speculum virginum* and Religious Reform', p. 266, emphasizes the differences in outlook between the *Speculum virginum* and Hildegard and Tenxwind.

[20] Griffiths, *Garden of Delights*, pp. 197–201.

[21] The illustrations are discussed by Klemm, 'Der Bilderzyklus im Hildegard-Gebetbuch', pp. 176–85.

[22] This association of the right hand of the Lord and virtue belongs to a tradition derived from Psalm 117. 16: 'Dextera Domini fecit uirtutem' (The right hand of the Lord has made virtue). *Virtus* can be translated as either virtue or strength, power. Both meanings are operative

The cursed display angry animal faces that protrude from their mouths; some figures carry symbols characterizing the vice they represent, such as a moneybag, spears, and swords.[23] The illustrations balance virtue with vice, coupling the poor in spirit with the proud, the meek with the angry, those who mourn with those who rejoice at the worst matters, those who hunger for righteousness with the miserly, the merciful with those who glory over others' adversities, the pure in heart with the malevolent, the peacemakers with the contumelious, those who suffer persecution with the persecutors.[24] The prayers on the facing pages ask for aid in practising virtue and avoiding vice.[25] The *Gebetbuch* further demonstrates the currency of this motif in spiritual art and literature from Hildegard's environment.

Hence, Hildegard's thought derives from the inward-looking spirituality of monasticism and its inheritance of the Platonic and Origenist notion of the conflict within the individual soul. E. Ann Matter signals the Alexandrian's impact on exegesis of the twelfth century: 'But it is Origen's sense of the drama of Christ and the soul that predominates in twelfth-century exegesis.'[26] How Hildegard develops that sense of drama in her exegesis will unfold in the remainder of this chapter. We begin with a brief summary of the characters, plot, and theme of the *Ordo uirtutum*.

---

simultaneously. Patristic and later exegetes associated the hand with Christ and the making of virtue. See Bouché, 'Spirit in the World', pp. 56–57.

[23] See Katzenellenbogen, *Allegories of the Virtues and Vices*, p. 7, on the Carolingian miniaturists that characterized the vices as 'weird powers of darkness' that 'give an immediate impression of violence and wildness'. On the iconography of the beatitudes, see Martin Gosebruch, 'Die Magdeburger Seligpriesungen', *Zeitschrift für Kunstgeschichte*, 38 (1975), 97–126; J. A. Harris, 'The Beatitudes Casket in Madrid's Museo Arqueológico: Its Iconography in Context', *Zeitschrift für Kunstgeschichte*, 53 (1990), 134–39; Géza Jászai, *Die Domkammer der Kathedralkirche Sankt Paulus in Münster* (Münster: Kapitel der Kathedralkirche St Paulus zu Münster, 1991); D. Kötzsche, 'Drei Seligpreisungen von einem Schrein', in *Per assiduum studium scientiae adipisci margaritam: Festschrift für Ursula Nilgen zum 65. Geburtstag*, ed. by Annelies Amberger and others (St Ottilien: EOS-Verlag, 1999), pp. 137–44; K. H. Usener, 'Sur le chef-reliquaire de Pape Alexandre', *Bulletin des Musées Royaux d'Art et d'Histoire*, 6 (1934), 57–63. I am grateful to J. Hamburger for these references.

[24] *Gebetbuch*, fols 32ᵛ, 33ᵛ, 34ᵛ, 35ᵛ, 36ʳ, 37ᵛ, 38ᵛ, 39ᵛ. See Klemm, 'Der Bilderzyklus im Hildegard-Gebetbuch', pp. 176–85.

[25] *Gebetbuch*, fol. 39ʳ. The prayer for Matthew 5. 9, avoiding discord, enumerates a list of vices to avoid.

[26] Matter, *Voice of My Beloved*, p. 39.

The Ordo uirtutum

The *Ordo uirtutum* opens with a presentation of the virtues to the Patriarchs and Prophets.[27] Souls placed in bodies lament their fall into the shadow (*umbra*) or darkness of sinners,[28] an indication of the work's strong neo-Platonic themes and a foreshadowing of Anima's fall into sin.[29] Felix Anima (the Happy Soul) sings joyously before sin weighs her down and she appears as Anima Grauata (the Soul weighed down).[30] The virtues encourage her to seek their help to overcome the Devil.[31] As the *Ordo* unfolds, most of the virtues introduce themselves; the chorus responds with praises and affirmation of the particular virtue's qualities.[32] The virtues lament the wandering of Anima from her master, and the penitent Anima engages in dialogue with them both singly and collectively, as she beseeches their aid. The Devil arrives in pursuit of Anima, who was once in his embrace. Anima stands firmly against him and pleads for aid from Humilitas, who calls upon Victoria and the other virtues. They bind up the Devil, and Victoria sounds forth a triumphant *Gaudete!*[33] Castitas and the other virtues resist the Devil's insults and appeal to God for continuing direction in leading his children to the heavenly Jerusalem. To complete the drama, the chorus of virtues and souls evokes the original greenness of creation and depicts a suffering but victorious Christ, the warrior or *uir preliator* (Is 42. 13),[34] who shows his wounds and appeals to all humans to reverence the Father and receive his outstretched hand.[35]

---

[27] *Ordo*, p. 505, lines 5–9.

[28] *Ordo*, pp. 505–06, lines 15–22.

[29] On the Platonism of the *Ordo*, see Dronke, *Poetic Individuality in the Middle Ages*, p. 172; and Richard Axton, *European Drama of the Early Middle Ages* (London: Hutchison, 1974), pp. 94–99.

[30] *Ordo*, p. 506, lines 24–40.

[31] *Ordo*, p. 507, lines 42–45.

[32] Innocentia appears after having been described by the chorus: 'Innocentia, que in pudore bono non integritatem non amisisti et que auariciam gutturis serpentis non deuorasti' (*Ordo*, p. 508, lines 77–79). Her appearance and reply constitute a bridge to the next group of virtues (*Ordo*, p. 512, line 154).

[33] *Ordo*, p. 519, line 311.

[34] *Ordo*, p. 519, lines 346–60. Is 42. 13: 'Dominus sicut fortis egredietur sicut uir proeliator suscitabit zelum uociferabitur et clamabit super inimicos suos confortabitur.'

[35] For an outline of the *Ordo*, see Audrey E. Davidson, 'Music and Performance: Hildegard of Bingen's *Ordo virtutum*', in *Ordo virtutum of Hildegard of Bingen*, ed. by Davidson, pp. 1–30 (pp.

Generally scholars identify seventeen virtues: Humilitas, Scientia Dei, Charitas, Timor Dei, Obediencia, Fides, Spes, Castitas, Innocentia, Contemptus Mundi, Amor Celestis, an unidentified virtue whose name is illegible in the manuscript, Verecundia, Misericordia, Victoria, Discretio, and Paciencia.[36] I argue that an eighteenth should be added: Virginitas, a key figure in Hildegard's exegesis, teaching, and preaching. At the centre of the play, a key passage engages the chorus with Castitas and Virginitas. Castitas addresses Virginitas with imaged language inspired by the Song of Songs, 'Virginitas, in regali thalamo stas' (Virginity, you stand in the royal bride-chamber). Virginity utters no reply, but the chorus sings:

> Flos campi cadit vento,
> pluvia spargit eum. O Virginitas, tu permanes in symphoniis supernorum civium:
> unde es suavis flos qui numquam aresces.[37]

[The flower of the field falls to the wind, the rain scatters it. O Virginity, you remain among the symphonies of the supernal citizens, whence you are a gentle flower who never becomes arid.]

This song, replete with imagery from the Song of Songs, constitutes the musical 'high point of the drama', for which Hildegard reserved her 'most lavish and florid setting'.[38] The chorus replies to Castitas and addresses Virginitas. The latter does not reply or introduce herself as do the other virtues.[39] Nonetheless, the voiceless Virginitas, addressee of songs from Castitas and the Chorus, arguably constitutes an eighteenth character even if she is off stage. Moreover, Hildegard cites the same line from Castitas to Virginitas in her epistolary lament on the death of Richardis.[40] If one considers Virginitas a voiceless character in the play, the suggestion

---

8–9). Peter Dronke analyzes themes and imagery in *Poetic Individuality in the Middle Ages*, pp. 167–79.

[36] All but two virtues, Verecundia and Paciencia, figure in some way in the *Expositiones*. Dronke assumes that the unnamed virtue is Disciplina but notes that the speaker's name is erased in the Riesenkodex. *Nine Medieval Latin Plays*, ed. and trans. by Peter Dronke (Cambridge: Cambridge University Press, 1994), p. 170. A passage similar to the *Ordo uirtutum* but shorter appears at the end of *Sciuias*. Dronke discusses this and scrutinizes textual parallels in 'Problemata Hildegardiana', pp. 100–06. Dronke, *LDO*, p. lxxix, contests the assumption of Carlevaris and Führkotter (*Sciuias*, pp. xiii, xxxi, li–lii) that the *Ordo* and related lyrics are derived from *Sciuias*, III.13.

[37] *Ordo*, p. 511, line 144; p. 512, lines 150–52.

[38] Davidson, 'Music and Performance', p. 14.

[39] *Ordo*, p. 511, lines 144–48.

[40] *Letters*, I, 13R, p. 30, lines 14–15. On the letters pertinent to this episode in Hildegard's life, see Ferrante, 'Correspondent', pp. 103–04.

that Hildegard composed the speech of Castitas in memory of Richardis takes on added poignancy.[41]

The Ordo *and the* Expositiones: *Vocabulary and Structure*

Do the *Ordo* and the *Expositiones* share significant vocabulary that signals thematic similarities? Hildegard equates the scriptural *multitudo miliciae celestis* (the multitude of the heavenly host) with *multitudo uirtutum* (the multitude of virtues) when she explains the significance of the heavenly host in her commentary on Luke 2. 13.[42] In the homily on the healing of the leper and the centurion's servant (Mt 8. 1–13), Hildegard explains that the soul with a great army of virtues (*tanta milicia uirtutum*) will enter the body and the senses, represented by the centurion's house.[43] In her commentary on John 10. 11–16, Jesus as the good shepherd, she glosses the biblical 'one flock', *unum ouile*, which represents the virtues, as *una milicia in Deo* (one army in God).[44] The term *militia* describes the ensemble of the virtues and emphasizes their solidarity and strength. Likewise in the *Ordo*, the virtues are *milites*, soldiers or knights. When Victoria engages in dialogue with other virtues, Humilitas calls Victoria to battle with her soldiers (*militibus tuis*) and to bind up the Devil. Victoria in turn calls the virtues *milites* ('O fortissimi et gloriosissimi milites') as she calls for their aid. The virtues reply that they will do battle gladly: 'nos libenter militamus tecum contra illusorem hunc' (We fight gladly with you against this mocker).[45] Hence, the military connotation of the word *militia* and of its cognomen *miles* conveys the combative role of the virtues in Hildegard's works, as in the *psychomachia* tradition. The *magistra* casts the host of virtues as

---

[41] Newman, *Sister of Wisdom*, p. 223. Holloway, 'Monastic Context', p. 70, describes the *Ordo* as the story of a 'prodigal daughter', inspired by Richardis, and as the 'celebration of Obedience', 'following upon a revolt'; and Gunilla Iversen, 'O Virginitas [...]: New Light on the *Ordo virtutum* [...]', *Early Drama, Art, and Music Review*, 20 (1997), 1–16.

[42] *Expo. Euang.*, 8, p. 209, lines 41–43: '*Et subito facta est*, ita quod cito erit, *cum angelo*, scilicet cum gratia Dei, *multitudo miliciae celestis*, id est multitudo uirtutum *laudantium Deum* in suauissimo sono *et dicentium* in ostensione: *Gloria in altissimis Deo.*'

[43] *Expo. Euang.*, 19, p. 239, lines 36–40: '*Et respondens*, reminiscendo sui, *centurio*, id est quinque sensus, *ait: Domine*, uidelicet anima, cui obedire debeo, *non sum dignus*, propter inconstantiam meam, sed parce, ne peream; *ut intres*, cum tanta milicia uirtutum, *sub tectum meum*, scilicet corporis mei.'

[44] *Expo. Euang.*, 31, p. 276, line 29.

[45] *Ordo*, pp. 518–19, lines 294–99, 301–04.

helpers to humankind on the arduous path to the performance of good works and the attainment of salvation. The virtues serve as knights under the ultimate command of the *uir preliator*, the triumphant Christ.

Beyond the crucial metaphors of *militia* and *miles*, does the structure of some *Expositiones* echo the play and reflect the struggle between virtue and vice? Hildegard's exegesis of the parable of the prodigal son (Lk 15. 11–32) demonstrates how the *magistra* makes the most of a biblical narrative that is itself clearly arranged as a drama.[46] The well-known tale bears repetition as Hildegard reconstructs it. The younger son, hungering for pleasure and evil knowledge, leaves home and spends his time recklessly with various vices (reckless living, Lk 15. 13). He makes an alliance with Malice (the citizen of another country, Lk 15. 15), who sends him to his farm (Lk 15. 15), where the young man may cultivate vices (the pigs and their food, Lk 15. 15–16) and nourish his wickedness.[47] Hildegard adapts the agricultural and nutritional imagery of the parable to describe the cultivation of vices: the younger son directs his work in the wrong way; he eats the wrong food; and he is left to feed vices (the husks, Lk 15. 16) to pigs, embodiments of wickedness. The son continues seeking to fulfill his desire with these evil practices. He wants to blame God, stating that God bears greater responsibility for his faults than he himself does. Hildegard interprets the unwillingness of anyone to feed the younger son (Lk 15. 16) as creation turning against him because of his accusation against God. The son's alienation is complete when all of creation rejects him, and he has no nourishment.[48]

Nevertheless, the younger son eventually remembers his Creator and becomes aware of the evils he did. He resolves to leave his wicked path, to follow the good road to his father, and to say to his Creator that he has transgressed with the heavenly breath in him, because despite knowing God, he still committed sins. On account of his wickedness, he is not worthy to be called God's son. He will ask to be one of the hired laborers (Lk 15. 19), those who fulfill God's will by their own blood and toil.[49] When the son resolves to convert and returns home (Lk 15. 20), the father exercises the virtues of Mercy, Love, Righteousness, and Charity. They stand in dramatic opposition to Malice's practice of vices. The repentant son then confesses that he sinned (Lk 15. 21) when, even while knowing God, he did not

---

[46] See Bovon, *L'Évangile selon saint Luc*, pp. 41–44, on the questions raised by modern exegetes concerning the three parts of the narrative.

[47] *Expo. Euang.*, 26, p. 261, lines 21–24.

[48] *Expo. Euang.*, 26, p. 261, lines 25–30.

[49] *Expo. Euang.*, 26, p. 261, lines 31–35.

refrain from sinning.[50] The confession marks a dramatic reversal of the son's tendency to blame God for his problems. The father's kiss (Lk 15. 20) unites the two and sets in motion the repentance the son has been planning. Hildegard interprets the son's return as a turning from vice to virtue, from union with Malice to the embrace and reception of Justice and Charity.[51]

As the forgiving father calls his servants (Lk 15. 22), so God summons the virtues. Hildegard explains that the virtues represent humankind's helpers in the work of serving God. God orders that the son be clothed with innocence and righteousness and be bestowed with the understanding of good works (the stole, ring, and shoes, Lk 15. 22). Thereupon, he will renounce the Devil and proceed on the straight path.[52] Hildegard asserts that the Son of God should be called upon. The fatted calf (Lk 15. 23) represents the Son; he brought heavenly fullness or anointing, and his martyrdom is repeated in that anointing. The taste for good works will then be consumed, and rejoicing will take place (the banquet, Lk 15. 23).[53] The restorative life-giving power of the Holy Spirit has blossomed in the repentant son (Lk 15. 24). Here Hildegard introduces the notion of *uiriditas* to describe the Holy Spirit's role in the Son's return, repentance, and redemption, and to usher in the vocabulary and concepts of rebirth.[54]

The older brother, in contrast to his younger sibling, possesses good knowledge and cultivates his heavenly inheritance. Reflecting on his ways, he approaches the mansion of virtues (the house, Lk 15. 25), which stands as the moral opposite of Malice's farm where his brother had gone. At the mansion of virtues, he hears the joy of the heavenly vision ascending on high as well as the beauty and glory that serves God (the music and dancing, Lk 15. 25).[55] Through his meditation, he calls upon Faith; through his searching for God's grace, he asks what awoke him. Faith (a servant, Lk 15. 27) answers his pondering, recognizing that he knows God, that he has made the right journey, and that the Creator has retold the passion of his

---

[50] *Expo. Euang.*, 26, pp. 261–62, lines 38–40.

[51] *Expo. Euang.*, 26, p. 262, lines 46–50.

[52] *Expo. Euang.*, 26, pp. 262–63, lines 55–61.

[53] *Expo. Euang.*, 26, p. 263, lines 61–65.

[54] *Expo. Euang.*, 26, p. 263, lines 65–70: 'uiriditas Spiritus Sancti in ipso refloruit; *quia hic filius meus* quem creaui *mortuus* fuerat, quoniam scientiam Dei non habebat, *et reuixit*, reuertendo ad me; *perierat* in memoria iusticie, quia saturitatem uitae non habuit, et *inuentus est* in uia iusticie. *Et ceperunt* epulare in congratulatione inuentae perditae ouis.'

[55] *Expo. Euang.*, 26, p. 263, lines 71–76.

son who brought fullness of life.[56] God warns the older brother to remain on the good course. In response to the elder son's jealous protestations, God admonishes him and assures him that it is fitting to rejoice in the renewing power (*uiriditas*) of the Holy Spirit and to celebrate the turning of evil knowledge to the good.[57]

What semantic or structural features of the *Ordo uirtutum* does the homily evoke? In both texts, the virtues inhabit a *mansio*. The older brother approaches the mansion of virtues (*mansioni uirtutum*), much as Anima in the *Ordo* invokes the virtues in their *mansio*: 'O you, royal virtues, how sweet is your dwelling place.'[58] The music of rejoicing accompanies repentance in the homily and the *Ordo*. The older brother hears the joy of the heavenly vision (*gaudium supernae uisionis*), occasioned by the repentant sinner's return. Similarly, the chorus in the *Ordo* hails the restoration of Anima. Moreover, *uiriditas*, the restorative life-giving power of the Holy Spirit, flowers in both works. It blossoms anew in the repentant son, 'the greenness of the Holy Spirit blossomed anew in him',[59] reflecting the restoration of the lost innocence of creation. The *Ordo* evokes that original blossoming of creatures: 'In the beginning all creatures were green, flowers bloomed in the midst; later greenness descended.'[60] The *uiriditas* that blossomed in creation and then withered from sin finally finds restoration through grace in human repentance.

The virtue of Fides plays a key role in both texts. When the older brother ponders the rejoicing over the younger son's return, he calls upon Fides, who explains that the younger brother has chosen the right path: 'Your brother, with the knowledge by which he knows God, has come, in that he has made the right journey.'[61] In the *Ordo*, Fides speaks authoritatively as well, explaining the mystery of faith to the other virtues: 'I am Faith, mirror of life. Venerable daughters, come

---

[56] *Expo. Euang.*, 26, pp. 263–64, lines 76–84.

[57] *Expo. Euang.*, 26, p. 264, lines 85–110.

[58] *Expo. Euang.*, 26, p. 263, lines 73–76: '*et* propinquaret, per bonam coniunctionem, *domui*, id est mansioni uirtutum, *audiuit*, ad superna ascendendo, *symphoniam*, scilicet gaudium supernae uisionis, *et chorum*, uidelicet decorem et gloriam in quibus Deo seruitur'. *Ordo*, p. 515, lines 220–27: 'O uos regales uirtutes [. . .] et quam dulcis est uestra mansio'. *Ordo*, p. 519, line 313 (praises).

[59] *Expo. Euang.*, 26, p. 263, lines 64–65: '*et epulemur*, in congratulatione, quia uiriditas Spiritus Sancti in ipso refloruit'.

[60] *Ordo*, p. 521, lines 343–45: 'In principio omnes creature uiruerunt, in medio flores floruerunt; postea uiriditas descendit.'

[61] *Expo. Euang.*, 26, p. 263, lines 80–81: '*Isque*, scilicet fides, *dixit illi*, respondendo cogitationi ipsius: *Frater tuus*, in agnitione qua Deum scit, *uenit*, in eo quod rectum iter fecit.'

to me and I will show you the spouting fountain.'[62] In the two works, Fides affirms
or promises to reveal the source for salvation, represented by the right path or the
spouting fountain.

These key images, biblical and classical in origin, convey a meaning replete with
Christian symbolism. The *rectum iter* recalls the *uia regia* (royal road) of Numbers
21. 22 and figures prominently in monastic literature to denote the path to salvation that requires living under obedience to the *Rule*.[63] The *fons saliens*, an image
from the Song of Songs as well as classical literature, occurs frequently in writings
inspired by the Song. The fountain waters, a standard element of the *locus amoenus*,
whether it be paradise or the courtly garden, represent the source and reflection of
life. The character of Fides in the *Ordo* also describes herself as the mirror of life
(*speculum uitae*), which constitutes the image par excellence of twelfth-century
symbolism and neo-Platonism.[64] The word *speculum* came to refer to the world and
the elements therein as a mirror or reflection of God.[65]

A powerful image of Christ occurs near the close of both works. In the homily,
Hildegard evokes the *uir preliator*, who represents Christ as the champion over evil,
changing bad knowledge into praiseworthy good.[66] Hildegard then takes on a
preaching voice when she extends the third person voice of God in the biblical text
(Lk 15. 32) to explain that the sinner or younger brother 'died in his wickedness,
was reborn' when he recognized God and became mindful of his true self; 'he
perished' when he valued deception, 'and was found' in true light.[67] In contrast, the

---

[62] *Ordo*, p. 511, lines 129–31: 'Ego, Fides, speculum uite: uenerabiles filie, uenite ad me et
ostendo uobis fontem salientem.'

[63] Leclercq, *Love of Learning*, pp. 102–05.

[64] On the images of fountain and mirror in Hildegard's visionary works, see Newman, *Sister
of Wisdom*, pp. 50–54.

[65] Alan of Lille (*c.* 1125–*c.* 1202) wrote: 'Omnis mundi creatura | Quasi liber et pictura | Nobis
est et speculum.' See Chenu, *Nature, Man and Society*, pp. 102, 117. On the *speculum* image, see
Herbert Grabes, *The Mutable Glass: Mirror-Imagery in Titles and Texts of the Middle Ages and
English Renaissance*, trans. by Gordon Collier (Cambridge: Cambridge University Press, 1982),
pp. 1–15.

[66] *Expo. Euang.*, 26, pp. 264–65, lines 109–13: 'Necesse est enim ut mala scientia ad bonum
redeat, ubi omnia bona Patris laudantur, et magnificantur in omni creatura; sicut uir preliator qui
superat inimicum, et inimicus postea erit amicus illius necessitate compulsus, quoniam ei resistere
non poterit, et ideo uictus in milicia sua laudandus est.'

[67] *Expo. Euang.*, 26, p. 265, lines 113–16: '*Quia frater tuus mortuus erat* in nequitia sua *et
reuixit* in agnitione Dei, suimet in causis suis recordatus; *perierat* in estimatione deceptionis *et
inuentus est* in uera luce.'

Ordo introduces the victorious warrior in the final chorus, recounting the words of the *uir preliator*, who sees the fall of humankind and knows that the golden number is still unfulfilled.[68] He looks upon the errant ways of humanity and reminds them of the coming judgement. In the *Ordo* then, the warrior stands at a different point in the course of salvation history, one that precedes the triumph depicted in the homily and looks back to the Fall. Nonetheless, the homily and the *Ordo* reflect the theme of *Christus Victor*, frequent in twelfth-century and earlier theology: Christ stands as conqueror of the Devil and of evil.[69]

A final parallel between the *expositio* on Luke 15. 15–32 and the *Ordo* emerges in the motif of rejoicing with great joy, such as that for a lost sheep now found (*in congratulatione inuentae perditae ouis*). Hildegard echoes the preceding parable of the lost sheep in the Lukan text (Lk 15. 3–7).[70] Likewise, the chorus of virtues in the *Ordo* alludes to the same parable when it laments the errancy of the soul and cautions it: 'Heu, heu, nos Virtutes plangamus et lugeamus, quia ouis domini fugit uitam!' (Woe, woe, let us virtues lament and mourn, because the sheep of the Lord flees from life); and 'Noli timere nec fugere, quia pastor bonus querit in te perditam ouem suam' (Do not fear or flee, because the good shepherd seeks his lost sheep in you).[71] The homily looks to the ultimate homecoming of the sheep, while the *Ordo* reminds the audience that the larger return of humankind has not occurred.

In summary, Hildegard's tropological interpretation of the parable of the prodigal son, like the *Ordo uirtutum*, focuses on the journey of the soul and reveals parallels in vocabulary, scriptural allusions, and theme with the *Ordo*. The biblical

---

[68] *Ordo*, p. 521, lines 346–47: 'Et istud uir preliator uidit et dixit: Hoc scio, sed aureus numerus nondum est plenus.' *Epistolarium*, I, 59, p. 141, lines 69–70. I am grateful to Audrey Pitts for locating this reference. Baird and Ehrman point out the use of the term in the *LDO* to refer to the company of martyrs in the early Church. Hildegard also uses the concept of the 'golden number' in one of her letters with a clear eschatological view; she writes to a congregation of monks and exhorts them to obedience so that God may count them in the 'golden number'. *Letters*, I, 59, p. 138. See *LDO*, III.5.33, p. 457, line 40. (Baird and Ehrman cite *LDO*, III.x.12, III.x.33.)

[69] See Hugh Feiss, 'Christ in the "Scivias" of Hildegard of Bingen', in *Angesicht*, pp. 291–98. *Epistolarium*, II, 223R, p. 494, line 153; *Letters*, III, p. 22 (translated as 'man of war'). The *uir preliator* does not necessarily designate a historical person other than Jesus. Kerby-Fulton, 'Prophet and Reformer', signals the image and translates it as 'crusader' without noting the biblical origin. *LDO*, III.5.12, p. 429, lines 1–12. She repeats the image later with a cross reference to *Sciuias*: III.5.33, p. 457, lines 39–47.

[70] *Expo. Euang.*, 26, p. 263, lines 69–70: '*Et ceperunt*, epulare in congratulatione inuentae perditae ouis.'

[71] *Ordo*, p. 515, lines 221–22; p. 516, lines 234–35.

parable involves a dramatic and thematic structure that moves from choice to sin to reconciliation and rejoicing. Hildegard' preserves and enhances the parable's structural outline in order to trace the spiritual journey and struggles of the human being in salvation history and in everyday life. She enunciates in both the homily and the *Ordo* fundamental elements of her theology of creation, Fall, and redemption. In two instances, Hildegard highlights different moments in the same story of salvation. The homily alludes to *uiriditas* to capture the repentance of the son, while the *Ordo* evokes the original greenness of creation. Moreover, the *uir preliator* in the homily stands at the moment of triumph, whereas in the *Ordo* he cautions that the final fulfilment, represented by the golden number, has not arrived. The two texts complement each other to fill out the complete story of salvation.

The homily includes an element of the human drama that lacks in the play: the *magistra* accords an active role to a vice in the homily when she assigns a dwelling to Malice and the vice draws the younger son further into sin. In the *Ordo*, the vices have no roles; the Devil takes the stage as the lone antagonist. Moreover, in the *Ordo*, Hildegard does not script the enactment of Anima's sins; they occur offstage. In contrast, the son's transgressions punctuate the narrative of the homily as they do the biblical story. These differences in plot and character representation between the homily and the *Ordo* make the texts complementary, with the homily re-creating the human struggle more fully.

Knowledge of Good and Knowledge of Evil

Does Hildegard recount the full struggle of the soul in other texts? The soul, endowed with the faculty of reason, must choose on a daily basis between good and evil. That problem of ethical choice begins the allegorical drama in one of Hildegard's Easter homilies (Mk 16. 1–7).[72] Mary Magdalene (Mk 16. 1), in accord with her medieval identity as a repentant sinner, represents at the same time knowledge of good and evil: as the sinful woman, she stands for knowledge of evil, and as the penitent, she denotes knowledge of good.[73] Mary, mother of James (Mk 16. 1), designates

---

[72] *Expo. Euang.*, 29, pp. 272–74. Jaehyun Kim discussed this homily in 'Hildegard of Bingen's Gospel Homilies and her Exegesis of Mark 16. 1–7', International Congress of Medieval Studies, Kalamazoo, Michigan, May 1999, and explained the complex symbolism of the stone and the tomb.

[73] *Expo. Euang.*, 29, p. 272, lines 1–3. See Katherine Jansen, *The Making of the Magdalen: Preaching and Popular Devotion in the Later Middle Ages* (Princeton: Princeton University Press, 2000); Beverly Mayne Kienzle, 'Penitents and Preachers: The Figure of Saint Peter and his

holy rationality, and Salome (Mk 16. 1) represents appropriate appetite of the flesh.[74] Together they put aside self-will and come to the very sweet gifts of the virtues, knowing God by Charity. Before evil takes root and before the heat of carnal desires arises, they seek Good Desire (the tomb, Mk 16. 2). Conferring with one another, they ask who will remove the weight of their resistance to doing good works (the stone, Mk 16. 3) and open them to Good Desire (the tomb, Mk 16. 3).[75]

Hildegard departs from the third person verb of the biblical text, 'Et dicebant' (And they were saying), to give the virtues of Knowledge, Rationality, and Taste a voice. They say to themselves: 'Who among angels or humans will remove from us, who lean towards the flesh, the hardness that we do not want to do good works?'[76] Hildegard explains that God's grace removes the stone; the human cannot move it alone.[77] With peaceful mind, the virtues enter good desire and see another life (the angel, Mk 16. 5) in the sphere of God's power, wrapped in heavenly desire (the white garment, Mk 16. 5); and they marvel at it. The angel advises them not to look back at the carnal desire they left behind.[78]

From this point on in the homily, Hildegard assumes the angel's voice from the biblical text and addresses her audience directly in second person plural:

> *You seek Jesus of Nazareth crucified*, looking for him who will make you holy. He was *crucified* for you in carnal desires so that you can do good works through good desires. *He has risen, he is not here*; he has not been buried in you because he was there first. *Behold the location*, the disquiet of your mind, *where he was placed*, thinking that you were not able to do good works through good desires. *But go* with good report, *tell his disciples and Peter*, announcing in his footsteps and example that you are firm now for doing our will. *He goes before you into Galilee*, preparing an eternal home for you, crossing over to life.[79]

Relationship to Saint Mary Magdalene', in *La figura di san Pietro nelle fonti del medioevo: Atti del convegno tenutosi in occasione dello Studiorum universitatum docentium congressus (Viterbo e Roma 5–8 settembre 2000)*, ed. by Loredana Lazzari and Anna Maria Valente Bacci, Textes et études du moyen âge, 17 (Louvain-la-Neuve: F.I.D.E.M., 2001), pp. 248–72.

[74] *Expo. Euang.*, 29, p. 272, lines 3–4.

[75] *Expo. Euang.*, 29, pp. 272–73, lines 4–12.

[76] *Expo. Euang.*, 29, p. 272, lines 13–17: '*Et dicebant*, conferendo, *ad inuicem*, scientia, racionalitas et gustus: *Quis*, angelorum uel hominum, *reuoluet*, id est auferet nobis tendentibus ad carnalia, *lapidem*, scilicet duriciam illam quod bona opera facere nolumus, *ab ostio*, uidelicet clausura, *monumenti*, scilicet boni desiderii.'

[77] *Expo. Euang.*, 29, p. 272, lines 20–21.

[78] *Expo. Euang.*, 29, p. 273, lines 27–28.

[79] *Expo. Euang.*, 29, p. 273, lines 28–38: '*Iesum quaeritis*, uidendo ad ipsum, *Nazarenum*, qui uos sanctos faciet, *crucifixum*, ita ut uobis crucifixus sit in carnalibus desideriis, ut per bona desideria

Hildegard preaches through the angel's voice, assuring her listeners that Christ has sanctified them and been crucified in them with their carnal desires. She exhorts them to do good works, to go forth in his paths, and to show his example in preparation for an eternal home. In this case Hildegard does not depict the moment of triumph, or the Christus Victor; rather she evokes the suffering of Christ, albeit in mild tones, and urges her audience to the imitation of Christ in daily life.

The Virtues

The Holy Spirit guides the human who faces the choice between good and evil and sends the virtues to assist. Certain *expositiones*, such as the above on Mark 16. 1–7, depict this moment of moral decision. Others employ virtues for description, such as the strongest strength (*fortissimae fortitudinis*) of Peter, or an exhortation to do good works with strong strength (*in forti fortitudine*).[80] Several virtues with parts in the *Ordo uirtutum* play a minor role in the *Expositiones*, including Innocentia;[81] Amor Celestis (Heavenly Love), who bears similar names in the *Expositiones*: Amor Celestium, Celeste Desiderium, and Spiritale Desiderium;[82] Contemptus Mundi (Contempt of the World), exemplified by monks and virgins;[83] Scientia Dei, known

---

bona opera facere possitis, *surrexit, non est hic,* quia modo in uobis non est sepultus, ut prius erat. *Ecce locus,* inquietudinis mentis uestrae, *ubi,* positus erat, putantes quia iusta et sancta opera facere non possetis. *Sed ite,* bono rumore, *dicite,* annunciantes, *discipulis eius,* id est uestigiis et exemplis eius, *et Petro,* quoniam nunc duri ad uoluntatem nostram estis, *quia precedet uos,* preparando uobis eternam mansionem, *in Galileam,* transeundo ad uitam.'

[80] *Expo. Euang.,* 4, p. 200, line 39; *Expo. Euang.,* 7, p. 207, line 43. These phrases demonstrate Hildegard's taste for *annominatio* (the repetition of a word in a different form or the use of a word's cognate in proximity to it). On Hildegard's fondness for superlatives and alliteration, see Dronke, *Poetic Individuality in the Middle Ages,* p. 155, who notes her 'excessive use of superlatives', and associates it with her 'mystical intensity'. Dronke, *LDO,* pp. xxv, xxxii, cites a few examples of *annominatio* and superlatives in that work.

[81] *Expo. Euang.,* 13, pp. 224–25, lines 50–56; *Expo. Euang.,* 21, pp. 243–44, lines 15–16; *Expo. Euang.,* 23, p. 250, lines 35, 41; p. 251, lines 59, 66; *Expo. Euang.,* 28, p. 271, line 43; *Expo. Euang.,* 36, p. 286, line 17; *Expo. Euang.,* 1, p. 188, line 26; p. 189, line 70; *Expo. Euang.,* 26, pp. 262–63, lines 57–58; *Expo. Euang.,* 27, pp. 267–68, lines 60–62; *Expo. Euang.,* 4, p. 199, lines 24, 27–28; *Expo. Euang.,* 11, p. 219, line 41; *Expo. Euang.,* 12, p. 221, line 53.

[82] *Expo. Euang.,* 4, p. 199, line 5; p. 200, lines 44–45. *Expo. Euang.,* 38, p. 293, lines 22–23; *Expo. Euang.,* 44, p. 308, lines 30–31, 46; *Expo. Euang.,* 55, p. 327, lines 55–56.

[83] *Expo. Euang.,* 3, p. 197, lines 76–80.

in the *Expositiones* by that name as well as the related *scientia bona*.[84] However, the most compelling representations of the virtues place them as personified characters in the action or dialogue of the homily. I shall explore the depiction of the key virtues of Fides, Humilitas Mentis, Caritas, Timor Domini, Virginitas, and Sapientia.

Fides (Faith): Shepherd of the Virtues

Fides plays a role in two of the *Expositiones* as well as in the *Ordo uirtutum*. As we observed above, the authoritative virtue addresses the older brother of the parable of the prodigal son (Lk 15. 11–32) and expounds the soundness of the younger son's choice to repent. I shall focus, however, on John 10. 11–16, where Hildegard casts the shepherd as Fides and sets the virtue, like the biblical shepherd, against the imminent danger of the wolf and the hired hand, who fails to protect the sheep. In contrast to Faith, the hired hand (Jn 10. 12) stands for unfaithfulness (*infidelitas*), which the *magistra* explains as the varied sorts of errors to which the virtues do not belong and are not inborn. In Hildegard's reading, the wolf (Jn 10. 12) represents danger to souls: as the wolf catches the sheep (Jn 10. 12), danger snatches the fruitfulness of virtues and saddens them. The *magistra* views the flight of the hired hand (Jn 10. 12) as the moment when unfaithfulness resounds among the good. Unfaithfulness, she asserts, has no good or holiness, but instead falseness, since no good things are bound to it.[85] On the other hand, Fides, as a sort of shepherd of the virtues, brings great benefit. She knows the virtues born from her, as the shepherd knows his sheep (Jn 10. 14),[86] and as Hildegard knew her sisters and took on the responsibility to protect them against the perils that threatened their souls. Hildegard reads the Father in the biblical text as eternity: the Father reveals Faith, and in turn, Fides (at once the shepherd and the Son) reveals eternity (the

---

[84] *Expo. Euang.*, 52, p. 321, lines 28–32.

[85] *Expo. Euang.*, 31, pp. 275–76, lines 6–17: '*Mercennarius*, id est infidelitas, *et qui non est pastor*, scilicet diuersus error, *cuius non sunt oues*, uidelicet uirtutes, *propriae*, quoniam ei non sunt innatae, *uidet lupum*, id est periculum animarum, *uenientem*, in errore, *et dimittit oues*, scilicet abiciendo uirtutes, quibus se per deceptionem coniunxerat, *et fugit*, se subtrahendo in adiutorio, quia possibilitatem adiuuandi in bono non habet. *Et lupus*, scilicet periculum animarum, *rapit*, fructuositatem uirtutum, *et dispergit*, uidelicet contristat, *oues*. Mercennarius autem fugit, ubi in bonis sonat, sed bona non habet, *quia mercennarius est*, mendacium habens, quoniam illi bona alligata non sunt. *Et non pertinet ad eum*, in sanctitate, *de ouibus*, id est uirtutibus.'

[86] *Expo. Euang.*, 31, p. 276, lines 18–20: '*Ego sum pastor bonus*, in magna utilitate, *et cognosco meas*, uirtutes quae de me natae sunt, *et cognoscunt me meae*, quia de me uenerunt.'

Father).[87] The Latin wording conveys the oneness of Father and Son in a mirror-like reciprocal revelation that underscores the eternal nature of Christ. Faith sends forth a call to the sheep (Jn 10. 16), which designate the other virtues.[88] As a dutiful shepherd, Fides keeps virtues from outside the flock (the other sheep of Jn 10. 16) under observation when enemies threaten. Fides affirms that she will cry out to the other virtues as the shepherd cries out to other sheep (Jn 10. 16). The virtues will come to lend aid with new miracles, and they will perceive Fides's admonition through many signs.[89] When Fides kills the enemies who want to destroy the virtues, she emits a 'sweet sound'.

The depiction of Fides in this homily recalls the *Ordo* in at least four respects. Like the virtues in the *Ordo*, Fides reveals her identity directly, albeit without allegory. Moreover, Faith's call to the sheep (Jn 10. 16), which designate the other virtues, parallels the summoning of the virtues in the *Ordo*.[90] Faith's sweet cry of victory brings to mind the character of Victoria in the *Ordo*, who exults at the binding of the Devil.[91] Faith intones sweetly on behalf of her flock of virtues, arguably taking a singing part in the homily as she does in the *Ordo*. One can imagine a musical representation of the theme that would echo Hildegard's preaching in this *expositio*.[92] Finally, Fides calls herself 'mirror of life' in the *Ordo*,[93] an explicit

---

[87] *Expo. Euang.*, 31, p. 276, lines 20–21: '*Sicut nouit me*, in ostensione, *pater*, id est eternitas, *et ego agnosco patrem*, quia eternitatem ostendo.' The Latin seems disjointed here. The Father and eternity do the revealing of Faith, as the Son and Faith likewise reveal eternity.

[88] *Expo. Euang.*, 31, p. 275, lines 2–5: '*Ego*, quae fundamentum sum uirtutum, *sum pastor*, id est fides, *bonus*, scilicet utilis. *Bonus pastor*, uidelicet fides, *animam suam*, id est uocem, *dat*, scilicet emittit, *pro ouibus suis*, uidelicet uirtutibus.'

[89] *Expo. Euang.*, 31, p. 276, lines 24–59: '*Et alias oues*, scilicet uirtutes, *habeo*, in obseruatione, *quae non sunt ex hoc ouili*, quia in his uirtutibus notae non sunt, *et illas oportet me adducere*, quando inimici eas destruere uolunt: illis clamabo, ut in magno auxilio et in nouis miraculis ueniant, *et uocem meam*, in admonitione per omnia, in multis signis, *audient*, percipiendo.'

[90] *Expo. Euang.*, 31, p. 275, lines 2–5.

[91] *Expo. Euang.*, 31, p. 276, lines 21–33: '*et animam meam*, scilicet sonum, *pono*, in dulcedine, *pro ouibus meis*, quia occido inimicos qui illas destruere uolunt'. *Ordo*, p. 519, line 311: Victoria: 'Gaudete, o socii, quia antiquus serpens ligatus est!'

[92] The personified Fides does not appear in the *Symphonia*. Fides as an attribute appears in 'O ecclesia', *Symph.*, 64, p. 464, lines 9–10: 'In uisione uere fidei | Ursula Filium Dei amauit'.

[93] This corresponds to the third technique of Hildegardian allegory that Dronke proposes, the direct self-revelation that occurs in the *Ordo uirtutum* when the personified virtues reveal their identity. For the fourth technique, in contrast, the allegorical figure explains herself by means of allegories that she expounds. Dronke, 'Allegorical World-Picture of Hildegard of Bingen', pp. 3–6.

mirror image that evokes the reciprocal mirroring and revelation of Father and Son in the homily.[94]

Does Faith in this homily or in the *Ordo* recall her depiction in the *Psycho-machia*? While the victorious Fides evokes in part the triumphant virtue in the *psychomachia* tradition, the Prudentian character displays a brutality that Hilde-gard's portrayal of the virtue does not even approach.[95] It is difficult to imagine that Hildegard would not have known the *Psychomachia*. I would argue that she retains the element of triumph but chooses not to follow the Prudentian model strictly. Instead she tones down the virtue's victory, perhaps intensifying the spiritual triumph, in accord with the general tenor of both the homily and the *Ordo* and in line with her message to her own flock, the sisters whom she guarded as shepherd. One can imagine that she uttered authoritatively the gospel text, 'I am the good shepherd', in order to remind her sisters of the appropriate roles of shepherd and flock.[96]

Humilitas Mentis (Humility of Mind): Mother of Good Works

Humilitas Mentis plays an active role in Hildegard's second exposition for the Birthday of Saint John the Baptist (Lk 1. 57–68).[97] The *magistra* interprets Eliza-beth, mother of John the Baptist, as Humility of Mind; as the biblical Elizabeth bore a son (Lk 1. 57), the virtue, after humbling herself, gives birth to holy works.[98] Hildegard explicates the rejoicing of Elizabeth's neighbours and relatives at her news (Lk 1. 58) as the exultation of the angels and saints at the accomplishment of Humilitas Mentis.[99] The *magistra* interprets the eighth day, the time for circum-cision in the biblical account (Lk 1. 59), as either the end of work or the death of

---

[94] *Ordo*, p. 511, lines 129–31. Fides promises to show the virtues the fountain, an image that signifies the source of life.

[95] See Nugent, '*Virtus* or Virago?', pp. 20–21, on the depiction of Fides in the *Psychomachia*.

[96] I am grateful to John F. Rhilinger for this insight on the homily.

[97] *Expo. Euang.*, 42, pp. 303–04.

[98] *Expo. Euang.*, 42, p. 303, lines 1–3: '*Elisabeth*, id est humilitatis mentis, *impletum est*, in perfectione, *tempus pariendi*, id est in processura operum humiliari, *et peperit filium*, scilicet quod produxit sancta opera.'

[99] *Expo. Euang.*, 42, p. 303, lines 4–7: '*Et audierunt uicini*, id est angeli, *et cognati eius*, uidelicet alii sancti, *quia magnificauit Dominus*, in ampliatione uirtutum, *misericordiam suam cum illa*, scilicet in inspiratione uirtutum, *et congratulabantur ei*, quia bonum fructum perfecit.'

the human. With the latter interpretation, the figure of Elizabeth inches towards
the broader identity that Hildegard gives her later when she reads Elizabeth as the
soul. Fittingly, Humilitas Mentis does not identify herself, as Fides does in the
homily just discussed; neither does she boldly enter the scene. Instead, she gains
confidence just as Elizabeth does.

The *magistra* sees the act of circumcision as the removal of the 'decay of ash' (*putredinem cineris*) by the angels and saints. Subsequently they sanctify the good works
of the human and call her holy, as the neighbours called the infant by his father's
name, Zachariah (Lk 1. 59).[100] When Elizabeth objects and says that the child will
be called John (Lk 1. 60), Hildegard gives a speaking part to the personification of
Humilitas Mentis. The virtue insists that her works ought not to be praised out of her
own merits but because of the grace of God.[101] As the neighbours and friends
indicate they wish to know Zachariah's opinion on the child's name, so the angels
and saints defer to God to decide what merit God wishes to give the soul.[102]

Hildegard's development of direct speech for Humilitas Mentis becomes clear
when the virtue responds to the protest that the neighbours and friends make to
Elizabeth (Lk 1. 61). Hildegard extends their words to give her character more to
say. The biblical text reads: 'And they said to her: there is no one known to you
who is called by this name.' In accordance with the *magistra*'s interpretation, the
angels and saints speak directly to Humilitas Mentis. Hildegard retains the second
person (*tua* in the scriptural verse) as she has the angels and saints explain:
'Nothing is found among your holy works [. . .] except that you be called a holy
soul.'[103] The *magistra* employs the second person forms *tuis* and *uoceris* and extends
the biblical text as she expands the identity of Humilitas Mentis to encompass the
holiness of the entire soul that results from the practice of good works. At this

---

[100] *Expo. Euang.*, 42, p. 303, lines 8–12: '*Et factum est in die octaua*, id est in fine operis, uel in morte hominum, *uenerunt*, angeli et sancti, *circumcidere*, scilicet auferre putredinem cineris, *puerum*, scilicet bona opera sanctificando, *et uocabant eum nomine patris sui*, uidelicet Dei de quo exierunt, *Zachariam*, id est sancta.'

[101] *Expo. Euang.*, 42, p. 304, lines 13–15: '*Et respondens mater eius*, uidelicet humilitas mentis, *dixit, Nequaquam*, de meritis meis opera mea laudanda sunt, *sed uocabitur Iohannes*, sed de gratia Dei.'

[102] *Expo. Euang.*, 42, p. 304, lines 19–20: '*Innuebant autem patri eius*, ita ut permittant in iudicium Dei, *quem uellet uocari eum*, scilicet quod meritum illi dare uelit.'

[103] *Expo. Euang.*, 42, p. 303, lines 16–18: '*Et dixerunt ad illam*, humilitatem mentis, *quia nemo est in cognatione tua*, id est non est aliud inuentum in sanctis operibus tuis, *qui uocetur hoc nomine*, scilicet nisi ut sancta anima uoceris.'

point Elizabeth no longer represents simply Humilitas Mentis, but she comes to designate the holy soul that practices good works with the aid of the virtue.

When Zachariah writes that the child's name will be John (Lk 1.63), the neighbours and friends are all astonished. According to Hildegard's reading of this, God affirms that the soul, equipped with the knowledge of good and evil, has made the right journey, and through God's grace, the soul has achieved holiness through good works.[104] Consequently, the biblical Zachariah breaks through the muteness that had held him, and his tongue begins to sing the canticle of praise. Hildegard interprets this as the manifestation of praise from the Father (the mouth of Zachariah) and Rationality (the tongue of the Father). Thereupon, the *magistra* relates that the whole assembly of saints marvels and rejoices before the soul's merits. A stupefying new noise-making comes about (*in noua concinnantia*).[105] All who heard these things understood the joy and longing for divine grace and exclaimed how blessed and holy the soul is in its deeds.[106] Divine aid shone in brilliant light and work. Hildegard's allegory then turns the canticle of Zachariah (Lk 1. 67) into God's voice, which backs the chorus and praises the soul. She interprets the biblical people of Israel in the canticle (Lk 1. 68) as the soul, snatched from its sins.[107]

What thematic and structural parallels does this *expositio* present with the *Ordo uirtutum*? The *magistra* accords an active role and a brief speaking part to Humilitas Mentis, the counterpart of Humilitas in the *Ordo*, although Humilitas Mentis

---

[104] *Expo. Euang.*, 42, p. 304, lines 21–25: '*Et postulans*, id est ostendens, *pugillarem*, scilicet in scientia boni et mali, quod rectum iter fecerit, *scripsit dicens*, in recto iudicio: *Iohannes est nomen eius*, ita ut per gratiam Dei sancta anima in bonis operibus sit. *Et mirati sunt*, in meritis illius, *uniuersi*, id est omnis turba sanctorum.'

[105] On Luke 1. 65, see *Expo. Euang.*, 42, p. 304, lines 29–31: '*Et factus est timor*, stuporis in noua concinnantia, quia in hoc quod ignotum est, homo primum stupet, *super omnes uicinos eorum*, scilicet angelos.'

[106] On Luke 1.66, see *Expo. Euang.*, 42, p. 304, lines 34–37: '*Et posuerunt*, notando, *omnes*, qui audierunt haec intelligendo, *in corde suo*, gaudium et suspirium propter diuinam gratiam, *dicentes*: *Quis putas*, cogitando, *puer iste erit*, in sanctitate? Hoc est: O quam felix et quam sancta anima ista in operibus suis est!'

[107] On Luke 1. 66–68, see *Expo. Euang.*, 42, p. 304, lines 37–45: '*Et enim manus Domini*, id est diuinum auxilium, *erat cum illo*, in fulgente luce et opere. *Et Zacharias pater eius*, id est Deus, *impletus est Spiritu Sancto*, scilicet in laude sanctitatis illius, *et prophetauit dicens*: *Benedictus Dominus Deus Israel*, in sanctitate, *quia uisitauit*, inspiratione et fecit in magnificentia redemptionem, scilicet ereptionem, *plebis suae*, uidelicet animae illius de peccatis, propter bona quibus eum semper inspexit.'

does not introduce herself in the homily.[108] Moreover, the joyous noises — the *noua concinnantia* — recall the scene in the *Ordo* where Humilitas animates the other virtues. However, as she summons the aid of her sister virtues and urges Victoria to tie up the Devil, the virtue in the *Ordo* takes a more aggressive role than Humilitas Mentis in the *expositio*. In the *Ordo*, after Humilitas enlists Victoria to conquer the Devil, Victoria announces the binding of the serpent and the soul's victory over the Devil with an unusually high *Gaudete*, whereupon the choir of virtues sings loud praises just before the drama's close. Overall the narrative that Hildegard constructs in the *expositio* advances with the animated and musical progression of a mini-drama.

While Humilitas in the *Ordo* displays more aggressivity than Humilitas Mentis in *Expositio* 42, Hildegard in both texts portrays a much less brutal Humilitas than do Prudentius and other works that follow his design.[109] In the *Psychomachia*, Mens Humilis decapitates Fraus (Fraud or Deceit). The *Speculum uirginum*, influenced by the Prudentian model, depicts Humilitas in the act of piercing Superbia (Pride) with a sword. The *Liber de fructu carnis et spiritus* portrays an equally violent Humility. Herrad of Hohenbourg probably drew inspiration from the latter and possibly from the *Speculum uirginum* for the depiction of virtues and vices in the *Hortus deliciarum*. She depicts a combative Humilitas at the head of seven virtues that oppose Superbia and an equal number of vices.[110] Whether Hildegard's milder-mannered Humilitas reflects her choice to tame the virtue or her lack of access to illustrations of this scene in the *Psychomachia* is matter for speculation. Given the

---

[108] Humilitas figures in *Symph.* 16, p. 391, lines 1–5: 'O quam magnum miraculum est | quod in subditam femineam formam | rex introivit. | Hoc Deus fecit | quia humilitas super omnia ascendit'; and 'O factura Dei', *Symph.* 72, p. 475, lines 1–5: 'O factura Dei | que es homo, | in magna sanctitate edificata es, | quia sancta diuinitas in humilitate | celos penetrauit.'

[109] Certainly, Hildegard was not following Prudentius closely in her milder portrayal of Humility. Yet the notion of the virtues' victory over vice remains, as does some military imagery. Dronke, *Poetic Individuality in the Middle Ages*, p. 169, notes in a similar vein that the *Ordo* 'shows no perceptible debt to Prudentius either in language or in details of content', even though he considers it 'unlikely that Hildegard should have no acquaintance at all with Prudentius's poem'.

[110] Katzenellenbogen, *Allegories of the Virtues and Vices*, pp. 2, 10–11, 16, Plate VII. Fiona Griffiths, 'Herrad of Hohenburg: A Synthesis of Learning in the Garden of Delights', in *Listen Daughter*, ed. by Mews, pp. 221–44 (pp. 233–34), remarks that Herrad may have known the *Speculum*, but her portrayal of the virtues and vices and in particular of Humility seems to draw more from the anonymous *On the Fruits of the Flesh and of the Spirit*, attributed incorrectly in the *PL* to Hugh of St Victor. Griffiths follows Katzenellenbogen, *Allegories of the Virtues and Vices*, pp. 10–11 who links the latter two works. See also Griffiths, *Garden of Delights*, pp. 187, 197–201.

wide influence of the *Psychomachia*, it would seem that Hildegard again opted to modify the Prudentian model in accord with her more delicate theological vision.

Caritas (Charity): Mother of Obedience

Caritas figures in several *expositiones* as Hildegard describes God's love or love for God. While Caritas more often denotes an abstract quality or a descriptive attribute,[111] the virtue takes an active role in an *expositio* on Luke 2. 1–14, a Christmas homily.[112] Hildegard's tropological interpretation of the pericope and her identification of the virtue with the character of the Virgin Mary provide fruitful material for comparison to the *Ordo*. The three major characters of the biblical story, Mary, Joseph, and the infant Jesus, represent respectively the virtues of Caritas, Bonum Desiderium (Good Desire), and Obedientia. The manger stands for Humilitas. The *magistra* reads the issuance of the edict throughout the world (Lk 2. 1) as the extension of the will through the whole body. Hence, she sees the first enrollment in the biblical text (Lk 2. 2) as the first extension of the will, which was made from the appetite of the flesh (*de gustu carnis*). Once the will moved away from carnal desire, virtues and vices turned themselves to their respective duties or properties (Lk 2. 3, *ad officium suum*).[113] Hildegard interprets Joseph's journey from Nazareth to Bethlehem (Lk 2. 4) as the ascent of Good Desire from Reason into the secret path to knowledge of God (*artam uiam agnitionis Dei*).[114] Bethlehem is equivalent to the city of David in the biblical text; in Hildegard's commentary Bethlehem represents the soul's salvation (*saluatio animae*), while the city of David designates the secret path to knowledge of God.[115] The *magistra* explains that Bonum Desiderium

---

[111] *Expo. Euang.*, 8, p. 208, lines 13–17; *Expo. Euang.*, 25, p. 260, lines 79–82; *Expo. Euang.*, 26, p. 262, lines 49–50; *Expo. Euang.*, 29, p. 272, lines 6–7; *Expo. Euang.*, 45, p. 309, line 18; *Expo. Euang.*, 50, p. 317, lines 14–16; *Expo. Euang.*, 57, p. 331, line 54.

[112] Dronke, 'Platonic-Christian Allegories', pp. 385–87, interprets this homily briefly as a 'psychological' or 'microcosmic' reading of the text. He identifies possible sources but gives no attention to the elements of drama or to the monastic theology present.

[113] *Expo. Euang.*, 8, p. 208, lines 2–7: '*Haec descriptio prima*, scilicet prima dilatatio, *facta est a preside Siriae Cyrino*, id est de gustu carnis. *Et ibant omnes*, scilicet uirtutes et uicia, *ut profiterentur*, se conuertendo, *singuli in suam ciuitatem*, uidelicet ad officium suum.'

[114] Literally, the 'habit' or 'culture it has in rationality'. *Expo. Euang.*, 8, p. 208, lines 7–9: '*Ascendit autem*, sursum, *et Ioseph*, id est bonum desiderium, *a Galilea*, scilicet a consuetudine, *de ciuitate Nazareth*, id est a cultura quam in racionalitate habet, *in Iudeam*.'

[115] *Expo. Euang.*, 8, p. 208, lines 10–11: 'in *ciuitatem Dauid*, uidelicet in artam uiam agnitionis Dei, *quae uocatur Bethlehem*, id est saluatio animae'.

has known good and evil from the time of creation. Once Bonum Desiderium has been bonded to Caritas, as Joseph was espoused to Mary (Lk 2. 5), the couple of virtues may have spiritual offspring, that is other virtues.[116] Hildegard reads the time Joseph and Mary spend in Bethlehem as Bonum Desiderium's dwelling with Caritas. When Mary gives birth, the splendour of good works shines forth. The *magistra* interprets the child in the manger (Lk 2. 7) as Obedientia, the first virtue and the offspring of the virtuous couple. Like a mother, Caritas embraces the baby-like Obedientia and places the infant virtue in Humilitas, because there is no room in Vanitas (the inn, Lk 2. 7).[117]

When the biblical text advances to the shepherds (Lk 2. 8), Hildegard introduces the human being's anxiety over accomplishing good things; like the shepherds, the human keeps watch with abstinence, prayer, and circumspection, turning away from sins in order to keep her good deeds untouched.[118] The angel of the Lord enters the biblical narrative at Luke 2. 9; Hildegard interprets the angel as God's grace, which surrounds the human's anxiety. The brilliance of God that glows from the angel represents God's sustaining aid. Yet, like the frightened shepherds (Lk 2. 9), humans fear; the *magistra* explains that they are anxious over how they will vanquish the Devil. Hildegard assures her audience that God's grace tells the human not to doubt, because the breath of life, common to all human persons, has *magnam uirtutem*, which can be understood as great power or virtue, or both at once. For the angels' announcement that a Saviour is born in the city of David, the *magistra* states that holy reason, which is Christ the Lord, comes from God and is born in humans as a fortification (*munitione*) for holiness.[119] This image of the fortified wall (*munitio*) recalls the text where Hildegard expresses her concern to fortify her community with the words of Scripture and the observance of monastic life.[120] She

---

[116] *Expo. Euang.*, 8, p. 208, lines 13–14: '*desponsata sibi*, scilicet coniuncta, *uxore pregnante*, parere uirtutes'.

[117] *Expo. Euang.*, 8, p. 208, lines 15–21: '*Factum est autem cum essent ibi*, uidelicet cum bonum desiderium cum caritate sic uersatur, *impleti sunt dies ut pareret*, scilicet ut splendor bonorum operum appareret. *Et peperit*, producendo, *filium suum primogenitum*, scilicet obedientiam, primam uirtutem, *et pannis eum inuoluit*, id est in amplexibus eum habet; *et reclinauit eum in presepio*, ponens in humilitate, *quia non erat eis locus in diuersorio*, quia nullum locum uanitatis habet.'

[118] *Expo. Euang.*, 8, p. 208, lines 22–26.

[119] *Expo. Euang.*, 8, pp. 208–09, lines 31–37.

[120] *V. Hild.*, II.12, p. 37, lines 29–32: 'At ego per ostensionem Dei eis hoc innotui ipsasque uerbis sanctarum scripturarum et regulari disciplina bonaque conuersatione circumfodi et muniui'; *Life of Hildegard*, p. 60. Silvas, *Jutta and Hildegard*, p. 174, translates the passage as 'I fenced them about and armed them', which overlooks the notion of digging (*circumfodere*).

assures her sisters that they may exert the divine gift of reason in order to participate in building the fortifications that Hildegard seeks to construct.

At the moment when the angelic host (Lk 2. 13) enters the scriptural text, Hildegard introduces the multitude of virtues (*multitudo uirtutum*). With God's grace, the
virtues, like the angels, sound forth with the sweetest sound (*suauissimo sono*) of
praise.[121] She explicates the glory that the angels proclaim 'in the highest' (Lk 2.
14) as God's power to do all things and to lead the sinner back to life, whenever God
becomes involved in earthly matters. The *magistra* affirms that amidst adversarial
storms of vanity, humans may find quiet when they do good willingly, unless they
stumble (*praepedirentur*) in their fragility. God will bring peace to such people.[122]

Hildegard's allegory skirts completely the issue of the Virgin birth that occupied
numerous commentators on this passage.[123] The espoused virtues produce another
virtue: their first-born son, Obedience. Hildegard's allegory directs her audience's
thoughts to the child, at once Obedience and Christ, who epitomizes the virtue
through his perfect obedience to the Father. She intends her sisters to dismiss
Vanity from their hearts and create a place of Humility in order to embrace Christ
through obedience to the *Rule* and to her as their spiritual mother. In this case,
Hildegard's concern for the tropological message overrides any reference to
theological controversy.

I discern various parallels between the homily on Luke 2. 1–14 and the *Ordo*.[124]
The first and least complex concerns the dramatic structure of the homily. At the
homily's conclusion, the angelic chorus, which represents the multitude of virtues,
emits sweet sounds that mirror the songs of rejoicing and praise that resound from
the *Ordo*'s choir of virtues upon the restoration of the soul. A second area of comparison relates to the identification of particular virtues in each. Three of the
virtues in the homily — Caritas, Obedientia, and Humilitas — play a role in the
Ordo. A fourth virtue in the *expositio*, Agnitio Dei, corresponds in some degree to

---

[121] *Expo. Euang.*, 8, p. 208, lines 42–43: '*multitudo miliciae celestis*, id est multitudo uirtutum,
laudantium Deum, in suauissimo sono'.

[122] *Expo. Euang.*, 8, p. 209, lines 46–49.

[123] See Bede, *In Lucae euangelium*, 1, 2, p. 48, lines 1163–65.

[124] One may see a tangential point of comparison in that both the homily and the *Ordo* establish a semantic link between Knowledge of God (Agnitio Dei in the homily, Scientia Dei in the
Ordo) and salvation of the soul. In the homily, Bonum Desiderium goes from Reason into the
secret path to knowledge of God (*artam viam agnitionis Dei*). Scientia Dei addresses Anima as
'daughter of salvation' in the *Ordo*, p. 507, lines 49–50: 'Vide quid illud sit quo es induta, filia
saluationis, et esto stabilis, et numquam cades' (See that with which you are clothed, daughter of
salvation; be firm and never fall).

Scientia Dei (Knowledge of God) in the *Ordo*, but Hildegard does not personify Agnitio Dei in the homily. In the *Ordo*, the *magistra* describes the three virtues of Caritas, Obedientia, and Humilitas with rich imagery from the Song of Songs. The three introduce themselves directly, which they do not do in the *Expositiones*. Caritas pledges to guide the virtues to the flowering branch; Obedientia promises to lead them to the king's kiss; and Humilitas describes herself as the Queen of Virtues who will nourish them to find the lost drachma (Lk 15. 8–10) and the crown of glory.[125] Third, with respect to the role of the virtues, the speech of Obedientia, Humilitas, and Caritas in the *Ordo* concerns their assistance to other virtues and ultimately to the soul on its journey. Similarly in the homily, Charity functions clearly to help the soul on the road to salvation, and the three stand as a holy family of monastic virtues, mirroring their status in the *Rule of Benedict*: Obedience and Humility occupy two of the opening chapters of the *Rule*; Charity guides the soul in fulfilling the precepts of the *Rule*.[126]

Another significant parallel lies in Hildegard's association of Caritas with the Virgin Mary in the homily and the *Ordo*. Hildegard's exegetical narrative depicts Caritas, representing Mary, as the mother virtue who embraces her first-born son, Obedientia, and places him in the manger of Humilitas.[127] Caritas holds the leading role in this trio of virtues, just as Mary worked as the agent of salvation by giving birth to Jesus. The *Ordo uirtutum* also presents Caritas as the allegorical leader of the virtues and associates Caritas with Mary as historical bearer of salvation. The imagery of the *Ordo* links the Virgin and Caritas, when she promises to lead the virtues into the bright light of the flowering branch: 'I am Charity, flower worthy of love. Come to me, virtues, and I will lead you into the bright light of the flowering branch.'[128] The brilliant light of the flowering branch recalls the splendour that surrounds the birth in the homily.[129]

---

[125] *Ordo*, p. 509, lines 88–90 (Obedientia), 94–97 (Humilitas), 104–06 (Caritas).

[126] Saint Benedict, *Regula*, pp. 1–10, 38–41, 43–57; *The Rule of Benedict*, trans. by Anthony C. Meisel and M. L. Del Mastro (New York: Doubleday Image, 1975), Prologue, Chapters 5 and 7, pp. 45, 54–55, 55–61.

[127] *Expo. Euang.*, 8, p. 208, lines 15–21: '*Factum est autem cum essent ibi*, uidelicet cum bonum desiderium cum caritate sic uersatur, *impleti sunt dies ut pareret*, scilicet ut splendor bonorum operum appareret. *Et peperit*, producendo, *filium suum primogenitum*, scilicet obedientiam, primam uirtutem, *et pannis eum inuoluit*, id est in amplexibus eum habet; *et reclinauit eum in presepio*, ponens in humilitate, *quia non erat eis locus in diuersorio*, quia nullum locum uanitatis habet.'

[128] *Ordo*, p. 509, lines 104–06: 'Ego Karitas, flos amabilis. Venite ad me, Virtutes, et perducam uos in candidam lucem floris uirge.'

[129] *Expo. Euang.*, 8, p. 208, lines 15–17.

The imagery and the theology of the *expositio* on Luke 2. 1–14 and the *Ordo uirtutum* correspond not only in each of these two texts; they reverberate throughout Hildegard's other works and indeed they pervade twelfth-century spirituality. Barbara Newman's *Sister of Wisdom* brought attention to the role of Caritas as the archetype of the Virgin Mary in Hildegard's theology of the feminine. Newman cites Hildegard's Letter 30, where the maiden Caritas utters the antiphon: 'I bore you from the womb before the morning star.' The same letter describes the virtue as the 'means and matrix of creation'. These characterizations of Caritas correspond to Hildegard's depictions of the feminine aspects of Wisdom.[130] The *expositio*'s interpretation of Mary as Mother Caritas places this text in the tradition Newman elucidates. However, the personification of Sapientia does not enter this homily on Luke 2. 1–14; instead, Caritas gives birth to Obedientia.[131] The highest monastic virtue dominates the scene, constituting the personification of the Christ child in the homily and the goal of imitation of Christ in the religious life.

Timor Domini (Fear of the Lord): Admonisher of the Soul

Fear of the Lord stands in for the Lord himself in a homily on Mark 16. 14–20, the reading for the feast of the ascension.[132] The *magistra* allegorizes Jesus's appearance to the disciples (Mk 16. 14) as Timor Domini's warning to the soul that punishments and the fire of hell await one who has not shown faith. Hildegard ascribes the following speech to Timor Domini, when the virtue urges the soul to purify itself: 'And Fear of the Lord said to them, "Go out" from uncleanness to cleanness.'[133] She extends the words of the biblical text (Mk 16. 15), keeping its second person plural form of address to frame the virtue's words. From Mark 16. 16a, 'One who believes and has been baptized will be saved', Hildegard has the virtue utter a promise: 'One who rejects evil and undertakes the good will be a friend of

---

[130] Newman, *Sister of Wisdom*, pp. 56–58, 63–64, considers the association of Sapientia, Caritas, Mary, and Christ in the context of the eternal predestination of Christ and, in some texts, like the *Speculum uirginum*, of Mary as well.

[131] *Expo. Euang.*, 57, names Caritas and Sapientia together with Bona Scientia and Humilitas, but this is the only association of the two virtues in the *Expositiones*. The phrase sister of wisdom does not occur. In *Expo. Euang.*, 7, Joseph represents Wisdom.

[132] *Expo. Euang.*, 33, pp. 278–79.

[133] *Expo. Euang.*, 33, p. 278, lines 9–11: '*Et dixit eis*, timor Domini: *Euntes*, de immundicia ad mundiciam.'

God.' In line with that reading, she interprets Mark 16. 16b, 'one who has not believed will be damned', to mean that 'one who returns to evil will be an enemy of God'.[134]

The *magistra* allegorizes the closing of Jesus's advice to the disciples and his subsequent ascension as the victory that Timor Domini achieves. As Christ ascends, good desires go up to heaven to prepare repose among the virtues for those who interiorize the virtue's attribute and accordingly fear the Lord.[135] Like the disciples, the once lazy souls actualize their new attitude and go out to preach: aided by Fear of the Lord and by Christ's sacrifice, they proclaim the merit of virtue. Finally, they confirm their message with good examples and signs of the rewards of eternal life (Mk 16. 17–18, 20).[136]

A broad structural parallel marks the two works: the proclamation of victory and the praise that Timor Domini utters in the *expositio* echo the praises and acclaim that the chorus in the *Ordo* sounds forth for Anima's restoration. Moreover, the warnings that Hildegard has Timor Domini issue in the homily correspond thematically to the admonitory role that Timor Dei (Fear of God) defines for herself in the *Ordo*. In the play, Timor Dei introduces herself as the one who will equip others to look upon the living God and not to perish: 'I, Fear of God, prepare you blessed daughters so that you look upon the living God and do not perish.' Therefore, she aids the soul in its journey to eternal life. Moreover, the virtues praise her for her assistance: 'You are greatly beneficial to us.'[137] This self-characterization by Timor Dei weighs against Hildegard's portrayal of Timor Domini in the homily, where the virtue, in dialogue with the soul, makes no self-introduction but describes the salvific outcome of her intervention. In this instance again, one may see the texts as complementary; the homily illustrates the outcome of the promise that the virtue makes in the drama: Hildegard skilfully puts into action the interiorization and implementation of the virtue. The lazy souls, once transformed, preach virtue, practise good deeds, and demonstrate signs. The homily dramatizes events of the soul's journey that take place outside the *Ordo*.

---

[134] *Expo. Euang.*, 33, p. 278, lines 12–13: '*Qui crediderit*, mala dimittendo, *et baptizatus fuerit*, bona incipiendo, *saluus erit*, id est amicus Deo appellabitur. *Qui uero non crediderit*, scilicet qui se ad malum reducit, *condempnabitur*, uidelicet inimicus Dei est.'

[135] *Expo. Euang.*, 33, p. 279, lines 23–26.

[136] *Expo. Euang.*, 33, p. 279, lines 27–31.

[137] *Ordo*, p. 510, lines 110–11, 113–14: 'Ego, Timor Dei, uos felicissimas filias preparo ut inspiciatis in deum uiuum et non pereatis'; 'ualde utilis es nobis'. Likewise, the seer depicts the virtue in *Sciuias* as a scrutinizing figure covered with eyes, *Sciuias*, I.1.2, p. 9. Cf. *Vite mer.*

Virginitas (Virginity)

Virginitas enters *expositiones* on three pericopes: the Magi's discovery of Mary and the child (Mt 2. 1–12); the resurrection narrative (Mk 16. 1–7); and the feast of the purification (Lk 2. 22–32), the only Marian feast included in the collection of *Expositiones euangeliorum*.[138] Hildegard comes the closest to personifying the virtue in the homily on Matthew 2. 1–12, where the biblical character of Mary denotes both *uirginitas* and *uirginalitas*. The *magistra* first interprets Mary as virginality (*uirginalitate*) in the discipline of the law that foretold the incarnation. She then explains that virginity (*uirginitas*) gives birth to innocence, the state that Cain lost by murdering his brother.[139] Hence the homicidal offspring of Adam and Eve contrasts with the innocent Christ who brought salvation through resurrection. *Virginalitas* indicates the possibility or quality of virginity contained in the prophecies, whereas *uirginitas* designates the virgin mother of God.

In the homily on Mark 16. 1–7, Hildegard reads the young man sitting in the tomb (Mk 16. 5) as the virile strength present in virginity and abstinence; through chastity, one enters the tomb that represents mortification and renunciation of the flesh. The whiteness of the man's garment (Mk 16. 5) designates the brilliance of virginity shining in strength and the original clothing of innocence.[140] Mary's virginity and motherhood of Christ (the new law and the time of grace) joins her observance of the law, which models the practices of mortification and renunciation of the flesh. The *magistra* delivers a congruent message but not a totally coherent allegory. Hildegard seems intent on teaching about the virtue of virginity and the necessary discipline required to maintain the virginal state.

---

[138] *Expo. Euang.*, 12, 28, 21, pp. 219–22, 269–72, 243–45.

[139] *Expo. Euang.*, 12, p. 222, lines 68–73: '*Et intrantes domum*, scilicet legem rectitudinis, *inuenerunt puerum*, uidelicet innocentiam, *cum Maria*, id est uirginalitate in disciplina legis, quae premonstrauit incarnationem Christi, *matre eius*, uidelicet innocentia, quia uirginitas profert innocentiam, quam Cain perdidit in effusione sanguinis fratris sui, unde postea innocens Christus ad saluandos populos surrexit.'

[140] *Expo. Euang.*, 28, p. 271, lines 35–44: '*Et introeuntes*, per castitatem, *monumentum*, scilicet mortificationem carnis, ubi se homines propter Deum mortificant, *uiderunt*, ab renuntiatione sui, *iuuenem*, id est uirilem fortitudinem, quae in uirginitate et in continentia est, ita quod homo hoc quod in carne est dimittit, et hoc in spiritu aggreditur quod in carne non est, manens in castitate sine macula et sine ruga, *sedentem*, ante tribunal Dei, *in dextris* potestatis Dei, ut dictum est: *Sede a dextris meis, coopertum* in circumcinctione, *stola*, scilicet prima ueste innocentiae, *candida*, in candore uirginitatis, *et obstupuerunt*, de irrisione diaboli et de strepitu mundi.'

In the purification homily, Hildegard first describes Virginitas abstractly. She offers a literal/historical explanation of purification rites for Mary (Lk 2. 22), a virgin, and then draws a moral lesson on virginity for her nuns. The *magistra* explains that Mary remained a virgin, unlike men and women, who are created from earth and water and who usually marry. Mary's womb was closed, she adds, although it could have been opened. With the latter remark, Hildegard seems to assert Mary's humanity, perhaps having in mind heretical views of the Virgin as apparently but not truly human.[141] The *magistra* continues and states that those who vow virginity bring Jesus to Jerusalem (Lk 2. 22), in that they may reach the vision of true peace and salvation.[142]

Ascent to Jerusalem applies as well to Hildegard's identification of Simeon, who was 'in Jerusalem', that is, in the vision of salvation. He designates the virginal person, looking at himself in a mirror and guarding himself lest the hawk attack.[143] Two of Hildegard's letters clarify the import of this image. She advises Philip, Archbishop of Cologne, that bishops should imitate the humble, Christ-like gaze of the dove and not the haughty and worldly view of the hawk. Similarly, the *magistra* instructs Helenger of Disibodenberg that hermits and pilgrims who yearn for the path to heaven know how to avoid the hawk, just as the dove flies away when it sees the hawk in the mirror of water (*in speculo aque*).[144]

---

[141] Beverly Mayne Kienzle, 'Mary Speaks Against Heresy: An Unedited Sermon of Hélinand of Froidmont for the Purification, Paris, B.N. MS. Lat. 14591', *Sacris erudiri*, 32 (1991), 291–308.

[142] *Expo. Euang.*, 21, p. 243, lines 1–12: '*Postquam impleti sunt*, id est peracti sunt, *dies*, in ueritate, *purgationis*, Mariae ita ut purgata sit ab omni contagione muliebris copulae, scilicet quod uirgo permansit, *secundum legem*, uidelicet ut uir et mulier coniungi solent, *Moysi*, qui et de terra et de aqua creati sunt; *tulerunt*, qui uirginitatem uouent bono exemplo, Iesum, id est uirginitatem, *in Iherusalem*, scilicet ad uisionem uerae pacis et salutis, *ut sisterent*, uidelicet ut adimplerent, *eum*, scilicet uirginitatem, *Domino*, quam uouerunt. *Sicut scriptum est*, id est secundum quod exemplum habebat, *in lege Domini*, scilicet de incarnatione Domini, quae sine macula fuit, *quia omne masculinum adaperiens uuluam*, ita ut uuluam aperire possit, si uelit, sed eam uiriliter clauserit.'

[143] *Expo. Euang.*, 21, p. 244, lines 18–21: '*Et ecce homo*, qui in uirginitate talis esse debet, *erat in Ierusalem*, scilicet in uisione salutis, *cui nomen Symeon*, uidelicet speculum, in quo se ipsum consideret et custodiat, ne accipiter super eum irruat.' The hawk appears in Leviticus 11. 16, Deuteronomy 14. 15, Job 39. 13, and Job 39. 26.

[144] *Epistolarium*, I, 17, p. 52, lines 24–28: 'Ipsos etiam excelsum templum per altam doctrinam episcopalis officii ascendere decet, quemadmodum et columba oculis suis in altum aspiciat et non secundum oculos accipitris, id est: non secundum mores huius seculi facere debent, qui uulnera quidem faciunt que oleo non unxerunt'; *Letters*, I, p. 68. *Epistolarium*, I, 77R, p. 174, lines 213–16: 'Et hi omnia transacta et preterita, que uel prospera uel aduersa fuerunt, inspiciunt, quatenus

The homily continues its moral instruction: Virginitas is virtuous and holy to God; it serves as a path for imitating the Lord's incarnation; Virginitas gleams and shines (*claret et lucet*) in its chastity before all the other virtues.[145] Hildegard interprets the 'Nunc dimittis' passage (Lk 2. 29–32) as Simeon's plea to take away inordinate desire so that he may rest in chastity and peace, freed from the Devil (*a diabolo solutus*). The light (Lk 2. 32) signals the dawn manifested to counter the carnal laws of those who live in carnal bonds; the glory of Israel (Lk 2. 32) refers to the singular reward for those who follow virginity.[146] As with the exegesis of Luke 2. 1–14, the *magistra* holds up the virginal life as the ideal for her community of nuns, but she does not enter into the historical theological controversy over Mary's perpetual virginity.[147]

The homily offers thematic and semantic parallels with the *Ordo uirtutum*. Virginity's gleam evokes the jewels that comprise the structure of the heavenly Jerusalem, an echo of the *Ordo* where redeemed sinners 'gleam (*lucent*) in heavenly goodness'.[148] Simeon's liberation from carnality, representative of the virginal soul, echoes the motif of Anima's release in the *Ordo*. Furthermore, the notion that Simeon or the flesh is released (*solutus*) from the Devil evokes antithetically the scene where the Devil is bound (*ligatus*), as Victoria exclaims: 'Rejoice, o friends, that the ancient

quomodo acerrimo accipitri se surripiant, precauerant, queadmodum columba ab isto fugit, cum ipsum in speculo aque uiderit'; *Letters*, I, p. 171.

[145] *Expo. Euang.*, 21, p. 243, line 13: 'uirginitas uirtuosa et sancta Deo est'; p. 244, lines 34–39: '*Et cum inducerent*, bene operando, *puerum Iesum*, scilicet uirginitatem quae pura esse debet, *parentes eius*, uidelicet bona exempla, *ut facerent*, parando, *secundum consuetudinem*, id est honorem, *legis*, scilicet incarnationis Domini, quam in uirginitate imitantur, *pro eo*, in sanctitate et laude'; p. 245, lines 49–50: 'uirginitas pre ceteris uirtutibus in castitate claret et lucet'.

[146] *Expo. Euang.*, 21, p. 245, lines 42–54: '*Nunc dimittis*, id est aufer, *seruum tuum*, scilicet seruile opus carnis meae et ardorem concupiscentiae, *secundum uerbum tuum*, uidelicet secundum honorem filii tui, qui nobis castitatem ostendit, *in pace*, ita ut in pace requiei, a diabolo solutus [...]. *Lumen*, scilicet auroram, *ad reuelationem*, in manifestatione, *gentium*, id est contra carnis iura illorum qui in copula carnali uiuunt, *et gloriam*, scilicet singulare pretium, *plebis tuae*, scilicet omnium, *Israhel*, qui in uirginitate subsecuntur.'

[147] Bede, *In Lucae euangelium*, I, ii, p. 62, lines 1690–96 (de uirginitate); Haymo of Auxerre, *Homiliae de tempore*, 14, *PL* 118: 100. Hildegard's other interpretation follows a typological framework: the purification of Mary represents the transformation of the old law into the new, as in Bede, *In Lucae euangelium*, I, ii, pp. 61–62, lines 1673–80 (*de antiqua lege*); cf. Bede, *Homeliarum euangelii libri II*, I, 18, p. 129, lines 29–35. Ambrosius Autpertus, *Sermo in purificatione sanctae Mariae*, 3, pp. 986–87, lines 10–30.

[148] *Ordo*, p. 520, line 335: 'qui nunc lucent in superna bonitate!'

serpent has been bound!'[149] Moreover, the Devil's last words to the virtues attack their renunciation of carnality, the physical barrenness of virginity. Castitas utters the last rebuke to the Tempter, asserting that she has brought forth the Redeemer.[150] One may see the homily as a complement to the *Ordo*, in that Hildegard extends her teaching on virginity beyond what the drama allows in Castitas's brief rebuke to the Devil. As in the *Ordo*, where Virginity plays no active role but is addressed off-stage, so in the *Expositiones* Virginity shines, nearly beyond reach.

How does this depiction of Virginity compare to prior exegesis of the pericope? Hildegard borrows little from the exegetical tradition on Luke 2. 22–32 beyond the identification of the turtledoves as innocence and chastity, and the standard reading of Jerusalem as the vision of peace.[151] A contemporary visual and textual witness to the depiction of the pericope, the *Hildegard-Gebetbuch*, reflects those same traditional elements as it illustrates the scene in the temple with the child Jesus blessing the turtledoves. The accompanying prayer emphasizes the purity of Mary, who although unspotted, nonetheless offered herself for purification out of humility. While exegetical themes similar to Hildegard's inform the *Gebetbuch*, its emphasis lies on the supplicant's willingness to accept the need for purification, rather than on praise of virginity.[152] Hildegard, in contrast, exalts virginity, an attainable ideal in the human flesh of Mary.

Overall, the *magistra*'s homilies on virginity advocate various practices necessary for the virginal life: namely, renunciation of the flesh and a hawkishly watchful eye. None of these homilies personifies Virginitas in a consistently active role. Rather the virtue remains more an abstraction. Yet Mary in the homily on Luke 2. 22–32 also represents Virginality, who seems like a Platonic ideal beyond the grasp of practice, perhaps like Virginity in the *Ordo*, standing out of reach.

---

[149] *Ordo*, p. 519, line 311: 'Gaudete, o socii, quia antiquus serpens ligatus est!'

[150] *Ordo*, p. 520, lines 322–24: Diabolus: 'Tu nescis quid colis, quia uenter tuus uacuus est pulcra forma de uiro sumpta — ubi transis preceptum quod deus in suaui copula precepit; unde nescis quid sis!' *Ordo*, p. 520, lines 326–29: Castitas: 'Quomodo posset me hoc tangere | quod tua suggestio polluit per immundiciam incestus? | Unum uirum protuli, qui genus humanum | ad se congregat, contra te, per natiuitatem suam.'

[151] Bede, *Homeliarum euangelii libri II*, I, 18, p. 129, lines 56–58: 'turtur indicat castitatem'. See other sources in *Expo. Euang.*, 21, apparatus fontium, p. 243. On Jerusalem in this pericope, Ambrosius Autpertus, *Sermo in purificatione sanctae Mariae*, 4, l. 21, p. 988.

[152] *Gebetbuch*, fols 16ᵛ–17ʳ.

Sapientia (Wisdom)

Sapientia occupies centre stage in an *expositio* for Christmas Eve (Mt 1. 18–21), where Hildegard allegorizes Mary as the faithful soul (*fidelis anima*) and Joseph as Wisdom.[153] The allegory of Mary as the soul assigns another feminine role to the Virgin, one with ample precedent in prior exegesis. Hildegard explicates the betrothal of Mary and Joseph (Mt 1. 18) as baptism, whereby the faithful soul (Mary) becomes the mother of Jesus and a member of Christ's body by accomplishing good deeds. Wisdom (Joseph) knows the good and resides in heaven and on earth, where it is found among people of the world who meditate on heavenly matters when instructed by the Holy Spirit.[154] Just as Joseph did not want to hand over (*traducere*) Mary publicly (Mt 1. 19), Wisdom does not want to relinquish the faithful soul to worldly things since it meditates on the heavenly; instead, it wishes to test for itself whether or not it can achieve what it began: not to fear (Mt 1. 20) to espouse the faithful soul, 'noli timere', but to lead it confidently to knowledge of God.[155]

Hildegard reads the angel as Inspiration (Mt 1. 20). When Inspiration (the angel) addresses Wisdom (Joseph), the *magistra* extends the scriptural 'noli timere' (Mt 1. 20) with more advice: 'confide eam ducere' (lead her confidently into marriage), retaining the second person singular form of the biblical text.[156] Wisdom (Joseph) will lead the soul (Mary) confidently to knowledge of God (the marriage), since the soul was united to it by baptism. The child born from this union (Mt 1. 21) represents the full and complete deed by which the soul will be saved. Jesus will free the faithful soul's thoughts, speech, and entire body from the snares of sin and lead it to God (Mt 1. 21).[157] That transferring (*translatio*) echoes but transforms Joseph's refusal to hand over Mary and Wisdom's denial to relinquish the soul to worldly matters.[158]

[153] One may have expected Mary to represent Wisdom, but as Barbara Newman points out, Sapientia was depicted by male and female figures in the twelfth century and other eras. See Newman, *Sister of Wisdom*, p. 43.

[154] *Expo. Euang.*, 6, p. 204, lines 1–9.

[155] *Expo. Euang.*, 6, pp. 204–05, lines 9–20.

[156] *Expo. Euang.*, 6, p. 205, lines 17–20: '*noli timere*, in ulla dubietate, *accipere Mariam coniugem tuam*, id est fidelem animam; sed confide eam tecum ducere ad illa quae in Deo sapis, quoniam ipsa tibi in sancto baptismo coniuncta est'.

[157] *Expo. Euang.*, 6, p. 205, lines 20–27.

[158] See Rahner, 'Die Gottesburt'.

What role does Wisdom play in other *Expositiones*? Hildegard personifies Wisdom in another gospel narrative that involves the holy family: Luke 2. 42–52, the story of Jesus teaching in the temple at age twelve.[159] In this instance, the allegorical identities of the characters change: Mary represents Wisdom, while Joseph stands for the Holy Spirit. Jesus designates *rationalitas*, the faculty that enables the human to discern good and evil, when aided by the admonition of the Holy Spirit (Joseph) and Wisdom (Mary). Jesus's age, twelve (Lk 2. 42), refers to the age of reason.[160] The three-day journey (Lk 2. 46) that Mary and Joseph undertake back to Jerusalem (Lk 2. 45) entails the will's decision to choose good works over evil, when it is admonished by virtue over vice. The days correspond to three aspects of performing the good: rationality, faith, and the will to do what is good.[161] The teachers in the temple (Lk 2. 46) designate the models of other holy persons. Wisdom (Mary) asks the human not to hide the treasure of good works, and the Holy Spirit's admonition (Joseph) joins Wisdom in asking the human to honour them.[162]

Overall the homily retains the pericope's narrative focus on the character of Jesus, but Hildegard nonetheless highlights the personification of Wisdom. The biblical text uses direct speech from mother to son (Lk 2. 48): 'Fili, quod fecisti nobis' (Son, what have you done to us?); and Mary refers to herself and Joseph with first person plural: 'querebamus te' (we were looking for you), including one first person singular reference: 'et ego' (and I). Hildegard retains that framework of discourse and expands Mary's words into a longer discourse as Wisdom speaks for both characters:

> Sed nolo ut thesaurum tuum abscondas, sed ut aperte in bonis operibus incedas. *Ecce pater tuus*, scilicet admonitio Spiritus Sancti, quae tibi bonum inspirauit, *et ego*, uidelicet sapientia quae te suauiter nutriuit, *dolentes*, si inhonorares nos, scilicet si opus nostrum sine utilitate portares, *querebamus te*, ita quod nolumus ut inhonores nos hoc modo, ne agnoscamur in te.[163]

> [I do not want you to hide your treasure but to enter in openly with good works. *Behold your father*, that is the admonition of the Holy Spirit that has inspired you to the good, *and I*, namely wisdom that has nourished you gently, *are sorrowful*. If you dishonoured us, that

---

[159] *Expo. Euang.*, 15, pp. 228–30.

[160] *Expo. Euang.*, 15, p. 228, lines 1–3.

[161] *Expo. Euang.*, 15, p. 229, lines 24–26: '*Et factum est*, id est cum admonitio ista sic completa fuerit, *post triduum*, quia homo racionalis est et fidem suscepit, et etiam uoluntatem bonum operandi habet.'

[162] *Expo. Euang.*, 15, p. 229, lines 29–31, 37–39.

[163] *Expo. Euang.*, 15, pp. 229–30, lines 38–44.

is if you carried our work without benefit, *we were looking for you*, because we do not want you to dishonour us in this way, that we not be recognized in you.]¹⁶⁴

Note that few words (eight of fifty-seven in the Latin) belong to the scriptural passage. Hildegard constructs the rest of Wisdom's address, admonishing the soul to good works, explaining the guidance of the Holy Spirit, and reminding Rationality that she nourished the child with gentleness. Rationality replies in the first person and focuses on the notion of walking openly in the good. She fears the vice of Vainglory: 'I fear that if I walk openly, Vainglory will impede me.'¹⁶⁵ Wisdom and the admonition of the Holy Spirit advise Rationality not to hide his good works but to let them shine discreetly. Hildegard first relates this advice in the third person, 'They did not want him to cast himself to the ground and so hide his good works', as in the biblical text: 'ipsi non intellexerunt' (Lk 2. 50, they did not understand). However, she then rephrases the ideas, introducing her paraphrase with 'quasi dicerent' (as if they said), and giving her characters a voice in the first person plural: 'Our task has been revealed, and we have not fallen. We want you to act in this way; and do not hesitate.'¹⁶⁶ Presumably it is Wisdom that speaks again for the two parents. Her voice this time is firm and admonitory, much as Hildegard's would have been when, as superior of her community, she urged her sisters to practice good works.

To complete the story, the *magistra* returns to the third person narrative. Just as Jesus heeded his parents (Lk 2. 51), the human puts aside his own will. As Jesus came to Nazareth (Lk 2. 51), he comes to evident models of good works. As Jesus grew in wisdom and knowledge (Lk 2. 52), so the human grows in good works. Wisdom keeps fear, anxiety, and obedience in her heart.¹⁶⁷ Hildegard exploits the dramatic and the pedagogical potential of the gospel passage by developing the scriptural discourse of Mary and Joseph into a longer utterance by Wisdom, who speaks on behalf of herself and the Holy Spirit.

The figure of Wisdom here takes on Marian and feminine characteristics that stem from the identification of the virtue with the Virgin. This second of two

¹⁶⁴ See Newman, *Sister of Wisdom*, p. 94, on Hildegard's interpretation of Jesus's remark to Mary in *Expo. Euang.*, 14.

¹⁶⁵ *Expo. Euang.*, 15, p. 230, lines 46–47: 'timeo, si aperte ambulauero, quod uana gloria me impediat'.

¹⁶⁶ *Expo. Euang.*, 15, p. 230, lines 55–56: 'nolebant, ita ut se in terram deiceret, et bona opera sua ita occultaret [. . .]. Opus nostrum apertum est, et non cecidimus. Sic etiam uolumus, ut tu facias, et non dubites.'

¹⁶⁷ *Expo. Euang.*, 15, p. 230, lines 59–68.

expositiones where Hildegard personifies Sapientia assigns a nourishing but admonitory role to the virtue. In the homily discussed above (Mt 1. 18–21), Joseph represents Wisdom and Mary stands for Caritas, who cares for the infant Obedientia. In that text, Caritas and not Sapientia takes the role of nurturer. Each homily contains a coherent allegory, but the features change. Nonetheless, in both homilies, one may imagine the voice of Hildegard as *magistra*. She teaches the value of obedience, the discarding of self-will, and the practice of good works — all essential components of the Benedictine *Rule*.

The Battle between Virtues and Vices

Does the antagonist of the virtues play a role in the *Expositiones*? Indeed the Devil enters the homilies just as he does the *Ordo*. Moreover, the vices, assistants to the Devil, figure in the *Expositiones* as well, while no Devil's helpers appear in the play. Jesus's birth in Bethlehem (Mt 2. 1) represents the birth of Christ in the penitent confession of the sinner, who is beset by the Devil's temptations.[168] The Magi (Mt 2. 1) signify knowledge of God, when the human turns towards God with spiritual joy from the birth of God's grace and comes to the vision of peace. Hildegard reiterates that Jesus is born in penitence through God's grace,[169] which is born as the star rising in the East (Mt 2. 2). With no direct reference to Augustine, she reads the phenomenon of the star as the indication that the Augustinian 'era of grace' has begun, both in Christ's birth and in the possibility of penitence and redemption for the human being. Penitence tramples the Devil in the abyss; like Bethlehem among the cities of Judah (Mt 2. 5), it stands great among the virtues, including Chastity, Continence, and Holiness, and from it, the Saviour issues forth.[170]

The process of repentance does not take place without opposition from the Devil and his right-hand vices, Vainglory and Pride. Once Hildegard introduces the Devil into her commentary, she begins to shape a lively dramatic narrative. As

---

[168] *Expo. Euang.*, 13, p. 223, lines 1–5.

[169] *Expo. Euang.*, 13, p. 223, lines 5–11: '*ecce magi*, id est cognitio Dei, ubi homo ad Deum conuertitur, *ab oriente*, uidelicet ab ortu gratiae Dei, *uenerunt*, in spiritali gaudio, *Iherosolimam*, scilicet in uisionem pacis, quia Deus penitentem hominem suscipit, *dicentes*: *Vbi est*, in gratia sua, *qui natus est*, per dona sua in penitentia hominis, *rex Iudeorum*, quia Deus potens est peccata dimittere illis qui ea confitentur?'

[170] *Expo. Euang.*, 13, p. 224, lines 34–37: '*Ex te enim exiet*, quia penitentia diabolum in abysso conterit, *dux*, saluator, peccata dimittens, *qui regat*, in celestibus et in terrenis, *populum meum*, quem ego tango, dicit gratia Dei, *Israel*, qui in uirtutibus Deum inspicit.'

Herod summons the Magi (Mt 2. 7), the Devil deceitfully calls upon Knowledge of God and asks for information (Mt 2. 8) — the beginning and intent of Good Report. The Devil sends this knowledge to Penitence, instructing Penitence first to rise up with Vainglory and ask how the human can wish to be innocent, and second, to join him (the Devil) by taking pride in his own holiness. After hearing the Devil's temptation, Knowledge of God scrutinizes Penitence; and Good Report stands in perseverance thanks to God's grace. Upon finding Innocence with unpretentious faith, Knowledge rejoices, as the Magi rejoice upon seeing the star (Mt 2. 10). Entering the room (the inn, Mt 2. 11) where the sinner makes his confession, Knowledge finds Innocence (the child Jesus, Mt 2. 11) and Holiness (Mary, Mt 2. 11). With praises for the Lord who worked repentance in the sinner, Knowledge brings three gifts that correspond to the three offerings of the Magi (Mt 2. 11): gold indicates that the human begins to know God; frankincense reveals that the human confesses his sins; and myrrh shows that he casts himself down in constraint (*se totum in constrictione prosternit*).[171] As the Magi returned not to Herod but to their own land (Mt 2. 12), so Knowledge returns to the righteousness in which the righteous person will hold an inheritance.[172]

One can imagine a drama enacted from this homily: Knowledge of God and the Devil would play the leading roles. Hildegard finds in her exegesis an avenue for developing the Devil's actions and opposition to specific virtues as well as his interaction with his vice-assistants. The active opposition of the Devil to the virtues recalls the Tempter's role in the *Ordo uirtutum*. Whereas the virtues bind the Devil in the drama, in the homily they trample him in the abyss. In the *Ordo*, the Tempter acts alone as the voice of evil; in the *expositio*, Vainglory and Pride work at his side to attempt deceit. The homily thus provides an episode in the struggle between virtues and vices, a sort of mini-drama that does not occur in the *Ordo* but could easily form part of a broader performance or constitute a dramatic representation on its own. As assistants to the Holy Spirit, the virtues take on a triumphant role and stage a scene in the narrative of salvation where Christus Victor ultimately overcomes evil.

---

[171] *Expo. Euang.*, 13, p. 225, lines 64–68: '*Et apertis* bona uoluntate *thesauris suis*, inicio operum suorum, *obtulerunt ei*, representando, *munera*, scilicet magnum meritum: *aurum*, quod homo incipit Deum cognoscere, *thus*, quod peccata sua in confessione aperit, *et mirram*, quod se totum in constrictione prosternit.'

[172] *Expo. Euang.*, 13, p. 225, lines 71–73: 'regressi sunt recte et bene uiuentes *in regionem suam*, id est ad iustitiam in qua iustus homo haereditatem habebit'.

In the above homily on Matthew 2. 1–12, Hildegard introduces the theme of the birth of Christ in the penitence of the sinner.[173] Similarly in her interpretation of the story of Zacchaeus (Lk 19. 1–10), Hildegard reads the entrance into another house (*domus*) as a story of Jesus entering the human heart. Jesus (Lk 19. 1) represents himself, the Son of God, while Zacchaeus (Lk 19. 2 and others) stands for the wicked person who transgressed commandments but later becomes righteous. Zacchaeus's small stature (Lk 19. 3) points to the wickedness of individual thoughts. The tax collector's ascent of the sycamore tree (Lk 19. 4) denotes the sinful human being's haste to follow her own desires and turn away from heavenly things. Jesus's reaching and calling Zacchaeus to come down (Lk 19. 5) stands for his seeing the sinner's evil way of life and calling the sinner to repentance by humbling himself. Hildegard interprets the Saviour's key words, 'in domo tua oportet me manere' (it is necessary for me to remain in your house, Lk 19. 5), as Jesus's entrance into the sinner's heart if she wants to be saved, where the house stands for the heart. Zacchaeus's climb down from the tree (Lk 19. 6) denotes humility, along with acts of repentance: putting aside sins, sighing, crying.[174]

The *magistra* reads the act of Zacchaeus standing (Lk 19. 8) as the sinner's stability in victory over sin. She interprets the tax collector's action of giving half his wealth to the poor (Lk 19. 8) as the human's decision to make himself small and poor. Consequently, Hildegard explicates the fourfold return of goods (Lk 19. 8) as four actions: vanquishing the self, putting aside bad habits, doing good works, and persevering to the end — an echo of the *Rule of Benedict*.[175] The house appears again (Lk 19. 9) as the heart and soul. Finally, the *magistra* interprets becoming a son of Abraham (Lk 19. 9) as being a victor over the Devil, and she adds that one vanquishes the Devil with the dove's simplicity.[176]

---

[173] *Expo. Euang.*, 13, p. 223, lines 1–3.

[174] *Expo. Euang.*, 58, p. 332, lines 24–31: '*Zachee*, qui prius preuaricator eras, sed modo iustificaberis, *festinans*, penitendo, *descende*, id est humiliare, ut a peccatis tuis abluaris, *quia hodie*, cum te requiro, *in domo tua*, scilicet in corde tuo, *oportet*, si saluari desideras, *me manere*, id est in te glorificabor sancta mansione. *Et festinans*, penitendo, *descendit*, quia homo ille per humilitatem peccata sua dimittere incipit, *et excepit illum*, in suspirio suo, *gaudens*, in lacrimis saluationis.'

[175] *Expo. Euang.*, 58, p. 333, lines 44–47: '*reddo quadruplum*, meipsum contra uoluntatem meam uincendo et malam consuetudinem meam dimittendo, et postea bonum opus perficiendo, et sic in eo usque in finem perseuerando'.

[176] *Expo. Euang.*, 58, p. 333, lines 48–53: '*Ait Iesus* in admonitione Spiritus Sancti *ad eum*, in penitentia illum suscipiendo: *Quia hodie*, ubi penitentiam egit, *salus*, in passione redemptionis omnium, *domui huic*, scilicet cordi tuo et animae tuae, *facta est*, quia uictor diaboli extitit, *eo quod ipse*, qui sic saluatus est, *filius sit*, per redemptionem, *Abrahae*, eterni regni in simplicitate columbae.'

Parallels between this homily on the Zacchaeus story and the *Ordo* are thematic and structural: the sinful human who hurries to follow her own desires corresponds to Anima and her fall. Jesus's call to Zacchaeus evokes the virtues' appeal to Anima. In order for Zacchaeus to climb down from the tree so that Jesus may enter his house, acts of humility and sounds of repentance prove necessary. The acts of putting aside sins, sighing, and crying allow Jesus to enter the human heart. These repentant actions and sounds recall the lament of penitent Anima and the chorus of virtues, as well as the appeal of Anima in the *Ordo* for Humilitas, 'true medicine', to intervene.[177] They also evoke the spirituality and the language of the Benedictine *Rule*. Humility leads the monk or sister to acts of repentance, performed with groaning and sighing.[178]

Does the soul's struggle end successfully in all the *Expositiones*? Two vices, Desire for Pleasure and Vanity, occupy centre stage and address each other directly in one homily on the parable of the great banquet (Lk 14. 16–24).[179] Vanity serves as desire's messenger (the servant, Lk 14. 17), who searches for humans (guests, Lk 14. 17) who will consent to desire (the master, Lk 14. 16). The reluctant invitees give three excuses for not attending the banquet (Lk 14. 18–20); Hildegard interprets them as the individual soul's struggle within itself. As the three men speak in

---

[177] *Ordo*, p. 515, lines 221–22: Virtutes: 'Heu, heu, nos Virtutes plangamus et lugeamus, | quia ovis domini fugit vitam!'; p. 517, lines 256–59: 'Et o vera medicina, Humilitas, prebe michi auxilium, | quia superbia in multis viciis fregit me, | multas cicatrices michi imponens. | Nunc fugio ad te, et ideo suscipe me.'

[178] Saint Benedict, *Regula*, 4, 57–58, p. 35: 'Mala sua praeterita cum lacrimis vel gemitu cotidie in oratione Deo confiteri'. The English translation by Meisel and Del Mastro, p. 53, renders this as confessing daily 'in humble prayer'.

[179] *Expo. Euang.*, 40, p. 300, lines 34–54: '*Tunc iratus*, in terrore, *paterfamilias*, scilicet dulce desiderium uoluptatis, *dixit seruo suo*, uanitati: *Exi cito*, id est ilico, *in plateas*, scilicet in communem populum, *et uicos*, uidelicet inpotentes, *ciuitatis*, plus quam potentum, *et pauperes*, armatos, *ac debiles*, ministros armatorum, *cecos*, id est pauperes, *et claudos*, scilicet pauperiores, *introduc huc*, uidelicet affer eos ad me, quoniam aliquem in his inuenio michi consentientem. *Et ait seruus*, uanitas: *Domine*, quia tibi seruio, *factum est ut imperasti*, scilicet temperamentum, *et adhuc locus est*, uoluntati tuae, quia sapientes et scientes ad te nondum uenerunt. *Et ait dominus*, desiderium uoluptatis, *seruo*, id est uanitati: *Exi*, te dilatando, *in uias*, id est in sapientes, *et* plateas, scilicet in im | plexos sanctitate, *et compelle*, uidelicet constringe admonendo, *intrare*, ad me, ita ut michi consentiant, *ut impleatur*, id est ut plena sit, *domus mea* scilicet desiderium meum. *Dico autem*, uidelicet annuntio uobis, qui mecum militatis, *quod nemo uirorum illorum*, scilicet nulla uis, *qui uocati sunt*, id est qui uocationem meam contempserunt, nec michi consentire uoluerunt, *gustabit*, tangendo, *cenam meam*, id est delicias meas, in ulla dulcedine et suauitate mearum concupiscentiarum, sed in amaritudine et dolore eos usque in finem exercebo.'

the first person singular, so the human soul relates three hesitations: 'me a vanis continere volo' (I want to restrain myself from vain things); 'in pauore michimetipsi resistentem' (I am resisting myself in fear); 'ignem concupiscentiae misi in carnem meam' (I put the fire of desire in my flesh).[180] The conflict ends without any victory of the virtues. On the contrary, Vanity asserts that it will not cease the battle: 'in amaritudine et dolore eos usque in finem exercebo' (I will test them until the end in bitterness and pain).[181]

The harsh ending to the homily leaves the soul's combat in suspense and the audience on guard. Hildegard's predominant insistence in the *Expositiones* on the drama of fall and restoration highlights the singularity of this homily on the parable of the great supper. Vanity's concluding threat leads one to imagine a tense situation at Rupertsberg and perhaps even a reflection of Hildegard's anger over the departure of Richardis and Adelheid.[182] Certainly, the menace of Vanity stands apart from the usual stream of the *Expositiones*.[183]

Conclusion

Semantic and structural comparisons between the *Expositiones* and the *Ordo uirtutum* demonstrate the vitality of the theme of the soul's struggle in Hildegard's teaching. Military imagery describes the virtues as *milites* or knights and the active ensemble of the virtues as a host or *multitudo*. Fourteen virtues appear in both works, fifteen if we count Virginitas. The soul seeks help from the virtues against the vices in the *Expositiones*, just as in the *Ordo uirtutum*, Anima beseeches the

---

[180] *Expo. Euang.*, 40, pp. 299–300, lines 19, 25, 27–28.

[181] *Expo. Euang.*, 40, p. 300, lines 53–54. On the history of the parable's interpretation, see Bovon, *L'Évangile selon saint Luc*, pp. 456–57; Wailes, *Medieval Allegories*, pp. 161–66. Hildegard echoes some exegetical features from Origen, Augustine, and Gregory the Great, as well as their general emphasis on bodily versus spiritual pleasures. However, other exegetes such as Ambrose and Augustine focus on the three excuses together as refusals made by heathens, Jews, and heretics, a theme Hildegard does not pursue.

[182] Holloway, 'Monastic Context', pp. 68–72; Iversen, 'O Virginitas'. Fassler, 'Composer and Dramatist', p. 150, says that the *Ordo* would always have been 'a play within a play, a mousetrap for conventual souls'.

[183] Superbia weighs down Innocentia in *Expo. Euang.*, 11 as in Matthew 2. 18, 'A voice was heard in Ramah', an allusion to Jeremiah 31. 15. *Expo. Euang.*, 11, p. 219, lines 40–41: '*Vox, miseriarum, in Rama*, id est sursum, *audita est*, ubi superbia innocentiam percutiendo depressit.' However, the vice is not victorious.

chorus of virtues to assist her against the Devil.[184] Many *expositiones* reveal a dramatic structure like the *Ordo*. The soul chooses between good and evil, experiences conflict, repents, and returns restored to God. Various *expositiones* conclude with rejoicing, which mirrors the jubilance of the chorus in the *Ordo*. Hildegard probes the spiritual, psychological process of exercising ethical knowledge or choosing between good and evil. Certain *expositiones* characterize the soul in a particular state, faithful (*fidelis anima*) or sinful (*homo peccator*), which correspond broadly to the character of Anima in the *Ordo*, first as Felix Anima and then as Anima Grauata. The soul, whether faithful or sinful, chooses between good and evil through the gift of the rationality (*rationalitas*) that God bestowed on the human being. Moreover, personifications of virtues such as Fides play active roles in the *Expositiones* as in the *Ordo*, and Hildegard addresses her community through their speaking roles to emphasize her responsibility to protect them from perils to their souls. The struggle between virtue and vice, like the *magistra*'s depiction of salvation history, takes place on multiple levels: within the person, the community, and the cosmos.

The 'textual community' of Rupertsberg must have been accustomed to an extraordinary exegetical drama in which Hildegard interpreted the Scriptures in multiple media and genres.[185] Nearly one half of the *Expositiones* depict some aspect of the soul's journey and in so doing incorporate commentary, dialogue, reported dialogue, and reported music.[186] The *Sciuias* presents vision with

---

[184] As Anima begins to fall, she cries: 'Succurrite michi, adiuuando, ut possim stare' (Assist me, helping, so that I may stand). When repentant, she calls for aid to resist the Devil: 'Nunc est michi necesse ut suscipiatis me, quoniam in uulneribus feteo quibus antiquus serpens me contaminauit' (Now it is necessary for you to assist me, because I stink from the wounds with which the ancient serpent polluted me). *Ordo*, p. 507, line 47; p. 516, lines 237–39.

[185] On the 'multimediality' of dramatic texts, see Manfred Pfister, *The Theory and Analysis of Drama* (Cambridge: Cambridge University Press, 1988), pp. 6–12; Kienzle, 'Medieval Sermons and their Performance'.

[186] The soul's struggle or the virtues and vices figure in twenty-two *expositiones*: *Expo. Euang.*, 2, on Luke 16. 1–9; *Expo. Euang.*, 6, on Matthew 1. 18–21; *Expo. Euang.*, 8, on Luke 2. 1–14; *Expo. Euang.*, 11, on Matthew 2. 13–18; *Expo. Euang.*, 15, on Luke 2. 42–52; *Expo. Euang.*, 17, on John 2. 1–11; *Expo. Euang.*, 19, on Matthew 8. 1–13; *Expo. Euang.*, 21, on Luke 2. 22–32; *Expo. Euang.*, 23, on Matthew 20. 1–16; *Expo. Euang.*, 25, on Matthew 4. 1–11; *Expo. Euang.*, 29, on Mark 16. 1–7; *Expo. Euang.*, 33, on Mark 16. 14–20; *Expo. Euang.*, 36, on John 3. 1–15; *Expo. Euang.*, 38, on Luke 16. 19–31; *Expo. Euang.*, 40, on Luke 14. 16–24; *Expo. Euang.*, 42, on Luke 1. 57–68; *Expo. Euang.*, 45, on Luke 5. 1–11; *Expo. Euang.*, 48, on Luke 19. 41–47a; *Expo. Euang.*, 50, on Mark 7. 31–37; *Expo. Euang.*, 52, on Luke 18. 10–14; *Expo. Euang.*, 56 on Luke 21. 25–33; *Expo. Euang.*, 58, on Luke 19. 1–10.

monologue and dialogue, followed by commentary, and ends with drama. The illuminations of *Sciuias* (I.4) depict the tribulations of the soul in a series of medallions, as well as the soul's evasion of the Devil's darts.[187] Various sections in *Sciuias* provide visual representations of the virtues,[188] including one scene in which laden with stones they ascend a ladder.[189] Inspired by the dream of Jacob (Gn 28. 10), the ladder figures in early Christian literature such as the *Acts of Perpetua and Felicity* and *The Shepherd* of Hermas and appears in the *Speculum ecclesiae* of Honorius Augustodunensis, the *Speculum uirginum*, and the *Hortus deliciarum*.[190] The ladder image from *Sciuias* depicts the virtues performing the sort of conduct that Hildegard urges on her sisters in the *Expositiones*.

Features of moral drama mark Hildegard's other works. In the hymn 'O ignee Spiritus', the soul flies about, encircled on all sides by clouds and desires. It rises upright with the aid of the Spirit, which compels rationality to obedience.[191] Like

---

[187] *Sciuias*, I.4.1, pp. 62–66, *Scivias* (Eng.), p. 109; *Sciuias*, I.4.4, pp. 67–72, *Scivias* (Eng.), pp. 112–16.

[188] *Sciuias*, III.3.3, pp. 375–76; *Scivias* (Eng.), pp. 343–54. See Liebeschütz, *Das allegorische Weltbild*, pp. 20–35; Katzenellenbogen, *Allegories of the Virtues and Vices*, pp. 42–44; and Caviness, 'Artist', pp. 119–20 on Hildegard's creative use of this building imagery. *Sciuias*, III.3.8, pp. 478–79; *Scivias* (Eng.), pp. 425–48. *Sciuias*, III.8.14, pp. 496–97; *Scivias* (Eng.), p. 436.

[189] *Sciuias*, III.8.14, pp. 496–97; *Scivias* (Eng.), p. 436.

[190] *Passio Sanctarum Perpetuae et Felicitatis*, in *The Acts of the Christian Martyrs*, ed. by H. Musurillo, Oxford Early Christian Texts (Oxford: Clarendon Press, 1972), pp. 106–30. Katzenellenbogen, *Allegories of the Virtues and Vices*, p. 25, argues that the miniaturist combines the dreams of Perpetua: the ladder and the wrestling match with the Egyptian. On ladder imagery, see Christian Heck, *L'Échelle céleste dans l'art du Moyen Âge: Une image de la quête du ciel* (Paris: Flammarion, 1997); and Eva-Maria Kauffmann, *Jakobs Traum und der Aufstieg des Menschen zu Gott: Das Thema der Himmelsleiter in der bildenden Kunst des Mittelalters* (Tubingen: Wasmuth, 2006). I am grateful to J. Hamburger for these references. *Sciuias*, p. 478, lines 62–63: 'oneratas lapidibus'. *Similitudo*, IX, *Le Pasteur*, ed. by R. Joly, SC, 53bis (Paris: Cerf, 1997), pp. 289–365. See Katzenellenbogen, *Allegories of the Virtues and Vices*, pp. 5, 43 on depictions of this motif. On Hildegard and *The Shepherd*, see Constant J. Mews, 'Hildegard of Bingen: The Virgin, the Apocalypse, and the Exegetical Tradition', in *Wisdom which Encircles Circles*, ed. by Davidson, pp. 27–42 (p. 30), and other scholarship cited there. Newhauser, *Treatise on Vices and Virtues*, pp. 157–58; Griffiths, *Garden of Delights*, pp. 205–07, on the Ladder of Virtues and the related images of garden and tree. Powell, '*Speculum virginum* and the Audio-Visual Poetics', pp. 122–26, discusses the key role of the trees of virtue and vice in the *Speculum uirginum*.

[191] 'O ignee Spiritus', *Symph.* 27, p. 408, lines 18–21: 'Quando nebula uoluntatem | et desideria tegit, | in quibus anima uolat | et undique circuit.' Newman, 'Poet', pp. 188–91, discusses it as a psychodrama, to be interpreted on levels of individual and salvation history. See also *Symphonia*, ed. and trans. by Newman, pp. 280–81.

the *Expositiones*, the hymn highlights the obedience necessary for observance of the Benedictine *Rule*, and the virtues assist the soul to perform good works and follow the path to salvation. The Holy Spirit sends the virtues as helpers to the soul in peril. The *Liber uitae meritorum* has been described as a 'drama of human life' in which 'human reason struggles permanently in its dilemma' between vice, or destructive self-centeredness, and virtue, the 'transcendence to exuberating fullness'.[192] The *Liber diuinorum operum* accords speaking roles to certain virtues; various letters convey Hildegard's advice in the form of parables of virtue and vice. A text of mixed genre, entitled *Carmina et meditationes*, incorporates the songs into a narrative framework, a mixture of prose and verse that literary scholars term *prosimetrum*.[193] The prevalence of the theme in the Hildegardian corpus invites further study.

[192] Meis, '*Symphonia Spiritus Sancti*', pp. 391, 424.

[193] *Epistolarium*, III, 390, pp. 164–72. See above, p. 59, note 157, on prosimetric hagiography.

HILDEGARD'S EXEGESIS
AND PREACHING AGAINST HERESY

There are some who deny the first beginnings, namely that God created all things and commanded them to multiply by germinating and growing. There are some who deny the Lord's beginning, namely that he appeared before the Ancient of Days, because the Word of God had to become human.[1]

Prima principia et dominicum principium *(The first beginnings and the Lord's beginning)*

Writing to the monks of St Martin in Mainz, Hildegard denounced certain persons who denied the *prima principia*, the creation of the world by God, and the Lord's eternal existence, the *dominicum principium*. Likewise, she explained in one of her *Expositiones*: 'the Creator is known through the creation, and it is understood that the highest has created it. [. . .] Visible objects are created by God'.[2] Around the same time, the *magistra* railed against enemies of God and apostates who were 'like the bowels of the Devil', working out Satan's plan and destroying the Scripture and doctrine inspired by the Holy Spirit.[3] These and other statements defending orthodoxy and attacking heresy derive from the body of writings that Hildegard composed and in some cases preached against

---

[1] *Epistolarium*, II, 169, p. 381, lines 82–86: 'Hi sunt qui prima principia negant, scilicet quod Deus omnia creauit et ea germinando et crescendo procedere iussit. Hi sunt qui dominicum principium negant, scilicet quod ante antiquitatem dierum apparuit, quoniam Verbum Dei homo fieri debuit.'

[2] *Expo. Euang.*, 25, p. 258, lines 34–36: 'per creaturam creator cognoscitur, et quod summus eam creauerit [. . .] uisibilia a Deo creata esse'.

[3] *Epistolarium*, III, 387, p. 152, lines 15–18.

the Cathar heresy between 1163 and her death in 1179. The seer's anti-heretical work proves larger and more complex than previously thought, comprising an 1163 treatise Hildegard sent to Schönau and the monks of St Martin in Mainz;[4] sermons delivered in Cologne and Kirchheim and preserved as letters;[5] some short texts published in the third volume of the *Epistolarium*; a portion of the commentary on the Athanasian Creed; and several of the *Expositiones euangeliorum*.[6] This chapter will survey the corpus of anti-heretical works and will bring to the fore the little-studied texts in the third volume of the *Epistolarium* and the *Expositiones*.[7] I shall investigate how the *magistra*'s exegesis undergirds her attack on heretical beliefs and practices. Finally, I will question whether the denunciation of heresy may have enhanced the *magistra*'s authority to address clerical corruption and schism, or vice versa.

The 1140s and Heresy in the Rhineland

When Hildegard wrote to the clergy at Mainz (Letter 169R), she looked back to a time twenty-three years and four months before her 1163 vision, when the four winds 'blown from the mouth of the black beast' wrought ruin in the four corners of the earth. The *magistra*'s account of the winds begins with those that blew forth

---

[4] *Epistolarium*, II, 169R, pp. 378–82. See also Raoul Manselli, 'Amicizia spirituale ed azione pastorale nella Germania del sec. XII: Ildegarde di Bingen, Elisabetta ed Ecberto di Schönau contro l'eresia Catara', in *Studi in onore di Alberto Pincherle*, Studi e materiali di storia delle religioni, 38 (Rome: Ateneo, 1967), pp. 302–13.

[5] *Epistolarium*, I, 15R, pp. 34–44 plus appendices; *Epistolarium*, II, 149, pp. 332–37. See among others, Elisabeth Gössman, 'Der Brief Hildegards von Bingen an den Kölner Klerus zum Problem der Katharer', in *Miscellanea Mediaevalia: Die Kölner Universität im Mittelalter: Geistige Wurzeln und soziale Wirklichkeit*, vol. XX, ed. by Albert Zimmermann (Berlin: de Gruyter, 1989), pp. 312–20.

[6] Philip Timko, 'Hildegard of Bingen against the Cathars', *American Benedictine Review*, 52 (2001), 191–205, sees statements against the Cathars in *Sciuias* as well, but the evidence is less compelling.

[7] This chapter extends the work in Beverly Mayne Kienzle, 'Crisis and Charismatic Authority in Hildegard of Bingen's Preaching against the Cathars', in *Charisma and Religious Authority: Jewish, Christian, and Muslim Preaching, 1200–1600*, ed. by Miri Rubin and Katherine Jansen (Turnhout: Brepols, forthcoming); Kienzle, 'Defending the Lord's Vineyard: Hildegard of Bingen's Preaching against the Cathars', in *Medieval Monastic Preaching*, ed. by Carolyn A. Muessig (Leiden: Brill, 1998), pp. 163–91; Kienzle, '*Operatrix in vinea Domini*: Hildegard of Bingen's Preaching and Polemics against the Cathars', *Heresis*, 26–27 (1997), 43–56.

from the East, site of the interchange or alternation (*uicissitudo*) of foul behaviour, while in the West there occurred blasphemy, neglect of God, and idol worship.[8] Does the *magistra*'s chronology correspond to identifiable events? The moment she places around 1140 occurred a few years before Everwin of Steinfeld wrote to Bernard of Clairvaux in the 1140s about heresy with Eastern roots. Prior of a Praemonstratensian community near Cologne, Everwin requested Bernard to provide written advice for dealing with groups of heretics in the Rhineland.[9] Everwin may have known Bernard already, having perhaps met him at the 1135 Council of Pisa or during the Abbot's journey to Germany in 1147. Uwe Brunn argues for dating the correspondence to 1147/48 and concludes that there were two incidents involving heresy in Cologne: one occurred in 1143, as recounted in the *Annals of Brauweiler*, and another in 1147.[10]

Everwin insists that the time has come for Bernard to draw the best wine (Jn 2. 10) against the heretics. The people whom Everwin describes share notable features with the heretics in I Timothy 4. 1–3, who will come at the end of time: attention to the teachings of demons, hypocrisy, opposition to marriage, and abstinence from certain foods.[11] The 'new heretics' are emerging everywhere and in

---

[8] *Epistolarium*, II, 169R, pp. 378–81, at p. 379, lines 24–34: 'Nam uiginti et tres anni ac quattuor menses sunt [. . .] in oriente uicissitudo squalidorum morum efflata est.'

[9] Everwin of Steinfeld, *Epistola* 472, *PL* 182: 676–80, is discussed by Anne Brenon, 'La Lettre d'Evervin de Steinfeld à Bernard de Clairvaux de 1143: un document essentiel et méconnu', *Heresis*, 25 (1995), 7–28. Bernard Hamilton, in Hugh Eteriano, *Contra Patarenos*, ed. and trans. by Janet Hamilton (Leiden: Brill, 2005), p. 30, states that 'no surviving medieval anti-Cathar writings show any knowledge of [Everwin's letter]', but I suggest that Hildegard implies that foul behaviour spread from the East to the other points and that this may indicate familiarity with Everwin's letter. As we shall see below, she seems to echo a few elements from Bernard's reply. Brunn, *Des contestataires aux 'cathares'*, pp. 155–60, argues that Ekbert of Schönau replies to points that Everwin raises, including the apostolic succession and the legitimacy of the Catholic hierarchy. In that case, Ekbert would have known Everwin's work and found Bernard's reply inadequate. In *Cistercians, Heresy and Crusade*, pp. 85–90, I present a detailed analysis of the correspondence, including points where Bernard does reply to Everwin.

[10] Historians have associated the events in the *Annals of Brauweiler* with those recounted by Everwin. See Brunn, *Des contestataires aux 'cathares'*, pp. 103–05, 124–50.

[11] Everwin of Steinfeld, *Epistola* 472, *PL* 182: 676B–677A: 'Laetabor ego super eloquia tua, sicut qui invenit spolia multa, qui nobis memoriam abundantis suavitatis Dei eructare in omnibus dictis et scriptis vestris soletis, maxime in Cantico [...] De hydra quantum, sanctissime pater, habes nobis modo propinare! De [. . .] quinta, contra haereticos circa finem saeculi venturos, de quibus per Apostolum manifeste Spiritus dicit: "In novissimis temporibus [. . .]." Jam tempus est ut de quinta haurias, et in medium proferas contra novos haereticos, qui circumquaque jam fere per

nearly all churches, rising up from the pit of hell. The prior appeals for the Cistercian to explicate Song of Songs 2. 15, 'Seize for us the little foxes that are destroying the vineyards', and distinguish all the elements of the heresy in order to provide arguments and authorities to combat them.[12] Debaters and preachers needed an outline they could adapt and employ when they confronted dissidents who frequently evidenced confident knowledge of the Scriptures.

After making the initial request of Bernard, Everwin recounts the events that have taken place in his region: the public examination of heretics, a three-day delay before punishment, and the subsequent seizure and burning of some number of persons by an angry mob, which Everwin opposed. Everwin writes as if he was among the interrogators: 'Duo ex eis [...] nobis restiterunt' (Two of them opposed us). Two of the dissidents, a bishop and his associate, had defended their beliefs with arguments from the Gospels and Pauline texts in the presence of the Archbishop of Cologne and high-ranking lords.[13] This would indicate some degree of collaboration between secular and ecclesiastical power against heresy, although the execution was carried out by a mob.[14] The prior also reports on the apostolic faith of the heretics, their disdain for the world and asceticism, and their liturgical practices — especially baptism by imposition of hands rather than water; and he describes their differences from another group of dissidents.[15] Some who were

---

omnes Ecclesias ebulliunt de puteo abyssi, quasi jam princeps illorum incipiat dissolvi, et instet dies Domini.'

[12] Everwin of Steinfeld, *Epistola* 472, *PL* 182: 677B.

[13] Everwin of Steinfeld, *Epistola* 472, *PL* 182: 677C: 'Duo ex eis, scilicet qui dicebatur episcopus eorum cum socio suo, nobis restiterunt in conventu clericorum et laicorum, praesente ipso domino archiepiscopo cum magnis viris nobilibus, haeresim suam defendentes ex verbis Christi et Apostoli. [...] rapti sunt a populis nimio zelo permotis, nobis tamen invitis, et in ignem positi, atque cremate.' See Robert I. Moore, *The Birth of Popular Heresy*, Medieval Academy of America Reprints for Teaching, 33 (New York: St Martin's Press, 1976; repr., Toronto: Medieval Academy of America, 1995), pp. 74–78; Moore, *The Origins of European Dissent*, Medieval Academy of America Reprints for Teaching, 30 (London: Allen Lane, 1977; repr., Toronto: Medieval Academy of America, 1995), pp. 168–72, 179; Malcolm Lambert, *The Cathars* (Oxford: Blackwell, 1998), p. 20; Kienzle, *Cistercians, Heresy and Crusade*, pp. 4, 82–84. There I state that three persons were burned, following Moore's translation of the *Annales Brunwilarenses*, *Birth of Popular Heresy*, p. 74, but Everwin's letter gives no exact number. Brenon, 'La Lettre d'Evervin de Steinfeld'.

[14] Brunn, *Des contestataires aux 'cathares'*, pp. 150–51, suggests possible scenarios for the events and concludes that the bishop's role was weak.

[15] Everwin of Steinfeld, *Epistola* 472, *PL* 182: 678C–D: 'Et talem baptismum per impositionem manuum debere fieri conati sunt ostendere testimonio Lucae, qui in Actibus Apostolorum

reconciled to the Church reported that they were a worldwide movement; the victims claimed that their faith had remained hidden in Greece and other lands since the times of the martyrs. According to Everwin, they called themselves apostles and had their own pope. Moreover, these 'apostles of Satan' hail apostolic models for living chastely with women, a claim that Everwin doubts.[16]

In response to Everwin, Bernard reflects on Song of Songs 2. 15 in Sermons 65 and 66, although topics relevant to heresy enter into the two preceding sermons as well.[17] In Sermon 64, the Abbot clarifies his position against the use of force: heretics should be captured by arguments and not by arms, 'capiantur, dico, non armis, sed argumentis'.[18] The Abbot also specifies the method a churchman should employ for persuading a heretic.[19] Just as Everwin requested a clear exposition of error supported by arguments and authorities, Bernard assumed that clear reasoning

---

describens baptismum Pauli, quem ab Anania suscepit ad praeceptum Christi, nullam mentionem fecit de aqua, sed tantum de manus impositione: et quidquid invenitur tam in Actibus Apostolorum, quam in Epistolis Pauli, de manus impositione, ad hunc baptismum volunt pertinere.' Everwin goes on to distinguish the *electi* who have received the baptism by laying on of hands and can thus baptize others, the *credentes*, and the *auditores* who can be received among the *credentes*, also by the imposition of hands.

[16] Everwin of Steinfeld, *Epistola* 472, *PL* 182: 679CD–680A: 'Noveritis etiam, domine, quod redeuntes ad Ecclesiam nobis dixerunt, illos habere maximam multitudinem fere ubique terrarum sparsam, et habere eos plures ex nostris clericis et monachis. Illi vero qui combusti sunt, dixerunt nobis in defensione sua, hanc haeresim usque ad haec tempora occultatam fuisse a temporibus martyrum, et permanisse in Graecia, et quibusdam aliis terris. Et hi sunt illi haeretici, qui se dicunt apostolos, et suum papam habent. [. . .] Isti apostolici Satanae habent inter se feminas (ut dicunt) continentes, viduas, virgines, uxores suas, quasdam inter electas, quasdam inter credentes; quasi ad formam apostolorum, quibus concessa fuit potestas circumducendi mulieres.'

[17] Sermons 65 and 66, *On the Song of Songs*, trans. by Kilian Walsh, 4 vols, vol. III trans. by Kilian Walsh and Irene Edmonds (Kalamazoo: Cistercian Publications, 1971–80), III, 179–206, and *SBOp*, II, 172–88. See Kienzle, *Cistercians, Heresy and Crusade*, pp. 85–90.

[18] Sermo 64.8, *SBOp*, II, 170: 'Simplex est sensus, ut haeretici capiantur potius quam effugentur. Capiantur, dico, non armis, sed argumentis, quibus refellantur errores eorum; ipsi vero, si fieri potest, reconcilientur Catholicae, revocentur ad veram fidem. Haec est enim voluntas ejus qui vult omnes homines salvos fieri et ad agnitionem veritatis venire (I Tm 2. 3).'

[19] Sermo 64.8–9, *SBOp*, II, 170–71: 'Itaque homo de Ecclesia exercitatus et doctus, si cum haeretico homine disputare aggreditur, illo suam intentionem dirigere debet, quatenus ita erratem convincat, ut et convertat, cogitans illud apostoli Iacobi [. . .] (Jas 5. 20). Nec propterea sane nihil se egisse putet qui haereticum vicit et convicit, haereses confutavit verisimilia a vero clare aperteque distinxit, prava dogmata, plana et irrefragabili ratione prava esse demonstravit, pravum denique intellectum, extollentem se adversus scientiam Dei, in captivitatem redegit.'

furnished the best method to achieve a heretic's conversion.[20] However, Bernard specifies what to do when a heretic does not bend to clarity after a second admonition: 'then, according to the Apostle, he is to be shunned as one who is completely perverted. Consequently I think it better that he should be driven away or even bound rather than be allowed to spoil the vines.'[21] In Sermons 65 and 66 Bernard levels various charges against the heretics, including suspicious secrecy and practising unspeakable obscene acts in private.[22] The Abbot assails the dissidents' view of the apostolic life.[23] He criticizes them for rejecting the Church's authority, its teaching on purgatory, and its practice of infant baptism, and he evokes negative biblical imagery to assail them as wolves, foxes, and dogs.[24] The Cistercian Abbot shows great anger at the dissidents' co-habitation with women.[25] He rails harshly against the dissidents' disregard for the Church's views on marriage and holds that the Cathar position, that only marriages between virgins are valid, constitutes an

---

[20] Bernard contradicts himself in Sermon 66.12, where he claims that heretics cannot understand logical argumentation. Sermo 66.12, *SBOp*, II, 186. See Kienzle, *Cistercians, Heresy and Crusade*, p. 86.

[21] Sermo 64.8, *SBOp*, II, 170: 'Quod si reverti noluerit, nec convictus post primam iam et secundam admonitionem, utpote qui omnino subversus est, erit, secundum Apostolum (Ti 3. 10), devitandus. Ex hoc iam melius, ut quidem ego arbitror, effugatur, aut etiam religatur, quam sinitur vineas demoliri.'

[22] Sermon 65.2, *SBOp*, II, 173: 'Quid faciemus his malignissimis vulpibus, ut capi queant, quae nocere quam vincere malunt, et ne apparere quidem volum, sed serpere [...]. "Non," inquiunt, "sed ne mysterium publicemus." Quasi gloria Dei non sit revelare sermonem. An Dei invident gloriae? Sed magis credo quod pandere erubescant, scientes inglorium. Nam nefanda et obscena dicuntur agere in secreto: siquidem et vulpium posteriora foetent [...]. Stat nempe Scripturae veritas: "Gloriam regum celare verbum, gloria Dei revelare sermonem." [...] Respondeant proinde Evangelio: "Quod dico", ait "in tenebris, dicite in lumine, et quod in aure auditis, praedicate super tecta" (Mt 10. 27).'

[23] Sermo 66.8, *SBOp*, II, 183: 'Nempe iactant se esse successores Apostolorum, et apostolicos nominant, nullum tamen apostolatus sui signum valentes ostendere.'

[24] Sermo 66.9, 11, *SBOp*, II, 183–85. Sermo 66.1, *SBOp*, II, 178: 'Hi sunt qui veniunt in vestimentis ovium, ad nudandas oves et spoliandos arietes [...]. Hi oves sunt habitu, astu vulpes, actu et crudelitate lupi.' Sermo 66.8, *SBOp*, II, 183: 'Videte detractores, videte canes.' See Kienzle, *Cistercians, Heresy and Crusade*, p. 87, and Kienzle, 'La Représentation de l'hérétique par l'imagerie animale', in *Les Cathares devant l'histoire: Mélanges offerts à Jean Duvernoy*, ed. by Anne Brenon and Christine Dieulafait (Castelnaud-la-Chapelle: L'Hydre, 2005), pp. 181–95.

[25] Sermo 65.4, *SBOp*, II, 175: 'Cum femina semper esse, et non cognoscere feminam, nonne plus est quam mortuum suscitare?'

attempt to tear apart the sacraments.[26] Moreover, Bernard attacks the dissidents' abstinence and compares them directly to Manicheans: in their 'insane manner' they find God's creation unclean.[27] Ekbert of Schönau was to continue and develop the false parallel with Manicheism twenty years later.[28] Bernard, like Everwin, depicts the rapid rise of heresy with alarm:

> Women have left their husbands, and husbands their wives, to join these people. Clerks and priests have left their people and their churches, the untonsured and the bearded have been found there among the weaver men and women. Is this not great havoc? Is this not the work of foxes?[29]

He threatens that if the heretics are dealt with negligently, their evil will escalate and grow like gangrene or a cancer (II Tm 2. 16).[30] Nonetheless, Bernard condemns the murder of heretics by mob actions, asserting in an often quoted sentence that faith is to be persuaded and not forced: 'fides suadenda est, non imponenda'.[31] He concludes with measures for 'trapping the foxes': separate the men from the

---

[26] Sermo 66.3, *SBOp*, II, 179–80. Sermo 66.4, *SBOp*, II, 180: 'Quidam tamen dissentientes ab aliis, inter solos virgines matrimonium contrahi posse fatentur. Verum quid in hac distinctione rationis afferre possint, non video: nisi quod pro libitu quisque suo sacramenta Ecclesiae, tamquam matris viscera, dente vipereo decertatim inter se dilacerare contendunt.'

[27] Sermo 66.7, *SBOp*, II, 182–83: 'At si de insania Manichaei praescribis beneficentiae Dei [...]. Vae qui respuistis cibos quos Deus creavit, iudicantes immundos et indignos quos traiciatis in corpora vestra, cum propterea vos corpus Christi, quod est Ecclesia, tanquam pollutos et immundos expuerit.'

[28] Hugh Eteriano, *Contra Paterenos*, ed. and trans. by Hamilton, p. 30, notes that Ekbert did not follow Everwin's lead in identifying the Eastern origins of the movement. However, Ekbert did follow Bernard's lead in his jump to associate Cathars and Manichees.

[29] Sermo 65.5, *On the Song of Songs*, III, 186; *SBOp*, II, 176: 'Mulieres, relictis viris, et item viri, dimissis uxoribus, ad istos se conferunt. Clerici et sacerdotes, populis ecclesiisque relictis, intonsi et barbati apud eos inter textores et textrices plerumque inventi sunt. Annon gravis demolitio ista? Annon opera vulpium haec?' Translation of the second sentence is mine.

[30] Sermo 66.1, *SBOp*, II, 179: 'sed non est, dico vobis, cum eis negligenter agendum: "Multim enim proficiunt ad impietatem, et sermo eorum ut cancer serpit."'

[31] Sermo 66.12, *SBOp*, II, 187: 'Approbamus zelum, sed factum non suademus; quia fides suadenda est, non imponenda.' Nonetheless, he says that he applauds the zeal of the mob and adds: 'It is better for them to be restrained by the sword of someone who bears not the sword in vain than to be allowed to lead others into heresy. One who avenges a wrong-doer for wrath is the servant of God (Rom 13. 4).' Sermo 66.12, p. 187: 'Quamquam melius procul dubio gladio coercerentur, illius videlicet qui non sine causa gladium portat, quam in suum errorem multos trajicere permittuntur. Dei enim minister ille est, vindex in iram ei qui male agit (Rom 13. 4).'

women, and then expel them if they refuse to comply.[32] We shall see to what extent these topics surface in Hildegard's critique.

1163: Collaboration with Schönau, the Mainz Treatise, and the Cologne and Kirchheim Sermons

Heresy and Schism in the 1160s

About twenty years after the 1140s correspondence between Everwin of Steinfeld and Bernard of Clairvaux concerning an alarming 'new' heresy,[33] Elisabeth of Schönau wrote to Hildegard and called for her to take leadership. 'The Lord's vineyard has no cultivator, the Lord's vineyard perishes, the Church's head has weakened and its limbs have died', lamented Elisabeth.[34] Schism had begun in 1159 when Emperor Frederick I, after the election of Pope Alexander III (1159–81), supported the first of three anti-popes. Rainald of Dassel, imperial chancellor (1156–67) and Archbishop of Cologne (1159–67), then Germany's largest city, directed the Emperor's policy, which included the control of Italian cities.[35] The *Chronica regia*

---

[32] Sermon 66.14; *SBOp*, II, 187: 'Quamobrem ut deprehendantur, cogendi sunt vel abicere feminas, vel exire de Ecclesia [. . .]. Hoc solo, etiamsi aliud non esset, facile deprehendis si, ut dixi, viros et feminas, qui se continentes dicunt, ab invicem separes, et feminas quidem cum aliis sui et sexus et voti degere cogas, viros aeque cum eiusdem proposito viris.'

[33] Everwin of Steinfeld, *Epistola* 472, *PL* 185: 676–80. See Brenon, 'La Lettre d'Evervin de Steinfeld'. Uwe Brunn's recent work calls into question the usual dating of this correspondence (1143/44) and argues for a date of 1147/48. *Des contestataires aux 'cathares'*, pp. 124–39.

[34] *Die Visionen der hl. Elisabeth und die Schriften der Äbte Ekbert und Emecho von Schönau*, ed. by F. W. E. Roth (Brünn: Verlag der Studien aus dem Benedictiner-und-Cistercienser-Orden, 1884), p. 74: 'O domina Hildegardis perfice opus domini, sicut usque nunc fecisti, quia posuit te dominus operatricem in vinea sua. Quesivit enim dominus operarios in vineam suam, et invenit eos omnes ociosos, quia nemo eos conduxit. Vinea domini non habet cultorem, vinea domini periit, caput ecclesie languit, et membra eius mortua sunt.' The letter is edited as two texts, *Epistolae* 202 and 203, in *Epistolarium*, I, pp. 455–58. For a comparison of Elisabeth and Hildegard, see Newman, 'Hildegard of Bingen: Visions and Validation', pp. 173–75. See Elisabeth of Schönau, *Complete Works*, pp. 142–47. The text comprises chapters 20–28 of Elisabeth's *Third Book of Visions*. Sections 20–24 focus on the Cathars; 25–27 address clerics; 28 adds a clarification to Section 24, explaining what Elisabeth meant by the 'sulfurous tongues' of the Cathars. See also Brunn, *Des contestataires aux 'cathares'*, pp. 263–74, who points out (pp. 262, 270) that Ekbert had Hildegard's text in hand when he suggested that Elisabeth have a similar vision.

[35] See Brunn, *Des contestataires aux 'cathares'*, pp. 26–29, on the importance of Cologne and its archbishops.

Coloniensis records the siege of Milan by imperial armies for the year 1162. The *Chronica* reports that in 1164, Rainald brought the relics of the Three Kings to Cologne in a celebration that the chronicler vaunts along with the victories in Italy 'for the perpetual glory of Germany'.[36] Persecution of heresy must have reinforced the assertion of power and orthodoxy: the Emperor promoted an aura of triumphant piety and orthodoxy in the face of his opposition to Alexander III.

Hildegard's opinion on the 1159–77 schism yields centre stage to her denouncement of heresy and call for reform of the clergy. She initially held in check her criticism of Emperor Frederick I. She commented in an 1163 letter to the Cologne clergy that she had 'kept quiet' because of the division in the Church.[37] Her friend Philip of Heinsberg, dean of the cathedral, became Archbishop of Cologne (1167–91), a powerful see that was closely allied with imperial power. Philip of Heinsberg supported the Emperor during the schism, as did many of the German prelates, but he later came into conflict with the Emperor over territorial rights.[38] It is possible that Hildegard's admonitions to clergy would not alienate either faction in the shifting conflict between emperor and papacy, because each group saw the other as corrupt. The worldliness of clerics was seen as fuel for the donatist views of the Cathars, who rejected the worth of the catholic clergy and the sacraments they performed.[39] However, in the view of Uwe Brunn, the Cologne

---

[36] *Chronica Regia Coloniensis*, ed. by Georg Waitz, MGH SS, 18 (Hannover, 1880), pp. 1–299 (pp. 109–112 for 1162; p. 115 for 1164): 'Itaque cum praefatis et illustrissimis donis in vigilia beati Iacobi Coloniam ingressus [Reinoldus], gloriose ac magnifice suscipitur, maxime pro reliquiis, quas ad perpetuam Germaniae gloriam Coloniae intulit.' Manfred Groten, *Priorenkolleg und Domkapitel von Köln im hohen Mittelalter: Zur Geschichte des kölnischen Erzstifts und Herzogtums*, Rheinisches Archiv, 109 (Bonn: Röhrscheid, 1980), p. 213, links the rising power of the cathedral chapter to the arrival of the relics. See Brunn, *Des contestataires aux 'cathares'*, p. 254.

[37] I am grateful to Zachary Matus for his work on Hildegard and schism, presented at the International Congress on Medieval Studies, Kalamazoo, Michigan, May 2005.

[38] *Epistolarium*, I, 15R, pp. 34–47. Philip of Heinsberg intervened in the dispute over the man buried at Rupertsberg and, according to Guibert of Gembloux, visited Hildegard 'rather often' ('eamque sepius uisitat'). Guibert of Gembloux, *Epistolae*, II, 26, p. 280, line 378. See Brunn, *Des contestataires aux 'cathares'*, pp. 253–55, 410–11. Philip's relationship with Emperor Frederick I shifted amidst conflicts over territorial rights. See Haverkamp, *Medieval Germany*, pp. 235–38, 276; *Jutta and Hildegard*, trans. by Silvas, p. 91; Flanagan, *Hildegard of Bingen*, p. 178.

[39] Haverkamp, *Medieval Germany*, pp. 43–44 (on Arnold of Brescia and Frederick I), pp. 228–34; Griffiths, *Garden of Delights*, pp. 110–11; Hugh Eteriano, *Contra Patarenos*, ed. by Hamilton, pp. 6–8, who asserts that the exchange of information about heretical groups was not possible between the factions during the schism, nor was the coordination of efforts against

sermon probably served Philip of Heinsberg well against the powerful rival clergy in the city whom Hildegard inculpated for the spread of heresy. Philip's support of the anti-pope would have prompted the supporters of Alexander III to label him as a heretic. Hildegard's decrial of heresy in the city would have deflected attention from the schism.[40]

In early August of 1163, dissidents were arrested in Cologne: six men, two women, and the three leaders, Arnold, Marsilius, and Theodoric, according to the *Codex Thioderici*. After a public interrogation and the heretics' refusal to accept the orthodox faith, they were condemned and burned.[41] Ekbert of Schönau's sermons, composed to assist Archbishop Rainald, attest to repeated efforts to root out and interrogate the heretics.[42] In the preface, Ekbert speaks of the frequent arrests of Cathars in the diocese of Cologne and looks back on the days in Bonn when he and a colleague named Bertolph debated often with the heretics.[43] Ekbert, a former canon and deacon at St Cassius in Bonn, applied the experience he gained debating heretics in Bonn to the Cologne interrogation.[44] Moreover, the *Vita Eckeberti*

---

heresy. Alexander III's backers would not have had access to the texts produced in the Emperor's circle and vice versa.

[40] Brunn, *Des contestataires aux 'cathares'*, pp. 254–56.

[41] Henri Maisonneuve dates the arrest on 2 August 1163 and the burning on 5 August 1163. See H. Maisonneuve, *Études sur les origines de l'inquisition*, 2nd edn (Paris: Vrin, 1960), pp. 111–12. An account appears in the *Chronica Regia Coloniensis*, ed. by Waitz, p. 114. Brunn, *Des contestataires aux 'cathares'*, pp. 200–07, brings to light the *Codex Thioderici*, a contemporary text: *Codex Thioderici Aeditui Tuitiensis*, ed. by O. Holder-Egger, MGH SS, 14 (Stuttgart, 1883), pp. 562–77, discussed in Brunn, ibid., pp. 286–87. Brunn signals (p. 413) that the *Chronica Regia Coloniensis* was composed as a work of imperial history around 1202, then followed a few years later by two different versions.

[42] Ekbert of Schönau, *Sermones adversus pestiferos foedissimosque Catharorum*, *PL* 195: 11–98. Walter Wakefield and A. P. Evans, *Heresies of the High Middle Ages: Selected Sources Translated and Annotated*, Records of Western Civilization Sources and Studies, 81 (New York: Columbia University Press, 1991), p. 722, n. 1, point out several passages (*PL* 195: 52, 84, 88). An additional reference appears in the preface, *PL* 195: 13. Brunn, *Des contestataires aux 'cathares'*, pp. 218–19, dates the transmission of the work to 1164, between the return of Dassel to Cologne on 23 July 1164 and the death of Elisabeth of Schönau on 18 June 1165.

[43] Ekbert of Schönau, *Sermones*, *PL* 195: 13: 'In vestra dioecesi frequenter contigit deprehendi quosdam haereticos, qui diebus istis plurimum notabiles sunt in erroribus suis. Hi sunt quos vulgo Catharos vocant [. . .] Cum essem canonicus in ecclesia Bunnensi, saepe ego et unanimis meus Bertolphus, cum talibus altercati sumus, et diligenter attendi errores eorum ac defensiones.'

[44] Ekbert was ordained priest in Rome in 1154 during the preparations for the coronation of Frederick I (1155) and at the point when Arnold of Brescia's revolt was being suppressed. After

confirms that Ekbert frequented the heretical communities in Bonn in order to know their errors more thoroughly. The *Vita* also recounts that Ekbert intervened against heretics in Mainz in the later 1160s.[45]

Ekbert reveals his familiarity with the Cathar ritual of *consolamentum*, which he calls 'catharizing' (*catharizare*), when he mocks the saving power of recent baptisms of this sort: the 'archiCathar' Arnold in Cologne with his associates (*complices*); and Theoderic and his companions (*socios*) in Bonn.[46] In the context of Cathar criticism of the worth of sacraments performed by unworthy clergy, the monk explains that he sets forth the teaching of the Fathers in order to enlighten unlearned people who listen to both catholic (*nostros*) and Cathar (*vestros*) sermons. Such a remark assumes the ongoing activity of Cathar preachers.[47] Later in the same context, Ekbert recalls questioning a prominent man who converted back from Catharism. He and the Archbishop of Cologne (probably Arnold I, 1138–51) interrogated the man about Cathar beliefs, notably their contempt for

---

returning from Rome, he entered the monastery of Schönau in 1155 and became abbot in 1166. See Brunn, *Des contestataires aux 'cathares'*, pp. 207–29.

[45] See Brunn, *Des contestataires aux 'cathares'*, pp. 212–16.

[46] Ekbert of Schönau, *Sermones*, PL 195: 52: 'Nonne sic nuper baptizavit Colonia archicatharum vestrum Arnoldum, et complices ejus, et similiter Bunna Theodericum et socios ejus, et continuo, ut dicitis, avolaverunt in coelum?' On the *consolamentum*, see Jean Duvernoy, *La Religion des Cathares, Le catharisme*, vol. I (Toulouse: Privat, 1976), pp. 151–52; Anne Brenon, 'Les Fonctions sacramentelles du consolement', in *Les archipels cathares* (Cahors: Dire Editions, 2000), pp. 129–52; Ylva Hagman, 'Le Rite d'initiation chrétienne chez les cathares et les bogomiles', *Heresis*, 20 (1993), 13–31; Bernard Hamilton, 'The Cathars and Christian Perfection', in *The Medieval Church: Universities, Heresy, and the Religious Life. Essays in Honour of Gordon Leff*, ed. by P. Biller and B. Dobson, Studies in Church History, Subsidia, 11 (Woodbridge: Boydell and Brewer, 1999), pp. 5–23 (pp. 12–13); Lambert, *The Cathars*, p. 33.

[47] Ekbert of Schönau, *Sermones*, PL 195: 83D–84A: 'O Cathari, hoc vos scire volo, quod ea quae varie dixi, de his quae in Ecclesia gesta sunt, et quae a Patribus statuta et dicta sunt in ea, non propter vos tantum dixi, sed magis propter nostros indoctos populos, qui pariter nostros et vestros aliquando percipiunt sermones, ut sciant rationabiles nobis sermones non deesse, sed reddendam rationem de his quae credimus et agimus in Ecclesia Dei.' On Cathar preaching, see Jean Duvernoy, 'Origène et le berger', in *Autour de Montaillou, un village occitan: Histoire et religiosité d'une communauté villageoise au Moyen Âge*, Actes du colloque de Montaillou, 25–27 aout 2000 (Castelnaud-la-Chapelle: L'Hydre, 2001), pp. 335–44; Anne Brenon, 'La Parole cathare: Une catéchèse de l'Evangile', in *Les Archipels cathares*, pp. 153–71. Anne Brenon, 'La Prédication cathare méridionale', in *Slavica occitania*, vol. XVI, *Bogomiles, Patarins et Cathares* (Toulouse, 2003), pp. 259–71; John H. Arnold, *Inquisition and Power: Catharism and the Confessing Subject in Medieval Languedoc* (Philadelphia: University of Pennsylvania Press, 2001).

catholic clergy.[48] A previous interrogation of one man in Bonn also pertained to donatist ideas among the Cathars.[49] The prevalence of this theme in Ekbert's sermons sheds light on Hildegard's tendency to chastize corrupt clergy and attack heresy in the same breath.

Other incidents involving dissidents with Cathar-like beliefs multiplied across northern Europe in the 1160s and 1170s. In 1162 the Archbishop of Reims prosecuted men from Flanders as Manicheans or Publicans.[50] In the early 1160s groups from Flanders or Germany journeyed to England. Prevostin, chancellor of the university of Paris from around 1206–09, may have gleaned his expertise on heresy from residence as a *scholasticus* in Mainz. Scholars have assumed that Prevostin's teaching about the Cathars in Paris was grounded on familiarity with Catharism in northern Italy. However, one of his Mainz sermons speaks of Cathars.[51]

The Mainz Treatise

These indications of heresy in Mainz lie behind the visionary treatise against heresy that Hildegard sent to Schönau and to the monks at St Martin in Mainz.[52] The

---

[48] Ekbert of Schönau, *Sermones, PL* 195: 84C: 'Memini vidisse aliquando in praesentia Coloniensis archiepiscopi Arnoldi, quemdam non parvi nominis virum, qui de schola Catharorum reversus fuerat ad suos, a quo dum inquireremus diligenter, quae essent haereses illorum, ita respondit: Brevi sermone ea de quibus interrogatis, concludam: "Omnia quae creditis, omnia quae agitis in Ecclesia, illi falsa et inania judicant."' Brunn, *Des contestataires aux 'cathares'*, p. 214, cites this passage to date Ekbert's intervention against heresy to the 1140s. In his view, Ekbert refers to the event Everwin of Steinfeld witnessed around 1147. He proposes that both men were involved in the same incident.

[49] Ekbert of Schönau, *Sermones, PL* 195: 88C: 'Fuit mihi concertatio de his rebus quadam vice in domo mea Bunnae, cum quodam viro qui suspectus erat nobis quod esset de secta Catharorum: et contigit ut incideremus ad loquendum de sacerdotibus malis, et dicebat ita de eis: Quomodo fieri potest, ut qui tam irrationabiliter vivunt, distribuant in Ecclesia corpus Domini?'

[50] Wakefield and Evans, *Heresies of the High Middle Ages*, p. 39.

[51] See Peter Biller, 'Northern Cathars and Higher Learning', in *The Medieval Church*, ed. by Biller and Dobson, pp. 25–51 (pp. 35–36 and nn. 44–45), and on the spread of Catharism from Francia, p. 41. A *Summa contra haereticos* that seems to refer to Italy has been attributed, but not on solid grounds, to Prevostin (of Cremona).

[52] *Epistolarium*, II, 169, p. 377, lines 19–26: 'A veridicis siquidem personis relatum est nobis quod quedam de errore Catharorum scripseritis, quemadmodum illa in uisione secretorum Dei uidistis. Que ut nobis transmittatis, omni deuotione expetimus, quoniam diuine ostensioni et responso magis credimus quam humano. Sanctis itaque orationibus uestris nos commendamus, petentes ut quicquid uobis sponsus uester Dominus Iesus de his reuelare dignabitur, nobis bona

role of Elisabeth of Schönau points to collaboration in the effort against heresy. Not only did Elisabeth urge Hildegard to complete the Lord's work, she composed her own visionary text and played some role in her brother Ekbert's composition of the *Sermones contra Catharos*, which were completed sometime before Elisabeth's death on 18 June 1165.[53] Elisabeth called upon the learned clergy to study the New Testament and to find material there to combat heresy.[54] Ekbert's sermons compile scriptural authorities suited to that task and conclude with excerpts from Augustine's *De Manichaeis*.[55]

Hildegard received another appeal for her views against heresy from the monks at St Martin in Mainz, who specifically requested the things that she had written about the errors of the Cathars.[56] Hildegard carefully dates this vision to July 1163

uoluntate, sicut uos decet, scribi faciatis'; *Letters*, II, 169, p. 122. See Brunn, *Des contestataires aux 'cathares'*, p. 258, on the question of the audience for the treatise. The vision and its influence are discussed in Manselli, 'Amicizia spirituale'.

[53] *Die Visionen der hl. Elisabeth*, ed. by Roth, p. 74. See ibid., p. xxxviii, on the dating of MS Pergam. 40 nr. 96, Dombibliothek von Merseburg, containing the 'Visio sororis Hildegardis contra Kataros' (fol. 110ʳ), addressed to Elisabeth. Brunn, *Des contestataires aux 'cathares'*, pp. 262, 270, argues out that Ekbert had Hildegard's text in hand and suggested that Elisabeth had a similar vision.

[54] Elisabeth wrote to Ekbert (*Die Visionen der hl. Elisabeth*, ed. by Roth, p. 76): 'Vos autem qui litterati estis, scrutamini libros de novo testamento, et recordamini verborum eius, qualem fructum inveneritis. Renovamini spiritu sancto et refocillate animas vestras in edificationem ecclesie, que est santificata in Christo Iesu, et illuminata per sancta evangelia, et dealbata de antiqua rubigine.' On Ekbert and his works, see Brunn, *Des contestataires aux 'cathares'*, pp. 207–30. On Elisabeth and Ekbert, see Anne Clark, *Elisabeth of Schönau: A Twelfth-Century Visionary* (Philadelphia: University of Pennsylvania Press, 1992), pp. 22–25; and Clark, 'Repression or Collaboration? The Case of Elisabeth and Ekbert of Schönau', in *Christendom and its Discontents: Exclusion, Persecution, and Rebellion, 1000–1500*, ed. by Scott L. Waugh and Peter D. Diehl (Cambridge: Cambridge University Press, 1996), pp. 151–67; and Manselli, 'Amicizia spirituale', pp. 302–13.

[55] Ekbert of Schönau, *Sermones*, PL 195: 13–14: 'Ego itaque operae pretium duxi errores describere, et adnotare auctoritates Scripturarum, ex quibus se defendunt, ac demonstrare quomodo sane intelligi debeant: simulque eas partes fidei nostrae, quibus se opponunt, proponere; et quibus Scripturae auctoritatibus, quibus vexationibus defendi possint, cum superno adjutorio demonstrare, ut qui ista legere et in memoria habere curaverint, aliquanto promptiores sint ad discrepandum cum illis, si quando, ut assolet, in populo fuerint deprehensi. Valde enim linguosi sunt, ac semper in promptu illis est quod adversum nos dicere possint. Et est non parva verecundia nostris, qui litteras sciunt, ut sint muti et elingues in conspectu illorum.' Brunn, *Des contestataires aux 'cathares'*, p. 218, argues that Ekbert's work represents the fruit of around two decades of involvement against heresy and that he began to write it after his arrival at Schönau, between 1155 and 1160.

[56] *Epistolarium*, II, 169, p. 377, lines 19–26; see note 52 above. Brunn, *Des contestataires aux 'cathares'*, pp. 258–59, underscores that the letter presumes that the monks knew of a text that

and locates the serpent's deceit at a point sixty years and twenty-four months earlier. This reference to the year 1101 bolsters Bernard Hamilton's argument that Catharism entered Europe in the aftermath of the First Crusade.[57] Hamilton's point may be supported by the chronicler Ekkehard of Aurach, who when writing of the First Crusade, captures the suspicions concerning the swirl of people, including pseudo-prophets, who attempted to corrupt the armies.[58] In an additional chronological reference, the *magistra* refers to ruin wrought by winds blowing from the four cardinal points, but first from the East, twenty-three years and four months before her 1163 vision: around 1140 then, a few (or several) years before Everwin of Steinfeld wrote to Bernard of Clairvaux about heresy with Eastern roots.[59] Hildegard may, therefore, have known this correspondence. On the other hand, Uwe Brunn suggests that Hildegard's dating may refer to the Second Lateran Council (1139) and Innocent II's call for the pursuit of *raptores* and *malefactores*

already existed. Marianna Schrader and Adelgundis Führkotter carefully establish the connections between Hildegard and the clerics of Mainz and other cities in *Die Echtheit des Schrifttums der heiligen Hildegard von Bingen. Quellenkritische Untersuchungen*, Beihefte zum Archiv für Kulturgeschichte, 6 (Cologne: Böhlau-Verlag, 1956). Rudolf Holbach devotes an important article to Hildegard's connections with the churches in Mainz, Cologne, and Trier: 'Hildegard von Bingen und die kirchlichen Metropolen'. On the twelfth-century archbishops, particularly those of Mainz, and their use of monasteries, see Haverkamp, *Medieval Germany*, pp. 156–57 and 231, 234, 277. *Epistolarium*, I, 20R, 21, 22R, 24, pp. 57–58, 59–60, 66–68; *Letters*, I, 20R, pp. 72–73 to Arnold; 21, 22R, pp. 73–75, to Conrad; 24 to Christian, pp. 80–82. Van Engen, 'Letters and the Public Persona of Hildegard', p. 390, asserts that the archbishops of Mainz treated Hildegard 'with caution and respect but at a distance'.

[57] Bernard Hamilton, 'Wisdom from the East: The Reception by the Cathars of Eastern Dualist Texts', in *Heresy and Literacy in the Middle Ages, 1000–1530*, ed. by P. Biller and A. Hudson (Cambridge: Cambridge University Press, 1996), pp. 38–60, uses Hildegard's dating to support his assertion that the appearance of Western Catharism occurred in the aftermath of the first crusade. He reaffirms that in the 'Introduction' to Hugh Eteriano, *Contra Patarenos*, pp. 61–63.

[58] *Ekkehardi Chronica*, I, in *Frutolfs und Ekkehards Chroniken un die anonyme Kaiserchronik*, ed. by Franz-Josef Schmale and Irene Schmale-Ott (Darmstadt: Wissenschaftliche Buchgesellschaft, 1972, pp. 124–208 (p. 144): 'His et huiusmodi signis tota creatura in Creatoris se militiam cohortante nil moratur inimicus ille ceteris etiam dormientibus semper pervigil bono illi semini zizania sua superseminare, pseudoprophetas suscitare, dominicis exercitibus falso fratres et inhonestas feminei sexus personas sub specie religionis intermiscere, sicque per aliorum hypocrisin atque mendacia, per aliorum vero nefarias pollutiones Christ greges adeo turpabantur, ut iuxta boni pastoris vaticinium etiam electi in errorem ducerentur.'

[59] On Evervin and Bernard, see Brenon, 'La Lettre d'Evervin de Steinfeld', and the dating proposed by Brunn, *Des contestataires aux 'cathares'*, pp. 124–39.

(robbers and evildoers).[60] I consider both hypotheses plausible and not mutually exclusive.

Establishing the longevity of the heretics' threat positions Hildegard solidly for her attack on Cathar beliefs. Hildegard speaks in the voice of the twenty-four elders seated around God's throne in Revelation 4. 4. The *magistra* moves between vivid images and theological critique. The sequence of images that characterizes the heretics includes the lion that threatens the heavenly queen (Rv 12. 1–6), the perversely breathing black beast, the deceptive serpent, and the menacing dragon. Hildegard warns that the serpent sends emissaries who resemble the Sadducees and the worshippers of Baal.[61] These phrases, 'Sadducees' and 'worshippers of Baal', appear in her other works as names for heretics. In this treatise, Hildegard unleashes a flow of negative images: the heretics resemble the crab, scorpions, and giant birds that reject their own eggs as if poisonous. The latter non-human images dehumanize the heretics and imply a reversal of the natural order, a common feature of antiheretical and polemical discourse.[62]

The *magistra* asserts that the heretics reject God's creation of all things and the eternity of the Word incarnate: the *prima principia*, the basis of Genesis 1, 'God created all things and ordered that they come forth by germinating and growing'; and the *dominicum principium*, the Lord's beginning, as spoken in John 1, 'He appeared before the ancientness of days; the Word of God was to become human.'[63] Thus she attacks the dualistic teachings and Docetism of the Cathars. Further, she states that the heretics are 'worse than the Jews'.[64] With this accusation, common in the polemical discourse that viewed heretics and Jews as enemies of Christ,[65]

---

[60] Brunn, *Des contestataires aux 'cathares'*, p. 259, n. 58.

[61] See Adso, *De ortu et tempore Antichristi*, p. 22, lines 9–16, where Antichrist will send heretical emissaries throughout the world.

[62] *Epistolarium*, II, 169R, pp. 378–81, esp. p. 381, lines 74–82. On animal images in polemical literature, see Kienzle, 'La Représentation de l'hérétique par l'imagerie animale'.

[63] *Epistolarium*, II, 169R, p. 381, lines 81–90, esp. lines 82–86. Ekbert of Schönau devotes Sermon 6, *PL* 195: 40–41, to the creation (third heresy, according to Ekbert's list), alluding at the opening to Genesis 1 and John 1. Sermon 12, *PL* 195: 94–96, concerns the humanity of the Saviour (ninth heresy).

[64] *Epistolarium*, II, 169R, p. 381, lines 81–90, esp. lines 86–88: 'Hi sunt uobis peiores Iudeis qui cecos oculos modo habent ad uidendam igneam formam que in sancta diuinitate nunc homo splendet.'

[65] See Beverly Mayne Kienzle, 'Inimici crucis: La théologie de la croix et la persécution du catharisme', in *Autour de Montaillou*, pp. 283–99; Sara Lipton, *Images of Intolerance: The Representation*

Hildegard takes aim again at Cathar Christology. She then returns to terrifying images of the heretics, comparing them to sulfurous fiery mountains, to the entrails of the most wicked beast. Finally, in language reminiscent of Bernard of Clairvaux, Hildegard exhorts the people in God's voice to cast out this 'impure and unholy people', to 'torture them with harsh and hard words', to expel them completely, and to chase them into their caves.[66] The costs of not treating the heretics in such a way are high: condemnation by God and widespread destruction.

Hildegard underscores her charismatic authority with the order given her by the surging voice (*torrentem uocem*) to write down these things and transmit them quickly to priests of the Church who worship God with pure faith. The clerics were then to preach to the people everywhere in their area (*ut illa ubique in circuiti suo populis predicent*) and keep them from the tricks of the Devil, which otherwise would take root and bring them to ruin.[67] The fact that this treatise from July 1163, designed for public preaching, precedes the events of early August in Cologne, demonstrates that the seer's authority served at a minimum to justify the pursuit of heretics.[68]

While Hildegard composed the Mainz treatise for widespread preaching, she herself delivered a sermon in Cologne sometime in the early 1160s. Philip, dean of the cathedral chapter of Cologne and later archbishop of that city (1167–91), wrote to Hildegard in 1163 acknowledging her Spirit-given power and requesting a copy of the sermon she had recently delivered *uiua uoce*.[69] The sermon's influence is attested by a 1220 reference to it from Gebeno, prior of Everbach, who wrote about the heretics to Hildegard's daughters at their request and who cites Hildegard's letter to Cologne as a point of departure for his own comments.[70]

---

of Jews and Judaism in the Bible moralisée (Berkeley: University of California Press, 1999), esp. pp. 82–111.

[66] *Epistolarium*, II, 169R, p. 382, lines 110–14: 'immundum et profanum populum a uobis proicite et cum asperis ac duris uerbis eos cruciate, et eos omnino in expulsionem ducite atque in infelices cauernas et speluncas eos ex toto effugate, quia uolunt uos seducere'.

[67] *Epistolarium*, II, 169R, p. 382, lines 114–32.

[68] This is also close to the opinion of Brunn, *Des contestataires aux 'cathares'*, p. 262.

[69] *Epistolarium*, I, 15R, pp. 34–47.

[70] Gebeno's *Pentachronon* is extant in hundreds of manuscripts, including Cambridge, Harvard University, Houghton Library MS Riant 90. I am grateful to Jeffrey Hamburger for pointing it out. On the diffusion of the *Pentachronon*, see Embach, *Die Schriften Hildegards von Bingen*, pp. 17–27 and others. Kerby-Fulton, *Reformist Apocalypticism*, pp. 28, 39.

The letter opens with the authority of God's voice in Revelation 1. 4: 'The one who was and is and is going to come.' Hildegard explains that verse as an affirmation of the truth of God's creation. God looks over the whole of created things from the firmament to the depths and proclaims that they are instruments for human edification and service.[71] Yet humans have failed to heed God's commands. The topic of heresy moves from the background to the foreground of the letter about two-thirds of the way through. Hildegard depicts the Devil working from backstage, plotting against the clergy and sending his ever-ready emissaries to bring ruin upon them. She again casts the heretics as non-human creatures, 'scorpions in their morals and snakes in their works', lurking behind the serene guise of 'wan faces' (*pallida facie*), black robes, and tonsure (*cappatus sub nigra ueste et recto modo tonsus*). Furthermore, they prize voluntary poverty and abstinence.[72] Yet Hildegard warns that this virtuous appearance disguises the Devil's work: 'through the spirits of the air' he deceives the heretics and permits their desire to be chaste.[73] How else to controvert Cathar adherence to the poverty, chastity, and abstinence that represented the ideals of apostolic life? Their chastity particularly disturbs Hildegard as *magistra* of religious women. She observes that the heretics 'do not love women, but flee from them'. Further, she fears that the heretics' chastity deceives women and leads them into error.[74]

To conclude, Hildegard underscores the diabolical force behind the seemingly virtuous heretics: 'These are people of no faith, seduced by the Devil.' They 'will be the scourge to discipline' the clergy 'severely'.[75] Finally, the seer predicts a horrific end for the heretics: 'after their perverse worship of Baal and their other depraved works are made known, princes and other great men will rush upon them, and like rabid wolves will kill them, wherever they can be found.' Hildegard

---

[71] *Epistolarium*, I, 15R, pp. 34–35, lines 1–35.

[72] *Epistolarium*, I, 15R, p. 40, lines 175–90.

[73] *Epistolarium*, I, 15R, pp. 40–41, lines 190–209.

[74] *Epistolarium*, I, 15R, pp. 41–42, esp. lines 204, 226–27. See Daniela Müller, *Frauen vor der Inquisition: Lebensform, Glaubenszeugnis und Aburteilung der deutschen und französischen Katharerinnen* (Mainz: von Zabern, 1996). Müller points out (personal correspondence) that, on the one hand, Hildegard does not seem to take seriously the views held by women involved in Catharism, while on the other, she does notice the strong influence that Catharism had on them.

[75] *Epistolarium*, I, 15R, p. 42, lines 248–51: 'Infideles autem homines isti, et a diabolo seducti, scopa uestra erunt ad castigandum uos, quia Deum pure non colitis, et tamdiu uos cruciabunt quousque omnes iustitie et iniquitates uestre purgentur.'

places this vision of the heretics' death before the 'dawn of justice' (*aurora iustitie*), implying that they must be destroyed before order is reestablished.[76]

Werner of Kirchheim wrote to Hildegard around 1170, praising the Spirit's gifts in Hildegard and asking her to send in writing what she had revealed for 'us and many more in Kirchheim about the negligence of priests in the divine sacrifice'.[77] The Kirchheim text opens with the well-known vision of the beleaguered Church whose first words are 'Foxes have holes, and the birds of heaven nests, [but the son of Man has no place to rest his head]' (Mt 8. 20), and it describes signs of doom that the Bollandists interpreted as portents of the upheaval provoked by sixteenth-century reformers.[78] After this dramatic vision of the Church suffering from the clergy's corruption, Hildegard predicts that princes and a 'bold people' will rise up against the clergy, denouncing their wayward living and reckoning their priestly office and consecration as nothing.[79] She seems to mean by *consecrationem uestram* the ordination of priests, but the Office (*sacerdotale officium uestrum*) certainly applies more widely to include the sacraments. Therefore, the *magistra* patently links clerical misbehaviour with donatist beliefs, probably those of the Cathars (the 'bold people'). While the Kirchheim letter attends less to heretics than the Mainz treatise or the Cologne sermon, it delivers a stinging indictment of clerical neglect and clearly holds the clergy responsible for provoking the donatist ideas that correspond to those of the Cathars.[80]

[76] *Epistolarium*, I, 15R, p. 43, lines 255–59: 'Sed tamen postquam ipsi in peruersitatibus Baal et in aliis prauis operibus sic inuenti fuerint, principes et alii maiores in eos irruent et uelut rabidos lupos eos occident, ubicumque eos inuenerint. Tunc aurora iustitie exsurget, et nouissima uestra meliora prioribus erunt.'

[77] *Epistolarium*, II, 149, pp. 332–33, lines 18–23; see p. 50, note 119. However, see Flanagan, *Hildegard of Bingen*, p. 172; Newman, *Sister of Wisdom*, pp. 241–42. Theodoric does not mention Kirchheim in the *Vita*.

[78] See Newman, *Sister of Wisdom*, pp. 241–42, and n. 113.

[79] *Epistolarium*, II, pp. 335–36, lines 71–75, 80–83: 'principes enim et temerarius populus super uos, o sacerdotes, qui me hactenus neglexistis, irruent et uos abiecent et fugabunt, ad diuitias uestras uobis auferent pro eo quod tempus sacerdotalis officii uestri non attendistis. [. . .] Nam permissione Dei super uos in iudiciis suis fremere incipient plurime gentes, et multi populi de uobis meditabuntur inania, cum sacerdotale officium uestrum et consecrationem uestram pro nihilo computant.'

[80] Brunn, *Des contestataires aux 'cathares'*, p. 244, asserts that I am alone in considering this text as an anti-Cathar writing. However, see Flanagan, *Hildegard of Bingen*, p. 172; and Newman, *Sister of Wisdom*, pp. 241–42.

The *Expositiones*

How prominently does the criticism of heresy figure in the *Expositiones*? Homilies on Luke 21. 25–33 and on Luke 5. 1–11 use the term 'heretics' or 'heresy'. Two of three *expositiones* on John 3. 1–15, the story of Nicodemus, counter beliefs that are heretical, although Hildegard does not use the word heretic in any of its forms. Similarly, one of the homilies on Matthew 4. 1–11 does not name heretics but lays out a clear theology of creation that directly opposes the belief of the Cathars. Moreover, in a few other texts Hildegard accents her theology of creation and her Christology; she moves beyond the narrative aspect of salvation history in such a way that she arguably has heresy in mind as she comments.

Expositio 54, the second of the four homilies on Luke 21. 25–33, names heretics and heretical ministers of Antichrist among the troubling portents that the biblical text foretells (Lk 21. 25). Hildegard identifies the 'signs in sun, moon, and stars' and the 'distress of nations on earth' (Lk 21. 25) with the coming of heretics who challenge the humanity of the Saviour and who will attempt to attack the Church.[81] She warns that priests, teachers, and spiritual people will turn away from the truth, and error will spread and contaminate other peoples and provinces. The Antichrist will send his heretical ministers through the world.[82] Bishops and leaders will be shaken and will withdraw rather than openly defend the Church and God's justice as they should.[83] The faithful will suffer for Christ's sake and those who deny the Antichrist will recognize the true nature of Christ, as God and human (*uerum Deum et hominem*).[84] After the tribulation of the saints, the fruit of good works will come and the righteous will receive the reward of eternal blessedness.[85]

Less elaborate and less rhetorically violent than the Mainz and Cologne texts, this homily nonetheless makes clear associations between weak clergy and heresy, and heretics and Antichrist. Here as in *Sciuias*, Hildegard draws on the evocative

---

[81] *Expo. Euang.*, 54, p. 323, lines 1–3: '*Erunt signa*, id est portenta, *in sole*, scilicet in Christo, ita ut errantes humanitati saluatoris resistant, *et luna*, uidelicet in ecclesia, cum heretici ecclesiam impugnare conabuntur.' On the development of Hildegard's apocalyptic thought, see Constant J. Mews, 'From *Sciuias* to the *Liber divinorum operum*: Hildegard's Apocalyptic Imagination and the Call to Reform', *Journal of Religious History*, 24 (2000), 44–56.

[82] *Expo. Euang.*, 54, pp. 323–24, lines 3–10.

[83] *Expo. Euang.*, 54, p. 324, lines 16–20.

[84] *Expo. Euang.*, 54, p. 324, line 26.

[85] *Expo. Euang.*, 54, pp. 324–25, lines 34–46.

power of literature and imagery on Antichrist.[86] A mixture of possible sources emerges for other elements of her interpretation, such as the meanings of the sun, moon, and stars, which have precedents in Ambrose and resemble the readings of Irimbert of Admont. Ambrose associates the sun with light and Christ; Irimbert stresses Christ as illuminator and Redeemer; Hildegard simply equates *in sole* and *in Christo*. She offers a similar interpretation in *Sciuias* while commenting on the same Lukan verses.[87] Ambrose, Irimbert, and Hildegard associate the moon with the Church, while the stars represent some category of virtuous people: for Irimbert the apostles; for Hildegard priests, teachers, and spiritual people; for Ambrose light-givers holding the word of life in the world.[88]

Despite these points where Hildegard's reading corresponds to that of earlier commentary on Luke, no previous text to my knowledge links the 'distress of nations on earth' (Lk 21. 25) with the coming of heretics who contest the human nature of Christ.[89] The *magistra* clearly refers in this *expositio* to Docetic beliefs that correspond to those of the Cathars, the 'heretics who challenge the humanity of the Saviour'. Her prediction pertaining to bishops mirrors other texts where she views the clergy as responsible for feeding the donatist views of the Cathars, and the notion of the assault on the Church echoes the Kirchheim letter. The *magistra*'s alarm over the number and identity of adherents to heresy, from priests to

---

[86] On Antichrist in Hildegard's *Scivias*, see Emmerson, 'Representation of Antichrist'. Antichrist seems to enter the tradition for this pericope with Bede, but several of his successors also include the ominous figure. Bede, *In Lucae euangelium*, vi, xxi, p. 369, line 244. See other sources in apparatus fontium, *Expo. Euang.*, 54, pp. 323–24.

[87] *Sciuias*, I.3, pp. 43–44, lines 5–6. See Ambrose, *Expositio euangelii secundum Lucam*, X, 37, p. 356, lines 355–61; Gottfried of Admont, *Homiliae dominicales*, 7, *PL* 174: 51.

[88] On the sun, see Ambrose, *Expositio euangelii secundum Lucam*, X, 37, p. 356, lines 355–63; Gottfried of Admont, *Homiliae dominicales*, 7, *PL* 174: 51; *Sciuias*, I.3, pp. 43–44, lines 5–6. On the moon and the Church, see Ambrose, *Expositio euangelii secundum Lucam*, X, 37, p. 356, lines 359–61; Gottfried of Admont, *Homiliae dominicales*, 7, *PL* 174: 52. On the stars, see Ambrose, *Expositio euangelii secundum Lucam*, X, 38, p. 356, lines 363–66; Gottfried of Admont, *Homiliae dominicales*, 7, *PL* 174: 52: *apostoli*. In contrast, Gregory the Great does not pause to interpret allegorically the sun, moon, or stars. Gregory the Great, *Homiliae in euangelia*, I, 1, p. 6, lines 19–21. The connection that Hildegard makes between the powers of heaven and the bishops and elders finds precedent in Haymo of Auxerre, *Homiliae de tempore*, 2, *PL* 118: 20.

[89] Brunn, *Des contestataires aux 'cathares'*, p. 244, n. 7, disagrees with my articles identifying this homily as an anti-Cathar writing. He asserts that numerous medieval authors use this passage to evoke heresy in no particular context, and that when Hildegard comments on it, she stays within traditional exegetical frameworks. He cites no other exegesis on the pericope, however. See the apparatus fontium, *Expo. Euang.*, 54, pp. 323–25, for other sources of comparison.

bishops, recalls the tenor of Everwin of Steinfeld's warning that a great multitude of heretics, including clerics and monks, extended in all directions.[90]

The first of the *magistra*'s three readings of Luke 5. 1–11, the miraculous catch, names heresy among the things that disciples must leave behind to follow Christ. In Hildegard's reading of the passage, the biblical Jesus stands for God the Creator, and the crowds (Lk 5. 1) represent the substance of created beings. The two boats (Lk 5. 2) designate the elements and other created things. The allegory moves with broad strokes through the Genesis account to focus on the typological theme of leaving the old and adhering to the new, the Gospel and Christ. The nets (Lk 5. 6) haul in vices and sorrow; the fishermen leave behind (Lk 5. 11) the old law, heresy, and the blame of sin (*ueteri lege et heresi ac propria causa in peccatis*).[91] Hildegard groups heresy with old beliefs, much as in other texts she situates the worship of idols in the time before the coming of Christ. She does not introduce any particular heretical belief or group.

In contrast, two of Hildegard's homilies on John 3. 1–15 include teachings that may be aimed against the Cathars even though the *magistra* does not name 'heretics' or 'Sadducees' as she does in other writings. In this difficult scriptural passage, Nicodemus, a Pharisee, comes to Jesus at night and asserts that he knows Jesus came from God as a teacher and that no one could perform the things Jesus does unless God is with him. Jesus replies that anyone must be born anew to see the kingdom of God (Jn 3. 3), and Nicodemus questions him about the meaning of being born again (Jn 3. 4). Jesus responds that unless someone is 'born from water and the Spirit, he can not enter into the kingdom of God' (Jn 3. 5). At the end of the pericope, Jesus asks how Nicodemus will believe what he says about heavenly things, when he does not believe him about earthly things (Jn 3. 12).[92]

Hildegard's first homily interprets Nicodemus as the false prophets who believe more in the invisible than the visible life. Jesus's instruction then aims at teaching them that they must know the visible before the invisible. The *magistra* explains that, as the Son of Man descended from heaven to earth and then ascended, so humans receive souls from heaven, perform good works on earth, and then return

---

[90] Everwin of Steinfeld, *Epistola* 472, *PL* 182: 679: 'et habere eos plures ex nostris clericis et monachis'.

[91] *Expo. Euang.*, 43, p. 306, lines 54–58: '*Et subductis ad terram nauibus*, sic ut genus et genus hominum, cum elementis et ceteris creaturis in terrenis uersarentur, usque dum Deum in humano corpore uiderent, *relictis omnibus*, scilicet ueteri lege et heresi ac propria causa in peccatis, *secuti sunt illum*, in fide et euangelio pacis.'

[92] *Expo. Euang.*, 34, pp. 279–82.

to heaven.[93] In the second homily, Hildegard comments on John 3. 12 and likewise maintains the necessity of knowing the visible before understanding the invisible. She further affirms that nothing exists unless it comes from 'the Son of Man who is in heaven' (Jn 3. 13).[94]

The two homilies expound Hildegard's theology on the origin of souls and the notion of procession and return. Moreover, she affirms the goodness of visible things and the identity of Christ as God and Creator. Jesus, representing God and the highest good, asserts in the second homily that all things take their life from him. Hildegard clearly asserts the role of Christ at the creation and the belief in creation ex nihilo. The notion of rebirth in water, which is expressed in John 3. 5, leads Hildegard to adduce Genesis 1. 2: that the 'Spirit of God was borne across the waters'. The *magistra* brings together the waters of Genesis, the gospel pericope, and the sacrament of baptism when she asserts that the human being, dried out from sin, is revived by the water of the Holy Spirit in baptism.[95] Thus water links creation and baptism and binds the role of the three persons of the Trinity in creation and redemption through the sacraments and good works. Moreover, for Hildegard, the life-giving power of God in the force of *uiriditas* holds a central function: it gives life, strengthens, and leads to eternal life.[96]

The *magistra* skilfully emphasizes fundamental tenets of her theology that implicitly oppose the views of the Cathars: she portrays God and Christ as one and Creator; she expresses the belief in creation ex nihilo; and she describes powerfully the necessity for the administration of baptism with water, a divine element that

---

[93] *Expo. Euang.*, 34, p. 282, lines 62–63: 'homines animas de celo accipiunt, quae ad celum per bona opera redeunt, cum etiam membra filii Dei sint'.

[94] *Expo. Euang.*, 35, p. 285, lines 63–66: 'nulla forma esse potest, nisi de me sit, *filius hominis qui est in celo*, quoniam creaturae primum inuisibiliter formari incipiunt, et de me uitam sumunt, quae uiror earum sum'.

[95] *Expo. Euang.*, 34, pp. 280–81, lines 27–33: 'Omnis creatura circuitum habet in aqua, ita ut absque aqua non sit, nec uiuat, *et Spiritu*, quoniam cum *Spiritus Domini ferebatur super aquas*, apparuit quod Spiritus Domini aquam efflauit et uiuificauit; unde et spiritus hominis in ea ad uitam resuscitatur in baptismo; *non potest introire in regnum Dei*, uidelicet quia solus homo est in ariditate a primo ortu propter inobedientiam Adae.' On Adam's sin, see Rupert of Deutz, *Commentaria in Euangelium Sancti Iohannis*, III, p. 139, line 818, p. 149, line 1181. More commonly exegetes in the line of Bede, whose Homily II.18 was read in Paul the Deacon's homiliary, insert discourses on baptism here. Hildegard refers only briefly to its life-giving force. See apparatus fontium, *Expo. Euang.*, 34, p. 281.

[96] *Expo. Euang.*, 35, p. 285, lines 70–73: 'ita etiam ascendit de me uigor et uiriditas ad confortationem ceterarum creaturam, *ut omnis qui credit, in ipso*, uidelicet ut cuncta creatura quae in uigore et in uiriditate sua constat, *non pereat*, id est ne diffluat'.

unites the world from its beginning and gives new life to the human. The Cathars, in contrast, assimilated nothingness and material creation, which they considered to be evil and the work of Satan. Moreover, they advocated one sacrament, a baptism not by water but by the Holy Spirit. When the Cathars read the same Johannine verse, John 3. 5 — 'unless anyone is born from water and the Spirit, he can not enter into the kingdom of God' — and cited it in their manuals for worship, they accented the power of the Spirit over the material element of water. The Dublin Cathar ritual employs John 3. 5 and implies that baptism by water is a first step, but that the second baptism, with the Spirit, assures salvation.[97]

Several elements of Hildegard's commentary on Nicodemus correlate with the interpretations of preceding expositors who discuss heresy and baptism in their readings of the same passage. Their principal concern remains rebaptism. Chromateius of Aquilea denounces heretics for denying the Holy Spirit: 'ausi sunt haeretici decem spiritum sanctum denegare'.[98] Following Bede, whose Homily on the Gospels, II.18, was read in the Cluny lectionary, various exegetes insert discourses on baptism into their commentaries.[99] Hildegard refers briefly to the life-giving force of baptism in connection to the waters of Genesis and the gospel pericope, but she does not discuss the sacrament at length. Other exegetes including Rupert of Deutz, discuss heretical and schismatic views on rebaptism in homilies that mention Nicodemus. They do not, however, attribute such views to Nicodemus, as Hildegard does.[100] For the homilies on John 3. 1–15, Hildegard apparently grounds her exegesis and views of contemporary heresy by drawing on older sources that deal with conflicting views on baptism and the role of the Spirit.

---

[97] The Dublin ritual, written in Occitan, is preserved in a fourteenth-century copy of an earlier text. According to Ylva Hagman, 'Le Rite d'initiation chrétienne chez les cathares et les bogomiles', the extant Cathar rituals preserve liturgical rites that correspond to earlier Bogomil texts. On the Cathar rituals and the formula from John 3. 5, see Brenon, 'Les Fonctions sacramentelles du consolament', pp. 132–36; and in general, Brenon, 'L'Église de l'Esprit saint: Étude sur la notion d'Esprit dans la théologie cathare', in *Les Archipels cathares*, pp. 111–27. See also Duvernoy, *La Religion des Cathares*, pp. 44–52, 343.

[98] Chromatius of Aquilea, *Sermones*, ed. by J. Lemarié, CCSL, 9A (Turnhout: Brepols, 1974), S. 18, pp. 83–84.

[99] See Étaix, 'Le Lectionnaire de l'office de Cluny', no. 2.51, p. 116. An additional reading was Gregory Nazianus, Hom. 4; Étaix, 'Le Lectionnaire de l'office de Cluny', no. 121, p. 106.

[100] Rupert of Deutz, *Commentaria in Euangelium Sancti Iohannis*, pp. 146, 154, 161. See also Hrabanus Maurus, *Homiliae in euangelia et epistolas*, 72, *PL* 110: 283A; Smaragadus, *Collectiones epistolarum et euangeliorum de tempore et de sanctis*, *PL* 102: 340; Haymo of Auxerre, *Homiliae de tempore*, 108, *PL* 118: 579.

Several *expositiones* that do not allude to contemporary heresy reflect historical controversies over the dual nature of Christ and indicate, like the *Explanatio Symboli Sancti Athanasii*, that Hildegard was well aware of the Arian controversies as well as other christological debates. In her exegesis of Luke 2. 42–52, the *magistra* accents Christ's human nature; the same theme enters her homily on Mark 16. 14–20. Hildegard affirms the eternal nature of Christ, Creator and Redeemer, when commenting on other pericopes, notably Luke 2. 42–52, John 1. 1–14, Matthew 4. 1–11, and John 2. 1–11.

The first homily on Jesus teaching in the temple at age twelve (Lk 2. 42–52) addresses the dual nature of Christ and emphasizes his humanity. Christological debates swirled around this pericope, particularly in the centuries of conflict over Arianism.[101] Hildegard establishes a salvation-historical framework for her reading: she begins with the incarnation and then introduces the time between the old and the new law. Joseph and Mary represent the Jewish people under the old law, who did not know that the Son of God was in human form.[102] Hildegard stresses the theme of signs that point not merely to Jesus's coming but to his coming in human form. She repeats the synonymous gloss, 'incarnatus in humanitate' or 'incarnatus Dei filius'.[103] In dialogue with his parents, Jesus asks if they did not see through signs that he would accomplish his Father's will in the flesh.[104] She specifies the signs of the ram in the thicket, the burning bush, and the words of Isaiah 7. 14: 'For behold, a virgin shall conceive.' When Mary and Joseph do not understand what Jesus said, Hildegard explains that they did not comprehend that the Word would become human, because they saw him not in the flesh but only imperfectly in the shadow (*umbra*). The seer uses this term here and elsewhere to designate the knowledge of prophecy.[105] The *magistra* then explains that Jesus's going down to

---

[101] See Kevin Madigan, *The Passions of Christ in High-Medieval Thought* (Oxford: Oxford University Press, 2006).

[102] *Expo. Euang.*, 14, p. 226, lines 12–14: '*et non cognouerunt parentes eius*, quia iudaicus populus in uetere lege nesciebat eum filium Dei in humanitate esse'.

[103] *Expo. Euang.*, 14, p. 227, lines 34–35: '*Fili*, incarnatus in humanitate'; line 39: 'incarnatus Dei filius'.

[104] *Expo. Euang.*, 14, p. 227, lines 30–31: 'quoniam ego, uerbum patris, uoluntatem eius in carne mea adimplebo?'

[105] *Expo. Euang.*, 14, p. 227, lines 45–47: 'quia uerbum patris non intellexerunt hominem esse, quoniam eum non in carne sed tantum in umbra significatum uiderunt'. *Expo. Euang.*, 12, p. 222, lines 78–80: '*Et responso accepto*, per salutarem inspirationem in ipso desiderio, *in somnis*, id est in umbra prophetiae, *ne redirent*, retro, *ad Herodem*, scilicet ad eresim quae a diabolo uenit.' The same

Nazareth and being subject to Mary and Joseph (Lk 2. 51) designates coming into humanity through humility and obeying the law.[106] Hildegard explicates the final verse of the pericope (Lk 2. 52), 'Jesus advanced in wisdom and age and grace with God and men', saying that at the fullness of time, 'all would know that Jesus was God and man'.[107] Similarly, the seer introduces the theme of the signs pointing to Jesus's humanity in her first ascension homily (Mk 16. 14–20). There she explains that signs were sent to the prophets, as to Abraham through the ram and to Jacob through the angel, in order to scourge their ignorance and to show that Christ was going to come in 'humanity'. Furthermore, the *magistra* asserts that Christ showed himself truly in the incarnation and manifested himself as God in the ascension, when he encompasses heaven and earth in majesty.[108]

Patristic commentators on Luke 2. 42–52 addressed the controversy over Christ's dual nature with pressing intensity in the midst of centuries of conflict over Arianism. Ambrose, with Bede following him, signals the heretical reading of Luke 2. 51 that Jesus was subordinate to the Father.[109] Hildegard does not raise this issue directly. However, she must have been aware of it, because she refers to Christ's human or dual nature several times.[110]

With respect to the divine and eternal nature of Christ, Hildegard articulates her theology of Creator and creation in various homilies within the context of salvation history. I have analyzed these in that framework and shall recall them here only briefly. The *magistra*'s exegesis of the parable of the labourers in the vineyard (Mt 20. 1–16) matches the events of the parable with the days and works of

---

image occurs in *Symph.*, 31, p. 417, lines 1–9: 'O spectabiles viri | qui pertransistis occulta, | aspicientes per oculos spiritus | et annuntiantes | in lucida umbra | acutam et viventem lucem | in virga germinantem, | que sola floruit | de introitu radicantis luminis.' Hildegard's usage of *umbra* follows the tradition of Augustine and numerous writers after him, cited in *Expo. Euang.*, 14, apparatus fontium, p. 227.

[106] *Expo. Euang.*, 14, p. 228, lines 48–50: '*Et descendit cum eis*, propter hominem de sinu patris in humilitate, *et uenit Nazareth*, id est in circumcisionem et legem, *et erat subditus illis*, uidelicet omnibus institutis legalium preceptorum.'

[107] *Expo. Euang.*, 14, p. 228, lines 54–57: '*Et Iesus proficiebat*, ad perfectionem, *sapientia*, id est prophetia, *et aetate*, uidelicet lege, ubi uenit plenitudo temporis, *et gratia*, in euangelio, *apud Deum*, id est diuinam fortitudinem, *et homines*, ita ut ab omnibus cognosceretur quod Deus et homo esset.'

[108] *Expo. Euang.*, 32, p. 278, lines 30–32: 'Christus ueraciter ostensus est in incarnatione, ut predictus fuerat, *et sedet*, Deus manifestatus, *a dextris Dei*, quia celum et terram in maiestate comprehendit.'

[109] Ambrose, *Expositio euangelii secundum Lucam*, II, 65, pp. 58–59, lines 844–56.

[110] I am grateful to Nicholas Cohen for pointing out these references.

creation, but her emphasis lies on the works of creation and the duties of the creatures. Hildegard interprets the edict from Caesar Augustus (Lk 2. 1) as God's ancient plan for the coming forth of all creatures.[111] The creation results from the Word and the Father, the Word being both the head of the entire process of creation (*caput omnis formationis*) and the one who was to be incarnated.[112] Each creature went forth in accordance with its own nature and properties, that is, by walking, swimming, or flying. The human was placed on high, above the other creatures; he comprehends everything since he possesses the faculty of reason (*rationalitas*). God created the human in his image and likeness, which means that the human went out from God at his creation and goes back to God upon his redemption — a concise statement of the theological theme of procession and return.[113] Hildegard views the human as generic being here and does not differentiate Adam and Eve, male and female. In fact, she introduces Eve into only four of the *Expositiones*, despite the many references she makes to Genesis.[114]

[111] *Expo. Euang.*, 7, p. 205, lines 2–4: '*Exiit edictum*, id est antiquum consilium, *a Cesare Augusto*, scilicet a superno patre, *ut describeretur*, id est ut procederet, *uniuersus orbis*, uidelicet omnis creatura.' See Dronke, 'Platonic-Christian Allegories', pp. 385–88.

[112] *Expo. Euang.*, 7, p. 205, lines 5–7: 'creatio, *facta est* [...] per uerbum patris, quod erat caput omnis formationis, et quod etiam incarnandum erat'.

[113] *Expo. Euang.*, 7, p. 206, lines 15–16: 'Deus illum *ad imaginem et similitudinem suam* creauerat; *ut profiteretur*, Deum, de quo creatus exiuit, et ad quem redemptus iuit.' See also *Expo. Euang.*, 34, lines 62–63: 'quia homines animas de celo accipiunt, quae ad celum per bona opera redeunt, cum etiam membra filii Dei sint'. On the theme of procession and return in the twelfth century, see Jaehyun Kim, 'Journey, Procession and Return in John the Scot, Eriugena' (unpublished doctoral dissertation, Princeton Theological Seminary, Princeton, New Jersey, 2003), esp. pp. 247–54.

[114] On the figure of Eve in Hildegard's visionary works and the implications of her depiction for Hildegard's anthropology and theology of the feminine, see Newman, *Sister of Wisdom*, pp. 89–120. In *Expo. Euang.*, 9, Hildegard likens the making of the Word into flesh to the sleep of Adam in sinlessness before the creation of Eve, while she compares the Word's dwelling among us to Eve's dwelling with Adam before the Fall, when evil had not yet entered them. After the Fall, no flesh could be in righteousness except the Christ child, conceived from heavenly wind (*uento Spiritus*) in the Virgin. *Expo. Euang.*, 9, p. 214, lines 95–102: '*Et uerbum*, scilicet idem uerbum quod carnem de terra formauit cum spiratione uitae, *caro factum est*, ita quod se indidit in integram carnem, et dormiuit simili dormitione, sicut Adam sine peccato dormiuit, cum ex eo alia caro facta est in mulierem. Sic *uerbum caro factum est*, et creuit homo, *et habitauit in nobis*, sicut Eua cum Adam, ante peccatum, quoniam in illis nulla uicissitudo erat, sed integri fuerunt, sicut Deus eos creauerat, et ideo malum illos nondum intrauerat.' See also *Expo. Euang.*, 5, p. 203, lines 1–7; *Expo. Euang.*, 16, p. 231, lines 1–6; *Expo. Euang.*, 16, p. 233, lines 53–60.

Hildegard interprets the theology of creation further in one of her homilies on Jesus's temptations in the wilderness (Mt 4. 1–11). She explains that Jesus's entrance into the wilderness represents the Word of the Father entering the substance of created beings through the power of the Holy Spirit. Jesus's reply to the first temptation (Mt 4. 3–4) provides the springboard for Hildegard to controvert Cathar teaching that Satan created the material world. In the *magistra*'s view, the Devil orders Jesus to create by his own command and thus be like God, when 'He commanded and they were made' (Ps 32. 9). Hildegard underscores her theology of the goodness of material creation in her interpretation of Jesus's response: 'the Creator is known through the creation, and it is understood that the Highest has created it. [. . .] Visible objects are created by God.'[115] This statement constitutes a clear refutation of Cathar beliefs. Moreover, if Jesus were to create on his own as Satan tempted him to do, he would perform a role like the Cathar bad god or the evil principle, which some Cathars held responsible for material creation.[116]

Likewise in her other homily on Matthew 4. 1–11, Hildegard envisions Christ as Creator before the creation. In the wilderness, no human or animal activity occurred and the Devil endeavoured to tempt Christ through hearing and tried to frighten Him away from the work of creation. The first temptation again provides an allegorical stepping stone for Hildegard to have Jesus voice her theology of creation. The *magistra* first explains that the Devil did not tell Christ to make bread from nothing, but to change a created thing into another, which is contrary to God's justice. In that way, He would know more truly if He was the God of creation. To clarify what is against justice and what is not, Hildegard asserts that Jesus's miracle of changing water into wine was not contrary to nature: wine is liquid just like water, and, therefore, the water changed only in taste.[117] If the stones had been made into bread, they would have lost their entire nature, as the loaves of bread

---

[115] *Expo. Euang.*, 25, p. 258, lines 34–36: 'per creaturam creator cognoscitur, et quod summus eam creaverit [. . .] visibilia a Deo creata esse'.

[116] On the Cathar beliefs about creation, see works of Brenon and Duvernoy cited above, as well as Peter Biller, 'Cathars and Material Women', in *Medieval Theology and the Natural Body*, ed. by P. Biller and A. J. Minnis, York Studies in Medieval Theology, 1 (Woodbridge: York Medieval Press, 1997), pp. 61–108.

[117] *Expo. Euang.*, 24, p. 254, lines 62–68: 'Et dixit: *Dic* solo uerbo, *ut lapides isti*, quia ibi presentes erant, *panes fiant*. Non dixit ut de nichilo panes faceret, sed ut creaturam in alium modum mutaret, ut tanto ueracius cognosceret, si ipse Deus creatura esset. Et quod contrarium iustitiae Dei erat, fieri persuasit, quia aduersus iusticiam Dei esset, si creaturam aliquam in alium modum mutaret, ut diabolus semper fieri persuadet.'

would have also.[118] Jesus's response to the Devil's first temptation leads Hildegard back to the creation: living not 'by bread alone but by every word that proceeds from the mouth of God' (Mt 4. 4) means that when God said 'Let there be light' (Gn 1. 3), lights and other created things were made.

The miracle at Cana (Jn 2. 1–11), adduced in the preceding exegesis of the Matthean temptation story, itself serves for reflection on the theology of creation. The wedding designates the creation of the human, and Hildegard interprets Jesus's words to his mother (Jn 2. 4) as God's command to the first humans. Christ speaks to his mother, humanity, as the Creator and the incarnate Word, stating, in Hildegard's words: 'All things were created through me', and 'humanity is present to me, so that I would create all things and that you would be my garment'.[119] This concept of Christ as Creator lies at the core of Hildegard's Christology and theology of the creation and it grounds in some way all her arguments against the Cathar heresy.

Hildegard's commentary on John 1 and, in particular, her explanation of the two possible meanings for John 1. 3–4 fall within a longstanding exegetical debate over this passage. For centuries, the Johannine passage lay at the heart of christological controversies and engaged the intellect and passion of patristic commentators. Augustine discussed the beginning of John's Gospel at length in the context of debates over Manichaean and Arian beliefs; subsequent commentators treated his texts as essential: Bede, John Scotus Eriugena, Heiric of Auxerre, to name a few.[120] The Cluny lectionary and the homiliary of Paul the Deacon prescribe the reading of a Bedan homily that is heavily indebted to Augustinian thought.[121] Hildegard offers only one expositio on John 1, but she comments on the passage elsewhere, notably in the *Liber diuinorum operum* and in her *Explanation of the*

---

[118] *Expo. Euang.*, 24, p. 254, lines 68–73: 'Sed quod filius Dei aquam in uinum conuertit, hoc naturae contrarium non fuit, quia uinum sicut et aqua madidum est et fluit, ei ideo aqua saporem suum tantum mutauit; lapides autem si panes facti fuissent, omnino naturam suam perdidissent: sed et idcirco panes, quia primus et fortior cibus esurientium est.'

[119] *Expo. Euang.*, 16, p. 231, lines 15–17: 'omnia per me creata sunt, *et tibi est mulier*, scilicet humanitas michi adest, ut omnia crearem, *et tibi*, ut indumentum meum esses'.

[120] The immense bibliography on Augustine's interpretation of John lies beyond the scope of our study. An excellent synthesis and bibliography can be found in the articles 'Anti-Arian Works' and 'Anti-Manichean Works', in *Augustine Through the Ages*, pp. 31–34 and 39–40.

[121] The homiliary of Paul the Deacon has Bede, *Homeliarum euangelii libri II*, I, 8, pp. 52–59; Grégoire, *Homéliaires liturgiques médiévaux*, p. 435; and the lectionary of Cluny has the same homily from Bede, according to Etaix, 'Le Lectionnaire de l'office à Cluny', p. 97. For the impact of Augustinian writings on the homily, see the apparatus fontium, *Expo. Euang.*, 9, pp. 209–15.

Athanasian Creed.[122] Hildegard's reading of John 1 proves foundational not only for the theology of the *dominicum principium* and the *prima principia* but also for the opposition to Catharism.[123]

Hildegard's interpretation of John 1 in the *Expositiones* corresponds closely in content to her commentary on the same pericope in the *Liber diuinorum operum*: she emphasizes the presence of the Word — logos, rationality, Son of God — at the creation. The *expositio* on John 1 concerns this relationship beween the two books and thus its composition correlates with the *Liber diuinorum operum* chronologically. However, the Johannine passage in the *Liber diuinorum operum*, with its brilliant overlay of images, corresponds to Hildegard's visionary style of writing, whereas the *magistra*'s homily on John 1 clearly stands in the genre of scriptural commentary. Whether the composition of the homily precedes the treatise, or vice versa, is a matter for debate. Dronke asserts that the homily reflects the 1163 vision and predates the more polished version in the *Liber diuinorum operum*.[124] However, Hildegard shows clear awareness of the competing interpretations for the pericope when she explains alternate readings of John 1. 3 and 1. 4 in her homily, something she does not do in the visionary work. It is unlikely that Hildegard received the vision complete with competing interpretations of two controversial verses. The homily shows a higher level of exegetical sophistication, if not theological reflection, than the *Liber diuinorum operum* and, therefore, may date from a period after the initial 1163 vision. It would then predate the completion of the *Liber diuinorum operum* and represent an intermediate stage in Hildegard's thought on this pericope, somewhere between 1163 and 1170. The manuscript evidence

---

[122] *Expl. Symb.*, p. 118, lines 250–60: 'Itaque ut praedictum est, increatus Pater est, Filius etiam increatus, sic et Spiritus sanctus increatus; quoniam hae tres personae unus Deus est, et omnes creaturae per eumdem Deum creatae sunt; *sed sine ipso factum est nihil.* Initium quippe, quod in initio creationis factum est, similitudinem illius qui sine initio est, habere uoluit, quod nullo modo fieri debuit, quia nihilum fuit, quoniam in Deo uita et ueritas est, in perdito uero angelo et in homine uanitas est, quam superbia inflauit, quae tanquam uentus pertransiit. Et quod per Deum et in Deo factum est, uita in ipso est, et Deus caput illius contriuit, qui praedicta mala primum arripuit, ac eum qui sine uita est, in infernum projecit.' *Expl. Atha.*, p. 43.

[123] On Cathar interpretation of John, see Duvernoy, *La Religion des Cathares*, pp. 49, 51–55; and Anne Brenon, 'Un monothéisme dualiste', in *Les Archipels cathares*, pp. 85–94.

[124] Final changes to the visionary treatise were probably finished in 1174, according to Dronke, and incorporated into the Gent manuscript. See *LDO*, pp. x–xii. Dronke points out that Hildegard states that she wrote (*scripsi*) the 'Librum diuinorum operum' after finishing the life of Disibod. He interprets this to mean that she 'continued or perfected the major work' from 1170 onward. See also Dronke, 'Platonic-Christian Allegories', p. 388.

indicates that the homily likely precedes 1170. With respect to the stylistic complexity of the texts, the didactic intent of the *expositio* may explain the relative simplicity of the style of the *Expositiones* vis-à-vis the *Liber diuinorum operum*. In other words, differences between the works may reflect conventions of genre and not different phases of Hildegard's understanding or of her poetic prowess.

The analysis of Hildegard's thought and her possible sources proceeds sequentially, that is following the verses of John 1 in order.[125] For John 1. 1–2, Hildegard explains that the Word is the beginning of all but is not called 'beginning' because he sounded forth the 'fiat'.[126] This concern for the Word's name has precedent in Augustine and others, notably Heiric, who explain why the Son is called 'verbum'. However, Augustine and Heiric state that the Father and Son are called 'beginning'.[127] Despite her differences with these predecessors, Hildegard returns to affirm in her own words the indivisibility of Father and Son. Equating the Word and Rationality, she declares that Rationality created all. Rationality has a starting point in the human and the angel, but in God has no point of origin, neither made nor created. Similarly, God and rationality are one and cannot be divided.[128] This notion of indivisibility echoes previous exegetes, notably Heiric, who is influenced by Eriugena when he asserts: 'There is one principle/beginning and not two, one God and not two.'[129] The identification of God in Christ with rationality has several precedents that bear on the interpretation of John 1. 4 as well. Bede, for example, uses the phrase *uitalis ratio*.[130]

For the controversial elements of John 1. 3–4, Hildegard offers two readings each. For John 1. 3a, 'Omnia per ipsum facta sunt' (All things through him were made), Hildegard proclaims that all things — heaven, earth, and all that are in them — were made when God uttered 'fiat'. Augustine specifies what 'all things'

---

[125] The works of several major exegetes may have influenced the *magistra*: Augustine, Bede, John Scotus Eriugena, Haymo, and Heiric of Auxerre. Analysis here is limited to those exegetes and to the interpretation of John 1. 1–4. Jaehyun Kim and I have a fuller study in preparation.

[126] *Expo. Euang.*, 9, p. 209, lines 1–4. Cf. *LDO*, I.4.105, p. 251, lines 84–96 and p. 252, lines 116–17.

[127] Augustine of Hippo, *In Iohannis euangelium*, I, 11, p. 6, lines 1–17; Heiric of Auxerre, *Homiliae*, I, 10, p. 82, lines 39–48; *Homiliae*, I, 11, p. 93, lines 93–108.

[128] *Expo. Euang.*, 9, p. 210, lines 5–9. On rationality, see *LDO*, I.4.105, p. 248, lines 4–5, p. 249, lines 21–22, p. 250, lines 77–78; on the notion of having no origin and being indivisible, see *LDO*, I.4.105, p. 250, lines 75–76, and *LDO*, I.4.105, p. 251, lines 79, 82, 90.

[129] Heiric of Auxerre, *Homiliae*, I, 10, p. 82, lines 52–53; *Homiliae*, I, 11, p. 93, lines 103–08.

[130] Bede, *Homeliarum euangelii libri II*, I, 8, p. 54, line 88.

include. He names spiritual creation — angels, archangels, thrones, dominations, powers, principalities (Ps 120. 1) — and natural creatures, everything that flies, moves, and so on, 'from the angel to the worm', and including the bothersome fly, which the Manicheans claimed to be the Devil's creation.[131]

For John 1. 3b, 'sine ipso factum est nihil' (without him nothing was made), Hildegard explains that *nihil* means contradiction, which was made without rationality in the Son. God made the angel rational, but the angel used reason to contradict, that is to act against God. God allowed this to happen but did not make it happen. Heiric of Auxerre gives a similar reading, when he interprets *nihil* as negation. Hildegard allows that this phrase may be understood in another way, namely that without the Son, *nihil* was made.[132] Here the *magistra* probably has Augustine in mind, where he equates *nihil* with what God did not make, sin and idols, as in I Corinthians 8. 4: *nihil est idolum*. Haymo of Auxerre follows Augustine on this, while Heiric equates *nihil* with evil, or with the negation of all things, the latter being similar to Hildegard's *contradictio*.[133] Hildegard herself explains *nihil* as evil and sin in the *Liber diuinorum operum*, thus following her predecessors more closely in that work than in the *Expositiones*. In the visionary treatise, she explains: 'without him nothing was made except evil, which is from the Devil', and that 'Rational man [...] committed sin [...] which comes to nothing.' The notion of contradiction or negation is implicit, but she does not discuss it explicitly, as she does in her homily.[134]

When Hildegard turns to John 1. 4, 'what was made in him' (*quod factum est in ipso*), she explains first that 'what was made' *in ipso* was made in rationality, in the Son of God incarnated. That 'was life' (*uita erat*), because the Son of God was

---

[131] *Expo. Euang.*, 9, p. 210, lines 10–13. Augustine, *In Iohannis euangelium*, I, 5, p. 3, lines 11–15; I, 9, p. 6, lines 24–26; I, 13, p. 7, lines 11–16; I, 13, p. 8, lines 35–42. On the fly, see *In Iohannis euangelium tractatus*, I, 14, p. 8, lines 1–22.

[132] *Expo. Euang.*, 9, p. 210, lines 13–19: '*Omnia*, uidelicet celum, terra et cetera quae in eis sunt, *per ipsum facta sunt*, in hoc quod Deus dixit *fiat*. *Et sine ipso*, scilicet sine racionalitate, id est sine filio, *factum est nichil*, quod est contradictio. Deus angelum racionalem fecit; sed quod racionalitas Deum in angelo contradixit, ipse non fecit, sed fieri permisit. Quamuis etiam alio modo intelligatur, ita quod sine filio nichil factum sit.' Heiric, *Homiliae*, I, 11, p. 95, lines 148–56; p. 95, lines 149–53 (*negationem*).

[133] Augustine, *In Iohannis euangelium*, I, 13, p. 7, lines 3–11; Haymo of Auxerre, *Homiliae de tempore*, I, 5, *PL* 118: 57; Heiric, *Homiliae*, I, 11, p. 95, lines 148–56; p. 95, lines 149–53 (*negationem*).

[134] *LDO*, I.4.105, p. 252, lines 139–40; Newman, 'Commentary on the Johannine Prologue', p. 25.

human.[135] Hildegard also asserts that *nihil* neither touched nor entered Christ, as it did the angel and humankind, a comment that relates back to *nihil* as the contradiction or disobedience of sin. She then introduces another meaning of the phrase with wording similar to her comment on the preceding verse, *sine ipso factum est nihil*. She states: 'quamuis etiam, *quod factum est*, aliter intelligi possit, quia omnia quae facta sunt, in Deo uitam habent' (All things which were made have life in God). 'Life,' Hildegard says, 'is the incarnation of God's son.'[136] For her interpretation of John 1. 4 in the *Liber diuinorum operum*, the *magistra* does not refer to disobedient humans or angels or the Devil.[137] In contrast, when she comments on the Athanasian Creed, Hildegard defines Satan as the one without life.[138] Moreover, in that work she includes both her interpretations of John 1. 4: that *nihil* could not pertain to God, and that all things have life in God.[139] She does not clearly differentiate the two as she does in the *Expositiones*. However, both commentaries (*Expositiones* and *Explanatio*) include the two readings, whereas the visionary work does not. This difference may relate to the genre of the works or possibly to increased knowledge of the exegetical tradition.

Augustine distinguished two readings of verse four, the first punctuated after *est*: *Quod factum est* [...]; the second after *illo*: *Quod factum est in illo* [...]. He rejected the second way of reading, stating that stones, for example, are made but are not life, as the Manicheans assert. Hildegard does not include the refutation of the Manichees, but she defines life in terms reminiscent of Augustine's definition of life as wisdom and reason (*sapientia* and *ratio*): 'est autem in ipsa sapientia spiritaliter

---

[135] *Expo. Euang.*, 9, pp. 210–11, lines 23–26: '*Quod factum est, in ipso*, id est in uerbo, scilicet in racionalitate, uidelicet in filio Dei, qui erat homo incarnatus, *uita erat*, quia filius Dei homo talis erat, quod nichil ipsum nec tetigit, nec intrauit, sicut in angelum et in hominem fecit.'

[136] *Expo. Euang.*, 9, pp. 210–11, lines 26–29: 'quamuis etiam *quod factum est* aliter intelligi possit, quia omnia quae facta sunt in Deo uitam habent. *Et uita*, id est incarnatio filii Dei'. In her commentary on the Athanasian Creed, Hildegard includes both interpretations of verse four: that *nihil* could not pertain to God, and that all things have life in God; but she does not overtly differentiate the two as in the *Expositiones*. *Expl. Symb.*, p. 118, lines 250–60. *Expl. Atha.*, p. 43.

[137] *LDO*, I.4.105, pp. 252–53, lines 147–81; Newman, 'Commentary on the Johannine Prologue', p. 25.

[138] *Expl. Symb.*, p. 118, lines 258–60: 'Et quod per Deum et in Deo factum est, uita in ipso est, et Deus caput illius contriuit, qui praedicta mala primum arripuit, ac eum qui sine uita est, in infernum projecit.'

[139] Newman, 'Commentary on the Johannine Prologue', p. 25. *Expl. Symb.*, p. 118, lines 250–60. *Expl. Atha.*, p. 43. Hildegard also treats the concept of nothingness in the *Vita*, where she remarks that Lucifer could not destroy God or the human being. *V. Hild.*, II.16, p. 44, lines 19–21; *Life of Hildegard*, p. 67. I am grateful to Charles Stang for pointing out this parallel.

ratio quaedam qua terra facta est'.[140] Bede's Homily I, 8 on John 1 also transmitted this view from Augustine.[141] Eriugena repeated Augustine's remarks on the two ways of reading this verse and included phrasing from *De Trinitate* and *De Genesi ad litteram* as well.[142] Heiric of Auxerre emphasized *ratio* more than Augustine and repeated it several times in the paragraph.[143] Heiric, following Eriugena, gave the second meaning of the phrase as 'all things created by God subsist in him'.[144]

From Hildegard's exegesis of John 1. 1–4, her awareness of complex theological issues and exegetical debates becomes clear. She neither follows nor cites any particular source, although her reading of the pericope, like that of other exegetes, reflects the influence of Augustine above all. Certainly, she shows herself capable of engaging in the complex task of linking the 'principial' texts, an important exegetical problem in the twelfth-century schools. Moreover, she demonstrates the same profound concern with the harmony of the *prima principia* in Genesis and the *dominicum principium* in John's Gospel that she evidences in other texts. In the *Vita Hildegardis*, she explains that she began her exegesis of the *Liber diuinorum operum* after comprehending the connection between John 1 and Genesis 1. This exposition on John 1. 1–14 reflects that advanced level of thought and must date roughly from the same period. Overall, the *magistra* seems to simplify complex theological arguments in the homily, giving her sisters a sort of 'crash course' on the controversy surrounding the passage. At the same time she affirms what she views as the best interpretation, one that conveys her Christology and theology of creation and that serves to counter the beliefs of the Cathars.

Anti-Heretical Writings from the 1170s

The third volume of Hildegard's *Epistolarium* includes two writings against heresy, one called *admonitio* and the other *sermo*.[145] In contrast to the *Expositiones*

---

[140] Augustine, *In Iohannis euangelium*, I, 16, pp. 9–10, lines 9–25; p. 19, lines 241–45; see p. 276, notes 135–36, 138 above.

[141] Bede, *Homeliarum euangelii libri II*, I, 8, p. 55.

[142] John Scotus, *Homélie*, p. 242.

[143] Heiric, *Homiliae*, I, 11, pp. 96–97, lines 183–96. Augustine emphasizes the eternal *sapientia* of God in *In Iohannis euangelium*, I, 16, pp. 9–10.

[144] John Scotus, *Homélie*, p. 244; Heiric, *Homiliae*, I, 10, p. 84, lines 92–109; I, 11, 11, pp. 96–97, lines 167–99, at p. 96, lines 177–78.

[145] *Epistolarium*, III, 381: *Sermo: De peruersa hereticorum doctrina*, pp. 139–44; *Letters*, III, 170–74; *Epistolarium*, III, 387: *Admonitio: Quid sit Dei uerbum contra hereticos*, pp. 151–52;

euangeliorum, both texts open with a visionary preface, which probably indicates that their intended audience lay outside the monastery at Rupertsberg. The twenty-line *Admonitio: Quid sit verbum Dei contra hereticos*, dated tentatively to 1173–77, begins with the voice of God, who utters verses from the opening of John's Gospel and affirms the unity of God the Creator and God the Son along with the life-giving power of the Spirit.[146] Hildegard then asserts that God bestowed on creation the possibility of praise, implicit evidence of its goodness. To defend it, the warrior (*signifer preliator*) of Isaiah 42. 13, the central image of the *Liber uitae meritorum* that represents God and Christ, stands against the enemies who ascribe to themselves what the Holy Spirit bestows.[147] Hildegard calls the enemies not only apostates (*apostate*) but also the bowels (*uiscera diaboli*) of the tyrant Devil, stripped of divine light. They destroy the Scripture and teaching that the Holy Spirit dictated.[148] This short series of invectives punctuates the affirmation of Trinitarian theology, beginning with Father and Son, and asserts in conclusion that 'the words of the Holy Spirit cannot be changed'.[149] Evidently Hildegard takes aim at the heretical interpretation of Scripture, possibly the Cathar reading of the Gospel of John.[150]

In contrast to the *admonitio*, the *Sermo: De peruersa hereticorum doctrina* contains a full exposition of Hildegard's anti-Cathar teaching. A preface establishes both the seer's wakefulness upon receiving the vision and her age of seventy-three, thereby dating the vision to 1171. As the living light instructed her, Hildegard asserts, she writes about God, Creator of the heavens and of the human in his own image. The *magistra* explains the impact of the elements, water, fire, and air, within

---

Letters, III, 181. A third, short text, *Epistolarium*, III, 352, p. 111, rails against Sadducees in the context of schism. *Letters*, III, 144–45.

[146] *Epistolarium*, III, 387, p. 151, lines 1–4: 'Mens omnipotentis Dei Filius suus est, cui adest opus scilicet omnis creatura, quoniam per Verbum Dei, quod Filius suus est, omnia facta sunt, que spiranti uita uiuificata sunt'; *Letters*, III, 181.

[147] *Vite mer.*, I, XXI, p. 21, lines 376–79. As Meis, '*Symphonia Spiritus Sancti*', p. 391, n. 22, points out, despite the similarities between the warrior of Isaiah 42. 13 and the *uir* of the *Vite mer.*, there is a 'marked difference in the articulation of the dynamic force of the acts of the two figures' ('una diferencia notoria en la articulación de la índole dinámica de la actuación de ambas figuras').

[148] *Epistolarium*, III, 387, pp. 151–52, esp. lines 17–18: 'et instigatione eiusdem tyranni scriptura, et doctrinam, quam Spiritus Sanctus dictauit, destruunt'.

[149] *Epistolarium*, III, 387, p. 152, lines 19–20: 'uerba Spiritus Sancti mutari non possunt'.

[150] On Cathar interpretation of John, see Duvernoy, *La Religion des Cathares*, pp. 49, 51–55; and Brenon, 'Un monothéisme dualiste'.

the human endowed with rationality. As flesh and blood are one, so body and soul unite with rationality in the human being. God is hidden fire, invisible to human eyes; the Word is the water of life, the river of Jesus's baptism, and the waters over which the spirit of the Lord moved at the creation. Thus Hildegard associates fire and water with Father and Son, creation and incarnation.[151]

The *magistra* then affirms the full humanity of Christ, who ate and drank so that human flesh and blood might take nourishment. Likewise, he gave his body and blood to his disciples in the bread and wine of the Eucharist, which Hildegard associates with the mustard seed and the wine in old wineskins, both of which, as the seer explains, grew through mystical grace (*per mysticam gratiam Dei*) without any reproductive process. The fire of the Father and the water of the Spirit fashioned the Son. The flesh and blood of the Son correspond to the offering of bread and wine, which is transformed into flesh and blood just as the mustard seed and wine change through the hidden power of *uiriditas* (*per gratiam Dei in uiriditate sua occulte crescendo*).[152] Hildegard extends her theology of the elements from creation, incarnation, and Eucharist to repentance. The human, washed by baptism, slides back into sin but through repentance and confession is cleansed in the wounds of Christ.[153]

After constructing this rich web of symbols that unifies creation and incarnation with the sacraments of baptism, Eucharist, and penance, Hildegard turns to the Cathars, whom she calls heretics and Sadducees (*heretici et Sadducei*). They deny the crux of the theological and symbolic universe she just elaborated, for they refuse the humanity of the Son of God and the sanctity of his body and blood in the Eucharist.[154] The *magistra* asserts that the Devil has blinded the heretics with unfaithfulness, so that they neither hope nor believe in the true God, and has bitten them like a viper, so that they follow him and disregard God.[155] Furthermore, they do not hold the soul and spirit of the human in right faith, because they attend to the carnal and tread upon the divine — a powerful reversal of the apocalyptic imagery of treading Satan underfoot.[156] Even more, the Devil has

---

[151] *Epistolarium*, III, 381, pp. 139–43; *Letters*, III, 171. On the concept of *uis ignea* in Hildegard's *LDO* and Cicero's *De natura deorum*, see Dronke, 'Problemata Hildegardiana', p. 111.

[152] *Epistolarium*, III, 381, pp. 140–42, esp. lines 61–81; *Letters*, III, 172–73.

[153] *Epistolarium*, III, 381, p. 142, lines 114–17; *Letters*, III, 173.

[154] *Epistolarium*, III, 381, p. 142, lines 119–20: 'sanctissimam humanitatem Filii Dei et sanctitatem corporis ac sanguinis sui, que in oblatione panis et uini est, negant'.

[155] *Epistolarium*, III, 381, p. 142, lines 123–28.

[156] *Epistolarium*, III, 381, p. 142, lines 129–34. Examples include *Sciuias*, II.7.25, p. 324, lines 588–91, 596–98; *LDO*, I.1, p. 47.

successfully tempted the heretics to follow their own law by disobeying the order
to be fruitful and multiply. He further tempts them to afflict their bodies with
fasting and to perform incest.[157] In sum, the heretics disobey the entirety of God's
commands and contaminate the entire earth.[158] Hildegard ends in an exhortation
to all Christian kings, dukes, princes, and men to expel the heretics and put them
to flight, but not to kill them, because they are in God's image.[159]

The layering of symbols in the first part of the *sermo* recalls the exegesis of
John 1 in the *Liber diuinorum operum*, with its juxtaposition of images of human
and cosmos.[160] The second section of the *sermo* contains indications that Hildegard
may have augmented her richly imaged thought with the arguments and invective
of Bernard of Clairvaux's letters to Everwin of Steinfeld and perhaps with the ideas
of Everwin and Ekbert of Schönau. The *magistra*'s emphasis on baptism echoes the
alarm of the three churchmen.[161] Her railing against incest recalls Bernard's accusation that the heretics' disregard for marriage makes them committers of incest,
among other sexual activities he viewed as impure.[162] Hildegard's charge of excessive fasting again brings to mind the denunciation of Cathar abstinence from
certain foods, as uttered by Bernard and Everwin, as well as Ekbert of Schönau.[163]
The Abbot of Clairvaux compares the heretics to vipers, and while that image
belongs to standard polemical and anti-heretical invective, Hildegard's word

---

[157] *Epistolarium*, III, 381, p. 143, lines 134–43. Compare with Ekbert of Schönau, Sermo V,
Circa primam haeresim de conjugio, PL 195: 33: 'Adhuc mihi dicite, popule stulte et insipiens, si,
sicut docti estis, viro prohibuit Deus mulierem, et mulieri virum, quomodo fieri potuit illud quod
dixit ad eos: *Crescite et multiplicamini, et replete terram?* (Gn 1) Quid debuerunt aut potuerunt
facere, ut crescerent et multiplicarentur, si debebant omnino ab invicem abstinere?'

[158] *Epistolarium*, III, 381, p. 143, lines 143–47.

[159] *Epistolarium*, III, 381, p. 143, lines 148–54, esp. lines 149–51: 'populum istum ab ecclesia
facultatibus suis priuatum expellendo et non occidendo effugate, quoniam forma Dei sunt'.

[160] *LDO*, I.4.105, pp. 248–64. Dronke, *Poetic Individuality in the Middle Ages*, p. 163, signalled
Hildgard's use of a 'composite image' in the sequence for St Ursula. Newman, 'Commentary on
the Johannine Prologue'.

[161] Sermo 66.9, 11, *SBOp*, II, 183–85; Everwin of Steinfeld, *Epistola* 472, PL 182: 678B–D;
Ekbert, *Sermones*, VII on baptism of infants (*PL* 195: 40A–51C) and especially VIII on baptism
with water (*PL* 195: 51B–55C).

[162] Sermo 66.3, *SBOp*, II, 179–80. Everwin of Steinfeld, *Epistola* 472, PL 182: 679: 'omne
conjugium vocant fornicationem praeter quod contrahitur inter utrosque uirgines [. . .]. Isti
apostolici Satanae habent inter se feminas (ut dicunt) continentes, uiduas, uirgines.'

[163] Sermo 66.7, *SBOp*, II, 182–83; Everwin of Steinfeld, *Epistola* 472, PL 182: 678A; Ekbert,
Sermo VI, *Contra secundam haeresim de esu carnium*, PL 195: 36D–40C.

choice, *uipereo more*, may echo Bernard's *dente uipereo* in Sermon 66.4.[164] The exhortation to expel and put to flight (*effugate*) the heretics recalls Bernard's Sermon 64.8, where he concludes that an unconverted heretic should be driven away (*effugatur*).[165] Finally, Hildegard's caution that heretics should not be killed recalls in thought if not in wording the Abbot's condemnation of murder by mob action and his often quoted 'fides suadenda est, non imponenda'.[166]

Hildegard again comments on the *dominicum principium* in her *Explanation on the Athanasian Creed*. She expounds the late fourth- or early fifth-century creed, whose affirmations countered Arian beliefs, with a view to twelfth-century heresy. Hildegard presents her theology of history, beginning with the creation and moving to the early Church and the time of Athanasius's battle against Arianism.[167] Athanasius, in the *magistra*'s words, trampled (*conculcavit*) on Arius after being strengthened by John the Evangelist, who suckled (*suxit*) the breast of Jesus, flew on high (*in altum uolauit*), and composed the Gospel with the mystical breath of divinity (*in mystico spiramine de diuinitate*).[168] Hildegard paraphrases the Athanasian Creed and affirms that God alone created the world, but through the Word, as John the Evangelist states. The *magistra* asserts the theological inseparability of the *prima principia* and the *dominicum principium*. She proceeds through the beginning of John's Gospel, employing imagery and analogy of fire, with its indivisibility, and the wheel: the Father is eternal like a turning wheel with no beginning or end; the Son, co-eternal, is like the sun, whose rays are undiminished when they reach earth; the Holy Spirit inspired movement in creation.[169] Hildegard's thought and imagery of fire and wheel recall the metaphors of fire and water in the *Sermo: De peruersa hereticorum doctrina* and the *Liber diuinorum operum*, which she had completed in 1174.[170]

In the exhortation that follows the *Explanatio*, Hildegard accuses the *magistri et doctores* of blindness and deafness to the inner meaning of the Scriptures. Their teaching should convey the knowledge of Scripture, analogous to the rays of the

---

[164] Sermo 66.4, *SBOp*, II, 180. A search of Everwin's letter and Ekbert's *Sermones* (*PL* 195: 11–98) shows no occurrences of *uipereo* or *dente*.

[165] Sermo 64.8, *SBOp*, II, 170. A search of Everwin's letter and Ekbert's *Sermones* shows no occurrences of *effugo* or any of its forms.

[166] Sermo 66.12, *SBOp*, II, 187.

[167] *Expl. Symb.*, pp. 111–15.

[168] *Expl. Symb.*, p. 115, lines 175–82.

[169] *Expl. Symb.*, pp. 115–27.

[170] See Dronke, *LDO*, p. xii.

sun, in order to illumine the darkness of errant people: Sadducees, heretics, and others known to them. The *magistra* calls upon the *magistri et doctores* to ruminate on the Scripture and rend the darkness of the errant and faithless. She instructs the teachers specifically on what to teach: that God created heaven, earth, and other creatures for the human, placed the human in paradise, and gave him a commandment that he transgressed, after which he was expelled. That disobedience showed that the human obeyed Satan and not the Lord, whereas it is more righteous to obey the Lord than a deceitful servant. Hildegard appeals to the teachers of Scripture to disseminate these words and fill the hearts of the righteous with them like an iron rod (*in uirga ferrea*) that prevents them from turning away from the Creator and falling into hell with Satan. Further, she calls upon them to check the worldly appetites that result in their keeping barely one eye on heavenly teaching.[171]

These admonitions remain consistent with the teaching on creation that Hildegard directed against the Cathars and with her criticism of clerical conduct. She affirms that God created the material world; the heretics' assignment of that work to Satan implies, in her view, the worship and obedience of Satan. Moreover, the worldliness of the clergy provided fuel for Cathar criticism of the Roman Church and the heretics' stance on the unworthiness of corrupt clergy and the sacraments they performed.

The uir preliator

Hildegard's theology of creation and incarnation undergirds these various writings against heresy, an attack unified in theme and image. Against heretics who reject her theology of Christ as Creator and Redeemer, she poses the figure of the *uir preliator* (Is 42. 13). Hildegard apparently knew the passage and its scriptural context well and she developed its themes to the fullest. Isaiah 42 contains the first 'servant song' that Christian exegetes read typologically to point to Christ. The voice of God identifies his servant, who will bring justice to the nations (Is 42. 1–4). The passage proclaims the coming of the new and the passing of the old; it hails God as Creator, the source of life, and the illuminator of history, who will lighten the darkness, keep his covenant, and free prisoners (Is 42. 5–9). The song of praise (Is 42. 10–13) lauds the warrior as the mighty defender against evil.

While Christian exegesis has drawn extensively on Isaiah, this particular phrase appears to have had little resonance among patristic and medieval exegetes.

---

[171] *Expl. Symb.*, pp. 127–29, lines 511–69.

Interestingly, two of Hildegard's German predecessors evoke the image: Rupert of Deutz and the author of the *Speculum uirginum*. Rupert of Deutz, in his commentary on the Gospel of John, calls on the image dramatically in the poignant setting of Christ's appearance before Pilate. Addressing Pilate directly, the author warns him that he will be judged and found guilty by God and humanity. Rupert warns that the one then subject to Pilate's power will ultimately triumph over him and other enemies of the Lord. Rupert also alludes briefly to the *uir preliator* in his commentary on Joshua, in the context of the Lord's appearance to Moses. The *Speculum uirginum* adduces the image along with other phrases from Isaiah in the context of the explanation of divine fortitude.[172] Of these three parallels, Rupert's use of the *uir preliator* in the Johannine commentary proves the most striking. Moreover, the ironic juxtaposition of crucifixion and triumph that the image embodies calls to mind Hildegard's use of the Isaiah phrase in the *Ordo uirtutum*.

The *magistra* depicts a suffering but victorious Christ in the *Ordo uirtutum*. The *uir preliator* shows his wounds and appeals to all humans to reverence the Father and receive his outstretched hand.[173] No semantic parallels confirm that Hildegard was remembering Rupert of Deutz when she devised this scene; however, the similar juxtaposition of cross and victory is all the more striking in view of the apparently limited usage of the Isaiah passage in twelfth-century writings. Moreover, the overall study of Hildegard's sources includes possible reminiscences of her learned predecessor's commentary on John.[174]

---

[172] Isaiah 42. 13: 'Dominus sicut fortis egredietur sicut vir proeliator suscitabit zelum vociferabitur et clamabit super inimicos suos confortabitur.' Rupert of Deutz, *Commentaria in Euangelium Sancti Iohannis*, XIII, p. 735, lines 946–49: 'Dominus namque qui nunc infirmus sub tua potestate tenetur sicut fortis egredietur sicut uir praeliator suscitabit zelum uociferabitur et clamabit super te et super omnes inimicos suos confortabitur.' For *De sancta trinitate et operibus eius, In Iosue*, p. 1139, line 794, Rupert's source in Isaiah is not noted in the apparatus biblicus. 'Moysi namque apparuit dominus in flamma ignis de medio rubi huic autem tamquam uir proeliator stans et euaginatum gladium tenens unicuique iuxta rerum sequentium proprietatem figuras uel formas competentes praeostendens illi uidelicet splendida facturo miracula ignis apparuit ut iam dictum est uidi inquiens afflictionem populi mei in aegypto et clamorem eius audiui et descendi liberare eum huic mox cruenta bella facturo euaginatum gladium tenens apparet: princeps inquiens ego sum exercitus domini et nunc uenio.' The *Speculum uirginum* also adduces Isaiah 42. 13, 44. 7, 48. 13, and 11. 2, in the context of an explanation of divine fortitude. *Speculum uirginum*, ed. by Jutta Seyfarth, CCCM, 5 (Turnhout: Brepols, 1990), XI, p. 324, lines 342–43.

[173] For an outline of the *Ordo*, see Davidson, 'Music and Performance', pp. 8–9. Dronke analyzes themes and imagery in *Poetic Individuality in the Middle Ages*, pp. 167–79.

[174] For additional references, see the apparatus fontium, *Expo. Euang.*, pp. 586–87.

How does the image function in Hildegard's other works? The opening vision of the *Liber uitae meritorum* describes the figure of a man, superimposed on the universe; he looks in four directions and describes what he sees. Hildegard explains that the man, the *uir preliator*, represents God and Christ.[175] In the *Liber diuinorum operum*, Hildegard introduces the warrior in an eschatological theme: he opposed the Devil and all wickedness and will scrutinize the iniquities of her day — a clear allusion to Christ coming at the Judgement.[176] In the *Admonitio*, Hildegard affirms that God bestowed the capacity for praise on creation; that capacity evidences the goodness of creation. To defend that goodness and the Spirit's power to give life, the warrior (*signifer preliator*) of Isaiah 42. 13 opposes the enemies who appropriate what the Holy Spirit bestows by denying the Spirit's power.[177] Despite the human form of the warrior, who might be taken as Father and Son alone, Father, Son, and Spirit form an inseparable triad: Father and Son assert the Spirit's power to give life and to inspire the immutable Scriptures.[178] Hildegard again introduces the figure of the warrior in *Expositio* 26 on Luke 15. 11–32, the parable of the prodigal son. Near the end of the homily, she evokes the *uir preliator* as the champion over evil. He works within the human being to change an enemy into a friend and bad knowledge into good:

> Just as the warrior who overcomes the enemy; and the enemy will later be his friend out of necessity, because he will not be able to stand up to him and, therefore, the one vanquished by the army is to be praised.[179]

[175] *Vite mer.*, I, XX–XXI, p. 21, lines 373–79; XXII, p. 22, lines 405–07. The explanation extends through the remainder of the first book. *Vite mer.*, I, XXI, p. 21, lines 376–79 reads: 'Qui iuste uire nominatur: quoniam omnis uis et omnia que uiunt ab ipso procedunt. Ipse etiam uir ille est, de quo Propheta dicit: Dominus sicut fortis egredietur; sicut uir preliator suscitabit zelum. Vociferabitur et clamabit, super inimicos suos confortabitur.' See *Expo. Euang.*, 26, pp. 264–65, lines 109–13: 'Necesse est enim ut mala scientia ad bonum redeat, ubi omnia bona Patris laudantur, et magnificantur in omni creatura; sicut uir preliator qui superat inimicum, et inimicus postea erit amicus illius necessitate compulsus, quoniam ei resistere non poterit, et ideo uictus in milicia sua laudandus est.' *Ordo*, p. 521, lines 346–47: 'Et istud vir preliator vidit et dixit: Hoc scio, sed aureus numerus nondum est plenus.'

[176] *LDO*, III.5.12, p. 429, lines 1–12. She repeats the image later in the *LDO* (III.5.33, p. 457, lines 39–47), and refers herself to *Sciuias*.

[177] *Epistolarium*, III, 387, pp. 151–52, esp. lines 17–18: 'et instigatione eiusdem tyranni scriptura, et doctrinam, quam Spiritus Sanctus dictauit, destruunt'.

[178] *Epistolarium*, III, 387, p. 152, lines 19–20: 'uerba Spiritus Sancti mutari non possunt'.

[179] See *Expo. Euang.*, 26, p. 263, lines 76–79: 'Necesse est enim ut mala scientia ad bonum redeat, ubi omnia bona Patris laudantur, et magnificantur in omni creatura; sicut uir preliator qui

The warrior, like Hildegard's exegesis overall, reveals more than one sense of interpretation. The typological reading signals the Trinity, and more particularly, the warrior represents Christus Victor and centres the attack on heresy. On the individual and moral level, the warrior takes a part in Hildegard's tropological reading of the pericope as the story of an individual soul that falls away from God and returns restored.

Conclusion

Hildegard's datable writings issue from a climate of crisis, which mirrors the alarm that was discernable around twenty years earlier in the correspondence between Everwin of Steinfeld and Bernard of Clairvaux, a correspondence that Hildegard probably knew. At least three of Hildegard's texts were disseminated beyond her monastery, and it is not unreasonable to assume that the others were circulated for reading elsewhere. The two sermon/letters (Cologne and Kirchheim) both resulted from Hildegard's preaching in those cities. The Mainz treatise, intended for others to preach, was circulated at least in written form as was the Cologne sermon: Elisabeth of Schönau was familiar with the Mainz vision and Gebeno of Everbach included both texts in his *Pentachronon*. All the texts with anti-heretical content except those from the *Expositiones euangeliorum* begin with a visionary preface.

In several *Expositiones*, Hildegard grounds her arguments against heresy on exegesis of key biblical passages as she defends the theology of creation, incarnation, the Trinity, and the sacraments. The Cathars saw the material world as the product of Satan, and Hildegard joined with Bernard of Clairvaux, Everwin of Steinfeld, and Elisabeth and Ekbert of Schönau to write or preach against their heretical teaching. In various works, the *magistra* continues the line of argumentation that she sets forth in the 1163 Mainz treatise: the heretics reject the *prima principia*, God's creation of all things, and the *dominicum principium*, the eternity of the Word incarnate. The exegesis of the 'principial' texts of Genesis and John grounds the articulation of faith and denunciation of heresy in the *Explanationes*. The autobiographical narrative in the *Vita Hildegardis*, dated around 1170, explains that she received a vision in the form of sweet raindrops that clarified the meaning of John's Gospel.[180] In the *Liber diuinorum operum*, composed between 1163 and 1174, the

---

superat inimicum, et inimicus postea erit amicus illius necessitate compulsus, quoniam ei resistere non poterit, et ideo uictus in milicia sua laudandus est.'

[180] *V. Hild.*, II.16, pp. 66–67.

magistra exegetes both the first chapter of the fourth Gospel and the creation story in Genesis. The relationship between those texts remains key to the understanding of her theology and her opposition to Catharism. It touches the core of her belief in the goodness of the wondrous cosmos she described so brilliantly. Moreover, the harmony of the *prima principia* relates to Hildegard's creative work and moral responsibility. She states in the *Liber diuinorum operum* that the duty of teaching involves 'singing righteousness into the minds of humans through the voice of rationality', and that one who teaches, like the Word that sounds forth, ought to let her voice resound 'with love and fear of God', to 'gather the faithful and put the faithless to flight'.[181] The faithful teacher or preacher, therefore, mirrors God's creative Word and holds the moral responsibility to sound it forth.

Hildegard's writings against heresy prove integral to her exegetical, teaching, and preaching mission, but how do they compare to the works of her contemporaries? There are a few indications in the vocabulary Hildegard uses that she may have recalled the sermons of Bernard of Clairvaux, that is, at least held them 'in the back of her mind' when she wrote. Clearly the *magistra* demonstrates familiarity with the major theological and moral arguments against the Cathars, as put forth by Bernard, Everwin of Steinfeld, and Ekbert of Schönau. Elisabeth of Schönau also denounces Cathar beliefs: the denial of God's creation of the material world, of Christ's incarnation, and of the sacraments. Hildegard's appeal to the teachers of Scripture in the text linked with the *Explanation of the Athanasian Creed* echoes Elisabeth in tone and content: both women call the clergy to greater responsibility. However, Hildegard's attack on the Cathars reveals more breadth and more exegetical grounding than Elisabeth's.

The Hildegardian writings against heresy, particularly the two letters that convey material preached earlier, are significant for their witness to monastic preaching by a *magistra*, as well as to monastic preaching both outside the monastery and focused on the outside world, the external vineyard.[182] In the early twelfth century, Benedictines in Cologne held responsibility for the *cura animarum*, but their role

---

[181] I am grateful to Jess Michalik for his interpretation of this passage in *LDO*, III.2.10, pp. 367–68, lines 43–50: 'Qui autem per doctrinam omnipotentis Dei officium suum exercent alios docendo, fistulis sanctitatis resonant, cum per uocem racionalitatis iusticiam in mentes hominum canunt; sicut etiam uerbum dictat et sonus resonant, et ut per sonum uerbum auditur et circumdatur, quatinus audiri possit. Et ut per fistulam uox multiplicatur, ita in timore et amore Dei uox doctoris in hominibus multiplicari debet, ubi fideles congregat et infideles fugat.'

[182] On the rarity of references to the outside world in preserved texts, see Kienzle, 'Twelfth-Century Monastic Sermon', pp. 306–12.

was diminished as Augustinian houses were founded.[183] At mid-century, monks were not authorized to preach in public unless expressly commissioned.[184] Bernard of Clairvaux described a monk's desire to do so as a temptation: 'a deceitful fox, evil disguised as good'.[185] Furthermore, Hildegard's writings against heresy are more numerous than those of Bernard of Clairvaux. Indeed, from years of Cistercian involvement against heresy, very few texts remain from which to ascertain what was actually preached during the campaigns. From Bernard's tour of southern France, we have literary sermons, letters, and reports narrated by other people.[186] Hildegard's two sermons preserved as letters are probably closer to a real preaching event than those texts of Bernard's. The invective of Bernard's sermons, directed largely against immorality, employs dense biblical imagery; however, Hildegard's apocalyptic framework and bold language is stronger than Bernard's.[187] Her intensity brings to mind later texts written by Henry of Clairvaux or Geoffrey of Auxerre and contemporaneous with Joachim of Fiore.[188]

Hildegard's anti-heretical message must have persuaded certain clergy to allow her greater and bolder expression. During the schism, her Cologne sermon doubtless aided Philip of Heinsberg against his rivals whom Hildegard blamed for the growth of heresy. The supporters of Alexander III probably labelled Archbishop Philip as a

---

[183] On the controversy over Benedictine preaching and Rupert of Deutz's role, see Brunn, *Des contestataires aux 'cathares'*, pp. 94–97; Van Engen, *Rupert of Deutz*, pp. 326–30.

[184] On the prohibition against monks' preaching, see Giles Constable, 'The Second Crusade as Seen by Contemporaries', *Traditio*, 9 (1953), 213–79 (pp. 276–77). Constable explains that the right to preach was controlled by diocesan bishops and the pope. As greater numbers of monks entered holy orders in the late eleventh and twelfth centuries, controversy over their preaching was heated and Gratian's *Decretum* includes the restriction under the heading 'Nullus monachus preter Domini sacerdotes audeat praedicare' (*Corpus Iuris Canonici*, I, ed. by Aemilius Friedberg (Leipzig: Bernhard Tauchnitz, 1879): Decreti secunda pars, causa XVI, quest. I, c. 19 (cols 765–66), <http://mdz.bib-bvb.de/digbib/gratian/text/>).

[185] Sermo 64.3, *SBOp*, II, 168.

[186] Kienzle, *Cistercians, Heresy and Crusade*, pp. 78–108.

[187] Kerby-Fulton, *Reformist Apocalypticism*, pp. 27–31, signals the increasing radicalization of Hildegard's apocalyptic ideology later in her life as her disgust with the established Church intensified. Kerby-Fulton, pp. 39–40, also points out that the heretics Hildegard presents as types of the false prophets (II Tm 3) are not the false prophets themselves but their forerunners. Consequently their appearance announces what Kerby-Fulton terms the 'end of an era for the corrupt clergy', rather than the end of the world. Kerby-Fulton further observes that Hildegard uses the pseudo-prophets to fill a 'symbolic slot in apocalyptic theology'.

[188] Kienzle, *Cistercians, Heresy and Crusade*, pp. 205–06.

heretic for his support of the anti-pope.[189] Hildegard's decrial of heresy in Cologne and Philip's persecution of it undoubtedly deflected attention from the schism.

With respect to the hierarchy of Mainz, the last ten years of Hildegard's life were certainly not without conflict. Archbishops Arnold (1153–60) and Christian of Mainz (1165–83) supported Frederick I during the schism. After Arnold's murder (24 June 1160) as a result of the city's rebellion against him,[190] his successor, Conrad I (1162–65), remained loyal to the pope, refusing to recognize the antipope Paschal III at the Diet of Wurzburg (1165). However, the Emperor replaced Conrad with Christian of Buch, who supported the anti-pope and led forces against Alexander III, whose legitimacy Hildegard upheld.[191] Hildegard later faced her own problems with Archbishop Christian in 1178–79 over a deceased man to whom she had granted burial at Rupertsberg while the Mainz prelates claimed that he was still excommunicated. Hildegard refused to have the body exhumed and suffered gravely under the interdict, which was imposed on Rupertsbrg and lifted not long before her death.[192]

In the face of such conflict with Mainz and the vacillating relationship between the Emperor and the archbishops of Cologne, Hildegard walked a tightrope in her pronouncements on schism but found sound footing for her denunciations of heresy. It would seem that denouncement of heresy solidified the already established charismatic authority that Hildegard earned as a visionary theologian and exegete. Certainly Hildegard deserves recognition with Bernard of Clairvaux as one of the leading ecclesiastical figures of the twelfth century who participated in the Church's campaign against heresy. Her writings belong alongside those of Bernard, Everwin of Steinfeld, and Ekbert of Schönau as a significant source for studying the Cathar heresy and the Church's reaction against it.

---

[189] See Brunn, *Des contestataires aux 'cathares'*, pp. 254–56.

[190] Baird and Ehrmann point out that Arnold owed his position to Barbarossa's patronage and accompanied the Emperor on his campaign in Italy. *Letters*, I, 72, and text of Letters 20 (Arnold to Hildegard) and 20R (Hildegard's response), pp. 70–73. On Hildegard and the archbishops of Mainz, see also Van Engen, 'Letters and the Public Persona of Hildegard', pp. 379–418.

[191] On Christian of Buch, see Haverkamp, *Medieval Germany*, p. 277, and *Letters*, I, 21, 22, 22R, pp. 73–75; notes, p. 82.

[192] Flanagan, *Hildegard of Bingen*, pp. 17–18, 22–26. *Letters*, I, 23, 24, 24R, pp. 76–83.

AGING, AUTHORITY, AND EXEGESIS

Afterwards he rushes to the time of old age, so that his marrow is filled with all knowledge [...] the transformation of age imbues him such that he knows the truth.[1]

ildegard reflects on the ages of human life and human history in an 1170 epistolary sermon to Abbot Helenger of Disibodenberg. She explains that a child sucks his mother's milk, next eats soft food, then makes choices and chews what he wishes to eat. After reaching maturity, the human's *medulle*, the marrow of brain and bone, are filled with knowledge of the truth. The *magistra* extends her reflection from the generic human being to parallel analogies, historical and contemporary: first, Moses, a man full in years (*uir plene etatis*), who taught wisdom and truth; and second, her audience for this letter and its earlier oral version, the abbot and the monastery of St Disibod. She advises them to work obediently under the *Rule*, which stands as a clear parallel to the Law of Moses.[2]

What of Hildegard's last writings during the 1170s? Does the spiritual fullness of marrow ground a stronger sense of authority as the sap begins to age? Scholars have examined textual evidence, namely the letters and the prefatory pieces to the visionary works, to argue that Hildegard's voice grew more confident as she progressed in her public writing career. The claim to divine revelation as justification for writing becomes shorter and less elaborate. Moreover, various studies have considered indications of Hildegard's growing sense of authority, from the assertion of her public persona dating back to the 1147 council in Trier, to the growing

---

[1] *Epistolarium*, I, 77R, p. 170, lines 78–81: 'Et postea ad etatem senectutis currit, ita quod medulle ipsius omni scientia plene sunt, et deinde lac et duas priores etates non sentit, sed mutata etas ipsum imbuit, ita quod ueritatem cognoscit.'

[2] *Epistolarium*, I, 77R, p. 170, lines 83–87; p. 172, lines 155–59.

power and fluidity of her Latin style, to the increasing boldness of her exegesis, as reflected in the proportion of exegetical material in her three visionary works.

This concluding chapter begins by tracing the theme of age and fullness as it relates to Hildegard's visionary mandates from *Sciuias* onward to reveal the mysteries of Scripture and to proclaim the story of salvation history. The organic unity of Hildegard's thought and language is such that one could accent any one of a number of word-concepts, images, or themes and argue that it constitutes the crucial point for charting Hildegard's allegorical universe.[3] Throughout the *magistra*'s works, theology and image interconnect and provide a non-linear coherence that reaffirms messages central to Christian theology and to the roles of the Father, Son, and Holy Spirit throughout history. Hence a recap of the book's major points risks becoming a widening spiral. I shall limit myself to a few remarks on Hildegard's theology and method of exegesis and its place alongside the works of Bernard of Clairvaux and among writings composed for a female audience.

The Fullness of Marrow

The seer, when full in years like Moses, apparently felt more confident in her teaching of wisdom and truth. Hildegard already employs the word *medulla* numerous times in *Sciuias*, notably in the *Protestificatio* when she describes the physical suffering that resulted from not revealing the understanding of Scripture; she had reached the age of forty-three and advanced from girlhood to fullness of fortitude. The *medulla* aches with hermeneutical pain. Similarly and nearly thirty years later in the *Vita Hildegardis*, the *magistra* describes her state before and after composing the *Vita Disibodi* in terms of blood and marrow, withered and then restored.[4]

In the early part of *Sciuias*, *medulla* proves a key image when the Voice of God calls upon Hildegard to speak what she sees, because the learned who see the *medullam* of sacred letters do not preach it. Instead they regard the preservation of righteousness with lukewarmness and dullness, and they timidly conceal the divine mysteries in a hidden field. Hildegard must unlock the enclosure for these mysteries.[5] Similarly the seer refers to the *medulla* of the Law as the core that was

---

[3] I am grateful to Kenneth Oliff for suggesting the concept of organic unity versus linear arrangement to describe Hildegard's thought.

[4] *V. Hild.*, III.24, p. 67, lines 16–17: 'atque uene cum sanguine, ossa cum medullis in me reparata sunt, quasi de morte suscitata fuissem'; *Life of Hildegard*, p. 93.

[5] *Sciuias*, p. 5, line 60: 'Ipse enim in medullis et in uenis carnis suae doluit, constrictum animum et sensum habens atque multam passionem corporis sustinens, ita quod in eo diuersa securitas non

transformed into the Gospel, like water into wine.[6] The transformable and trans-
formative potential of *medulla* appears also in imagery likening humans and trees;
medulla is part of the life-constituting sap that makes trees grow, while in the
human it receives the pouring out of God's wisdom and brings spiritual growth:
the greenness of the marrow and the veins and all the members of the body.[7]
Clearly then the motif of *medulla* provides a nexus for themes of age, authority,
and scriptural interpretation. The *medulla* represents the hidden, inner spiritual
meaning of Scripture as well as the place in the human body where God infuses
revelation and which feels pain from not revealing the understanding that results
from the visionary infusion. *Medulla* also takes on a monastic context: obedience
to the monastic rule as to God's law promotes spiritual growth.

During the tumult of the 1170s, when the pro-imperial Archbishop Christian
of Buch ruled in Mainz, Hildegard completed the *Liber diuinorum operum* and
other key works where she asserts her exegetical confidence. Moreover, the *magistra* wrote herself into the *Liber diuinorum operum* in order to legitimate her earlier
work. In a skilful literary manoeuvre, she has *Caritas* speak in Book III (Vision 3,
Chapter 2) to affirm the authority of her spokesperson: 'and from this shadow the
book *Sciuias* came forth by means of a woman who was herself a shadow of health
and strength, because these forces were lacking in her'.[8] Hildegard takes up the
theme of age, marked by changes in marrow, in a letter from around 1170

---

latuit, sed in omnibus causis suis se culpabilem aestimauit.' *Sciuias*, I.1, pp. 7–8, lines 30–37: 'Et ecce
idem qui super montem illum sedebat fortissima et acutissima uoce clamabat dicens: "O homo,
quae fragilis es de puluere terrae et cinis de cinere, clama et dic de introitu incorruptae saluationis,
quatenus hi erudiantur qui medullam litterarum uidentes eam nec dicere nec praedicare uolunt,
quia tepidi et hebetes ad conseruandam iustitiam Dei sunt, quibus clausuram mysticorum resera
quam ipsi timidi in abscondito agro sine fructu celant."'

[6] *Sciuias*, III.11.24, p. 589, lines 487–93: 'Quid tunc? Ipse enim ueniens medullam legis aperuit,
ubi aquam legis in uinum euangelii conuertit, ubi et maxima fluenta uirtutum emanare fecit, quod
tam tempestiue ueniens compleuit, ut ecclesiasticae uirtutes quas Spiritus sanctus incendit firmis
radicibus in hominibus confortarentur, et ut uirginitas quam in semetipso attulit dignissima
germina florum suorum dilatare posset.'

[7] *Sciuias*, I.4.16, p. 78, lines 579–85: 'et etiam cerebrum hominis tangit: quia in uiribus suis non
solum terrena sed etiam caelestia sapit, cum Deum sapienter cognoscit; ac se per omnia membra
hominis transfundit, quoniam uiriditatem medullarum ac uenarum et omnium membrorum toti
corpori tribuit, uelut arbor ex sua radice sucum et uiriditatem omnibus ramis dat'. *Symph.*, 49, 'O
Ierusalem', p. 437, 4a, lines 23–26: 'O tener flos campi | et o dulcis uiriditas pomi | et o sarcina sine
medulla, | que non flectit pectora in crimina.'

[8] *LDO*, III.3.2, p. 380, lines 25–27: 'De umbra hac scriptura Sciuias processit per formam
mulieris, quê uelut umbra fortitudinis et sanitatis erat, quoniam uires istê in ea non operabantur.'

concerning the *Liber diuinorum operum*.[9] The imagery of the fullness of marrow serves to ground Hildegard's praise of Ludwig of Trier: he has the necessary wisdom for undertaking the important task of correcting her work.[10]

It was also in the 1170s that Hildegard began organizing the writing of her *uita*,[11] and composed the *Life of St Disibod*, the *Solutiones*, and the *Explanation on the Athanasian Creed*.[12] The *Vita Disibodi* follows the thematic course of her other works with a discourse on the creation, the proper order of creatures, sin, and repentance with the aid of the Holy Spirit.[13] Themes of salvation history from Genesis to John dominate the *Solutiones*.[14] Thirteen of the thirty-two solutions concern Genesis; one explicates the Johannine theme of procession and return and relates back to Genesis.[15] A few comment on Adam's loss of spiritual vision at the Fall — a theme that joins Hildegard's discussion elsewhere of Adam's loss of voice and the infusion of soul into his marrow at the creation.[16] In the *Explanation on the Athanasian Creed*, Hildegard addresses the sorrow of her daughters at her coming death. As she prays for the Holy Spirit to guide them and preserve them from quarrels when they have lost her voice, she looks back to the Spirit's infusion at the creation. God, wisdom and artisan (*faber*), instilled the soul into the veins and marrow of human flesh.[17] Hildegard employs a similar image in the *Cause et cure*: the breath of life (*spiraculum uitae*) enlivens the soul.[18] From the composition of

---

[9] *Epistolarium*, II, 215, 217, pp. 474, 476–78 (p. 477); *Letters*, II, 196–97, 198–99.

[10] See *LDO*, pp. lxxxvi–xcvii.

[11] *Jutta and Hildegard*, trans. by Silvas, p. 122.

[12] *Epistolarium*, I, 77, 77R, pp. 166–75; *V. Disib.*, *PL* 197: 1093–1116.

[13] *V. Disib.*, *PL* 197: 1109–10.

[14] On the text, see Bartlett, 'Commentary, Polemic and Prophecy', pp. 153–65; and on the genre, see Häring, 'Commentary and Hermeneutics', p. 177.

[15] *Quaestiones* I, II, IV, V, VI, VII, VIII, IX, X, XXV, XXVIII, XXIX, XXXVI; XXIII on procession and return (John 8 and 15).

[16] *Solut.*, I–VI, *PL* 197: 1040B–1042, on the creation story.

[17] *Expl. Symb.*, p. 111, lines 64–71: 'Unde et sapientia faber recte dici potest, quoniam coelum et terram circuiuit, et aequali pondere ponderauit. Caro autem hominis, cum anima in uenis et medullis pleniter perfusa est, ita ut caro per animam semper suscitetur; et quia etiam homo creaturas per animam cognoscit, ipsas in iucunditate et gaudio habet. Sic namque homo in carne et anima uelut de misericordia et charitate amabilis est, quemadmodum sapientia et charitas unum sunt.' See *Expl. Atha.*, p. 8. *Epistolarium*, II, 195R, pp. 445–47; *Letters*, II, 169–71.

[18] *Cause*, p. 71, lines 16–22: 'Et cum deus spiraculum uite in eum misit, material eius, que ossa et medulla ac uene sunt, per idem spiraculum confortata sunt; et illud in eandem massam ita se

Sciuias to the 1170 letter to Abbot Helenger, the relationship between age, authority, and scriptural understanding remains clear in Hildegard's works.

Do other texts from the 1170s reflect Hildegard's confidence in her exegetical knowledge? Two letters with a salvation-historical framework date from the last four or so years of Hildegard's life. In one, dated around 1175–77, Hildegard advises Philip, Count of Flanders, before he embarks on crusade to Jerusalem. Two events of salvation history constitute the letter's theological framework: Adam's sin and Christ's redemption. Hildegard urges Philip to repent of his sins and not to kill unjustly. However, if the infidels attempt to destroy the 'fountain of faith', then Philip should, in the *magistra*'s words, 'resist as much as he can'.[19] The cross takes on powerful meaning as the locus of Christ's suffering, the symbol of what the Count will protect as well as the emblem that will safeguard him and ensure that his sins will be forgiven when he dies.

A well-known letter (23) deals with the interdict imposed on Hildegard's monastery in 1178–79.[20] The seer boldly asserts that God implanted the authorizing vision for the letter in her soul before her birth. Her comprehension of Adam's transgression in the plan of salvation history grounds her determination of what constitutes obedience and disobedience. Adam disobeyed and lost the divine voice of Spirit that he shared with the angels. God, however, renews the hearts of the elect whom he commands to praise him with music. Voices and instruments aid the restoration of the soul to its heavenly condition, and the ability to hear the celestial symphony becomes manifest when the community sings.[21] The prelates

---

distinxit, ut uermis in domum suam se intorquet et ut uiriditas in arbore est; et etiam ita confortata sunt, ut argentum in alium modum fit, cum illud faber in ignem proicit; et sic in corde eius sedit. Tunc etiam in eadem massa de igne anime caro et sanguis facta sunt.'

[19] *Epistolarium*, III, 324R, pp. 83–84; *Letters*, III, 122. See Miriam Rita Tessera, 'Philip Count of Flanders and Hildegard of Bingen: Crusading against the Saracens or Crusading against Deadly Sin?', in *Gendering the Crusades*, ed. by Susan B. Edgington and Sarah Lambert (New York: Columbia University Press, 2002), pp. 77–93.

[20] *Epistolarium*, I, 23, pp. 61–66; *Letters*, I, 76–83. See the detailed study of Wolfgang Felix Schmitt, 'Charisma gegen Recht? Der Konflikt der Hildegard von Bingen mit dem Mainzer Domkapitel 1178/79 in kirchenrechtsgeschichtlicher Perspektive', in *Hildegard von Bingen 1098–1998*, special issue, *Binger Geschichtsblätter*, 20 (1998), 124–59. On Hildegard and the archbishops of Mainz, see also Van Engen, 'Letters and the Public Persona of Hildegard'; Flanagan, *Hildegard of Bingen*, pp. 17–18, 22–26.

[21] See Stephen D'Evelyn, 'Heaven as Performance and Participation in the *Symphonia armonie celestium revelationum* of Hildegard of Bingen', in *Envisaging Heaven in the Middle Ages*, ed. by Putter and Muessig, pp. 155–65.

who prohibit singing endanger their souls. It is they who are truly disobedient to God's command. Within the frame of her defiance, Hildegard defines herself as obedient while showing that the interdict disobeys God's order. Likewise, she asserts that the Eucharist, which she and her sisters had been denied, is necessary for cleansing from sin and for sanctification of the body. In this perhaps last letter, Hildegard's voice resounds strongly, confident in her decision not to obey the prelates' order to disinter the body and in her assertion of their disobedience, not hers, to God's law.

Hildegard's writings of the 1170s reveal a confident teacher who speaks from a broad comprehension of Scripture. The understanding of Genesis — creation and transgression — contributed to strengthening Hildegard's confidence in her authority as an exegete. The image of marrow unifies the themes of salvation history with the progress of human life and wisdom, and the seer's own aging. In numerous shorter works from the last decade of her life, Hildegard offered instruction on Scripture and the sacrament of the altar, and she addressed the problems of her day, articulating the tenets of faith, and denouncing heresy and clerical laxity. To use her own terminology, she attained the fullness of confident wisdom that began over forty years earlier with the infusion of scriptural understanding into the marrow of her body and soul. When the marrow withered in death, her merit showed forth in the miracles attested by her nuns and included in the *Acta inquisitionis*.[22]

Hildegard's Theology and Method of Exegesis

Hildegard received a solid monastic schooling, which she absorbed along with the pedagogical approach of glosses on Psalms, hymns, and sequences. The seer adapted those brilliantly to create a novel method of biblical commentary. First educated in the monastery, she embarked on an auto-didactic course of continuing education that produced dazzlingly creative results. The *magistra* imbibed her theology of exegesis as well as her knowledge of patristic commentaries from the Benedictine liturgy and the intellectual exchange that occurred through conversations and written texts. Hildegard employed various types of glosses and incorporated them into a continuous and largely coherent narrative that reveals the structural and dialogic characteristics of drama: a dramatic narrative exegesis. This sense of drama accords with the *magistra*'s preference for the allegorical and especially the tropological

---

[22] *Acta inquisitionis*, ed. by Bruder.

sense of Scripture over the literal. The *Glossa Hildegardiana*, the incorporation of glossing into narrative, differs substantially in form from the usual practice of marginal and interlinear glossing and from nearly all other contemporary commentary on the Gospels. Moreover, the seer enhances the dramatic features of her narratives with the development and extension of the voice of biblical characters in her own words: the *Vox Hildegardiana*. Among her contemporaries, only Bernard of Clairvaux, to my knowledge, approaches her genius for exegetical storytelling.

Hildegard's method of exegesis reflects Origen's theology of the transformation of Scripture through spiritual interpretation and the role of the Spirit and even the Trinity in the authorship of the Scriptures. For Hildegard, exegetical technique and theology of exegesis are indivisible. The *magistra* emphasizes the continuity of history in visions that stretch from creation to the patriarchs and prophets to the incarnation and the Gospel. Jesus transformed the old law into the new, and the doctors of the Sacred Scripture interpreted the old law spiritually in order to continue that transformation. In the era of grace, the Holy Spirit guides the soul and assists it with the aid of virtues in performing good works. The process of exegesis continually reaffirms the message of grace; every passage of the Gospel that Hildegard exegetes points to some aspect if not the whole of salvation history.

Hildegard's theology of salvation history finds its roots in Augustine. The great Bishop influenced Hildegard's contemporaries as well, notably Rupert of Deutz, who stands as the foremost precedent for visionary exegesis in her cultural *milieu*. In *De sancta trinitate et operibus eius*, Rupert presented the mystery of the Trinity through the works particular to Father, Son, and Holy Spirit: the creation, redemption, and renovation. Furthermore, Rupert saw the Spirit's work in history as manifest in three ages: creation to the Fall; the Fall to the passion of Christ; the resurrection to the end of time and the general resurrection. Although Hildegard does not follow Rupert strictly on these points, his general influence on her thought seems undeniable. Hildegard's Trinitarian reading of texts compares with the threefold and Trinitarian themes of her visionary trilogy. Various homilies deal with three acts of salvation history: the time from creation to incarnation; the role of Christ as Redeemer; and the work of the Spirit in contemporary time.

Hildegard's theology of the Trinity in the text and illustrations of *Sciuias* and the *Liber diuinorum operum* sheds light on her thought and method in the *Expositiones*. As Bernard McGinn asserts, Hildegard was fascinated with 'the economic Trinity, that is, the Trinity revealed in history', but she had 'little interest in the inner life of the Trinity'.[23] This same concept of the 'economic Trinity' dominates the *Expositiones*. Moreover, for Hildegard the Trinity's revelation in history extends to the cosmos. The figure of the Creator, Father and Son as one, animates the unity of the cosmos and the hope of cosmic redemption. Hildegard represents the unity of Father and Son and of the Trinity with a rich use of visual image, metaphor, and expansion of semantic field.

Admonitions Outside and Inside the Monastery

Hildegard's opposition to heresy unifies certain writings from 1163 onwards and stems from the exegetical visions that drive her interpretation of the 'principial' texts. The notions of *prima principia* and *dominicum principium* undergird the *magistra*'s theology and rest upon her exegesis of Genesis 1 and John 1. Hildegard asserts that the heretics reject the teaching of both Genesis 1, God's creation of all things, and John 1, the eternity of the Word incarnate. In the 1163 Mainz treatise, she states that the heretics deny the *prima principia*, the basis of Genesis 1: 'God created all things and ordered that they come forth by germinating and growing.' Moreover, they spurn the *dominicum principium*, the Lord's beginning, as spoken in John 1: 'He appeared before the ancientness of days; the Word of God was to become human.'[24] Hildegard devotes one lengthy homily to John 1. 1–14 and treats the opening of the fourth Gospel in the *Liber diuinorum operum* and a brief *meditatio* as well.[25] Hildegard's interpretation of John 1 in the *Expositiones* corresponds to her commentary in the *Liber diuinorum operum*: she accents the presence of the Word — logos, rationality, Son of God — at the creation.[26] In the *Vita Hildegardis*, she recounts how the vision of John the Evangelist compelled her to 'explore every statement and word of this Gospel regarding the beginning of the work of God', and she indicates the connection between John 1 and Genesis 1: 'I

---

[23] McGinn, 'Theologians as Trinitarian Iconographers', pp. 187–95.

[24] *Epistolarium*, II, 169R, p. 381, lines 81–90, esp. lines 82–86. Ekbert of Schönau devotes Sermon 6, *PL* 195: 40–41, to the creation (third heresy, according to Ekbert's list), alluding at the opening to Genesis 1 and John 1. Sermon 12, *PL* 195: 94–96, concerns the humanity of the Saviour (ninth heresy).

[25] The *meditatio* is in *Epistolarium*, III, 374, p. 130.

[26] On *rationalitas* in Hildegard's works, see Chávez-Alvarez, *'Die brennende Vernunft'*, and on rationality in the *Liber uitae meritorum*, see Meis, *'Symphonia Spiritus Sancti'*, pp. 391, 424.

saw that the same explanation must apply to the beginning of the other Scripture which was not yet revealed.'[27]

It is significant but not altogether surprising that Hildegard introduces her anti-Cathar views into monastic homilies. Her preaching against the Cathars from the scriptural base of John 1 and Genesis 1 calls to mind Augustine's preaching about John 1 and looking over his shoulder at the Donatists, or the exegesis of Genesis that he directed against the Manicheans. In twelfth-century monastic writings, there is a discernable pattern for the relationship of genre and content: homilies and sermons tend to offer material for meditation instead of commenting on events of the world or entering into polemics. Liturgical sermons characteristically do not view the events of the outside world. Bernard of Clairvaux revised his liturgical sermons to exclude references to happenings outside the monastery.[28] In contrast, exegetical treatises may reflect the events of the day and letters certainly do. Bernard railed against heresy in several of his *Sermons on the Song*; in his letters, his voice engaged fully and at times vehemently in contemporary issues. The sermons he and other twelfth- and early thirteenth-century Cistercians preached against heresy have not, for the most part, been preserved. From Bernard's tour of southern France, we have letters and reports narrated by other people.[29] Overall, very few texts remain from years of Cistercian involvement against heresy that allow us to ascertain what was actually preached during the campaigns.

Hildegard's denunciation of heresy enters into only a few *Expositiones*, which keeps with the pattern of twelfth-century liturgical sermons to focus on the inner life. Her strongest attacks on heresy are tied to preaching but are preserved in letters, a *sermo* and an *admonitio*. The two letters of Hildegard that convey material preached earlier are, therefore, significant not only for their evidence of preaching by a *magistra*, but also for their witness to monastic preaching that took place outside the home monastery and that focused on the outside world.[30] Hildegard's two sermons preserved as letters constitute important parallels to the letters of Bernard addressing heresy in southern France. Moreover, Hildegard's texts may even stand closer to the real preaching event than Bernard's letters. Furthermore, Hildegard's

---

[27] *Life of Hildegard*, pp. 61, 67.

[28] Kienzle, 'Twelfth-Century Monastic Sermon', pp. 310–12.

[29] Kienzle, *Cistercians, Heresy and Crusade*, pp. 78–108.

[30] On the rarity of references to the outside world in preserved texts, see Kienzle, 'Twelfth-Century Monastic Sermon', pp. 306–12.

writings against popular heresy outnumber Bernard's.[31] Bernard's invective, directed largely against immorality, employs dense biblical imagery and skilled figures of speech. However, Hildegard's language surpasses Bernard's in intensity by virtue of its apocalypticism and boldness. Her writing brings to mind later texts written by Henry of Clairvaux or Geoffrey of Auxerre and contemporaneous with Joachim of Fiore.[32]

As interesting as Hildegard's anti-heretical writings are, the majority of her *Expositiones* belong to the predominant mode of monastic preaching that focuses on the inner life. Monastic spirituality, as articulated in the *Rule of Benedict*, itself a work of exegesis and a guide for lived exegesis, inspires and unifies the *Expositiones* and the other writings and lyrics. Hildegard emphasizes the implementation of good works in the continuing human drama — a process that begins with the rationality endowed by the Creator, restored by the Redeemer, and illumined by the Spirit with the aid of the virtues. Nearly one-half of the *Expositiones* deal with some aspect of the soul's inner struggle, a consistent theme in monastic literature that derives from Origen's use of Platonism. In those homilies, Hildegard shares the monastic predilection for interpreting Scripture according to the tropological sense. Exegesis and practice go hand in hand: the interpretation of the Gospel is not merely an intellectual exercise; it encompasses a whole way of life. When Hildegard focuses on the interior struggle of monastic observance, she expounds the gospel texts in such a way as to create dramatic readings that engage the virtues and vices in conflict and dialogue. The tropological readings of Scripture instruct her audience on how to live according to the ideals of the Benedictine *Rule*. The *magistra* stresses the key virtues of humility, charity, and obedience. Several homilies, such as those on Luke 16. 1–9 and Matthew 20. 1–16, emphasize the importance of obedience to a superior, whether Adam to the Creator or the other creatures to Adam.

Hildegard's *Expositiones* again merit comparison with the writings of Bernard of Clairvaux, notably the sermons where he addresses specific behaviours that hinder progress in observance of the *Rule*. He warns against vices such as aloofness or singularity, false humility, envy. His self-reflection focuses on his responsibilities as abbot.[33] In the *Expositiones*, Hildegard does not identify herself as the superior

---

[31] Kienzle, *Cistercians, Heresy and Crusade*, pp. 78–108.

[32] Kienzle, *Cistercians, Heresy and Crusade*, pp. 205–06.

[33] See Beverly Mayne Kienzle, '*Verbum Dei et Verba Bernardi*: The Function of Language in Bernard's Second Sermon for Peter and Paul', in *Bernardus Magister: Papers Celebrating the*

as Bernard does in his sermons. Nonetheless, the *magistra*'s voice of responsibility carried over into the homilies, even if she does not make her duty as explicit as Bernard does in reflections on his abbatial responsibilities. It is likely that Bernard's obligation as abbot moved him to reflect on his office and to reproach his monks in a more deliberate way than Hildegard did as a *magistra* subject to the rule of an abbot. Bernard's sermons often take an eschatological turn, which derives in part from his responsibility for the souls of his monks at the Judgement. The relative absence or weaker presence of such a theme in Hildegard's *Expositiones* may again reflect the different weight of responsibility and authority that each bore.[34]

The Expositiones *and Works for a Female Audience*

Hildegard must have felt 'at home' in the exegesis she develops in the *Expositiones* and felt no need to preface them with a claim for visionary authority. One may wonder if they were not intended for wider circulation. They were copied in the Riesenkodex and stand beside other works that both circulated and included a visionary preface. The lack of an opening vision for the *Expositiones* most likely indicates that Hildegard uttered her interpretations comfortably at Rupertsberg in the accustomed venue of the chapter house and wrote or oversaw the writing of the *Expositiones* for the same audience. Her authority there needed no reinforcement of its visionary derivation. Four of the homilies indicate that she possibly did the same at Disibodenberg. A glance back at the homilies from Admont recalls the multi-part structure that reflects the responsibility and approach of a male preacher who had the duty of placing the gospel reading in its Eucharistic context. The preacher's introductory preface on the profundities of Scripture corresponds to some degree to the visionary prefaces with which Hildegard opened her more 'public' writing in treatises and letters. In the *Expositiones*, she felt no such obligation. Within the bounds of her leadership of a women's community, she aimed to enrich the Divine Office with her homiletic, hagiographic, and musical compositions. Hildegard had moved to her own monastery, and the male provost was her secretary.

Nonacentenary of the Birth of Bernard of Clairvaux, ed. by John R. Sommerfeldt (Kalamazoo: Cistercian Publications, 1992), pp. 149–59.

[34] See the previous note and pp. 151–54 above, and Kienzle, 'Twelfth-Century Monastic Sermon'. I am grateful to the students in my fall 2006 course, especially Matthew Cressler, for raising this question.

To what extent do the *Expositiones*, a work composed by a woman largely for women, speak to a gendered audience? Most of the homilies address souls, both male and female, calling them to conversion of life and advising them on the struggles of living under the Benedictine *Rule*. Nonetheless, the concerns of a female audience appear in Hildegard's praises for the ideal of virginity. In that regard, the 'domestic' focus of the *Expositiones* joins them to the *Ordo uirtutum* and its drama of the soul. The accent on virginity ties the *Expositiones* to other twelfth-century works written for a female audience. The *Speculum uirginum*, a guide in the form of dialogue and illustration, incorporates extensive verbal imagery from the Song of Songs and includes illustrations of the virtues and vices that follow traditional models for text and image more closely than Hildegard does.[35] The Anglo-Norman cultural milieu, which lies outside the scope of this volume, provided substantial literature for women in the religious life. Much of it was written by men for female audiences and accented the themes of virginity and chastity.[36] Finally, the *Hortus deliciarum* of Herrad of Hohenbourg, written by a woman for a female audience, provides a manual for religious women. Its introductory poem accents the theme of chastity, but the wide-ranging *Hortus* contains more than eleven hundred excerpts from various authors, which Herrad identified for the most part and described as the 'diverse flowers of Sacred Scripture and philosophical writings'.[37]

The *Expositiones* stand apart from Hildegard's visionary texts and their more evident accent on the female and the feminine. The figure of Wisdom, which plays a key role in the visionary works, occupies only a minor part in the *Expositiones*. The same can be said for the Virgin Mary and for Eve. Instead, the *Expositiones* reveal both an experiential monastic theology and a theology of exegesis in which all persons of the Trinity play a role: God the Creator resounds from Genesis through the Gospels; Christ, Redeemer and Creator, occupies the central place through the gospel text; the Holy Spirit guides the human along the path to salvation. Hildegard echoes the creative Word, teaches the message of redemption, and instructs on the virtues necessary for the religious life. The traditional themes and practice of monastic homilies on the Gospels undergird the innovative method of Hildegard's exegesis.

---

[35] See the fine essays in *Listen Daughter*, ed. by Mews, and Figs 2 and 3 in the same volume.

[36] See Vera Morton, trans., and Jocelyn Wogan-Browne, *Guidance for Women in Twelfth-Century Convents* (Woodbridge: Boydell and Brewer, 2003).

[37] I am grateful to Fiona Griffiths's observation (in personal correspondence) that the excerpts in the *Hortus* are not 'by and large gender specific'.

Nonetheless, the *magistra*'s status as a self-taught woman allows her freedom of creativity. The visionary texts and letters draw the authoritative parameters for the exegesis, teaching, and preaching that Hildegard implements in the *Expositiones*: the voice of God authorizes 'a person in female form', 'a person not versed in the Scriptures and not instructed by an earthly teacher' to 'speak new secrets' and 'many deep meanings', to 'sing righteousness into human hearts'.[38] The *Expositiones* are, therefore, feminine exegesis directed primarily to a female audience but extending to multiple audiences. They are remarkable for their authorship by a medieval woman and for the extraordinary exegesis Hildegard developed to instruct her sisters about personal *conuersio* (conversion) and *conuersatio* (way of life). That message encompasses each soul, including her own, the entire community of her sisters, all of humankind, and the cosmos. Hildegard's concept of exegesis and her performance of it encompass a blending of voices — teaching, preaching, and song — in a symphonious harmony that conveys and mirrors the sound of the creative Word.

---

[38] *Epistolarium*, III, 280, p. 33; *Sciuias*, III.11, p. 586, lines 379–91; *LDO*, III.2.10, pp. 367–68, lines 43–45.

REVIEW OF RELEVANT SCHOLARSHIP

ildegardian studies extend across various fields, including theology, history, literature, spirituality, history of art, medicine, and music. A review of scholarship relevant to the *Expositiones euangeliorum* will prove useful for readers who may be entering the field through the present volume. Studies of Hildegard's works have focused, for the most part, on her visionary writings and to a lesser degree her letters, as the critical editions and translations have become available. Moreover, beyond the editions of the visionary works, there has been little discussion of the *magistra*'s use of sources. The translation by P. S. Holdener, *Auslegung einiger Evangelien*, made the homilies more accessible to German-speaking readers.[1] Important studies of Hildegard's works incorporate references to the *Expositiones*, but scholars' access to the texts was limited by the absence of a critical edition. The new edition of the *Expositiones euangeliorum* joins the editions of the *Ordo uirtutum*, the *Symphonia*, the *Explanation on the Athanasian Creed*, and the *Explanation on the Rule of St Benedict*, in a volume that brings together texts that relate to various dimensions of the liturgy at Rupertsberg.

Paleographical analysis was once necessary to dispel doubts about the authenticity of Hildegard's writings. It continues to prove essential for appreciating the seer's view of authorship, her process of composition, the extent of collaboration with her secretaries, and the production of manuscripts at Rupertsberg. Hans Liebeschütz initiated the study of the manuscripts of Hildegard's writings in his *Das allegorische Weltbild der heiligen Hildegard von Bingen* in 1930.[2] They have

---

[1] *Auslegung einiger Evangelien: Explanationes quorumdam Evangeliorum*, trans. by P. S. Holdener (Landshut, 1997).

[2] Hans Liebeschütz, *Das allegorische Weltbild*; Dronke, 'Allegorical World Picture of Hildegard of Bingen', pp. 1–14.

since been the subject of painstaking paleographical and codicological analysis, grounded with the volume of Marianna Schrader and Adelgundis Führkotter: *Die Echtheit des Schrifttums der Heiligen Hildegard von Bingen. Quellenkritische Untersuchungen* (1956). Führkotter and Angela Carlevaris extended the findings of *Die Echtheit* in the critical editions of *Sciuias* and *Liber uitae meritorum*. For the *Hildegardis Epistolarium*, Monika Klaes added the third volume to the preceding two edited by Lieven van Acker. Albert Derolez and Peter Dronke made an extensive study of the manuscripts for the edition of the *Liber diuinorum operum*. Franz Staab's edition of the *Vita Juttae* contributed to the elucidation of Hildegard's early years and the culture of female religious life.[3]

Hans Liebeschütz in his pioneering work, *Das allegorische Weltbild der heiligen Hildegard von Bingen*, established that allegory constitutes far more than a literary device for Hildegard; it lies at the core of her view of the world. Liebeschütz placed Hildegard in the line of visionary Old Testament prophets and of *The Shepherd* of Hermas, who received the divine revelation both of images and their interpretation. In her writings and didactic visions, or *Lehrvisionen*, the tradition of teaching allegory in the schools converges with the tradition of the unlearned saints such as the desert fathers. In addition, Liebeschütz recognized the extensive use of allegory among Hildegard's contemporaries as well as their recourse to the theme of microcosm and macrocosm. He signalled other major motifs of the seer's visionary works, such as building imagery and virtues and vices. He also recognized that Hildegard possessed a wealth of learning, whose sources he began to uncover, and that her awareness of the erudition in her works motivated her to portray herself as one who was taught only by divine inspiration. Moreover, Liebeschütz maintained that Hildegard's use of knowledge, literary methods, and theological themes that were prevalent in the twelfth century remained distinctive and at the same time essential to her image of the world.[4]

The scholarship of Peter Dronke not only extended and corrected Liebeschütz's findings but called the attention of English-speaking readers to Hildegard among

---

[3] *Vita domnae Juttae inclusae*, ed. by Franz Staab, in 'Reform und Reformgruppen in Erzbistum Mainz: Vom *Libellus de Willigisi consuetudinibus* zur *Vita domnae Juttae inclusae*', in *Reformidee und Reformpolitik im Spätsalisch-Frühstaufischen Reich: Vorträge der Tagung der Gesellschaft für Mittelrheinische Kirchengeschichte vom 11. bis 13. September 1991 in Trier*, ed. by Stefan Weinfurter, Quellen und Abhandlungen zur Mittelrheinische Geschichte, 68 (Mainz: Selbstverlag der Gesellschaft für Mittelrheinische Kirchengeschichte, 1992), pp. 119–87, Appendix II, pp. 172–87.

[4] Liebeschütz, *Das allegorische Weltbild*, pp. 20–30, 35–38, 86–106 (Der Kosmosmensch), pp. 111–16.

other *Women Writers of the Middle Ages*, to borrow the title of Dronke's 1984 book. Dronke's 1992 article on the *Expositiones*, 'Platonic-Christian Allegories in the Homilies of Hildegard of Bingen', proposes the distinctions of microcosmic or psychological interpretations, and macrocosmic or cosmological.[5] Dronke includes in 'Platonic-Christian Allegories' the early fruits of his research on Hildegard's sources in the *Liber diuinorum operum*. He uncovers hints of her interpretations from earlier texts and verifies the list of works against the holdings of libraries near Rupertsberg. He asserts that Hildegard 'constructs fables of the creation of the world and of mankind, in the fabulatory mode that she knew from the Chalcidian *Timaeus*'; and she 'constructs fables of the microcosm' in a mode that she knew through the works of 'early Christian Platonists, such as Ambrose and Origen'. Dronke identifies specific works that probably or possibly influenced the *Liber diuinorum operum* and thus probably the *Expositiones*. He concludes from various examples that 'Hildegard's allegorical exposition of the Hexameron owes much to Origen's *Homeliae in Genesim*', a text among others available at the library of St Maximin in Trier.[6] Dronke's 1981 article, 'Problemata Hildegardiana', also points to Hildegard's mention of Origen in one of the *Expositiones* and signals the possible influence of *De principiis* on her cosmology.[7] Dronke notes that 'hints' of Hildegard's interpretations could be found in earlier works. He allows for Hildegard's reliance on 'traditional allegorical meanings that go back to [Origen and Ambrose] or else to Gregory the Great or Bede',[8] but he does not explore the influence of the liturgical reading of such sources and thus of Hildegard's aural reception of the texts. In contrast, Sr Angela Carlevaris's study on 'Ildegarda e la patristica' asserts the importance of readings that Hildegard would have heard in the Office.

Dronke extends his analysis of sources and manuscript copies available to Hildegard in various later publications, notably in the edition of the *Liber diuinorum operum*. Stephen D'Evelyn's commentary on the *Symphonia* extends Dronke's work and explores in depth the sources for Hildegard's lyrics.[9] Dronke looks again at the *Expositiones* briefly in 'The Allegorical World Picture of Hildegard', where he proposes five techniques of Hildegard's allegory: (1) establishment of allegorical

---

[5] Dronke, 'Platonic-Christian Allegories', p. 391.

[6] Dronke, 'Platonic-Christian Allegories', p. 384, n. 11.

[7] Dronke, 'Problemata Hildegardiana', p. 114.

[8] Dronke, 'Platonic-Christian Allegories', p. 384.

[9] Stephen D'Evelyn, 'A Commentary with Translations and Emended Text of Hildegard of Bingen's *Symphonia armonie celestium revelationum*, carm. 1–50' (unpublished doctoral dissertation, University of Cambridge, 2003).

correspondence; (2–4) self-revelation: gradual, direct, and allegory within allegory; and (5) allegoresis — allegorical reading of the sacred text. For the first technique, Dronke cites the simple explanation of details in the visionary works; and for the second, he looks at the gradual dramatic revelation that images make about themselves in the visionary works. He discerns a third technique of direct self-revelation in the *Ordo uirtutum* where the personified virtues reveal their identity. In the case of the speech of Caritas in the *Ordo*, the allegorical figure explains herself by means of allegories that she expounds. Dronke separates that as a third manner of self-revelation or a fourth technique of allegory. The fifth technique of allegory, allegoresis, is evident in the *Expositiones*.[10]

In 1989 Barbara Newman published her groundbreaking *Sister of Wisdom: St. Hildegard of Bingen's Theology of the Feminine*, which was reissued in 1997. As a reviewer remarked, Newman's 'construction of Hildegard will remain the touchstone for future research'.[11] Newman's analysis of Hildegard's works draws on the *magistra*'s written and visual oeuvre to elucidate Hildegard's theology and her accent on the feminine. Newman's book grounded and stimulated the thereafter burgeoning literature on Hildegard and other women mystics of the Middle Ages. Newman places Hildegard's thought in the current of sapiential theology, which she defines as 'the perennial school of Christian thought that centres on the discovery and adoration of divine Wisdom in the works of creation and redemption'. Sapiential theology accents 'divine beauty, the feminine side of God, the absolute predestination of Christ and Mary, the moral and esthetic ideal of virginity and the hope of cosmic redemption'.[12] At the same time, Newman points out that the mystery of the incarnation lies at the centre of Hildegard's theology; the incarnate Word is both the 'center and final cause of creation — predestined by God "from before the foundation of the world"', as stated in Ephesians 1. 4.[13] The centrality of the incarnation and the eternal oneness of Creator and Redeemer are essential concepts for comprehending the theology of the *Expositiones*. Newman's grasp of Hildegard's theological mindset and its twelfth-century context proves invaluable for understanding all the *magistra*'s complex works and imagery. With respect to Hildegard's preaching, Newman analyzes the letters to Cologne, Kirchheim, and

---

[10] Dronke, 'Allegorical World Picture of Hildegard of Bingen', pp. 3–6.

[11] Anne L. Clark, Review of Barbara Newman, *Sister of Wisdom: St. Hildegard of Bingen's Theology of the Feminine, Speculum,* 74 (1999), 801–02.

[12] Newman, *Sister of Wisdom*, pp. xxi, 45.

[13] Newman, *Sister of Wisdom*, p. 45.

Trier; these represent the written product of an oral address to congregations.[14] Newman alerts readers to the understudied *Expositiones euangeliorum* and draws on three of them in her analysis.[15] Moreover, Newman, in an earlier article, called attention to the 'wide reading [...] evident' in Hildegard's works.[16] Newman's articles on Hildegard after the appearance of *Sister of Wisdom*, notably on Hildegard's 'auto-hagiography', as well as her edition of the *Symphonia* and *Voice of the Living Light*, have made priceless contributions to the study of Hildegard's works. Moreover, Newman's scholarship continues to elucidate Hildegard's place as 'Mother of Mystics', to borrow Newman's term, within the broader context of medieval women's mystical writings that she explores in her recent works.[17]

Other works published in the late 1980s or 1990s provide valuable context for the study of the *Expositiones*. Numerous biographies of the seer have been published in German, English, and other languages. Among them, Sabina Flanagan's work, released in a second edition for 1998, devotes attention not to the *Expositiones* but to the epistolary sermons as well as to Hildegard's network of contacts and her relationship with her secretaries — all vital pieces for understanding Hildegard's exegetical work.[18] Authors have focused on one theme in Hildegard's theology and incorporated the *Expositiones* into their analysis. Fabio Chávez-Alvarez uncovers the concept of *rationalitas* at the core of Hildegard's theology.[19] Hildegard Gosebrink includes passages from the German translation of the *Expositiones* in her study of Hildegard's Mariology.[20] The vast reception of Hildegard's works is now elucidated in Michael Embach's *Die Schriften Hildegards von Bingen: Studien zu ihrer Überlieferung und Rezeption im Mittelalter und in der Frühen Neuzeit*.

---

[14] Newman, *Sister of Wisdom*, pp. 27–28, 234, 239, 241–42.

[15] Newman, *Sister of Wisdom*, pp. 94–95 on John 2. 4; pp. 171–72 on John 1. 14; p. 184 on Matthew 1. 18–21.

[16] Newman, 'Hildegard of Bingen: Visions and Validation', p. 166.

[17] Newman, 'Commentary on the Johannine Prologue'; Newman, 'Hildegard and her Hagiographers'; Newman, 'Three-Part Invention'. Newman's works on medieval religious women and their works include *From Virile Woman to WomanChrist* (Philadelphia: University of Pennsylvania Press, 1995); *God and the Goddesses*.

[18] Flanagan, *Hildegard of Bingen*. See the reservations of Caviness, 'Hildegard of Bingen: Some Recent Books', pp. 113–14. Caviness concludes, p. 114, that Flanagan 'is not cautious enough about the cultural gap between us and Hildegard'.

[19] Chávez-Alvarez, *'Die brennende Vernunft'*; review by John Van Engen, *Speculum*, 69 (1999), 757–58.

[20] Gosebrink, *Maria in der Theologie Hildegards von Bingen*.

Various volumes that result from conferences held in 1998, the 900th anniversary of Hildegard's birth, advanced the research in various areas, including her cultural milieu. Those include *Hildegard of Bingen: The Context of her Thought and Art*, edited by Charles Burnett and Peter Dronke; *Hildegard von Bingen in ihrem historischen Umfeld*, edited by Alfred Haverkamp; and *'Im Angesicht Gottes suche der Mensch sich selbst': Hildegard von Bingen (1098–1179)*, edited by Rainer Berndt. Franz Felten, who contributed valuable articles to these anniversary volumes, assesses the contributions of the anniversary research in a 2003 article.[21] Other collections of scholarly merit aim at a more general audience and place the seer in the broader context of mystical theology.[22]

Recent research on the libraries, education, and writings of medieval religious women, particularly in the Empire, vastly enrich our knowledge of their intellectual environment. I signal three studies in English that include contributions and bibliography from international scholars. Constant Mews's 2001 volume, *Listen Daughter: The 'Speculum virginum' and the Formation of Religious Women in the Middle Ages*, introduces the rich cultural environment of the *Speculum virginum* and of Hirsau monasticism. Alison Beach uncovers the writings, scribal practices, and library holdings of religious women, and particularly Benedictines, in German-speaking lands. Her 2007 volume, *Manuscripts and Monastic Culture: Reform and Renewal in Twelfth-Century Germany*, extends that work with the contributions of other scholars working on women's monasteries and libraries within the broader context of twelfth-century monastic culture in Germany. Fiona Griffiths explores the *Hortus Deliciarum*, or *Garden of Delights*, compiled by the Augustinian canoness Herrad of Hohenbourg. Herrad gathered and structured excerpts from authors read in the curriculum at cathedral schools in order to provide an unparalleled manual for religious women.[23]

Still, the Hildegardian opus and, in particular, the written evidence of her exegesis and preaching stand out among the accomplishments of medieval religious women. Yet in works focused on Hildegard, references to the *Expositiones* are few. From the 'anniversary' volumes, significant articles by Bernard McGinn and Joop van Banning stand out, in addition to the previously cited study of Angela Carlevaris.

---

[21] Felten, 'Hildegard von Bingen, 1098–1998'.

[22] See notably *Hildegard von Bingen in ihrem Umfeld — Mystik und Visionsformen in Mittelalter und früher Neuzeit. Katholizismus und Protestantismus im Dialog*, ed. by Änne Bäumer-Schleinkofer (Würzburg: Religion und Kultur Verlag, 2001).

[23] *Listen Daughter*, ed. by Mews; Beach, *Women as Scribes*; *Manuscripts and Monastic Culture*, ed. by Beach; Griffiths, *Garden of Delights*.

Bernard McGinn signals the importance of Hildegard as an exegete. He compares Hildegard's view of exegesis as *intelligentia spiritualis* and her place as 'visionary exegete' with that of Joachim of Fiore and his successors Bonaventure and Peter John Olivi. McGinn's survey of Hildegard's visionary works finds that the percentage of passages containing exegetical material increases in the *Liber diuinorum operum*, and much of it becomes focused rather than 'piecemeal' commentary.[24] McGinn also considers Hildegard in his essay 'The Spiritual Heritage of Origen in the West'.[25] There he signals a few references that Hildegard makes to Origen and concludes, as does Angela Carlevaris, that the one passage where Hildegard refers to Origen by name alludes to the legend of his fall.[26] McGinn also points out that Elisabeth of Schönau clearly knew of Origen and his works. Hildegard's contemporary and sister visionary recounts that she asked the Virgin Mary whether Origen, 'that great doctor of the Church', had been saved or not. The Virgin replied that Origen's error did not derive from malice but from an excess of fervour for exegesis and of desire for scrutinizing divine secrets. Mary remembered the exegete with a special showing of light on her feast days and, according to a vision Elisabeth received from John the Evangelist, the Virgin herself would determine Origen's fate.[27]

Joop van Banning's 'Hildegard von Bingen als Theologin' explores Hildegard's exegesis in the light of patristic biblical interpretation and the concerns of modern interpreters of Scripture. Van Banning discusses allegory as concept and technique and then moves quickly through the *Expositiones*, selecting several to illustrate Hildegard's use of a particular sense of Scripture, according to the classification he makes of the level of scriptural interpretation that predominates in each of the *Expositiones*.

Finally, Uwe Brunn's 2006 book, *Des contestataires aux 'cathares': Discours de réforme et propagande antihérétique dans les pays du Rhin et de la Meuse avant l'Inquisition*, delves into the ecclesiastical network of writers who engaged in debates over reform and heresy in Cologne and nearby areas. Brunn brings to light unstudied documents and calls into question the dating of important events and texts in the Rhineland that relate to the rise of dissent and the Church's response. Brunn examines in detail two of Hildegard's writings against heresy and scrutinizes

---

[24] McGinn, 'Hildegard of Bingen as Visionary and Exegete', p. 343.

[25] McGinn, 'Spiritual Heritage of Origen in the West', pp. 279–82.

[26] McGinn, 'Spiritual Heritage of Origen in the West', p. 280.

[27] McGinn, 'Spiritual Heritage of Origen in the West', pp. 263–64.

her interaction with Elisabeth and Ekbert of Schonau. He includes a brief reference to one of the *Expositiones*.

The Abbreviations List above and Select Bibliography below include these and other studies of Hildegard's works as well as numerous patristic sources cited in the notes. Many additional sources are also cited in the notes. Readers who seek further parallels for particular exegetical trends in the Middle Ages may consult the extensive apparatus fontium of the *Expositiones euangeliorum*.

SELECT BIBLIOGRAPHY

For Hildegard of Bingen's works and other frequently cited volumes, see the Abbreviations. Many other published sources and manuscripts are cited in the footnotes of the volume.

Primary Sources

Acta inquisitionis de uirtutibus et miraculis S. Hildegardis, ed. by Petrus Bruder, *Analecta Bollandiana*, 2 (1883), 116–29

Adso Deruensis, *De ortu et tempore Antichristi*, CCCM, 45 (Turnhout: Brepols, 1976)

Ambrose of Milan, *Expositio euangelii secundum Lucam*, ed. by M. Adriaen, CCSL, 14 (Turnhout: Brepols, 1957)

Augustine of Hippo, *De doctrina christiana*, ed. by J. Martin, CCSL, 32 (Turnhout: Brepols, 1962)

Augustine of Hippo, *De Genesi ad litteram libri duodecim*, ed. by J. Zycha, CSEL, 28.1 (Vienna, 1894)

Augustine of Hippo, *Enarrationes in psalmos*, ed. by E. Dekkers and J. Fraipont, CCSL, 38–40 (Turnhout: Brepols, 1956)

Augustine of Hippo, *In Iohannis euangelium tractatus CXXIV*, ed. by R. Willems, CCSL, 36 (Turnhout: Brepols, 1954)

Augustine of Hippo, *Quaestionum euangeliorum*, ed. by A. Mutzenbecher, CCSL, 44B (Turnhout: Brepols, 1980)

Augustine of Hippo, *Sermones*, PL 38–39 (1845–46)

Ps.-Augustine of Hippo, *Sermo 136*, PL 72 (1849): 771–73

Bede the Venerable, *Homeliarum euangelii libri II*, ed. by D. Hurst, CCSL, 122 (Turnhout: Brepols, 1955)

Bede the Venerable, *In Lucae euangelium expositio*; *In Marci euangelium expositio*, ed. by D. Hurst, CCSL, 120 (Turnhout: Brepols, 1960)

Saint Benedict, *Regula*, ed. by R. Hanslik, CSEL, 75 (Vienna: Hoelder-Pichler-Tempsky, 1977)

Bernard of Clairvaux, *Sancti Bernardi Opera*, 8 vols (Rome: Editiones cistercienses, 1957–77)

Biblia latina cum glossa ordinaria: facsimile reprint of the *Editio princeps*, Adolph Rusch of Strassburg 1480/81, intro. by Karlfried Froehlich and Margaret T. Gibson, 4 vols (Turnhout: Brepols, 1992)

Ekbert of Schönau, *Sermones adversus pestiferos foedissimosque Catharorum*, *PL* 195 (1855): 11–98

Elisabeth of Schönau, *The Complete Works*, trans. by Anne L. Clark, Classics of Western Spirituality (New York: Paulist Press, 2000)

Elisabeth of Schönau, *Die Visionen der hl. Elisabeth und die Schriften der Äbte Ekbert und Emecho von Schönau*, ed. by F. W. E. Roth (Brünn: Verlag der Studien aus dem Benedictiner-und-Cistercienser-Orden, 1884)

Everwin of Steinfeld, *Epistola Everwini*, 472, *PL* 182 (1855): 676–80

Gottfried of Admont, *Homiliae dominicales*, *PL* 174 (1854): 21–632

Gottfried of Admont, *Homiliae in diuersos Scripturae locos*, *PL* 174 (1854): 1059–1133

Gottfried of Admont, *Homiliae in festa totius anni*, *PL* 174 (1854): 633–1059

Gregory the Great, *Homiliae in euangelia*, ed. by R. Étaix, CCSL, 141 (Turnhout: Brepols, 1999)

Gregory the Great, *Homiliae in Hiezechihelem prophetam*, ed. by M. Adriaen, CCSL, 142 (Turnhout: Brepols, 1971)

Gregory the Great, *Moralia in Iob Libri I–IX*, ed. by Marcus Adriaen, CCSL, 143–143B (Turnhout: Brepols, 1979–85)

Guibert of Gembloux, *Epistolae quae in codice B. R. Brux. 5527–5534 inueniuntur*, ed. by A. Derolez, E. Dekkers, and R. Demeulenaere, CCCM, 66, 66A (Turnhout: Brepols, 1988–89)

Haymo of Auxerre, *Homiliae de tempore*, *PL* 118 (1852): 11–746

Heiric of Auxerre, *Homiliae per circulum anni*, ed. by R. Quadri, CCCM, 116, 116A, 116B (Turnhout: Brepols, 1992–94)

Hrabanus Maurus, *Homiliae in euangelia et epistolas*, *PL* 110 (1852): 35–468

Irimbert of Admont, *see* Gottfried of Admont

Jerome, *Commentariorum in Matheum Libri IV*, ed. by D. Hurst and M. Adriaen, CCSL, 77 (Turnhout: Brepols, 1969)

Jerome, *Epistulae*, ed. by I. Hilberg, CSEL, 54, 55, 56 (Vienna, 1910–18) (editio altera supplementis aucta, 1996)

Jerome, *Liber interpretationis hebraicorum nominum*, ed. by P. de Lagarde, CCSL, 72 (Turnhout: Brepols, 1959)

John Scotus, *Homélie sur le prologue de Jean*, ed. by E. Jeauneau, SC, 151 (Paris: Cerf, 1969)

Origen, *Commentarius in Matthaeum*, ed. by E. Klostermann and E. Benz, *Origenes Werke*, vols X.1, XI, Die Griechischen Christlichen Schriftsteller der ersten Jahrhunderte, 40, 41.1 (Berlin: Akademie-Verlag, 1935; Leipzig: J. C. Hinrichs, 1941)

Origen, *De principiis*, ed. by P. Koetschau, *Origenes Werke*, vol. V, Die Griechischen Christlichen Schriftsteller der ersten Jahrhunderte, 22 (Leipzig: Hinrichs, 1913)

Origen, *De principiis*, ed. by H. Crouzel and M. Simonetti, in *Origène. Traité des Principes*, vol. III (Books 3 and 4), SC, 268 (Paris: Cerf, 1980)

Origen, *Homélies sur la Genèse*, ed. by Henri de Lubac and Louis Doutreleau, SC, 7 bis (Paris: Cerf, 1976)

Origen, *Homélies sur l'Exode*, ed. and trans. by Marcel Borret, SC, 321 (Paris: Cerf, 1985)

Origen, *Homélies sur Ézéchiel*, ed. and trans. by Marcel Borret, SC, 352 (Paris: Cerf, 1989)

Otloh of St Emmeram, *Liber de admonitione clericorum et laicorum*, *PL* 146 (1853): 244–62

Otloh of St Emmeram, *Liber visionum*, ed. by Paul Gerhardt Schmidt, MGH, Quellen zur Geistesgeschichte des Mittelalters, 13 (Weimar: Nachfolger, 1989), pp. 31–115

Otto of Freising, *Chronicon seu rerum ab initio mundi ad sua usque tempora 1146 libri VIII*, sive *Historia de duabus civitatibus*, ed. by Adolf Hofmeister, MGH SS, 20 (Hannover, 1868), pp. 1–457

Rupert of Deutz, *Commentaria in Euangelium Sancti Iohannis*, ed. by Rhaban Haacke, CCCM, 9 (Turnhout: Brepols, 1969)

Rupert of Deutz, *De gloria et honore Filii hominis super Mattheum*, ed. by Rhaban Haacke, CCCM, 29 (Turnhout: Brepols, 1979)

Rupert of Deutz, *De glorificatione Trinitatis et processione Spiritus Sancti*, PL 169 (1854): 13–202

Rupert of Deutz, *De sancta trinitate et operibus eius*, ed. by Rhaban Haacke, CCCM, 21–24 (Turnhout: Brepols, 1971–72)

Rupert of Deutz, *De uictoria Dei*, ed. by Rhaban Haacke, MGH, Quellen zur Geistesgeschichte des Mittelalters, 5 (Weimar: Herman Böhlaus Nachfolger, 1970)

Rupert of Deutz, *Liber de diuinis officiis*, ed. by Rhaban Haacke, CCCM, 7 (Turnhout: Brepols, 1967)

Speculum uirginum, ed. by Jutta Seyfarth, CCCM, 5 (Turnhout: Brepols, 1990)

Trithemius, Johannes, *Catalogus illustrium uirorum*, *Johannes Trithemii Opera historica*, vol. II, ed. by Marquand Freher (Frankfurt, 1601; repr. Frankfurt/Main: Minerva, 1966)

Vita domnae Juttae inclusae, ed. by Franz Staab, in 'Reform und Reformgruppen in Erzbistum Mainz: Vom *Libellus de Willigisi consuetudinibus* zur *Vita domnae Juttae inclusae*', in *Reformidee und Reformpolitik im Spätsalisch-Frühstaufischen Reich: Vorträge der Tagung der Gesellschaft für Mittelrheinische Kirchengeschichte vom 11. bis 13. September 1991 in Trier*, ed. by Stefan Weinfurter, Quellen und Abhandlungen zur Mittelrheinische Geschichte, 68 (Mainz: Selbstverlag der Gesellschaft für Mittelrheinische Kirchengeschichte, 1992), pp. 119–87, Appendix II, pp. 172–87

Secondary Literature

Arduini, Maria Ludovica, *Rupert von Deutz (1076–1129) und der 'status Christianitas' seiner Zeit: Symbolisch-prophetische Deutung der Geschichte* (Cologne: Böhlau, 1987)

Axton, Richard, *European Drama of the Early Middle Ages* (London: Hutchison, 1974)

Bartlett, Ann Clark, 'Commentary, Polemic, and Prophecy in Hildegard of Bingen's "Solutiones triginta octo quaestionum"', *Viator*, 23 (1992), 153–65

Beach, Alison I., 'Listening for the Voices of Admont's Twelfth-Century Nuns', in *Voices in Dialogue: Reading Women in the Middle Ages*, ed. by Linda Olson and Kathryn Kerby-Fulton (Notre Dame: University of Notre Dame Press, 2005), pp. 187–98

Beach, Alison I., ed., *Manuscripts and Monastic Culture: Reform and Renewal in Twelfth-Century Germany*, Medieval Church Studies, 13 (Turnhout: Brepols, 2007)

Beach, Alison I., 'The Multiform Grace of the Holy Spirit: Salvation History and the Book of Ruth at Twelfth-Century Admont', in *Manuscripts and Monastic Culture*, ed. by Beach, pp. 125–37

Beach, Alison I., 'Voices from a Distant Land: Fragments of a Twelfth-Century Nuns' Letter Collection', *Speculum*, 77 (2002), 34–54

Beach, Alison I., *Women as Scribes: Book Production and Monastic Reform in Twelfth-Century Bavaria* (Cambridge: University of Cambridge Press, 2004)

Bell, David, *What Nuns Read: Books and Libraries in Medieval English Nunneries*, Cistercian Studies, 158 (Kalamazoo: Cistercian Publications, 1995)

Biller, Peter, 'Northern Cathars and Higher Learning', in *The Medieval Church: Universities, Heresy, and the Religious Life. Essays in Honour of Gordon Leff*, ed. by P. Biller and B. Dobson, Studies in Church History, Subsidia, 11 (Woodbridge: Boydell, 1999), pp. 25–51

Böckeler, Maura, *Wisse die Wege. Scivias: Nach dem Originaltext des illuminierten Rupertsberger Kodex* (Salzburg: Müller, 1928)

Bouché, Anne-Marie, 'The Spirit in the World: The Virtues of the Floreffe Bible Frontispiece: British Library, Add. Ms. 17738, fols 3^v–4^r', in *Virtue and Vice: The Personifications in the Index of Christian Art*, ed. by Colum Hourihane (Princeton: Princeton University Press, 2000), pp. 42–65

Boynton, Susan, 'The Didactic Function and Context of Eleventh-Century Glossed Hymnaries', in *Der lateinische Hymnus im Mittelalter: Überlieferung-Ästhetik-Ausstrahlung*, ed. by Andreas Haug, Monumenta Monodica Medii Aevi, Subsidia, 4 (Kassel: Bärenreiter, 2004), pp. 301–29

Boynton, Susan, 'From the Lament of Rachel to the Lament of Mary: A Transformation in the History of Drama and Spirituality', in *Signs of Change: Transformations of Christian Traditions and their Representation in the Arts, 1000–2000*, ed. by Nils Holger Petersen, Claus Clüver, and Nicolas Bell, Studies in Comparative Literature, 43 (Amsterdam: Rodopi, 2004), pp. 319–40

Boynton, Susan, 'Latin Glosses on the Office Hymns in Eleventh-Century Continental Hymnaries', *Journal of Medieval Latin*, 11 (2001), 1–26

Boynton, Susan, 'Orality, Literacy, and the Early Notation of the Office Hymns', *Journal of the American Musicological Society*, 56 (2003), 99–167

Boynton, Susan, 'Ricerche sul breviario di Santa Giulia (Brescia, Biblioteca Queriniana, ms H VI 21' (co-authored with Martina Pantarotto), *Studi medievali*, 42 (2001), 301–18

Boynton, Susan, *Shaping a Monastic Identity: Liturgy and History at the Imperial Abbey of Farfa, 1000–1125* (Ithaca: Cornell University Press, 2006)

Boynton, Susan, 'Training for the Liturgy as a Form of Monastic Education', in *Medieval Monastic Education*, ed. by G. P. Ferzoco and C. A. Muessig (London: Leicester University Press/ Continuum, 2000), pp. 7–20

Brenon, Anne, 'La Lettre d'Evervin de Steinfeld à Bernard de Clairvaux de 1143: Un document essentiel et méconnu', *Heresis*, 25 (1995), 7–28

Brunn, Uwe, *Des contestataires aux 'cathares': Discours de réforme et propagande antihérétique dans les pays du Rhin et de la Meuse avant l'Inquisition*, Collection des Études Augustiniennes: Moyen Âge et Temps Modernes, 41 (Paris: Institut d'Études Augustiniennes, 2006)

Carlevaris, Angela, 'Ildegarda e la patristica', in *Angesicht*, pp. 65–80

Carlevaris, Angela, 'Sie kamen zu ihr, um sie zu befragen: Hildegard und die Juden', in *Umfeld*, pp. 117–28

Caviness, Madeline, 'Artist: "To See, Hear, and Know All at Once"', in *Voice*, pp. 110–24

Caviness, Madeline, 'Hildegard as Designer of the Illustrations to her Works', in *Context*, pp. 29–62

Caviness, Madeline, 'Hildegard of Bingen: Some Recent Books', *Speculum*, 77 (2002), 113–20

Chávez-Alvarez, Fabio, *'Die brennende Vernunft' Studien zur Semantik der 'rationalitas' bei Hildegard von Bingen* (Stuttgart-Bad Cannstatt: Friederich Frommann, Günther Holzboog, 1991)

Chazan, Robert, *In the Year 1096 [. . .] The First Crusade and the Jews* (Philadelphia: Jewish Publication Society, 1996)

Chenu, Marie-Dominique, *Nature, Man and Society in the Twelfth Century: Essays on New Theological Perspectives in the Latin West*, ed. and trans. by Jerome Taylor and Lester K. Little (Chicago: University of Chicago Press, 1968)

Clark, Anne L., *Elisabeth of Schönau: A Twelfth-Century Visionary* (Philadelphia: University of Pennsylvania Press, 1992)

Clark, Anne L., 'Repression or Collaboration? The Case of Elisabeth and Ekbert of Schönau', in *Christendom and its Discontents: Exclusion, Persecution, and Rebellion, 1000–1500*, ed. by Scott L. Waugh and Peter D. Diehl (Cambridge: Cambridge University Press, 1996), pp. 151–67

Constable, Giles, 'Hildegard's Explanation of the Rule of St. Benedict', in *Umfeld*, pp. 163–87

Constable, Giles, 'The Ideal of the Imitation of Christ', in *Three Studies in Medieval Religious and Social Thought* (Cambridge: Cambridge University Press, 1995), pp. 143–248

Constable, Giles, *Letters and Letter Collections*, Typologie des Sources du Moyen Âge Occidental, 17 (Turnhout: Brepols, 1976)

Constable, Giles, *The Reformation of the Twelfth Century* (Cambridge: Cambridge University Press, 1996)

Constable, Giles, 'The Second Crusade as Seen by Contemporaries', *Traditio*, 9 (1953), 213–79

Davidson, Audrey E., 'Music and Performance: Hildegard of Bingen's *Ordo virtutum*', in *The Ordo virtutum of Hildegard of Bingen: Critical Studies*, ed. by A. E. Davidson (Kalamazoo: Medieval Institute Publications, 1992), pp. 1–30

Derolez, Albert, 'The Manuscript Transmission of Hildegard of Bingen's Writings: The State of the Problem', in *Context*, pp. 17–28

D'Evelyn, Stephen, 'Heaven as Performance and Participation in the *Symphonia armonie celestium revelationum* of Hildegard of Bingen', in *Envisaging Heaven in the Middle Ages*, ed. by Ad Putter and C. A. Muessig, Routledge Studies in Medieval Religion and Culture (London: Routledge, 2006), pp. 155–65

Dronke, Peter, 'The Allegorical World Picture of Hildegard of Bingen: Revaluations and New Problems', in *Context*, pp. 1–16

Dronke, Peter, *Dante and Medieval Latin Traditions* (Cambridge: Cambridge University Press, 1986)

Dronke, Peter, 'Hildegard's Inventions: Aspects of her Language and Imagery', in *Umfeld*, pp. 299–320

Dronke, Peter, 'Platonic-Christian Allegories in the Homilies of Hildegard of Bingen', in *From Athens to Chartres: Neoplatonism and Medieval Thought: Studies in Honour of Edouard Jeauneau*, ed. by Haijo Jan Westra (Leiden: Brill, 1992), pp. 381–96

Dronke, Peter, 'Problemata Hildegardiana', *Mittellateinisches Jahrbuch*, 16 (1981), 97–131

Dronke, Peter, *Women Writers of the Middle Ages: A Critical Study of Texts from Perpetua (d. 203) to Marguerite Porete (d. 1310)* (Cambridge: University of Cambridge Press, 1984)

Duvernoy, Jean, *La Religion des Cathares, Le catharisme*, vol. I (Toulouse: Privat, 1976)

Elvert, C., 'Die Nokturnenlesungen Klunys im 10–12 Jahrhundert', in *Corpus consuetudinum monasticarum*, 7.4, ed. by C. Hallinger (Siegburg: Schmitt, 1986), pp. 37–126

Embach, Michael, *Die Schriften Hildegards von Bingen: Studien zu ihrer Überlieferung und Rezeption im Mittelalter und in der Frühen Neuzeit* (Berlin: Akademie, 2003)

Emmerson, Richard, 'The Representation of Antichrist in Hildegard of Bingen's *Scivias*', *Gesta*, 41 (2002), 95–110

Étaix, Raymond, 'Le Lectionnaire de l'office à Cluny', *Recherches augustiniennes*, 11 (1976), 91–159

Fassler, Margot, 'Composer and Dramatist: "Melodious Singing and the Freshness of Remorse"', in *Voice*, pp. 149–75

Faust, Ulrich, 'Gottfried von Admont', *Studien und Mitteilungen zur Geschichte des Benediktinerordens und seiner Zweige*, 75 (1964), 273–359

Feiss, Hugh, 'Christ in the "Scivias" of Hildegard of Bingen', in *Angesicht*, pp. 291–98

Felten, Franz J., 'Hildegard von Bingen, 1098–1998 — oder Was bringen Jubilaen fur die Wissenschaft?', *Deutsches Archiv für Erforschung des Mittelalters*, 59 (2003), 165–94

Felten, Franz J., 'Zum Problem der sozialen Zusammensetzung von alten Benediktinerklöstern und Konventen der neuen religiosen Bewegung', in *Umfeld*, pp. 189–235

Flanagan, Sabina, *Hildegard of Bingen, 1098–1179: A Visionary Life*, 2nd edn (London: Routledge, 1998)

Gibson, Margaret T., 'The Twelfth-Century Glossed Bible', in *Studia patristica*, XXIII, Papers Presented to the Tenth International Conference on Patristic Studies held in Oxford, 1987, ed. by Elizabeth A. Livingstone (Leuven: Peeters, 1989), pp. 232–44

Gosebrink, Hildegard, *Maria in der Theologie Hildegards von Bingen* (Würzburg: Echter, 2004)

Grégoire, Réginald, *Homéliaires liturgiques médiévaux: Analyse de manuscrits* (Spoleto: Centro italiano de studi sull'Alto Medioevo, 1980)

Griffiths, Fiona, *The Garden of Delights: Reform and Renaissance for Women in the Twelfth Century* (Philadelphia: University of Pennsylvania Press, 2006)

Grönau, Eduard, *Hildegard von Bingen 1098–1179, Prophetische Lehrerin der Kirche an der Schwelle und am Ende der Neuzeit* (Stein am Rhein: Christiana, 1985)

Grundmann, Herbert, *Religious Movements in the Middle Ages: The Historical Links between Heresy, the Mendicant Orders, and the Women's Religious Movement in the Twelfth and Thirteenth Century, with the Historical Foundations of German Mysticism*, trans. by Steven Rowan (Notre Dame: University of Notre Dame Press, 1995)

Hamburger, Jeffrey F., 'Before the Book of Hours: The Development of the Illustrated Prayer Book in Germany', in *The Visual and the Visionary: Art and Female Spirituality in Late Medieval Germany* (New York: Zone, 1998), pp. 149–95

Hamburger, Jeffrey F., 'Gebetbuch der Hildegard von Bingen', in *Krone und Schleier: Kunst aus Mittelalterlichen Frauenklöstern*, Kunst- und Ausstellungshalle der Bundesrepublik Deutschland, Bonn und dem Ruhrlandmuseum Essen (Munich: Hirmer; Bonn and Essen: Kunst- und Ausstellungshalle der Bundesrepublik Deutschland, Bonn und dem Ruhrlandmuseum Essen, 2005), pp. 311–12

Hamburger, Jeffrey F., *St John the Divine: The Deified Evangelist in Medieval Art and Theology* (Berkeley: University of California Press, 2002)

Hamburger, Jeffrey F., 'Vision and the Veronica', in *The Visual and the Visionary: Art and Female Spirituality in Late Medieval Germany* (New York: Zone, 1998), pp. 350–70

Hamilton, Bernard, 'The Cathars and Christian Perfection', in *The Medieval Church: Universities, Heresy, and the Religious Life. Essays in Honour of Gordon Leff*, ed. by P. Biller and B. Dobson, Studies in Church History, Subsidia, 11 (Woodbridge: Boydell and Brewer, 1999), pp. 5–23

Hamilton, Bernard, 'Wisdom from the East: The Reception by the Cathars of Eastern Dualist Texts', in *Heresy and Literacy in the Middle Ages, 1000–1530*, ed. by P. Biller and A. Hudson (Cambridge: Cambridge University Press, 1996), pp. 38–60

Haverkamp, Alfred, *Medieval Germany 1056–1273*, trans. by Helga Braun and Richard Mortimer, 2nd edn (Oxford: Oxford University Press, 1992)

Haverkamp, Alfred, 'Tenxwind von Andernach und Hildegard von Bingen', in *Institutionen, Kultur und Gesellschaft im Mittelalter, Festschrift für Josef Fleckenstein* (Sigmaringen: Thorbecke, 1984), pp. 515–48

Holbach, Rudolf, 'Hildegard von Bingen und die kirchlichen Metropolen Mainz, Köln und Trier', in *Umfeld*, pp. 71–115

Holbrink, Shelley Amiste, 'Women in the Premonstratensian Order of Northwestern Germany 1120–1250', *Catholic Historical Review*, 89 (2003), 387–408

Hotchin, Julie, 'Female Religious Life and the *cura monialium* in Hirsau Monasticism, 1080 to 1150', in *Listen Daughter*, ed. by Mews, pp. 61–78

Hotchin, Julie, 'Women's Reading and Monastic Reform in Twelfth-Century Germany: The Library of the Nuns of Lippoldsberg', in *Manuscripts and Monastic Culture*, ed. by Beach, pp. 139–90

Katzenellenbogen, Adolf, *Allegories of the Virtues and Vices in Medieval Art* (Toronto: University of Toronto Press and Medieval Academy of America, MART repr. 1989)

Kerby-Fulton, Kathryn, 'Prophet and Reformer: "Smoke in the Vineyard"', in *Voice*, pp. 70–90

Kerby-Fulton, Kathryn, *Reformist Apocalypticism and Piers Plowman* (Cambridge: Cambridge University Press, 1990)

Kienzle, Beverly Mayne, *Cistercians, Heresy and Crusade (1145–1229): Preaching in the Lord's Vineyard* (Woodbridge: Boydell and Brewer, 2001)

Kienzle, Beverly Mayne, 'Constructing Heaven in Hildegard of Bingen's *Expositiones evangeliorum*', in *Envisaging Heaven in the Middle Ages*, ed. by Ad Putter and C. A. Muessig, Routledge Studies in Medieval Religion and Culture (London: Routledge, 2006), pp. 34–43

Kienzle, Beverly Mayne, 'Crisis and Charismatic Authority in Hildegard of Bingen's Preaching against the Cathars', in *Charisma and Religious Authority: Jewish, Christian, and Muslim Preaching, 1200–1600*, ed. by Miri Rubin and Katherine Jansen (Turnhout: Brepols, forthcoming)

Kienzle, Beverly Mayne, 'Defending the Lord's Vineyard: Hildegard of Bingen's Preaching against the Cathars', in *Medieval Monastic Preaching*, ed. by Carolyn A. Muessig (Leiden: Brill, 1998), pp. 163–91

Kienzle, Beverly Mayne, 'Hildegard of Bingen's Exegesis of Luke', in *Early Christian Voices in Texts, Traditions, and Symbols: Essays in Honor of François Bovon*, ed. by David H. Warren, Ann Graham Brock, and David W. Pao (Boston: Brill, 2003), pp. 227–38

Kienzle, Beverly Mayne, 'Hildegard of Bingen's *Expositiones evangeliorum* and her Exegesis of the Parable of the Prodigal Son', in *Angesicht*, pp. 299–324

Kienzle, Beverly Mayne, 'Hildegard of Bingen's Teaching in her *Expositiones evangeliorum and Ordo virtutum*', in *Medieval Monastic Education*, ed. by G. P. Ferzoco and C. A. Muessig (London: Leicester University Press/Contiuum, 2000), pp. 72–86

Kienzle, Beverly Mayne, 'Medieval Sermons and their Performance: Theory and Record', in *Preacher, Sermon and Audience in the Middle Ages*, ed. by Carolyn A. Muessig (Leiden: Brill, 2002), pp. 89–124

Kienzle, Beverly Mayne, 'Performing the Gospel Stories: Hildegard of Bingen's Dramatic Exegesis in the *Expositiones euangeliorum*', in *Visualizing Medieval Performance: Perspectives, Histories, Contexts*, ed. by Elina Gertsman (Aldershot: Ashgate, 2008), pp. 121–40

Kienzle, Beverly Mayne, dir., *The Sermon*, Typologie des Sources du Moyen Âge Occidental, 81–83 (Turnhout: Brepols, 2000)

Kienzle, Beverly Mayne, *Women Preachers and Prophets Through Two Millennia of Christianity*, co-ed. by Pamela J. Walker (Berkeley: University of California Press, 1998)

Kihlman, Erika, '*Expositiones sequentiarum*': *Medieval Sequence Commentaries and Prologues: Editions with Introductions*, Acta Universitatis Stockholmiensis, Studia Latina Stockholmiensia, 53 (Stockholm: Stockholm University, 2006)

Klemm, Elisabeth, 'Der Bilderzyklus im Hildegard-Gebetbuch', in *Hildegard-Gebetbuch: Faksimile-Ausgabe des Codex-latinus monacensis 935 der Bayerischen Staatsbubkiothek, Kommentarband* (Wiesbaden: Reichert, 1987), pp. 80–356

Klemm, Elisabeth, 'Das sogenannte Gebetbuch der Hildegard von Bingen', in *Jahrbuch der Kunsthistorischen Sammlungen in Wien*, 74, n.s. 38 (Vienna: Verlag Anton Schroll, 1978), pp. 29–78

Krone und Schleier: Kunst aus Mittelalterlichen Frauenklöstern, Kunst- und Ausstellungshalle der Bundesrepublik Deutschland, Bonn und dem Ruhrlandmuseum Essen (Munich: Hirmer; Bonn and Essen: Kunst- und Ausstellungshalle der Bundesrepublik Deutschland, Bonn und dem Ruhrlandmuseum Essen, 2005)

Leclercq, Jean, *The Love of Learning and the Desire for God*, trans. by C. Misrahi, 3rd edn (New York: Fordham University Press, 1982)

Leclercq, Jean, *Women and St. Bernard* (Kalamazoo: Cistercian Publications, 1989)

Liebeschütz, Hans, *Das allegorische Weltbild der heiligen Hildegard von Bingen* (Leipzig, 1930; repr. with Nachwort, Darmstadt: Wissenschaftliche Buchgesellschaft, 1964)

Lobrichon, Guy, 'Une nouveauté: les gloses de la Bible', in *Le Moyen Âge et la Bible*, ed. by Pierre Riché and Guy Lobrichon, Bible de tous les temps, 4 (Paris: Beauchesne, 1984), pp. 95–114

Longère, Jean, *La Prédication médiévale* (Paris: Études augustiniennes, 1983)

Lubac, Henri de, *Exégèse médiévale: Les quatre sens de l'Écriture*, 3 vols (Paris, 1959–64); English translation: *Medieval Exegesis*, vol. I, trans. by Mark Sebanc (Grand Rapids: Eerdmans; Edinburgh: T. and T. Clark, 1998); *Medieval Exegesis*, vol. II, trans. by E. M. Macierowski (Grand Rapids: Eerdmans; Edinburgh: T. and T. Clark, 2000)

Lutter, Christina, 'Christ's Educated Brides: Literacy, Spirituality, and Gender in Twelfth-Century Admont', in *Manuscripts and Monastic Culture*, ed. by Beach, pp. 191–213

Lutter, Christina, *Geschlect und Wissen, Norm und Praxis, Lesen und Schreiben: Monastische Reformgemeinschaften im 12. Jahrhundert* (Vienna: Oldenbourg, 2005)

Manselli, Raoul, 'Amicizia spirituale ed azione pastorale nella Germania del sec. XII: Ildegarde di Bingen, Elisabetta ed Ecberto di Schönau contro l'eresia Catara', in *Studi in onore di Alberto Pincherle*, Studi e materiali di storia delle religioni, 38 (Rome: Ateneo, 1967), pp. 302–13

Matter, E. Ann, *The Voice of My Beloved: The Song of Songs in Western Medieval Christianity* (Philadelphia: University of Pennsylvania Press, 1990)

Mayr-Harting, Henry, *Ottonian Book Illumination* (London: Harvey Miller, 1999)

McGinn, Bernard, 'Hildegard of Bingen as Visionary and Exegete', in *Umfeld*, pp. 321–50

McGinn, Bernard, 'The Originality of Eriugena's Spiritual Exegesis', in *Iohannes Scottus Eriugena: The Bible and Hermeneutics, Proceedings of the Ninth International Colloquium of the Society for the Promotion of Eriugenian Studies, Leuven and Louvain-la-Neuve, June 7–10, 1995*, ed. by Gerd Van Riel, Carlos Steel, and James McEvoy (Leuven: University Press, 1996), pp. 55–80

McGinn, Bernard, *The Presence of God: A History of Western Christian Mysticism*, vol. II: *The Growth of Mysticism* (New York: Crossroad, 1996)

McGinn, Bernard, 'The Spiritual Heritage of Origen in the West', in *Origene maestro di vita spirituale. Milano, 13–15 settembre 1999*, ed. by Luigi F. Pizzolato and Marco Rizzi (Milan: Vita e Pensiero, 2001), pp. 263–89

McGinn, Bernard, 'Theologians as Trinitarian Iconographers', in *The Mind's Eye: Art and Theological Argument in the Middle Ages*, ed. by Jeffrey F. Hamburger and Anne-Marie Bouché (Princeton: Princeton University Press, 2006), pp. 186–207

Meier, Christel, 'Eriugena im Nonnenkloster? Überlegungen zum Verhältnis von Prophetum und Werkgestalt in den figmenta prophetia Hildegards von Bingen', in *Eriugena redivivus: Frühmittelalterliche Studien* (Berlin: de Gruyter, 1985), pp. 466–97

Meier, Christel, 'Ildegarde di Bingen: profezia ed esistenza letteraria', *Cristianesimo nell storia*, 17 (1996), 271–303

Meier, Christel, 'Prophetentum als literarische Existenz: Hildegard von Bingen (1098–1179); ein Portrait', in *Deutsche Literatur von Frauen*, vol. I: *Vom Mittelalter bis zum Ende des 18. Jahrhunderts*, ed. by Gisela Brinker-Gabler (Munich: Beck, 1988), pp. 76–87

Meier, Christel, 'Scientia divinorum operum: Zu Hildegards von Bingen visionär-künstlerischer Rezeption Eriugenas', in *Eriugena redivivus: Zur Wirkungsgeschichte seines Denkens im Mittelalter und in Übergang zur Neuzeit: Vorträge des V. Internationalen Eriugena-Colloquiums, Werner-Reimers-Stiftung Bad Homburg, 26.–30. August 1985*, ed. by W. Beierwaltes (Heidelberg: Carl Winter Universitätsverlag, 1987), pp. 89–141

Meis, Annelies, 'Symphonia Spiritus Sancti: Acercamiento al dilema de la razón humana en LVM de Hildegard von Bingen (1098–1179)', *Teología y Vida*, 46 (2005), 389–426

Mews, Constant J., 'From *Scivias* to the *Liber divinorum operum*: Hildegard's Apocalyptic Imagination and the Call to Reform', *Journal of Religious History*, 24 (2000), 44–56

Mews, Constant J., 'Hildegard and the Schools', in *Context*, pp. 89–110

Mews, Constant J., 'Hildegard of Bingen: The Virgin, the Apocalypse, and the Exegetical Tradition', in *Wisdom which Encircles Circles*, ed. by A. E. Davidson (Kalamazoo: Medieval Institute Publications, 1996), pp. 27–42

Mews, Constant J., 'Hildegard, the *Speculum virginum* and Religious Reform', in *Umfeld*, pp. 236–67

Mews, Constant J., 'Hildegard, Visions and Religious Reform', in *Angesicht*, pp. 325–42

Mews, Constant J., ed., *Listen Daughter: The 'Speculum virginum' and the Formation of Religious Women in the Middle Ages* (New York: Palgrave, 2001)

Mews, Constant J., 'Monastic Educational Culture Revisited: The Witness of Zwiefalten and the Hirsau Reform', in *Medieval Monastic Education*, ed. by G. P. Ferzoco and C. A. Muessig (London: Leicester University Press/Continuum, 2000), pp. 182–97

Moore, Peter, 'Mystical Experience, Mystical Doctrine, Mystical Technique', in *Mysticism and Philosophical Analysis*, ed. by S. Katz (New York: Sheldon, 1978), pp. 101–31

Moulinier, Laurence, 'Abbesse et agronome: Hildegarde et le savoir botanique de son temps', in *Context*, pp. 135–56

Muessig, Carolyn A., 'Learning and Mentoring in the Twelfth Century: Hildegard of Bingen and Herrad of Hohenburg', in *Medieval Monastic Education*, ed. by G. P. Ferzoco and C. A. Muessig (London: Leicester University Press/Continuum, 2000), pp. 87–104

Newhauser, Richard, *The Treatise on Vices and Virtues in Latin and the Vernacular*, Typologie des Sources du Moyen Âge Occidental, 68 (Turnhout: Brepols, 1993)

Newman, Barbara J., 'Commentary on the Johannine Prologue translated and introduced by Barbara Newman', *Theology Today*, 60 (2003), 16–33

Newman, Barbara J., *From Virile Woman to WomanChrist* (Philadelphia: University of Pennsylvania Press, 1995)

Newman, Barbara J., *God and the Goddesses: Vision, Poetry, and Belief in the Middle Ages* (Philadelphia: University of Pennsylvania Press, 2003)

Newman, Barbara J., 'Hildegard and her Hagiographers: The Remaking of Female Sainthood', in *Gendered Voices: Medieval Saints and their Interpreters*, ed. by Catherine M. Mooney (Philadelphia: University of Pennsylvania Press, 1999), pp. 16–34

Newman, Barbara J., 'Hildegard of Bingen: Visions and Validation', *Church History*, 54 (1985), 163–75

Newman, Barbara J., 'Poet: Where the Living Majesty Utters Mysteries', in *Voice*, pp. 176–92

Newman, Barbara J., 'Possessed by the Spirit: Devout Women, Demoniacs, and the Apostolic Life in the Thirteenth Century', *Speculum*, 73 (1998), 733–70

Newman, Barbara J., *Sister of Wisdom: St. Hildegard of Bingen's Theology of the Feminine* (Berkeley: University of California Press, 1997)

Newman, Barbara J., 'Sybil of the Rhine', in *Voice*, pp. 1–28

Newman, Barbara J., 'Three-Part Invention: The *Vita S. Hildegardis* and Mystical Hagiography', in *Context*, pp. 189–210

Nikitsch, E. J., 'Wo lebte die heilige Hildegard wirklich? Neue Überlegungen zum ehemaligen Standort der Frauenklause auf dem Disibodenberg', in *Angesicht*, pp. 47–56

Pernoud, Régine, 'The Preaching Peregrinations of a Twelfth-Century Nun', in *Wisdom which Encircles Circles*, ed. by A. E. Davidson (Kalamazoo: Medieval Institute Publications, 1996), pp. 15–26

Pernoud, Régine, 'Die predigten Hildegards von Bingen', in *Tiefe des Gotteswissens — Schönheit der Sprachgestalt bei Hildegard von Bingen. Internationales Symposium in der Katholischen Akademie Rabanus Maurus, Wiesbaden-Naurod vol. 9. bis 12. September 1994*, ed. by Margot Schmidt (Stuttgart: Frommann-Holzboog, 1995), pp. 181–92

Pfau, Marianne, 'Music and Text in Hildegard's Antiphons', in Newman, *Symphonia*, pp. 89–93

Powell, Morgan, 'The *Speculum virginum* and the Audio-Visual Poetics of Women's Religious Education', in *Listen Daughter*, ed. by Mews, pp. 111–35

Roitner, Ingrid, 'Das Admonter Frauenkloster im zwölften Jahrhundert: Ein Musterkloster des *Ordo Hirsaugiensis*', *Studien und Mitteilungen zur Geschichte des Benediktinerordens und seiner Zweige*, 15 (2005), 199–289

Saurma-Jeltsch, Lieselotte E., *Die Miniaturen im Liber 'Scivias' des Hildegard von Bingen: die Wucht der Vision und die Ordnung der Bilder* (Wiesbaden: Reichert, 1998)

Schiewer, Hans Jochen, 'German Vernacular Sermons', in *The Sermon*, dir. by Kienzle, pp. 861–961

Schmitt, Wolfgang Felix, 'Charisma gegen Recht? Der Konflikt der Hildegard von Bingen mit dem Mainzer Domkapitel 1178/79 in kirchenrechtsgeschichtlicher Perspektive', in *Hildegard von Bingen 1098–1998*, special issue, *Binger Geschichtsblätter*, 20 (1998), 124–59

Schrader, Marianna, and Adelgundis Führkötter, *Die Echtheit des Schrifttums der heiligen Hildegard von Bingen. Quellenkritische Untersuchungen*, Beihefte zum Archiv für Kulturgeschichte, 6 (Cologne: Böhlau-Verlag, 1956)

Seeberg, Stephanie, 'Illustrations in the Manuscripts of the Admont Nuns from the Second Half of the Twelfth Century: Reflections on their Function', in *Manuscripts and Monastic Culture*, ed. by Beach, pp. 99–121

Seyfarth, Jutta, 'The *Speculum virginum*: The Testimony of the Manuscripts', in *Listen Daughter*, ed. by Mews, pp. 41–57

Sheingorn, Pamela, 'The Virtues of Hildegard's *Ordo virtutum*; or, It *Was* a Woman's World', in *The Ordo virtutum of Hildegard of Bingen: Critical Studies*, ed. by A. E. Davidson (Kalamazoo: Medieval Institute Publications, 1992), pp. 52–57

Silvas, Anna, trans., *Jutta and Hildegard: The Biographical Sources* (University Park: Pennsylvania State University Press, 1999)

Smalley, Beryl, *The Study of the Bible in the Middle Ages* (Oxford: Oxford University Press, 1952; repr., 1985)

Suydam, Mary A., 'Background: An Introduction to Performance Studies', in *Performance and Transformation: New Approaches to Late Medieval Spirituality*, ed. by Mary A. Suydam and Joanna E. Zeigler (New York: St Martin's Press, 1999), pp. 1–26

Suzuki, Keiko, *Bildewordene Visionen oder Visionserzählungen: Vergleichende Studie über die Visionsdarstellungen in der Rupertsberger 'Scivias' — Handschrift und im Luccheser 'Liber divinorum operum' — Codex der Hildegard von Bingen*, Neue Berner Schriften zur Kunst, 5 (Bern: Lang, 1998)

Tessera, Miriam Rita, 'Philip Count of Flanders and Hildegard of Bingen: Crusading against the Saracens or Crusading against Deadly Sin?', in *Gendering the Crusades*, ed. by Susan B. Edgington and Sarah Lambert (New York: Columbia University Press, 2002), pp. 77–93

van Banning, Joop, 'Hildegard von Bingen als Theologin', in *Angesicht*, pp. 243–68

Van Engen, John, 'Abbess: "Mother and Teacher"', in *Voice*, pp. 30–51

Van Engen, John, 'The "Crisis of Cenobitism" Reconsidered: Benedictine Monasticism in the Years 1050–1150', *Speculum*, 61 (1986), 269–304

Van Engen, John, 'Letters and the Public Persona of Hildegard', in *Umfeld*, pp. 379–89

Van Engen, John, *Rupert of Deutz* (Los Angeles: University of California Press, 1983)

Waddell, Chrysogonus, 'The Liturgical Dimension of Twelfth-Century Cistercian Preaching', in *Medieval Monastic Preaching*, ed. by Carolyn A. Muessig (Leiden: Brill, 1998), pp. 335–49

Wailes, Stephen L., *Medieval Allegories of Jesus's Parables* (Berkeley: University of California Press, 1987)

Wieland, Gernot Rudolf, *The Latin Glosses on Arator and Prudentius in Cambridge University Library, MS Gg.5.35* (Toronto: Pontifical Institute of Mediaeval Studies, 1983)

SUBJECT INDEX

Medieval and modern authors are generally cited when mentioned in text or in notes. If a reference occurs in the text and in the note(s) on the same page, only the page is cited. Names and topics cited in the Preface are not included in the index.

The index is extensive but not exhaustive. For the major topics of the book — Hildegard of Bingen, exegesis, the *Expositiones euangeliorum*, and other works by Hildegard — please consult the chapters. For references to works by B. M. Kienzle, please consult the chapters and the bibliography.

SCRIPTURAL INDEX

MEDIEVAL WOMEN: TEXTS AND CONTEXTS

All volumes in this series are evaluated by an Editorial Board, strictly on academic grounds, based on reports prepared by referees who have been commissioned by virtue of their specialism in the appropriate field. The Board ensures that the screening is done independently and without conflicts of interest. The definitive texts supplied by authors are also subject to review by the Board before being approved for publication. Further, the volumes are copyedited to conform to the publisher's stylebook and to the best international academic standards in the field.

Titles in series

Household, Women, and Christianities in Late Antiquity and the Middle Ages, ed. by Anneke B. Mulder-Bakker and Jocelyn Wogan-Browne (2006)

The Writings of Julian of Norwich: 'A Vision Showed to a Devout Woman' and 'A Revelation of Love', ed. by Nicholas Watson and Jacqueline Jenkins (2006)

Les Cantiques Salemon: The Song of Songs in MS Paris BNF fr. 14966, ed. by Tony Hunt (2006)

Carolyn P. Collette, *Performing Polity: Women and Agency in the Anglo-French Tradition, 1385–1620* (2006)

Mary of Oignies, Mother of Salvation: Texts and Studies, ed. by A. B. Mulder-Bakker (2007)

Anna M. Silvas, *Macrina the Younger: Philosopher of God* (2008)

Thomas of Cantimpré: The Collected Saints' Lives. Abbot John of Camtimpré, Christina the Astonishing, Margaret of Ypres, and Lutgard of Aywières, ed. by Barbara Newman (2008)

Virgins and Scholars: A Fifteenth-Century Compilation of the Lives of John the Baptist, John the Evangelist, Jerome, and Katherine of Alexandria, ed. by Claire Waters (2008)

Jennifer N. Brown, *Three Women of Liège: A Critical Edition of and Commentary on the Middle English Lives of Elizabeth of Spalbeek, Christina Mirabilis, and Marie d'Oignies* (2008)

Suzanne Kocher, *Allegories of Love in Marguerite Porete's 'Mirror of Simple Souls'* (2008)